Music

THROUGH THE AGES

MUSIC

AN INTRODUCTION TO MUSIC HISTORY

MARION BAUER AND ETHEL R. PEYSER

Through The Ages

EDITED AND REVISED BY

ELIZABETH E. ROGERS, Ed.D.

Third Edition, Completely Revised

G. P. Putnam's Sons, New York

*We dedicate this book
to the students and music lovers
who have been impelled
by a curiosity about music
to open its covers.*

*And if there come the singers and the dancers
and the flute players,—buy of their gifts also.
For they too are gatherers of fruit and
frankincense, and that which they bring,
though fashioned of dreams, is raiment and
food for your soul.*

From THE PROPHET
Kahlil Gibran.

Editor's Preface

In undertaking the task of revising and editing MUSIC THROUGH THE AGES as an instructional implement to the study of music history I have worked along certain guidelines which I would like to share with the reader, so that he may have a notion of the philosophy underlying this volume. It is my hope that the result would have pleased the original authors.

It has become a truism needing no elaboration that one cannot "teach appreciation" nor can a book further such an ambition, insofar as motivation or curiosity is lacking. There is no argument to counteract this statement, but if one trusts entirely to direct experience, one finds that the years yield a rather sparse harvest. A mass of information and inviting suggestion can telescope the time factor very effectively, condensing several lifetimes of empirical knowledge into a malleable span. Without the aid of such vicarious experience it is as if one observed lightning, even endured its impact, yet remained ignorant of the basic phenomenon of electricity in nature.

Too often a text serves only as a pretense for displaying the erudition of the author; it becomes cluttered with the debris of his personal researches and burdens the music lover with paraphernalia so bulky that it impedes his intellectual probings. Equally often, a volume claims a comprehensiveness far beyond its capacity and asserts a tacit position of sagely providing all the answers if only the reader would follow blindly the course of its pages. Unfortunately often, American musicology is but a pale reflection of the thinking of a German school who dryly analyze and dissect the corpse of music as if in a physiology laboratory, rather than treat music as living, exciting, meaningful matter, to be received by the listener eagerly and in terms of his unique personality, leavened with a healthy skepticism and a sense of humor as well.

In my opinion, there is entirely too much of a hands-off, museumish attitude toward the masterworks of music which, after all, are far from fragile. Music can and has survived quite a bit of manipulation through the ages. One who tussles with it actively, by virtue of energy expended, is much more likely to incorporate its beauty into himself and gain insights denied the more passive devotee.

As a consequence of this line of thought, I have endeavored to vivify the data in *Music Through The Ages* to its logical limits, without falling into the easy expedient of being merely anecdotal or condescendingly over-simplified. I have attempted whenever tenable to link past with present and have kept technicalities to a minimum. For instance, the reader will not find a skeletal outline of the elements of music or an illustrated catalogue of musical instruments for the simple reason that these topics are adequately dealt with elsewhere and, in abbreviated form, are often meaningless or superfluous to the tyro. I have also omitted scores, again incomprehensible to many laymen and in any case now happily available in publications such as those listed at the conclusion of each chapter.

No foreign publications or periodical references are included in "Suggestions for Further Reading" because they too are often inaccessible to the average person, important as they may be to such a study. Softcover editions of books about various aspects of music, on the other hand, are extensively noted, as a supplementary benefit comes to him who can economically build an individual reference library. The largely chronological sequence of the original edition has been maintained as it is as serviceable a format as any other. After each chapter is a selected bibliography, a discography, a list of projects and an itemization of technical terms found in that segment. I realize that the "Opportunities for Study in Depth" often present prospects of doctoral proportions, but the reader is free to pursue these to the extent of his competence and interest. If one discerns repetition, it is in the service of reinforcement of learning. The numerous illustrations are meant to act as visual points of reference to certain facets of each division.

While I have tried to allow ample exposure to all significant aspects of the history of music in Western civilization, I naturally have revealed subjective points of emphasis. These I gladly confess and leave to the critic his own evaluation of their validity. Moreover, some effort ought to be left to instructor or student in the name of individuation and also in recognition of the fact that learning involves a strenuous reorientation if it is to be achieved. A triologue between reader and instructor and, most important of all, living music, should always prevail.

Lastly, I come to the pleasant task of acknowledging assistance from a number of sources: from Misses Joanna Messerschmidt, Kay Weber and Marguerite Lansing for materials dealing with Roman Catholic liturgy; from the Free Public Library of Trenton, N.J., Veronica Carey,

Director, for cheerful aid in tracking down elusive bits of information; to Dr. Muriel Eldridge and Edith Dunn Hartman, M.A., for invaluable typing and proofreading; to Fred B. Rogers, M.D., for generous field-work; to Olga Gratch Gorelli and Anna-Marie Chirico, M.D. for translations; to Drs. Roger McKinney of Trenton State College, Christopher Hatch of Columbia University and Gordon Myers of Columbia College, Columbia, S.C., for helpful comments; to two decades of students who taught me much; and to my editor, Mr. Richard H. Miller of G. P. Putnam's Sons, who was ever cooperative.

Elizabeth E. Rogers
Trenton, N.J.
January, 1967.

Preface

TO THE SECOND EDITION

In our introduction to the first edition of *Music Through The Ages* (1932) we said:

"Music Through The Ages is designed as a tool for the student to pick out the salient points in the long and vivid story of music, with no intention to be encyclopedic. Although primarily for the student, it is written also with the idea of enticing the layman and stimulating him to acquire information about the varying phases of music since its genesis through the era in which he lives; and to leave with him some inkling as to what may come in the future."

This is still our purpose but we would add that we want this book to assist readers in their understanding of radio, recorded, and concert-hall music and to be an effective textbook in the classroom and in the home.

We hope that we have succeeded in proving that music has had its "ups and downs," sometimes rising to great heights and sometimes lapsing to uninspired "lows." Every art has a beginning, its period of experiment, its highest flight, its decline, followed by a wholesome, if sometimes unwelcome, birth of new ideas, which form the nucleus of new procedures. It is the way of all healthy and lusty art. This can be plainly witnessed and traced in poetry and painting even in a most elementary study of classicism and realism to an inevitable adaptivism (a happy mixture of digestible elements in any art).

Because music stretches into the future before the ears and eyes of those who can hear, we have related music to life. We have given it practical as well as aesthetic values in order to proclaim its stamina throughout the ages as a living, progressive, and essential art . . . despite its ever recurring and wholesome surface and later-to-be-discarded "queernesses." Its queernesses are like the awkwardness of youth, uncomfortable, clumsy today, forgotten tomorrow. You will have this revealed to you as you become familiar with this book. In this way we hope, among other things, to help our readers to a tolerance of the new and a willingness to listen and to wait. We also hope to convince our readers of the importance of the early stages of music history.

The scope of this book may be amplified by making use of the lists of suggested reading at the end of each chapter, as we have used them for our bibliography.

It is not necessary to read *Music Through The Ages* from cover to cover, although we hope you will. You may progress chronologically from section to section according to the subject under discussion, in the classroom or out of it, and in this way achieve the progressive unity at which we have aimed.

Finally, we leave *Music Through The Ages* to you, as a key to unlock some of the infinite chambers of the most elusive of the arts. Should you succeed in this the authors will rejoice.

A word of thanks is due Robert Haven Schauffler whose *Beethoven: The Man Who Freed Music* has been a valuable source book. Most stimulating, too, was *The Unknown Brahms: His Life, Character and Works, Based on New Material.* In addition we are indebted to Mr. Schauffler for permitting us to use information from his *Florestan: The Life and Work of Robert Schumann.* We canont end the annals of our gratitude without expressing our profound appreciation to Curt Sachs for permitting us to quote and use information from his altogether fascinating books, packed with new material: *World History of the Dance, The History of Musical Instruments, The Rise of Music in the Ancient World East and West.* To Gustave Reese we wish to proffer our thanks for his able book *Music in the Middle Ages,* from which we have quoted occasionally, and to Paul Henry Lang for his encyclopedic *Music in Western Civilization.* Also to Cyr de Brant do we give thanks for his wisdom in counsel on such matters as concern the lives and works of Orlando Lasso, Palestrina, and material concerning the music of the early Christian era. *The International Cyclopedia of Music and Musicians* (Oscar Thompson, editor) has proved invaluable. And we thank Cecily Lichtenstadt for timely suggestions.

A new chapter on Latin-American music will prove, we hope, to be a timely addition. We must thank the Thomas Y. Crowell Company for its generosity in lending us the proofs of Nicolas Slonimsky's *Music in Latin America,* which was invaluable as source material; also in granting us permission to quote from its pages. The chapter was enhanced in value by material from the National Broadcasting Company's handbooks of the University of the Air, *Music of the New World: Music in American Cities* and *Folkways in Music.* We are grateful for permission to quote from them. We also thank Gilbert Chase for his kindness in lending us the proofs of his bulletin *Guide to*

Latin American Music, and for permission to quote from his published writings, the NBC handbooks, and his illuminating book, *The Music of Spain,* published by W. W. Norton.

We thank Aaron Copland, one of our American composers who is an authority on contemporary conditions, and his publisher, Whittlesey House, for quotations from *Our New Music.*

We also wish to point out that the name of this book was suggested by *Art through the Ages,* Helen Gardner's most admirable book, and that Noel Payne, eminent radio technician, has been kind enough to give us many an idea for our radio chapter.

MARION BAUER AND ETHEL PEYSER

MacDowell Colony, Peterborough, N. H.,
and New York City

Acknowledgments

The editor gratefully acknowledges permission to reproduce quotations from the following books and articles:

Henry Adams. *Mont Saint Michel and Chartres*. Houghton Mifflin Co. © 1905, 1933.

A. L. Bacharach, ed. *Lives of the Great Composers*. Vols. II and III. Penguin Books Ltd. © 1935.

Anthony Baines, ed. *Musical Instruments through the Ages*. Penguin Books Ltd. © 1961.

Arthur H. Benade. *Horns, Strings and Harmony*. Doubleday and Co., Inc. © 1960.

Hans von Bülow-Richard Strauss Correspondence. Boosey Hawkes G. m. b. H. Bonn. © 1953. English translation © 1955 by Hawkes and Son (London) Ltd.

Paul Collaer. *A History of Modern Music*. The World Publishing Co. © 1961.

Aaron Copland. *Music and Imagination*. Harvard University Press. © 1952, by the President and Fellows of Harvard College.

Alfred Einstein. *A Short History of Music*. Alfred A. Knopf, Inc. © 1937, 1938, 1954.

Alfred Einstein. *Music in the Romantic Era*. W. W. Norton and Co., Inc. © 1947.

Hayes M. Fuhr. *Fundamentals of Choral Expression*. University of Nebraska Press. © 1944.

Kahlil Gibran. *The Prophet*. Alfred A. Knopf, Inc. © 1923.

Peter S. Hansen. *An Introduction to Twentieth-Century Music*. Allyn and Bacon, Inc. © 1961.

Friedrich Heer. *The Medieval World*. Tr. by Janet Sondheimer. The World Publishing Co. © 1963.

Paul Hindemith. *A Composer's World*. Harvard University Press. © 1947, by the President and Fellows of Harvard College.

Heinrich Eduard Jacob. *Felix Mendelssohn and His Times*. Tr. by Richard and Clara Winston. Prentice-Hall, Inc. © 1963.

Arthur Jacobs, ed. *Choral Music*. Penguin Books Ltd. © 1963.

Bernard Jacobson. "The 'In' Composer." *High Fidelity.* © 1966.

Irving Kolodin. *The Composer As Listener.* Horizon Press. © 1958.

Susanne K. Langer. *Feeling and Form.* Charles Scribner's Sons. © 1956.

René Leibowitz. *Schoenberg and His School.* Philosophical Library. © 1949.

Irving Lowens. *Music and Musicians in Early America.* W. W. Norton and Co., Inc. © 1964.

Joseph Machlis. *Introduction to Contemporary Music.* W. W. Norton and Co., Inc. © 1961.

Leonard B. Meyer. *Emotion and Meaning in Music.* The University of Chicago Press. © 1956.

Edna St. Vincent Millay. *Collected Poems.* Harper and Row, Inc. © 1928, 1955 by Edna St. Vincent Millay and Norma Millay Ellis.

Robert Nathan. *The Green Leaf and Other Poems.* Alfred A. Knopf, Inc. © 1950.

Carl Parrish. *A Treasury of Early Music.* W. W. Norton and Co., Inc. © 1958.

Reinhold Pauly. *Music in the Classic Period.* Prentice-Hall, Inc. © 1965.

Ezra Pound. *The Spirit of Romance.* J. M. Dent. © 1932.

Robertson, Alec, ed. *Chamber Music.* Penguin Books Ltd. © 1957.

Alec Robertson and Denis Stevens, eds. *Pelican History of Music.* Vols. II and III. Penguin Books Ltd. © 1960, 1963.

Curt Sachs. *Our Musical Heritage.* Prentice-Hall, Inc. © 1955.

Lew Sarett. *Covenant with Earth.* University of Florida Press. © 1956 by Alma Johnson Sarett.

Marcel Schneider. *Schubert.* Tr. by Elizabeth Poston. Grove Press. © 1959.

Harold C. Schonberg. "Books in Review." *The New York Times.* © 1966.

Madame Anil de Silva, Professor Otto von Simson, Roger Hinks and Philip Troutman, eds. *Man through His Art: Music.* Vol. II. New York Graphic Society. © 1964.

Igor Stravinsky. *The Poetics of Music.* Harvard University Press. © 1952, by the President and Fellows of Harvard College.

Gerhart von Westerman. *The Concert Guide.* Tr. by Cornelius Cardew. Arco Publishing Co., Inc. © 1963.

Jack A. Westrup. *An Introduction to Musical History.* London: Hutchinson University Library. New York: Harper and Row. © 1955.

Contents

CONTENTS

Part VII: MUSIC OF EARLY ROMANTICISM

CONTENTS

26

PART IX: MUSIC OF THE UNITED STATES

CONTENTS 29

Prelude

M USIC through the ages has had a universal appeal because of
its intimate relationship with social, religious, scientific, political
and aesthetic facets of life. Through the ages music has been a document of human experience—recorded in movement and sound. Although the beginning is shrouded in that period which antedates man's
annals, it seems reasonable to assume, on the basis of such evidence as
we have for study and formation of hypotheses, that shortly after the
man-ape descended from the trees and discovered elementary means of
survival on earth, he pursued his curiosity about the functions of sounds
—his own, those he heard and those he produced. An eminent scholar,
Curt Sachs, has classified relics of musical instruments as belonging to
the Stone Ages.

In delving into the misty pre-history of music, we also may deduce
that the "sources of musical imagery," to use Machlis' excellent phrase,
are relatively constant. To whatever extent our present preoccupation
with music as a species of entertainment and a source of potential self-
knowledge blinds us to the utilitarian role of music in the life of early
man, we perceive that human existence through the ages has a curious
commonality. From studies of folksong and music of contemporary
primitives we can discern fundamentals of what music is "about" and,
perhaps, has always been. Music through the ages has been closely involved with all phases of life: birth and death; the past, present and,
sometimes, the future; love, work, religion, play, war and peace—as
well as the myriad other occurrences that arouse emotions within us,
be they joyous, comedic or tragic. An infinite variety of difference ever
reveals itself, but a variance in degree of sophistication or abstraction,
not necessarily dissimilarity in the musical "subject matter" itself.

A long road but a direct one led from savage rites, by way of pagan
ceremony, to church ritual as we know it. Until less than three centuries ago, organized religion directed the trend of music even as it

influenced sculpture, painting and literature. Dionysian hymnody, Hebrew psalms, plainsong, the motets and Masses of Palestrina and others of the Italian and Franco-Belgian schools provide convincing examples. Vocal music predominated.

Traveling along a parallel highway, the music of the people has come down through the ages. Their songs and dances have formed the basis of all secular music and of practically all instruments and instrumental forms. Out of the accompaniment for dancing came the classical suite of Bach and his contemporaries, which gave way to the sonatas of Haydn, Mozart and Beethoven. In turn, when the revolt against Classicism produced Romanticism, music, following in the wake of the other arts, fell into smaller and more integrated forms, better adapted to the need of a more subjective expression, such as we find in Chopin, Schumann and Debussy.

We are now living in a time of experimentation and transition comparable to such momentous periods as the fifteenth century when *organum* gave way to *ars nova*; the end of the sixteenth century, leading to the birth of opera; and, again, the beginning of the nineteenth century, when the declaration of personal independence burst forth as the Romantic movement. Realizing that the story of music is a record of mutations, we should be prepared for the inevitability of change taking place under our own ears, and, furthermore, to understand the normality of present-day trends. Instead of being discouraged at what seems to be shattering of tested musical customs, we should be stimulated, and acknowledge the fact that art grows by adapting itself to its own era.

*   *   *   *   *

How does one approach the study of music, spanning as it does such a length of time and a multiplicity of events? How can one hope to gain insight and understanding of so vast a literature, abounding with problems of intent, style and technicalities of performance? One can embark on the long voyage of attaining control and skill upon a musical instrument, savoring as much music as he can upon what may well be a lifetime adventure. Indeed, music-making is the most direct route to music itself. On the other hand, one may choose to immerse himself in the very elements of musical substance—melody, harmony, rhythm, sound production, form and dynamics—the *theory* of music. Analysis and solution of innumerable musical logarithms will undoubtedly lead to enlightenment and the possession of keen-edged tools of musical artisanship. Yet neither of these avenues, granting an unlikely perfection is reached, can alone suffice for a comprehensive study of music.

One must also listen. Susanne K. Langer writes that listening is the "primary musical activity."

> The real basis of music appreciation is the same as of music-making: the recognition of forms in virtual time, charged with the vital import of all art, the ways of human feeling . . . Anything [the listener does or thinks of] that helps concentration and sustains the illusion—be it inward singing, following a half-comprehended score, or dreaming in dramatic images—may be one's personal way to understanding.

But, one may reply, we all listen. In fact, it is difficult to escape from listening, with the static of the automobile radio, the blare of the sidewalk transistor and the token nods of television networks assaulting our ears from every direction, competing with the highly audible emanations of high-fi and stereo phonograph and tape mechanisms. Do we, however, in reality hear the music at all? Or do we rather passively accept these organized sounds as just another component of our noisy, throbbing modern civilization?

Musical listening is a complex affair including many levels of perception. "What most people relish is hardly music· it is rather a drowsy revery relieved by nervous thrills," as philosopher Santayana puts it. By analogy, the effects of music on a listener are often comparable to those of a warm bath at the end of day, or the caress of a gentle, cooling breeze on a steamy evening. That this is so does not imply that there is anything wrong with such a reaction. In fact, it is a completely natural one, as our physical sense equipment is finely tuned and responsive to the phenomenon of sound, as is that of many animals.

Who has not observed a pet dog howling at the stimuli of certain pitches? Why did the cowboy persist in his droning croon except that it seemed to have a sedating influence on his restless herd? Similarly, why should the military establishment bother to maintain countless brass bands except that their stirring martial airs affect the legs and disciplined reflexes of the troops? Why does one's favorite restaurant supply with each culinary offering a sauce of subdued instrumental music, but that it is salutary in aiding one's digestive juices? Sound, working through the agency of the sympathetic nervous system, does induce specific physiological changes in our bodies. That fact is incontestable.

If, however, we limit our musical responsiveness to the solely physical or sensory (which, it happens, is literally impossible), we make ourselves immune to the riches music can bring. Another level of musical response, often termed emotive or associative, true of most of us most of the time within the periphery of some sort of music, is acknowledged by such remarks as "that reminds me of . . ." or "that makes me feel . . ." In the course of this kind of reaction, a listener is adding his emotional inventory to that of the music, either through fantasy or memory, thereby involving himself on a personal stratum of feeling with the composed material. He is selecting, by means of his own personality, elements of music that are meaningful to him—"dreaming in dramatic images." It is on the emotive or associative plane that music therapy often works wonders with deeply disturbed or withdrawn victims of mental illness. It is on this basis, moreover, that many of us may express a preference for program music which offers the listener extra-musical stimulation. Our emotive responses are as varied as we ourselves. "To some people music is like food; to others like medicine; to others like a fan."

We can add another order of response to music which augments our comprehension and enjoyment that is intellectual in essence. A listener may utilize resources of his knowledge of music, of its history, of its conventions, of its structure, to invest the activity with a more profound significance. He may proceed augustly across St. Mark's Square in Venice to the cadence of Gabrieli's brasses; he may regard with awe the masterful economy and resultant unobstructed tension as Beethoven manipulates his famous four-note theme in the first movement of the *Fifth Symphony*; he may apprehend vicariously something of savagery through Stravinsky's masterful orchestration of *The Rite of Spring*. By developing an "educated" ear, the informed listener is able to superpose an entirely new and powerful measure to his relationship with music.

Ideally, listening to music requires all three categories of responses: the physical, emotional and intellectual. Nor is there any rigid separation between them, save for the necessity of putting them down on paper. Total listening enmeshes them simultaneously, more or less, depending upon the individual and those capacities he submits to the musical experience.

To return, however, to our initial question—do we really hear the music that is all around us? Byron wrote in *Don Juan* that "there's music in all things, if men had ears." Listening to music, nevertheless, requires far more of us than ears alone. It demands concentration and the ability and willingness to "sustain the illusion." In return for these we are enabled to gain access to yet another set of comments on the accumulated data of human existence. We "develop a sense of values about art," indicates Norman dello Joio, "and learn about another dimension of reality previously hidden."

A common disillusionment encountered by a student of music history occurs when he discovers that learning about music is not such an easy matter as he may have previously imagined. Robert Schumann wrote truly when he stated that "the study of the history of music and the hearing of masterworks of different epochs will speediest of all cure you of vanity and self-adoration." An enormous literature in score, a unique technical vocabulary and the very sublime abstraction of music which "begins where words end" all serve to baffle the tyro. "Music is the vapor of art," says Victor Hugo. "It is to poetry what reverie is to thought, what fluid is to liquid, what the ocean of clouds is to the ocean of waves." A variety of problems would seem to arise, not the least of which is that "the differences between the music of one age and the next are not simple." Sir Jack Westrup comments:

> There are differences in technique, in approach, in environment. Music is affected by the circles for which it is intended: it may be written for a cultured aristocracy, for the great public of music-lovers, or for a mutual admiration society. Though its appeal is the same for every age, there is always a difference in the terms in which emotion is expressed. In consequence, though it may continue to give delight to music-lovers of succeeding ages, it can never mean exactly the same to them as it did to those who first heard it. Our environment, our reactions, our first impressions are different from those of our forefathers. The music which comes to us from the past has to pass through the veil of our own experience.

*   *   *   *   *

Music Through the Ages is designed to aid the serious student—be he in a college class, a conservatory, a secondary school or his own living-room armchair—to meet and wrest with some of the issues posed by the study of the history of music. We make no claim to be encyclopedic, a false claim that can at best only result in superficiality. Nor, moreover, do we pretend that any book can substitute for actual listening, in concert performances or through recordings. A text can serve, however, to telescope experience, to suggest stimulating challenges and to provide pertinent information that heightens a listener's awareness of one of the most profound and meaningful arts.

PART I
Primitive and Ancient Music

Chapter 1.

MUSIC OF PRIMITIVE MAN

Over and under
The shaking sky,
The war-drums thunder
When I dance by!—
Ho! a warrior proud,
I dance on a cloud,
For my ax shall feel
The enemy reel;
My heart shall thrill
To a bloody kill,—
Ten Sioux dead
Split open of head!—

Look! to the West!—
The sky-line drips,—
Blood from the breast!
Blood from the lips!
Ho! when I dance by,
The war-drums thunder
Over and under
The shaking sky.
Beat, beat on the drums,
For the Thunderbird comes.
Wuh!
Wuh!

—LEW SARETT, *Iron-Wind Dances*

GENESIS OF MUSIC

The genesis of music as a form of human activity is as yet unexplained and probably will remain hidden in the mysterious eons of a fathomless past. Lingering notes of the tunes have long since died; the instruments of cane, wood or horn have disintegrated and the dancers have been stilled. Aside from a few durable artifacts, whose age and function are subject to dispute, little else remains. Fortunately, however, all primitive peoples seem to share the same general experiences and we have been able to learn something of the earliest stages of music through studying the savage wherever we find him. In this age, which we are wont to call ultramodern, all phases of civilization are represented, from the primitive to the sophisticated. The Bushman of Africa exists in the same world which has produced the learned university professor, and the professor comes from stock which was once as primitive as the Bushman. This overlapping of eras gives us the opportunity to discover traits common to early man in all periods.

ETHNOMUSICOLOGY

Scholars in the field of **comparative musicology** or **ethnomusicology**, as this study is sometimes called, range through undeveloped areas all over the world, recording, notating and observing the music and the musical behavior of peoples still dwelling in conditions similar to those of the Stone Age. Remote from civilization until only recently, these tribes may be able to guide us to a better understanding of the origins of music. With the penetration now made possible by swift means of transportation, however, we have arrived at a point where some sort of cultural conservation is imperative. In much the same manner as the newly independent African nations are striving to preserve from extinction the fast-disappearing flora and fauna of their countries, so researchers are avidly at work gathering data before inevitable adulteration distorts and destroys these primary sources of primitive music-making and music-use.

We do know that the materials out of which music is made are thousands of years old. Scales, instruments and notation are the results, not of fixed and deliberate development, but of centuries of experimentation and application of processes sometimes with purpose, but as often accidental. Much time passed before man succeeded in organizing language and in understanding the forces of nature. Think of the terror of primitive man in the face of natural phenomena which we accept as ordinary occurrences. Consider how long it was before music was anything but crude rhythmic patterns and equally raw snatches of melody. The savage gave vent to his feelings of joy and grief in bodily motions, and accompanied them by rhythmic noises. What he enacted in pantomime or expressed in grunts and shouts gradually became dance and song. Long before music was subjected to codification, it was man's means of spontaneous emotional expression. Before it could become either an art or a science, a musical language had to be developed. This language has varied greatly among different peoples and at different periods.

MUSICAL TONE

Because we are concerned here with beginnings and fundamental bases of the art of music, it might be well to digress for a moment from our discussion of the music of primitive man to a consideration of the stuff of music itself—**tone.** What is tone? How is it defined? How is it perceived? How is it produced and reproduced?

Tone is the result of **vibration,** which Webster defines as "periodic motion of the particles of an elastic body or medium in alternately opposite directions from the position of equilibrium when that equilibrium has been disturbed . . ." This concept may be visualized in the common illustration of a pendulum, which is no more than a weight suspended from a rod or string. When the weight, through the application of a force, is set into motion, it swings back and forth in a regular manner. Because of the quality of *regularity,* the speed of *oscillation* (the complete swing) is measurable, and such measurement of cycles is termed *c.p.s.* (cycles per second) or **frequency.** The distance the vibrating surface covers from its point of equilibrium is known as **amplitude.** It follows that the more energy used to disturb the equilibrium, the greater the amplitude; the faster the cycles per second, the greater the frequency.

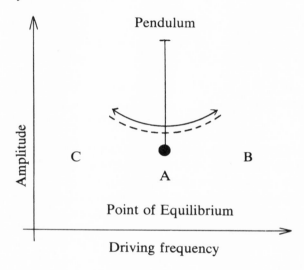

A vibrates between B and C

Fig. 1. Illustrating the action of a pendulum (*see text*).

The pendulum is not, of course, a musical instrument. Nor is tone such a simple matter as the foregoing elementary explanation may imply. Within each musical tone, if we dissect it, we discover a cluster composed of a *fundamental* and an infinite series of *partials, harmonics,* or *overtones* (synonymous terms for our purposes), not necessarily audible to the human ear, but physically demonstrable. An engineer, Arthur H. Benade, makes the following comment:

> A complex system can vibrate in a whole set of different ways, called modes of vibration. We generally rank these in order of increasing vibrational frequency, and the frequency of the lowest mode is often called the "fundamental" frequency. If the system is such that its higher modes vibrate at frequencies which are integral multiples of the fundamental, we can say that these higher frequencies are *harmonics* of the fundamental.

In other words, any tone generates a series of overtones which exist in an inexorable order that the following notation illustrates. A simple experiment will confirm the existence of overtones. Depress the second, third, fourth and fifth partials silently on a piano. Keeping the keys down, strike the fundamental C with some force. Listen to the result. Depending on the resonance of the instrument, all five partials will be audible.

Overtone Series

Partials 1   2   3   4   5   6   7   8   9 10 11 12 13 14 15 16
Fundamental

Fig. 2. Overtone series.

Some scholars have used the phenomenon of the overtone series to explain the entire history of musical materials; and there is certainly some truth in such a generalization, although like all preconceived theories it suffers from needs of qualification and omission. The perfect intervals of octave, fifth and fourth would seem to predate the interval of a major third in historical musical usage; and basic harmonic materials would seem to follow the overtone through the sixth partial. The parenthesized seventh, eleventh, thirteenth and fourteenth partials do not, however, coincide with the pitches of our tempered scales. As Persichetti notes, "The acoustician's observations are useful to the composer only if blended with artistic intuition."

Webster's Dictionary defines musical tone as "sound having such regularity of vibration as to impress the ear with its individual character." It is distinguished from its parent, sound, by regularity of vibration (usually transmitted through the medium of air), and from its stepbrother, noise, by the fact that it is measurable and dependable, rather than random and varied.

In order to experience the sensation of hearing, our aural organ, the ear, is essential. Hearing is an enormously complicated process, explanations of which are best left to experts in physics, medicine and psychology. For our purposes, however, we may say that sound vibrations enter the outer, mechanical organ which, in turn, alters and selects among these vibrations before they are converted into nerve impulses conveyed to the brain. The "educated" ear is responsible for transforming the physical properties of tone—frequency, amplitude and vibration mixture—into the corresponding musical properties of **pitch** (location of a tone in relation to height or depth of sound), **volume** (the loudness or softness of a tone) and **tone color** or *timbre* (the individual quality of a tone). Needless to say, a fourth tonal property is mandatory, that of **duration** (the length of time vibration is maintained).

All of us free from severe physical impairment possess a very special instrument for producing sounds and musical tones. That instrument is the voice. We set the vocal cords in vibration through the impulse of our breath. Fuhr notes: "It is one of the natural wonders of this fascinating mechanism that these slim bands in the larynx can, through the coordination of ear, mind and larynx, execute the correct number of vibrations per second to produce instantaneously single tones or scales of great rapidity." Resonation is supplied by means of bony cavities with which we have been endowed, "against which the speaking and singing voice may resound and be reinforced."

It is but a short step from producing sounds with our voices to creating percussive noises by clapping the hands, slapping the knees or stamping the ground. Yet another elementary extension is required to seize upon convenient materials of nature lying about us which can, through simple manipulations, create sound or musical tones. Several well-known examples will suffice to illustrate this point.

There are very few children who at one time or another have not stretched a blade of grass in their cupped hands and produced a sound by blowing upon it. This primitive procedure demonstrates in essence the principle of a vibrating reed. Who has not at one time or another tried blowing across the aperture of a soft-drink bottle? Vibrations are effected in the body of the vessel which result in sound. Stretch a rubber band to a point of tension and pluck it. A dull but recognizable tone can be heard. Stretch it farther and a higher tone follows. Allow it to go slack and nothing is heard, for the reason that the amplitude is insufficient to stimulate a response from the human hearing apparatus, of which meaningful reception of amplitude or intensity is limited in range; that is, a whisper measures 10 to 20 decibels, while sounds over 130 decibels are painfully unpleasant.

The extreme range of human hearing is approximately from 16 cycles to 15,000 or 16,000 per second. This is called the audible or audio range. Sixteen cycles per second give us the lowest register of sound vibrations that we can perceive. This would be a bit below the range of a thirty-foot organ pipe which is measured at about 16.15 cycles. The latter tone and those lower are "felt," not heard. They wrack the ear, so slow are the vibrations. (One probably remembers hearing an organ tone in church which was distinctly disturbing.) In the realm of from 15,000 to 16,000 cycles we get the squeak of a door or the chirp of an insect. These high vibrations are most essential in the reproduction of harmonics. They give music its natural vitality and richness and in all ranges effect differences in instrumental *timbres*.

Sixteen cycles is far below A_4, 27.50 cycles or the fourth A below middle C (256 cycles, vibrations or audio-frequencies). Sixteen thousand cycles is much higher than c^4 or four C's above middle C. It might be interesting to say here that our orchestras tune themselves to A, or 440 cycles, usually given to them by oboe. This is called **international pitch**. The frequency range of the orchestra is from contrabassoon (B_4, 30.87 cycles) to piccolo (d^4, 4,186 cycles), not counting the harmonics or overtones.

WHAT CAME FIRST

One enters an arena when he commences to speculate about what element of music "came first." It is far easier to contradict the theoretical arguments advanced for this or that than it is to agree upon a decisive answer. For instance, Charles Darwin, whose theory of evolution evoked whole new lines of thought in the nineteenth century, hypothesized that the origins of music lay in modes of courtship, possibly based upon the mating songs of birds. Studies of bird song, however, indicate that birds sing for many reasons. This, in addition to the dearth of love songs among primitives, would seem to negate such an argument. Bücher's idea that music originated among workmen who utilized its stimulus to ease the burdens of labor is apparently obviated by the fact that work songs among primitives are comparatively rare, and oftentimes do not exist at all. The relationships of the origins of music to the intonations of language also seem cloudy when tested by fact. We simply do not yet know whether rhythm preceded melody, whether vocal music arose before instrumental music, whether it happened simultaneously or was indeed the benevolent gift of the gods.

It is possible that prehistoric man made noises much as a child does, and finding them pleasing or curious, he repeated them until he was almost hypnotized by the sound of his own voice. He may have relayed them for the criticism of his fellows. If they liked the sounds, they may have joined him in singing, and thus a relationship between the tones may have developed, based on the ease with which they could be sung. It is natural to suppose that the first musical instruments were those which marked rhythm, for, after all, early man could not have been wholly insensitive to the wealth of rhythm in his natural world—the rhythm of the seasons, of the winds, of the waters and of his own breathing.

As already noted, nature has given us two sets of percussion instruments, our hands and our feet; we have evidence of their early usage.

The next step might have been to knock pieces of wood together; then to hollow out a tree trunk and to stretch an animal skin across the top to make a drum. "Rhythmic patterns of movement, the plastic sense of space, the vivid representation of a world seen and imagined," writes Curt Sachs in his *World History of the Dance,* "these things man creates in his own body in the dance before he uses substance and stone and word to give expression to his inner experiences."

CHARACTERISTICS OF PRIMITIVE MUSIC

One feature of the music of primitive man on which all authorities seem at one is its nonaesthetic nature. Both instruments and songs reflect its magical and functional *raison d'être* in the life of early peoples. The concept of music as entertainment was reached only after a long journey through the ages. Another general characteristic of the music of primitive man is its lack of a theoretical system and, of course, of a means of notation. It is characterized both by spontaneity and improvisation and, at the same time, by reliance upon a miniscule repertory of *formulae* or tribal traditions. Perhaps for the latter reason, yet another feature is its singular repetitiveness, to our ears often resulting in monotony.

On the affirmative side, however, we can discern clues, sometimes remarkably unmodified, of threads used in the tapestry of Western music as we know it today. The endless singsong of tribal chanters, encompassing as it does but two or three tones and completely subordinated to the focus of the text, is reminiscent of early Christian chanting, as well as the rope-jumping dronings of American sidewalks. The alternation of solo and refrain is discovered again in the singing of psalms of the Roman liturgy as well as on that all-American favorite, the community sing. The question and answer technique of combining phrases appears in the *ouvert* and *clos* of medieval dances as well as in the imperfect and perfect cadences of standard harmonic practice.

PRIMITIVE MUSICAL INSTRUMENTS

Perhaps most significant, however, is the formulation of the rudiments of musical instruments. Practically all types of instruments existing today can be traced from those of savages and ancient nations. These fall into three distinct classes grouped according to the means of tone production: percussion (beaten or struck) instruments; wind (blown) instruments; and stringed (plucked or bowed) instruments.

Associated with responding to or underlining bodily movements of the ritualistic dance, as well as with communication, percussion instruments as found in primitive cultures range from the very crudest to moderately complex varieties. They include many species of rattles, utilizing dry seeds, seashells and twigs; scrapers of bone, horn and gourds; "ground" instruments in which a hole in the earth acts as resonator; slabs of rocks used as drums or gongs; xylophones of stone, bamboo and hollow tree-trunks; and a wealth of drums, including single-skin drums, double-skin drums, frame drums (such as the tambourine) and friction drums (in which a flexible surface is rubbed).

Primitive wind instruments are found in the forms of flutes, trumpets and reeds. There are even examples of phenomena resembling the Aeolian harps of the nineteenth century (suspended mechanisms of strings and sound-boxes whose vibrations are set in motion by the wind). Bone flutes have been discovered that date back to the earliest Stone Age, although we do not know whether the holes were fingered or merely ornamental. Flutes are often strongly associated with magic beliefs. Wachsmann writes, "Even in the small area around Lake Victoria the following roles are played by flutes: preventers of storms, makers of rain, encouragers of the flow of milk from the cow's udder during milking, symbols of defloration, givers of life to the divine ruler, and voices that are personal possessions and must not be imitated."

Trumpets include a whole array of horns and conchs (instruments utilizing large spiral seashells of several *genera*), again closely associated with magico-religious functions, although used largely for signaling purposes much as bugles are today. We know of the existence of bands of trumpets through the explorer Vasco da Gama's notes of his reception when he landed on African shores. Primitive reed instruments have been found in Africa and from Arabia to the Far East.

Among primitive peoples, stringed instruments are the least developed group. This is understandable when we remember that the preponderantly vocal and rhythmic character of aboriginal music does not necessitate the development of melodic instruments; also, the more perishable stringed instruments are too fragile for savage use. There are, however, zithers, harps, lyres and lutes in plenty, all of which are probably descended from the prototype of the hunting bow as a musical instrument. There is extant a cave painting in France, dating from approximately 15,000 B.C., in which a man disguised under a buffalo skin holds a bow to his face, apparently "playing" it. Whether the hunting bow or the musical bow was the progenitor of the other, or each developed independently, is not certain, but its antiquity is unquestioned.

Before closing our discussion of the music of primitive man, it will be of interest to take a closer look at the music of American aborigines, of which there are numerous families, each with its own spoken language, songs, instruments and traditions; yet, even without a common

Fig. 3. Cree singer Buffy Sainte-Marie playing the mouth bow. Whether the hunting bow or the musical bow as the progenitor of the other is uncertain, but its antiquity is unquestioned. (Courtesy Arthur Schatz, *Life* Magazine © Time Inc.)

system, all tribes disclose similar traits characteristic of primitive music in general and of the red man in particular. Revealing the inner life of a primitive man, the Indian's song is a record of birth, marriage and death; of his gods and of his entire experience. He has ceremonial songs, dream songs, weather and medicinal incantations, war, hunting and children's songs, personal narratives, chief and council songs, songs of legends and heroic individuals, and dance and game songs.

MUSIC OF THE AMERICAN ABORIGINES

In general, the primitives of the extremes of North and South America have the sparsest musical resources. It is reported that the inhabitants of Tierra del Fuego have no instruments as such. Instead, they pound the ground with poles, bellow into their hands cupped against the earth, blow into the windpipe of a bird or simply beat sticks against the frame of the festival hut.

In contrast, among the Eskimo, we do find accounts of a *kilaut,* or frame drum, constructed by stretching the viscera of whale, walrus or deer over a bone frame. This tambourine-like instrument is attached to a handle of carved and painted bone, and beaten with a whalebone drumstick (*kentum*). The explorer Charles Hall writes:

When the drum is played, the drum-handle is held in the left hand of the performer, who strikes the edge of the rim, opposite to that over which the skin is stretched. He holds the drum in different positions, but keeps it in a constant fan-like motion by his hand and by the blows of the *kentum* struck alternately on the opposite side of the edge. Skillfully keeping the drum vibrating on the handle, he accompanies this with grotesque motions of the body, and at intervals with song, while the women keep up their own Innuit songs, one after the other, through the whole performance.

Eskimo songs may be roughly divided into two groups: one comprises folk songs, game songs and magic songs, which are handed down unchanged through generations; and the other, dance songs or "topical" songs which are popular for a short time and then disappear.

Among the aborigines of Canada and the United States, music as an extension of tribal life was always present, but never achieved any degree of sophistication or independence. Artifacts on display in museums throughout the country show that Indian musical products were more decorative than aurally satisfying. Their most important use was as accompaniment to the gyrations of the *shaman,* or medicine man. Rattles of hundreds of shapes, sizes and materials have existed; the Chippewa used birchbark; the Yaquis, cactus rib; the Pima, palm seeds; the Zuni, parts of deer; the Plains Indians dried and looped buffalo tails. Flutes, whistles, bull-roarers, whizzers and scrapers are found in abundance; and, more rarely, mention is made of horns (the Mimacs of New Brunswick), musical bows (among the California Indians) and rudimentary fiddles (the Apaches). The drum, however, played almost as large a role in Indian life as it did in African music. It assumed forms of single, double-skin and frame drums and was manufactured of the most diverse materials, including logs, pottery, turtle shells, closely woven grass and dried hides. Water drums were common. Many savages believed that a drum, large or small, had the power of prediction, so its uses were manifold. George Catlin, in his *Memoirs* (1848), describes the following scene:

> Sioux women sing with the men during dancing-songs. At gatherings of the Sioux, one man acts as the leader of the singers who sit around the drum. The number at the drum vary with the size of the gathering. If many are dancing, the singers sit as close as possible around the drum, each man beating the drum as he sings. Sometimes ten men can sit at a drum. If a singer at the drum becomes tired, he lays down his stick and someone who has been dancing or looking on takes his place. Most songs may be repeated any number of times, the leader giving the signal for the end by sharp taps on the drum, after which the song is sung only once more.

An Indian's love for his drum is proverbial. When the Ojibways traveled, for instance, they always carried a hidden drum with which to entertain themselves during rest periods. Rivalry among gifted drummers of the tribe once led to contests that were akin to the medieval competitions of *Minnesingers* in the German Middle Ages. Because drumbeat and voice do not always synchronize, Indian rhythms often seem complicated to us. It has not been decided whether this is due to a superior rhythmic sense or a defective one.

From the old men and women who are his teachers, an Indian boy learns the history of his tribe and its songs at the same time. The leading tribal drummer and singer, often second to the chief in importance, is regarded as official historian. The Indian's musical scale has not been shaped by centuries of learning nor has he an instrument of the string type (such as a monochord) to help him establish pitch. His scale usually contains five tones—the pentatonic scale of many primitive races, similar to that of the Chinese, Japanese, ancient Greeks, Hindus, Irish, Scots and Anglo-Saxons. Its appearance in widely separated localities, eras, races and stages of civilization substantiates the belief that the range of human experience manifested in ritual and art is universal.

The Indians' music, like that of other primitive music-makers, gradually descends in pitch so that in most songs the final tone is the lowest. The vocal range often covers two octaves and the interval of a fourth is characteristic. Although Indian melodies may sound alike to us, typical intervallic and rhythmic figures distinguish different kinds of songs. An Indian would never mistake, for example, a begging song for a game song, or a buffalo-hunt song for a warpath song. Natalie Curtis comments:

> Also it should be borne in mind that Indian music is essentially for singing. . . . The actual melody can be recorded with its rhythmic accompaniment of drum or rattle. But the rendering of the song,—the vocal embellishment, the strange gutturals, slurs and accents that make Indian singing so distinctive,—all this is altogether too subtle and too much a part of the voice itself to be possible of notation.

When we survey the music of primitive men in Mexico, Central America and South America, we come into contact with much more highly developed cultures than those to the north. The Spaniards reported the existence of a rich native music which was used in sacred ceremonies and secular festivals. As so much of it was cult music and heathenish, early Christian religious teachers attempted to do away with it and to substitute their own in its place. They even destroyed the native instruments. Nicolas Slonimsky writes, in *Music of Latin America:*

Despite this persecution, native music survived, and eventually found its way into community life, and even into the church itself. . . . Christianity and religious primitivism are combined [today] . . . in the festivals and street parades celebrated in Latin-American towns and villages.

This amalgamation of Hispanic and Indian sources is found in different countries as, for example, in a Nicaraguan mystery play and in Peruvian hymns where "Inca chants and Gregorian melodies are sung in alternation."

Mexico City was the center of the Aztec confederacy, a powerful political body for at least two hundred years before Cortes conquered the country, in 1521. The historian William Prescott gives the following account of the overture to Cortes' invasion:

> As the Spaniards drew near, the Indian sentinels took the alarm and fled. The priests, keeping their night-watch on the summit of *teocallis,* instantly caught the tidings and sounded their shells, while the huge drum in the desolate temple of the war-god sent forth those solemn tones, which, heard only in seasons of calamity, sounded through every corner of the capital.

Although the Aztecs used music in their religious and secular ceremonies, it seems to have been somewhat limited in scope. Because of their warlike nature, the Aztecs leaned toward the drums of war and the hunting horn; yet whistles, flutes and pipes, many of terra-cotta and molded into the forms of animals and deities, are abundant (and available at tourist shops today), as well as bells of precious metals and gems.

The Mayan empire extended through Mexico and Central America, dating from about 3000 B.C. It was perhaps the most advanced culture in the Americas, particularly in the field of science. The Mayas were especially interested in astronomy and devised a most accurate calendar, as well as highway systems and great monuments. Unfortunately, the haze of history has obscured evidence of their musical precocity, although they assuredly used music in connection with religious and special rites, with drama and possibly as an art of itself. Drums, rattles, nose and mouth flutes, shell-trumpets and scrapers remain as mute relics of a dispersed civilization now submerged in the greedy tropical rain jungle. Gisèlle Freund writes that:

> Diego Durán (an early Spanish missionary), in his *Historia de las Indias,* tells us that in every city, next to the temples, there stood large houses called *'cuicacalli'* or 'Houses of Song,' where professors of music, song and dance trained young people in these arts so that they might have the professional finish required of the ballet and choral groups that partici-

Fig. 4. "Procession of Musicians"—detail from a wall painting, Bonampak Temple, Mexico, eighth-ninth century A.D. In this Mayan victory procession, we see the percussion section featuring large rattles and drums of turtle shells.

pated in the constant rituals and celebrations. There were songs and dances of great solemnity, with a rhythm measured and austere; others, for less serious occasions, were lighter and sang of love and happiness. Most elaborate of all were those that accompanied the floral offerings to the gods. The richness of the costumes imitating fruits and flowers, birds and animals; the grace of the dancers representing the gods and their worshippers; and the strange and stirring music; all made Durán declare that this was 'the most beautiful and solemn dance this nation possessed', and he never expected to witness again anything more wondrous.

Before Mexico City and Lima, Peru, became cultural centers of the Hispanic period, the ancient cities of Cuzco and Quito had a history that reached far into a mythical past. Cuzco, high in the Andes, was the capital of the vast Incan empire which extended from northern Ecuador to middle Chile. "Within its mighty walls," Gilbert Chase writes, in *Music in American Cities,* "stood the temple of the Sun. . . . There in 'The Golden City' of Cuzco the worshippers gathered to sing the *Hymn to the Sun,* while musicians played the *quenas* (flutes), *antaras* (panpipes), ocarinas, conch-shell trumpets, and drums covered with hide." The most advanced musical system of the early American continent was the Peruvian.

At the height of its prosperity, the empire of the Incas comprised a population of some 10,000,000 persons and a superb agrarian culture. Beatrice Edgerly comments, "With the murder of Atahualpa by Piz-

Fig. 5. Peruvian whistling jar. Whistling pottery jars were typical Incan instruments. (Courtesy The Metropolitan Museum of Art, The Crosby Brown Collection of Musical Instruments, 1889.)

zaro, the glory of the Inca after five hundred years of splendor and after uncounted previous centuries of culture and achievement was at an end." Effectively silenced were the medicinal drums, the whistling pottery jars and the conch-shell horns. Still to be heard, however, are the shepherd pipes consisting of reeds—perhaps seven in number—cut in graduated lengths and laced together; they are rather like the *syrinxes* on view in the British Museum, which might indicate that the ancient Peruvians had an instrumental music built on intervals similar to those of Asiatic countries, much more advanced than the music of the North American Indian. "Those simple, ancient pipes were blown by the shepherds of the Andes long before Plato was charmed to tears by the sweet ecstasies of Marsyas' flute and the pipes of Pan."

Next in importance among the cities of the Inca empire was Quito, the present capital of Ecuador. It has a rich store of folk and popular music and native dances. The Spaniards introduced some of their own songs and dances which were called *danzas criollas,* but Ecuador has remained Indian country.

INFLUENCE OF AMERICAN PRIMITIVE MUSIC

Before concluding this chapter, we shall pose a final question—what influence has the music of American primitives had upon American music in general? The answer is easy—very little! Perhaps because of its fragmentary nature, perhaps because the lure of faraway exoticism is more attractive, perhaps because successive European invasions did such a thorough job of annihilating and debilitating the native American inhabitants—for these or other reasons, native primitive music exists quite apart, in most cases, from the mainstream of creativity. We do find traces of influence in such works as Edward MacDowell's (1861-1908) "From an Indian Lodge"; Henry Kimball Hadley's (1871-1937) *Azora, Daughter of Montezuma;* in the works of Arthur Farwell (1872-1952), who did considerable research among American Indians and who supplied Puccini with a Zuni folk melody for his opera, *The Girl of the Golden West;* in Harvey Worthington Loomis' (1865-1930) "Lyrics of the Redmen"; in Charles Wakefield Cadman's (1881-1946) opera *Shanewis,* produced by the Metropolitan Opera House in 1918, and in his popular song "From the Land of the Sky-Blue Water"; in Charles Sanford Skilton's (1868-1941) *Indian Dances,* an opera, *The Sun Bride* and *Suite Primeval;* in Arthur Nevin's (1871-1943) opera, *Poia,* which was produced in Germany, and his *A Daughter of the Forest,* performed by the Chicago Opera Company in 1918; and in Thurlow Lieurance's (1897-1963) well-known song "By the Waters of Minnetonka."

The contributions of Latin America to music, notably in the form of dances, are very real, but the styles are fusions of Indian, Spanish and Negro influences, with the latter two most obvious. Slonimsky analyzes the ingredients thus:

> The Indians adhere to short phrases, with long pauses and a monotonous drum beat for accompaniment. The Colonial rhythms are prevalently Spanish, and are typified by the dual meter of three-four and six-eight, resulting in characteristic cross-rhythms in the middle of the measure. The Negro influence brings syncopation within an almost unchanged two-four time.

An illustration of this intermixture may be cited to make the matter more clear. Some of our recent popular dances, such as the *tango, rumba* and *conga,* are of Latin American origin. The *tango* and the *habanera* are closely related through their rhythms. Gilbert Chase quotes Carlos Vega, an Argentine student of folk music, as stating that "the Argentine tango reached Buenos Aires from Andalusia via the *zarzuela,*" a form of popular musical play of the seventeenth century. Slonimsky writes that "the word [*tango*] is of Negro origin and was formed as an imitation of the drum beat." He traces it back to the English country dance of 1650, or *contradanza* of Spain, 1750. It was imported into Cuba where it became the *danza habanera* (the dance of Havana) and was carried back to Spain as *habanera.* "During the Spanish-American War," Slonimsky continues, "a popular dance, called *Habanera del Cafe* appeared, which was the prototype of the tango."

In the music of one twentieth-century American composer, Carlos Chávez (1899-   ), of Mexico, Indian material does play an integral and significant role. Chávez is a *mestizo;* that is, his mother was an Indian. By the time he was twenty he had written his first symphony, after having tried his hand at piano pieces. In 1922 he left Mexico, went to Europe and later spent some time in New York. During these years he became interested in the modern European trends. In *Our New Music,* Copland writes:

> He has faced in his music almost all the major problems of modern music: the overthrow of Germanic ideals, the objectification of sentiment, the use of the folk material in its relation to nationalism, the intricate rhythms, the linear as opposed to vertical writing, the specifically 'modern' sound images. It is music that belongs entirely to our own age.

Copland tells of Chávez's "Mexicanness" as being the result of his annual visits to the Indians and of hearing ritualistic music that was little known even in Mexico. His ballet, *El Fuego Nuevo* (*The New Fire*), was the first work in which he experimented with native material and native percussion instruments. Next came *Sonatinas* for violin and piano, 'cello and piano and piano solo. These seem to be an amalgamation of his studies of European methods with the Indian music, of which there is no direct quotation. While Copland finds "perhaps a recognizably native turn of phrase," as a whole, "the folk element has been replaced by a more subtle sense of national characteristics." It is this characteristic that dominates Chávez's later works—his music has "caught the spirit of Mexico"—and he has created a Mexican tradition.

Works in which the two trends are visible are *Sinfonia Antigona* and *Sinfonia India*. The first was written as incidental music for Sophocles' *Antigone,* later reworked into symphonic form. Chávez said that the score was not subordinated to any program. "Stark and elemental, this music can be made expressive only by laconic strength, just as primitive art can be exalted only by power that is also primitive." In the *Indian Symphony,* Chávez has used actual Indian tunes and has tried to express the Mexican Indian's soul. He has added native instruments to the standard symphony orchestra.

Chávez's influence has been not only as a composer, but as a teacher, director of the National Conservatory, where he modernized methods of instruction, and as conductor of the *Orquesta Sinfonica de Mexico,* which was founded by him in 1928, and has done much to make Mexico City an important music center. He has performed the scores of younger Mexicans, several of whom are his pupils. Among these is Daniel Ayala (1908-   ), an Indian, who is at the head of the contemporary movement in Mérida, Yucatan, and who uses ancient Mayan folklore as a basis of modern expression.

In the music of primitive peoples we find harbingers of many of our more refined forms and instruments. In the next chapter we shall discover that ancient civilizations added to our musical resources, especially in terms of instruments and systematized theory.

SUGGESTIONS FOR FURTHER READING

Baines, Anthony, ed., *Musical Instruments Through the Ages.** Baltimore, Penguin, 1961.
Benade, Arthur H., *Horns, Strings and Harmony.** Garden City, Doubleday, 1960.
Bessaraboff, Nicholas, *Ancient European Musical Instruments.* Cambridge, Harvard University Press, 1941.
Bowra, Cecil M., *Primitive Song.* London, Weidenfeld & Nicolson, 1962.
Chase, Gilbert, *A Guide to the Music of Latin America.* Washington, Pan American Union, 1962.
Coleman, Satis N., *The Drum Book.* New York, John Day, 1931.
Curtis, Natalie, *The Indian Book.* New York, Harper, 1923.

* Available in paperback edition.

Edgerly, Beatrice, *From the Hunter's Bow*. New York, Putnam, 1942.

Kunst, Jaap, ed., *Ethnomusicology*. The Hague, Nijhoff, 1959.

Kurath, Gertrude P., *Iroquois Music and Dance*. Washington, Smithsonian Institution (Bureau of American Ethnology), 1964.

Meggers, Betty J., and Evans, Clifford, *Aboriginal Cultural Development in Latin America*. Washington, Smithsonian Institution, 1963.

Merriam, Alan P., *The Anthropology of Music*. Evanston, Northwestern University Press, 1964.

Morley, Sylvanus G., *The Ancient Maya*. Stanford, Stanford University Press, 1956.

Nettl, Bruno, *Folk and Traditional Music of the Western Continents*.* Englewood Cliffs, Prentice-Hall, 1965.

———— *Music in Primitive Culture*. Cambridge, Harvard University Press, 1956.

———— *Theory and Method in Ethnomusicology*. New York, Free Press, 1964.

Prescott, William H., *The History of the Conquest of Mexico*.* Chicago, University of Chicago Press, 1967.

Roberts, Helen H., *Musical Areas in Aboriginal North America*. New Haven, Yale University Press, 1936.

Sachs, Curt, *The History of Musical Instruments*. New York, Norton, 1940.

———— *The Wellsprings of Music*.* New York, McGraw-Hill, 1965.

———— *World History of the Dance*.* New York, Norton, 1937.

Stevenson, Robert, *The Music of Peru, Aboriginal and Viceroyal Epochs*. Washington, Pan American Union, 1959.

A SAMPLER OF SUPPLEMENTARY RECORDINGS

N.B. We are fortunate today to have at our disposal a treasury of ethnic recordings, available on the commercial market, and purportedly authentic. Those listed below are but a very few of the many one may wish to hear. If, however, any of the following are out of press, acceptable substitutes can easily be found by consulting a catalog such as that issued monthly by W. Schwann, Inc., 137 Newbury Street, Boston, Mass. 02116.

American Indian Music

Indian Music of the Southwest	Folkways 4420
Sioux and Navajo	Folkways 4401
Songs and Dances of the Great Lakes Indians	Folkways 4003
Song of the Indian	(10") Canyon 6050
Anthology of Brazilian Indian Music	Folkways 4311
Indian Music of the Canadian Plains	Folkways 4464
Indians of Mexico	Folkways 8851
Yaqui Dances	(10") Folkways 6957

African Music

African Music	Folkways 8852
Bantu Folk Music	Columbia KL-213
Ekonda	Washington 709
Face of Africa	London 91204
Songs of West Africa	Continental 1519
Watusi Songs of Ruanda	Folkways 4428

Tribal Music and Dances, Senghor, Sonar	Counterpoint 513
Folk Music of Ethiopia	Folkways 4405

Miscellaneous Collections

Aborigine Music of Australia	Columbia KL-208
Maori Songs	Folkways 4433
African and Afro-American Drums	2-Folkways 4502
Man's Early Musical Instruments	2-Folkways 4525
Primitive Music of the World	2-Folkways 4581

Composed Works of Interest

Cadman, Charles W., *American Suite*	Dorian 1008
Chávez, Carlos, *Sinfonia India*	Columbia ML-5914
MacDowell, Edward, *Woodland Sketches*	Westminister 9310
Milhaud, Darius, *Création du monde*	Victor LD-2625
Stravinsky, Igor, *Sacre du printemps*	*

OPPORTUNITIES FOR STUDY IN DEPTH

1. Prepare a bibliography of periodical literature about one aspect of the music of primitive man. *The Reader's Guide,* available in reference departments of libraries, will prove most helpful.

2. Construct a primitive musical instrument, utilizing as guides suggestions found in such books as Coleman's *The Drum Book* (see "Suggestions for Further Reading").

3. Visit a nearby museum and examine its collection of primitive instruments and artifacts. Be sure to secure a catalog and a few postcards.

4. Make a study of one tribe of primitive man, placing its music in the context of its social and spiritual life.

5. After delving into the subject of African music, make a comparison between an authentic recording of primitive music-making and the "primitive" features included in such a composition as Milhaud's *Création du monde.*

6. Experiment with glasses or bottles and a pitcher of water, adding liquid until a "tuned" set is produced. The piano may be used to countercheck pitches.

7. Try improvisation of Indian dances, using the black keys of the piano (which comprise a pentatonic scale). Keep in mind the melodic tendency to descend, the feature of thematic repetition and the strong rhythmic beat of untuned drums. One player might serve as drummer, beating upon low E flat and B flat (an interval of a fifth). Another might be the vigorous warrior whose gutteral song is spun spontaneously in the middle register of the instrument. Such improvisation is great fun and very easy to do.

8. Examine the contents of an elementary school rhythm-band kit. Note the correspondences between these instruments for children and the instruments of primitive man.

---

* If no record company is designated, it means that there are many recordings of the work from which to choose.

Vocabulary Enrichment

ethnomusicology
cultural conservation
tone
vibrations
frequency
amplitude
partials
harmonics
overtones
fundamental
c.p.s.
perfect intervals

pitch
volume
tone color or *timbre*
larynx
resonation
vibrating reed
decibels
nonaesthetic
pentatonic scale
shepherd's pipes
habanera
tango

Chapter 2.
MUSIC OF ANCIENT CIVILIZATIONS

Praise the Lord!

Praise him with trumpet sound;
  praise him with lute and harp!
Praise him with timbrel and dance;
  praise him with strings and pipe!
Praise him with sounding cymbals;
  praise him with loud clashing cymbals!
Let everything that breathes praise the Lord!

Praise the Lord!

                                —Psalm 150

CRADLE OF CIVILIZATION

When one seeks the cradle of civilization, he is directed by scholars to the barren area of modern Iraq, land lying between the Tigris and Euphrates rivers, a once fertile plain that provided the home for man's earliest-known social culture, existing some six thousand years ago. Nearby in time lay the marvelous dynasties of the Upper Nile Valley and the legendary wonders of China, separated by that mysterious area now known as India. In each of these regions man emerged from savagery to a state characterized by progress in the arts, sciences and statecraft, which sharply differentiated him from his primitive fellows. Just why this happened is a matter of conjecture; perhaps an abundance of food, resulting from richness of soil and sound methods of agriculture, gave him leisure to contemplate the earth and the heavens, thereby uncovering knowledge that he put to use in skills. Whatever the reason, however disparate the sites, man developed unique forms of communal organization, in each of which music had a place.

SOURCES OF INFORMATION

Although our present-day knowledge is punctuated with yawning gaps of ignorance, we are fortunate to know more of ancient civilizations through the tireless curiosity and labor of archaeologists who during the last hundred years have opened vast areas of exploration into mankind's past. Until this relatively recent time, our history of remote antiquity was based almost wholly upon two sources of information: the Bible and the writings of the Greek historian Herodotus—occasionally interspersed with fragmentary data from seafarers, daring merchants such as the Venetian Polo family, and warriors.

To these we now add large libraries of documentation preserved by means of arid climates (as is the case with Egyptian *hieroglyphics*) or durability of the writing medium (as in the case of Mesopotamian *cuneiform*). We now can view representation of ancient life in friezes, tomb paintings and excavated artifacts. And, as a result, we can better relate today's remnants to yesterday's roll of goods. A general aid to the study of ancient ways of non-Occidental civilizations is their ideological climate, which discourages novelty and enforces compliance to tradition, thus embalming forms from much earlier eras for our perusal.

In beginning a survey of the music of ancient civilizations, a few words of caution are in order. First, we must keep in mind the fact that we are dealing with thousands of years of time, as well as with wide geographical spaces, some of which are relatively unknown to us. Secondly, we should not be dismayed by the complexities of semantic confusion which we meet at every turn, in the form of phonetic spellings, alien languages and dialectal variations. Thirdly, we cannot expect to find clear-cut lines of development or derivation, for a dazzling intermixture was constantly occurring through the wanderings of nomads, the mutual flow of trade and frequent invasions, annexations and defeats. Lastly, we again have to emphasize the paucity of information (due to the lack of ancient written music and our inability to decipher certain lingual relics) as well as the disputed nature of much data and the inevitable distortions of time.

Why, then, is it important to learn something of the music of ancient civilizations? The answer is that we are in many ways heirs of these peoples, obliged to them for threads in our modern tapestry. As the historian L. J. Cheney writes: "And if anyone is so hasty as to think that these long-forgotten men and women of far-off antiquity do not matter to him, let him know that we reckon our days in hours of sixty minutes each of sixty seconds because that was the way the ancient Babylonian astronomers worked it out." Not to mention such commonplaces of everyday life as Arabic numerals, gunpowder and spaghetti! Musically, too, we are indebted to ancient civilizations—as we shall see—for the putative ancestor to violins, for contributions to Greek musicology, for the development of **idiophones** (instruments that sound by their own nature, without added tension—such as gongs, cymbals and bells), for rudimentary methods of musical notation and for much of the Judaic-Christian tradition of musical observance which has loomed so large in music through the ages.

MESOPOTAMIAN MUSIC

The land between the Tigris and Euphrates Rivers was dominated by a succession of cultures beginning with the Bronze Age Sumerians (4000-2040 B.C.) and followed by Babylonians (2040-1750 B.C.), Hittites (1740-1160 B.C.) Assyrians (1160-625 B.C.), Persians (583-

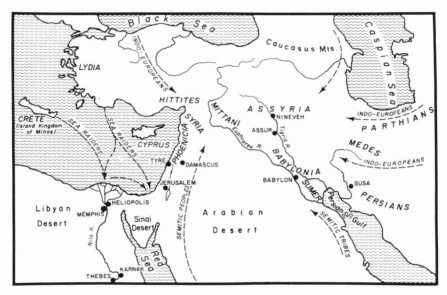

Fig. 6. The ancient Near East.

331 B.C.), and the Greeks and Romans thereafter. Sumerian cities existed before the year 3000 B.C.—cities supported by a planned agrarian economy, with copper tools, oxen and canals to control the rivers' flood-waters. In each city a square and massive temple rose, its stepped tower leading to the holy place of the gods, whose priest was the king. From words which have survived we know that each temple practiced well-organized liturgies chanted in the techniques of **solo and response** (between priest and choir) and **antiphony** (between choir and choir). Each set of words had its appropriate tune and was felt to have a quality peculiar to a particular god or a specific effect of magic.

Whether instrumental music existed independent of vocal music we do not know, but the Sumerians possessed many instruments including reed pipes (associated with the breath of their thunder god, Ramman) and hourglass drums (assigned to the god of the flood, Ea) as well as tambourines, kettledrums and flutes. From the celebrated excavations of the Royal Tombs at Ur—diggings supervised jointly by the Museum of the University of Pennsylvania and the British Museum—we find evidence of magnificent harps and lyres, apparently sacred instruments of social as well as spiritual uses.

About the year 2500 B.C., a conqueror from the north named Sargon made himself master of Mesopotamia; his forces were in turn overrun by another group of Semites who in 2000 B.C. became the new overlords of the plain and ruled from Babylon. The *Code of Hammurabi* and numerous accounts on clay tablets tell us of the richness and elaborate organization of this empire. About 1830 B.C. Indo-Europeans, the Hittites and the Mittani (who introduced the horse to Asia), swarmed into the land. During this time of rule from Babylon, music of the temple services evolved from simple chanted hymns to a complete liturgical service including from five to twenty-seven selections, interspersed with instrumental music. The practice of using a certain melody for a certain poem-type seems to have originated here, thence adopted into Jewish tradition and further perpetuated in early Protestant psalters.

With the weakening of the Babylonian Empire, the Assyrians, a Semitic tribe dwelling high up on the river Tigris, moved southward and mercilessly conquered the territory, ruling with an iron hand from their capital, Nineveh. On a bas-relief of Sennacherib's palace we see a picture of a victory procession of instrumentalists and singers, fifty-two in number. A line of instrumentalists precedes the singers; it includes both men and women or eunuchs, playing harps of many strings, double pipes, a drum and a *santir* (resembling a European dulcimer, consisting of strings stretched over a hollow case, pressed with the left hand and beaten with a small hammer held in the right hand) and cymbals. The singers are women and boys, all clapping as they proceed and one has her hands at her throat, apparently thus producing the characteristic *tremolo* peculiar to singing in the Near East today. Sir Henry Layard, who restored the ruins at Kouyunjik for the British Museum, wrote: "The whole scene, indeed, was curiously illustrative of modern Eastern customs. The musicians portrayed in the bas-relief were probably of that class of public performers who appear in Turkey and Egypt at marriages, and on other occasions of rejoicing. . . ."

Several items are significant when interpreting the above-mentioned bas-relief: women are included among the performers; there is evidence of an orchestra of sorts, as well as a chorus; there seems to be a union of dancing and music; the musical personnel, by Layard's implication, are professional; in A. Z. Idelsohn's opinion, the modest percussion forces indicate a tendency toward musical refinement; and lastly, the occasion is a secular one, which helps to correct the perspective we derive from records of temple officials. Peter Crossley-Holland comments:

> [Music] was important in the various festivals, and musicians were attached to the royal households. The court minstrel was held in high regard, and musicians performed not only for the royal household at banquets and on other occasions but also gave public performances which the people at large could hear, and played for martial occasions. Such performances no doubt influenced music in its more popular forms.

In 612 B.C. the Chaldeans, another Semitic people, seized the Babylonian government. To them we owe much of our early knowledge of the stars; and to them we ascribe the relationship of music to astrology and mathematics with "numerous cosmic correspondences demonstrated by the harmonic divisions of a stretched string."

> Thus the primary divisions of a string-length gave four intervals which can be expressed in mathematical ratios as follows 1:1 (unison); 1:2 (octave); 2:3 (fifth); and 3:4 (fourth). These they correlated with the four seasons (spring, summer, winter, autumn). The properties of particular numbers were also important, especially those of the number 4 and the number 7—the latter being most probably the number of notes in the ancient Chaldean scale.

The modern reader is familiar with the Chaldeans through their famous emperor, Nebuchadnezzar, who, having rebuilt Babylon, captured Jerusalem in 597 B.C. and carried off large numbers of the Jews, whose plight in captivity is most movingly presented in Psalm 137:

> By the waters of Babylon, there we sat down and wept, when we remembered Zion. On the willows there we hung up our lyres. For there our captors required of us songs, and our tormentors, mirth, saying, "Sing us one of the songs of Zion!"

We also have an account of Nebuchadnezzar's "band" in the biblical book of Daniel, Chapter 3, where at a dedication ceremony a herald proclaims: ". . . when you hear the sound of the horn, pipe, lyre, trigon, harp, bagpipe, and every kind of music, you are to fall down and worship the golden image that King Nebuchadnezzar has set up."

In 538 B.C. a Persian king, Cyrus, overthrew the Chaldean rulers and mercifully released the imprisoned Jews. His successors, notably Darius I, stretched the limits of the Persian empire as far as India on the east, Ethiopia on the south and the Black Sea on the north. Indeed,

Persia ruled the entire civilized world. Yet we know very little about the Persians, especially about their music. It is likely that they absorbed the musical resources of others and that more sensuous elements of music were emphasized, as their style of living was indeed luxurious. The worshipers of Zoroaster, the god of light, however, remain in darkness.

Before examining the music of the ancient civilizations of Egypt and Israel, we might pause a moment to reflect on the reasons for presenting the materials above at such length. After all, we do not know how any of this music sounded, nor how the instruments were played. We can, however, form some valuable inferences. First, we can scan the successive cultural and ethnic changes in the same land area over a temporal panorama of several thousand years. Secondly, we can recognize certain aspects of the music of ancient Mesopotamia as they appear in the music of contiguous civilizations. Lastly, from the site of man's earliest known civilization we can trace influences extending to Egypt, Palestine, Greece, Islam, India and perhaps even as far east as China.

Egyptian Music and Instruments

Egypt was a leader among nations of antiquity to whom music was a part of life in war and peace, in the marketplace and in the temple. It influenced Hebrew, Greek and early Christian Church music by way of various national and international conquests and migrations. Like many early peoples, the Egyptians personified nature in their gods: Osiris, god of the underworld, died each year to be born again as the grain was harvested and the seed planted; Ra was the sun god. As with many early peoples, moreover, musical instruments were intimately associated with deities: Osiris related to bells and flutes; Isis, his wife, goddess of fertility, to the *sistrum* (a strung rattle); Thoth, the moon god, to the lyre. Intricate ceremonies of worship were devised, in which the human voice was the primary supplicant, chanting alone or accompanied by instruments in unison. Music was also an integral part of state celebrations, festivals, martial events and daily diversion.

Egypt's vitality is apparent in her ability to adopt and adapt instruments of other nations, as she apparently had few that were indigenous. We know of the existence of one-handed clappers, probably derived from utilitarian devices of crop protection which, with double percussion sticks, came to be associated with agrarian fertility dances. During the numerous dynasties of the Old and Middle Kingdoms, that is, until about 1570 B.C., the standard Egyptian instruments consisted of a vertical flute, a double clarinet and, most importantly, the arched or bow harp. The latter had a lower sound chest or bowl and a sloping neck, but lacked the supporting pillar found on our modern instruments. The tuning is thought to have been pentatonic, with possible semi-tones, and its pitch rather deep, because of the flexibility of the neck. Through the years, Egyptian harps varied in size and in the number of strings, but rarely in popularity.

Fig. 7. "Egyptian Female Musicians"—Theban tomb painting, *c*. 1420-1411 B.C. Looking from left to right we find an arched harp, a lute, a double oboe and a lyre.

The phenomenon of the blind harper is interesting, frequently appearing on tomb paintings and friezes where, with flutists and others, he accompanies a consolatory song for the departed. The text of one such song, dating from 1370 B.C. and found on a relief from the tomb of Pa-aten-em-heb, at Memphis, concludes with the following cynical refrain:

> Make holiday, and weary not therein!
> Behold, it is not given to a man to take his property with him.
> Behold, there is not one who departs who comes back again!

Toward the end of the Middle Kingdom, nomadic tribes brought to Egypt new musical resources, including drums, castanets and a Semitic lyre (with two asymmetric, divergent arms), similar in appearance to the classic Greek instrument. With the lyre may have come a long-handled lute, whose origin is uncertain. An Oriental influence permeated Egypt during the time of the New Kingdom, about 1500-1000

B.C., owing to the forages of militant Pharaohs into the Near East. Asiatic instruments were introduced and assimilated into the culture. Among these were the double oboe, a straight metal trumpet and an angular harp with an upper sound-chest. Following the Greek conquest (c. 332 B.C.) cymbals appeared and are still used in Coptic religious services.

In the Old Kingdom a typical instrumental ensemble consisted of a wind player and a harpist accompanying a singer. During Cheop's reign, the group included harps, tenor and alto flutes and single pipes. By the much later time of Cleopatra, we find Plutarch, the Roman historian, describing "her barge in the river of Cyduus, the poop whereof was of gold, the sails of purple, and the oars of silver, which kept stroke in rowing after the sound of the music of the flutes, howboys (oboes), citherns (harps), viols (lutes or tambouras), and such other instruments as they played . . ."

There is evidence to support the assumption that music was used to facilitate physical labor in ancient Egypt. One painting shows the moving of a colossal statue, with an overseer clapping his hands, apparently to the measured cadence of a song. Another portrays workers in a vineyard, singing and dancing. One of the oldest metrical songs of Egypt exhorts:

> Thrash ye for yourselves,
> Thrash ye for yourselves, O oxen,
> Thrash ye for yourselves,
> Thrash ye for yourselves,
> The straw which is yours,
> The corn which is your master's.

As the Egyptians became more pleasure-loving and cosmopolitan, the rich harp gave way to the tambourine and the dancing girl, imports from subject monarchs of Semitic nations in Asia Minor. The slow and solemn dances of earlier days were replaced by livelier, faster ones, and there is reason to believe music was more sensuous that formerly. Trumpets were used on martial occasions, and the dulcimer, imported from Assyria and Babylon, gradually took the place of the small harp. In the twenty-second dynasty the flute became the prince of instruments. Its popularity may be ascribed to the fact that the flute, unlike the diatonic harp, lent itself to chromatics and so fulfilled the current demands made upon music.

The cosmopolitan Egyptians were great instrument-makers and might have gone much further in musical development had not the state been so rigid in proscribing new musical activities. Strict rules governed the music education of ancient Egypt, and an almost inescapable caste-system consigned to music those whose fathers had been musicians. It is interesting to note, however, that the invention of the water organ (*hydraulus*), usually credited to Greece, was actually the work of an Egyptian, Ctesibius of Alexandria (230 B.C.).

HEBRAIC MUSIC AND INSTRUMENTS

Unlike other theocratic civilizations, the ancient Hebrews were not exponents of the arts. Their music sprang up as an expression of the soul of a people whose everyday life, nomadic or sedentary, had become religiously ordered. They were forbidden in the Commandments to make "graven images" and like the Moslems, developed no pictorial arts or architecture. Their first temple was little more than a tent, until Solomon summoned a foreigner to build one of fitting dignity. Music was supposed to be of heavenly origin, like that of the Egyptians and the Assyrians. "The morning stars," says Job (Job 38:7) "sang together and all the sons of God shouted for joy." Much of our knowledge of the presence of music in the life of the ancient Hebrews is gained from the Old Testament, corroborated by Egyptian, Assyrian and Arabian records which give us evidence of the melody, structure and compass of Hebrew music.

Naturally the Exile in Egypt affected Hebrew music deeply. Moses must have studied music while a disciple of the Egyptian priesthood, because he was "learned in all the wisdom of the Egyptians." Moreover, he was commanded by the Lord while the Children of Israel were in the wilderness: "Make thee two trumpets of silver; of a whole piece shalt thou make them; that thou mayest use them for the callings of the assembly and for the journeyings of the camps" (Numbers 10:2).

The Book of Psalms (Songs of Praise) contains 150 religious lyrics of the Hebrew people, undoubtedly influenced by Egyptian, Babylonian and Canaanite examples, but including, as the Hebrews themselves recognized in their reiteration of the words "new song," an element peculiarly their own. The texts themselves were impassioned and developed into a parallelism of sentences or phrases which still inspire, because of their tremendous power, and still persist in worship—Christian as well as Hebrew.

The song sung by Moses and the Children of Israel is a beautiful example of parallel verse which was probably sung responsively somewhat like this:

Moses: "I will sing unto the Lord, for he hath triumphed gloriously."
C. of I.: "The horse and his rider hath He thrown into the sea."
Moses: "The Lord is my strength and my song."

C. of I.: "And He has become my salvation."
Moses: "He is my God, and I will prepare him a habitation."
C. of I.: "My father's God, and I will exalt Him."

It is possible to infer from this type of statement and amplification that our antiphonal choruses stem from poetry of the Old Testament, contributed by many writers and brought to lyric and bardic perfection by the royal minstrel, King David himself.

The Hebrews credited to music curative and inspirational powers, for we see David playing to heal Saul, and Elias stimulating himself, by music, to ecstatic prophecy. Furthermore, in the Song of Solomon, that radiant secular hymeneal of the Bible, we see the bridal processions accompanied by music, and realize how great was its power in the life of the ancient Hebrew man and woman.

Owing to the regimentation of living, most Hebrew songs were religious. Because the line between the religious and the secular was often thin, it is sometimes difficult to tell them apart. That not all were religious is evidenced in the lovely folk song from Joel 3:13:

> Put in the sickle for the vintage is ripe:
> Come, tread, for the winepress is full,
> The vats overflow.

In temple music, the songs used in religious ceremonies seem to have been sung to secular tunes. For example, the directions to the musicians on Psalms 57, 58, 59 and 75 suggest the use of the vintage tune "Destroy It Not." This custom of joining the secular and religious in sacred music flourished for ages until it was extirpated during the Protestant Reformation and the Catholic Counter-Reformation. Withal, rhythm rather than melody was the major element in Hebrew music. The instrument merely supplemented the voice as an accompaniment. The melodies, according to logical deductions from Arab analogies and from the effect of Egyptian influences, were short in compass and were reiterated with hypnotic rhythmic power.

Power rather than sensuous sweetness seems to have been the essence of Hebrew music, and simplicity, the result of the welding of the nomadic and religious life. The close racial relationship between the Arabs and the Hebrews leads more than one authority to believe that Hebrew music was similar to that of the ancient Arab which has persisted through the ages. Therefore, what we know of the music itself can be gleaned from a study of Arabic music. The nasal *timbre* of Arab singing is similar in quality to that heard in the intoned prayers and the singing of the cantor in an orthodox synagogue.

Jubal, according to an ancient Spanish record (Mexico), was the first singer among the Hebrews. He realized differences in pitch by listening to the strokes on the anvil, and imitated them with his voice. In Genesis it is written that Jubal was "the father of all such as handle the harp [kinnor] and organ"—probably pipe or flute, akin to their *ugab*. David played on the *kinnor,* a lyrelike instrument similar to the Greek *kithara* and Roman *cithara.* It was plucked and used to accompany a singer.

It is difficult to classify instruments in use thousands of years ago. Names have undergone changes. The *psaltery* or *psalterion* may be like the *dulcimer* of Assyria, the Arabian *kanoun* or Persian *santir.* *Nevels* were probably psalterions, a type of harp, lyre or lute; they were plucked. *Asors,* also, were stringed instruments. *Magrepha* is the Hebrew word for the water organ. The instrument may never have been used by the Hebrews, but the name was seized upon by later writers, who mistook it for pipes (*syrinx*) or even bagpipes.

There were also cymbals small and large, bells or jingles and small drums (*tabrets, timbrels* and *tofs*). Of drums, the *tof* is the most familiar. Yet the *timbrel* and *tabret* are most used in the English version of the Bible: "Miriam, the prophetess, the sister of Aaron, took a timbrel in her hand; and all the women went out after her with timbrels and with dances" (Exodus 15:20). The *shofar* or ram's horn, five thousand years old and still used in Jewish rituals, is the only typical Hebrew instrument that has come down to us. (The ram was a sacrificial animal and the *shofar* was held sacred.) Ironically, it is the least musical of all. The metal trumpet had its conventional usage ordained by the Lord. It proclaimed war, religious ceremonies and festivals. In Joshua 7:20 we read that a trumpet blast blew down the walls of Jericho. Later the trumpet was introduced in the temple services.

Liturgical music was fostered by King David and the Levite priesthood with a regime akin to a school (I Chronicles 24:1-7) which influenced the music of the times. Four thousand musicians were employed in the service of the temple, of whom 288 were "instructed in the songs of the Lord"; the rest were assistants and pupils. (David was the Saint Gregory of the Jews.) Women were not permitted to sing in the temple, but took part in choruses unliturgical in character. They were forbidden to sing solos, until long after A.D. 70 (the destruction of the temple). The liturgy included dancing, playing of instruments and choral singing. A demonstration of religious dance was David's penance before the Ark of the Covenant. The liturgical dance was prohibited later by the Christians but it has remained to our time in Spain.

Despite the religious orientation, a garish secular music, introduced by aliens and enjoyed by the wealthier classes, gradually developed. Isaiah characterizes the frivolous rich (5:12), saying: "And the harp and the viol, the tabret and pipe, and wine are in their feasts."

After Titus' celebrated victory (A.D. 70) the Hebrews were scattered over the world. They were absorbed by other nations, were "sore harassed" and saddened, but transmitted their spiritual heritage to those with whom they came in contact. They have always been the great executants of music. Although records of their ancient music have passed away, enough remains of the spirit of aspiration to relay the religious fervor and poetic insight of the ancient Hebrew people, whose music was their ritualistic speech and their secular need.

ARABIAN MUSIC, INSTRUMENTS AND THEORY

Arabian civilization goes back to the time of King Solomon. As Arabia was the seat of culture in the benighted Dark Ages of Europe, its influence was great and far-flung. Large universities flourished in Bagdad and Damascus long before the Christian era, and they attracted scholars from Greece and Rome. The nomadic Arabs were preeminent in science and mathematics; they gave the name to algebra, built unique buildings, introduced the *arabesque,* and, like the Greeks, delighted in theoretical treatises on music. Scientifically minded, musically avid, and the most cultured people of their day, they absorbed much Persian music and made it over into a better fabric. Moreover, before the Mohammedan conquest (A.D. 700-800), Arabian music, well planned and organized, spread as the Arab went on his conquering way—in Egypt, Morocco, Greece, Italy and Spain.

In the time of Mohammed (A.D. 570-632), the Arabs were at the height of their vitality and power. They invaded Europe, drove out the Goths and settled in Spain, but were prevented by Emperor Charlemagne from entering the Frankish Empire. During the Crusades (1095-1271), in which European nations struggled to wrest the Savior's tomb from the Mussulman, every nation meeting the Arab learned much from him of science, music, design, architecture, manufacture and human character. For besides being a conqueror, the ancient Arab was loyal, proud, courageous, courtly and honest.

The rhythm of Arabian music, its most prominent feature, is very difficult for a Western listener to grasp. For example, we interpret 9/4 meter as 3×3; the Arab musician is free to take it as 3×3 2's or in other subdivisions. Melodies are accompanied by drum or string in a repeated or continuous figure. The air and accompaniment may coincide in simple pieces but the Arabs like cross rhythms which are very difficult for us to produce. The drum usually takes a rhythm different from that of the melody and maintains it throughout.

Unlike the Hebrew, Arabian music did not express exalted utterances nor was it based on religious instinct. In fact, Mohammed said, "Your prayers, if music be a part of them, will end in piping and hand-clapping." Under his ruling, instrumental music was prohibited, a "bootlegged" art, for the practice of which Arabs were arrested. Not until the reign of Harun al-Rashid (A.D. 764?-809) were instruments legally permitted. The court musicians became prominent, and prizes were awarded for skill in composition and in playing.

Arabian music is sad and plaintive, and to our ears sounds "out of tune" and rhythmically intricate. Thirds of a tone and quarter-tones are common. Harmony is not used, although today the Arabs (who in many regions are still uncontaminated by modern café music, jazz and the phonograph) show a native ability to "answer" and "join in" extemporaneously, like the popular use of antiphony by the Hebrews. They retain the fundamentals of a rich past, and their music can be studied as examples of the ancient art. An unusual nasal quality of singing is still evident, as in Sennacherib's time (705-681 B.C.).

It is difficult to determine how many scales or modes exist, for the slightest change in a step creates a new mode. It is maintained by some that there are thirty-four; by others, twenty-four, one for each hour of the day: and some claim four modes for the elements: fire, water, earth and air; or twelve for the signs of the Zodiac and seven for the planets. The vivid names given to each mode add flavor to the system. Baron d'Erlanger, an English composer and scholar, believed two distinct systems to be in use, one derived from Asia, the other from the Pharaohs of Egypt. He thought if we were to lower, very slightly, the third and seventh of our major scale, it would result in the simplest form of the Pharaoh's scale. The others can be played on instruments with no fixed tuning, such as the violin or the Arabian prototype of the European lute.

Eerie effects are made in Arabian music by the *gloss* or trill-like ornament, grace notes, slidings, leaps and descending rather than ascending tones. Much of its distinction, allure and charm, is obtained by the frequent wanderings from triple to duple and from duple to triple time. Arabian composers are limited to traditional musical formulae called *maqamāt* (singular: *maqām*), which in Oriental fashion restrict creators to age-old patterns of music-making.

When the Arabs overran Persia, they adopted the many instruments found there. Foremost among these was the *al-ud* (whence our word, lute), plucked with the talon of an eagle and often mentioned in *The Arabian Nights*. Next in importance was the *rabab,* a distant ancestor of the violin, played with a bow; the *qanun,* a trapezoidal zither; *kissars,* lyres, drums and brasses, spike fiddle, flute and wooden oboe. An

Fig. 8. "A Festive Scene"—illumination of Maqsud, mid-sixteenth century. In this elegant scene, the central male figure is playing an *al-ud,* while to his right, a woman accompanies him with a *chang,* a harp-like device. Below her is the tambourinist. (Courtesy Imperial Museum, Teheran.)

angular harp was about the only instrument of the Near East not to enter Europe during the Middle Ages.

That there was no musical notation among the Sumerians, Egyptians, Assyrians, Hebrews and early Arabs is vivid testimony of the inherent strength of their musical systems, which persisted from father to son and thence from nation to nation in their diverse developments since 3000 B.C., the time of the building of the pyramids.

INDIAN MUSIC, INSTRUMENTS AND THEORY

Over a period of six thousand years successive waves of migrants and invaders entered the vast area of central Asia now known as India, merging with and often dominating the previous cultures or pushing the original inhabitants southward toward the sea. As a result, India now has no less than fourteen major languages and numerous tribes, as well as vestiges of various world religions in addition to the dominant Hinduism. The country also exhibits a very definite cultural, ethnic and social dichotomy between North and South, dramatized even in our time by the dispute over Kashmir waged between Moslem Pakistan and India.

Negritos, Australian aborigines, a neo-Sumerian people, Aryans, Persians and Greeks, all came to India in ancient days. Remains of the Indus Valley culture include an ideograph of a Sumerian type of harp (2000 B.C.) and other artifacts. About 1500 B.C., Aryan tribes pushed into the land from the west. (Hinduism embodies the traditions of these people.) Following the conquest of India by Darius I, of Persia, in 518 B.C., came that of Alexander the Great of Macedon, in 327 B.C. At about the same time Buddhism was adopted as an Indian religion, not to be relinquished until early in the seventh century A.D.

The Hindus ascribed the origin of music to a heavenly source. To Nareda is attributed the *vina,* their most popular instrument, and to Saraswati (wife of Brahma) the scale. She is the goddess of music and of speech. Krishna, the beloved god of pastoral life, is thought to have invented the flute with which he is always associated. Throughout Hindu myth and music, nature and deity go heart to heart. Music is still used to please and appease the gods and to bring sunshine or rain. In fact, whatever the occasion, the religious element is not far distant in performances of Indian music.

In the literature of India, the importance of music in the temple ritual and religious ceremony is constantly stressed. A holy book says that "Indra rejects the offering made without music." The sacred knowledge of the ancient Aryans was written down about 1000 B.C. in four books known as the *Vedas;* hymns were collected in the oldest of these, called the *Rigveda;* the *Samaveda* includes religious chants. From the sixth century B.C. onward came the epics of the *Ramayana* and the *Mahabharata* with frequent comments about music. The oldest specific book about music dates from 200 B.C. and codifies practices already well-established. Its author, Bharata, is considered the founder of Hindu classical music.

The famed Bengalese poet, Rabindranath Tagore, has offered a word of explanation about the spirit of India's classical music, which may help to clarify its essence:

> It seems to me that Indian music concerns itself more with human experience as interpreted by religion, than with experience in an everyday sense. For us, music has above all a transcendental significance. It disengages the spiritual from the happenings of life. It sings of the relationship of the human soul with the soul of things beyond. . . . At the very root, nature is divided into two, day and night, finite and infinite. We men of India live in the realm of night; we are overpowered by the sense of the One and Infinite. Our music draws the listener away beyond the limits of everyday human joy and sorrow, and takes us to that lonely region of renunciation which lies at the root of the universe.

Music also has a secular significance—in the courts of princes, in the humbler homes, for festivals, in the marketplaces, for drama, snake charmers and dancing girls. The instrumental ensembles vary in size (although orchestras as such are rare) and the dances are lively and vigorous, rarely languorous. Here, as in Japan, a class of musician-dancers, called *bayadères* or *nautch* girls, has developed. The singing of poems has always been popular. It is interesting to note, however, that differences between secular and sacred music are definitely distinguished, one from the other.

The Indians have a carefully organized system to their music, one which is exhaustive in its theoretical ramifications. It has one fascinating feature—an almost complete reliance upon *patterns* for music-making. We in the Western world call a creator of music a composer, a designation derived from the Latin *componere,* to put together. In India, as in Arabian countries and ancient Israel, a musician quite literally builds his music from already defined pattern-blocks which allow him little freedom of self-expression and yet give him opportunities for ingenious extemporization. That this kind of creativity has not altogether been lost in our Western culture is underlined by Curt Sachs:

> It left its traces in the Gregorian chant, in the Lutheran chorale, the Calvin psalter, the art of the *Meistersinger,* and the folksong of all countries. Indeed, Wagner's principle of piecing together an unending melody out of *leitmotives,* particularly in the *Ring des Nibelungen,* is tech-

nically, though not spiritually, the principle of ancient Jewish cantillation.

The Indians use a melody pattern called a *rāga* on which songs and tunes are based. The word itself means color, emotion or passion, which gives us a clue to its intent as well as its content. A *rāga* is assigned to every one of the eight watches (of three hours) of the day and to each of the six seasons; it is associated also with moods, zodiacal signs, planets, colors, periods of the life span, calls of birds and many other phenomena. It has been estimated that there have been over 11,000 known *rāgas,* although the number in use is considerably smaller. Each *rāga* comprises a melody package with many characteristics: from the *srutis* (the twenty-two microtonal divisions of the octave), *gramas* (scales) are selected; tones of particular emphasis are noted; pitch range is defined; typical melodic lines are suggested; the types of ornaments are given; the frequency of certain intervals and tones is prescribed; the emotional atmosphere is indicated.

Each *rāga* is associated with a *tala* or rhythmic pattern, which denotes *tempo* (pace—slow, medium or quick) and the organization of beats in various multiples, through duration as well as through our means of stress. While some *talas* are relatively short and simple, many are complex and bewildering to Western ears. In general, musical time is intimately related to word rhythms and lacks the pulsatile repetition of Occidental meters. To complete the musical materials of an Indian performer, a third element is required—*kharaja*—a drone tone which is sustained and acts as a modal center or guide throughout a selection.

Musical education is relatively lengthy in India, rarely less than six years, at the end of which a musician has at his command the repertory of *rāgas* and *talas* and the technical competence which he requires. His song falls into three main sections: a slow prelude without words or drumming; announcement of the theme of the song; and finally the body of the work in which a drum sets the *tala* and the executant continues in medium or quick tempo to develop the *rāga* with all the subtlety at his command. There is no stated time limit; thus a performance may last from fifteen minutes to an hour or two.

Indian music is predominately vocal, yet it is accompanied by numerous types of portable instruments. These include percussion (many kinds of drums, tambourines, castanets, cymbals and gongs), winds (flutes, oboes, bagpipes, horns and trumpets), specialized instruments used by itinerant beggars and dancing girls, as well as various types of stringed instruments.

Among the strings is the *vina,* often decorated with a peacock or elephant. This is a favorite instrument of Southern India and consists of a long cylindrical body of wood reinforced by gourd resonators, with six or seven strings and movable frets. Held as a guitar or banjo, it is plucked with the fingernails of the right hand or with *plectra* (picks). The *sitar* or lute is more favored in the North; and the *sarinda* or *sarangi* is a variety of viol played with a bow. The *tambura* (Persian, *tanbur*) is an unfretted long lute used to provide the *kharaja* "pedal tone."

The protean music of India has exerted an influence upon its neighbors and even upon the West, to some extent. The concept of "composed" music appeared in India a thousand years before it was utilized by ancient civilizations of the Near East. Buddhist music, although little studied, undoubtedly took Indian elements with it when it moved eastward into China. And Gypsies, those colorful nomads, brought to Europe Indian influences which contributed to folksong and dance, and later to art music.

CHINESE MUSIC, INSTRUMENTS AND THEORY

Contemporary with Sumerian rule in Mesopotamia and the Old Kingdom in Egypt was the rise of civilization in China. From the Shang dynasty (1766-1122 B.C.) come the earliest surviving musical relics —singing stones (*ch'ing*) and globular flutes (*hsüan*). The *Book of Songs* (*Shih Ching*) compiled during the twelfth century mentions the existence of drums (*ku*) and bells (*chung*) as well as the use of music during various agricultural festivals. Other sources of information about ancient Chinese music include the *Book of History* (*Shu Ching*), the *Record of Rites* (*Li Chi*) and the *Book of Changes* (*I Ching*). The bases of Chinese musical theory were formulated from the time of Confucius (551-479 B.C.) to the third century, when the source-book *Lü Shih Ch'un Ch'iu* (of Lü Pu-wai) was written. We might know much more had not a soreheaded "destroyer of precedents," the Emperor Shih-huang-ti, in the third century B.C. ordered all instruments and books demolished except those pertaining to medicine, agriculture and magic.

The Chinese word for music is *yuo*. The word for serenity is *lo* and the symbol for both is the same. The Chinese musical system is deepset in philosophy and in the feeling for qualities of sound in stone, metal, wood, silk and bamboo. According to legend an emperor of the third millennium B.C. sent an emissary to the mountains of Northwest China to cut a pitch pipe of bamboo which would provide a basic tone (*huang chung*) that would serve a triple purpose—as a sacred eternal principle, as the basis of the state and as a measure of definite pitch for music. From this fundamental tone was derived, whether through imitation of the tones of the phoenix bird or through cutting other bamboo tubes in accordance with the magical numbers two and three, a series of pitches in intervals of fourths and fifths, resulting in twelve tones, arrived at through a **cyclic** rather than **harmonic** (as in Sumeria) method.

By rearranging the first five tones above, we can establish a **pentatonic scale** (an ordered succession of different tones within the octave), including three whole tones (F-G, G-A, C-D) and two minor thirds (A-C, D-F), the predominant Chinese scale, used throughout the Far East and prevalent in the music of the Eskimos and American Indians, who are also of Mongoloid extraction. Because Chinese ritual required that music be attuned to each of the twelve months, as well as the twelve hours, constant **transposition** (change of tonic) was necessary, so that each of the twelve tones at one certain time of the year served as a *tonic* or starting pitch for its own scale.

As expressed in Chinese music, time and space were but differing aspects of the Great Heart or Great One that reconciled the polar universal principles, *Yang* and *Yin*. Cosmological connotations were attached to the tones of the scale as illustrated below.

Notes	F (*Kung*)	G (*Shang*)	A (*Chiao*)	C (*Chi*)	D (*Yü*)
Cardinal points	North	East	Center	West	South
Planets	Mercury	Jupiter	Saturn	Venus	Mars
Elements	Wood	Water	Earth	Metal	Fire
Colors	Black	Violet	Yellow	White	Red

The Chinese separated their four seasons into musical intervals. The note F was Autumn, C was Spring, G was Winter, and D was Summer. At one time the names of the their notes were Emperor (F), Prime Minister (G), Loyal Subject (A), Affairs of the World (C) and Mirror of the World (D).

To our ears Chinese melodies wander aimlessly; the instruments seem to improvise freely, while the voice rises and falls in nasal twangings, which the Chinese think beautiful because they are supported by centuries of tradition. It is true that Oriental music is often incomprehensible to the listener steeped in expectations wholly outside it. If, however, he suppresses his prejudices and learns something of the metaphysical elements implicit in the music, he may discover that the alien quality of what he hears changes to one of interest. In Chinese music we often find a high degree of integration among words, music and the dance. As the *Record of Rites* notes: "Poetry expresses the idea; song prolongs the sounds; dance enlivens the attitudes." From ancient rituals grew secular puppet shows and, finally, the Chinese music drama.

We can also discern in Chinese music a more prominent place given to instrumental music and to a concept of orchestras. Dating from the time of Confucius and Tao, the Chinese developed unique instruments in the stone chime (*pien-ch'ing*), a series of L-shaped stone plates suspended in a frame, the bell chime (*pien-chung*), a comparable set of bells and the reed mouth-organ (*shêng*) which served as a prototype for our harmonica. The Chinese orchestra uses drums of all kinds and sizes (one drum is raised on a pedestal six feet high); bells; single stones beaten with mallets; cymbals; wooden clappers; rows of tuned stones; series of copper plates strung up to be hammered; and wooden tubs, some beaten from the outside and others from the inside. The wind instruments are globular flutes and flutes of clay, bamboo and metal, and the *koan-tsee,* an instrument of twelve pipes of bamboo bound together.

In the first-century A.D. Buddhist monks arrived in China from India and introduced a more flexible type of music on a native stringed instrument they adopted, called the *ch'in*. This is a type of zither, with five to seven strings, stopped by studs along the fingerboard, and lending itself to an impressionistic style, characterized by all manner of ornaments including twenty-six kinds of *vibrato* (a wavering in pitch produced by muscular action). Another popular type of zither is called *shê*. The Persian harp entered China following the conquest of Turkestan in A.D. 384. A short lute (*p'i-p'a*) originally from central Asia, became a favorite instrument of the T'ang (A.D. 618-907) poets, soon rivalling the *ch'in* in popularity.

Orchestras, maintained by the Royal Court and by the nobility as well as the temples, were supposed to be sound bridges between the gods and ancestors and living people. As with the tones of the scale, each instrument was associated with a substance, an element, a cardinal point, a season and a planet. For instance, the flute represented East, Spring and bamboo. The musical resources of ancient China often reached elaborate proportions; for one shrine, in addition to the singers, there were 120 *ch'in,* a like number of *shê,* 200 *shêng* and twenty oboes plus the percussive forces. Apparently a choir sang a measured hymn, resembling medieval *cantus firmus,* while the winds and bell chimes played in unison and the mouth organs and zithers added a quicker measured rhythm, sometimes accompanying the melody with intervals of fourths or fifths, similar to crude *organum*. The resulting beauty lay in the subtle blend of tone qualities, rather than in intellectual intricacies. It is written in the *Yok-Kyi*:

> Music holds the place of the great original principle, Heaven: the rites hold the place of created beings, Earth. In showing itself without repose music is like heaven, which is in perpetual motion: in showing themselves immovable, the rites resemble earth, which is without motion.

*   *   *   *   *

Limitations of space prevent us from examining the music of Tibet, Japan and the mainlands and islands of Southeast Asia. Students interested in Lamaistic music, Japanese *Nō* plays, *Kabuki* entertainments, *Shinto* rituals, the *koto* and *samisen,* Japanese and Indonesian variants of the Chinese pentatonic scale, and other such matters, are referred to the bibliography below. It comes as no surprise, however, to find the Sinic influence extending north, south, east and west. In each area, moreover, one discovers the contributions of Hindu, Buddhist and Moslem cultures, mixed in differing proportions with the indigenous and Chinese elements to produce uniquely individual civilizations and music.

CHARACTERISTICS OF ANCIENT EASTERN MUSIC

Before concluding our discussion of the music of ancient peoples of Africa, the Near East and the Far East, we might, in summarizing, cite some common characteristics, allowing, of course, for falsehoods of generalization. Ritual music in ancient civilizations was usually professional and rarely if ever enlisted the active participation of the entire community, as is the case with primitive peoples. Ancient music and its theory rested squarely upon religious and cosmological pillars, steadied by mathematical speculation. It was predominantly vocal and **monophonic** (single-voiced), emphasizing melody and rhythm with only occasional **heterophony** (accidental interweaving of musical lines). Because of its relationship with philosophy and metaphysics, music, once systematized, was closed to revision or experimentation and attained a traditional format that persisted. Rudiments of notational efforts survive, but they are undeveloped and particularly weak in rhythmic direction.

INFLUENCES ON THE WEST

What influence did this music of the East exert upon that of our Western world? Subsequent chapters will throw more light on the many contributions of music from the ancient Near East to the development of European music. We shall mention but two facets here.

The first is the curious popularity of Turkish military music and its instrumentation that found an enthusiastic response in eighteenth-century Europe, where Mozart, Haydn and Beethoven, as well as lesser composers, incorporated features of it into their works, including Mozart's opera *Die Entführung aus dem Serail* (*The Abduction from the Seraglio*), in which he uses bass drum, cymbals and triangle, Haydn's *"Military"* Symphony (No. 100 in G), and Beethoven's "March" from *The Ruins of Athens* (*Op.* 113).

Fig. 9. "Masquerade in Naples"—Raphael Morghen, 1778. In eighteenth-century Europe, Turkish military music found an enthusiastic response. Gradually Europeans assembled their own "Turkish" bands, often used in fantastic fashion, as seen here. Our military bands stem from the Turks. (Courtesy The Metropolitan Museum of Art.)

A second area of Oriental influence appears strongest in works of twentieth-century composers, although it may date from Weber's overture, *Turandot,* written in 1809. This demonstrates an interest in exotic features of tone quality inherent in the idiophonic instruments we have mentioned. Claude Debussy's (1862-1918) excitement on hearing a *gamelan* (classic Indonesian chime orchestra) at the Exposition Universelle in Paris in 1889 is well known. The same composer was inspired by the discovery of "finger" cymbals in an Egyptian tomb to include these "ancient cymbals" in scoring his tone poem, *L'Après-midi d'un faune* (*The Afternoon of a Faun*). Debussy's colleague, Maurice Ravel (1875-1937), also made use of them (*crotales*) in *Daphnis and Chloë.* Puccini (1858-1924) used the Far Eastern gong-chime in his operas *Madame Butterfly* and *Turandot.* Other selected examples are:

Albert Roussel's (1869-1937) opera-ballet *Pâdmâvatî*; Gustav Holst's (1874-1934) opera *Savitri* and setting of *Hymns from the Rig-Veda*; Benjamin Britten's (1913-   ) ballet, *Prince of the Pagodas*; Henry Cowell's (1897-1965) *Homage to Iran* and *Persian Set*; Lou Harrison's (1917-   ) *Suite for Violin, Piano and Small Orchestra*; Alan Hovhaness' (1911-   ) *Koke no niwa*; and William Walton's (1902-   ) *Belshazzar's Feast*; also Paul Hindemith's (1895-1964) Burmese puppet show *Das Nusch-Nuschi*; Bernard van Dieren's (1884-1936) *"Chinese" Symphony*; and John Alden Carpenter's (1876-1951) *Watercolors*.

SUGGESTIONS FOR FURTHER READING

Edgerly, Beatrice, *From the Hunter's Bow*. New York, Putnam, 1942.

Engel, Carl, *The Music of the Most Ancient Nations*. London, Reeves, 1929.

Fox-Strangways, A. H., *The Music of Hindoostan*. London, Clarendon, 1914.

Galpin, Francis W., *The Music of the Sumerians and Their Immediate Successors, the Babylonians and Assyrians*. Strasbourg, Strasbourg University Press, 1955.

Graham, David C., *Songs and Stories of the Ch'uan Miao*. Washington, Smithsonian Institution, 1954.

Halson, Elizabeth, *Peking Opera: A Short Guide*. New York, Oxford University Press, 1966.

Idelsohn, A. Z., *Jewish Music in Its Historical Development*. New York, Holt, 1929.

Kunst, Jaap, *Music in Java*. The Hague, Nijhoff, 1949. 2 vols.

Le May, Reginald, *The Culture of South-East Asia*. London, Allen & Unwin, 1954.

Malm, William P. *Music Cultures of the Pacific, the Near East, and Asia.** Englewood Cliffs, Prentice-Hall, 1967.

Powell, Hickman, Cape, Jonathan, and Smith, Harrison, *The Last Paradise*. New York, Cape, 1930.

Pritchard, James, ed., *Ancient Near East Texts*. Princeton, Princeton University Press, 1955.

Ribera, Julian, *Music in Ancient Arabia and Spain*. Stanford, Stanford University Press, 1929.

Rothmuller, Aron Marko, *The Music of the Jews.** New York, Barnes, 1960.

Sachs, Curt, *The Rise of Music in the Ancient World, East and West*. New York, Norton, 1943.

Scott, A. C., *The Kabuki Theatre of Japan*. New York, Barnes & Noble, 1964.

Stainer, John, *The Music of the Bible*. London, Novello, 1914.

Stevens, Denis, and Robertson, Alec, eds., *The Pelican History of Music,* vol. 1.** Baltimore, Penguin, 1960.

Woolley, C. Leonard, *Ur of the Chaldees*. New York, Scribner, 1930.

A SAMPLER OF SUPPLEMENTARY RECORDINGS

Music of the Near East

Classical Arab-Andalusian Tunisian Music	Folkways 8861
Arabic and Druse Music	Folkways 4480

* Available in paperback edition.

Santur Recital	Lyric 135
Kurdish Folksongs and Dances	Folkways 4469
Folk Music of Palestine	Folkways 4408
Music and Songs of Lebanon	Philips 200063
Folk and Traditional Music of Turkey	Folkways 4404
Bulos — Lebanon, Syria, Jordan	Folkways 8816

Music of the Far East

Exotic Sounds of Bali		Columbia ML-4618
Folk and Traditional Music of Burma		Folkways 4436
Chinese Classical Instrumental Music	(10″)	Folkways 6812
Chinese Songs and Opera		Folkways 8880
Through China in Song and Dance		Bruno 50114
Chinese Drums and Gongs		Lyric 102
Classical Indian Music		London 9282
Drums of India		World 1403
Morning and Evening Ragas		Angel 35283
Ravi Shankar in Concert		World 1421
Folk Music of Indonesia		Columbia KL-210
Azuma Kabuki Musicians		Columbia ML-4925
Art of the Koto		Elektra 234
Japanese Temple Music		Lyric 117
Japanese Folk Music		Folkways 4429
Malaysian Dream Music		Folkways 4460
Folk Music of Pakistan		Folkways 4425
East of the Urals		Monitor 316

Composed Music of Interest

Cowell, Henry, *Persian Set*	Composers Recordings, Inc. 114
Beethoven, Ludwig, *Ruins of Athens:* Incidental Music	Angel 35509
Hába, Alois, *Fantasy for Violin Solo in ¼ Tones*	Folkways 3355
Harrison, Lou, *Suite*	CRI 114
Hovhaness, Alan, *Koke no niwa* ("Moss Garden")	CRI 186
Honegger, Arthur, *Le Roi David*	Vanguard 1090
Walton, William, *Belshazzar's Feast*	Columbia ML-6267

OPPORTUNITIES FOR STUDY IN DEPTH

1. Make an intensive study of the ancient music of one country or area, investigating its uses, theory, instruments and forms.

2. Visit a museum and examine its collection of musical instruments from throughout the world, seeking examples of those mentioned in the text and noting their sizes and construction.

3. Make a comparison, by means of recordings, between authentic Iraqi or Iranian music and such a work as Henry Cowell's *Persian Set,* noting what elements of the indigenous folk music the composer chose and how he handled them.

4. Experiment with the tone qualities of various natural and synthetic materials and set forth findings of the experimentation.

5. Using the black keys on the piano keyboard (which form a pentatonic scale, as explained earlier), improvise "Chinese" dances, utilizing such concepts as high pitch, thematic repetition, lively tempo, the drone and imitations of plucked and struck instruments and occasional parallelism to characterize the music. One player might alternate the treble tones G flat and D flat at regular rhythmic intervals. Another, working above the resulting drone, might sound double tones, selected by omitting an intervening black key, at a quicker pace.

6. Prepare, with aural and visual aids, a unit for teaching children of the middle grades about the music of India, China or Japan.

7. Read one of the great religious books of the Orient and lead a class discussion of its contents and its relationship to cultural forms of art and music. One subject could be the *Jataka* and the Ajanta cave temples of India (see G. Yazdani, *Ajanta*. Oxford, Oxford University Press, 1930).

8. Experiment with the so-called "Oriental minor" scale, used to produce exotic effects in film music and found in Arabic-Jewish centers in Eastern Europe. This scale is constructed of two tetrachords, each featuring an interval of the augmented second; *i.e.,* a descending C scale would read — C, B, A flat, G, F sharp, E flat, D, C.

VOCABULARY ENRICHMENT

idiophones	*tala*
solo and response	*srutis*
antiphony	tempo
tremolo	*plectrum*
cosmology	fret
harmonic division	scale
cyclic division	*vibrato*
gloss	monophonic
maqamāt	heterophony
rāga	

Chapter 3.

MUSIC OF THE GREEKS AND ROMANS

Orpheus was the son of Apollo and the Muse Calliope. He was presented by his father with a lyre and taught to play upon it, which he did
to such perfection that nothing could withstand the charm of his music.
Not only his fellow-mortals but wild beasts were softened by his strains,
and gathering round him laid by their fierceness, and stood entranced
with his lay. Nay, the very trees and rocks were sensible to the charm.
The former crowded round him and the latter relaxed somewhat of their
hardness, softened by his notes.

—Thomas Bulfinch, *The Age of Fable*

The Greek contribution to the world, at the height of her attainment,
marked not only the turning point in Western history but the starting
point of modern language and of the arts. Probably the basic reason for
the preeminence of ancient Greece was that a fundamental of Greek
life was freedom; its greatest ideal, beauty; its means of attainment,
simplicity and directness; and its desire, harmony—a balanced many-
sidedness. All these qualities had play with few or no obstacles from the
state. The good fortune of the Greeks was that there was no religious
tyranny to combat, their gods being conceived in their own image, not
to frighten, but to be lived with in fellowship and humanized intimacy.
The greatness of Greece was founded on philosophy and respect for
reason. From their early dramatists to Euripides and Plato, the Greeks
produced poetry, sculpture and architecture never excelled, and a science of music of rich import to future generations.

MUSIC IN GREEK LIFE

Music, the word which the Greeks handed down to many nations,
was far more inclusive to them than it is to us. The word itself is derived
from the *Muses,* the nine daughters of Zeus who were, so to speak, the
matron saints of the arts. In the music schools, singing, playing, dancing,
oratory and allied subjects were taught. The two main branches of
learning were music and gymnastics. Like other ancient peoples, the
Greeks used melody, probably without harmony. From the writings of
Pythagoras, Terpander, Timotheus, Aristoxenos, Aristotle, Plato the
poet and Plato the philosopher, it can be inferred that Greek melody

had greater passion and sensuousness than ours. This was due, no doubt, to a richer, broader tonal variety in the use of modes, and of tones smaller than our half-steps. The presence of microtones may be evidence that Greek music had its genesis in the Orient of Asia Minor.

The Greeks had no Bible as such but as they imbued their gods with human attributes, the result was an anthropomorphic religion—one of the richest mythologies in the world. To Pan they ascribed the pipes of Pan or the *syrinx*; to Apollo the *lyre*; and such myths as that of Orpheus grew up in profusion. Therefore, in common with other young civilizations, Greece ascribed music to divine sources.

In the taxation system of Athens were five *liturgies* (taxes). One, a supertax, was paid by a rich man, called the *choregus,* whose obligation it was to equip the chorus for the drama festivals in honor of Dionysius. The audience and judges chose the winning dramatist, and the event was of religious and national significance. It was celebrated in high revels, for the worship of Dionysius had nothing grave about it. Monuments built to commemorate the prize-winning play were inscribed with the names of the *choregus,* the flute player, the dramatist and the date. The *choregus* was responsible for the training of the chorus and all its expenses, which were tremendous.

At the height of drama in Athens the tragic chorus numbered fifteen, having decreased from an earlier fifty. (The comic chorus numbered twenty-four.) The Greek chorus in its most interesting era consisted of masked singer-actor-dancers, who in many ways took the place of our printed libretto, and made up in gesture and posture for the scant scenic effects of a primitive stage. In the outdoor amphitheaters they danced in the orchestra, a space in front of the stage buildings. (Dance in Greek was *orchesis,* hence our word which came into common usage with the activities of the Florentine *camerata* in the late sixteenth century.) The drama was a perfect synthesis of music, poetry and the dance. Dramatists were not only poets, but composers who had devoted much of their time to the study of music.

The Greeks were a gay people. R. W. Livingstone, in *The Greek Genius and Its Meaning to Us,* calls them "amiable ruffians." They reveled in feasts, drinking and sports, as well as in *symposia* (after-dinner discussions), oratory, the arts and philosophy. Their festivals commemorated all their interests. The most famous, no doubt, were the Olympic Games, held every four years, from 776 B.C., which date became the basis of their calendar. Besides this sports festival, there were the city *Dionysia,* the rural *Dionysia* and the *Lenaean*; moreover, every town held its own contests and competitions. Most famous of these were the Pythian Games, in honor of the Delphic Apollo, at Delphi, dating from 586 B.C.; the Isthmian and Nemean competitions in music and poetry; and the music contests held at the Panathenian festivals. All classes and conditions of men witnessed and took part in these celebrations. Holidays were observed for each, and the altars of the gods in every theater were lavishly revered.

In countless writings about Greek dance there is nothing to tell us exactly *how* it was done. All we have are the static records on vases, statuary, tablets and monuments; quotations from orations and poetry; and directions in the plays for the chorus. It originated in the *goat dance* in honor of Dionysius. Later the goat dance or goat chorus was part of the drama of Thespis, the first tragedian of Athens. "Tragedy" comes from *tragodia,* Greek for "goat (*tragos*) song." (From Thespis, we get our word for actor, thespian.)

The function of the Greek dance was to represent objects and events by posture and gesture, and to illustrate the words of poetry. Poetry and the dance grew up almost as the same art. Indeed, the smallest division of verse was called "foot." Livingstone explains, "A verse two feet long was styled *basis* or a 'stepping.' The words *arsis* and *thesis,* which denoted the varying stress of the voice in singing, originally referred to the raising up and placing down of the foot in . . . dancing." This identical terminology indicates the intimate union of dance, music and poetry in ancient Greece.

The dance, in the time of Thespis and before, was mostly of the legs. Later, it became far more a dance of the arms. Ovid, in his *Art of Love,* when advising a young lover in the ways of wooing, suggested that he should dance "if his arms are flexible." It was not considered humiliating as it was later, in Rome, for men of high caste to dance. In fact, as a youth, Sophocles himself danced naked in public.

Hypokrites or "one who answers" was the Greek word for actor. (From this our term "hypocrite" is derived.) In the earliest drama there was only the chorus. In Aeschylus' time (524-456 B.C.) there was one actor, and he introduced a second. Later there were three in tragedy, whence it became less lyric and more dramatic. The drama included speech, recitative and song of some sort. The type of verse form and its place in the drama determined the medium. Often in the play an actor would go directly from speech to song. This was simpler in Greek than in English, for Greek was accented tonally—that is, inflected—rather than by stressing the syllable. This doubtless gave a singing character even to everyday speech. The accompaniment was played by a single flute or occasionally a harp, as nothing was permitted to obscure the value of the words.

Plato reported the various classes and styles of music: *hymns,* which were prayers to the gods; *dirges*; *paeans,* originally choral dances of healing; *dithyrambs,* dances dedicated to the cult of Dionysius and *nomes.* Gustave Reese in his *Music in the Middle Ages* states that the *nomos* "was a sung strain as distinguished from a recitation." As the word means "law," the *nomoi* seem to have been formulae of " 'law-giving,' fundamental and rhythmic types which might be worked over by musicians into something more or less new." The *nomoi* were said to have been introduced by a Phrygian, Olympos, in 900 B.C., as bases for the music of the reed pipe, or *aulos.* As all Phrygians came to Greece from Asia Minor and as the "laws" seem to have been melodic formulae for music-making, strong reasons exist for acknowledging Egyptian and Oriental influences upon the music of ancient Greece.

GREEK MUSICAL RELICS

While Greek treatises and philosophic speculations about music are in abundant supply, examples of the actual music are rare indeed. Less than twenty relics are known to us and all but one of these are of vocal music. Included are two hymns to Apollo, found carved in stone at Delphi, dating possibly 200 B.C., a time at which Greece was already feeling twinges of the might of Rome, and a time when Greek music had disregarded classic ideals in favor of more vulgar motives; a *skolion* or drinking song of Seikilos, engraved on the tomb of his wife at Aidin, Turkey; a fragment of the lost score of *Orestes* by Euripides; and several hymns by Mesomedes from the second century A.D. (The "Pythic Ode" of Pindar is now considered spurious.) In any case, these fragments cannot tell us very much about the kind of music that enthralled the great Greek writers, for music, even in the Golden Age of Greece, had already degenerated to a point that obliterated the great ideals of the past, a return to which Plato proposed.

GREEK MUSICAL THEORY

Although examples of actual music are rare, enough was written about the theory of Greek music for present-day musicologists to reconstruct the system. The basic principle of this system was related to the **tetrachord** (meaning "four strings"). The two outer tones, which measured a perfect fourth in our nomenclature, were fixed, and the intermediate tones were movable. The tetrachords were varied according to the position of the intermediate tones. "In theory, of course," Barry writes, "the possible forms of the tetrachord were infinite, yet in practice, their number was limited to certain recognized differences of *genus, shade* and *species.* This limitation was based on the usage of musicians."

According to Aristoxenos (fourth century, B.C.), tetrachords were of three *genera* or classes: **diatonic,** in which the intervals were arranged in two whole steps with only one half-step; **chromatic,** in which the intervals were arranged to include two half-steps and a minor third, or two half-steps and an augmented second; and **enharmonic,** in which intervals smaller than half steps, such as quarter-tones and one-third tones, were used with a sharpened major third. While we speak in terms of our intervals, the three *genera* had many shades in which the ratio of the intervals differed from ours. Aristoxenos, in addition to the three types of tetrachords, indicated others, the steps of which do not exist in our tuning.

In the following table, in terms of our system, the half steps are indicated with a slur. We build our scales from the lowest to the highest tones, but the Greeks built theirs downward.

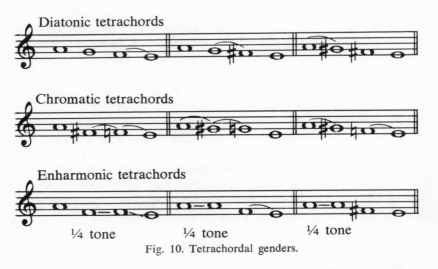

¼ tone   ¼ tone   ¼ tone

Fig. 10. Tetrachordal genders.

Primary species derive their names from the confederacies of Dorian, Ionian and Aeolian cities on the western coast of Asia Minor (which also lent their names to Greek architectural styles, that, interestingly enough, connote, in addition to the familiar capitals, the general plan of the building, its proportions, its particular friezes and cornices, rather analogous to the melody packages of the *rāgas* and the *nomoi*) and the inland Phrygian and Lydian territories. Of these, Gustave Reese states that the Dorian species was the only octave that had a "modal life." The other species were keys (*tonoi*) without the implications we give either to medieval or modern modes. The Dorian, Phrygian and Lydian are but different aspects of the principal, or Dorian mode.

Dorian:	e	d	c͡b	a	g	f͡e
Phrygian:	e	d͡c♯	b	a	g͡f♯	e
Lydian:	e͡d♯	c♯	b	a͡g♯	f♯	e

Fig. 11. Diatonic species.

Species are formed of two adjacent tetrachords similarly constructed and joined together in one of two ways. The **disjunct** method creates an eight-tone scale. The **conjunct** method occurs when the two tetrachords overlap, resulting in a seven-tone scale, with the middle note as tonic, final or *mesē,* thus (in the Dorian mode):

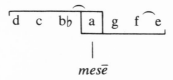

mesē

To complete the octave, a step was added in late antiquity, combining a species of fifth (*pentachord*) with that of the fourth (*tetrachord*). In ascending, conjunct order this resulted in seven *tonoi,* according to Ptolemy and to Gaudentios in the second century A.D. Reese shows that the *mesē* is always reckoned according to the intervals of the Dorian mode:

Mixolydian:	e f		g	a b♭	c	(d)	e
Lydian:	e	f♯	g♯ a	b	(c♯)	d♯ e	
Phrygian:	e	f♯ g	a	(b)	c♯ d		e
Dorian:	e f		g	(a)	b c		d	e
Hypolydian:	e	f♯	(g♯)	a♯ b		c♯	d♯ e
Hypophrygian:	e	(f♯)	g♯ a	b	c♯ d		e
Hypodorian:	(e)	f♯ g		a	b c		d	e

Fig. 12. Diatonic octachords.

Each primary species had its secondary species distinguished by the prefixes, *hypo* (below) and *hyper* (above). The primary Dorian mode had associated with it the *Hypodorian,* or *Aeolian* species, and the *Hyperdorian,* or *Mixolydian* species, also the *Ionian.* The *Phrygian* had as secondary species the *Hypophrygian* and the *Hyperphrygian,* or *Locrian.* The *Lydian* had as its related species the *Hypolydian* and the *Hyperlydian.*

After the time of Aristoxenos (about 320 B.C.) the enharmonic species became obsolete, unfortunately, as both the enharmonic and the chromatic genus had given emotional color to Greek music. Cecil Torr, in the *Oxford History of Music,* says: "The Greeks gave melody a perfection that the Europeans cannot understand . . . small intervals are not unknown in Oriental music even now, but the modern Oriental has not the genius of the ancient Greek for taking full advantage of them, nor has the Modern European any such capacity."

ETHOS

We have already seen that the interconnection of music with mystic power was a common phenomenon among primitive and ancient peoples. Important in the magical bag of tricks was the use of music to heal the ravages of disease, incomprehensible then except as a scourge of the gods. How often must the medicine man have harassed the dying with his leaping, drumming and doleful chanting! That the Greeks did not make an entirely original contribution to claims for the powers of music is obvious; but perhaps they made the best statement of an age-old belief in the psychological and physiological effects of music upon the human being in their theory of *ethos.*

The Greeks claimed ethical meaning for the various scales. Various writers stated that Dorian mode was virile, energetic, and proper for the perfect citizen; Phrygian was ecstatic, religious, and affected the soul; Lydian (our major scale?) induced effeminacy and slack morals; the Mixolydian was fit for lamentations; and the Hypolydian was dissolute and voluptuous. Sachs writes, "The famous term *ethos* denoted the emotional power of melodies according to their scales." Apparently pitch, range, rhythm, tempo, type of melody and metaphysical symbolism were also ingredients in the ancient alchemy.

GREEK MUSICAL SCIENCE

While we have inherited much from Greek music indirectly, the experiments of Pythagoras (*c.* 585-*c.* 479 B.C.) in measuring the relationship of tones are a concrete contribution. With a background of study in Babylonian and Egyptian temples, Pythagoras is supposed to have gathered the Greek modes into a definite system, to have invented the science of acoustics and to have increased the number of strings of the lyre. He also founded a brotherhood based on music as a means of life, education and moral uplift.

By means of an instrument of one string, a precursor of the medieval **monochord,** Pythagoras presented a principle that is the basis of acoustical theory. By dividing the string into two equal parts, the tone produced was an octave above that of the entire length. In addition to the octave, he established the ratio of the fifth, the fourth, the twelfth and the double octave. Carrying Pythagoras' theory into the science of acoustics, the numerical ratio of intervals shows the octave as 1:2; the fifth as 2:3; the fourth, 3:4; the twelfth, 1:3; the double octave, 1:4; the major third, 4:5; the minor third, 5:6; the major second (wholestep), 8:9; the minor second (half-step), 10:11; as illustrated in the overtone series.

About 500 B.C. Pindar's teacher, Lasos of Hermione, discovered that vibrations were the cause of sound. Archytas of Tarentum, one hundred years later, found that two kinds of vibrations were necessary for hearing, stationary waves within the instrument and moving waves in the air surrounding the ears.

It was Euclid, however, in the fourth century B.C., who described the Perfect System of scales which were probably the outgrowth of Pythagoras' theories. The *kithara* theoretically covered a two-octave range in a pentatonic arrangement which corresponded to the *Greater Perfect System.* This consisted of four tetrachords organized from a center tone a, called the *mesē,* with an added tone A below, called the *proslambanomenos.* Each degree and each tetrachord has its name, and the scale is the Dorian (e'-d'-c'-b-a-g-f-e), which occupied the center of the system with a conjunct tetrachord below. (The Greeks called low the pitch we designate as high.) The tetrachords named from the top down were: *hyperbolaen* (extreme) a'-g'-f'-e'; *diezeugmenôn* (disjunct) e'-d'-c'-b; *mesôn* (middle) a-g-f-e; *hypatôn* (upper) e-d-c-B, to which was added A.

The *Lesser Perfect System* had a compass of eleven tones from d' to the added A. It consisted, as reckoned from below upward, of the *proslambanomenos* and the *hypatôn* and *mesôn* tetrachords, to which was added a conjunct tetrachord *synemmenon* (hooked).

One difficulty in understanding Greek music is the confusion of terms, started by the Greeks themselves. "The tangle of Greek systems, scales, keys, and modes is unbelievable," says Sachs. Mixing up the words *tonos* (key) and *modus* (the Latin translation of *tonos*) led to inverting the naming of the medieval ecclesiastical modes. Boëthius

(c. A.D. 480-524) tried to reinterpret the Greek theory conscientiously, but a tenth-century treatise, *Alia musica,* misinterpreting Boëthius, reversed the order of the Greek octave species.

GREEK MUSICAL INSTRUMENTS

Greek instruments can be classified into two general categories— string and pipe, or **lyre** and **aulos.** Our knowledge of them comes from representations on monuments, vases, statues and friezes and from the testimony of Greek authors. The lyre was the national instrument and included a wide variety of types. In its most antique form, the *chelys,* it is traced back to the age of fable and allegedly owed its invention to Hermes. Easy to carry, this small lyre became the favorite instrument of the home, amateurs and women, a popular accompaniment for drinking songs and love songs, as well as more noble kinds of poetry. Homer had written of Achilles:

> How he comforts his heart with the sound of the lyre— Fairly and cunningly arched and adorned with a bridge of silver— Stimulating his courage, and singing the deeds of heroes. . .

Professional Homeric singers used a *kithara,* a larger, more powerful instrument, which probably came originally from Asia Minor, perhaps from Egypt. The *kithara* had a flat wooden sound-box and an upper horizontal bar supported by two curving arms. Within this frame were stretched strings of equal length, at first but three or four in number. Fastened to the performer by means of a sling, the *kithara* was played with both hands. We are not sure in just what manner the instrument was used to accompany the epics. It may have been employed for a pitch-fixing prelude and for interludes, or it may have paralleled or decorated the vocal melody in more or less free fashion.

Sachs claims that the lyre "was pentatonic without semitones and preserved its archaic tuning even when the number of its strings was increased beyond five." Two types of tuning were used: the **dynamic,** or pitch method, naming the degrees "according to function"; and the **thetic,** or tablature, naming them "according to position" on the instrument.

As early as the eighth century B.C., lyres of five strings appeared. Terpander (fl. *c.* 675 B.C.), one of the first innovators, is said to have increased the number of strings to seven. He is also supposed to have completed the octave and created the Mixolydian scale. (Born in Lesbos, he was called to Sparta to quell an uprising, by means of his music.) Aristoxenos claimed that the poetess Sappho, in the seventh century B.C., in addition to introducing a mode in which Dorian and Lydian characteristics were blended, initiated use of the *plectrum* or pick. At the time of Sophocles (495-406 B.C.), the lyre had eleven strings.

Another harplike string instrument was the *magadis,* whose tone was described as trumpetlike. Of foreign importation, it had twenty strings, which, by means of frets, played octaves. As some of the strings were tuned in quarter-tones, it was an instrument associated with the enharmonic mode. Smaller versions, the *pectis* and the *barbitos,* were also tuned in quarter-tones. Greek men and boys had a style of singing in octaves that was called *magadizing,* after the octave-playing instruments.

The *kithara* was identified with Apollo and the Apollonian cult, representing the intellectual and idealistic side of Greek art. The *aulos* or reed pipe was the instrument of the Dionysians, who represented the unbridled, sensual and passionate aspect of Greek culture. Although translated as "flute," the *aulos* is more like our oboe. Usually found in double form, the pipes set at an angle, the *aulos* was reputed to have a far more exciting effect than that produced by the subdued lyre. About 600 B.C. the *aulos* was chosen as the official instrument of the Delphian and Pythian festivals. It was also used in performances of the Dionysian *dithyramb* as well as a supplement of the chorus in classic Greek tragedy and comedy, as our account of the drama has mentioned.

Fig. 13. "Aulos and Clappers"—vase painting. *Music* was a word which the Greeks handed down to many nations. Notice the *phorbeia* about the cheeks of the *aulete.* (Courtesy British Museum.)

There was a complete family of *auloi* covering the same ranges as human voices. One authority names three species of simple pipes and five varieties of double pipes. (The double pipe was the professional instrument.) An early specimen was supposed to have been tuned to the chromatic tetrachord D, C sharp, B flat, A, a fact that points to Oriental origin. Elegiac songs called *aulodia* were composed in this mode to be accompanied by an *aulos*. Although the first wooden pipes had only three or four finger-holes, the number was later increased so that the Dorian, Phrygian and Lydian modes might be performed on a single pair. Pictures of *auletes* show them with a bandage or *phorbeia* over their faces; this may have been necessary to hold the two pipes in place, to modulate the tone or, perhaps, to aid in storing air in the cheeks for the purpose of sustained performance.

We have already spoken of the *syrinx* or pipes of Pan, a possible forerunner of the pipe organ and of Pythagoras' monochord. There were, in addition, a few Greek war trumpets, and a small parchment hand drum called the *tympanon* as well as *krotola,* wooden or metal castanets.

GREEK NOTATION

The Greeks had two systems of notation, instrumental and vocal, with which to indicate the twenty-one degrees lying within the octave. In the older **instrumental system,** the letter names were chosen from a Phoenician alphabet and the scale moved in upward succession, with each of the seven tones accompanied by two stopped notes. In the so-called **vocal system,** letters of the Greek alphabet were used to denote tones in descending order. These tones were not arranged successively, however, but were grouped in threes, that is, *alpha beta gamma,* each triad belonging to one string of the lyre. In other words, both forms of notation were really **tablatures,** scripts devised for an instrument, indicating fingering rather than pitches. As the singer was expected to accompany himself upon a lyre, it is quite understandable that tablature notation would serve his purpose.

The rhythms of Greek music leaned heavily upon the contrast of short-long which underlay the rhythm of Greek poetry whose terminology, as we have seen, originates from that of the dance. That the principal Greek meters are still in use today is but another testimony to the contribution ancient Greece made to the world. These basic meters included the *pyrrhic* (short-short), the *iamb* (short-long), *anapest* (short-short-long), *spondee* (long-long), *trochee* (long-short) and the *dactyl* (long-short-short). These were combined in twos, threes and fours to produce more varied movement patterns. Curt Sachs provocatively notes that the theme of the second movement of Beethoven's *Seventh Symphony* might serve as an example of the idea of dactyl-spondee dipody—long-short-short long-long, long-short-short long-long. Rhythm, governed largely by versification, also had a code to indicate duration of sound.

*   *   *   *   *

The course of music in Greece during more than a millennium of its history exemplifies the vagaries of development and decline. Following the Heroic Age of absorption and formulation came the age of epic poems attributed to Homer and sung by privileged bards to the simple accompaniment of a lyre. Music was also the property of the community at large, in its feasts and games. Secular lyrics by poet-musicians gradually became popular, to be preempted during the sixth and fifth centuries by the musical drama. With Aristophanes (*c.* 444-380 B.C.), we find, in his parodies, that classical austerity had succumbed to laxities. Chromaticism and intimacy led to a separation of creator and performer. Vulgarity resulted in a cleavage between the professional executant and the proper citizen, with social implications that remain to the present day. Music had fallen from its lofty position of former times to that of a debased kind of casual entertainment.

ROMAN MUSIC

Rome—conqueror, jurist and engineer—took from vanquished Greece its musical resources, with little or no modification, together with much of its mythology and its arts. But to meet the demands of a martial, acquisitive and noise-loving organization, it used, in addition to modified Greek and Egyptian instruments, what we call brasses, and a primitive organ. Inconsistently, Rome developed the *mimus* and the *pantomime;* consistently, it reveled in showy processions, blares of trumpets, overelaborate exhibitions and bloodcurdling gladiatorial combats. Therefore, the importance of Roman music lies in its having been the bridge between the old Egyptian, Hebrew and Greek, and the *new,* the early Christian music, with its genesis in Rome itself.

Just as today we have a theater of the absurd, ancient Rome had its own in verity, with one of the chief actors the Emperor Nero himself, he who proverbially "fiddled" while Rome burned. If indeed he made music under such an exciting stimulus, it was probably upon the *tibia* (pipe or bagpipe) or the *cithara,* since the fiddle was then unknown in Rome (although there was in Hadrian's time a *tamboura,* the plucked lute of two or three strings). The mad-sad Nero, however, exemplifies several aspects of Roman musicians.

Early Romans had been much too busy conquering and administer-

Fig. 14. The Forum at Rome. Rome, conqueror, jurist and engineer, took from vanquished Greece its musical resources, modifying them to meet the demands of a martial, acquisitive and noise-loving organization. (Photograph by the editor.)

ing their empire to bother with such an ephemeral pursuit as music. This they left to slaves. But as Rome grew and matured, the bright hard core of the Roman citizenry lost its luster and purity, the government became corrupt and insecure and the populace clamored increasingly for larger and more lascivious entertainments to lull its discontent. A "star" system developed among performers, who were much in demand, handsomely paid and whose caprices were of great interest. Nero conceived himself the greatest of these; he practiced assiduously, performed to captive audiences as often as he could and is credited with originating that venerable institution among temperamental artists, the *claque,* a group of professional applauders, who followed after the great one. So far had Nero's delusions gone that his reputed last words were, "What an artist the world is losing in me!"

Although the Romans adopted and adapted Greek instruments, including the *auloi* (*tibia*) and *kithara* (*cithara*), they centered their attention chiefly on the *tuba* (trumpet) for the infantry; the *lituus,* like the J-shaped trumpet or *shofar* used in the Hebrew ritual; and the *buccina,* a progenitor of the sackbut and trombone. The *buccina* was twelve feet long, and passed around the player's body, with the bell over his left shoulder, as our circular bass (brass) does now. These instruments were probably never played in harmony, nor could a performer play more than three or four blatant notes on them.

Naturally the noise-loving, soldierly Roman people had percussion instruments. Among these were the *tympanum,* much like a tambourine and beaten with the hands; the *scabillum,* two hinged metal plates which were fastened under the foot and stamped upon to mark rhythm; the *cymbali,* similar to our cymbals; and the *crotola* and *crusmata,* approximating the castanet. From Egypt came the *sistrum.* Romans used the *tintinnabula,* metal bells set in intervallic progression, sometimes on a hoop.

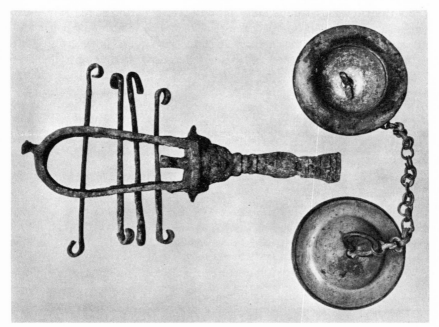

Fig. 15. Roman cymbals and sistrum—Pompeii. Roman instruments reflected the scope of Roman domination; but *sistrum* and cymbals reflect borrowings from the Near East. (Courtesy National Museum, Naples.)

The *cithara* inspired a Roman *citharoedic chant,* usually addressed to a god or goddess. In many of these chants, Greek texts persisted until A.D. 300, but Roman poets such as Horace and Catullus were masters of the form in Latin and regaled many a festive occasion by singing them.

Of all the Roman instruments, the **organ,** because of its place in later Christian music, may be of most significance. There had been evidence of a water *aulos* (*hydraulus*) in writings of Philo of Alexandria (200 B.C.); Vitruvius, an architect in Augustus' reign (c. A.D. 25), and Hero of Alexandria also mention the instrument. This evidence was substantiated in 1885 when a pottery model made by Possessoris in A.D. 100 was uncovered. The Romans had a pneumatic organ as well. Both instruments were apparently available in portable forms and used for revels and coarse and gaudy circuses. Because of its pagan and profane associations with excesses of the later Roman Empire, the organ, as well as other instruments, was banned from early Christian observances.

* * * * *

It is not possible to write a comprehensive history of ancient Greek (and Roman) music until more information is forthcoming. However, our legacy in written theory, acoustical data, the doctrine of *ethos* and musico-drama cannot be underestimated. The Greeks have given more to modern music than any other ancient people, because for the first time music had attained the dignity of an art, with all its aesthetic, emotional and moral significance, with its complicated theory, its sophisticated technique, consciously employed to give pleasure and to uplift the mind of man.

SUGGESTIONS FOR FURTHER READING

Anderson, Warren D., *Ethos and Education in Greek Music: The Evidence of Poetry and Philosophy*. Cambridge, Harvard University Press, 1966.

Bowra, Cecil M., *Greek Lyric Poetry from Alcman to Simonides*. Oxford, Oxford University Press, 1936.

———— *The Greek Experience.** New York, World, 1957.

Edgerly, Beatrice, *From the Hunter's Bow*. New York, Putnam, 1942.

Haigh, A. E., *The Attic Theatre*. Oxford, Clarendon, 1907.

Hamilton, Edith, *The Greek Way to Western Civilization.** New York, Norton, 1930.

———— *Mythology.** Boston: Little, Brown, 1942.

———— *The Roman Way to Western Civilization.** New York, Norton, 1932.

Lippman, Edward A., *Musical Thought in Ancient Greece*. New York, Columbia University Press, 1964.

Livingstone, R. W., *The Greek Genius and Its Meaning to Us*. Oxford, Oxford University Press, 1915.

Macran, H., *Aristoxenus*. Oxford, Oxford University Press, 1902.

Marrou, H. I., *A History of Education in Antiquity.** New York, Sheed & Ward, 1956.

Reese, Gustave, *Music in the Middle Ages*. New York, Norton, 1940.

Sachs, Curt, *The Rise of Music in the Ancient World*. New York, Norton, 1943.

* Available in paperback edition.

Stevens, Denis and Robertson, Alec, eds., *The Pelican History of Music*, vol. 1.*
Baltimore, Penguin, 1960.
Strunk, Oliver, ed., *Source Readings in Music History.** New York, Norton, 1950.

A SAMPLER OF SUPPLEMENTARY RECORDINGS

"Seikilos Song" and "Hymn to the Sun"   Decca 20156
"Skolion of Seikilos" (*2000 Years of Music*) Folkways 3700

Related Works of Interest

Euripides, *Medea*
Debussy, Claude, *Syrinx for Unaccompanied Flute*
Handel, G. F., *Julius Caesar*
Homer, *Selections*
Ravel, Maurice, *Cinq Mélodies populaires Grecques*
Satie, Erik, *Trois Gymnopédies*
Sophocles, *Oedipus Rex*
Stravinsky, Igor, *Apollon Musagète*
            Oedipus Rex

N.B.: Musical scores in modern notation for the "First Delphic Hymn," Mesomedes' "Hymn to the Sun" and the "Seikilos Song" are available in Davison
and Apel, *Historical Anthology of Music*, vol. 1. (Cambridge, Harvard University Press, 1949). The "Skolion of Seikelos" is also given in both modern
and Greek letter notation in Starr and Devine, *Music Scores—Omnibus*,
Part 1. (Englewood Cliffs, Prentice-Hall, 1964).

OPPORTUNITIES FOR STUDY IN DEPTH

1. Prepare a demonstration of the methods and results of Pythagoras' experimentation in the field of acoustics. Present it in class, using models constructed, as far as possible, upon primary source materials.

2. Read one of the ancient Greek tragedies and make a set of stage directions for
   a concert production, utilizing what is known about the roles of music, dance
   and speech in Greek drama.

3. Read what Plato has to say about the concept of *ethos* in the ideal state. Then
   scan modern music-therapy literature. Compare the underlying ideas, drawing
   parallels, if any, discussing differences in theoretical approach and presenting personal inferences.

4. Listen to Erik Satie's *Gymnopédies* and analyze these "Greek" dances in terms
   of the elements and style of classic Greek music, as we know it. What has the
   composer tried to accomplish? What is he suggesting? What is non-Greek
   about these compositions?

5. The German nineteenth-century philosopher Friedrich Wilhelm Nietzsche divided art between the polarities of Apollonian and Dionysian ideals. State an
   opinion on this dichotomy. Is it defensible?

6. Compile a detailed outline of the cultural borrowings of Rome from the civilization of ancient Greece, noting modifications and differences in the social
   contexts of the two nations.

7. Make a study of the Greek musical theorists, drawing upon translated excerpts

to be found in such volumes as Strunk's *Source Readings in Music History* (see "Suggestions for Further Reading").

8. Note the function of rhythm as an organizing force in poetry and music. Two books that deal with this topic, although not specifically focused upon Greek materials, are Curt Sachs' *Rhythm and Tempo* (New York, Norton, 1953) and Grosvenor Cooper's and Leonard B. Meyer's *The Rhythmic Structure of Music* (Chicago, University of Chicago Press, 1960).

VOCABULARY ENRICHMENT

music	conjunct
choregus	*mesē*
chorus	*ethos*
orchestra	Pythagoras' theory
Dionysia	perfect systems
tragedy	*magadis*
nomoi	*phorbeia*
aulos	tablature
kithara	verse meters
tetrachord	*claque*
diatonic	tuba
chromatic	*lituus*
enharmonic	*buccina*
disjunct	*hydraulus*

PART II

Music of the Church

MUSICA SACRA

Chapter 4.

MUSIC OF THE EARLY CHRISTIANS

Song awakens the soul to a glowing longing for what the song contains;
song soothes the lusts of the flesh; it banishes wicked thoughts, aroused
by invisible foes; it acts like dew to the soul, making it fertile for ac-
complishing good acts; it makes the pious warrior noble and strong in
suffering terrible pain; it is a healing ointment for the wounds suffered
in the battle of life; St. Paul calls song the "sword of the spirit" because
it protects the pious knight against the invisible enemy; for "the word
of God" if sung in emotion has the power to expel demons. All this gives
the soul the force to acquire the virtues of devotion and is brought to
the pious by ecclesiastical songs.

—ANON., *c.* A.D. 370

THE DARK AGES

The first thousand years of the Christian era were indeed Dark Ages
in contrast to the periods of enduring culture in Greece and Rome.
They form an age when the barbaric tribes—the Ostrogoths, Visigoths,
Vandals, Franks, Huns, Celts, Saxons, Vikings and Slavs—were evolving from primitive peoples into nations which were later to rule the
world. Many of these tribes overran the Roman Empire, conquered it
and in turn were themselves conquered by its learning and institutions.

The Dark Ages, however, were less black than they have been
painted, because the ancient civilization was not extinguished but was
infused with new forces, new power, new enthusiasms—new soil
through which would burst the hardier seedlings of its culture. A potent
factor in molding modern civilization was Christianity. The emblem of
power shifted from the Emperor to the Pope of Rome, and the Church
developed institutions, directed world policies and encouraged learning.
The altruism of Christian doctrine had direct bearing on architecture,
painting, sculpture, literature and music. The Gregorian chant, one of
the greatest musical developments of all time, was a product of this
climate.

As the barbarian hordes descended upon Rome, they were gradually
converted to the Christian faith, and subsequently the fathers of the
Church went to the far corners of Europe to preach the new word. So
modern civilization is like a basket woven out of the treasures of Greek

and Roman antiquity; the Hebraic religious doctrines and moral precepts which influenced the early Christian fathers; the masterful spirit of the Celts, Teutons and Slavs; and the wisdom of the Arabs, who, through conquests and the later Crusades, came in contact with this younger civilization.

EARLY CHRISTIAN OBSERVANCES

That light was not completely lost to the world during the early centuries of the Christian era is due to small bands of humble, often untutored folk, the faithful followers of Jesus Christ, many of whom were converted Jews. We know very little about them and their doings. Several factors aid in explaining this obscurity: early Christian observances were completely decentralized and nonformal—no such body as a "Congregation of Rites" was available to pronounce what should or should not be done; early Christians were firm believers in an imminent Second Coming of Christ, and while they worshiped and prayed, they waited for the anticipated Day of Judgment and exit from this world (St. Paul wrote, "The appointed time has grown very short" [I Corinthians 7:29]). As Jesus welcomed all to his teachings, early Christians were Jews, Greeks, Egyptians, Syrians, Italians, Franks and Gauls, among others, with little in common except their new faith.

We may assume from Paul's instruction to the Corinthian converts, "When you come together, each one has a hymn, a lesson, a revelation, a tongue or an interpretation" (I Corinthians 14:26), that early Christian observances were communal in nature and followed the general procedures of the nonsacrificial synagogue-ritual of prayers, psalms and scriptural readings (*synaxis*). Meetings were held in the homes of wealthier converts, in the fields and, during the Roman persecution, in the underground caverns of the Catacombs. Here the psalms were intoned, possibly in the manner of Hebrew cantillation. Here hymns were sung, probably based upon Hellenic-Roman models. One Christian hymn to the Holy Trinity, written in Greek alphabetic notation (the Oxyrhynchus Manuscript) has been discovered, dating from the third century A.D. in Egypt. In fact, the *Skolion* of Seikilos was itself converted into a *Hosanna filio David*. From the Jewish liturgy the *Kadosh, Kadosh, Kadosh* became the thrice *Sanctus*, while *Baruch atā Adonoi* endures as *Gratias agimus tibi*.

In Antioch, St. Ignatius (A.D. 49-107) is said to have introduced antiphonal singing, the course of which may be traced in the Hebrew Psalm singing, the Greek chorus and the Roman citharoedic chants. St. Ambrose (A.D. 340-397) introduced the custom in the West. Early Christian music was entirely vocal, as instruments, regarded as debasing symbols of paganism, were forbidden. Originally, the Jewish cantor may have served as solo *psalmista;* all participated in intoning the psalms and singing hymns. Later, however, women were gradually excluded from taking part, and, apparently the congregations, knowing less and less of the psalms, responded only with an *Amen* or *Alleluia,* until all these functions finally became vested in professional ecclesiastic choirs. Meanwhile, another order of service, that of the *Eucharist,* drawn from the Last Supper, became a unique part of Christian rite; during the fourth century, the *synaxis* and *Eucharist* merged to presage the celebration of the Mass, which was still incomplete in the tenth century.

DIVINE OFFICES

Another quite different aspect of Christian worship also developed, again from a Jewish practice—that of going to the Temple to pray at specified hours of the day. This was the *Offices* or *Canonical Hours,* held eight times a day, including *Matins, Lauds, Prime, Terce, Sext, None, Vespers* and *Compline.* The journal of a Spanish abbess, the *Peregrinatio Etheriae* or *Pilgrimage of Etheria,* written in the fourth century and quoted by Egon Wellesz, describes "the regular singing of hymns and psalms, and antiphons at Matins and of psalms and hymns at the sixth and ninth hours, and of psalms, hymns and antiphons (suitable to the day and place) at Vespers," adding that "it was customary to translate the lessons, where they were read in Greek, into Syrian and Latin for the benefit of those who did not understand the language." The various orders of monasticism rigidly observe the Canonical Hours to this day, inspired by the pioneer *opera Dei* of St. Benedict (*c.* A.D. 480-550).

It is interesting to note that among the early Roman converts to Christianity was a young noblewoman, who was martyred *c.* A.D. 229. She was later canonized as St. Cecilia, tutelary saint of music and musicians. In her honor, music festivals were held and societies formed in different countries.

PSALMODY AND HYMNODY

Psalmody and **hymnody** formed the bases of early Christian musical practices. Eusebius, Bishop of Caesarea (A.D. 260-340), wrote, "The command to sing psalms in the name of the Lord was obeyed by everyone in every place: for the command to sing psalms is in force in all Churches which exist among the nations, not only for the Greeks but also for the Barbarians." In addition to the psalm repertoire were the canticles, including *Benedictus* (*Song of Zachariah*), *Magnificat* (*Song of the Virgin*) and *Nunc Dimittis* (*Song of Simeon*). Hymns, on the other hand, were based on freely-invented, metric, nonscriptural texts and were more simple and accessible to congregations. An early hymn, attributed to St. Ambrose, was the *Te Deum laudamus* (*Lord, We Praise Thee*).

* * * * *

In A.D. 313 Constantine made Christianity the national religion of Rome. When he removed the seat of government of the Roman Empire to Constantinople, it became, with Rome, Antioch, Alexandria and Jerusalem, a center of Church rule. In Constantinople, the Eastern Church developed the Byzantine service. Thus, the early hymns were a bridge between Oriental, Greek and Roman monody and the dawning polyphony of Europe. The influence of the Byzantine service is still visible in Russian music. Tillyard and Egon Wellesz have done much in the revival of these chants, which probably developed from the Greek liturgy used by St. Basil in Palestine (fourth century).

VARIETY OF RITES

During the fifth century, the Roman Empire commenced to succumb to the invasions of northern barbarians. As it slowly crumbled, the Christian Church grew in strength and offered to the continent of Europe at least a semblance of stability in an otherwise shaken world. Unanimity was hardly a natural characteristic of the Church, however; it was an attribute which was achieved only after much time, labor and determination were expended. Coexisting at about the same time and in some cases still present in today's world were various rites and liturgies, jealously preserved and slow to bend to the will of Rome. These included the Ambrosian, the Sarum, the Mozarabic and the Gallican forms, as well as those of the Eastern Catholic Church.

We have already mentioned St. Ambrose, Bishop of Milan, in connection with hymnody. He desired to regulate tonality and the way of singing sacred music, so he replaced the heretical hymn with the Christian hymn, trying thus to eliminate the music of popular street songs that had found its way into the sanctuary. Also associated with his name is a collection of chants, developed from the fourth through the twelfth centuries, combining original derivations from early Eastern liturgies with popular elements and later Byzantine and Gregorian modifications. Fortunately, most of the Ambrosian chant is available to us, as it is still used at the Cathedral of Milan; unfortunately, its manuscripts date back no further then the 1100's. Carl Parrish writes of "such characteristically Ambrosian traits as the melodic rhyme at the ends of the various phrases, the actual repetition of long sections of the melody in the whole structure . . . and the repetition of a motive

Fig. 16. The Cathedral at Milan. Ambrosian chant is still used here today. (Photograph by the editor.)

within phrases with subtle variations. . . ." Alec Robertson, however, notes that "Ambrosian chant has not the sobriety or the symmetry of the Roman chant and it inclines more to the dramatic." In general, it seems more florid and Eastern in nature than Roman plainsong.

The Sarum rite is one that was in use in the British Isles and represents a local medieval modification of Gregorian liturgy as practiced at Salisbury Cathedral, whence it was imposed in 1543 upon "the whole province." Some of it is included in the music of the Anglican Church today.

The Mozarabic liturgy of Spain is allegedly ancient in origin and still celebrated in the Cathedral of Toledo. Unfortunately, its music is locked in undeciphered notation which has yet to yield its secrets. Only a few sixteenth-century examples are available. Despite the name, this chant does not seem to show any special Arabic influence.

The Gallican liturgy and chant were developed by the converted Visigoths after they conquered parts of France and Spain in the fifth century. No complete copy of this chant survives, although parts of it were incorporated into the Roman, for instance, the *Improperia* of the Mass for Good Friday. When Charlemagne was crowned Emperor of the West (A.D. 800), so thoroughly did he believe in Pope Gregory's plan "for creating a united church by means of a common music," that he ordered all the Gallican songbooks destroyed and directed the attention of his empire to Rome. Despite this suppression, elements of Gallican chant undoubtedly entered the Roman compilation through the exhaustive work of French monasteries and their schools.

For, as Christianity expanded and its evangelism spread, it gradually assumed the form of an institution. Monasteries became centers of learning and their schools included those for the training of choirs. As the music became more florid, it was too difficult for congregational chanting and had to be sung by trained choirs. In A.D. 367 congregational singing was banned.

In the monasteries of Syria and Egypt, the liturgy first became definite in form, and schools of singing similar to the *Scholae Cantorum* in the Latin churches of the seventh and eighth centuries were developed in Greek churches at Antioch and Alexandria, in the fourth century. Early in the same century a school of chant was established in Rome. In the fifth century trained singers of Syria were employed as cantors in Italian churches. For generations the melodies were handed down orally from master to pupil. The task of learning the growing repertory by heart was arduous, but as Isidore of Seville (seventh century) lamented, "Unless retained by the memory sounds perish, for they cannot be written down."

GREGORIAN CHANT

It is paradoxical that the sixth century should have given birth to two men as widely separated in thought as Mohammed (570-632) and Pope Gregory I (the Great, 540-604), for they were to shape destiny in quite antithetical fashions. Gregory, a pupil of Benedict, ascended the throne of St. Peter in 590, and to him is ascribed the building of Christendom, toward which the followers of Mohammed were to remain implacable foes. Although Gregory's role is increasingly open to question, and documents relating it date only to the ninth century, we do know that before becoming Pope he had been governor of Rome and was an able administrator; that he wrote books on religion and sent letters far and wide to his clergy regarding Church matters; and that he was responsible for St. Augustine's mission to Britain.

The Venerable Bede (673-735) gave a description of St. Augustine's entry into England with forty monks, singing a hymn which converted King Ethelbert. In 1897 the same Gregorian hymn was sung at Canterbury in celebration of the coming of St. Augustine 1500 years before. After Gregorian music had reached England, monks were sent to the *Schola Cantorum* in Rome. Bede himself did much to spread the Gregorian tradition, and wherever a monastery was founded, a music school was started.

What concerns us here is that Pope (later Saint) Gregory I or his successors were responsible for the collecting and standardizing of the eclectic chant and expanding schools of singing to establish the authenticity of the music which over a period of some four hundred years became the first great literature of Western music—one various, moving and aesthetically satisfying that we can hear today in approximately its medieval form—*Gregorian chant.*

To St. Gregory has been ascribed the reorganization of the *Schola Cantorum,* a Roman school of singing, founded by Pope Sylvester (A.D. 314-335), and, some biographers claim, supervised personally by Gregory. Gevaert says in *Les origines du chant liturgique de l'église latine,* "By the seventh century we are in the presence of an advanced art, conscious of its principles, with rules and formulas for each class of composition." The *Schola Cantorum* directed training of singers and teachers throughout the Christian world. Nine years were required to complete the curriculum, and all the chants had to be memorized.

Although our discussion of this music must perforce to be somewhat superficial, we shall begin by considering some general characteristics. "Gregorian music," writes one churchman, "is wide in its range of emotional expression, majestic, spiritual, and austere beyond all other forms of the art, exquisitely spontaneous and pure in its melody, and extremely subtle and sophisticated in its technical perfection." In musical terms, Gregorian chant (also known as plainsong and *cantus planus*) may be described as (1) modal; (2) monodic; (3) developed through the use of formulae; (4) formal only in a melodic sense; (5) often stepwise in movement, with few intervallic leaps beyond that of the fifth; (6) limited in tonal range to eight or nine notes; (7) responsive to word rhythms for musical rhythm; (8) dependent upon Latin text; (9) set down in a definite repertoire; and (10) wholly dedicated to the greater glory of God.

Several of these characteristics require further explanation. Before the year 1000, a system of modes was codified, based on Gregorian music. Its terminology is a scramble, and definition of exact pitch is almost nonexistent. Its theory, however, shows its debt to medieval understanding—or misunderstanding—of the classic Greek orientation.

To the four **authentic** scales or modes, frequently attributed to St. Ambrose, four **plagal** forms, often called Gregorian modes, were added. The word "plagal" comes from the Greek, *plagios,* meaning oblique. So the plagal modes were oblique or collateral, in that every authentic mode had its related plagal mode, lying a fourth below it. Emulating Greek terminology, the plagal modes were given the prefix *hypo.*

Below is a table of the eight ecclesiastical, or Church, modes:

AUTHENTIC MODES

I. Dorian:
    d ef g a bc d

II. Hypodorian:
    a bc d ef g a

III. Phrygian:
    ef g a bc d e

IV. Hypophrygian:
    bc d ef g a b

PLAGAL MODES

V. Lydian:
    f g a bc d ef

VI. Hypolydian:
    c d ef g a bc

VII. Mixolydian:
    g a bc d ef g

VIII. Hypomixolydian:
    d ef g a bc d

Each mode has its *finalis,* or final, and its "dominant." The final acts as a base toward which melody proceeds as its energy is spent. The dominant tends to characterize and individualize the mode. A treatise, *Enchiridion musices* (*Handbook on Music*), until recently attributed to Odo, Abbot of Cluny from 927 to 942, lays a clear theoretical background for the tonal system of chant melody:

Mode I. Dorian—the final is d, dominant a.

Mode II. Hypodorian—the final is d, dominant f.

Mode III. Phrygian—the final is e, dominant c.*

Mode IV. Hypophrygian—the final is E, dominant A.

Mode V. Lydian—the final is F, dominant C.

* Notice that the dominant C in Mode III is a departure from the scheme. This was made in order to avoid the *diabolus in musica,* that is, the **tritone** (three whole steps) formed between F natural and B natural.

Fig. 17. "Pope Gregory and Three Scribes"— ninth-century ivory relief. Although Pope Gregory's role in formulating Gregorian plainsong is increasingly open to question, we know that he and his successors were responsible for standardizing the various chants which bear his name. (Courtesy Museum of Art, Vienna.)

Mode VI. Hypolydian—the final is F, dominant A.
Mode VII. Mixolydian—the final is G, dominant D.
Mode VIII. Hypomixolydian—the final is G, dominant C.

Each of the eight ecclesiastical modes corresponds roughly to one of the **psalm tones,** which provides the priest with a formula for intoning each double verse of a psalm. This formula includes an ascending beginning, a repeated tone (*tenor,* that is, sustained) and a variety of endings, known as *differentiae,* indicated by the code, *euouae,* derived from the vowels in the phrase *sEcUlOrUm AmEn* which concludes each psalm in the Catholic liturgy. Generally, the psalm is preceded and followed by the singing of an *antiphon,* or refrain. A ninth possibility, the *tonus peregrinus* or traveling tone, allows the psalmist two reciting tones.

The rhythms of Gregorian chant are neither metrical nor for the dance but reflections of word-rhythms of the Latin text. This in itself has posed a problem, for the Greek quantitative measure, in the opinion of some authorities, clashed with the accentuated features of popular Roman poetry. In any case, over a period of years the concept of long-short gave way to that of stress and nonstress of equal pulses. Davison and Apel, for example, in the *Historical Anthology of Music* present the Ambrosian hymn, *Aeterne Christi munera,* both in notes of equal value (as found in today's *Antiphonary*) and in a short and long pattern of three beats, reported by St. Augustine as the proper interpretation of an iambic foot—thus underlining the existing ambiguity.

The Latin texts of Gregorian chant are set in three declamatory styles which are significant in terms of performance. These are (1) the **syllabic,** which places one tone to one syllable; (2) the **neumatic,** in which two or three tones are used for each syllable of the text; and finally, (3) the **melismatic,** where many tones, often more than a breath can sustain, allow a syllable to soar to wondrous heights of expression.

1. Syllabic
2. Neumatic
3. Melismatic

Responsible for the difficulties of authentic presentation which now face us is the inadequate nature of early musical notation, once the chants were written. In Byzantine schools, the critics and grammarians, attempting to preserve inflections of the rapidly disappearing Greek language, invented a system of signs by which it was written and read for centuries. The West borrowed these acute and grave accents from the Alexandrian Greeks as a practical means of indicating the rising and falling inflection of the singing voice in its chants, which were little more than exaggerated speech.

The notation was called **neumatic** from the Greek word *neuma,* meaning nod or sign. (It must not be confused with the word, *pneuma* [breath], which was also used to indicate phrasing.) Gradually the system took on various combinations of dashes, curves and dots, and in time became a complete music notation, without, however, indicating definite pitch, size of intervals or rhythm.

Fluctuations in rhythm were indicated, if at all, by the most rudimentary means, that is, by using one of several Roman letters, such as *b* for *bene* (much) or *e* for *expectare* (hesitate). Techniques of singing were sometimes shown in *neumes* signifying *tremolo* or *quilisma,* interpreted by most scholars as denoting a slight *vibrato* on a certain note. Toward the end of the first millennium A.D., scribes commenced to group and space the *neumes,* giving some further notion of pitch; but a really revolutionary step was the introduction of a single red line of reference (for F) above or below which the signs were placed. The exact pitch of F, however, remained a matter of doubt and the rhythms were still largely ignored on the score.

We may imagine a small choir of monks clustered about a single large manuscript, utilizing it as more of a memory aid than anything else. As the chants grew in number, the dependence upon memory weighed heavily. Possibly an urge toward creativity also contributed to a practice which sprang up in the ninth century—that of **troping,** making textual additions and musical insertions to already established chant. Sometimes this took the form of setting words to melismatic portions of the plainsong, thus making them syllabic and easier for the Western singer, to whom the elaborate cantillations of Jewish liturgy were alien.

Notker Balbulus, librarian of the monastery of St. Gall (*c.* A.D. 890), in the preface of his *Liber Ymnorum* describes his delight on learning of the possibility of adding words to the highly melismatic *alleluias,* a kind of trope which came to be known as **sequence.** (St. Augustine had written that the seemingly spontaneous vocalization of the final syllable of *alleluia* was a "song of joy without words." When textual additions were appended to this *melisma,* they were called *jubilus,* to connote a joyous mood.) Notker industriously added reverential texts. Through the centuries other monks joined him, until a substantial group of *sequences*

Fig. 18. Neumatic notation and crwth-player—St. Martial Tropes, eleventh century. An example of neumatic notation without lines, a system of combinations of dashes, curves and dots of rather ambiguous character. A crwth is a type of cittern played with a bow. (Courtesy Bibliothéque nationale, Paris.)

was in use, gradually altering and diluting the purity of Gregorian chant. Finally, the Council of Trent, meeting from 1545 to 1563, stepped in to contain the situation, removing all but four *sequences* from the *Missal*. The four that remain include the *Dies Irae* (in the

Mass for the Dead, thirteenth century), *Victimae paschali* (Easter poem possibly attributable to the monk Wipo of Burgundy [d. 1048]), *Lauda Sion Salvatorem* (Corpus Christi text by St. Thomas Aquinas [d. 1274]) and *Veni Sancte Spiritus* (Pentecost poem by Stephen Langton [d. 1228]). A fifth *sequence,* the *Stabat Mater dolorosa* (used on Friday before Palm Sunday and of uncertain authorship, thirteenth century) was restored to the Mass in 1727.

From tropes composed in the latter half of the first Christian millennium sprang the seeds of liturgical drama which were to blossom subsequently in Passion plays and still later in secular music drama and opera. The earliest of these was of the question and answer variety, attached to the Mass of Easter. It is found in tenth-century manuscripts and was actually staged at Winchester Cathedral, England. The text reads:

> *Question:* Whom do you seek in the Sepulchre, servants of Christ?
> *Answer:* Jesus of Nazareth who was crucified, celestial ones. He is not here, he is risen as he foretold; go, announce that he is risen from the Sepulchre.

Robertson comments, "The plays, with the introduction of secular as well as clerical performance, moved inevitably from the sanctuary of the church to the porch, and so out into the marketplace, and eventually into the theatre."

Gregorian chant had in many ways won the battle and lost the war. As Curt Sachs writes, "If the Gregorian version was able to conquer its rival versions, the Ambrosian chant in Milan, the Gallican in France, and the Mozarabic in Spain, it was unable to keep its own tradition." Vagueness of notation and the constancy of change led to indecision regarding performance and often a deplorable lack of discipline on the part of members of individual *Scholae Cantorum.* Toward the end of the nineteenth century, the Benedictine monks of Solesmes Abbey, France, took on the enormous task of restoring Gregorian chant to its original form through study of manuscripts from the ninth, tenth and eleventh centuries. In 1904 the first volume (*Graduale*) of the *Editio Vaticana* appeared and this edition is the official version of the chant today, even though much bitter controversy has centered about the Solesmes method of making all tones equal in length, albeit some are more equal than others.

BYZANTINE MUSIC

We have already mentioned the debt owed by the West to the East in various phases of Church affairs. No visitor to Italy will forget the black-and-white-striped "Byzantine" churches of St. Cosmas and St. Damian in Rome, St. Vitale at Ravenna or the Cathedral at Orvieto, not to mention the fantastic Basilica of St. Mark in Venice. Nor is Greek a complete stranger to the Latin Mass which has retained the *Kyrie eleison* of a distant time as well as the *Trisagion,* which is sung in both Greek and Latin, as Carl Parrish notes, "a last vestige of a practice that was once apparently widespread in the Middle Ages of singing certain texts in both languages on important feasts." Nor is it possible to forget that the ancient liturgies and literature of Antioch and Alexandria are in many ways parents of both the Roman Catholic and the Greek Orthodox Churches.

After the Emperor Constantine had moved the seat of government from Rome to Constantinople, the site of Byzantium, and now named Istanbul, a liturgy and chant developed that both conserved ancient ways and, at the same time, bore unique tendrils of its own. The Basilica of St. Sophia, constructed between 532 and 537 under the Roman emperor Justinian I, dates from the same epoch as the initial growth of the Byzantine liturgy. This liturgy differs from Roman Catholic observance in the greater emphasis on hymnody to the neglect of psalmody and in its dramatic celebration of the Mass. Several poetic forms are represented in the Byzantine hymns: (1) the fourth- and fifth-century *troparia,* originally inserts in psalm recitation; (2) the seventh-century *kontakia,* homilies of many stanzas, sung by a soloist and answered by a choral refrain; and (3) the eighth-century *kanon,* a cycle of nine hymns of praise. There are eight Byzantine modes or *echoi,* each a melody package (similar to the Arabian *maqamāt*) rather than a scale formation. Orthodox music is completely vocal and professional.

Unlike the music of the West, Orthodox music never grew beyond monody; and such modern settings as those of Tchaikovsky, Gretchaninov and Rachmaninov are more Italianate or Russian than the authentic music of the early Eastern Christians. Yet Byzantine liturgy and music is significant, if not so well understood, for the fact that it is the ancestor of all musical services of Eastern European churches, and their counterparts throughout the world.

INSTRUMENTAL DEVELOPMENT

Instrumental development during the early Christian period was relatively barren, due to the interdict against instruments as inimicable to the sweet strains of choirs. A monochord, described in Boëthius' résumé of ancient music, *De Musica* (c. A.D. 500), was devised. A *cymbala,* tuned bells on a horizontal bar, struck with hammers, is known to have existed. Yet a third instrument was the organ, which by the tenth century had permeated many cathedrals and abbeys.

The medieval *positive,* a bellows-driven organ utilizing air rather than water as its source of power, reentered Europe from Byzantium. Organs were noted in Spain as early as the fifth century, in England in the eighth and France in the ninth, when Byzantine diplomats presented an instrument to Charlemagne at Aix-la-Chapelle, possibly generating increased interest in the art of organ construction.

A famous English organ which aroused curiosity, wonder and pride was built in the tenth century at Winchester Cathedral. From an account by the monk, Wulstan (d. 963), we learn that by means of twenty-six bellows, numerous men pumped air into the 400 pipes, "governed" by two organists at separate manuals. "They strike the seven differences of joyous sounds, adding the music of the lyric semitone [the seven diatonic intervals as represented by the white keys of the piano with a B flat added]. The music is heard throughout the town, and the flying fame thereof is gone out over the whole country."

While contemporary literature eulogized the organ as an instrument that could produce a great variety of sounds, from the roar of thunder to the sweetness of bells, from the facility of the lyre to the call of pipes, we would doubtless find the medieval *positive* a raucous and seldom persuasive mechanism. As Sachs mentions in his *History of Musical Instruments,* the bellows' lack of contrivances for stabilizing the air pressure resulted in sudden booms and disquieting fadeouts. The larger organs, such as Winchester's, "had several pipes on the same key, either in unison or in fifths, octaves, twelfths and double octaves, which sounded at once; no stop existed to disconnect some of them and to change volume or timbre." In fact, a contemporary poem has it that one paused to stop with his hand "his gaping ears, being in no wise able to draw near and bear the sound."

The instruments were very awkward to play, for apparently no keyboard as such existed until the thirteenth century. Instead, **sliders,** that is, horizontal wood-strips were used. When a slider, or tongue (*lingua*), was drawn, air entered the corresponding pipe or pipes. As there was no automatic return, the manipulation of sliders was unwieldy, to say the least. Although the performers probably attempted to simulate vocal technique, we may ruefully conclude that the tonal production was usually blaring and uncertain of intonation. Indeed, the first organ with a keyboard in the modern sense of the term had keys three inches wide which had to be pounded with hammers to produce sounds.

GUIDO OF AREZZO

We may appropriately conclude our discussion of the music of the first thousand years of Christian music with an examination of the contributions of an eleventh-century Benedictine French monk who spent most of his lifetime in Italy and who stood on the musical threshold between the freely disordered Middle Ages and the potential creative surge which was to follow—Guido of Arezzo (*c.* 995-1050). To Guido have been credited, accurately or otherwise, many valuable innovations; but he did write an extremely influential book, the *Micrologus de disciplina artis musicae,* that was a collation of everything known about music at that time; he did have a hand in developing staff notation; he did introduce to the West the pedagogical device of **solmization,** creating a rudimentary system of *solfège* and providing the basis for a visual-tactile learning aid, later known as the Guidonian Hand; and he did offer a primary source of our knowledge of *organum,* a musical development to be discussed in the next chapter.

Fig. 19. Statue of Guido Monaco (d'Arezzo). It is to this eleventh-century French Benedictine monk that we credit many valuable innovations. (Photograph by the editor.)

We have already mentioned that by a stroke of genius, anonymous scribes in the eleventh century helped to bring order out of chaos by drawing a red line across the page and marking it F, a line which now carries our bass clef. To them we are beholden for the concepts of staff and clef. The *neumes* were written on and above and below the line, indicating higher and lower pitch from the arbitrary F. This method was so successful that a second line, usually yellow in color, was employed to signify middle C.

Although *neumes* had superseded the Greek alphabet in written notation, there was still a need for an alphabet to express fixed pitch relationships. In the tenth century Latin letters replaced the Greek symbols but the position of the tone was the same as the Greeks had used and the syllable A was given to the *proslambanomenos,* the first tone of the Greek scale. For some time, both *neumes* and Latin letters were employed.

Guido perfected a four-line staff in which both lines and spaces were utilized, giving definite position, if not pitch, to each scale degree. His use of a **staff notation** made it possible for singers to read a melody without the teacher's aid, abolishing the time-consuming education by monochord and establishing our modern system. Instead of writing the script on the staff, the *neumes* themselves were placed on the lines and in the spaces. (Four lines form the standard plainsong staff to the present day.) *Neumes,* however, continued to be written without a staff in Germany as late as the fourteenth century, while staves of one, two and three lines frequently occur in twelfth- and thirteenth-century manuscripts.

"The influence of a perfected diastematic (intervallic) notation on the development of music was enormous," writes Gustave Reese. "Not only was the ecclesiastical singer freed from the necessity of laboriously committing to memory the whole liturgical repertoire, but the existence of a dependable notation made possible the rapid spread of new and original compositions such as tropes and sequences." Guido himself is quoted as stating, "Should anyone doubt that I am telling the truth, let him come, make a trial, and hear what small boys can do under our direction, boys who have until now been beaten for their gross ignorance of the psalms."

Many theorists built their scales in tetrachords, but Guido, probably as an outgrowth of the mnemonic device of solmization, conceived them in groups of overlapping **hexachords** (six tones). This conception he called the **gamut,** because a tone was added below the *proslambanomenos,* beginning on the lowest line of our grand staff, and was given the Greek name for G, *gamma.* The syllable, *ut,* designated the first degree of the scale for Guido, so *gam-ut* really means a scale starting on G.

Guido's hexachords were as follows:

1. molle					F	G	ab♭	c	d)	
2. naturale			C	D	E̲F̲	G	a⌣		)	These were repeated, starting an octave higher.
3. durum	G	A	B̲C̲⌣	D	E				)	

(Read from the lowest line up.)

A hexachord was *molle* (soft) if it contained B flat; *durum* (hard) if it contained B natural; and *naturale* if it contained neither B flat nor B natural. "Soft" and "hard" did not refer to any *ethos* of the hexachord but rather to the form the B took upon the page. Our symbols for flat and natural derive from the signs of B flat and B natural, a rounded soft B and a square hard B, which gradually were transformed into ♭ and ♮ . (The origin of our symbol for sharp, #, is still uncertain.)

Guido is also credited with bestowing the syllable names *ut, re, mi, fa, sol* and *la* on the six tones of the hexachords which could be mutated, one to another. These syllables were adapted from an eighth-century hymn composed by one Paul the Deacon to St. John the Baptist, each line of which began on successive degrees of the hexachord, inspiring Guido with the idea of naming each tonal degree by the first syllable of the Latin hymn, thus:

UT queant laxis,	(That with enfranchised voices
REsonare fibris,	thy servants may be able to proclaim
MIra gestorum	the wonders of thy deeds,
FAmuli tuorum,	remove the sin of [their] polluted lips,
SOLve polluti	O holy John.)
LAbii reatum,	
Sancte Ioannes.	

Ut was later changed to *do,* and a seventh syllable, *si,* added.

Guido's system initially proved difficult for choir singers and students, so he or his followers created the Guidonian Hand, a visual-tactile aid which allotted various positions on the fingers to the hexachords. While seemingly complex to us, his achievement was considered a pedagogical triumph for centuries to come.

SIGNIFICANCE OF EARLY CHRISTIAN MUSIC

Whether or not it is true that Gregory the Great, in the words of John the Deacon, "collected the sacred music of the Church and had it written in a book called the *Antiphonary,* which was chained to the

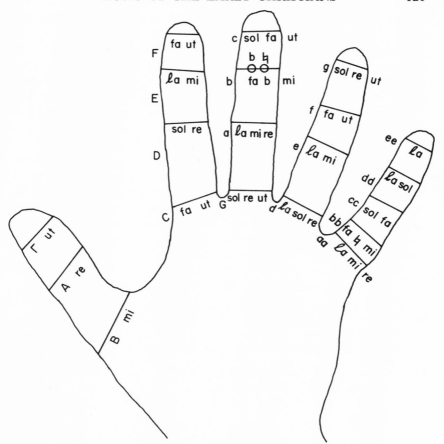

Fig. 20. The Guidonian Hand.

altar of St. Peter's as a model of what music should be," it cannot be denied that from the sixth century through the late Middle Ages, a collection of over 2500 compositions connected with the Roman Catholic services accumulated, organized in a coherent system and with a style uniquely its own—the unaccompanied, unison singing of haunting melody *ad majorem Dei gloriam*. This repertoire was to provide the foundation for unparalleled future developments in music through the ages, as we shall subsequently see. With both ups and downs of fortune, it has rarely been completely absent from the musical scene and, following the *motu proprio* of Pope Pius X (1903), has again been placed in the forefront of favored Roman Catholic music. Plainsong has provided the bases for many Protestant hymns, such as the Advent favorite, "O

Come, O Come, Emmanuel," as well as the Jewish melody of the *"Kol Nidre,"* drawn at least in part from Gregorian sources.

Composers have been inspired to use the melodies of plainsong in contemporary contexts. Anton Bruckner's (1824-1896) *Mass in E Minor* is worked on Gregorian themes. Among others, Hector Berlioz (1803-1869) and Sergei Rachmaninov (1873-1943) have used the *"Dies Irae"* theme effectively in *Symphonie fantastique* and *The Island of the Dead,* respectively. More modern works which reflect the influence of plainsong are Ottorino Respighi's (1879-1936) *Violin Concerto in Gregorian Mode;* Gustav Holst's (1874-1934) *"Hymn of Jesus";* Arthur Honegger's (1892-1955) *Symphony No. 3;* Charles Martin Loeffler's (1861-1935) *Hora Mystica,* a choral symphony for orchestra and men's voices; and Goffredo Petrassi's (1904-   ) setting of *Psalm 9.* The indirect importance of Gregorian chant has been immense, and the texts of the liturgy, of course, have afforded composers materials for sublime compositions in every succeeding epoch.

SUGGESTIONS FOR FURTHER READING

Apel, Willi, *Gregorian Chant.* Bloomington, Indiana University Press, 1958.

Bettenson, Henry, ed., *Documents of the Christian Church.* London, Oxford University Press, 1963.

Bukofzer, Manfred, *Studies in Medieval and Renaissance Music.* New York, Norton, 1950.

Davison, Archibald T., and Apel, Willi, *Historical Anthology of Music,* vol. I. Cambridge, Harvard University Press, 1949.

Ferand, Ernest T., *Improvisation in Nine Centuries of Western Music.* Cologne, Arno Volk, 1961.

Fremantle, Anne, ed., *The Age of Belief.** Boston, Houghton Mifflin, 1954.

Goodrich, Norma L., *The Medieval Myths.** New York, New American Library, 1966.

Liber Usualis. Tournay, Desclée, 1950.

Messenger, Ruth E., *The Medieval Latin Hymn.* Washington, Capitol Press, 1953.

Parrish, Carl, *The Notation of Medieval Music.* New York, Norton, 1959.

——— *A Treasury of Early Music.** New York, Norton, 1958.

Parrish, Carl, and Ohl, John F., *Masterpieces of Music before 1750.* New York, Norton, 1951.

Reese, Gustave, *Music in the Middle Ages.* New York, Norton, 1940.

Riemann, Hugo, *History of Music Theory.* Lincoln, University of Nebraska Press, 1962.

Robertson, Alec, *The Interpretation of Plainchant.* London, Oxford University Press, 1937.

Seay, Albert, *Music in the Medieval World.** Englewood Cliffs, Prentice-Hall, 1965.

Steuart, Dom Benedict, *The Development of Christian Worship.* New York, Longmans Green, 1953.

* Available in paperback edition.

Stevens, Denis, and Robertson, Alec, eds., *The Pelican History of Music,* vol. 1.*
    Baltimore, Penguin, 1960.
Strunk, Oliver, ed., *Source Readings in Music History.** New York, Norton, 1950.
Velimirovic, Milos, ed., *Studies in Eastern Chant,* vol. I. New York, Oxford Uni-
    versity Press, 1966.
Vollaerts, J. W. A., S.J., *Rhythmic Proportions in Early Medieval Ecclesiastical
    Chant.* Leiden, E. J. Brill, 1958.
Wellesz, Egon, *Eastern Elements in Western Chant.* Oxford, Oxford University
    Press, 1947.
———— *The Music of the Byzantine Church.* Oxford, Oxford University Press,
    1959.
Werner, Eric, *The Sacred Bridge.* New York, Columbia University Press, 1959.
Young, Karl, *The Drama of the Medieval Church.* Oxford, Clarendon, 1933.
    2 vols.

A Sampler of Supplementary Recordings

N.B. Special benefit will be derived from the use of recordings which are matched
to scores in modern notation. Several sets are available, including:

Masterpieces of Music before 1750	Haydn 9038/40
(Parrish and Ohl, *Masterpieces of Music Before 1750.* New York, Norton, 1951.)	
Treasury of Early Music	Haydn 9100/3
(Parrish, Carl. *A Treasury of Early Music.* New York, Norton, 1958.)	
Ten Centuries of Music	DGG KL-52/61

Collections

Early Medieval Music	Victor LM-6015
Music of the Middle Ages	Lyric 85
2000 Years of Music	Folkways 3700
Laudate Dominum	Columbia ML-4394
Gregorian Chant	Period 569, 570
Catholic Hymns	Gregorian Institute LAY-539
Russian Orthodox Christmas	Cook 1095
8 Introits in 8 Modes	(10″) Gregorian Institute LL-111
Informal Discourses on Spirit and Technique of Gregorian Chant	Gregorian Institute EL 1
Sunday Vespers and Compline (Solesmes Choir)	London 5597
Chants of the Church	World Library of Sacred Music 7

Composed Music of Interest

Bruch, Max, *Kol Nidre for Cello and Orchestra, Op.* 47
Foss, Lukas, *Echoi for 4 Soloists*
Rachmaninov, Sergei, *Isle of the Dead, Op.* 29
Schroeder, Hermann, *Missa Gregoriana*

Opportunities for Study in Depth

1. Visit a museum and examine examples of medieval manuscript. Notice, in addition to the notation and size of the volumes, the beautiful and often fanciful initial ornamentation. (It may also be possible to find in the margins comments made by the scribes as they worked silently for long hours in un-heated rooms.)

2. Attend a High Mass of the Roman Catholic Church, noticing the use of chant. Or visit a Greek Orthodox cathedral, observing how music is used in worship and also the altar arrangement, which differs from that of other denominations. After the service, speak to the choirmaster or the cantor, who will probably be happy to share his special knowledge.

3. Obtain a copy of the *Liber Usualis* (available at libraries and at all Catholic bookstores) and examine this comprehensive collection of plainsong, with the older notation, Solesmes rhythmic signs and Latin texts. Read the preface and try to interpret the notation.

4. Read Chapter 10 of Howard Boatwright's *Introduction to the Theory of Music* (New York, Norton, 1956) and experiment with composing Gregorian melodies as he suggests.

5. Listen to recordings of Gregorian chant, correlating the information offered in this chapter with the actual music. Write a summary report of what has been gained through the experience.

6. Examine any standard Catholic or Protestant hymnal, noting the sources of texts and tunes. Compile a list of those which are attributed to plainsong sources. One might commence with "Of the Father's Love Begotten" (Aurelius Clemens Prudentius, 348-413, twelfth-century plainsong, Mode V) or "O Trinity of Blessed Light" (plainsong from the *Sarum Antiphonal* with sixth-century text).

7. Listen to, play and/or sing the popular Advent hymn, *"Veni Emmanuel"* ("O Come, O Come, Emmanuel"), marking the musical features that authenticate its Gregorian origin. Listen to, play and sing the *"Kol Nidre,"* a Jewish melody associated with Yom Kippur, again seeking its possible relationship to plainsong.

8. Make a study of the early Middle Ages, placing the Roman Catholic Church in its historic and social context. Supplement this with an investigation of how all arts were used to glorify God.

Vocabulary Enrichment

synaxis

Eucharist

psalmnody

hymnody

Offices or Canonical Hours

canticles

Ambrosian chant

Sarum chant

Mozarabic chant

Gallican chant

Schola Cantorum

Gregorian chant or plainsong

ecclesiastical modes

psalm tones

syllabic declamation

neumatic declamation

melismatic declamation

quilisma

neumes
troping
sequence
troparia, kontakia, kanon
echoi
monochord

cymbala
positive
gamut
hexachord
solmization
Guidonian Hand

Chapter 5.

THE RISE OF POLYPHONY

Could you but hear one of these enervating performances executed with all the devices of the art, you might think it a chorus of Sirens, not of men; and you would be astounded by the singers' facility, with which indeed neither that of the parrot or nightingale, nor of whatever else there may be that is more remarkable in this kind, can compare. For this facility is displayed in long passages running up and down, in dividing or in repeating notes, in repeating phrases, and in clashing together of voices, while in all this the high or even the highest notes of the scale are so mingled with the lower and lowest, that the ears are almost deprived of their power to distinguish.

—John of Salisbury,
twelfth-century cleric.

What indeed, we may ask, happened to the reverent serenity of Gregorian chant to prompt John of Salisbury to write his extraordinary complaint? Actually, musical events of the later Middle Ages were quite momentous, and added new and pregnant dimensions to music through the ages. These, in turn, reflected changes in power and outlook in both Europe and the Near East that were laying a foundation for the unmatched burst of the Renaissance to come; for the philosophic and economic climate of Europe was subtly affected by a combination of circumstances that was to project the relatively young Western civilization into a cultural adolescence. A review of several aspects of the Middle Ages will provide us with a matrix from which to observe what was happening in the development of sacred music.

HISTORICAL BACKGROUND

The Turks had conquered Persia and sacred Christian sites of the Holy Land, even threatening the capital city of Constantinople. This pagan power drive caused great consternation in Western Europe, resulting in a series of Crusades or Holy Wars, which accomplished little in the long run, although certain coastal cities were captured by the Christian knights, only to be lost again. Feudalism as it is pictured in the popular mind flourished, with fortified cities and countless liege barons the norm. Abbots and bishops had become, in fact, members of the nobility, wielding great secular as well as spiritual power because of the Church's extensive land holdings.

The late Middle Ages witnessed the Norman Conquest of England, the establishment of universities—bodies of students and scholars—first in Italy, then at Paris, Oxford and Cambridge, with control gradually moving from clerical to secular masters. This was a time of Inquisition excesses and of the establishment of powerful monastic orders by St. Dominic, St. Bernard and St. Francis of Assisi. It also marked a transition from the Byzantine-Romanesque styles of architecture to that of the soaring Gothic, the first great example of which was the Cathedral of St. Denis, near Paris, commenced in 1140, to be followed by those at Paris, Chartres, Amiens and Beauvais.

Fig. 21. Chartres. During the twelfth century many musical centers, including Chartres, were contributing *organa* to sacred music literature. (Photograph by the editor.)

The centuries preceding 1300 were also distinguished by the calling of the first English Parliament, the revival of free cities, the organization of craft guilds and the commercial rovings of Venetian merchants to the Far East. Gimpel, in *The Cathedral Builders,* draws a novel parallel between eleventh- and twelfth-century Europe and the development of the Far West in nineteenth-century America.

A most significant force in the late Middle Ages was the evolution of a cult of the Virgin Mary—a sacred expression of the concept of chivalry—which, although not particularly encouraged by Rome, exerted tremendous influence upon the religious thinking of the *bourgeoisie.*

Another fateful factor was the Christian recapture of Castile and Aragon, pushing the Moors to the very tip of Spain. Despite claims to relative peace, however, there was in this medieval world a constant coming and going, a leavening of the dough of thought, that would provoke a shift from otherworldliness to a realization of the material blandishments of this earth, stimulating learning but insidiously undermining the absolute authority of the Church.

THE MASS

It was during the eleventh century that the principal ceremony of the Roman Catholic Church—the *Mass*—achieved its complete form. Because of the inspiration the Mass has been to composers ever since, it is well to review something of its overall structure.

The Mass

SYNAXIS
- I. PREPARATION
  - * a. Introit
  - b. *Kyrie*
  - c. *Gloria*
  - * d. Collect
  - * e. Epistle
  - * f. Gradual
    - *Alleluia* or Tract
  - * g. Gospel
  - h. *Credo*
- II. OFFERING
  - * i. Offertory

EUCHARIST
- III. SACRIFICE
  - j. *Sanctus*
- IV. COMMUNION
  - k. *Pater noster*
  - l. *Agnus Dei*
  - * m. Communion
- V. CONCLUSION
  - * n. Closing prayers
  - o. Dismissal (*Benedicamus Domino* or *Ita missa est,* from which the Mass gets its name)

The five sections, *Kyrie, Gloria, Credo, Sanctus* and *Agnus Dei,* make up the **Ordinary** of the Mass, that is, those parts of its text that are invariable. The parts designated by asterisks form the **Proper,** or those sections of its text that are exchangeable in accordance with the celebrations of the Church calendar. For each of the Ordinary texts several chants are available, while the Proper chants are numerous because of the number of different feasts. To the remarkable Frenchman Guillaume de Machault goes the distinction of composing the first complete polyphonic version of the Ordinary, which came to be established as the unit for the composition of Masses.

Apart from Masses that follow the prescribed Catholic usage there subsequently developed a repertoire of "concert" Masses, examples of which include Bach's *B Minor Mass* and Beethoven's *Missa solemnis,* among many others. These works are liturgically unacceptable to the Church because of their length, elaboration and individual interpretation of the text. In them, however, the composers explore and express vital and fundamental sentiments of the religious drama inherent in the structure.

A special type of Mass, the mournful *Missa pro defunctis* (*Mass for the Dead*), is well known to music lovers through settings by Mozart, Berlioz and Verdi. It opens with the Introit prayer, *Requiem aeternam dona eis* ("Grant eternal rest"), omits both the *Gloria* and *Credo* and includes the Doomsday sequence, *Dies Irae* ("Day of Wrath") in place of the *Alleluia.*

BIRTH OF POLYPHONY

During the very time that Gregorian chant was enjoying its Golden Age of development, a musical phenomenon appeared which was to become one of the most far-reaching in Western music. This was the idea of **polyphony,** the art of matching tone for tone simultaneously in a combination of several melodies, called *voices* because of their vocal origin. While isolated examples of rather accidental polyphony (*heterophony*) can be found in music of the Far East and other locales, no organized, notated collection of polyphonic music existed anywhere until the late Middle Ages in Europe.

The tenth century has been regarded by some historians as a period of decadence. Plainsong had reached the pinnacle of its possibilities and attempts to preserve it revealed weaknesses that led, through striking innovations, to its passing. But out of the decadence of one period rises the phoenix of a new art. The ninth-century lack of fixed notation activated a tenth-century search, which eventuated in mensural and polyphonic compositions with all their implications for the future. As F. Ll. Harrison notes, "The impulse which created Romanesque architecture by elaborating the basic plan of the early Christian basilica also created new liturgical and musical forms by elaborating the basic framework of the services . . . Polyphony was a purely musical method of festive decoration."

The actual origins of polyphony are lost in history but it is probable that they lie with the improvising performer. Polyphony may have been an offspring of Greek magadizing. Perhaps it was Nature's way of re-adjusting singing so that those with voices of medium register struck a balance between the high and low of the octave sung by men and women in unison. On the other hand, it may have come from folk music or resulted from the experiments of philosophers working with simultane-ous interval performance. Whatever its origins, the technique of **counter-point** had arrived upon the musical scene by the eighth century. A note was called a "point," so *punctus contra punctum,* from which our term is derived, signifies "note against note."

To a *cantus firmus* (fixed song) taken from Gregorian chant and later called the *tenor* (from the Latin, *teneo,* to hold) was added a second part, at a distance of a fourth or fifth (both considered con-sonant intervals). These parts were named *vox principalis* and *vox organalis*—the principal voice and the organal voice, respectively. The style was called *organum* or *diaphony* (two sounds). At some time the second voice may have been played on the organ, hence *organum.*

Hucbald (840-930), a monk of St. Amand in Flanders, wrote trea-tises which described the state of music in his day. Many innovations for which he was long given credit have been disclosed as those of others and there is strong reason to believe that they may have been merely codifications of already existing practices. A famous source of information, *Musica Enchiriadis* (*Handbook of Music*) has been at-tributed to Hucbald but authorities do not agree as to its real author-ship. The *Enchiriadis* contains the first technical description of *organum,* although the style had already been referred to in earlier works.

Simple *organum* was two-voiced, but there was also a composite *organum* of three or four voices, resulting from the doubling of the two voices in octaves.

nos qui vi - vi - mus be - ne- di - ci - mus Do - mi - ne

(x)

In the eighth chord (x) are the forbidden intervals of the tritone, the *diabolus in musica,* mentioned previously. As theorists of the tenth century admitted only "concords," that is, perfect fourths and fifths, the appearance of the tritone points to an early use of *musica ficta,* the insertion of accidentals without special indication. It is not known at what date these "false" tones were first used but a fourteenth-century theorist wrote, "Music is called *ficta* where we make a tone to be a semitone, or, conversely, a semitone to be a tone." Its most obvious example is that of changing B natural into B flat to make it conform to the rule of "concords."

A decided step forward was made when, instead of keeping the second voice at a parallel distance, different intervals were introduced. In the tenth century this was done by means of oblique movement, that is, the *vox organalis* remained stationary for several syllables.

Te hu - mi-les fa- mu- li mo- du-lis ve - ne- ran-do pi- is.

In the next three centuries great progress was made in the art of combining a given melody with another; contrary motion in voice-leading and the crossing of parts was permitted. *Descant, discant* or *discantus* (Latinized forms of the Greek word, *diaphony*) were names given to this more advanced polyphony in which the temporal element first enters as a conscious factor in music.

Before continuing to trace the further development of *organum,* we might pause to consider several elements that make listening to this rudimentary polyphony more meaningful. First of all, it is necessary to realize that medieval composers were not free, in the modern sense of the word, to do just anything that their creative instincts prompted. The second Council of Nicaea in 787 had flatly stated:

> The substance of religious scenes is not left to the initiative of the artists; it derives from the principles laid down by the Catholic Church and religious tradition . . . His art alone belongs to the painter, its organization and arrangement belong to the clergy.

Analogously, the Church laid down limits to the "organizing" a composer might do to plainsong; *organum* was used in celebrating the more important feasts and only the *antiphon* of a psalm, for instance, might be given the new setting, although at first the antiphons and

Ordinary sections of the Mass were not the most likely candidates for polyphony. Troping, of course, was flourishing during this period. In fact, an almost absurd point was reached when the tropes themselves were troped. Yet the medieval composer had not yet donned the guise of creativity we ascribe to artists today. He was still responsive to authority. He was an *organista.*

Another problem appeared with the birth of polyphony, that of the quality of intervals, which involves the twin concepts of **consonance** and **dissonance.** It is important to remember that definition, in this case, is a purely relative matter; what one considers consonant, another may regard as dissonant. Hucbald had written, "Consonance is the calculated and harmonious mixture of two notes which occurs only when these two notes, produced from different sources, are combined into one musical entity, such as when a boy and a man sing together." The consonant intervals of the Middle Ages were those with the simplest mathematical ratios, the so-called *perfect* intervals of unison, fourth, fifth and octave. We have seen that the tritone, forming diminished or augmented intervals, was regarded with horror and that our imperfect consonant intervals, thirds and sixths, were conspicuous by their absence in early medieval sacred music. Thus, when we hear *organum,* many of us notice a rather stark bareness which is not immediately congenial.

Formerly, it was almost impossible for listeners to enjoy music from earlier than the fourteenth century, as it sounded crude and ugly to ears accustomed to the suave harmonies of the nineteenth century. It was claimed that the early works showed an ignorance of musical laws. Today, however, we recognize that writers of *organum* and *discant,* unconscious of practices not yet formulated, were nevertheless method-bound. And until recently, unaware of their processes and indifferent to them, we regarded their systems as barbarous and unmusical. The greatest drawback, it would appear, was not that they were unscientific, but rather that they were too scientific. It was not until the fifteenth century that the mathematical and the musical mind become distinct, separate entities.

A modern listener, moreover, is faced with two additional considerations. The music of the late Middle Ages was written for "equal voices" —that is, voices lying within almost the same general range or *tessitura,* so that crossings were inevitable and often resulted in a tangled web of musical texture such as John of Salisbury describes. Also, as John implies, there were peculiarities of performance with which we cannot be familiar today, owing to the inadequate state of notation and the obliteration of the tradition. The "repeating notes" to which he refers, for instance, may have been the practice of *hoketus,* which Walter Odington defines as "a truncation . . . over the tenor . . . (made) in such a way that one voice is always silent while another sings."

However surreptitious the route, *organum* gradually found its way into every facet of Church musical observance, much to the dismay of conservatives who cried out against it. The eleventh-century *Winchester Troper,* a collection of 150 *organa,* unfortunately is notated in *neumes* and consequently not susceptible of precise transcription. Yet even here Marc Pincherle points to evidence of "a remarkable relaxation of the rules of *organum* in which contrary movement was already tolerated."

John Cotton, of the early twelfth century, who first justified the use of contrary motion, was one of those responsible for the "new *organum,*" shortly to become *discant.* The development of discant "was the subject of a continuous effort extending apparently from the beginning of the twelfth century to the second half of the thirteenth, and carried on both in France and England, but chiefly in France, and at first especially by the musicians of Paris," writes H. Ellis Wooldridge.

Meanwhile, in the cult of Mary, medieval man had found a divinity to love rather than one to fear. His devotion to the Virgin, which became so widespread that the phrase, *Notre Dame,* was almost synonymous with "cathedral," inspired clerics to write songs of adoration, now included in the Divine Offices and in many choral and solo settings. One of these poet-musician monks was Hermann the Cripple (Hermannus Contractus, 1013-1054) from the monastery of Reichenau. It was he who composed two of the four Marian antiphons—*Alma redemptoris mater* ("Kind Mother of the Savior") and *Salve regina mater misericordiae* ("Homage to Thee, O Queen of Compassion")—which exemplify the religious fervor of the eleventh century.

During the twelfth century many musical centers, including those at Paris, Chartres, Compostela, Padua and St. Gall were contributing *organa* to sacred music literature. Each center had its own style. A most interesting one was that of the Abbey of St. Martial at Limoges where the principal voice or *tenor* very much prolonged each tone of the Gregorian *cantus firmus* while the upper organal voice projected florid *melismas,* producing a total effect of an ethereal free-floating melody sounding against sustained pedal tones.

ARS ANTIQUA

From the middle of the twelfth century and through the thirteenth the focus of musical activity shifted to the Paris Cathedral, and its musical production has come to be known as *ars antiqua* (old style) to differentiate it from the *ars nova* (new style) of the fourteenth century.

However spurious the former term may be, it provides a convenient phrase and is so used here. Two chief representatives of Parisian *ars antiqua* were Leoninus (or Léonin) and Perotinus (or Pérotin), choirmasters at the church which was rebuilt in Pérotin's time as Notre Dame. Leoninus composed the *Magnus Liber,* a cycle of works for the services of an entire year, which Perotinus revised and rewrote in part.

Fig. 22. Notre Dame, Paris. Leoninus and Perotinus were the chief representatives of *ars antiqua* as choirmasters of Notre Dame, Paris. (Photograph by the editor.)

We know very little about the personalities of these two men, although they were respected as masters of their craft, Leoninus having been called "excellent organist" (*optimus organista*), which probably meant organizer of *organum,* as there is no mention of Notre Dame's having an organ at the time. Leoninus advanced the concepts of St. Martial, enriching his works with sweeping coloraturas and a remarkable use of variable rhythms. As Sachs remarked, "The dimensions had grown." We see in his work too the pressures of mensural music, for the rhythmically free *organum* is interrupted by *clausulae* or *copulae* in *discant* style, that is, in modal meter, with each of the two parts in the same basic rhythm. Performance of Leoninus' *organa* followed the usual practice of a soloist singing the upper part or *duplum,* while another singer or an instrumentalist rendered the lower *tenor* of plainsong.

In Perotinus a worthy successor was found to the older master. Perotinus rewrote selections by Leoninus, introducing richer *clausulae* and placing the music into more regular measure. In other words, this thirteenth-century composer tightened up the vast output of his predecessor as well as adding a third (*triplum*) and even a fourth (*quadruplum*) part to the music. He is also credited with the earliest Western use of *imitation,* a device which was to have importance in the development of polyphonic music, leading toward increased coherence and cleaner articulation.

It is not difficult to believe that from such a flourishing musical center as Paris should come, not only modification of *organum,* but also new forms. One of these was **conductus.** *Conductus* is distinguished from *organum* by several characteristics. Its musical materials were not derived from Gregorian chant but consisted of an original melody to which was added an original *duplum* (and possibly other voices). There was similarity of rhythm in all parts and the rhythm was a relatively simple one with regular stresses, a sort of sacred march, for *conductus,* as the name implies, was used during processionals from altar to choir and also in churchly doings outside the sanctuary proper. It had a single text.

A more curious phenomenon of the school of Notre Dame recalls the words of Henry Adams: "One seems easily at home in the Renaissance; one is not too strange in the Byzantine; as for the Roman, it is ourselves; and we could walk blindfolded through every chink and cranny of the Greek mind; all these styles seem modern, when we come close to them; but the Gothic gets away." The **motet,** a form or style of musical composition prominent in the *ars antiqua* of the twelfth and thirteenth centuries, was in its early appearances a very strange creation. In Sachs' words, it could be "polyphonic, polyrhythmic, polytextual and polyglot." Like the Gothic cathedrals with their asymmetry and combination of all sorts of dissimilar elements, the Gothic motet was "unified in the spirit rather than in appearance."

Every choral part of the service, except the *Credo* of the Mass, was written as a motet, and it survived all the other discarded forms. The word is derived either from *mot* (word) or from motion. *Motetus,* according to *Grove's Dictionary,* "sang the chief text, while the *tenor* held on, the *triplex* being the third voice (whence is derived our modern 'treble')." The *cantus firmus* of a motet was a plainsong tune with a familiar text, with which were combined other texts and tunes, often popular, or other secular songs with words in the vernacular. Early motets were crude but later the art of combining melodies, of creating smoothly moving parts, beautiful harmonies and well-balanced compositions brought into being some of the greatest works of the fifteenth and sixteenth centuries.

OTHER MANIFESTATIONS

In addition to the works of the Notre Dame school, we find other types of sacred music coming to the fore in the late Middle Ages. A twelfth-century bishop claimed an English origin for **canon,** a specific type of counterpoint in which a melody is so constructed that it is repeated in different voices, each entering a few bars after the other has started. The *Reading Rota,* "Six Men's Song," is a canon or round for six voices, to the text, *Sumer is icumen in* (*c.* 1240). Its authorship is unknown, although it has been variously attributed to John of Fornsete and Walter Odington.

The English theorist Walter Odington, a Benedictine monk at Oxford early in the fourteenth century, made studies of thirteenth-century rhythm; admitted the imperfect concords, thirds and sixths; defined *motet and rondeau,* new types of vocal compositions; used the word *harmony* in place of *discant;* and discussed *gymel* and *fauxbourdon.* **Gymel** (twin song) was a form of discant used by the early Britons, in which two-part writing with imperfect concords was employed. When a voice was inserted between the *cantus firmus* and the bass, creating intervals of thirds, the bass was sung, transposed an octave higher. Thus it was a "false bass" or **fauxbourdon.** Gustave Reese writes: "During the first twenty years of the fifteenth century English discant was to begin to appear on the Continent and alongside of it the earliest examples of *fauxbourdon* proper, with the *cantus firmus* in the highest voice."

We must also make mention of the musical side of the popular religious revivals which swept Europe during the thirteenth century. In many ways, the Roman Catholic Church had closed in upon itself, notably in that the clergy alone had direct access to Christ and in that the prohibition of translation of the Bible into vernacular languages made the great writings of the Church inaccessible to the people. Numerous small bands of "poor men of Christ" sprang up, and a mania developed for miracles and the spectacular. St. Francis of Assisi in the thirteenth century inspired many by his self-embraced poverty and unquestioning love for living things. He encouraged the composition of popular songs of praise called *laudi spirituali*. These works had texts in the language of the people and simple musical structures suitable for devotional singing. The style is distinctly Italianate in its lyricism and through the *laudisti* indirectly led to the oratorio of the seventeenth century.

NOTATION

A problem to be solved before tenth-century musicians could make further progress was that of notation. While the *neumes* indicated roughly whether a melody rose or fell, they failed to tell by what intervals it moved. Had not the schools handed down traditions orally— the notation merely aiding the memory—the music might have been lost altogether.

In the eleventh century a notation called *Daseian* was used. (This form was credited to Hucbald.) A Greek sign shown in different positions, resembling our F, indicated the first, second and fourth notes of each tetrachord. The third was shown by other signs. For beginners it was combined with horizontal lines marked *T* and *S,* which indicated the intervals of the tetrachords as whole tones or semi-tones. These staves varied from six to eleven lines depending on the range of the songs, and only spaces were employed. Frequently the *Daseian* notation was written alongside of the intervallic indication, and in place of *neumes* the words were written in script. When *organum* was well established, Hermannus Contractus in the eleventh century invented a system for indicating intervals by means of letters: *e* showed a unison; *s,* a semitone; *t,* a whole tone; *ts,* a minor third, *tt,* a major third, and so on.

As men did most of the singing in the Middle Ages, music was notated in the lower range: C was middle c and F was in the bass clef. When the range of a melody did not coincide with the compass of a staff, a necessity arose for changing the names of the lines, and the custom of placing letters at the beginning of the staff was introduced. These *claves signatae,* or **clefs,** were, according to the theorists, "the *keys* by which the secrets of the stave are unlocked."

The three clefs in use today are derived from these letters. The number of lines to the staff was not settled until the close of the sixteenth century, when four were used for plainchant and five for secular music. In the parchment manuscripts so marvelously illuminated by medieval monks, we sometimes see four-lined and sometimes six-lined staves. While we speak of our staves as having five lines each, they are actually part of a grand staff of eleven lines, the sixth line of which is middle C.

The clefs developed as follows:

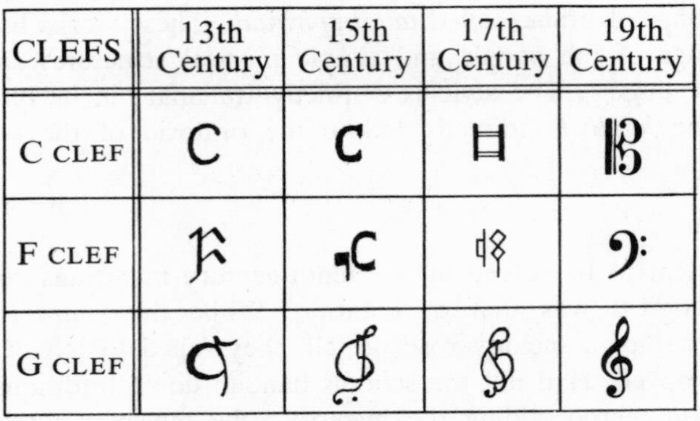

CLEFS	13th Century	15th Century	17th Century	19th Century
C CLEF				
F CLEF				
G CLEF				

(from Vincent d'Indy's *"Cours de Composition Musicale"*)

Fig. 23. Showing the development of the clefs.

The very earliest forms of *organum* which we have discussed did not require radically new notation, for the *tenor* sustained its tone until the *melisma* above it was completed, and then continued on. With additional elaborations, however, new problems arose, both in the metric setting of words and in evaluation and interpretation of rhythmic notation. When composers combined not only different voice parts but different meters as well, scribes were hard put to perpetuate their efforts. Somehow an equivalency had to be reached. Between 1150 and 1300 this was accomplished, rather arbitrarily, by establishing six rhythmic modes based on a unit of three.

Mode I — trochaic

Mode II — iambic

Mode III — dactylic

Mode IV — anapestic

Mode V — spondaic

Mode VI — tribrachic

This scheme applied only to the recording of *organa, conductus* and motets.

The "three degrees of length" is *triple* meter. *Tempus perfectum,* three *breves* to the measure, was indicated by a perfect circle O, the symbol of the Holy Trinity and, therefore, of perfection. To the medieval mind, music was inseparably a part of religion. The musician complicated things unnecessarily by holding almost superstitiously to the multiple of three as the standard unit. (*Duple* meter—two *breves* to the measure—was imperfect and was indicated by an incomplete circle C, from which is derived our sign for common time.)

Franco of Cologne, of the later thirteenth century, was the first to discuss notation in which notes have a more-or-less exact time value. Although he has been regarded as the inventor of time signatures, it has also been pointed out that he speaks of measured music as a thing already in existence. He probably gathered up and assembled early experiments into a comprehensive system. He may have been a mathematician interested in music, for, as cited earlier, the medieval musician was in essence a scientist (in the university curriculum, music was part of a *quadrivium* composed of the disciplines of arithmetic, geometry and astronomy; the theorist was far more esteemed than the performer). Whatever the case, Franco's researches were of such importance that the system was called Franconian notation. The principles on which his system is based underlie present-day notation.

Thirteenth- and fourteenth-century theorists accepted Franco's statement in his influential treatise, *De musica mensurabili,* that the two or more melodies in discant are made equal in time values by the use of sounds in three degrees of length—*longa, brevis* and *semibrevis*—which together with the *maxima* became more or less equivalent to our whole, half, quarter and eighth notes. Somewhat later a Frenchman, Petrus de Cruce (Pierre de la Croix, *c.* 1300), further subdivided the breve into twelve semibreves, confusingly retaining the breve writing-symbol but obviously expressing the composers' desire for shorter time values.

A glance at the diagram below will convey some sense of the evolution of rhythmic notation.

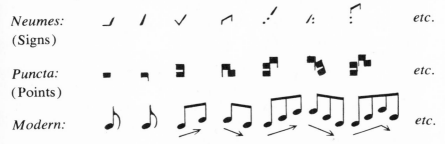

Neumes: (Signs)

Puncta: (Points)

Modern: etc.

To remedy the inconsistencies of the system three devices were employed—the dot, coloration of notes, and time signatures. The dot was a "point" or "prick of perfection" and made a *long, breve* or *semibreve* perfect by giving it a threefold count, the origin of our dotted note. The dot was also used above the staff as the first indication of a bar line. The use of red, yellow, green and black has been discussed in connection with staff development. Early manuscripts show notes filled in with black or red ink to indicate a change of value.

In our notation, the metric signatures were:

$$\odot = \tfrac{9}{8} \qquad \bigcirc = \tfrac{3}{4} \qquad \in = \tfrac{6}{8} \qquad C = \tfrac{4}{4} \qquad \mathbb{C} = alla\ breve$$

(*Alla breve* meant that that the standard time value was cut in half.)

Attempts to explain the meaning of such terms as mood, time, prolation, perfection, imperfection, major and minor, led to the construction of enormous time charts, many examples of which are found in medieval treatises. Mensural notation did not reach its ultimate development with Franco, for it was the subject of practically all treatises on theory for at least three hundred years.

LITURGICAL DRAMA

During the late Middle Ages liturgical drama had advanced from the "sanctuary of the church to the porch," proliferating from the brief dialogue of the Easter *"Quem quaeritis"* trope, mentioned earlier, into more ornate Easter scenes as well as plays devoted to the Christmas story, such as the late eleventh-century *Play of Three Kings* (*Infantem vidimus*), numerous "Herod" and "Rachel" dramas and the celebrated twelfth-century *Play of Daniel.* (The latter is available to us in a transcription of the Egerton Manuscript [thirteenth-century] in the British Museum, by Rembert Weakland, O.S.S. and the late Noah Greenberg.)

The Play of Daniel is far more complex than its troped-plainsong predecessors, as it includes nearly fifty melodies and a large cast of characters. It is monodic in texture and written in plainsong notation. We know its genesis from the prologue:

Ad honorem tui, Christe,	(To your honor, Christ,
Danielis ludus iste,	This play of Daniel
In Belvaco est inventus,	Was created in Beauvais,
Et invenit hunc juventus.	The product of our youth.)

Father Weakland, in his introduction, notes the use of ecclesistical modes as well as the popularity of the Ionian, the major mode of later times. He cites the secular-liturgical blending of musical ingredients as well as the vigor of medieval monophonic songs. "The intricacies and freedom of their meters and rhythm and the intensity of their feeling show that this type of Latin song was far from dead, even after the rise of polyphony." The Egerton Manuscript does not specify instrumentation, but there seems no doubt that instruments were used together with voices in presenting the play.

Fig. 24. Page from an antiphonary—thirteenth century. Problems of notation had to be solved before musicians could make further progress. On this page we discern an advance in notational accuracy. (Courtesy Laurentian Library, Florence.)

INSTRUMENTS

The earliest Western instruments actually surviving in today's museums date from the sixteenth century; thus a gap in our knowledge exists and we are referred to illuminations and written records for our information. We have already mentioned the use of the organ to supplement and sustain singers of the liturgy. Early in the twelfth century the Netherlands had evolved an organ with two manuals and a pedal arrangement. Smaller chamber instruments, called *portatives,* on which a player used one hand to operate the bellows and the other to perform

Fig. 25. "Virgin and Child"—Perre Serra, Spanish, fourteenth century. The angel-musicians surrounding the Virgin are playing (from top left) recorder, lute, portative organ, (from top right) psaltery, fiddle and harp. (Courtesy Museo de Arte Cataluña, Barcelona.)

the music, also became popular, especially in the realm of secular music. Buchner cites a Cambridge document that contrasts those instruments permitted by the Church with those outlawed. Among the favored were the harp, organ, zink or cornet (a horn with fingerholes) and chimes. It seems likely that Europe imported almost all her instruments through the ages from Asia, although we do not know just when. An independent instrumental music, however, did not exist within sacred confines during this period.

JEWISH MUSIC

We have indicated the early Christian debt to Jewish music. Paradoxically, a reciprocal contribution took place during the Middle Ages. Beside the synagogue cantillation that paralleled Near Eastern musical practices, another form of fixed chant arose, influenced by Christian plainsong and the ecclesiastical modes. This was especially true among the Jews of Central Europe. As the grasp of the Roman Catholic Church relaxed and secularism grew, Jews came directly into contact with European music. Salomone Rossi, a contemporary of Monteverdi, wrote polyphonic music for the Jewish service. Instrumental music was introduced into German synagogues about 1700. Reformation *chorales* were adapted to Jewish words, and one Hasidic arranger went so far as to borrow a tune from Verdi's *La Traviata*.

THEORISTS

A philosopher, mathematician and musician of the fourteenth century, Jean de Muris, probably of Norman birth, but Paris residence, left books containing valuable information about the music of his day. He was long believed to be the author of *Speculum musicae,* but musicologists have since proved it to be the work of Jacques de Liége, who was reactionary, while de Muris was an advocate of the new art. *Grove's Dictionary* records: "The seventh book deals with mensurable music, and is remarkable for the protest it contains against modern divergence from the theory and practice of Franco and his school, against innovations in notation, exaggerated sentiment in descant, the liberties taken by singers in the matter of embellishment, the excessive use of discords and the abandonment of the old organum and conductus in favor of motet and cantilena."

Another theorist, Johannes de Grocheo, writing in the year 1300, dared to discuss *musica vulgaris* (music of the people) with *musica sacra* (music of the Church). For the first time a scholarly nod had been made toward the existence of a secular music, of which we had formerly been aware only through the negative outcries of ranting clergy. That composers turned to writing secular music extensively may have been caused in part by the decree of Pope John XXII issued at Avignon in 1322, banning practically all kinds of polyphony from the Church's services. It was too late, however, to stem the tide.

The "moderns" against whom de Liége leveled his shafts were headed by Philippe de Vitry, Bishop of Meaux (1291-1361), French poet, theorist and composer. This revolutionist, who so soon took his place in history as an evolutionist, wrote treatises entitled *Ars Nova* and *Liber musicalium.* The "new style" summed up the procedures of his predecessors and added some innovations of importance. A reaction had set in, perhaps due to troubadours and advances in secular music, against the rigid discipline of church music. It resulted in greater harmonic and rhythmic freedom; more liberty in part-writing; the use of duple meter in sacred composition; and most amusing of all, a ban against consecutive fifths and octaves, which had been the basic principle of the old order. Although many of de Vitry's compositions have been lost, his theories are exemplified in the works of Guillaume de Machault, a contemporary of singular importance because he is the link between *ars antiqua,* as the motets of the late thirteenth century were sometimes designated, and *ars nova.*

GUILLAUME DE MACHAULT

Guillaume de Machault (1300-1377) was among the first to use music as a source of artistic expression. Formerly he was regarded as a leading poet of his age, and his music was considered primitive and unschooled. But Amédée Gastoué, in *Three Centuries of French Medieval Music,* speaks of the music of the fourteenth century "which reached its finished form in the compositions of the greatest master of this period, Guillaume de Machault."

De Machault left great quantities of manuscripts, many of which are in the *Bibliothèque nationale de Paris* (National Library). Gastoué gives a comprehensive list which illustrates the innovations introduced by the *ars nova.* The composer writes both sacred and secular music; secular music has pushed itself to the fore as an art product; the Mass (*Messe Notre Dame*), probably composed for the coronation of Charles V at Reims, where de Machault was a canon of the cathedral, is the first known in four parts; instrumental preludes and postludes, alternating with vocal passages, are brought to our notice; lays, motets, rondels, ballads and *chansons balladées,* or monodies with refrains, are current forms; Latin and French texts are used simultaneously; in some of the manuscripts only one line carries words, and the other voices are presumably played by instruments, showing that de Machault was influential in the use of instrumental accompaniments.

The last of the French poets to compose music for his own poems, an intimate of royalty, a nobleman himself, diplomat and spiritual leader, medieval prototype, as was de Vitry, of the many-sided Renaissance figure to come, de Machault synthesized the traditional with the new. He was the fourteenth-century master of the *isorhythmic* motet (one involving a repetition of both melodic and rhythmic pattern) and yet audaciously employed syncopation, the extended device of *hoquet* (in which a melody is divided between two or three voices in very short fragments) and individualistic rhythms and vocal coincidences.

* * * * *

The "mills of the gods" had ground out piece by piece the necessary equipment for the Age of Polyphony. In the background were the *déchanteurs* (discant singers) of Notre Dame de Paris; the troubadours and *trouvères,* whose influence resulted in greater rhythmic and melodic freedom in sacred music; the Crusaders, who stimulated an interchange of culture—all generating in the heart of man a slowly awakening recognition of his need for beauty.

The *art* of music was not the aim of early centuries; music was an accessory of the Church. The early Christian fathers fashioned materials out of which they built a science of music. A conscious desire for art pushed forward toward a Renaissance, however. It was not without reason that *ars nova* received its name. It was deliberate action—no flag of truce, but rather, a declaration of independence.

SUGGESTIONS FOR FURTHER READING

Adams, Henry, *Mont-Saint-Michel and Chartres.* Boston, Houghton Mifflin, 1933.

Apel, Willi, *The Notation of Polyphonic Music.* Cambridge, Medieval Academy of America, 1949.

Carpenter, Nan Cooke, *Music in the Medieval and Renaissance Universities.* Norman, University of Oklahoma Press, 1958.

Davison, Archibald T., and Apel, Willi, *Historical Anthology of Music,* vol. 1. Cambridge, Harvard University Press, 1949.

Gimpel, Jean, *The Cathedral Builders.** New York, Grove, 1961.

Heer, Friedrich, *The Medieval World.** New York, New American Library, 1963.

Male, Emile, *The Gothic Image: Religious Art in France of the Thirteenth Century.** New York, Harper, 1958.

Nettl, Paul, *The Book of Musical Documents.* New York, Philosophical Library, 1948.

Parrish, Carl, *The Notation of Medieval Music.* New York, Norton, 1957.

―――― *A Treasury of Early Music.** New York, Norton, 1958.

* Available in paperback edition.

Parrish, Carl, and Ohl, John F., *Masterpieces of Music before 1750*. New York, Norton, 1951.

Reese, Gustave, *Music in the Middle Ages*. New York, Norton, 1940.

Riemann, Hugo, *History of Music Theory*. Lincoln, University of Nebraska Press, 1962.

Seay, Albert, *Music in the Medieval World*.* Englewood Cliffs, Prentice-Hall, 1965.

Starr, William J., and Devine, George F., *Music Scores—Omnibus*, Part 1.* Englewood Cliffs, Prentice-Hall, 1964.

Strunk, Oliver, ed., *Source Readings in Music History*.* New York, Norton, 1950.

Trumble, Ernest, *Fauxbourdon*, vol. 1. Brooklyn, Institute of Medieval Music, 1959.

A Sampler of Supplementary Recordings

Collections

Treasury of Early Music	Haydn 1900/3
Music of the Middle Ages	Lyric 85
Masterpieces of Music before 1750	Haydn 9038/40
2000 Years of Music	Folkways 3700
800th Anniversary Notre Dame	Philips 500039
Ten Centuries of Music	DGG KL-52/61
Chansons and Motets of the Thirteenth Century	DGG ARC 3051
Early Medieval Music	Victor LM-6015
Court Dances of Medieval France	Turnabout 4008
French Ars Antiqua	Expériences Anonymes 35
Notre Dame Organa	Expériences Anonymes 21
The Play of Daniel	Decca DL 9402
The Play of Herod	Decca DX 187

Related Works of Interest

Bach, J. S., *Mass in B Minor*
Beethoven, Ludwig, *Missa solemnis in D, Op*. 123
Castiglioni, Niccolo, *Gymel for Flute and Piano*
    Tropi
Haydn, Joseph, *Mass No. 9 in D*
Langlais, Jean, *Mass in Ancient Style*
    Suite Medieval
Liszt, Franz, *Missa solemnis*
Stravinsky, Igor, *Mass*

Opportunities for Study in Depth

1. Examine the American national anthem, "The Star-Spangled Banner," and relate its rhythmic structure to the medieval practice of isorhythm.

2. Listen to Claude Debussy's piano prelude "The Engulfed Cathedral" (*La Cathédrale engloutie*) and Igor Stravinsky's ballet suite *Petrouchka*, citing any parallels between these two dissimilar works and the principles of *organum* and *fauxbourdon*.

3. Prepare a medieval liturgical drama for classroom performance, utilizing instruments as they might have been employed, improvising when necessary.

4. Attend a High Mass of the Roman Catholic Church. Listen to recordings of polyphonic settings of the Mass. Comment on the articulation of parts, as outlined in this chapter.

5. After more intensive reading and investigation, prepare an oral report on the two Gothic transition artists Guillaume de Machault and the famous Italian painter Giotto (*c.* 1266-1337).

6. Discuss the social position of the artist—plastic, visual and musical—in the panorama of the late Middle Ages. What distinguished him from his earlier and later colleagues?

7. Correlate the great Gothic architecture and music of the period, noticing the impress of Christian tradition and the vagaries of the less and less anonymous craftsmen.

8. Make a study of the late Middle Ages in Europe, concentrating particularly on those facets which lead to or presage the coming of a Renaissance.

VOCABULARY ENRICHMENT

Mass	*duplum*
Concert Mass	*triplum or triplex*
Requiem Mass	*conductus*
polyphony	motet
voices	canon
counterpoint	gymel
cantus firmus	*fauxbourdon*
tenor	*laudi*
vox principalis	Daseian notation
vox organalis	clefs
organum	rhythmic modes
musica ficta	*tempus perfectum*
discant	*quadrivium*
consonance	*alla breve*
dissonance	*portative*
equal voices	*musica sacra*
hoketus, hoquet, (*hocket*)	*musica vulgaris*
Marian antiphons	*ars nova*
ars antiqua	isorhythmic motet
clausulae	

PART III

Music of the People

MUSICA VULGARIS

Chapter 6.

THE MUSIC OF TROUBADOURS AND FOLK

Well pleaseth me the sweet time of Easter
That maketh the leaf and the flower come out.

And it pleaseth me when I hear the clamor
Of the birds' bruit about their song through the wood;

And it pleaseth me when I see through the meadows
The tents and pavilions set up, and great joy have I
When I see o'er the campana knights armed and horses arrayed.

—BERTRAN DE BORN
(Translated by Ezra Pound)

Thus did Bertran de Born, a twelfth-century petty nobleman of Hautefort, take a straightforward look at the world about him and rather ingenuously fashion his pleasures of spring, bird song and the panoply of medieval tents and warriors into a *chanson,* full of zest for living and noticeably lacking in reference to either the Church or the virtues of austerity. This wily troubadour is also reputed to have been partially responsible for the rebellion of young Henry III against his more illustrious brother, Richard the Lionhearted, for Bertran excelled in writing topical verses, full of wit and venom, that served as propaganda against both Church and temporal powers.

In previous chapters we discussed the development of musical liturgy in the Roman Catholic Church, momentarily setting aside the fact that concurrent with this important and comparatively orderly growth there were significant musical developments of entirely different nature, originating from a profusion of sources. At the same time that the art of music was purposefully evolving, song—a universal human instinct—was spontaneously recording the life of the times—of peasant, lover, warrior and nobleman. We shall devote this chapter to an examination of the varieties of secular monody and folksong.

ITINERANT MUSICIANS

The itinerant musician, whether bard, troubadour or *Minnesinger,* like bird and bee, was an agent for transmitting the pollen of secular melody, effecting an international cross-fertilization to enrich the native music of those countries through which he passed. Ultimately, this "bird of passage" influenced the further development of Church music and works of the Netherlands schools.

In Homeric times and among the ancient Celts, bards were heartily welcome, because there was no Christian Church to combat the influence of pagan story and instrumental frivolity. In early Britain the Celtic bards of the Druids held sway, as they did in Brittany (France), where the religion and language were similar. (In Brittany today some people still hang the sacred mistletoe of the Druid over their doors.) Priests were the bards, whose instrument was the *crwth,* a crude harp. (The ancient Eisteddfod and other Druidical contests have been revived in Wales, where they are now popular tourist attractions.) From the Druids we gain a sense of correspondence between the microcosmos of men and the macrocosmos of nature which is recognized in twelfth-century romances as a new insight into the world. (Vincenzo Bellini's popular opera *Norma,* though quite fictitious, is of interest here in that its plot concerns the love of a Druid princess for a Roman warrior in early Britain.)

Long before the medieval age, Norsemen and Vikings in Norway, Iceland and Finland had their *skalds* or *saga-men,* who detailed in song and verse stories of their gods. Their *eddas* and *sagas* were handed down orally from generation to generation until they were recorded. From these the modern skald Richard Wagner took the theme for his *Nibelungen Ring,* and Jan Sibelius has often drawn upon the Finnish *Kalevala* as inspiration for his music.

From improvised boast-songs of Germanic warriors gathered in hall or camp have come the archetype for the epics of the Middle Ages. Tacitus documented the wild singing, on the eve of battle, of these fierce fighters to whom the silent Roman legions listened as they awaited dawn. From the seventh to the tenth centuries improvised *cantilenae* flourished, in which warriors sang of their bold deeds without any professional services of accompanists.

Later came the *harpers* and *gleemen* of Britain, after its conquest by the Angles, Jutes and Danes. These gleemen used a small harp which was passed from guest to guest at the banquets to which they were welcomed. The gleemen, accepted everywhere, were exempt from military duties and were held inviolate even by the enemy, so as spies they performed secret service with musical *obbligato.*

From early times there appeared the "wandering minstrel," who spread secular music. Without newpapers, airplanes, radio, telegraph, railroads or regular mail channels, the populace would have been bereft indeed had it not been for the minstrels. Minstrels sang in marketplace and bazaar, before peasants and in the halls of the mighty. They delivered news and gossip entertainingly in song and poetry, and sowed seeds of popular romance as well as preposterous fiction. Inveterate travelers, they enlivened, nourished and stimulated people in widely separated territories. They wrested livings from both rich and poor in proportion to their musical skills and their power of pleasing or flattering. They knew most of their songs by heart, but the few who could read carried parchments with them in little wallets.

The *clerici vagantes* (wandering clerics), or *goliards,* so named because of their mythical founder, Bishop Golias, were not, strictly speaking, minstrels, because they were members of the minor clergy. Edward J. Dent says:

> They wandered all over Western Europe during the twelfth and part of the thirteenth centuries. They appear to have risen about the time of Charlemagne, and they are not much heard of after about 1225, the period at which the great medieval universities became systematically organized. They were of all nationalities, united by the common use of Latin as an international language. . . . Although technically ecclesiastics . . . they were classed socially with the minstrels, actors and acrobats who descended from the Roman *mimus,* and were generally regarded as vagabonds and notoriously immoral persons. . . . Their favorite subjects are either wine and women or satire of ecclesiastical authority. . . . It is mainly to the *goliards* that we owe the first notation of secular music.

The *goliards* set Horatian and Virgilian poetry to music in *neumes* and often included references to musical learning in their songs. More information about these raggle-taggle ex-clerics may be found in Helen Waddell's brilliant study, *The Wandering Scholars.* Twentieth-century composer Carl Orff (1895-   ) has set selected verses of the *Carmina Burana,* both the medieval vernacular and popularized Latin, in an appropriately vigorous and rowdy style. Only one authentic piece of *goliard* music exists in letter notation—the love song *O admirabile Veneris idolum.* This example suggests the use of major mode and a simple repeating form, although the rhythm remains a moot point.

With the Battle of Hastings (1066) came great changes in the arts, language, learning and in life itself. William, the Norman conqueror, brought his heritage to England. France had been a part of continental exploits of which she had sung thrillingly. She celebrated the mighty valors of the Age of Chivalry, the era when knight and horse, *chevalier* and *cheval,* not yet displaced by gunpowder, went forth to perform "doughty deeds" for the "liege lord," for his "ladye" or for the Church. Long before Hastings, France had woven in her *chansons de geste* tales of Charlemagne's victory over the invading Moors from Spain. The greatest of these was the *Chanson de Roland,* a glamorous series of song paintings. It is the leading French contribution to the epics of the Middle Ages and pictures the rugged idealism of the period.

In eleventh-century Europe, with Rome's power broken and paganism in abeyance, the Christian hosts raised, in gratefulness as well as self-protection against the still wandering tribes and robber barons, great cathedrals and mighty turreted castles. These settlements, widely isolated, fortified against the enemy and suspicious of the stranger, welcomed a minstrel. He was their diversion from the clangors of battle, their solace and reporter in a rigorous period. "Noblemen use not to make suppers, without harpe or symphony," says Bartholomaeus Anglicus. In fact, it was a common practice to perform secular music in the scattered medieval courts following mealtime.

Although the Church, with some reason, frowned upon the minstrel, to the extent of denying him all sacraments including that of marriage, and governments scowled, denying him civil redress for wrong in the courts and even the privilege of wearing trousers—eventually even monasteries came to extend him hospitality. No court was without its musicians, no noble without his singers. We see Philip the Bold, Duke of Burgundy, a typical feudal lord, glorying in his *ménestrels de bouche* —men and women singers, "as well as boys for his chapel at Dijon, and players on the gittern, harp, psaltery and *eschiquier,* a zither-like stringed instrument. Others played viols and rebecks; wind instrumentalists were represented by an organist, and two players each of *challemelle* (double reed pipes) and *cornemuse* (bagpipe). Towns also had their permanent minstrels; in Germany they formed very important corporations," writes E. J. Dent.

Yet, as frequently happens, minstrels became so numerous and so unequal in talents that bad performers began to crowd out the good. For this reason, in the fourteenth century, associations controlled by princes and guilds sprang up among the *bourgeoisie,* very much like our own music unions, with leaders called *kings of the jugglers.* During Lent, when they were forbidden to appear in public, the *jongleurs* went to schools of minstrelsy, corporate conclaves for the exchange of information about singing and playing.

CRUSADERS AND PILGRIMAGES

The Crusades (1095-1271), in which nearly every European nation joined, probably constituted the most important influence in medieval life and culture. The West met the East. Interchange of dialects and contacts made profound changes in language. Romance languages had stemmed from the Roman Latin. The influence of the rougher dialects of Frankish and Gothic tribes effected the mixture—a rustic Latin, or *Romanse rustique*—out of which developed French, Spanish, Italian, Portuguese and Roumanian. The Crusaders also brought home Arabic rhythms and new ways of singing, as well as the guitar and *al-ud* (called lute, in western Europe).

In these days it was the custom for armor-clad knights and squires to make pilgrimages both for their souls' sakes and to bring back trophies of their daring exploits. As Chaucer (*c.* 1340-1400) says in the prologue to his *Canterbury Tales*:

> Whanne that April with his shoures sote
>   The drought of March hath perced to the rote . . .
> Than longen folk to gon on pilgrimages . . .

To the tomb of the Savior they journeyed; they took part in tourneys and jousts, so that the medieval warrior and minstrel carried learning wherever they went and returned enriched with alien customs, story and song.

In an early *roman,* or medieval vernacular verse narrative, William of Saint-Paur describes pilgrims traveling musically toward the shrine of Mont-Saint-Michel. In Henry Adams' translation:

> The day was clear, without much wind,
> The maidens and the varlets
> Each of them said verse or song;
> Even the old people go singing;
> All have a look of joy.
> Who knows no more sings *Hurrah,*
> Or *God help,* or *Up and On!*
> The minstrels there where they go
> Have all brought their viols;
> Lays and songs playing as they go.

JUGGLERS AND MINSTRELS

After the first Crusade, the roads were alive with strolling singers, jugglers, mountebanks and players. They gave the world color as clad in brilliant hues, beribboned and befeathered, they trudged from town to town. Every tavern was regaled with their fun and fancy. Country fairs lured them, and the country girls awaited them with coquetries. These music makers came from every rank; gay scions who had squandered their fortunes, impoverished craftsmen, and even monks, tired of the discipline of the monastery—all took to the road and gave it the effect of "gay motley."

Fig. 26. "Eleventh-Century Musicians"—unknown artist. Minstrels and players were an indelible part of medieval life. Here we note (from left to right) three musicians playing small cymbals, a ten-stringed harp-like instrument and a fiddle (still bowless). The instrument in the foreground is probably a modification of the older monochord, now a hexachord. (Montecassino, Abbazia, Ms. 1896.)

Many and diverse were their accomplishments. This is verified by the statement of Robert le Mains, a wandering entertainer of the time:

> I can play the lute, the violin, the pipe, the bagpipe, the *syrinx*, the harp, the *gigue*, the *gittern*, the *symphony*, the *psaltery*, the *organistrum*, the *regals*, the *tabor* and the *rote*. I can sing a song well, and make tales and fables, I can tell a story against any man. I can make love-verses to please young ladies, and can play the gallant for them if necessary. Then I can throw knives into the air and catch them without cutting my fingers. I can do dodges with string most extraordinary and amusing. I can balance chairs and make tables dance. I can throw a somersault, and walk on my head.

Of most interest in his list is mention of the violin (*vielle,* fiddle), a new instrument of that time, for which we owe much to the minstrel, as its source is still somewhat a mystery. Among the other instruments mentioned by Le Mains are the *gigue,* a small type of violin to which the people danced *jigs;* the *gittern,* a small guitar strung with catgut; the *psaltery,* an oblong lute plucked with the fingers; the *regals,* portable

organs; the *rote,* a small portable instrument in the fo.
with many strings, much like the harp, but more square
Then there was the *organistrum,* a lute or guitarlike ins,
wire or gut strings and a set of keys, worked by a wheel. ꓹ
names, such as *Bauernleier* (peasant lyre), *Bettlerleier* (begg,
or hurdy-gurdy. Other instruments used were the *trumpet mc.*
rich-sounding monochord, the *cymbalum, cithara* and great horn.

* * * * *

TROUBADOURS AND TROUVÈRES

The first great bloom of secular music occurred during the twelfth
century, when the scope of knightly arts was expanded beyond hunting, warring and drinking to encompass a stylized worship of the gentle-
woman and formal manners expressed in poetry and song. Probably
never before in the history of Europe has such an aura surrounded the
musician as enveloped the *troubadour* of Provence (southern France)
and the *trouvère* from northern France. Even the names, from *trobar* (to
compose) and *trouvère* (to find), have romantic glints. Happily for us
the composers recorded their melodies in the notation of plainsong,
even though they rarely noted the accompaniments that were improvised on lute, guitar and *vielle* by a juggler or *jongleur* who traveled
with the troubadour. (Jules Massenet's opera, *Le Jongleur de Notre
Dame,* is founded on Anatole France's story of such a medieval *jongleur.*)

The first known troubadour was Guillaume, seventh Count of Poitiers
and ninth Duke of Aquitaine (1071-1127), a lusty gentleman who,
although he had taken part in the Crusades, nevertheless incurred the
wrath of the Church because of his passionate verses, which echoed both
Ovid and Moorish Spain. Friedrich Heer says: "In Guillaume's love-
songs the vocabulary and emotional fervor hitherto ordinarily used to
express man's love for God are transferred to the liturgical worship of
woman and vice versa." From Guillaume's time to that of his illustrious
granddaughter, Eleanor of Aquitaine, wife and mother of kings, the
art of the troubadour blossomed largely but not exclusively among the
aristocracy, increasingly refining its lofty concept of love, that private
relationship between a man and woman, which outweighed the powers
of both Church and state, as illustrated in the actual contemporary
relationship between the teaching monk, Abelard, and his abbess, Hel-
oise, who were castigated, as was Eleanor, by a very concerned and
busy St. Bernard of Clairvaux.

The troubadours have left us a legacy of some 200 tunes, possibly
in the beginning derived from *conductus* or from tropes and notated in

umes (meaning that rhythmical interpretation is dependent on metrical poetic modes) and 2600 texts, conceived in a Provençal language called *langue d'oc*. In elaborate *chansonniers* we find examples of *sirventes,* topical songs of praise, blame and war, such as de Born's; *planhs* (*plaintes*), musical elegies; *pastorelles,* in which the hero and heroine were always engaging shepherds and shepherdesses; *chansons de toile,* songs narrating the thoughts of women left behind to spin flax while their menfolk were away; *reverdies* or spring songs; *serenas* or serenades sung in the evening to the beloved; and *albas,* morning songs by which the lovers were to be aroused before they should be discovered, perhaps by her husband. There was an interesting argumentative song called the *tenson,* a contest vehicle in which a debate was carried on in the form of question and answer—often in more than one language. Bits of the troubadours' songs found their way into sacred music and as often Church melody crept into these secular monodies.

Eleanor of Aquitaine married Louis VII—a teen-age match arranged through motives of politics rather than on the existence of any mutual affection—and with her she carried the gay inventions of troubadours in the sunny land of *langue d'oc* to a chilly, squalid and suspicious Paris, then dominated by an ecclesiastical establishment (Louis himself had hoped to be a priest before the death of his older brother made this impossible). The northern counterpart of the troubadour was the *trouvère,* whose works were more dignified and formal and whose influence was more apparent in the Church music of the French and Flemish schools.

The *trouvères* collected tales from Normandy and Brittany, songs of the reign of Charlemagne and other valuable musical material. Among their ranks were kings, such as Thibaut IV of Navarre; aristocrats, such as Blondel de Nesles (1150-1200) and Richard the Lionhearted, son of Eleanor by her second marriage to Henry Plantagenet; and members of the *bourgeoisie,* such as Adam de la Halle (1220-1287), whose pastoral play, *Le Jeu de Robin et Marion,* a series of little love songs between a shepherd and a shepherdess, performed in Naples in 1285, is regarded as the first comic opera. Paul Hindemith uses a *trouvère* melody, *"Ce fu en mai,"* by Moniet d'Arras (thirteenth century), in his *Nobilissima Visione.*

The music of troubadours and *trouvères* is quite attractive to the modern listener, as it is simple, metric and less archaically modal than some plainsong. It also has a quality of naïve *joi de vivre,* perhaps more closely attuned to a modern viewpoint. In it, too, we find some semblance of formal organization in the modern sense of repetition and variety.

The *trouvère* repertoire falls into four main categories. (1) There is a strophic or stanza-by-stanza sort, such as that used in modern hymns. Examples include the *vers* and *canzo*. Often this followed the strophic structure A A B, as does the *chanson* of de Born, in which the first two lines are sung to an original tune, the next two lines to the same tune and the remainder to a different melody. (2) There is a litany type in which each line is sung to the same music. Epics or *chansons de geste* followed this format, their lengthy sections repeating over and over again until a concluding cadence was reached. (3) There is a sequence organization in which one phrase of melody is assigned to each two lines of the verse, *ad finitum*. The *lai*, a narrative or contemplative poem, is an example. Finally (4) there is a refrain or round-dance type in which leader and dancers respond according to a pattern, for to lead the dance was to lead the singing. In the words of one old English ballad:

> Sum [sang] ryng-sangis, dansys ledis, and roundis,
> With vocis schill, quhill all the dail resoundis;
> Quharso thai walk into thar carolyng,
> For amorus lays doith the Rochys ryng.

The combination of song, dance and instrument was called *balerie* or *ballade,* whence is derived our word *ballet*. In addition to the *ballade,* other forms of this type include the *virelai,* with an embryonic A B A structure, and the *rondeau,* which at this time consisted of an alternation of A and AB between leader and group. Altogether we know of some 1400 tunes and 4000 poems composed by the *trouvères*.

The flowering of secular monody was not confined to France. It spread, through pilgrimages to the shrine of St. James at Compostela (Santiago), to Spain, where King Alfonso the Wise (1221-1284) collected 400 *villancicos* (Spanish modification of *virelai*), some reputedly of his own composition, in volumes entitled *Cantigas de Santa Maria*. The troubadours and *trouvères* made little impression on Italy although the *laudi* or popular devotional hymns show some relationship. In England, too, even though Eleanor of Aquitaine assumed the title of Queen after the death of Henry, the most important monophonic songs were not French in genesis, but Anglo-Saxon, as examples ascribed to St. Godric illustrate.

MINNESINGERS

Another royal marriage, that of Beatrice of Burgundy to Frederick Barbarossa (Emperor Frederick I), brought the work of the *trouvères* into Germany, where, after initial paraphrasing, there developed another group of singers who celebrated love (*Minne,* in the old tongue). Like the troubadours they were of the nobility, but unlike them they sang and accompanied as well as composed their songs. *Viels,* or viols, and lutes were their instruments.

Although not as lighthearted as their French brothers-in-song, the *Minnesingers* were often fanciful and humorous. They used a marked rhythm and beauty of form and composed with conspicuous and meticulous simplicity. A dramatic quality in their song lent power to tales of Norse heroes and heroics. The story was their main object and they often incorporated the stern plainsong of the Church, pointing the way to Protestant music of the sixteenth century.

Fig. 27. "Tannhäuser"—Manesse manuscript. Tannhäuser, in the white cloak of the Knights of the German Order, who has been made known to us by Richard Wagner, was a famous *Minnesinger,* who took part in a song contest at the Wartburg.

Tannhäuser, made known to us by Richard Wagner, was a famous *Minnesinger* who took part in a song contest in 1206. Wolfram von

Eschenbach, another contestant, not only gave Wagner the idea for *Tannhäuser,* but wrote the poem from which Wagner took the story of *Parsifal.* Another famous *Minnesinger* was Walter von der Vogelweide, one of whose tunes has come down to us in the Protestant hymn *Old Hundred* ("All People That on Earth Do Dwell"). Von der Vogelweide was the greatest lyric poet of the German Middle Ages, and historian Friedrich Heer has stated, "The folk inspiration of Walter's love-songs remained unmatched until it was recaptured in the bell-like timbre and purity of Goethe." The list would not be complete without mention of an earthier and less ponderous *Minnesinger,* Neidhart von Reuenthal, who, as Sachs says, "added a healthier infusion of brisk and simple tunes from the countryside."

It is interesting to note that at this time new-old narrative materials were making an appearance—materials from which succeeding centuries would draw heavily. The *Minnesinger* Gottfried von Strassburg wrote a German version of the story of Tristan and Isolde. A *trouvère,* Chrétien de Troyes, whose patroness was a daughter of Eleanor of Aquitaine, presented stories of King Arthur and the Knights of the Round Table in masterly *romans courtois* (courtly romances). He anticipated the encyclopedic Lancelot-Grail epics compiled between 1220 and 1235. The legendary Robin Hood would soon become the subject of ballad literature. William Langland would in the meantime write his monumental poem, *Piers Plowman.*

MEISTERSINGERS

The *Minnesingers* in many ways presaged the collapse of the Holy Roman Empire; the last of them vanished about 1300. A revival, however, occurred among the burghers of fifteenth-century Germany, when big towns set up schools of singing and organized guilds that stimulated music by prize competitions. Strict rules abounded and a hierarchy of membership was established, ranging from the *Schüler* (pupil), who could scarcely read music at all, to the *Meistersinger* (master), who could read, write, sing and compose. It is alleged that Heinrich von Meissen, known as *Frauenlob* (Praise of Women), founded the *Meistersinger* system.

A splendid picture of the guild system at work is presented in Wagner's comic opera, *Die Meistersinger von Nürnberg,* in which figures the most celebrated one of all, Hans Sachs, who lived at Nuremberg from 1494 until 1576. His *Preislied* ("Prize Song") is written in the *Minnesinger* and *Meistersinger Barform* of A A B. The *Meistersinger,* however, was an anachronism in his own time, for by the fifteenth and sixteenth centuries, secular monody was a thing of the past and an advanced vocal polyphony reigned supreme in the rest of Europe.

INSTRUMENTAL MUSIC

From the short preludes played on the *vielle* by *jongleurs* before songs and accompanying dances were to come the first independent instrumental pieces of the Middle Ages. To accompany *carols,* a dance form called the *estampie* was used, often played by a trio consisting of shawm or bagpipe, bombard (large oboe) and trumpet. Its structure stemmed from the vocal sequence and gives evidence of the musical punctuation of half (*ouvert*—open) and full (*clos*—closed) cadences. A companion dance, the rapid *ductia,* was also popular. Incidentally, both dances were recommended by Johannes de Grocheo as counterforces to juvenile delinquency, dimly echoing the Greek concept of *ethos* and reminding us that anxiety for the adolescent is not a solely modern concern.

FOLK MUSIC

Despite wars, prejudice and hardship so prevalent in the Middle Ages, troubadours and *trouvères,* the gallant singing composers and reporters, gave us the glamor of chivalry and the beginnings of later forms. They made secular music acceptable as an independent branch of the art. Before, during and after them, however, another secular music undoubtedly existed, but because of the limitations imposed by lack of notation, it is difficult to pin it down to any exact period. This music is commonly known as folk music or folksong.

Folksong is a spontaneous music rooted in the soil of its national origin. It uses materials of its own environment and resolves them into forms that attain a timeless and generalized quality. Folk music is not necessarily of remote ages alone; it is still being made. It differs from the music of primitive peoples that we have already discussed in that it exhibits a balance of phrases and a system of tonal organization. It contrasts with art song in that it is usually of anonymous origin, less dependent upon accompaniment, less complex (in the sense of musical development) and more casual in emotional content.

Sir C. Hubert Parry, in the *Evolution of the Art of Music,* writes:

> The difficulty of introducing expression without spoiling the design was felt as much by the makers of folk-tunes as by composers of more advanced music; and the way in which nations looked at expression and design is the source of the most deep-seated differences between the different national products. Indeed the whole of the folk-music of the world may be broadly classified into two comprehensive divisions.

On the one hand, there are all those tunes whose ostensible basis of intelligibility is the arrangement of characteristic figures in patterns; and on the other, all those which by very prominent treatment of climaxes imply a certain excitement and an emotional origin.

Despite any compartmentalizing of folk music, every nation has had the same sort of songs, among which are songs of childhood, games and cradle songs; songs for religious ceremonies, festivals, holidays (Christmas carols); love songs; drinking, humorous, political and satirical songs; dance tunes; funeral and mourning songs; and narratives, ballads and legends.

We can only regret that no written folksong of the ancient Greeks has come down to us, nor the songs of the Germanic tribes of the first century, of which Tacitus speaks, and rejoice that our own forms have profited by the rhyming stanza developed by singers in the age of minstrelsy. But long before the Christian era, the Hebrews and Egyptians had folk music. And through the mass of folksong we are aware of the steady accretion of a secular branch of music, which evolved steadily while the conscious music of ritual and Church grew. Today can be heard "sung poetry" made centuries ago, much of which has fortunately been collected and analyzed. This collecting of folksongs is due to searchings of anthropologists and composers for material and to a desire to know the sources of widely different national musical inspirations.

ENGLISH FOLK MUSIC

The English folksong, like the English language, is without superfluous ornament and irregular or excessive accent, and has a directness and simplicity in common with other northern countries such as Germany, Holland, Norway and Sweden. Rarely wild, gay or muscular, English folk music is jolly, lilting, rhythmic, humorous, contented, but occasionally colored with an eerie melancholy. Throughout, the tunes are definite in design and order. The most familiar form, akin to German melodies, is the **A B A design,** or statement (A), contrast (B) and repetition of statement (A); or more frequently, A A B A, where the statement is repeated before moving on to the contrasting phrase.

Many of the English folksongs date from a very respectable antiquity, for their structure is modal not only in the form of the scale chosen but in other details. All the Church modes are represented in the folksongs of Great Britain, and most of them in purely English form. "Bristol Town," for example, is purely Dorian, while "There Is an Alehouse" is strictly Ionian. Although the English have nature songs, they are more interested in songs about people, things and occupations, and, like the Scots and southern Europeans, in love songs. However, the English love song is never impassioned, but quaintly tender.

This reasonable race sings much of action, freedom of country, political events, hunting, sailing, poaching and even of hangings and murders. But among the most beautiful songs are those of the Nativity and Christmas carols. Their naïveté, reverence and intimacy make them an indispensable part of the holiday season. In ancient Britain, drinking songs were a great part of banquet ceremonies. In connection with them the *wassail* bowl is frequently mentioned. This title is derived from the greetings of Rowena to her father, Hengist, *"Was hail hla, on cyning,"* which translated from Anglo-Saxon means, "Be of health, Lord King."

Fig. 28. Morris dancers with unicorn. The Morris dance, popular in the fifteenth century, was a sort of pageant, frolicsome and colorful, with gay costumes. (Photograph by the editor.)

The dance song, or round and ballad, taken from the French *rounde* and *ballet,* holds a distinguished place in English folk music. (One that has come down to us is "Sellenger's Round" from the *FitzWilliam Virginal Book.*) The *morris dance,* derived from the *moresque,* flourished in fifteenth-century England. The name originated in Spain as

Morisco, that is, a Christianized Moor. The dance, part of the May festival, was a sort of pageant, frolicsome and colorful with gay costumes. (A similar dance is found in France and Spain.)

The May festival, mentioned in relation to the *morris dance,* emphasizes again the reappearance of ancient customs through the ages. In England, as in every other country, the celebration of the rites of spring is but a survival of an unbroken line of ceremonies, dating from about 800 B.C. in Greece up to our own day—from Dionysius to Stravinsky. The songs, "The King and Queen of the May," "Maypole Dances" and "Jack in the Green," in England; the Thuringian "Little Leaf Man"; the Russian "Tree"; the "Dukes of May" in Florence and the burning of *"La Vecchia"* (the Old-Lady Doll) as a symbol of the annihilation of winter—all take as their protagonist the spring. Because of their ancient roots in the *Floralia,* a Roman festival, the Maypole dances of England were abolished in 1644 as a "heathenish vanity generally abused to superstition and wickedness." Later they drifted back into popular use and are still informally presented.

With the advent of printing, ballads became abundant. Everyone wrote them, and they were carried in baskets and sung and sold in the streets. Most of these were destined for dance tunes and never reached the dignity of bardic song. In keeping with the nature of the English, so many of their printed songs partook of lampooning and political satire that both Henry VIII and Queen Mary issued edicts forbidding the printing of books, ballads or rhymes. Elizabeth I removed the ban, and many of these dances and songs are now found in Shakespeare and sung in concerts as examples of genuine English folksong.

Two sources of English folk tunes are the early seventeenth-century music collected in the *FitzWilliam Virginal Book* and Playford's *English Dancing Master,* published about 1650. The lovely tunes of "Sally in Our Alley," "Bonny Dundee," "Greensleeves," "Lilliburlero" and "Over the Hills and Far Away" were included by John Gay in *The Beggar's Opera* (1728), the earliest English musical comedy. (Adam de la Halle in the thirteenth century had done a similar thing with French melodies in his *Jeu de Robin et Marion.*) Not to be overlooked are the English lullabies, such as "Bye, Baby Bunting," "Rockabye Baby" and many others, rich in the flavor and charm of true English folksong.

IRISH, SCOTTISH AND WELSH FOLK MUSIC

No folk music in the world is so replete with imagination, so illumined with keen humor, so flecked with superstitions, so rich in poetry, as that of the Irish. The rhythms of their jigs, reels, spinning tunes, plow songs, croons and a long list of others show their delight in gaiety and their capacity for sadness. In design alone, the folksongs demonstrate the deep emotional power and the inherent art of the Irish people. Theirs are models of what simple song form has been for centuries. For example, the "Londonderry Air" illustrates the Irish grasp of mounting emotion and the value of climax.

The Scots and Welsh also have as their heritage a wealth of song and ballad, rich in beauty of melody. These peoples use simple musical designs that might well be called their autographs. One of these is the Scottish "snap," a distinctive badge of Caledonian music employed by such diverse composers as Beethoven, Mendelssohn and Edward Mac-Dowell. The music of the Highland Scots is a product of Gaelic tribes and can be traced back to prehistoric days. For one of the most valuable researches into Scottish song literature, we can thank the poet Robert Burns, who said, "I have collected, begged, borrowed and stolen all the songs I could meet with."

Welsh tunes date from earliest antiquity and have been more or less associated with the Scottish until recent collections were made. Though not as "snappy" as the Gaelic, they yet share many of their characteristics. Possessed of a cooler beauty, they are sensitive and lyric and have affected the songs of both Britain and Brittany. Bards used a crude harp, or *crwth,* as a means of accompaniment. The Welsh today are still recognized among the foremost ministers of song. Some familiar Welsh melodies are "All Through the Night," "Men of Harlech" and "The Ash Grove."

As in other countries, the dance in England, Ireland and Scotland has been an integral part of folk music. Neither languorous nor wild, like the dances of Southern and Middle Europe and of Russia, nonetheless, British dances are incisively rhythmic, jolly rather than hysterical, happy rather than sensuous. The gay, rapid jig of Ireland; the Highland Fling of Scotland, with its obvious accent and robust enthusiasm; the round dances of England and her vigorous hornpipe—all are typical of the heart of British revelry.

Gypsy and Hungarian Folk Music

Gypsies have spread over Europe and America, carrying with them in their colorful caravans an eclectic musical mixture of old and new. They have absorbed the characteristics of nations they have adopted and, in turn, vitalized their music. Rarely has the music been notated, for Gypsies have uncanny memories. They graft their own peculiarities onto the folk music of other nations, giving it a dazzling individuality, a strange madness and a poignant sadness not found in other music.

So effectively have the Gypsies melded with Hungarian music, for instance, that many people think that Gypsy music is Magyar (the racial name for about one-quarter of Hungary's population) and that Magyar is Gypsy. The Magyar-Gypsy music has provided inspiration for many composers, among whom are Liszt, Brahms, and even Haydn and Bach. One of the characteristic dances of the Gypsy is the *czardas,* well-marked in syncopated rhythms, with many ornaments, strong accents and two well-contrasted parts, *lassan* (slow) and *friska* (very fast).

Gypsies have extraordinary instrumental virtuosity. As violinists they excel in natural skill and feeling. Spanish Gypsies play the guitar and castanets with a contagious rhythm and an infectious mood. No Gypsy orchestra is complete without the *cembalo.* Strung with metal strings, covering a range of four octaves, it is played with two small limber hammers. This *cembalo* is a descendant of the ancient dulcimer and psaltery, and the highly ornamental music apparently stems from the Arab *gloss* and other *fioritura.*

Probably Béla Bartók and Zoltán Kodály were the first investigators to make it clear that Gypsy music was not Hungarian folk music. The Gypsies have been performers of Hungarian music, and on it they have superimposed ornament, in trills, *glissandos* and grace notes, but so far as actually influencing the native folksong itself, they have contributed little.

Probably no other folk music is so dependent on language as is the Hungarian. The syllables and their accent are the bases of rhythm, which is fundamentally that of dance music. When greater stress is needed, the grace note is characteristically used, or often an ejaculation is prefixed to a first phrase, both in dance and song. But unlike the Gypsy music, Hungarian folk tunes are undecorated, strongly syncopated and abounding in amazing rhythms.

Besides the old or native music, Hungary has a newer style typical of music of the old regime yet different from any other folk music. Bartók thinks his is the only nation that has ever been able to unite new folksong with the old and still retain ancient character and archaic features. Hungarian melody is based to a large extent upon modality, the Dorian and Aeolian, as well as modern major tonalities.

Hungarian dances are spirited and gay, forcefully accented and very stirring. Some of them are the *czardas;* the *körtánez,* or society dance; and the *kanásztáncz,* or swineherder's dance, performed only by country people. The peasants use a shepherd's flute, violin, clarinet, *tütlöck* (a swineherder's horn), *puszata,* hurdy-gurdy and the *tárogató* (a type of English horn), on which a lament for the hero Rakoczy was played in its original form before its assimilation by the Gypsies and before it became a national Hungarian air, later grandly orchestrated by Hector Berlioz.

RUSSIAN FOLK MUSIC

Among the most beautiful and varied folksongs in the world are those of heterogeneous Russia. The melodies mirror the history of the Russian peoples from primitive times through the centuries of Mongol domination, during the long conflict between pagan and Christian supremacy, through the period of imposed feudalism and serfdom, in their struggles against nature, internal strife and in their longings toward peace and unity—an incomparably indelible record of the human condition. Despite the mosaic of structure of the tribes and peoples of this amalgamation called Russia, there is, underlying the thousands of folksongs, a similar sense of unity, variety, contrast, balance and design.

Usually the melody progresses diatonically and is often based on modal scales. There is, however, a decided shading toward half and quarter-tones in the interpolation of passing tones, most certainly an Oriental souvenir. The songs are generally simple and close with a restful unison or octave. Rhythm is dependent, as is the rhythm of all folksongs, on inflections of the language. Therefore, Russian folksongs differ intrinsically from tunes of the Latin or Celt and are infused with a more biting accent and a more engrossing emotional content, which gives Russian music its often frenetic quality.

The only Russian music prior to the nineteenth century was folksong and the liturgy of the Greek Orthodox Church—an amazing situation that has had interesting effects. Never has the classic order of a nation been so imbedded in folk sources as that of Russia. Glinka, Moussorgsky and others, inspired by the poet Pushkin, have made glorious use of the folk resources and mythology of Russia in their compositions and have given them to the world in impressive settings. (These adaptations are very striking in *The Fair at Sorotchinzk,* by Moussorgsky; in *Prince Igor,* by Borodin; *The Nutcracker Suite* by Tchaikovsky; and *The Rite of Spring* by Stravinsky.) They sing of their virgin forests, the once-prevalent beggar, rivers and seasons. From among the multitudinous songs we have such lovely things as *"Birchen Brand,"* "The Cossack's Lament," "Rushes and Roars the Wide Dnieper" and "Stenka Razin" (a pirate of the Volga).

Much of the unique quality of Russian music is the result of instruments which have come down from earlier times. The familiar *balalaika,* dating from the thirteenth century, is not unlike a triangular guitar with three or four strings. Another characteristic instrument, a descendant of the Greek psalterion, is the *gusli.* Resembling a zither, it consists of a hollow sound-box, over which are stretched from seventeen to twenty-four strings, which are plucked. Since the sixteenth century, blind minstrels have played a lute or *bandoura;* there is also the *jaleika,* a species of wooden clarinet with a mournful sound.

SPANISH FOLK MUSIC

The folk music of Spain is full of variety, teeming with warmth, passion and gesture, united in a general feeling of abandon and impulsiveness, or in an engulfing sensuousness and sentimental melancholy. The tunes are modal, highly individual and filled with a relish of rhythm molded on that of the onomatopoetic Spanish language. Andalusian songs and dances have an indolent insouciance so alluring and rhythms so enchanting that even Spaniards consider them the typical folk music of their country.

J. B. Trend writes, in *Manuel de Falla and Spanish Music:*

> *Cante Hondo* is the name given to a group of Andalusian folksongs the type of which Falla, Spain's foremost composer, believes to be the so-called *siguiriya gitana (Gypsy Seguidilla)* (from which are derived other types of melody)—for example, *polos, martinetes* and *soleares* (solitude songs) which still exist and which preserve certain characteristics of the highest musical interest, distinguishing them from the more modern songs commonly called *flamenco.* Strictly speaking, however, that name should only be applied to the more modern group, comprising *malagueñas, granadinas, rondeñas* (from which the first two are derived); *sevillanas, peteneras,* and others, which are also derivations from those already mentioned.

These may have come from India. *Cante Hondo* rarely exceeds in compass the limits of a sixth, plus enharmonic enrichments, repetitions of a note or phrase almost to the point of mania (as in Ravel's *Boléro*), passionate outbursts of emotion and the cries of *olé, olé,* supposed originally to have been *Allah, Allah,* in praise of the Mohammedan deity. Today, however, the beautiful *Cante Hondo* is losing ground to the *flamenco* with its reduced tonal compass, artificial ornaments and decreased flexibility. It is possible, asserts J. B. Trend, to trace the style through the *villancicos* of street and Church music "to the little pieces sung by shepherds in the dramatic entertainments of Juan del Enzina . . . (1483-1494)." The remote ancestors of Spanish folksong are the Byzantine liturgical modes and the music of the Arab and the Gypsy. (Nevertheless, Spanish music did not crystallize until the eighteenth century, probably through a reaction to the influx of Italian music.)

The music of Spain can be divided into four groups: the Basque, music of Biscay and Navarre, irregular in rhythm, with the *jota* as the characteristic dance; that from Galicia and Castile, with gay, bright, strongly marked rhythms, such as the *bolero* and *seguidilla;* that of Andalusia, perhaps the most beautiful of all; and the Catalonian, whose music is intense, somber and less Spanish than the others because of the influence of its French neighbors. The most important instrument is the guitar. Castanets are particularly Spanish, although they are of ancient Oriental origin. They express well the clipped, continuous accent, the marked gesture and the gay abandonment to emotional impulse.

The folk music of Spain has exerted a powerful effect on her composers, such as Albéniz, Granados and de Falla. It has influenced foreign composers as well. Bizet's *Carmen* is a classic example of Spanish music written by a Frenchman, and his fellow countryman Emmanuel Chabrier composed one of the most Spanish-seasoned works we know, *España*. Among others affected by the idiom were Rimsky-Korsakov and Tchaikovsky, as well as Ravel and Debussy, whose Spanish feeling, paradoxically, worked upon Albéniz and de Falla in return.

French, Italian and German Folk Music

France has a beautiful, limpid and romantic collection of folksongs; gay street songs abound, and tunes were inherited from the troubadours and *trouvères,* from Brittany and other highly distinctive provinces. A grace and a silver glow make them unique and enchanting. Particularly appealing are her lullabies and children's songs. The beautiful *Noëls* (Christmas carols), many of which come from Burgundy, are among the most exquisite songs in the world. From Normandy come the matter-of-fact workaday songs. Most unusual tunes come from Brittany, of Celtic and ancient modal origins. Of these, Jean-Jacques Rousseau said, "The airs are simple, not snappy, they have, I know not what of an antique and sweet mood which touches the heart. They are simple, naïve and often sad, at any rate they are pleasing." (A visit to Brittany to attend the music and religious festivals [*Les Pardons*] is one of the most satisfying experiences.) It is ironic that students of French folksong often find it in its most pristine form among the French-Canadian inhabitants of the New World. (We have seen this musical conservation, too, in Southern mountain regions of the United States, where old English song has been preserved.)

Italian music is colorful, highly-rhythmic, garish and florid. The best-known tunes are Neapolitan street songs. The Venetians have their boat songs, worksongs, serenades and other love songs, but these have a happy lack of decoration, a simple charm and beauty. Sicily has one of the richest folksong aggregations of all Italy because of early Norman, Saracen, Greek and Angevin influences. She has a rich collection of *ciuri, canzuni* and *arias.* There are still Greek-speaking peasants in Calabria and they have not only folksongs of their own, but many early Greek temples, to indicate Hellenic origins. In addition to the ancient influences that have enriched Italy's folk music, France, Austria and Spain have added to it through medieval conquests. One of the characteristic Italian dances is the very energetic *tarantella,* said to have been used to induce sufficient perspiration to throw off the poison caused by the bite of a tarantula.

"Much in little" might be a motto used to typify German folksong, because of the expert way in which melody, emotion and range of feeling are blended simply and rhythmically in effective design. The effect of the folksong on art music has been potent in Germany, from the hymns of Luther through and beyond the monumental beauties of Bach, Beethoven and Brahms. Furthermore, the folksong of Germany did much to place the major scale on a firm basis, after long domination of Church modes.

There is a homely, intimate quality about German folksongs that endears them to everybody. They have a vigor and accent that reflect the old Teuton character. Where sentiment is exaggerated, it seems a natural reaction. Wholeheartedness and wholesomeness linked with feeling are ancient qualities of folk music. Such songs as *"O Tannenbaum"* and *"Mus'i denn"* typify these. No songs are more virile and striking than the yesteryear student and stein songs of German university youth. Nearly every town has had its *Stadt Pfeifferei,* where the peasant boys played the fiddle and the shepherd boys, the *schalmey* (a kind of oboe). German festivities were rich in music and in merriment, and the country dances were jolly and good-humored. Nowhere have Christmas celebrations such a garniture of song and dance as in Germany.

*   *   *   *   *

Through the Middle Ages and later we have noted an artful as well as a folk development of secular song and dance. We shall have occasion to return to folk music when we discuss musical nationalism in the nineteenth century. (American folksong will be examined in another chapter.) Our journey in music through the ages now leads us to the surge of complex polyphony culminating in the compositions of Renaissance musicians throughout Europe, especially in the Lowlands and in Italy.

SUGGESTIONS FOR FURTHER READING

Adams, Henry, *Mont-Saint-Michel and Chartres.* Boston, Houghton Mifflin, 1913.
Aubrey, Pierre, *Trouvères and Troubadours.* New York, Schirmer, 1914.

Bartók, Béla, *Hungarian Folk Music*. London, Oxford University Press, 1931.

Boatwright, Howard, *Introduction to the Theory of Music*. New York, Norton, 1956.

Davison, Archibald T., and Apel, Willi, *Historical Anthology of Music,* vol. 1. Cambridge, Harvard University Press, 1949.

Fleming, Arnold, *The Troubadours of Provence*. Glasgow, Maclellan, 1952.

Geiringer, Karl, *Musical Instruments*. New York, Oxford University Press, 1945.

Gummere, Francis B., *The Popular Ballad.** New York, Dover, 1959.

Heer, Friedrich, *The Medieval World.** New York, New American Library, 1963.

Nettl, Bruno, *Folk and Traditional Music of the Western Continents.** Englewood Cliffs, Prentice-Hall, 1965.

Parrish, Carl, *A Treasury of Early Music.** New York, Norton, 1958.

Parrish, Carl, and Ohl, John F., *Masterpieces of Music before 1750*. New York, Norton, 1951.

Reese, Gustave, *Music in the Middle Ages*. New York, Norton, 1940.

Sachs, Curt, *The History of Musical Instruments*. New York, Norton, 1940.

Seay, Albert, *Music in the Medieval World.** Englewood Cliffs, Prentice-Hall, 1965.

Starr, William J., and Devine, George F., *Music Scores—Omnibus,* Part 1.** Englewood Cliffs, Prentice-Hall, 1964.

Taylor, Archer, *The Literary History of Meistergesang*. New York, Modern Language Association of America, 1937.

Trend, J. B., *Manuel de Falla and Spanish Music*. New York, Knopf, 1935.

Waddell, Helen, *Medieval Latin Lyrics.** New York, Penguin, 1952.

———— *The Wandering Scholars.** New York, Barnes & Noble, 1949.

A SAMPLER OF SUPPLEMENTARY RECORDINGS

Collections

Masterpieces of Music before 1750	Haydn 9038/40
Treasury of Early Music	Haydn 9100/3
2000 Years of Music	Folkways 3700
Ten Centuries of Music	DGG KL-52/61
Early Medieval Music	Victor LM-6015
Music of the Middle Ages	Lyric 85
Spanish Medieval Music	Decca 4196
Folksongs of the Old World	Capitol PBR 8345
French Troubadour Songs	Westminster 9610
Troubadour and Trouvère Songs	Expériences Anonymes 12
Cantigas de Santa Maria	E A 23
Folk and Cradle Songs	DGG 19462
Welsh Folk Songs	London 5172
Anthology of Spanish Folk Music	Monitor 370
Evening with Gypsies	Bruno 50098
Folk Music of Canada	Folkways 4482
Chansons de Noël	Vanguard 497
Music of the Medieval Court and Countryside	Decca 9400
The Festive Pipes	Kapp 9034
English Medieval Songs	E A 29

* Available in paperback edition.

Works by Individual Composers

Sachs, Hans, *Weisen: 5 Songs*	DGG ARC-3222
De la Halle, Adam, *Le Jeu de Robin et Marion*	DGG ARC-3002

Related Works of Interest

Bartók, Béla, *Hungarian Folk Songs*
Bellini, Vincenzo, *Norma*
Brahms, Johannes, *Academic Festival Overture*
Britten, Benjamin, *A Ceremony of Carols*
Canteloube, Joseph, *Songs of the Auvergne*
Gay, John, *The Beggar's Opera*
Hindemith, Paul, *Noblissima Visione* ("St. Francis")
Orff, Carl, *Carmina Burana*
Vaughan Williams, R., *English Folk Song Suite*
Wagner, Richard, *Die Meistersinger*
        Tannhäuser

OPPORTUNITIES FOR STUDY IN DEPTH

1. Study Chapter 13 of Howard Boatwright's *Introduction to the Theory of Music* (New York, Norton, 1956). Write several *chansons* patterned on troubadour and *trouvère* models, following the author's instructions. Have the class sing them.

2. Examine de la Halle's pastoral play, *Le Jeu de Robin et Marion,* using both score and recording. Prepare a classroom performance of the work, with an explanatory prologue.

3. Amplify with reasons and examples the statement in this chapter: "Folk music is not necessarily of remote ages alone; it is still being made."

4. Historians agree that there were political and radical social motivations underlying the seemingly artless and lofty music of the troubadours, *trouvères* and *Minnesingers.* Heer, for example, in *The Medieval World* (see "Suggestions for Further Reading"), is definitely of this opinion. As a result of supplementary reading, write a paper substantiating such a concept, citing examples to demonstrate this thesis.

5. Make an investigation of either English or American materials in which differentiation is drawn between authentic folk music, music retaining some authentic elements and pseudo, or fake, folk music. Delineate what is discovered.

6. If it is practical in the locality, try "collecting" some music retained in the memories of older, untrained singers. A portable tape recorder would be a great help for this project. Analyze the results as far as possible.

7. It is generally accepted as a truism that Spanish music through its South American modifications has contributed a great deal to the development of American jazz. In what measure and how was this accomplished? Aaron Copland, in *Our New Music* (New York, Whittlesey House, 1941), expresses some interesting ideas on the subject.

8. The Soviet Union has elevated music to a prime position as an arm of political propaganda and a factor for national unity. What role does Russian folk music play in this? What are the Russian antecedents for such a concept?

Vocabulary Enrichment

skalds
eddas and sagas
gleemen
clerical *vagantes* or *goliards*
chansons de geste
jugglers or *jongleurs*
vielle
gigue
gittern
psaltery
regals
rote
organistrum
troubadour
langue d'oc
sirventes
planhs
pastorelles
chansons de toile
reverdies
serenas
albas
tenson

trouvère
lai
ballade
virelai
rondeau
villancico
Minnesinger
roman courtois
Meistersinger
barform
carole
estampie
ductia
wassail
morris dance
Scottish "snap"
czardas
cembalo
balalaika
Cante Hondo
flamenco
tarantella

Chapter 7.

MUSIC OF THE *ARS NOVA*
AND THE RENAISSANCE

Panis angelicus fit panis hominum:
Dat panis caelicus figuris terminum:
O res mirabilis! manducat Dominum,
Pauper, servus, et humilis.

(Lo! angels' bread is made
   The bread of mortal man;
Shows forth this heavenly bread
   The ends which types began;
O wondrous boon indeed!
Upon his Lord now can
A poor and humble servant feed!)

—St. Thomas Aquinas (1225-1275), *Sacris solemniis*

Angels' bread was fast becoming the sustenance of mortal man in a far more literal sense than that expressed by the great Dominican intellectual Thomas Aquinas who, with Roger Bacon and Bonaventura, participated in the seething university circles of Paris during the thirteenth century, an era when rigid scholasticism was gradually giving way to Aristotelian concepts that would dominate the thinking of the Renaissance and, indeed, the philosophy of humanists, such as Jean-Paul Sartre and the late Albert Camus, to our present day. As viewed by its observers the world was becoming increasingly anthropomorphic—man-centered—and materialistic—matter-centered.

The office of the papacy had degenerated to a plaything of temporal rulers. During the 1300's there were two popes, one at Avignon, France, and the other in Italy, both controlled by powers outside the Church. The Hundred Years' War raged, and the Plague, or Black Death, decimated whole populations.

Nevertheless, the fourteenth century was an epoch of great prosperity in the Low Countries. The individual enjoyed more freedom than he had ever had before. Merchants were public-spirited, magnificent Gothic buildings were erected and the arts flourished. Perhaps as a consequence of this background Lowland musicians subsequently were to travel to

Italy, France, Spain and Germany, filling positions in the churches and teaching. (Tinctoris, for example, founded the school of Naples before 1500; Willaert started the Venetian school soon afterwards; and Orlando Lasso went to Munich a few years later.) All in all, the fourteenth century was both a period of decline and a time of impending explosion.

It will be helpful to bear in mind as one studies the following material several significant general influences: (1) the part played by secular music as a seedbed for national styles; (2) the path of interaction from France to the Lowlands to Italy and thence northward again; (3) the impact of humanism, especially as it radiated from Florence; and (4) the profound changes brought about by the invention of printing.

Ars Nova

Ars nova, the "new style," labeled by Philippe de Vitry, flourished from 1310 to about 1430. The term itself refers specifically to methods of notation and to French music, but it is generally applied to most "modern" music of that period. Two composers are closely associated with *ars nova.* We have already introduced Guillaume de Machault as a great French transitional poet-musician who retained characteristics of the older style while utilizing newer musical elements in his motets, *ballades, rondeaux* and *virelais.* In Italy a further freeing of music from its medieval bonds was occurring, even as a parallel liberation was producing the literary masterpieces of Boccaccio (*The Decameron*), Petrarch (*Canzoniere*) and Dante (*The Divine Comedy*), as well as the personalized paintings of Giotto and the naturalistic sculptures of Nicola and Giovanni Pisano.

While the motet was a creation of French composers, the **madrigal,** a secular part-song, was an Italian contribution in the fourteenth century. It reflects the influence of troubadour art and *conductus.* (The much-discussed name may have come from a medieval Latin word, *matricale,* meaning a rustic song in the mother tongue.) Other Italian *trecento* forms included: the **caccia,** a unison canon with an instrumental supporting line, whose subject was either market scenes, sports or street cries, portrayed in a curiously realistic way, with musical openwork somewhat analogous to the traceries of Gothic sculpture; and the **ballata,** with a number of stanzas set to sections of music forming an unbalanced A B A pattern.

Francesco Landini

Representative of this more spontaneous polyphony is the work of an Italian composer, Francesco Landini (1335?-1397). Born in Fiesole, near Florence, and blind since childhood, Landini became an outstanding organist and composer of *ballatas, madrigals* and *caccias*. Written in two and three voices, these compositions are conspicuous for their lyricism (a quality we link with Italian music in general), the absence of a plainsong *cantus firmus* and in an easygoing freedom of motion. Landini's name is lent to an *ars nova* cadence formula, certainly used before as well as after him, in which the upper voice moves from the seventh to the sixth tone of the diatonic scale before resolving to the tonic.

Fig. 29. Ending of ballata, *"Chi piu le vuol sapere"*—Francesco Landini, transcribed by Ellinwood. 1-partial signature, 2-multiple of duple meter, 3-parallel fifths, 4-"Landini cadence," 5-*musica ficta,* 6-equal voices.

MUSICAL SCHOOLS

The Parsian composers and theorists who practiced the contrapuntal polyphony of *ars antiqua* really formed the first musical "school," that is, a body of disciples of a teacher or a system, having more or less uniform opinions, methods and aims. Throughout the Renaissance we encounter informal groups of composers comprising the so-called Netherlands schools of polyphony, variously known as the Burgundian, Flemish and Franco-Flemish, and, when their influence reached Italy, the Venetian and the Neapolitan. Actually there was no such political entity as the Netherlands at this time and the designation is used to include geographically much of what is now northern France, Belgium and Holland. For instance, the powerful Philip the Good (1419-1467) was lord of Flanders and Artois, of Holland, Zealand, Hainault and Friesland, of Namur, Luxemburg, Brabant and Limburg. The culture of these diverse regions was of mixed Teutonic and Latin persuasion, strongly flavored by that of neighboring France.

JOHN DUNSTABLE

Apart from, but influential upon, the Burgundian school (possibly through Burgundy's alliance with England in the Hundred Years' War) stands the Englishman John Dunstable (c. 1370-1453), an astronomer and mathematician who was named by Johannes Tinctoris (1436-1511), a Flemish theoretician, as the foremost musician of England. Dunstable wandered widely and among his contemporaries were the founders of the Burgundian school, Dufay and Binchois, who benefited from his erudition. Dunstable's music, said to be among "the most beautiful specimens of the age," employed thirds and sixths as consonant intervals and often gave an original *cantus firmus* to the soprano instead of to the tenor—practices that became commonplace in Renaissance music. He also added a musical element of unity to the five sections of the Ordinary of the Mass, either by commencing each part with the same theme or by retaining a single *cantus firmus* throughout.

GUILLAUME DUFAY AND GILLES BINCHOIS

Guillaume Dufay (c. 1400-1474) was a member of the Burgundian school that bridges the Paris Gothic period and the sixteenth-century Netherlands school. Highly regarded by his co-workers, he traveled extensively, serving as a chorister in the Papal Choir in Rome, as Canon of Cambrai and as music tutor to the son of Philip the Good, whose court was a distinguished cultural center. Dufay introduced the use of secular melodies in place of Gregorian *cantus firmi* and was the first composer to include the popular folksong *"L'Homme armé"* ("The Man in Armor") in the structure of a Mass. In his hands the device of canon became a thing of beauty instead of an arid contrapuntal manipulation.

Gilles Binchois (c. 1400-1460), another leading composer of the Burgundians, was also educated at Cambrai and served as *chaplain-chantre* to Philip the Good. Although he wrote sacred music, he is best known for his secular works, including simple songs for solo voice accompanied by two instrumental parts. Pupils of Dufay and Binchois extended their teachings and, in turn, became instructors of those who developed the succeeding Netherlands school.

Dufay, Binchois and their colleagues prepared the way for changes which resulted in bringing the art of counterpoint to a high degree of perfection. Fourteenth-century methods were still in use, of course, but there was a tendency toward enhanced tonal expressiveness and greater realization of vocal resources. In the churches, singing was brought to such a peak of performance that many Lowland vocalists were engaged, as was Dufay, as choristers in Rome. (By way of illustrating the contrast

Fig. 30. Dufay and Binchois with portative organ and harp—Martin Lefranc, fifteenth century. Guillaume Dufay and Gilles Binchois were co-founders of the Burgundian school which flourished in the fifteenth century. (Courtesy Bibliothéque nationale, Paris.)

between the situation in Rome and the Low Countries, the following data speak for themselves. The Papal Chapel [Choir] in 1436 had but nine members; by 1500 it had grown to include twenty-four singers. On the other hand, when Ockeghem was at the Cathedral of Our Lady in Antwerp [1443], his choral forces totaled fifty-one; there were twenty-five singers of polyphony and twenty-six who performed the plainsong.)

An innovation of the early Renaissance was that of **choral polyphony,** as opposed to the medieval practice of one singer to each part. As a consequence of this, composers increasingly refined their treatment of dissonance and began to show a new respect for setting words to music, both in terms of prosody and in attention to the emotional meaning— an idea that later was called the "doctrine of affects," exerting great influence on Renaissance madrigals and on most music through the time of Richard Strauss (in the twentieth century).

JAN OCKEGHEM AND JACOB OBRECHT

An outstanding master of the Netherlands school was Jan Ockeghem (*c.* 1425-1495). Possibly a pupil of Dufay when the latter was at Cambrai, Ockeghem served some forty years at the courts of three French kings. Completely adept at Flemish counterpoint, he composed Masses, motets, *chansons* and canons with astounding facility and unparalleled powers of invention. One of his works, for example, a *Deo gratias,* is a canon for thirty-six different voices.

As was the fashion, Ockeghem wrote puzzle, or "riddle," canons as vehicles of technical bravura. Flaunting a composer's ingenuity, these enigmas of the Netherlands school were "crossword puzzles" for highly skilled musicians. Composers indicated canons by "inscriptions." The object was to make solution as difficult as possible, and subjects were presented in the guises of crosses, circles, squares, chessboards, rainbows and other fantastic designs. An inscription, in addition, contained a *guida,* a short quotation from a proverb or the Bible that provided a hint for solution.

Perhaps more significant was Ockeghem's consistent use of the technique of imitation and his construction of final cadences which already have a firm, dominant-tonic feeling that seems quite modern. Moreover, he aided the development of *augmentation* and *diminution,* through which a theme can be varied by changing proportionately the temporal value of the notes. Under Ockeghem's guidance vocal polyphony became more sophisticated; many forms, such as the medieval rondo, ballad and accompanied secular art song, were relegated to the background, and, in time, disappeared.

A contemporary of Ockeghem was Jacob Obrecht (*c.* 1452-1505). When the noted scholar Erasmus was a choir boy at Utrecht, Obrecht was his teacher. Obrecht also taught at Cambrai, Bruges and Ferrara, where he transmitted the secrets of Flemish contrapuntalists to his Italian students. An extremely ready composer, his Masses, motets and secular creations show an eclectic mastery and a deepened harmonic sensitivity. His last years were spent as chapel master of the Antwerp Cathedral.

JOSQUIN DES PRÉS

Ockeghem's greatest pupil was Josquin des Prés (*c.* 1442-1524), a Fleming, who might be considered the leader of another Netherlands school that could more accurately be called Franco-Flemish, as many French composers belonged both chronologically and stylistically to this faction. A singer at St. Quentin, in the chapel choir of Milan and at the Sistine Chapel (founded by Pope Sixtus IV in 1473), des Prés spent much time in the ducal courts of Milan, Florence and Ferrara. After his Italian sojourn, he lived at the French court of Louis XII. A sympathetic person, des Prés had a keen sense of humor and love for his fellow men. A prodigious worker, he left an enormous output of secular songs, motets and Masses that were written in all the varieties of his day: Masses built on liturgical *cantus firmi;* Masses constructed on secular *cantus firmi,* including two on the melody *"L'Homme armé";* Masses structured on original themes; and parody Masses, in which the whole of existing songs or motets were incorporated as bases of the compositions.

Heightened stimulation of the arts during the fifteenth century resulted in seeking beauty in melodic line and in harmonic freedom. Josquin, who experienced the development of arts at home and in Italy, participated in the movement toward a new appreciation of the creative mind. Having lived when printing was first invented and having been the idol of all Europe, Josquin found his Masses and motets "sung in every chapel in Christendom," as well as his secular songs in constant demand by the earliest publishers of music.

NICOLAS GOMBERT, JACQUES CLÉMENT AND JEAN MOUTON

Des Prés bequeathed his artistic creed to several pupils who in turn became famous musicians. Nicolas Gombert (*c.* 1490-*c.* 1556) followed Josquin's precepts and endeavored to vary the character of the music according to the character of the text. He was particularly successful as a composer of secular music, showing a love of nature in his choice of pastoral subjects. After service as chapel master to Charles V, Gombert in 1537 went to Spain and held office in the imperial chapel in Madrid.

Jacques Clément (*c.* 1510-*c.* 1556), called "Clemens non Papa," possibly to distinguish him from the reigning pope or another musician, was a composer who projected his aims with sincerity and nobility of purpose, striving to use new ideas to produce well-balanced polyphony, fresh and pleasing melodies and lucid harmony. Equally true is this of

Clément Janequin (*c.* 1485-*c.* 1560), who achieved stature as a writer of secular music; in fact, he might be thought of as the first exponent of program music because of his imitative descriptions in tone. He attempted to represent the sounds of birds in a chanson *"Le Chant des oiseaux"* ("Song of the Birds"); others of his more than 275 polyphonic songs include *"Caquet des femmes"* ("Cackle of Women"), *"Cris de Paris"* ("Cries of Paris") and *"Le Bataille de Marignan"* ("The Battle of Marignan"), which, by means of only four voices, depicts quite realistically episodes in the victory of François I.

Jean Mouton (*c.* 1470-1522) is a link between Josquin, his teacher, and Adrian Willaert, his pupil. A court musician to Louis XII and François I of France, Mouton was also Canon in the Collegiate Church of St. Quentin. Among his works, available in early editions of published music, are Masses, motets, psalms and a few *chansons,* which, in contrast to the "learned" style of many Lowlanders, are relatively light in texture, simple rhythmically and leaning toward vertical harmony.

A CHANGED WORLD

The Western world of 1500 was a vigorous one. The Moors had been driven from Granada in 1492, the same year that Christopher Columbus was commissioned by the Spanish monarchs Ferdinand and Isabella to set forth on a transatlantic voyage of exploration. The Portuguese were growing rich from penetration and exploitation of Africa—their maritime adventures made possible by the inventions of compass and astrolabe as well as a new type of sailing rig. With the election of Martin V at the Council of Constance (1419), the papal schism had finally been resolved. Henry V of England had led his forces to victory over the French at Agincourt. And the three medieval cultures—Greek Christian, Latin Christian and Arab—were contributing to a richer, more homogeneous civilization.

Sacred music was still a dominating factor, but aegis for inspiration came increasingly from royal chapels and cathedral schools, as we have seen, rather than from monasteries. Minstrels were occasionally found in courtly entourages, acting as heralds in times of war and supplying domestic music for peaceful moments. Musical interest in numerical relationships survived; witness the isorhythmic motet and the Franco-Netherlandish "artifices" of Ockeghem and others. Yet dancing had become very popular. We find mention of the *tedesca, branle, schiavo, round dances, zingaresca* and *pavane,* to list but a few. And humanistic trends were making themselves manifest in an extended use of vernacular languages and the actual recognition of composers who now signed their manuscripts, thereby personalizing what had hitherto been anonymous products.

With the fall of Constantinople (1453), its scholars, versed in Greek and Latin classics, migrated to Western Europe and brought with them the long-obscured learning of the past, and, more important to the musician, the Hellenic alliance between music and drama. The Medici family made Florence such a magnet for classic studies that it came to resemble another Athens. Academies for discussion and reading were founded, in addition to institutions like the University of Pisa, for the pursuit of Greek. Almost every phase of life reflected and was motivated by Greek influences. Buildings were erected from Greek and Roman designs and even pageants and carnivals were modeled on ancient patterns. The Medici instituted a system of patronage by means of which the arts and sciences flowered. From such soil were to come many of the great figures of the Renaissance: Leonardo da Vinci, Michelangelo Buonarroti, Raphael and Titian, in Italy; Cervantes, in Spain; Erasmus and Martin Luther, in Germany; Edmund Spenser and William Shakespeare, in England.

Into this burgeoning period came the invention of printing. Johan Gutenberg first used movable type, about 1450. Another German, Ulrich Hahn, experimented with printing music (Rome, 1476). Following partially successful efforts on the parts of Aldus, Gardane and Octavianus Scotus (Venice, 1481), Ottaviano dei Petrucci, early in the sixteenth century, arrived at an excellent musical typography and issued, in 1501, *Harmonice musices odhecaton A,* a collection of ninety-six Franco-Flemish polyphonic *chansons.*

In France, printing equipment was installed at the Sorbonne by Charles VII. Pierre Attaignant published (*c.* 1527-1549) the works of leading composers of the Franco-Flemish school. (Many of these have been reprinted by Henri Expert in his series, *Les maîtres musiciens de la Renaissance Française.*) About 1540 the house of Ballard was established and until 1788 it maintained a near monopoly on music publishing in France. The Psalms of Clément Marot and operas of Lully were printed by the Ballards.

William Caxton, the pioneer English printer, published Higden's *Policronicon* (1482), containing a musical illustration of eight notes, filled in, however, by hand. Wynken de Worde printed these notes in a later edition; in 1509 de Worde issued a missal and in 1530 he published the first English songbook.

Thus, music printing became a reality in the Renaissance. Its initial impact was more limited than might be supposed, due to the high cost of the volumes, which were set up (after 1525) in single-impression

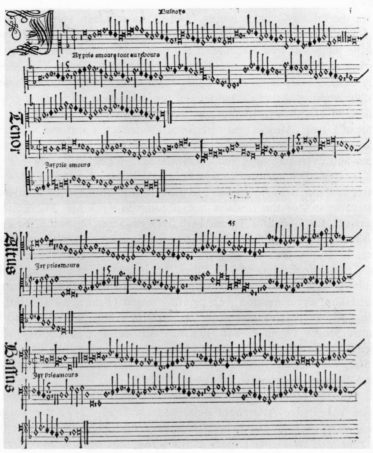

Fig. 31. *"Ay pris amour"* by Antoine Busnois, from *Harmonice Musices Odhecaton,* printed by Ottaviano dei Petrucci. Petrucci was revolutionary in inventing a method of music printing with moveable type, which he used in publishing his collection of Franco-Flemish *chansons,* including this example.

type, that is, each symbol was placed on its individual segment of staff. We might also note that vocal music was usually printed in parts, as seen in the Busnois example, rather than in full score, that is, with the elements presented vertically as a whole, a practice previously utilized by the school of Notre Dame and one which was to become the norm following the Renaissance. There was, of course, no copyright protection afforded the composer at this time; his claims to compensation were not established until several centuries later. As printing became more widespread, however, costs decreased and toward the end of the six-teenth century, printed music was being widely disseminated throughout Europe.

Adrian Willaert and the Venetian School

In Adrian Willaert (*c.* 1485-1562) we have yet another representative of the extension of Northern musical practice to the sunny climes of Italy. In his works we find a marriage between Flemish concepts of polyphony and the indigenous materials he found in Venice, where he was appointed chapel master of St. Mark's in 1527. A pupil of Mouton, Willaert is considered the founder of a Venetian school of composers among whom were Zarlino, Andrea Gabrieli and Cypriano de Rore, his successor at the Cathedral of the Doges.

Because St. Mark's was equipped with twin organ lofts and had al-ready experimented with music for alternating choruses, Willaert had the opportunity of systematizing composition for antiphonal choirs, a procedure he developed to a degree which left little even for Palestrina to improve upon. Another of his innovations is contained in a narrative of Susannah, set for five voices, which in its declamatory style fore-shadows oratorio. In his mature years Willaert also helped shape the sixteenth-century madrigal, of which we shall speak presently. His com-positions are characterized by boldness of modulation, an imaginative use of chromaticism and a peculiarly Venetian vigor of attack. Included among his works are Masses, motets, madrigals, *canzone* and *fantasie e ricercari,* the last precursors of fugue. A volume of his motets and madrigals, *Musica nova,* was published in 1559.

Another Lowlander, Jacob Arcadelt (*c.* 1505-*c.* 1560), is often as-sociated with the Venetian school because his six books of five-part madrigals, perhaps his finest works, were printed in Venice between 1538-1556. One volume of these short, refined pieces was so popular that it was reprinted sixteen times in the succeeding thirty years. As a young man, Arcadelt sang at the court of Florence, was singing-master to the choirboys at St. Peter's in Rome and a member of the Papal Chapel. The second half of his life was spent in Paris in the service of the Duc de Guise.

As a consequence of Greek influences upon Renaissance thought, prevailing musical practices were often examined in the light of Greek musical theory and attempts made to reconcile the two. Erasmus in-veighed against "the noisiness of modern music." Richard Pace tried to discover what ancient music really sounded like. Heinrich Glareanus, in his *Dodecachordon* (1547), suggested adding four modes to the exist-ing eight ecclesiastical modes—authentic and plagal forms of Ionian (our major) and Aeolian (our minor). But such endeavors were doomed to frustration, for Greek monody and Renaissance polyphony were essentially different phenomena and could not be homogenized.

Gioseffo Zarlino (1517-1590), a pupil and successor of Willaert, took a more realistic tack in three treatises that reveal the trends of advanced counterpoint and the beginnings of harmony as a science. More than a century before it came into vogue, Zarlino urged equal temperament, a method of dividing the octave into twelve uniform semitones. As a working composer, he recognized and noted the duality of the third in defining modes, thus contributing to the eventual formulation of our major-minor key organization. "From Zarlino," writes Curt Sachs, "the road of harmonic theory led directly to Jean-Philippe Rameau and his *Traité de l'Harmonie* of 1722." It is interesting to observe, however, that Zarlino's *Dimostrationi harmoniche* (1571), after the Greek fashion, is written in the form of dialogues between Willaert, the master, and Claudio Merulo (1533-1604) and Francesco Viola, members of the Venetian school.

SIXTEENTH-CENTURY MADRIGAL

At the risk of distorting our chronology we shall turn our attention for a moment to the emergence of the **sixteenth-century madrigal** and its ramifications through various "national" schools. The madrigal, an archetype of which had appeared in the fourteenth century, had been lost to music for a time, but survived as poetry in more or less its original structure and meaning. As secular music developed, out of the *frottola, villanescha, ballata* and *canzonetta* came a revivified form—the sixteenth-century madrigal. Nurtured in Italy by the expatriated Flemish composers, the madrigal soon engaged the attention of musicians in France, the Netherlands, Germany, Spain and England, forming part of a frame of reference from which elements of national styles would evolve.

The *frottola* was a cheerful song with often frivolous words, set in a deliberately simple style reminiscent of folk song. It was performed either by four unaccompanied voices or by a solo voice to the accompaniment of a lute or other instruments. In the madrigal, as a gesture against the *frottola,* poets tried to offer composers aristocratic verses, possibly influenced by French *chansons*. Subjects ranged from the amorous to political satire. Edward J. Dent asserts:

> . . . the whole life of the later Renaissance is mirrored in them. Jacques du Pont, organist at Rome, shows us the street seller of roast chestnuts; Giovanni Croce of Chioggia teaches us to play the game of the Goose,

still popular with Italian children today; Striggio describes the chatting of the women washing clothes in the river . . .

Madrigals became "the musical expression of the highly cultivated life of the small Italian courts." They were composed for weddings and other ceremonial events. The quantity written by major and minor composers was enormous (Philippe de Monte [1521-1603] wrote eleven hundred), and the quality surprisingly high. A standard voicing was for five singers, although parts varied from three to six or more, designed to be sung by individuals in their own homes; madrigals constituted, in fact, a form of vocal chamber music, to be experienced rather than to be heard passively, a condition that directed composers' compositional techniques. Instruments were sometimes added; perhaps a lute, for instance, to play the melody with the voice. A further step was for instruments to play preludes and interludes to the madrigals, called *ritornellos*. Motets, before the beginning of the seventeenth century, also had their *ritornellos*. These marked the dawn of instrumental chamber music, especially when the voices were omitted entirely and the madrigals and motets played by instruments alone.

The first designated madrigals in the new form were published in 1530 by Valerio Dorico of Rome. The Fleming Philippe Verdelot (d. *c.* 1550) shared the honors with Constanzo Festa (*c.* 1490-1545), as initiator. Choirmaster of the Papal Chapel at Rome from 1517 until his death, Festa enjoyed the distinction of being the only native Italian to hold so high a position. His madrigals, simpler than those of foreign masters, had a certain grace and elegance. He influenced other madrigal schools, notably that of the English.

Willaert and his pupils were significant in bringing the madrigal to a successful point in Venice. Their works exhibited a characteristically Venetian love of color and a search for expressiveness in harmony and textural contrasts, to emphasize the verbal content rather than the rhyming scheme or poetic line, one main differentiation between the madrigal and the *chanson*. Cypriano de Rore (1516-1565) and Constanzo Porta (*c.* 1529-1601) were innovators of a freer style; their use of chromaticism helped to disintegrate the dying modal system. De Rore was born in Antwerp but spent most of his life at the courts of Ferrara and Parma. Porta was an Italian choirmaster at Padua. Both united the learning of the Netherlanders with the rhythmic lyricism of the Italians. Andrea Gabrieli (*c.* 1520-1586), member of a family famous in the musical life of Venice, was also a composer of madrigals, but his most important historical achievements were those of instrumental composer and teacher of such stellar students as his nephew, Giovanni

Gabrieli (c. 1555-1612), Hans Leo Hassler (1564-1612) and Jan Sweelinck (1562-1621), the last great Netherlander of the post-Renaissance and an outstanding organist.

ITALIAN COMPOSERS

Three famous names (in addition to those of Lasso and Palestrina) grace the mature period of Italian madrigals: Luca Marenzio, Gesualdo, Prince of Venosa and Claudio Monteverdi. In the words of *The Compleat Gentleman,* by Henry Peacham (1622), "For delicious Aire and sweete Invention in Madrigals, Luca Marenzio excelleth all other whatsoever, having published more Sets than any Authour else whosoever." Peacham speaks of "Songs, the Muses themselves might not have been ashamed to have had composed." Born about 1553, Marenzio died in 1599. He was court musician to the king of Poland and later, until his death, organist of the Papal Chapel in Rome.

Like those of other composers, Marenzio's madrigals were intended for the private performance of amateur gentry. The texts were set phrase by phrase in separate sections, conceived more harmonically than contrapuntally. In the madrigal, *"S'io parto, i'moro"* ("If I Leave I Die"), for example, we find a rich five-voice texture with a vocal distribution resembling that used today.

"Equal voices" had gradually been discarded during the Renaissance in favor of wider range. The subsequent trio format of *cantus, contratenor* and *tenor* was further enlarged, in that the *contratenor* was divided into two parts, *contra altus* (high) and *contra bassus* (low), terminology still retained in our musical vocabulary. Dufay is credited with first extending the bass part to D below the staff, and in the cited Marenzio madrigal, the voice ranges span bass clef lower F to treble higher E flat, the five voices including two tenor strains.

Additive composition, that is, the method by which a composer first sketched a *cantus firmus,* then wrote out the entire *tenor* and lastly the *contratenor,* had been displaced by a more integrated system, in which the voices were balanced in prominence and the whole weighed against the parts, perhaps as a reflection of the classical ideal of the golden mean. Pietro Aron writes in a treatise of 1523, "the music of the moderns is better than that of the older composers because they consider all parts together and do not compose their voice-parts one after another."

Don Carlos Gesualdo, Prince of Venosa (c. 1560-1613), was one of the most daring composers in musical history. He was a skilled lutenist and well-schooled in contemporary methods of writing. His madrigals, the first volumes of which had gained popularity during his lifetime, were often harmonically radical and dramatically expressive. Tasso, Ariosto and Guarini supplied Gesualdo with literary backgrounds for the latest attempts to translate emotion into tonal form. Experiments which his colleagues were turning toward opera Gesualdo undertook in terms of the madrigal.

After being implicated in the murder of his unfaithful wife, her lover and a child whose paternity was uncertain, Gesualdo fled to Ferrara where he became part of an illustrious circle at the court of Duke Alfonso II d'Este. It was at Ferrara that he discovered a forty-year-old chromatic harpsichord that had been constructed in an effort to solve the enigmas of ancient Greek intonation. Perhaps influenced by this instrument, Gesualdo started composing madrigals in a new and unique style, full of strange chromatic harmonies conceived in unrelated blocks of sound with sudden, illogical modulations quite unthought of by his fellow musicians. Denis Arnold comments:

> He chose verses full of paradox and erotic imagery (something rather like that of the metaphysical poets in England), and set it in a kind of inspired improvisation. The phrases are short, the texture usually homophonic. There is no attempt at contrapuntal flow. Each line, sometimes each word of the poem suggests a new musical motive. Violent changes of tempo and even more violent changes of key . . . give a nervous discontinuity. There is little sheer ease of enjoyment for the singer, for this is virtuoso music, nor is there time for musical word-painting of the conventional kind. But it is undeniably effective in its neurotic stimulation, the era's final word in passion and continuous excitement.

The phrase "neurotic stimulation" is especially interesting as it has been used to describe a work written some three hundred and fifty years later—a work whose opening chords almost literally follow those of Gesualdo in his madrigal *"Moro lasso"* ("I Die, Alas!"). The work is the opera *Tristan und Isolde,* by Richard Wagner. Gesualdo's innovations were much admired by his colleagues but no one attempted to continue his chromatic explorations.

Although Claudio Monteverdi's greatest contribution to music lies in the domain of opera, his madrigals were definite experiments in harmonic combinations which sounded harsh to sixteenth-century ears. (In 1604, Artusi, a musician and theoretician who devoted his life and pen to combating the "imperfections of modern music," wrote that Monteverdi's work was against all natural musical laws.) In the first three books (Book I appeared when the composer was only sixteen years old), we can find examples of all the chief Renaissance styles of madrigal writing. In Book IV Monteverdi added a further element of drama to the madrigal, turning it toward the *cantata da camera* (a *salon* song), in which one singer recounts a short play or story in verse, accompanied by an instrument. *Basso continuo* appears in Book V, indicating, as does his treatment of dissonance, that Monteverdi was entering a wholly new realm of musical adventure.

The popularity of the madrigal, although it did not abruptly pass from favor, was eclipsed in seventeenth-century Italy by the *stilo recitativo,* which heralded the beginnings of opera. Madrigals, however, were occasionally written by Italian opera composers such as Stradello, Alessandro Scarlatti and Lotti.

FRENCH COMPOSERS

French music during the sixteenth century was enriched by an intermixing of Italian and Flemish with native styles, for, as we have seen, the ambiguous "Netherlands schools" often included composers who had been born in France and educated in Flanders, and others who were born elsewhere and led their professional lives at French courts or churches, including many of Josquin des Prés' pupils. Thanks to François I's enthusiasm for Italian arts, many Italian musicians were employed in France. The cultural interaction resulted, naturally, in a certain international sharing of forms and styles. But French poetry and a concern for setting the French language to music induced composers to write music different in character from that of other groups.

The poems of Clément Marot (1496-1554), short colloquial stanzas, had offered composers an opportunity to turn from Flemish complexities to a simpler kind of music modeled on the verse structure. Claudin de Sermisy (*c.* 1490-1562) and Clément Janequin wrote *chansons* in which the form often follows the rhyming scheme. Pierre de Ronsard (1524-1585), a member of a group of poets and musicians known as *Les Pléiades,* patterned after the Florentine Academies, sought to avoid Marot's provincialisms, substituting classical styles that would "glorify and ennoble" the French language, and beyond this, cultivating the Greek ideal of union between words and music. "Without music, poetry is almost without grace," he said, and invited the leading composers to set his sonnets. Janequin, Pierre Certon (*c.* 1510-1572), Muret and Goudimel composed music—each for the same ten sonnets—which was published by the poet in his first volume of verse.

Guillaume Costeley (William Costello, *c.* 1531-1606) used Ronsard poems for his *chansons.* An Irish musician living in France, he was organist and *valet de chambre* to two French kings. He was also the president of a society in honor of St. Cecilia, whose first prize contest was won by Orlando Lasso. Costeley wrote many four- and five-part *chansons,* subtle in their delicacy.

Claude Goudimel (*c.* 1505-1572) lived in Paris, writing secular and sacred music (for the Catholic services) until about 1557, when he associated himself with the Huguenots in Metz. For them he composed music for Marot's metrical psalms. He also made two four-part settings of the entire *Genevan Psalter,* the second of which (1565) followed the colonists to America and influenced their early hymns. Goudimel was a victim of the St. Bartholomew's Eve massacre of French Protestants at Lyons.

In 1570, another member of *Les Pléiades,* Antoine de Baïf, founded the *Académie Française de poésie et de musique,* which we shall have occasion to mention again in the next chapter. An aim of this Academy was *musique mesurée,* that is, music which mirrored exactly the long and short syllables of what Baïf called measured verse. Among composers who carried out Baïf's ideas were Jacques Mauduit (1557-1627) and the impressive Claude Le Jeune (*c.* 1530-*c.* 1600), whose large output in all current forms is comparable to that of Lasso. Both Catholic Mauduit and Huguenot Le Jeune composed polyphonic settings of metrical psalms written by Baïf.

German Composers

A school of writers of vocal polyphony developed in Germany during the fifteenth and sixteenth centuries, although Germany's place in Renaissance music is relatively modest. The first German composers whose works might be compared with those of Franco-Flemish masters were Heinrich Finck (1445-1527) and the engaging Heinrich Isaak (*c.* 1450-1517). Isaak, of Flemish birth, lived at the court of Lorenzo the Magnificent in Florence, where he was known as "Arrigo Tedesco." Later he became the center of a German group that included Finck, Paul Hofhaimer (1459-1537) and Ludwig Senfl (*c.* 1490-*c.* 1543), a Swiss assistant to Isaak and an acquaintance of Martin Luther. One of the most famous German madrigalists was Hans Leo Hassler of Nuremberg. A student of Andrea Gabrieli in Venice, Hassler wrote both German and Italian madrigals, as well as motets and organ works.

During the sixteenth century it was customary for German courts to employ musicians from the Netherlands and Italy, rather than from Germany. German secular music, however, was very much influenced by music of the Lutheran Reformation. As a German contribution to the Renaissance we might mention settings of classical Latin poems, such as the *Odes* of Horace. "They were written for use in schools and it was only in Germany that this musical aid to classical education was systematically practiced." Also peculiarly German was the *quodlibet,* whose polyphony combined themes of many songs in a humorous vein.

SPANISH COMPOSERS

During the fifteenth century, composers in Spain were in close touch with the Netherlands. During the following century, many *villancicos* and some madrigals were composed. Spanish musicians, however, tended to devote more time to sacred than to secular composition. In fact, many of the sacred melodies were borrowed for secular use, reversing the usual sequence. Among the best-known Spanish Renaissance composers are Juan del Encina (*c.* 1468-*c.* 1530), Francisco Guerrero (1527-1599) and Cristóbal de Morales (*c.* 1500-1553).

Most outstanding was the priest, Tomás Luis de Victoria (or Vittoria, *c.* 1549-1611). He, along with Guerrero and Morales, is often rather artificially assigned to a Roman school associated with Palestrina, for all three spent some years in Rome, and Victoria was a friend of Palestrina and of Giovanni Maria Nanini (*c.* 1545-1607). The Spaniards' style, however, according to Marc Pincherle, has an unmistakable national flavor "similar to that which marked the romances and ballads of the preceding century, alternating as they did between asceticism and the violent expression of sombre passions or no less exalted joys." Victoria's works, confined entirely to Church music, include Masses, motets and psalms, all exhibiting a freedom of melody, a richness of harmony and a dramatically mystic power which is immensely moving.

ENGLISH COMPOSERS

The recent revival of interest in Tudor music reveals that England had a school comparable to those on the Continent. With few men of genius among the number, the high average of talent, nevertheless, was extraordinary and the list of composers a long one. One chauvinistic authority asserts, "While the Roman and Venetian schools, for example, arose directly out of the Flemish school and only gradually attained to distinct individuality and independence with Palestrina and Gabrieli, the English school began with a distinct individuality and gradually came more under the Flemish influence." Be this as it may, it is worth pointing out that musical development in Renaissance England tended to lag behind that of the Continent and it was only after foreign influences made themselves felt that English music moved toward its Golden Age.

The "Three T's"—John Taverner (1495-1545), Christopher Tye (1500-1572) and Thomas Tallis (1505-1585)—were transitional composers between John Dunstable and William Byrd and the English madrigalists. Taverner composed eight Masses in a remarkable contrapuntal style and used a plainsong theme from one of them, *Gloria tibi Trinitas* (an *In Nomine Domini*), as the basis for a curious instrumental composition which persisted to the time of Purcell. Tye is said to have composed the first **anthem,** a form that replaced the motet when England withdrew from the Roman Catholic Church. The Anglican anthem used an English text and was written in a chordal, rather than polyphonic style, except when designed for "Great Services." Tallis, sometimes referred to as the father of English cathedral music, was the composer of a gigantic motet with forty voice parts in eight choruses which suggested a similar work by his Italian contemporary, Alessandro Striggio (*c.* 1535-*c.* 1595). One of his psalm tunes has been popularized in the Vaughan Williams' setting for string orchestra.

When Elizabeth I ascended to the throne (1558), Taverner had died and Tye and Tallis were already in their fifties. A young Lincoln organist, William Byrd (*c.* 1543-1623), was destined to be the new star on the English horizon. Byrd, whom critics compare to Palestrina, Lasso and Victoria, was blessed with an enviable versatility; he was equally at home in composing Roman Masses and motets, Anglican Services and anthems, madrigals, solo songs, fantasies for strings and music for the virginals. With Tallis (1575) he was given a twenty-one year grant from an admiring queen to print, import and sell music, from which issued many famous collections, including his *Psalmes, Sonnets, and Songs of Sadness and Piety* (1588). In Byrd's music is combined contrapuntal skill, expressive use of dissonances and a rhythmic incisiveness which is distinctly English.

From about 1560 England had been invaded by Italian madrigals that captured the fancy of the upper classes. In 1588, *Musica transalpina,* a collection of Italian madrigals (including two of Byrd's), was published by Nicholas Young, followed two years later by another set of foreign pieces, mostly Marenzio's, but again including two by Byrd. It was in 1594, however, that the first book of exclusively English madrigals appeared, Thomas Morley's *Madrigalls to Foure Voyces;* these were supplemented by numerous issues of numerous composers through 1630—works that comprised England's Golden Age.

Morley (1557-1602), a pupil of Byrd and a learned musician, introduced the vocal *ballet* (with its fa-la-la refrain) and composed in a style that superimposed an English mold upon the Italian forerunners. Through his *Plaine and Easie Introduction to Practicall Musicke* (1597) we gain valuable insights into musical practices of his day. As next holder of the queen's grant to print and publish, Morley was responsible for several volumes, including a collection of madrigals in praise of Elizabeth, *The Triumphs of Oriana* (1603), and the first English book of ensemble music (for a "broken" consort, that is, a group of different instruments—in this case, treble and bass viols, cittern, pandore, lute and recorder—1599).

Of the many madrigalists we shall mention but a few. John Dowland (1562-1626) was a gifted composer of madrigals as well as of *ayres,* solo and polyphonic songs, with lute or viol accompaniment. John Milton (*c.* 1563-1647), father of the poet, contributed to several famous collections. Orlando Gibbons (1583-1625) wrote some beautiful examples, such as "The Silver Swan." Richard Deering (*c.* 1580-*c.* 1630) along with Gibbons and Weelkes, used the "Cryes of London" as inspiration for madrigals. Perhaps most significant were John Wilbye (1574-1638) and Thomas Weelkes (*c.* 1575-1628), of whom Eric Blom writes, "They had the kind of genius for combining atmosphere and characterization with unfailing technical and formal mastery which Mozart was later to display in opera." Thomas Ravenscroft (*c.* 1590-*c.* 1633), an anthologist of tavern songs, rounds and catches, is alleged to have discovered the immortal "Three Blind Mice."

Another facet of England's Golden Age, which we shall investigate more fully later, lay in the field of instrumental music. If madrigals were derived from Flemish and Italian prototypes and *ayres* from French sources, music for virginals was an original English contribution, disdaining the Continental practice of vocal transcription in favor of dance and variation forms. Byrd's music in *My Lady Newell's Book* (1591) marks him as a leader; the *FitzWilliam Virginal Book,* dating from not earlier than the 1620's, contains specimens by composers such as John Bull (*c.* 1562-1628), Morley, Byrd, Gibbons, Giles Farnaby (*c.* 1560-1640), Tallis and Sweelinck.

Orlando Lasso and Palestrina

Although musical development, like general historical change, is not wrought by individual geniuses but is rather the resultant expression of social and intellectual circumstances in a given time, place and condition, the work of certain composers, either because of striking originality or high quality of output, can be viewed in our musical journey through the ages as definitive of at least part of the spirit of the times. Borrowing from and adding to sixteenth-century music, yet towering like twin peaks above their fellow composers, were Orlando Lasso (1532-1594) and Palestrina (*c.* 1525-1594). Almost exact contemporaries, as were Bach and Handel one hundred and fifty years later, Lasso and Palestrina may analogously be used to illustrate differing aspects of the ultimate in Renaissance music.

The music of both Lasso and Palestrina exhibits general features of sixteenth-century practices; neither composer was a radical innovator. Each used modifications of the Flemish contrapuntal style; each conceived his compositions primarily in melodic terms; each was confronted with fluctuations of modality and considerations of the treatment of dissonance; each was aware of problems of prosody; each was hailed by his contemporaries as *Princeps Musicae*; each wrote both secular and sacred music; each was prolific.

Yet Lasso was a cosmopolitan person who traveled widely through Italy, the Netherlands, France, England and Germany; Palestrina never strayed far from Rome. Lasso was the intimate of royalty, decorated by a pope and ennobled by Emperor Maximilian II; Palestrina was an employee of the Papacy and, at one time, a fur merchant. Lasso's style tended toward the dramatic exuberance of the Venetians; Palestrina's style was one of exalted abstraction and serenity. Lasso composed extensively in secular forms, including madrigals, *Lieder* and *chansons*; Palestrina, although he wrote Italian madrigals of high quality, was primarily a composer of sacred music. Lasso was accustomed to working with and utilizing instrumental resources, as shown in the print of the Bavarian Chapel; Palestrina confined his compositions to the limitations of *a cappella* performance, as that was the accepted manner of the Sistine Chapel. Lasso was a man of the world; Palestrina was, for a period, a priest of the Catholic Church.

Lasso—Epitome of the Netherlands Schools

Lasso (or Orlandus Lassus) began life in Mons, Belgium. His extraordinary gifts were recognized from early boyhood, when he was kidnaped three times while a chorister at St. Nicolas', because of the beauty of his voice. After the third abduction, he entered the service of Ferdinando Gonzaga of Sicily, and after that he spent time in Naples, Rome (as choirmaster of St. John Lateran), England, France, Antwerp and finally Munich, where he had a generous, devoted patron with whose encouragement he produced a prodigious amount of music. Duke Albert founded the Royal Library of Munich, in which are many valuable manuscripts, including Lasso's famous *Seven Penitential Psalms* (*c.* 1565).

Lasso's first publications (Antwerp, 1555)—collections of madrigals to poems of Petrarch and madrigals and motets to Italian, French and Latin texts—proclaimed his precocious musical maturity and his versatility. Over the years he published *Canzoni villanesche alla Napolitana,* simple songs from Naples, turned into an art form with the rustic style retained, along with the consecutive fifths characteristic of *organum*; a *Symphonie à six,* an early example of independent instrumental music;

Fig. 32. Orlando Lasso and the Bavarian Court Chapel—Mielen Codex. The "Prince of Musicians" is seated in the center front, surrounded by instrumentalists and singers of the Duke of Bavaria. (Courtesy Bavarian State Library, Munich.)

and six books of German *Lieder,* the titles of which, *Neue deutsche Liedlein mit fünff Stimmen welche ganz lieblich zu singen und auf allerly Instrumenten zu gebrauchen,* designate that the new little German songs for five voices were meant to be sung and used on all sorts of instruments.

Many authorities think that Lasso surpassed Palestrina in his motets, which have a "singularly compelling style." Cyr de Brant states that "the chromatic element is encountered more frequently in Lasso and none knew better than he, how to employ this sensitive feature of fluctuating harmony." By the sixteenth century, as Anthony Milner explains:

> The term "motet" covers not only motets properly so-called but includes polyphonic settings of the Proper Mass and Office texts, the canticles, and the psalms. The "classical motet style" of the sixteenth-century motet developed in all these forms, but while the motet proper was always polyphonic throughout, the settings of Proper chants and psalms generally involved alternate use of chant sections. Many motets were divided into two parts, each part being complete in itself; the second part often began with a change from duple to triple time.

Lasso's (and Palestrina's) motet-style settings of the *Offertories* are of historical importance as the first composed without a basis of plainsong.

The last years of Lasso's life were clouded with melancholia. After his death, his sons published 516 of his motets, in six volumes entitled *Magnum Opus Musicum O de Lasso* (1604). These are but part of the over 2000 Lasso compositions that exist, either in print or in the Munich Archives.

REFORMATION AND COUNTER-REFORMATION

Early in the sixteenth century an event took place that was to rock Europe to its very foundations. The catalyst of this quake was a German priest named Martin Luther; his world-shaking deed was an attack upon the prevailing corruption of the Roman Catholic Church. Like Columbus, who discovered a continent when searching for a new route to India, Luther founded (with the organizational aid of John Calvin) a new church when seeking only to reform the old.

Ecclesiastical music, despite the efforts of many dedicated composers, had fallen into bad ways. For the most part musical invention had become an arid contrapuntal exercise, where the melody obscured the contrapuntal device or where the counterpoint obscured the melody. And everything tended to obscure the words. We have seen that it was common practice for one part of a choir to sing religious words in Latin to plainsong themes, while another used popular tunes with profane and often lewd words in the vernacular. Although composers disguised the street songs by elongating the value of each tone, there was still a very questionable rationale underlying the procedure.

Luther recognized the incongruity of the situation. A musician himself, he realized that the congregation heard little and understood less of what was happening in the musical liturgy. This he deplored, as he felt strongly that music should serve God in the lives of the people. In fact, he stated, "After theology I accord to music the highest place and the greatest honor." To make popular participation a reality, Luther encouraged adaptation of dignified and edifying words to simple melodies and urged a return to the early Christian custom of communal singing.

What plainsong was to Catholicism, the **chorale** or Lutheran hymn was to German Protestants. Its effect on music was profound and far-reaching. *Chorales* were harmonized in four parts. They were usually sung in unison with the accompaniment of the organ or a group of instruments. This great change or revolt broke the backbone of polyphonic music, freed the spirit of the people and first brought into use modern scales as we know them.

Meanwhile, in England, Henry VIII's lust for Anne Boleyn, and the Pope's refusal of his request for a divorce from Catherine of Aragon, unwittingly precipitated the headstrong monarch into a separatist movement of his own, which resulted in the establishment of the Anglican Church. The first English translation of the New Testament was made in 1538 and shortly thereafter, psalms were translated into metrical verse. The Mass was replaced by the "Service" and the motet by the anthem.

Luther's charges against the Church and the popular reaction to him and his reforms, in turn, set in motion a Counter-Reformation, during which the Roman Church, with generous assistance from the stake, militant propaganda from the newly formed (1540) Society of Jesus and extensive soul-searching, set about ordering its own house and stemming the rising tide of Protestantism. In the process, it benefited from the works of a composer known to us as Palestrina.

PALESTRINA

The bare facts of Palestrina's biography can be quickly recounted. Born Giovanni Pierluigi in the small town of Palestrina, southeast of Rome, he was educated as a choirboy and occupied successive posts as organist and choirmaster of the Cathedral of Palestrina, maestro of the Julian Choir in Rome, choirmaster of St. John Lateran and of Santa Maria Maggiore, music director of a Roman seminary, member of the staff of Cardinal d'Este and then back to the *Cappella Giulia,* a position he retained until his death. In 1554 he published his first book of Masses and dedicated it to Pope Julius III, an unusual act in that day for any but foreign composers. In recognition of the dedication, however, Palestrina was appointed a member of the Papal Choir, only to be dismissed by Julius' successor, because of petty jealousies (he had not taken the entrance examination) and because he was a married man. After the death of several sons and of his wife, he was admitted briefly to the priesthood, but he relinquished the tonsure to marry (in 1581) the wealthy widow of a fur merchant, whose business he helped manage while composing some of his most sublime works.

Was Palestrina the heroic savior of polyphonic music as his virtual canonization in the annals of Catholic tradition would seem to imply? Did the "Prince of Music" single-handedly reform liturgical composition? Was his noble *Missa Papae Marcelli* responsible for changing the minds of members of the Council of Trent as has been alleged? The answers to all three questions are negative.

The Council of Trent had been convened to solidify Catholic doctrine against attacks by the Reformers and to correct abuses in Church administration. Music and its place and function in celebrating the liturgy was but one of many topics of deliberation, perhaps overemphasized in histories of music. The Council did, however, as we mentioned, earlier, abolish troping and eliminate all but four sequences from the liturgy. Moreover, in a decree of 1562, it redefined the official attitude toward music, stating that "All things should be so ordered that the Masses, whether they be celebrated with or without singing, may reach tranquilly into the ears and hearts of those who hear them, when everything is executed clearly and at the right speed." A minority of the Council favored a return to unadorned Gregorian chant, but the majority were concerned only that the use of secular *cantus firmi* and the techniques of counterpoint not exceed its true purpose within the Church.

Because the musical issues were left somewhat unresolved, the Pope appointed a commission of eight cardinals and eight singers from the Papal Chapel to pursue the subject. Palestrina was not among them. In 1576, however, Pope Gregory XIII ordered a revision of the *Gradual* and selected Palestrina and Annibale Zoilo to undertake "the task of reviewing, and as it shall seem expedient to you, of purifying, correcting, and reforming" the contents, bestowing upon the two "full and free permission and authority" and granting them the privilege of choosing other helpers "skilled in music." Palestrina commenced work on "The Proper of the Season" and Zoilo undertook "The Proper of the Saints." For rather vague reasons, Palestrina abruptly abandoned the project in 1578, leaving it unfinished, although his version was published after his death as the *Medicean Gradual* (1614).

What then does account for Palestrina's unquestioned position as one of the greatest composers of all time? Simply the fact that he composed music which of its kind reached the heights of near perfection and which in its spirit was in complete agreement with the ideals restated by the Church. There was no element of revolution in his work;

his polyphony was almost as modal as plainsong. He followed traditional Roman lines and such changes as he made were of the logic of genius, not of the experimenter. Palestrina's music has none of the sensuousness of Renaissance art; rather it echoes medieval mysticism and is full of the passionless fervor of a religious ecstatic. As Richard Terry writes, "His was the larger vision of the liturgist as opposed to the rubrician" —that is, the artist as opposed to the draftsman. He had an unerring instinct for rightness down to the smallest details. One critic comments, "For classical restraint and noble simplicity combined with a contrapuntal virtuosity that has ever since been regarded as flawless, Palestrina stands unsurpassed by any composer of his age."

Among Palestrina's compositions are 105 Masses, 280 motets, hymns, *Offertories, Lamentations, Litanies, Magnificats* and madrigals. Some of the most popular are the lofty *Missa Papae Marcelli,* the motet *Assumpta est Maria* and an *Improperia* that was sung every year in the Sistine Chapel on Good Friday, through 1870.

*   *   *   *   *

Palestrina died in 1594 and was honored by burial in St. Peter's at Rome. Orlando Lasso also died in 1594. The two composers in many ways represent the limits of aspiration which Renaissance music attained. *Grove's Dictionary* states:

> There is the spirit of the Renaissance already in the music of both Palestrina and Lassus, perhaps more manifest in the latter than the former. Both start from the same ground of the secular madrigal, but their paths and their aims diverge. While Palestrina for general grace and beauty of style has been compared to Raphael and Mozart, Lassus in his depth of thought has been considered to belong to the lineage of Michelangelo and Sebastian Bach.

Although the Renaissance marked a period of intensive musical activity, in music alone among the arts was there no real break from earlier lines of development or any dependence on Greek models. Even Palestrina, who represented polyphonic music at its meridian, did little more than apply Renaissance polish to well-worked extensions of embryonic medieval ideals. But soon, however, music, poised for a forward flight, would grasp for its advancement the Greek learning and through it evolve into a broader and more humane art.

SUGGESTIONS FOR FURTHER READING

Apel, Willi, *French Secular Music of the Fourteenth Century*. Cambridge, Medieval Institute, 1950.

Bukofzer, Manfred, *Studies in Medieval and Renaissance Music.** New York, Norton, 1950.

Dart, Thurston, *The Interpretation of Music.** New York, Longmans Green, 1954.

Davison, Archibald T., and Apel, Willi, *Historical Anthology of Music,* vol. I. Cambridge, Harvard University Press, 1949.

Donington, Robert, *The Interpretation of Early Music.* London, Faber & Faber, 1963.

Einstein, Alfred Mendel, Arthur, and Sessions, Roger, *The Italian Madrigal.* Princeton, Princeton University Press, 1949. 3 vols.

Fellowes, E. H., *William Byrd.* London, Oxford University Press, 1948.

Gray, Cecil, and Heseltine, Philip, *Carlo Gesualdo.* New York, Dial, 1926.

Greenberg, Noah, ed., *An English Songbook.** Garden City, Doubleday, 1963.

Jeppesen, Knud, *Counterpoint, the Polyphonic Vocal Style of the Sixteenth Century.* New York, Prentice-Hall, 1939.

Kerman, Joseph, *The Elizabethan Madrigal: A Comparative Study.* New York, American Musicological Society, 1962.

Morley, Thomas, *A Plain and Easy Introduction to Practical Music.* New York, Norton, 1952.

Naylor, Edward W., *Shakespeare and Music.* New York, Da Capo, 1965.

Newman, Joel, *Renaissance Music.** Englewood Cliffs, Prentice-Hall, 1967.

Parrish, Carl, *A Treasury of Early Music.** New York, Norton, 1958.

Parrish, Carl, and Ohl, John F., *Masterpieces of Music before 1750.* New York, Norton, 1951.

Reese, Gustave, *Music in the Renaissance.* New York, Norton, 1959.

Starr, William J., and Devine, George F., *Music Scores—Omnibus,* Part I.** Englewood Cliffs, Prentice-Hall, 1964.

Stevens, Denis, *Tudor Church Music.** New York, Norton, 1961.

Stevenson, Robert, *Spanish Cathedral Music in the Golden Age.* Berkeley, University of California Press, 1961.

Strunk, Oliver, ed., *Source Readings in Music History.** New York, Norton, 1950.

A SAMPLER OF SUPPLEMENTARY RECORDINGS

Collections

Masterpieces of Music before 1750	Haydn 9038/40
Treasury of Early Music	Haydn 9100/3
2000 Years of Music	Folkways 3700
Ten Centuries of Music	DGG KL-52/61
Ars Nova and Renaissance	Victor LM-6016
Sixteenth-Century Music	Victor LM-6029
Court and Ceremonial Music	Nonesuch 1012
Gothic and Early Renaissance Music	Allegro 9019
Maximilian I Imperial Chapel Repertoire	DGG ARC-3223
Music of the Renaissance	Lyric 86
Music from the Court of Henry VIII	Vox 950
15th-Century French and Italian Song	Nonesuch 1010
Elizabethan Ayres, Madrigals and Dances	Decca DL-9406
Triumphs of Oriana	Wal-212

* Available in paperback edition.

Music by Individual Composers
   Binchois, Gilles, *Music of Gilles Binchois*
   Des Prés, Josquin, *Missa Pange Lingua*
   Dowland, John, *Lute Songs*
   Dufay, Guillaume, *Hymns, Choruses and Songs*
   Dunstable, John, *Sacred and Secular Music*
   Gabrieli, Giovanni, *Processional Music*
   Gesualdo, Don Carlo, *Italian Madrigals*
   Gibbons, Orlando, *Short Service*
   Janequin, Clément, *Chansons*
   Landini, Francesco, *Songs from Codex of Squarcialupi*
   Lassus, Orlandus, *Seven Penitential Psalms*
   Marenzio, Luca, *Madrigals*
   Monteverdi, Claudio, *Madrigals*
   Morales, Cristóbal, *Magnificat*
   Morley, Thomas, *Elizabethan Madrigals*
   Ockeghem, Johannes, *Chansons*
   Palestrina, Giovanni, *Missa Papae Marcelli*
   Senfl, Ludwig, *Songs*
   Sweelinck, Jan, *Psalms*
   Tallis, Thomas, *Lamentations of Jeremiah*
   Victoria, Tomás, *Motets*
   Wilbye, John, *Madrigals*

Related Works of Interest
   Hindemith, Paul, *Mathis der Maler*
   Stravinsky, Igor, *Monumentum pro Gesualdo*
   Vaughan Williams, R., *Fantasia on a Theme by Tallis*
                         Five Tudor Portraits

OPPORTUNITIES FOR STUDY IN DEPTH

1. As noted in this chapter, the secular melody, *L'Homme armé,* was used by a number of great and lesser composers as a *cantus firmus* for Mass settings. Make a study of several of these, indicating how the tune was modified for sacred use and how different composers handled it. Excerpts in Davison's and Apel's *Historical Anthology of Music,* vol. 1 (see "Suggestions for Further Reading"), will provide a starting point.

2. Assemble a collection of paintings by Renaissance artists, containing musical subject matter. Annotate the representations. A model for this project may be found in Chrisman, Jo, and Fowler, Charles B., "Music Performance in a Renaissance Painting," *Music Educators Journal,* Nov.-Dec., 1965, vol. 52, no. 2, pp. 93-98.

3. Make a study of the songs used by William Shakespeare in his plays, suggesting the original manner of performance. List selected settings of these songs by various composers.

4. Investigate intensively the role of music in the early days of the Reformation, evaluating the ideas of Martin Luther, John Calvin and John Knox, among others.

5. Prepare for class performance several English madrigals, singing them in such a way and in such a setting as they were originally performed. Preface each selection with an oral program note.

6. Select Masses by Machault, Dufay, Ockeghem, Lasso and Palestrina. On the basis of listening and, if possible, score-study, write a report discussing the evolution of musical techniques over the several centuries involved and the impress of the individual composer as evidenced in his particular work.

7. Read the modern edition of Thomas Morley's *Plaine and Easie Introduction to Practicall Musicke* (see "Suggestions for Further Reading") and lead a structured discussion based upon his material and ideas.

8. Examine several madrigals of the Renaissance period, noting the devices by which composers attempted musical word-painting. For instance, Marenzio, in his *Cedan l'antiche,* depicts pillars and arches of old Roman architecture with chords and ascending and descending scales.

Vocabulary Enrichment

ars nova	*frottola*
madrigal	*ritornello*
caccia	*contratenor*
ballata	*contra altus*
Landini cadence	*contra bassus*
choral polyphony	*cantata da camera*
Franco-Netherlandish artifices	anthem
augmentation	*chorale*
diminution	Service
double choruses	motet

Chapter 8.

THE BEGINNINGS OF OPERA AND ORATORIO

Why cause words to be sung by four or five voices so that they cannot be distinguished, when the Ancients aroused the strongest passions by means of a single voice supported by a lyre? We must renounce counterpoint and different kinds of instruments and return to primitive simplicity.

—VINCENZO GALILEO, *Dialogo della musica* (1581)

On our journey in music through the ages we have had occasion, rather incidentally, to cite manifestations of attempts to unite music with drama and dance in some meaningful relationship. Indeed, ancient Greek plays were performed as semimusic dramas, and their interpretation after the Roman conquest, although degenerate, contained all the elements of today's musical comedy. The Oxyrhynchus Manuscript contains fragments of a "mime opera"; songs came to be strung together with passages of spoken dialogue, after the fashion of Adam de la Halle in *Le Jeu de Robin et Marion.*

Within the Roman Catholic Church we have mentioned the early triologue of *Quem quaeritis?,* the Easter trope, which over the centuries led to more elaborate liturgical music dramas based upon situations inherent in the rituals and Offices. Examples include *The Three Marys,* a five-character play featuring the three Marys, an angel and the guardian of Christ's sepulchre; and the parable of *The Wise and Foolish Virgins,* including both Provençal songs and Gregorian chant. *Laudi,* the devotional hymns, assumed a dialogue aspect, as did motets and their secular reflections, madrigals.

ANTECEDENTS OF OPERA

During the birth throes of the young Western nations, music, gentlest of the arts, was an avocation of the nobility and a consolation of the people, inevitably becoming part of dramatic observance. But music was preceded by pantomime, and speech was the last element to be conjoined. As in Greece the drama stemmed from religious ceremonies in the worship of Dionysus, so in our own civilization the theatre had its origin in Christian mystery, miracle and morality plays of the Middle

Ages. Thus, the immediate background of opera and oratorio lay in the *devozione,* the *maggi,* and the *sacre rappresentazione* of Italy, where the concepts were born and brought to fruition.

Mystery plays dealt with the Annunciation, the Ascension and with Christ's Passion according to the various accounts of the Apostles. These were announced by musical processions and employed songs in the course of the action. (The Passion Play of Oberammergau, first produced in 1633, has been revived, with few exceptions, every following decade.) The deeds of saints and biblical miracles provided the substance around which miracle plays were spun. Morality plays, in which allegory was a prevailing element, personalized vices and virtues, using chanting and some music. Well-known examples include the English *Everyman,* and its German counterpart, *Jedermann,* the latter performed annually at the Salzburg Music Festival, on the porch of the Cathedral.

In Italy, before the fourteenth century, *devozione,* akin to mystery plays, became popular. In addition to these dramas exploring sacred story for the purposes of education and edification were the festivals of May (*maggi*), celebrating, as did earlier pagan rituals, the fruitfulness of spring. Out of the *devozione* and *maggi,* and concurrently with them, developed the *sacre rappresentazione,* which combined music and speech. Under the guidance of Lorenzo the Magnificent the *sacre rappresentazione,* celebrating St. John, patron saint of Florence, attained tremendous proportions. Lorenzo and Poliziano, his poet friend, spent months preparing these spectacles in which they combined Greek legend, biblical pageantry and masque-like musical interludes.

They might have been advertised thus:

A PLAY—THE ASCENSION OF THE SAVIOR
A Biblical Miracle
Play by Lorenzo de' Medici
Poem by Poliziano
Scenery by Brunelleschi
Technicolor by Tintoretto
Scenery painted by Raphael and Leonardo da Vinci
Music by Alfonso della Viola

Scene: The streets of Florence are seething with people. Shops are closed and houses are locked up. Everyone is dashing hither and yon for good vantage points from which to see the sacred representation, about to begin. Little playhouses have been built on nearly every street and square. Each cardinal has his own theatre with which to entertain the Pope, who is in town for the day. The principal square is a mass of white and blue, and street arches are decked in wreaths of greens and flowers. On every pillar stands a young angel singing holy chants. In the center of the square is the tomb of Jesus, around which sleeping soldiers lie, and angels nearby guard the group. Then an angel singing the "Song of Resurrection" descends from the "sky" on a rope attached to the roof of a tent. After the song, intense silence fills the square . . . when . . . *crack!* . . . an explosion of powder shatters the peace. The soldiers awake. Christ arises from the tomb and sings in Italian of the salvation of the world He died to save. Angels bear Him heavenward, more music is played and the play is over.

(Adapted from R. Rolland)

Every imaginable mechanical device was used to enhance the effect: rumblings of thunder; shatterings of buildings by lightning; great stages rising skyward, representing the apotheoses of saints ascending into heaven; and conflagrations, often frighteningly real. In addition to the engineering triumphs, artists of first rank contrived the stage sets. "Up to this time," comments Romain Rolland, "the drama had all the elements of opera, save dramatic declamation. It had accented and continuous song, importance of machinery, the mixture of tragedy and fairy-tale, the interludes and ballets introduced without purpose." (Rolland deduces that among the madrigalists and composers of the time were some, such as the aforementioned Alfonso della Viola [1508-1570] at Ferrara, who may have attempted musical recitative).

It is a common trait of any era to turn away from the one just preceding it; in this the Renaissance was true to type. During the middle of the sixteenth century people who were steeped in classic learning began to disregard the *sacre rappresentazione,* immersing themselves instead in the Latin comedies of Plautus and Terence. Humanism had triumphed. Laymen, prelates, nobles and even Pope Leo X (Giovanni de' Medici) reveled in plays which threw all reverence to the winds. Nothing was too sacred to escape the pen of the satirists. Dance, song, ballet and instrumental music were inseparable from *il commedia,* and rarely, if ever, was it presented without music, elaborate stage sets and costumes. Quite irrelevant *intermedii* were inserted between acts to entertain the spectators.

From 1480 to 1540, Rome, Mantua, Venice, Florence and particularly Ferrara were the centers of comedy. Ariosto directed the building of a theater, holding 5000 people, for the celebration of the marriage of Lucrezia Borgia to Alfonso, son of Ercole d'Este (1502). Torquato Tasso's father, Bernardo, directed the plays in Mantua. Somewhat later (1597), Orazio Vecchi (*c.* 1550-1605) wrote *L'Amfiparnaso,* a madrigal-comedy of fifteen numbers modeled on an older form, the *commedia dell'arte,* which in turn was fashioned from ancient models and had been presented by strolling players (and is survived today by the comic figures of Pierrot, Pierrette and Harlequin).

Attune to contemporary thought and taste, Lorenzo de' Medici, with Angelo Poliziano and "Arrigo Tedesco" (Henry the German, or Heinrich Isaak) began to modify the *rappresentazione*. Born in Brabant, Heinrich Isaak spent many years in Florence as choirmaster of San Giovanni. While there he gained renown as a composer of *canzone,* including one about gingerbread venders and the beautiful *San Giovanni e Paula,* in which the engaging but ill-fated Giovanni de' Medici took part.

Never had music been so much an auxiliary of the arts of painting, sculpture and literature. It is said that even Leonardo da Vinci first presented himself to the Duke of Mantua as a lutenist rather than as a painter. Da Vinci was the product of an age of versatility and regarded himself as a gentleman and scientist as well as an artist and engineer. As defined in Castiglione's famous manual of manners, *The Courtier* (1528), a gentleman had also to be a musician. "I am not pleased with the Courtier," wrote Castiglione, "if he be not also a musician, and besides his understanding and cunning upon the book, have skill in like manner on sundry instruments."

Following the sack of Rome by Charles V in 1527 and the humiliation of Florence in 1530, Italy suffered a "moral convulsion." By 1540 the Italian Renaissance was effectively shackled. Fear possessed everyone; painting was suspect; life was as throttled as it had been free hitherto. The *sacre rappresentazione* and, of course, the ribald *commedia* were banned, save in absolute privacy. But the Italians used their chains as ladder rungs to another level of preopera development —the *dramma pastorale* or pastoral drama.

While Poliziano's *Orfeo* (1472—with scenery painted by Raphael) was a first approach to adapting methods of medieval morality plays to classical mythology subject matter, Beccari's *Sacrificio* (Ferrara, 1554), with music by della Viola, took the definite form of a play with legendary and pastoral aspects in which a mere excuse for a plot was bolstered by song, *balletto* and spectacle, and the musical resources included a revived kind of monody in which the singer accompanied himself with a lute.

Two other pastorales captured the attention of aristocratic audiences in sixteenth-century Italy. One was *Aminta* (Belvidere, 1573) by the brilliant poet-musician, Torquato Tasso (1544-1595), friend of Gesualdo, acquaintance of Palestrina and supplier of texts to many composers, including Monteverdi. The other was *Il Pastor fido* (*The Faithful Shepherd*), by Giovanni Guarini, which, with *Aminta,* served as a precursor of the earliest opera *librettos,* plays written to be set to music.

By 1598 the *dramma pastorale* was prevalent everywhere. A critic of the time, Angelo Ingegneri, said that these works "were intermediate between tragedy and comedy . . . give great delight . . . and it must not be forgotten that music should be a rest and not a fatigue." Thus, once again, the shepherds and their maids frolicked joyfully among the hills and dales of Arcady.

With roots in Church liturgy and classic learning and embued with the new tendency toward melody sung by one voice with an instrumental accompaniment, prefiguring harmony, the stage was set for raising the curtain on opera itself. As we have seen, the concept of opera did not occur without antecedent, but was the product of centuries of fragmented forms to which a new element, that of musical declamation, was added. For this we must look toward the city of Florence in Italy.

Fig. 33. Ponte Vecchio, Florence. With the encouragement and patronage of the Medicis, Florence became the center of the Renaissance and the birthplace of opera. (Photograph by the editor.)

THE CAMERATA

When we approach the pre-Classical or **Baroque period** of music, extending from *c.* 1600 (the birth of opera) to 1750 (the death of Bach), we enter a transition world lying between that of the Renaissance and that which we characterize generally as modern. We confront two dominant themes: (1) an interest in direct communication in which the listener for the first time becomes a significant factor for the composer; and (2) an absorption in formalization, resulting in the crystallization and codification of new forms of composition, both vocal and instrumental. From Galileo's words, quoted at the beginning of this chapter, we sense a need for simplification which, once accomplished, was grafted to the Renaissance heritage to hybridize in a final grandiose richness at the apogee of the impulse.

A compulsion to create a theatrical form like the ancient Greek drama was the impelling motive of a group of *literati* and musicians who formed the *camerata,* one of the many neo-Platonian Academies that had sprung up in Italy due to the revival of classical learning. This particular group first met in the home of Count Bardi of Florence and represented many facets of opinion in regard to what should be done. Some felt that the old polyphony should be retained; others that it ought to be abandoned in favor of the new monody; while still others suggested a combination of old and new. From the conflict of opinion was to come valuable advances.

Members of the *camerata* included the learned musician Jacopo Peri; the young singer Giulio Caccini of Rome; Emilio Cavalieri, inspector-general of artists in Florence and composer of ballets; Luca Marenzio, the Florentine madrigalist; Cristofero Malvezzi, who, with Marenzio, collaborated on Bardi's *intermezzi* to *L'Amico fido* (1589); and liberals and modernists who were out of sympathy with the "Goths," as Galileo called the contrapuntalists. Among the poets were numbered Laura Giudiccioni, Ottavio Rinuccini and Strozzi.

The *camerata* realized that music made poetry more poignant, especially when it was not allowed to ride roughshod over the verse. To understand opera, this is an essential starting point. Although few composers have successfully achieved the ideal blending of words and music, Debussy probably came closest in *Pelléas et Mélisande* and Gluck and Wagner made worthy attempts. The problem that faced the Florentines was removal of all musical impediments to the projection of word meanings, a concern that we have noted in many quarters during the late sixteenth century. The youthful Monteverdi asserted in his *Scherzi musicali* (1607), *"L'orazione sia padrona dell' armonia e non serva."* ("The text should be the master of the music, not the servant.") How was the aim to be accomplished?

Drenched in Aristoxenos' theories and avid to recreate Greek drama as they imagined it to have been, the Florentine musicians hit upon a tenable solution in a technique variously termed *stilo rappresentativo* (representational style), *musica parlanti* (musical speech) or *recitativo.*

This type of musical declamation was a most distinctive point of departure in the creation of opera. Although far from Greek dramatic practice in actuality, it provided the nearest approximation possible, with sixteenth-century modality and with a language radically different from ancient Greek.

Recitative followed the natural rhythms and inflections of Italian speech, allotting one syllable to one tone. It presented sentences in such a manner that minor words and syllables were hastened while important parts of the speech structure were prolonged, resulting in a dramatic presentation of narrative materials. As Sachs comments, "The road away from the Renaissance that the *camerata* opened led to emotionalism, individualism, illusionism and the disintegration of music as an end in itself." The ideals of polyphony were abandoned.

With selection of the solo voice as a means of musical expression, resources had to be marshalled to provide a tonal support. The lute of the Renaissance, essentially an accompanying instrument, had reinforced in *frottole, villanelli* and *madrigale* the construct of melodic line with harmony, as distinct from the old vocal-instrumental polyphony. What was developed came to be known as thorough bass or *basso continuo,* the conception of a functional bass line, over which simultaneous voice parts were grouped as *chords* (vertical groups of related tones perceived by the ear as an entity).

Rather naturally, performance of this accompanying substructure depended upon instruments which could handle such an assignment; these included the keyboard instruments and lutes. Because the composer could not know in advance the specific capabilities of these diverse instruments, he did not complete the harmonies but left their voicing to a player whose dependence upon the written score was supplemented by excellent improvisational skills. At first, the harmonies were only implied, and the performer was free to inject those that he felt suitable to the emotional mood. Later, however, the composer employed a system of musical shorthand, called *figured bass,* wherein the bass line was further notated with symbols (such as numbers and accidentals) to clarify his harmonic intentions. So important was the "realization" of the *basso continuo* that the keyboard player (*maestro al cembalo*) acted as conductor of the entire performance, a procedure maintained well into the eighteenth century.

Yet another musical aspect of *La nuove musiche* (the new music) concerns the establishment and stabilization of functional tonality as opposed to modality. The Renaissance composer, although using what we would call triads and first inversions, conceived of them as coincident melodic concords, not as successions of chords operating according to accepted rules of behavior. If we find the sounds of sixteenth- and seventeenth-century music somewhat strange at first, it is due to the absence of the functional and tonal patterns that dominate music from Bach to Wagner. Throughout the seventeenth century the concepts of tonality and chordal relationships were explored and refined, to be codified by Rameau (1722) in a form that differs very little from today's nonexperimental harmonic system.

Among the earliest attempts to reproduce ancient Greek drama were *Oedipus Rex* of Giovanni Gabrieli, and Marenzio's *Combat of Apollo and the Dragon.* Not satisfied with the Hellenic flavor of these, Galileo, with Bardi, composed Dante's *Lament of Ugolino, in stilo rappresenta-tivo,* for solo voice and instrumental accompaniment. But Caccini (*c.* 1546-1618), more gifted and adroit than either Bardi or Galileo, began to write *canzone* approximating a *cantilena* over a thorough bass. Although in *La nuove musiche* (1602) Caccini claimed for himself the creation of Italian monodic style, and although his daughter, a charming *cantatrice,* gave his *arias* wide currency, it is to Jacopo Peri (1561-1633) that the innovation properly belongs, as found in his epoch-making *Daphne* (1597). Unfortunately, only the libretto remains, but the work reputedly contained examples of recitative, chordal writing and ensemble accompaniment in its pastoral prologue and six scenes.

In 1600, Peri and Rinuccini were commissioned to produce an entertainment for the marriage of Marie de' Medici and Henry IV of France. An opera, *Euridice,* was the result. Its score, in *basso continuo,* contained figures indicating the harmonies. The vocal parts included long and, to us, tiresome stretches of monody. At the first performance, members of the *camerata* performed in an orchestra of sorts—a harpsichord, three *chitarrone* (large guitars), *viola da gamba* (related to the the violoncello), *theorbo* (double lute) and three flutes. (Euridice proved a durable damsel; she and her mate, Orpheus, have inspired more music than any other Greeks. In 1602 Caccini also composed a *Euridice,* but his was more of a pastorale.)

ORATORIO AND CANTATA

Differences between opera and **oratorio** in the seventeenth century were initially minimal; both utilized the same musical resources in much the same way. Predecessors of the oratorio were the spiritual madrigals which related sacred stories. Palestrina and others anticipated the new style and for a while spiritual drama reverted to its original home, the Church. But gradually, a distinction was made; oratorio used biblical subject matter and was performed in the Church oratory (a side chapel for private prayer), while opera, more and more, employed secular themes and was presented in the homes of nobles and in theaters.

Forty-two years before Cavalieri's important opera-oratorio, Saint Filippi (Filippo Neri), a friend of Palestrina's, laid the groundwork when he inaugurated religious meetings in the oratory of S. Maria Vallicelli in Rome. Predating *Euridice* by several months was Emilio Cavalieri's (1550-1602) mystery-devotion, *La rappresentazione dell' anima e del corpo,* on a text by Laura Giudiccioni, using *basso continuo* and recitative as well as monodic songs (*canzonette spirituali*). Characters in this *Play of the Soul and the Body* were allegorical—Life, the Body, Pleasure—and the plot was woven about the successful resistance of the Soul to various temptations. The didactic nature of the work showed an influence of the Counter-Reformation which made its first presentation in Rome most appropriate. The oratorio was sumptuously mounted, however, with staging, costumes, machinery and a ballet, in addition to an orchestra placed in the wings. Apart from its religious theme, it differs very little from *Euridice*.

Cavalieri's prefatory remarks exemplify the close relationship between opera and oratorio and, indeed, provide an excellent summary of opera to this day.

> The instrumentation should change according to the emotion expressed. An overture or instrumental and vocal introductions are of good effect before the curtain rises. The *ritornelle* and *sinfonie* should be played by many instruments. A ballet, or better, a singing ballet, should close the performance. The actor must seek to acquire absolute perfection in his voice . . . He should sing with emotion . . . as it is written . . . he must pronounce his words distinctly. . . . The performance should not exceed two hours . . . Three acts suffice and one must be careful to infuse variety, not only into the music but also the poem and even the costumes.

As opera advanced, so did oratorio, which, toward the middle of the seventeenth century, discarded operatic trappings and assumed an identity of its own. Following Cavalieri was the Roman composer Giacomo Carissimi (1605-1674), who wrote sixteen *Historiae sacrae,* including oratorio and a shorter form of more limited scope, the *cantata da chiesa* (church cantata). Carissimi used a narrator or *historicus* as coordinator in his dramatic works and enlarged the part of the chorus. A scene from *Judicium Salomonis* (*The Judgment of Solomon*) illustrates Carissimi's use of dramatic monody and also the subordinate position of the sustained and rather bare *continuo*. Succeeding Italian opera composers also worked in the medium of oratorio. Notable among these are Alessandro Stradella (*St. John the Baptist*) and A. Scarlatti (*Assumption Oratorio*). In France, Marc-Antoine Charpentier (1634-1704) carried on Carissimi's ideals, often using the same subjects. In Reform Germany, as we shall see, composers were to absorb the cantata and oratorio, raising them to places of unparalleled prominence.

CLAUDIO MONTEVERDI

The first great opera composer and perhaps the greatest composer to his day was Claudio Monteverdi (1567-1643). Born in Cremona, he became singer, viol player and conductor at the court of Mantua, which he left in 1613 for the post of director of music at St. Mark's in Venice, where he died. When he first began to write *favola* in music, later called opera, the form was a hothouse plant, delicate and charming, for the few in palace and court. But he left opera warm and humanized, able to survive popular enthusiasm. Whereas Peri, Caccini and Cavalieri represented the new in opera, Monteverdi gave it a method and a power of expression unknown to his contemporaries. He realized in the struggle against counterpoint that new riches had to be brought to music. "He found them in harmony, in the expressive accent of monodic chant and in the variety of instrumentation," notes *A Narrative History of Music.*

Monteverdi came from a cultivated Cremona family and early became the pupil of Marc' Antonio Ingegneri (1545-1592), talented composer and choirmaster of the Cremona Cathedral. Monteverdi's first book, *Madrigali spirituali* (1582), before the *Canzonette* (1584) and *Madrigali* (1587), was full of previously prohibited progressions. Dissonance he loved, frequent use of the seventh in suspension and other "unpleasantnesses." It is doubtful that Monteverdi unaided discovered the dominant seventh chord, that stalwart of harmony, as examples of unprepared sevenths have been found in compositions of William Byrd, but it is true that Monteverdi did make more extensive use of it than had his predecessors.

Due to the emotional quality and popularity of his music, he attracted the attention of Vincenzo di Gonzaga, Duke of Mantua, who engaged him as court musician (1590) and took him traveling with him, even into battle. After the publication of his fifth book of madrigals while he was still *maestro di cappella* at Mantua, Giovanni Maria Artusi hurled shafts of criticism against the progressive Monteverdi in his *Imperfections of Modern Music* (*Delle imperfettioni della moderna musica,* 1604), saying in part: "Though I am glad to hear of a new manner of composition, it would be more edifying to find in these

Fig. 34. "Monteverdi with His Bass Viol"—seventeenth century, Italian. The first great opera composer was Claudio Monteverdi whose range of expression extended from luminosity to somber horror. (Courtesy Ashmolean Museum, Oxford.)

madrigals reasonable *passagi,* but these kinds of air-castles and chimeras deserve the severest reproof. . . . Behold, for instance, the rough and uncouth passage in the 3rd example . . ."

Of all Monteverdi's contributions to music, his greatest lay in the field of opera, a form that he did not attempt until he was forty years old. His operas include *Orfeo* (1607); *Arianna* (1608); *Il ritorno d'Ulisse in patria* (1630, reworked in 1641); and *L'Incoronazione di Poppae* (1642). Of his *modi operandi,* Monteverdi gives us a clue to his thoughts in a letter written to his librettist concerning a script which was submitted to him:

Further I note that the Winds—that is, the northern and western winds —also have to sing. But how, dear sir, can I ever imitate the speech of winds when they do not speak! And in this way how should I ever be able to move the emotions? Arianna was moving because she was a woman, and Orfeo because he was a man, not a wind. Melodies represent people and not the noises of winds, nor the bleating of sheep . . .

Orfeo, composed to a libretto by Alessandro Striggio, is noteworthy for its great range of expression, extending from luminosity to somber horror; its structure is carefully planned and we find an association of instrumental coloring with dramatic character. In *Orfeo,* Monteverdi creates an emotional intensity and liveliness that far outshadow the earlier attempts of Peri, Caccini and Cavalieri. His effects were particularly heightened by his orchestra, which in *Orfeo* had over thirty pieces, including two *gravicembali* (harpsichords or spinets), two *contrabassi de viola* (double basses), one *arpa doppia* (double string harp), two *violini piccoli alla francese* (treble violins), ten *viole de braccio* (ten arm viols, discant or tenor viols), two *chitarroni,* two *organi de legno* (organs with wooden pipes), three *bassi da gamba* (bass *viole da gamba*), four *cornetti* (old instruments with cup-shaped mouthpieces and finger holes), one *flautina alla vigesma seconda* (flute at the twenty-second, equivalent to three octaves), one *clarino* (trumpet, eight feet long, in C) and three muted trumpets.

The only thing left of *Arianna* (*Ariadne*) is the *Lament* over the loss of Theseus. This is typical of Monteverdi's style and in its day was sung in nearly every household of Italy. In a way, Monteverdi molded a form for laments, which originated in polyphonic settings of the "Lamentations of Jeremiah," continued through the compositions of Galileo and provided ideal opportunities for the musical projection of emotion to many composers. In Monteverdi, we find the tragic mood heightened by means of chromatic intervals, dissonance and wide leaps, as well as abrupt contrasts in harmonic properties of the *basso continuo.* Later Monteverdi arranged the *Lament* as a five-part madrigal wherein his mastery of polyphonic technique is convincingly exhibited.

Many years separate the composition of *Orfeo* from that of *The Coronation of Poppea.* In the nonce composition of opera was activated in Rome and we can be sure that Monteverdi was fully apprised of contemporary developments. In his last opera he deftly combines counterpoint and harmony with almost modern orchestral color. Thus, this great man shows a sane eclecticism, in keeping the old upon which he grafted the new. Monteverdi tells the very dramatic story of Nero and Poppea as have few others. Here too is seen an advance in the independent part-writing for orchestra. At the same time, we may note the shift from a mythological to an historical subject and a facile handling of comic scenes. Pincherle writes, "Indeed, in the air all in half-tints like that of the page: *Sento un certo non so che* ('I feel something but I know not what') it is possible to see more than a similarity of situation with the *Voi che sapete* ('Say, ye who know Love's witching spell') of Mozart's Cherubino with which it is often compared."

Monteverdi was among the first to turn the madrigal into the *cantata da camera* (chamber cantata), which became almost as important for the seventeenth century as the madrigal was for the sixteenth. He wrote a dramatic scene, *Il Combattimento di Tancredi e Clorinda* (*The Combat of Tancred and Clorinda*, 1624), on a poem from Tasso, in which his creation of a *stilo concitato* (agitated style) is remarkable. He also used string *tremolo* to increase the effect of the *concitato*. To the two ways of playing string instruments, he added *pizzicato* (plucking the strings). Whereas in his earlier *Orfeo* the orchestration was thick, in *Il Combattimento* he arrived at a better balance of instrumentation and dramatic action, showing increasing musical discrimination.

Monteverdi was one of the first to declare the independence of instruments and to make use of their individual traits in writing for them separately. He also introduced orchestral effects which mark him one of the important innovators in music. Monteverdi realized that trumpets, trombones and drums were effective in battle, flutes in pastoral, and viols and lutes in love scenes. In this way he strengthened characterization, integrated tonal color with his new harmonies and gave the orchestra an importance which it has claimed ever since.

In 1630 Monteverdi became a monk, in gratitude for having escaped the Black Plague in Venice, where at a San Cassiano theater (the first opera house in Europe) many of his greatest works were presented. He died in Venice and was given a funeral worthy of the achievements of one who translated human feelings and ideas into tone, and paved a road on which music was destined to travel.

ROMAN OPERA

Our discussion of the genesis of Italian opera would not be complete without following the trail leading through the seventeenth century from Florence to Rome to Venice to Naples; for after the first decade of the century Florence lost its primacy in the field and the once-acclaimed recitative of the *camerata* was described as "tedious." Drama through music (*dramma per musica*) was straining to grow.

In the operas of Roman composers we find a distinction being worked out between recitative and *aria* (a formal song). *Arioso,* an intermediate between the two, appeared in the shape of a more melodic recitative or a less fixed song. We also can discern an extension of interest in the visual aspects of performance. Moreover, the first biographical opera, *Il Sant' Alessio,* was composed by Stefano Landi (*c.* 1590-*c.* 1655) in 1632; the first comic opera, *Chi soffre, speri* ("Those Who Suffer, Hope") by Marco Marazzoli (1619-1662) and Virgilio Mazzochi (1597-1646) on a libretto by Giulio Respigliosi, the author of *Il Sant' Alessio* (and later Pope Clement IX), appeared in 1639. Yet another Roman innovation was the concerted *ensemble* ending an act which eventually became a convention of operatic composition.

During the papacy of Urban VIII (1623-1644) opera flourished in Rome, albeit of a more moral and religious persuasion than that of Florence, as appropriate to the center of the Counter-Reformation. In addition to composers already named is the singer Luigi Rossi (1598-1653), whose *Il Palazzo incantato d' Atlante* (*The Enchanted Palace of Atlantis*) was such a success in 1641 that he was invited to produce his *Orfeo* in Paris, thus injecting an Italianate infusion into the French musical scene. After 1650, however, Rome ceased to be the center of opera, owing to the apathy of succeeding popes and to the exaggerated theatricalism of the genre itself which was basically secular.

VENETIAN OPERA

It was in the sparkling Republic of Venice that opera entered the public domain; in fact it was there that the term "opera" was first used, about 1650. The first opera house in Europe opened its doors in the San Cassiano section of the city in 1637, drawing upon a paying clientele which included all classes of society. This had important consequences involving the assertion of popular taste and the need to balance a budget. While the élite continued to enjoy monody operas, the Venetian citizens leaned toward spectacular scenes and clear-cut melodies. In Monteverdi's first public opera, *Il Ritourne d'Ulisse in patria* (*The Return of Ulysses to His Country*), in the revision of 1641 there is a profusion of *arias,* comic scenes, *ensembles* and spectacles with a dearth of choruses and a smaller, more homogeneous orchestra than that of *Orfeo.* In the operas of Venice's first popular opera composer, Francesco Cavalli (1602-1676), we find reduced participation of the orchestra and frequent elimination of the chorus altogether.

In catering to the taste of the public, two elements developed in Venetian opera. One was a tendency toward farfetched and complicated plots, interspersed with all sorts of stratagems—masquerades, elopements and intrigues—and a dependence on fantastic effects—sea monsters, flying horses and double staging. Another was the increasing domination of the musical resources by *arias* and solo singers. The

Fig. 35. The Teatro Fenice, Venice—eighteenth-century engraving. One of the first public opera houses in Europe opened its doors in the San Cassiano section of Venice in 1637. Behind the present view is a gondola entrance.

aria was enlarged, given external form, lyricism (the *bel canto* style) pervaded its contours, the meter was usually triple and the harmony more or less centered about one key. In addition, composers exploited a single emotional strain in each *aria,* sometimes assuring its perception by the audience through use of a motto phrase at the beginning, from which ensuing material was derived. There was, then, little contrast of musical idea within the *aria,* variety being supplied by differing key relationships.

Venetians preferred high voices to low ones and consequently the main operatic roles were written for soprano or tenor. Almost always the hero's part was consigned to a *castrato* (an adult male soprano) whose boylike purity and mature power enchanted his listeners. From Monteverdi's *Poppae* well into the eighteenth century, Italian opera retained *castrati* roles. In his heyday, a *castrato* enjoyed the prestige and remuneration of today's film star and was often a thorn in the side of the serious composer. The cult of the *virtuoso* singer had been reborn.

Among prominent composers of Venetian opera are numbered Cavalli, and Marc' Antonio Cesti (1623-1669) "who brought to Italian music a melodic sense impregnated with a sensual beauty which already foreshadows the art of the eighteenth century," according to Pincherle. Cesti's *Orontea* was a great success in Venice, while his *Il Pomo d'oro*

(*The Golden Apple*) scored a hit in Vienna in 1667. Later Venetian composers included Carlo Pallavicino (1630-1688), Pietro Andrea Ziani (1620-1684), Giovanni Legrenzi (1626-1690) and Carlo Francesco Pollarolo (1653-1722).

NEAPOLITAN OPERA

In 1650, Naples, a pleasure resort for centuries, modestly entered the opera arena and became the main center of activity several decades later, when she outgrew Venetian influences. An early Neapolitan musician was Francesco Provenzale (*c.* 1627-1704) who is survived by two of the eight operas he composed. Neapolitan opera discarded much of the superficiality of Venice, concentrating upon a centralized plot and narrative simplicity, favoring abundance and richness of song materials—so much so that Neapolitan opera was contemptuously described by its detractors as "a bundle of arias." Supporting this vocal emphasis were four municipal conservatories and many private schools which through strenuous training prepared the leading singers of the period, including the arrogant *castrati*. These singers were thoroughly schooled not only in vocal techniques but also in practical music, so that they were able to embellish an *aria* and improvise in a skillful manner.

One of the most important men of his time was Alessandro Scarlatti (1659-1725), from Palermo, who in 1684 was appointed musical director of the Spanish Viceregal Chapel (Naples then being an appendage of Spain). Although astonishingly prolific, writing for the harpsichord and composing *sinfonie,* sonatas, suites, concertos for different instruments, nearly seven hundred cantatas, oratorios and other church music, Scarlatti's fame rests on his operas, of which he wrote more than a hundred. His efforts resulted in a variety of contributions.

He revamped the uninterrupted recitative (*recitativo secco*) which had deteriorated to a hasty and perfunctory patter accompanied by a few chords on the harpsichord. He refined accompanied recitative (*recitativo stromento*), often employing an appropriate solo instrument in obbligato to the melody. His desire to escape monotony and the dreariness of some operas induced him to vary the recitative by a constant interposition of instrumental accompaniments. In his musico-dramatic compositions he came to use the *aria da capo* form almost exclusively. This structure, almost synonymous with what we consider as Baroque *aria,* was an A B A pattern and had been employed by Cavalli. Scarlatti was able to adapt it to a variety of types ranging from the *aria bravura,* or *virtuoso aria* to the *aria cantabile,* a *bel canto aria* which was smooth and ideal for the conveyance of sentimental emotion.

Alec Harman writes that in his operas before 1702, Scarlatti exhibited four noteworthy features:

> The first feature is the 'mixed scene' in which either one or two characters express different emotions. The second is the accompanied recitative which came to be reserved as an introduction to the emotionally climactic arias. The third is the introduction of two comic figures—usually an old woman (sung by a tenor) and an old man (bass)—who often have a scene to themselves at the end of Acts I and II, nearly always finishing with a duet. The fourth, the so-called Italian overture or *sinfonia* that precedes the opera, normally consisting of three movements—quick, slow, quick, and is, like the Neapolitan opera as a whole, fundamentally homophonic in texture.

OPERA IN FRANCE

When Baïf in 1570 secured a patent from Charles IX for his *Academy of Poetry and Music,* he and his colleague, Thibaut de Courville, were in many ways merely formalizing the neo-Florentine philosophies of members of *Les Pléiades,* who sought to unite all the arts into an organic whole, a line of thought that led toward the lyric theater. We have already mentioned Baïf's conception of measured verse set to measured music, a practice that helped shake off the trammels of plainsong. While the Italians developed the recitative, the French were evolving a rich rhythmic song, *musique mesurée à l'antique* (music in ancient meter).

As an extension of the Academy's theories of aesthetics, and in keeping with the rational temper of the French mind, Baïf and his friends created a theatrical formula combining music and dance in a magnificent spectacle which enjoyed great success. This was a *Ballet comique de la Reine,* or Court Ballet, entitled *Circe* (1581), organized by an Italian resident of France, Balthazar de Beaujoyeulx. In it Beaujoyeulx combined features of the native ballets and masquerades with those of the pastorales and Italian interludes, to arrive at a distinctly French product which influenced English *masques* somewhat later. Despite the vicissitudes of a shrinking treasury and political upheavals, France persisted in these costly and elaborate entertainments in which nobles, princes and even kings took part.

So, by way of Italy, France developed her own *ballet comique.* With Marie de' Medici's arrival in France, Italianate pressures were increased and possibly because of Caccini's presence at the French court, the *récits* which originally had been spoken were set in Italian monodic style. Cardinal Mazarin encouraged the production of Italian operas, including Luigi Rossi's *Orfeo* and Cavalli's *Serse,* but they were not entirely to the Parisian taste, except for the dancing and the scenery designed by Giacomo Torelli.

A decade after Cardinal Mazarin had introduced Italian opera to Paris, the Abbé Pierre Perrin wrote a pastorale with music by Robert Cambert (c. 1628-1677), a pupil of Jacques Chambonnières (c. 1602-1672). Perrin and Cambert aimed to build opera for the French on the Italian plan. Presented in 1659, their *pastorale* was described as the first French musical comedy. The music of this work has been lost, but that of *Pomone* (1671), which was an immense success, has been preserved. *Pomone* was performed at the opening festivities of the *Académie royale de musique,* under whose charter Perrin was authorized to produce and perform "operas and other stage presentations with music and verse in the French language similar to those that are given in Italy." Poor Perrin fell victim to diverse adversities and was forced to relinquish his privileges almost immediately to an ambitious and powerful musician of the court of Louis XIV, Jean-Baptiste Lully.

Twenty years older than Alessandro Scarlatti, Lully (1632-1687) was brought to France as a boy from his native Italy by the Duc de Guise, who had spotted him playing a guitar with a group of itinerant musicians in Florence. He spent his formative years in the household of Mlle. Montpensier, cousin to the King. With no background, but of natural wit and intelligence, Lully, desiring to know more about music, set himself to studies which he rapidly assimilated. He watched Italian opera in Paris, disliked it heartily and went his own way. An excellent mimic, dancer, actor and violinist, Lully at twenty joined the entourage of Louis XIV, whom he had known as Dauphin. Through his avidity for music and his abilities as a manager and director, he was able to ingratiate himself with the King and rise to a most commanding position, becoming the virtual czar of music in France. In 1652 he became one of the King's violinists; in 1653 he was appointed Court Composer for instrumental music; in 1661 he was promoted to Superintendent of the King's Music; and in 1672, Director of the *Opéra*. With his *Psyché* (a ballet, 1671) and thirteen subsequent operas, Lully was undoubtedly the most popular musician at court.

His first works were comedy ballets. One was written for the performance of Cavalli's *Serse* given at Versailles at Cardinal Mazarin's invitation. Lully did not turn to opera until it was opportune and then he devoted himself to it with a vengeance, composing an opera a year and taking full charge of its production. He closed a rival opera house. Indeed, opera could not be performed in France without his permission and an accompanying fee. And he managed to secure his powers for his heirs.

Despite the fact that his secretaries filled out his scores, as was customary at the time, Lully's contribution to the art of opera was real and lay largely in his realization of recitative or declamation. Living in the brilliant days of Molière, La Fontaine, Corneille, Boileau, Racine and Quinault (his librettist), Lully attained to something between music and declamation, cutting out the encumbrances that had grown up in the Italian *bel canto*. It was a forward move, even though it may often seem labored and monotonous to us, and rarely intensely emotional. Lully suited rhyme, verse and note to each other. "The recitative became not an artificial bond between airs and choruses, but the main burden of the opera, as it should be; and in this respect he is . . . akin to Monteverdi and Gluck . . . ," comments Romain Rolland. "The imitation of declaimed speech, the imitations of the rhythms of the voice and of things, the imitation of Nature—all these were Lully's realistic sources of inspiration and the instruments with which he worked."

Lully was a man of great vehemence and aspiration, unscrupulous and irascible in the extreme. He allegedly said he would kill anyone who called his music poor; he supervised all concerts and was very careful and discriminating when engaging vocalists and instrumentalists. If a violinist even suggested that he knew more than Lully, the latter would not hesitate, according to his biographer, Lecerf de la Viéville, to break his violin over his back. Then, afterward, Lully would "pay him three times the value of the instrument and take him out to dine." No hint of scandal ever attached itself to the *Opéra,* as Lully ruled with a firm and aloof hand.

Nevertheless, in his adaptation of recitative to the French language and preference, Lully made a solid contribution to the development of French opera. His operatic ideals, chiefly concerned with glorifying the King by allegorical means, were carried to logical conclusions, although his vocal writing was inferior to that of the Italians. His orchestra was richer, however, and his use of dances more extensive than that of his former compatriots. It was he who endowed French opera with a characteristic overture, much admired since he introduced it in the ballet, *Alcidiane,* in 1658. Lully's French overture consisted of a slow, massive opening section followed by a lively polyphonic part, after which another slow section might ensue. In the initial portion are to be found the dotted rhythms which help characterize the style.

OPERA IN ENGLAND

England's earliest forms of drama were miracle-mystery plays and *drolls,* songs of coarse texture, which, because they were enacted by common people, did not influence opera, basically an aristocratic art.

These "poor relations," as E. J. Dent calls them, became obsolete in the sixteenth century. Semiclassical tragicomedies performed by the Children of the Royal Chapels are mentioned during the reign of Henry VIII; *Damon and Pythias* was parodied by Shakespeare in the Pyramus and Thisbe frolic (*A Midsummer Night's Dream*).

"Disguisings" and "mummings" were popular in England in the fourteenth and fifteenth centuries. Processions of masked men, singing carnival songs, very much resembled processions under the Medici in Italy. From Italian entertainments, the court *masque* developed, with its poetry, vocal music, scenery, machinery and costumes, all at the disposal of aristocratic personnel.

Great *masques* were written in the reign of the Stuarts (seventeenth century) by Ben Jonson, Beaumont and Fletcher; Milton's *Comus* and Shakespeare's *Tempest* were set to music in this form. While Italy was experimenting with the music drama, England was entertaining itself with the *masque,* from which some time later her opera evolved. The transition from ballet to opera in France was much easier than in England. Opera, coming later there, did not proceed as rapidly as it did in Italy. England for a glorious period was rightly well content with her brilliant poets.

Early English opera was presaged by Henry Lawes (1596-1662) with his *Comus* based on Milton's *masque,* and *The Siege of Rhodes,* in which a woman appeared on the stage for the first time in England. During the interregnum period music did not flourish. After the Restoration, however, music once more came out of hiding. Matthew Locke (*c.* 1630-1677), a friend of Purcell, wrote *Psyche,* and *The Tempest* and *Macbeth* on Shakespearean texts. John Blow (*c.* 1648-1708) affected by Pelham Humphrey's (1647-1674) teachings after he came back from Italy, wrote the *masque, Venus and Adonis,* and tried many new experiments.

It is to the last of the English composers for the musical stage, Henry Purcell (1658-1695), to whom we should have looked for a developed operatic art had he lived longer. He was one of Captain Cooke's Children of the Royal Chapel Choir and became interested through Humphrey and Locke in dramatic works. His dramas were not operas in the modern sense but they were the nearest to which England arrived before the Italians came. Among other works, Purcell put to music plays of Dryden, Beaumont and Fletcher; he was the first to use Italian musical terms on his scores and one of the first composers, with Byrd, to write compositions of three and four movements for two violins, viola and violoncello—precursors of the string quartet.

Gustav Holst says ". . . the Royal love of the masque and opera

. . . helped to produce one of the few supreme dramatic musicians of the world." The ultimate result of this regal stimulus, albeit it was commissioned by a girls' school, was Purcell's *Dido and Aeneas*. "Written about the year 1689 . . . it is one of the most original expressions of genius in all opera. Mozart remains the greatest prodigy . . . but he was brought up . . . in opera, as well as other music. In England there was not then, nor has there ever been, any tradition of opera. . . . Yet . . . he wrote the only perfect English opera ever written. . . ." Holst proceeds to say that it "is performed as a whole for the sheer pleasure it gives as opera. . . . Probably the English language has never been set so perfectly, either before or since." The English publisher John Playford said of Purcell, "He had a peculiar genius to express the energy of English words." Purcell excelled in every form in which he wrote. His sacred music, *masques* and opera are works of genius.

OPERA IN GERMANY

Germany too had her background of opera in the miracle plays. These were given outside the churches on saints' days when the Passion songs were sung in Latin. Later, German was used in the play itself while Latin was used in the songs. By 1322 *Das Spiel von den Zehn Jungfrauen* (*The Play of the Ten Maidens*) was written entirely in the vernacular. Plays like this in Worms, Nuremberg and Augsburg soon became vulgar and increasingly obscene, until in the sixteenth century Hans Sachs and Jakob Ayer gained control of the output, introducing better music and more fitting words, and so inaugurated the German musical stage.

The word *Singspiel* for three hundred years designated a dramatic-musical representation given by the people. But the first genuine *Singspiel* was presented as a strong reaction against the people's plays by Jesuit students. The Jesuit plays were in Latin, with musical interludes provided with German words, and were the only thing in Germany that can parallel the seeds of opera in other countries. For a short time Germany followed Italian conventions in opera. A *Daphne* (1627), with words by Martin Opitz and music by Heinrich Schütz, was obviously fundamentally Italian in inspiration.

In 1644 the first purely German *Singspiel* appeared in *Seelewig* (*Eternal Soul*), a sacred *Freudenspiel* (comedy) by Sigmund Gottlieb Staden (1607-1655) for private performance and written for three trebles (violins), three flutes, three reeds and large horn, the bass being taken throughout by a theorbo. No two voices were heard at the same time and the instruments had short symphonies to themselves. The early German *Singspiel* flourished in Hamburg until 1678, when German opera *per se* began, culminating in the work of Reinhard Keiser (1674-1739). Thus we see that Germany for the most part seems to have used her own resources (more than France and far more than England), and moved more directly to opera than either of the others.

PENETRATION OF ITALIAN OPERA

Elsewhere in Europe Italian opera captured the stages, although in seventeenth-century Spain the *zarzuela* was popular. This was a native form, combining Spanish songs, dances and speech, usually in one act, rather informal and often insignificant. The most notable of *zarzuela* composers was Juan Hidalgo (*c.* 1600-1685) who worked from plays by Calderon. In Teutonic countries it is ironic that the only places for performances of German *Singspiel* were the Italian opera houses, Vienna's, built in 1651 and Dresden's, in 1667. Italian operas were first performed in Salzburg in 1618, Vienna in 1626 and Prague in 1627. Leading Italian composers were attached to the Viennese court, including Antonio Bertali (1605-1669) and Antonio Draghi (1635-1700). Neapolitan opera penetrated as far north as St. Petersburg, Russia, where a permanent opera house was established in 1734, again served by distinguished Italian composers such as Baldassare Galuppi (1706-1785), immortalized in Robert Browning's poem.

*   *   *   *   *

Opera began in the strivings of the *camerata* and in the flowering of Monteverdi's mastery. It progressed, through works of Cavalli and the Venetian school, to Alessandro Scarlatti, who bridged antiquarian and Classic opera. We shall return to its further development in a subsequent chapter. Meanwhile it is time to investigate the evolution of musical instruments and their repertoire—a significant aspect of Baroque music.

SUGGESTIONS FOR FURTHER READING

Arnold, Denis, *Monteverdi*. New York, Farrar Straus Cudahy, 1963.
Arnold, F. T., *The Art of Accompaniment from a Thorough-Bass*. London, Holland, 1961.
Bukofzer, Manfred F., *Music in the Baroque Era*. New York, Norton, 1947.
Cannon, Beekman, *Johann Mattheson*. New Haven, Yale University Press, 1947.
Davison, Archibald T., and Apel, Willi, *Historical Anthology of Music,* vol. II. Cambridge, Harvard University Press, 1950.
Dent, Edward J., *Alessandro Scarlatti*. London, Arnold, 1905.
———— *Foundations of English Opera: A Study of Music Drama in England during the 17th Century*. Cambridge, Cambridge University Press, 1928.
———— *Opera.** Baltimore, Penguin, 1965.
Fokine, Michael, *Book of the Dance*. New York, Putnam, 1934.

* Available in paperback edition.

Grout, Donald J., *A Short History of Opera*. New York, Columbia University Press, 1947.

Henderson, W. J., *Some Forerunners of Italian Opera*. New York, Holt, 1941.

Holland, A. K., *Henry Purcell: The End of a Musical Tradition*.* London, Penguin, 1948.

Loewenberg, Alfred, *Annals of Opera*. Cambridge, Heffner, 1955.

Parrish, Carl, *A Treasury of Early Music*.* New York, Norton, 1958.

Parrish, Carl, and Ohl, John F., *Masterpieces of Music before 1750*. New York, Norton, 1951.

Robinson, Michael L., *Opera before Mozart*.* London, Hutchinson, 1966.

Romain Rolland's Essays on Music.* New York, Dover, 1959.

Sachs, Curt, *World History of the Dance*.* New York, Norton, 1937.

Schrade, Leo, *Monteverdi, Creator of Modern Music*. New York, Norton, 1950.

Starr, William J., and Devine, George F., *Music Scores—Omnibus*,* Part 2. Englewood Cliffs, Prentice-Hall, 1964.

Strunk, Oliver, ed., *Source Readings in Music History*.* New York, Norton, 1950.

Westrup, J. A., *Purcell*. New York, Farrar Straus, 1960.

Worsthorne, S. T., *Venetian Opera*. Oxford, Oxford University Press, 1954.

A Sampler of Supplementary Recordings

Collections

Masterpieces of Music before 1750	Haydn 9038/40
Treasury of Early Music	Haydn 9100/3
2000 Years of Music	Folkways 3700
Ten Centuries of Music	DGG KL-52/61
Opera and Church Music	Victor LM-6030
Music of the Pre-Baroque	Lyric 109

Music of Individual Composers

Arne, Thomas, *Comus* (A Masque)

Carissimi, Giacomo, *Jepthe*

Cavalli, Pier Francesco, *Giudizio universale* (An Oratorio)

Charpentier, Marc-Antoine, *Médée*

Izaak, Heinrich, *Music for the Court of Lorenzo the Magnificent*

Locke, Matthew, *Music of Matthew Locke*

Lotti, Antonio, *Crucifixus*

Lully, Jean-Baptiste, *Operatic Arias*

Monteverdi, Claudio, *Combat of Tancredi and Clorinda*
        Incoronazione d'Poppea
        Orfeo

Scarlatti, Alessandro, *San Filippo Neri*
        Scipione nelle Spagne
        Arias
        Su le Sponde del Tebro

Stradella, Alessandro, *S. Giovanni Battista*

Opportunities for Study in Depth

1. Make a study of the contributions made to the art of orchestration by early opera composers. How were instruments utilized to enlarge the expression of emotional values? Of what significance was this?

2. After supplementary reading, prepare a report on the part played by famous English men of letters in the development of the *masque* and other English dramatic works. Cite examples and quote excerpts.

3. Compare several settings of operas based upon the myth of Orpheus and Euridice, noting how the story line was organized and how each composer arranged the musical structure. Make a schematic diagram of the findings.

4. Investigate the role of Italian opera composers in the development or lack of development of dramatic music in seventeenth-century northern Europe. Cite any parallels to this situation that are relevant.

5. Prepare a demonstration of scenic stage sets designed by well known artists for opera productions, utilizing whatever visual aids are available. Also reproduce examples of seventeenth-century stage machinery. Present this information to the class.

6. Discuss the hypothesis that Venetian interest in emotionalism through color, as seen in paintings of Titian and Veronese, is present, analogously, in works of the Venetian school of opera composers.

7. How did the oratorio and *cantata da chiesa* support the aims of the seventeenth-century Counter-Reformation in Italy? Were these musical forms important factors in reaffirming the faith of Roman Catholics in Europe?

8. Act as resource person in a symposium concerning the concept of public opera in the context of seventeenth-century Venice, including political, economic and social aspects.

VOCABULARY ENRICHMENT

devozione	*aria*
sacre rappresentazione	*arioso*
commedia dell'arte	*bel canto*
dramma pastorale	*castrato*
libretto	*recitativo secco*
camerata	Italian overture
stilo rappresentativo	*ballets de cour* or Court Ballet
basso continuo	French overture
chords	*masque*
figured bass	*Singspiel*
oratorio	*zarzuela*
cantata da chiesa	allegory
cantata da camera	*aria da capo*
dramma per musica	*stile concitato*

PART IV

Music for Instruments

Chapter 9.

THE DEVELOPMENT OF MODERN INSTRUMENTS

> Here you come with your old music, and
>   here's all the good it brings.
> What, they lived once thus at Venice where
>   the merchants were the kings,
> Where St. Mark's is, where the Doges used to
>   wed the sea with rings?
>
> What? Those lesser thirds, so plaintive,
>   sixths diminished, sigh on sigh,
> Told them something? Those suspensions,
>   those solutions—'Must we die?'
> Those commiserating sevenths—'Life might
>   last! we can but try!'
>
> So, an octave struck the answer. Oh, they
>   praise you, I dare say!
> 'Brave Galuppi! that was music! good alike
>   at grave and gay!
> I can always leave off talking when I hear a
>   master play!'
>
> *A Toccata of Galuppi's*—Robert Browning

In his pensive and rather melancholy lyric, Browning evokes the soulless gaiety of bygone Venice in the time when Galuppi "sat and played Toccatas, stately at the clavichord." An independent instrumental music had indeed become a reality by the middle of the seventeenth century. This fact, of course, presupposed the existence of mechanisms capable of projecting the musical thinking of "serious" composers. While the human voice has remained a constant in music through the ages, and is matchless in many respects, such is not the case with other instruments.

As we have seen, both primitive and ancient Oriental cultures had evolved a variety of instruments, often the objects of superstitious and religious awe, valued more for their symbolic qualities than for aesthetic ones. The importance of instruments as adjuncts of vocal music is obvious through the frequent references in ancient Greek and Roman literature. A setback to the development of instruments occurred during the dark early Middle Ages due to the prohibition of their use in

Christian Church ritual. That instruments coexisted at this time in secular life, however crude and obscure, is known to us through the invectives hurled against them by the Church Fathers. Only with the gradual secularization of European life and with certain technicological advances could instruments be improved and take their rightful places in the musical scene. This was a long time coming, but not, as we have noted, without precedents. Untidily and in straggling order they came singly and in groups to take their seats at the musical table.

SIXTEENTH- AND SEVENTEENTH-CENTURY INSTRUMENTS

It is difficult to allocate special instruments to either the sixteenth or the seventeenth century because many appear in both periods. During the sixteenth century besides the keyboard instruments, harpsichord, clavichord and organ, there were the lute, the theorbo and the arch lute; viols (tenor and bass), hackbrett or dulcimer, *psaltery* or zither harp and rebec; wind instruments included recorder, hautboy (oboe), cromorne, trumpet, clarion, trombone, schalmey and flute. In addition, there were a number of percussives—drums and others. Agricola's *Musica instrumentalis deudsch* (1529) and Praetorius' *Syntagma musicum* (1615-1620) give excellent accounts of contemporary instruments. The lute was most popular but in the seventeenth century its vogue waned with the advent of the violin. Lutes remained in use, nevertheless, up to the eighteenth century.

The early seventeenth century favored the harp, lyre, *psaltery,* dulcimer, mandolin, rebec, a guitar akin to the Russian *balalaika,* the Italian guitar, looking like the modern instrument and the *cittern* or English guitar, with an almost spherical body and a short neck. The wind instruments of this century approximated those of the sixteenth, with a few refinements such as the *Schalmei* (oboe, German; schalmey, English), which became *chalumeau* (from *calamus,* a reed), the precursor of the clarinet.

The popularity of accompanied monody, with its corollary, *basso continuo,* greatly accelerated the evolution of instruments suited to performing it, thereby exercising a selective function upon the multiplicity available in Renaissance reserves. On the one hand, some instruments were discarded altogether, because of their inability to encompass a wide range of tone with dynamic flexibility. The wind-cap shawms (*Rauschpfeife*) of Germany, dull and colorless, made a permanent exit. *Pommers, sorduns* and *rankets* all died out before the end of the seventeenth century. The *cromorne,* especially popular in France, was radically altered. Instruments such as the mandolin, guitar and bagpipe were relegated gradually to a limited position of folk or nationalistic

Fig. 36. "Mary, Queen of Heaven"—Master of the St. Lucy Legend. The variety of musical instruments was gradually expanding as we notice in this painting of Mary surrounded by fifteen singers and thirteen instrumentalists holding harps, recorders, soprano shawms, lutes, an alto shawm, a dulcimer, a vielle, a trumpet and a portative organ, performing *Ave regina celorum*. (Courtesy National Gallery of Art, Washington, D.C., Samuel H. Kress Collection.)

significance. The hurdy-gurdy descended to the hands of an organ grinder with his mendicant monkey.

On the other hand, the *recorder* (vertical flute), relatively minor during preceding centuries, was elevated to a place of prominence in scores of Scarlatti, Handel and Bach and was finally superseded in the eighteenth century by its transverse relative. Keyboard instruments— the organ in ecclesiastical music and the harpsichord in secular— assumed a new level of importance due them for their role in realizing the figured bass. Members of the violin family were grouped together to comprise the *corpus* of early orchestras. The need for volume, nuance and facility all played a part in determining which instruments should survive and which should be born.

Keyboard Instruments

A most prominent class of instruments that rose to importance in the seventeenth and eighteenth centuries was that with keyboards, a category which can be further subdivided into three groups: spinet, virginals and harpsichord; clavichord and pianoforte; and finally, apart from the stringed varieties, the organ.

The stringed keyboard's remote ancestors were the *psaltery,* dulcimer and monochord. The monochord, first used by Pythagoras (*c.* 550 B.C.), served in the Middle Ages to give pitch. "It was tuned with a movable bridge or fret pushed back and forth under the strings and fingers. First it was stretched with weights hung at one end. It was a simple matter to add strings to produce more tones, later tuning pins were added and finally a keyboard," the latter an accomplishment never achieved by Oriental civilizations. We first hear of stringed keyboard instruments in Jean de Muris' *Musica speculativa* (1323), in which several are described. The turn from mazal polyphony to a more vertical conception of music, occurring in the fourteenth century, apparently inspired the creation of keyboards, with music notated in tablature form.

Spinets, virginals and harpsichords, all probably developed from the psaltery, have in common **jack action,** wherein the strings are plucked by a *plectrum* of quill or leather, motivated by keys. Within the resonance box of a typical harpsichord are tuning pins with three sets of strings, two tuned in unison, one an octave higher ("four foot" pitch). Beyond this point are placed the jacks, one for each string. Extending back from the keyboard the strings pass over a soundboard and several bridges which aid amplification. At the end of each key is found a wooden jack, five to eight inches high into which a piece of hardwood, called a "tongue," is inserted and held by a pivot pin. Into the upper part of the tongue is placed the *plectrum,* and attached to the jack is a piece of felt which acts as a *damper.* Raymond Russell explains:

> When the key is depressed, the jack rises, and the plectrum plucks the string as it forces its way past on its upward journey. When the key is released, the jack falls back, the plectrum comes in contact with the string again, and this pressure causes the tongue to turn back on its pivot so that the plectrum can pass the string without plucking it again. The jack arrives back at its position of rest, the hog's bristle spring returns the tongue to the upright position, the plectrum is once

more beneath the string in readiness to attack it again, and finally the damper silences the vibrations on coming once more into contact with the string.

A large harpsichord would have two keyboards or *manuals,* each five octaves in length, and four stop levers, which could move the rows of jacks laterally causing variation in tone when the keys are depressed. Stops might include a lute-register, a harp-tone and the four-foot octave elevation. In addition, a "machine" and "Venetian swell," both operated by foot pedals, were added to later models, striving to increase the expressiveness of the instrument and making it competitive with the newly-invented *fortepiano* and the organ.

Two other features are worthy of mention. One is the *coupler* with which the upper manual eight-foot jacks are engaged with those of the lower manual, allowing the lower keyboard to play the keys and stops of the upper. The other concerns the "short octave" of the bass, which although continuing downward in visual regularity, actually skips several tones, in the interest of economy, being tuned to those most commonly used. As music became more chromatic, it was necessary to add the omitted accidentals. This was done in a fashion designed to cause as little confusion as possible to the standard harpsichord technique; each short key was divided into a front and a back half, thus allowing for two more notes without altering the overall design of the instrument.

The harpsichord, known variously as *clavicembalo, clavecin, Clavier, cembalo, gravicembalo* and *arpsicordo,* resembled a slender grand piano; its body suggested the contours of a harp. It was a stationary instrument, capable of considerable sound and contrast, albeit no dynamic nuances such as *crescendo* and *decrescendo.* Eighteenth-century musicians regarded it as the backbone of the orchestra. Carl Philipp Emanuel Bach writes in his *Essay on the True Art of Playing Keyboard Instruments* (1753):

> When the harpsichord quite rightly stands surrounded by all the participating musicians, its tone can be distinctly heard by everyone . . . Already entrusted with leadership by our ancestors, the keyboard instrument is thus in the best position to assist, not only the basses, but the entire ensemble as well in maintaining an even measure.

The spinet and virginals (the plural referring to the portable instrument with its stand, in the sense we speak of a "pair of scissors") were smaller, simpler instruments utilizing the jack action principle. The former was a "leg-of-mutton" in shape, the latter oblong. Each had a single keyboard and a single string for each key, with no assisting mechanical devices. Like the harpsichord, they were constructed of cypress wood and often placed into ornately painted and inlaid outer cases. Schools of instrument makers issued from Italy, the Low Countries (*i.e.,* Antwerp—Hans Ruckers (*c.* 1550-*c.* 1620)), England (Jacob Kirckman, 1710-1792) and Germany (*i.e.,* Hamburg—the Hasses —and Johann Silbermann (1727-1799) of Strasbourg). In an inventory of the great Bach's possessions at the time of his death, we find listed five harpsichords, one spinet and a lute-harpsichord, together with sundry stringed instruments.

The clavichord, derived from the monochord by way of a *polychord* (many strings) with stopping tangents, is an older instrument than the harpsichord. By the fifteenth century it had developed into an instrument of ten strings with a chromatic keyboard and was used as a practice and teaching supplement, except in Germany, where its peculiar tone and capabilities were appreciated well into the nineteenth-century. C. F. D. Schubart (1739-1791) comments in his *Ideen zu einer Aesthetik der Tonkunst* (*Ideas for an Aesthetic of Musical Art*):

> Clavichord, instrument of solitude, of melancholy, of unexpressible sweetness . . . He who does not like noise, outbursts, and tumult, he whose heart seeks tender effusiveness will turn away from the harpsichord and the fortepiano and will choose a clavichord . . .

The mechanism of a clavichord is based on the principle of **tangent action,** wherein the key drives a metal tangent against a wire string and is held there. The tone is dependent on the place that the tangent strikes the string. In earlier models called *gebunden* (fretted), one string was used by several keys. In post-1750 instruments an attempt was made to give each key its independent string; these were called *bundfrei* (unfretted). In either model, in sound boxes ranging in dimension from three feet by one to five feet by two, the strings were stretched horizontally from right to left in an oblong case. **Dampers** consisted of strips of cloth woven around the strings, which deadened the vibrations of that part of the string away from the tangent. A single manual was used.

The effect of the clavichord's tone made it an ideal instrument for the *style galant* or "gallant style" of the Rococo, characterized by elegance and sentimentality. Its loudest tone was soft but clear, and endowed with minute dynamic shadings. In addition, the instrument was capable of a violin-like *vibrato,* called *Bebung.* This was obtained by use of a varying pressure on the depressed key, resulting in a changing tension of the string, giving the tone a soulful character. The far-away quality lent the clavichord an expressiveness that made it especially adaptable to intimate performance. C. P. E. Bach's clavichord works, published between 1779 and 1787, are probably the most idiomatic compositions written for the instrument.

During the latter half of the eighteenth century, interest increasingly centered about the manufacture of a stronger, more responsive instrument. A combination of the best points of harpsichord and clavichord, together with more dynamic variety, greater volume of tone and more resistance, was sought. Many men worked toward this end. Pantaleone Hebenstreit's dulcimer with a double system of strings, played with hammers, produced a louder tone but lacked sweetness. After hearing it, Christoph Gottlieb Schröter (1699-1782), a German musician, decided that in order for the harpsichord to meet the new demands, it required hammer action, which, according to his own assertion, he invented in 1721.

Fig. 37. Piano forte, 1720—maker: Bartolommeo Cristofori. This "harpsichord with soft and loud" replaced quills with striking hammers, allowing a flexibility of dynamics previously unknown to keyboard instruments. (Courtesy The Metropolitan Museum of Art, The Crosby Brown Collection of Musical Instruments, 1889.)

Twelve years earlier, however, in 1709, Bartolommeo Cristofori (1665-1731), a Florentine, had constructed what he called a *gravi-*

cembalo col piano e forte, known as *fortepiano* until about 1800, when it became **pianoforte.** Cristofori's instrument differed from both the harpsichord and the clavichord in that the direct route from finger to key to string was interrupted by the action of a hammer. Through constant experimentation Cristofori had worked out the essentials of modern piano action by 1726, although he failed to interest anyone very much at the time.

Others continued to experiment, refining and reinforcing the resources of the piano. A Frenchman, Marius, created a harpsichord with hammers (*clavecin à mallets*). Silbermann, who built Frederick the Great's instruments, fashioned a type resembling our grand piano. In 1760 Christian Friederici invented a square piano, which Sébastian Érard was manufacturing in Paris in 1777. It is claimed that John Bach's demands for a pianoforte stimulated production in London where Burkhardt Tschudi and his Scottish partner, James Broadwood, established a firm which is still in operation. In 1776 Johann Zumpe, a German in Tschudi's employ, exhibited one of the first small pianos, "the shape and size of the virginal," according to Dr. Burney. The light and pleasing "Viennese" action praised by Mozart was the result of work done by Johann Andreas Stein (1728-1792) in Augsburg. Of Stein's instrument, Mozart wrote in 1777: "I can do with the keys what I like; the tone is always equal; it does not tinkle disagreeably; it has neither the fault of being too loud nor too soft, nor does it fail entirely."

Although Mozart used both harpsichord and pianoforte, he did much to popularize the latter instrument. Beethoven relied solely on the piano. Stein's daughter, Frau Streicher, inherited her father's business and moved to Vienna, where she was a close friend of Beethoven, supplying him with pianos, watching his health and helping him in his domestic arrangements. In 1818, Tschudi's partner, then the head of James Broadwood & Sons, sent Beethoven a piano equipped with both damper and soft pedals, by means of which the tones could be further varied. (A third pedal, the *sostenuto* or *pedale de prolongement,* was invented by Montal in 1862.)

America comes into the history of the pianoforte in 1800 when John I. Hawkins patented an upright piano; Alpheus Babcock patented an iron frame in a single cast in 1825; and Jonas Chickering of Boston, the first American manufacturer, invented the complete iron frame for the concert grand, which could stand a strain of thirty tons. In the middle of the nineteenth century the firm of Steinway & Sons was founded by Heinrich Englehard Steinweg, formerly of Hamburg.

During the nineteenth century the pianoforte rudely unseated its previous rival, the harpsichord, which often was unceremoniously demoted to serve as a desk or linen chest, or to gather dust as a museum exhibit. The pianoforte had definite advantages over the earlier instrument; it was easier to construct, simpler and surer to tune, more durable and cheaper. It also provided the Romantic composers, who took it to their bosoms and whose demands resulted in its developmental improvements, with an appropriately powerful instrument in an era of bigness and of *Sturm und Drang*. Even as it was struggling to gain a foothold on the musical scene, however, that "king of instruments," as de Machault had called it, was entering its Golden Age.

Until the fourteenth century, the organ, one of the most important of all instruments, had been used only as a guide for singers of plainsong. Through much experimenting from the time of the ancients, its increasing richness, power, sonority and flexibility infused composers with the desire to write for it. Before this time it had had no dynamic elasticity, but in the fourteenth century, and particularly the fifteenth, the organ proclaimed itself a solo instrument. By the sixteenth century organ-playing had made rapid progress, and many cathedrals in the Netherlands, France, Spain, England and Italy were known by the great organists associated with them. Furthermore, it was Germany's composers and players of the organ (and *Klavier*) that gave the nation impetus and set her on the way to becoming the leading musical force in the eighteenth and nineteenth centuries.

We have already mentioned the existence and development of organs through early Christian times in Europe, stemming from the Roman *hydraulus* described by Vitruvius, with its balanced keyboard and four stops. From banishment to the Middle East the practice of organ building returned to Europe in the eighteenth century, although in a crude and primitive form. Keys replaced the clumsy sliders in the thirteenth century. By the end of the next century some organs had solo stops, double manuals and a pedal keyboard as well. During the 1400's the organ embraced the "short octave," previously mentioned, in response to a compositional trend downwards which required deeper bass tones. The pedals became increasingly important and a dichotomy appeared between Italian and North European instruments, the former leaning toward mixtures while the latter preferred contrasting solo stops and multiple manuals. In 1491 the earliest *tremulant,* an interesting device to produce an emotional *vibrato* effect, was added to an organ in Alsace. "Reed" pipes were also an innovation of the time. In the eighteenth century, tuning was adjusted to tempered pitch and the swell pedal was added afterwards in an effort to increase the dynamic flexibility of the instrument.

The "king of instruments" is a complicated machine consisting of (1) the pipe mechanisms or *stops,* (2) the air devices and (3) the action. For each desired tone there must be at least one pipe; a row of pipes with the same *timbre* is called a "register" or "rank," and is controlled by one stop. As every organ has at least several registers, each producing a separate tone color, there is a rich variety of sound available. Pipes are constructed in several ways: there are *labial* pipes whose tone is the result of a vibrating column of air; there are also *reed* pipes, in which a free-moving tongue of metal produces the tone which the air within the pipe amplifies. Registers are designated by foot lengths, including eight-foot, sixteen-foot (one octave lower) and thirty-two foot (two octaves lower). A four-foot rank is an octave higher, while a two-foot register emits a tone two octaves higher than the eight-foot. By combining several ranks, overtones are emphasized.

The action mechanism, controlled from the keyboard, permits a performer to operate the air devices, which may be mechanical, pneumatic or electro-pneumatic. When a key is depressed, certain vents are opened, allowing air to enter the desired pipes. Various combinations of on and off are controlled by the organist by means of pulling or pushing stop pistons. A *coupler* enables the performer to combine several manuals or manuals to pedals. The larger the number of registers, the more keyboards there are likely to be. Modern theatre organs demonstrate the gigantic proportions to which this instrument may rise. For playing the bass line a pedal keyboard is included, which is operated by both feet.

There is no such instrument as the Baroque organ. In fact, all pipe organs tend to be built to individual specifications, although American organ builders have evolved a successful all-purpose instrument. There are, however, many kinds of Baroque organs united by some common characteristics. Between 1650 and 1750 the organ had reached a peak of popularity and artistic prominence. Two schools of organ building existed at this time: that of the French was highly stereotyped and full of finesse; the German and Dutch group, on the other hand, produced more sturdy and varied instruments, those capable of inspiring Buxtehude and Bach.

Baroque organ music relied for its expressiveness on strong contrasts rather than dainty shadings and a suitable instrument was devised to furnish a range of divergent effects. Choruses of numerous ranks of pipes, colored homogeneously by a basic *diapason timbre,* offered unusual possibilities of blending. Mixture stops, too, played an essential role. In these many pipes are devoted to each tone, enhancing and defining the bass and further empowering the treble with a richness of overtones. Mixtures had the peculiarity of producing different types of sound at different spots of the gamut and were not supposed to be used in musical figurations covering a wide compass. Lastly, a Baroque organ was supplied with a "bite" or attack, comparable to wind tonguing or string bowing, which articulated each tone cleanly. Each manual and the pedal keyboard was voiced with a complete chorus. Cecil Clutton writes, "A good Baroque chorus is bright, clear, and ringing, and is fairly powerful, though neither so loud that it rapidly palls nor so bright that it screams."

In performing such works as trio sonatas (Bach wrote six), in which each part is played on a different keyboard, the Baroque organist employed a combination of stops. Instead of individual solo stops, he relied upon an accretion of neutral tones at various pitches. In addition, he had at his disposal *mutation stops,* sounding at intervals of a twelfth, fifteenth, seventeenth, nineteenth or twenty-second above the unison. Clutton comments, ". . . By combining them in different ways, a number of highly colourful, quasi-synthetic effects were achieved." Combining was facilitated by the fact that all stops were approximately equal in power and thus could be discriminately used without endangering the balance of sound.

During the nineteenth century the organ met with mixed fortunes. It grew and grew in size, a case of musical *elephantiasis,* which attracted such eminent composers as Mendelssohn, Liszt, Franck and Reger to add to the literature in a flamboyant Romantic style. Its dominance as a solo instrument gradually declined, however, and the organ, as today, became the backbone support of sacred musical observances, and, in a miniature version, a popular instrument for the parlor.

BOWED STRING INSTRUMENTS

Writing about the ancestry of the violin creates the same feeling as one might have in a court of law where everything one says may be held against you. Authorities write glibly about the subject and then amiably contradict their own statements. Suffice it to say that the direct ancestry is confused and lies among many probable progenitors, including the rebec, *lira da braccio* and viol. Instruments of the violin family made their appearance in Europe during the sixteenth century, and were initially associated with the performance of dance music. As interest in instrumental music increased, the violin and its relatives—the viola, violoncello and double bass—gradually assumed the aristocratic position they now hold.

Viol is a generic English name for the bowed instruments that succeeded the medieval (and far from "respectable") fiddle, and preceded, as far as literature is concerned, if not in actual fact, the violin family. The viol appeared in the fifteenth century and passed out of general use in the eighteenth. It differed from instruments of the violin family in several significant ways, although superficially it resembles them and certainly shares the same remote common ancestry. In the beginning, bowed instruments were built in human voice ranges and were called treble or discant viol (with the range of a modern viola), tenor (an octave below the violin), bass (with the range of a 'cello) and double bass, each of different size and power. The six or seven strings were tuned like a lute, the fingerboard was fretted, the short and rigid bow was held palm up and, most distinctively, the instrument was positioned either vertically upon the knee or between the legs—hence the designation, *da gamba*. England was especially fond of its "Chest of Viols," residents in every gentleman's home. Samuel Pepys, the diarist, speaks of his "Chest," from which host and guests would extract instruments with which to regale the "companie."

Among the loveliest of the old viols was the *viola d'amore* (literally, viol of love), a tenor instrument with two sets of strings: one which was bowed and the other, lying beneath, which set up sympathetic vibrations that enriched the silvery *timbre*. The tuning was variable, the usual practice being to tune in the key of the work to be performed. The *viola bastarda,* a bass viol from which evolved the *baryton,* for which Haydn wrote so many compositions, was another of the many varieties found in the voluminous annals of the bowed instrument families. In Bach's scores, we find the *viola pomposa,* which Sachs defines as a viola with "the e^2 of the violin as a fifth string."

The *viole da braccio* (arm viols) provided a point of departure for our modern string family, although even the early violins were held against the breast and later against the collarbone, instead of under the chin. While France and Poland have claimed priority for the violin, the honors clearly belong to Italy, albeit one of the first violin makers was Gaspar Tieffenbrucker (*c.* 1514-1571), a Bavarian trained in Italy and naturalized in France. From Brescia came Gasparo Bertolotti da Salò (*c.* 1542-1609) and his pupil, Giovanni Paolo Maggini (1580-*c.* 1630). Da Salò's violins were characterized by rugged strength and are somewhat plump and large. Maggini improved on his master's work, enhancing the functional and aesthetic varnishing with elaborate ornamentation on the back.

From Cremona came the great families of Amati, Stradivari and Guarneri, whose workshops were side by side. From about 1560 to 1760 their passion was to create instruments of beauty in both appearance and tonal perfection, a feat never superseded. The first of the Amati dynasty was Andrea, a sixteenth-century craftsman whose birth and death dates are uncertain, although several of his violins are dated.

The greatest of the Amatis was his grandson, Niccolò (1596-1684), the teacher of Antonio Stradivari (*c.* 1644-1737) and Andrea Guarneri (*c.* 1625-1698), in whose family was the outstanding Giuseppi Bartolomeo or Giuseppi del Gesù (1698-1744).

Violin makers also produced other stringed instruments. The earliest known violas, in varying body lengths, were made by Andrea Amati and Gasparo da Salò, while one of the first violoncellos was the work of Andrea Amati (1572). Carlo Bergonzi (*c.* 1683-1747) constructed very successful 'cellos, constantly experimenting to achieve a finer tone and power, and benefiting from the tutelage of Stradivari, his mentor.

Outside Italy, the most prominent violin maker was Jacob Stainer (1621-1683), who built important instruments in the tranquil confines of the Tyrol, while the Thirty Years' War raged elsewhere. Among English artisans we find Benjamin Banks of Salisbury (1727-1795). In France, as in England, all violin makers imitated the Italians. Included in their number were Nicolas Lupot (1758-1824) and J. B. Vuillaume (1798-1875). But to France we owe the perfection of the modern bow. François Tourte (1747-1835) has been called the Stradivari of bow makers, and it was he who perfected the mechanism regulating the tension of the hairs.

Although Stradivari standardized the body pattern of the violin and gave its design an elegance which remains a model, his was not the last word. New musical tastes and new requirements necessitated modifications, and most of the precious extant Amati, Stradivari and Guarneri instruments have been altered since their manufacture. Over the years since 1700 the bass bar and the soundpost have been lengthened and thickened, respectively. The neck and fingerboard has been elongated and tilted. The former gut strings have been replaced by wire and overwrapped nylon. A chin rest has been added and the bridge raised. Whatever the value of these changes, it should be noted that the tone quality we hear today differs considerably from that of the originals.

Composers from Gabrieli through Boulez have exploited the flexibility of bowed string instruments, which can produce many effects with which we ought to be familiar. Members of the violin family excel in playing a sustained *legato* (as does the organ). In the Baroque period, *vibrato,* a fluctuating quality achieved through a performer's left-hand finger vacillating back and forth ever so slightly from the required position on the fingerboard, became popular. We have already mentioned that Monteverdi used the techniques of *pizzicato,* plucking rather than bowing a string, and *tremolo,* a rapid repetition of a single tone resulting from short up and down bow movements, to underline expressive effects. The *trill,* an alternation of contiguous tones, gives a birdsong effect. Use of a *mute,* a three-pronged clamp slipped over the bridge, muffles string tone. By lightly stopping the string at certain pre-defined points, it is possible to produce *harmonics,* high, clear, pure overtones of a glacial quality. *Double or multiple stopping* involves bowing two or more strings. Among the many other possibilities of string variety are *glissando,* in which a player slides along the fingerboard; *spiccato,* in which the bow is bounced on the string; and *col legno,* where the wood of the bow is used.

WOODWIND INSTRUMENTS

Woodwind instruments have had a rather harum-scarum history, achieving their modern forms fairly late. The term, woodwind family, is justified only by tradition, as most of the instruments are no longer wooden, nor do they show much family resemblance either in their very individual *timbres* or their means of sound production, which involve three different processes. From an enormous variety of pipes and horns, four instruments have come to form the standard woodwind group—the flute, the oboe, the clarinet and the bassoon. These are roughly equivalent to human voice ranges of coloratura soprano, soprano, soprano-alto and tenor-bass.

Historically, the *oboe* was the first instrument to appear in more or less modern guise, an invention (*c.* 1660) of Jean Hotteterre and Michel Philidor, members of the *Grande écurie du roi* of Louis XIV (for whom Lully acted as Superintendent of Music). Unlike the shawm, the oboe was made in three joints, with smaller bore, smaller bell and smaller fingerholes, as well as a narrower and longer double-reed mouthpiece. From the skill lavished on a favorite French bagpipe, the *musette,* came the craftsmanship necessary to create the new instrument. In its early years the "new" French oboe acquired popularity both as the principal upper woodwind orchestral instrument and as a solo vehicle for *virtuosos.* This popularity accounts for the large oboe concerto literature compiled in the century following its inception. Louis' *Douze grands hautbois du roi* ("Dozen Eminent Oboists of the King") in which the bass was provided by two bassoonists, was the prototype of a Baroque military band.

The *bassoon,* derived from the *curtal,* was originally conceived as a bass for the oboe, yet it has a highly sensitive and unique tone of its own, heavy and viscous in the low register, dry and nutlike in the middle and reedy and nasal in the upper. Usually made of maple or pear wood with its U-bend and angled fingerholes, the bassoon ventured forth in company with the oboe, achieving a companion popularity much overshadowing that of the violoncello in the initial century.

The *flute,* probably also a creation of members of the Versailles Court, was actually a remodeling of an earlier cylindrical instrument. Made in three or four joints, often beautifully stained and decorated at the joints with ivory, it leaned toward the key of D major and was less flexible in fingering and intonation than the recorder which was dominant until mid-eighteenth century. It has been cited that Johann Joachim Quantz (1697-1773), teacher of Frederick the Great and author of an early "method" of flute-playing as well as a composer for the instrument, warned that performers should avoid solos in difficult keys, unless the listeners were fully apprised of the hazards. The flute, however, had an unmistakably personal tone and became part of the equipment of the drive toward expressiveness. James A. Macgillivray writes: "A century earlier it had been held a disadvantage of the flute that it expressed the player rather than the music, but changing tastes had now made this a decisive advantage."

The *clarinet,* with its single reed, was the invention of a German instrument maker named J. C. Denner (1665-1707) who, in working upon the *chalumeau,* a one-register, seven-holed pipe, devised this popular instrument. At first the *embouchure* (lip position) we know today was reversed, in that the reed was controlled by the upper lip of the performer, but by Mozart's time, the reed faced downward and it is to this composer's perspicacity that we owe the introduction of the clarinet to a large musical audience. It entered the orchestra as an instrument in C but from the middle of the eighteenth century the warmer B flat clarinet became the favorite it has remained until today.

In Beethoven's time (early nineteenth century) a new phase of woodwind construction commenced with emphasis placed upon the addition of keys in order to obviate the difficulties we have mentioned in attaining true and facile chromaticism. With Theobald Boehm (1794-1881), a jeweler and flutist, came marked improvements resulting in the redesigning of the flute on entirely new principles derived from his exhaustive acoustical studies; his fingering system, with slight modifications, is still in use today. To the clarinet Boehm, with Hyacinthe Klosé (1808-1880) of the Paris Conservatory, contributed larger holes and more logical spacing, as well as improved keywork. The modern oboe was steadily but unspectacularly improved during the nineteenth century by French and German instrument makers, collaborating with acousticians. The bassoon, however, was not radically changed from its earlier form. To Berlioz we must credit the addition of piccolo to flute, English horn to oboe, bass clarinet to *B* flat clarinet and double bassoon to bassoon in the modern symphony orchestra complex. To Adolphe Sax (1814-1894) we may look for improvements in the clarinet as well as invention of the saxophone (1846) and the special tuba, on which he worked in Paris for Wagner's *Ring des Nibelungen* orchestra.

BRASS INSTRUMENTS

Members of the brass family, in common with those of the wood-wind group, play a dual role as executants in both the modern orchestra and the military, symphonic and jazz bands. Although their variety is great, because of limitations of space we shall confine ourselves to the basic orchestral instruments of French horn, trumpet, trombone and tuba. Students wishing further information are urged to utilize the excellent histories listed in "Suggestions for Further Reading" at the end of this chapter (as is the case for all the instruments we have mentioned, as well as those omitted).

Fig. 38. French horn—eighteenth-century French etching by Adam van der Meulen. The modern French horn evolved from a simple hunting horn like this. About 1815 valves were invented which allowed the performer to play an entire scale. (Courtesy The Metropolitan Museum of Art.)

Aside from primitive and archeological instruments, the predecessor of the modern *French horn* would seem to be the helican horn of the sixteenth century (often known as a hunting horn), which had a bugle-like bore and bell and a funnel mouthpiece. Little evidence of musical use of horns exists before the eighteenth century, although Lully (*La Princesse d'Élide,* 1664) and Cavalli (*Le Nozze di Tito e di Pelei, The Marriage of Titus and Pelea,* 1639) each used horns in fanfares during hunting scenes. A new type of horn of much smaller bore and in the form of a coiled hoop appeared about 1650 in France. To Germany, however, we must turn for the musical development of the instrument. The earliest known score using horns as integral members of the orchestra is Keiser's opera *Octavia* (1705).

In form the French horn is a conical tube, coiled to make its length more manageable, and expanding at the end to form a flared bell. Its length determines its pitch; a natural horn, *i.e.,* without mechanical devices, could sound only those overtones of the harmonic series above its fundamental. This meant that the performer was forced to use a different size horn for each tonality, an awkward situation for a musician. An improvement was made about 1715 when the *crook system* was devised. By use of two *mastercrooks* fitted with mouthpieces and several auxiliary crooks of various length of pipe, one horn could be extended to the required lengths for various keys. In 1750 Anton Joseph Hampel discovered that pushing the hand into the bell of the horn (hand-stopping) increased the number of pitches available and smoothed the tone of the instrument. Because the older crook system made reaching the bell almost impossible in some keys, Hampel created crooks fitting into the hoop, thus restoring a fixed mouthpiece. With this instrument grew up a series of virtuosos, one of whom prompted Mozart to write four horn concertos and other music for the instrument.

The next step forward occurred after the turn of the nineteenth century with the invention of the *valve,* which allowed a player to combine hand with valve technique and cover the disparity between open and hand-stopped tones. The *F/B flat double horn* used by most players today was first introduced in 1899, combining two instruments into a single one with one or two extra valves that allowed the performer to switch, with pressure from the thumb, from one tonal situation to the other. This facilitated the playing of the higher register and improved general intonation. The hand still exercises control of the instrument in a certain kind of muting as well as in raising the pitch a semi-tone. Separate mutes are also used for particular effects. It is interesting to note that the earliest horns, only eight inches in diameter, were held in a baldric with the small bell pointing upward. When larger horns became the fashion, the instrument was held shoulder-high. This dramatic posture was maintained through the eighteenth century, at which time hand-stopping forced the horn to descend to its present position across the chest of the player with the bell extending laterally at waist level.

Another practice which implies a peculiarity of the instrument is the tendency of hornists to specialize, developing an *embouchure* either for high (*cors-alto*) or low (*cors-basse*) horn parts.

Trumpets of one type or another have been with us from the earliest times, used for sounding alarms and providing royal accolades. The player, forcing his breath through a cupped mouthpiece, sets a tubular column of air vibrating. On a "natural" instrument, only a certain number of harmonics are possible, depending on the length of the tubing. The task of brass instrument makers was to solve the problem posed by this physical fact. One attempt, the *cornett* (not the modern band instrument), applied the system of woodwind fingerholes to a horn of cowhorn or wood and leather (but not metal). With this expedient a range of two and a half octaves of semi-tones was available. Bach, Handel and Gluck all made some use of this instrument.

The trumpet's typical form was achieved by 1500, that of some seven feet of tube coiled in one long loop, with pitch placed at C (at the old high pitch) which sounded D in eighteenth-century concert pitch, a factor that Bach and Handel took into account when scoring these instruments. German trumpet guilds developed the *clarino* technique, specializing in the use of upper harmonics including that of the eighteenth, for which such masters as Purcell, Bach and Handel wrote. This technique had disappeared by the time of Beethoven. Its reproduction on today's brilliant trumpet is somewhat difficult, both because of the strain involved and because the older trumpet was softer and richer in tone quality, thus producing a far different effect in terms of orchestral and vocal ensemble.

Meanwhile, the struggle toward chromatization continued, with a key trumpet, introduced in 1801 and briefly immortalized by Haydn's well-known concerto. A slide trumpet appeared now and then, but it made little headway against that supplied with crooks, as horns were, to allow the instrument to change key. At last, in Germany in 1815, Heinrich Stölzel and Friedrich Blühmel invented valves by which the player, controlling three pistons with his right hand, could adjust the length of tubing brought into play in such a way that a chromatic scale was possible, even if a bit sharp in intonation. It was not until the time of Richard Strauss, however, that the trumpet was accepted as a complete instrument in itself.

The slide, rather unsuccessful on treble instruments, proved quite the opposite when combined with trumpet-like tubing to form the tenor *trombone*. At first the telescopic slide was attached to a mouthpipe; the player steadied the mouthpiece with one hand while manipulating the entire extra-tubing along the mouthpipe with the other, a somewhat tricky procedure, but possible if the music was confined to slow rhythms. An improvement was made when the whole first loop was made to move while the rest of the instrument remained immobile. By 1500 the trombone achieved its basic form. Its tone quality, however, was much gentler and sweeter than that of today, a fact that should be taken into consideration by modern performers when playing older music. Only with Berlioz was the trombone discovered to be "menacing and formidable." Later, valves were also used on the trombone but with less success than slides, although valve trombones appear in European military bands and in modern jazz ensembles.

The progenitors of the *tuba* were the *serpent,* a bizarre-looking instrument, often complete with wagging tongue and dragon head, and the bass bugle or *ophicleide.* It was not until the invention of valves that a way was open to develop the lowest register of the brass instruments. The Stölzel-Blühmel creation was followed by that of a rotary valve, patented by Joseph Riedl in 1832. Both modern piston and rotary valves are equally efficient, although the former is preferred in the United States. There is little standardization among tubas to the present day. The orchestral tuba in use in America has the bell pointed upward and is known as a key of F instrument. The so-called Wagner tuba was built to the composer's specifications by Sax, as noted above, and designed to be played by horn players. It has rarely been called for by other composers, although examples occur in works by Bruckner, Richard Strauss and in the original score of Stravinsky's *The Firebird.* Parenthetically, we may take notice of the *Sousaphone,* first produced by G. C. Conn of Elkhart, Indiana in 1908, for use in John Philip Sousa's band.

Percussion Instruments

Percussion instruments, made of a variety of materials, ancient and exotic in origin, and producing sound either by shaking or striking, fall into two general classes: those with indefinite pitch and those that are tuned. As these valuable instruments are probably the most accessible to music lovers, we shall merely list representatives of each class and note those which played a part in music of the pre-Classical or Baroque period. Among the instruments of indefinite pitch we find the side or snare, tenor and bass drums, cymbals, gongs, tam-tam, triangle, tambourine, castanets, wood block, whip and cowbell as well as the Latin-American "battery." Percussion instruments of definite pitch include kettledrums or tympani, *glockenspiel,* xylophone, marimba and vibraphone, tubular bells or Cathedral chimes, Korean temple blocks and *celesta.*

Kettledrums which entered Europe by way of the Ottoman Empire in the fifteenth century were used initially by the cavalry, in combination with trumpets. During the seventeenth century they were equipped with screws to increase or lessen the tension of the vellum heads, tuned to the key of the trumpets and to its dominant, a fourth below. In the orchestras of Bach and Handel, the tympani were these same cavalry drums put to more refined use but still retaining the tonic-dominant tuning in trumpet keys of C and D. As they were struck by hard-headed sticks, their sound was far from delicate. The side or snare drum's original use was also military, employed in combination with the fife, as our famous trio of American Revolutionary soldiers demonstrated. These drums were occasionally employed in early operas and enjoy a spot in Handel's *Royal Fireworks Music*.

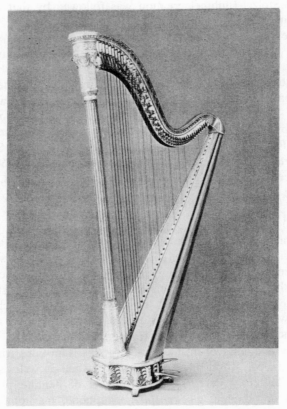

Fig. 39. A double-pedal harp. This Érard Freres' instrument was made about 1850 when the harp achieved its basic modern form. (Courtesy National Museum, Prague.)

HARP

With the *harp* we conclude our brief survey of the development of modern orchestral instruments. The modern harp differs markedly from its ancient archetypes in that it has a fore-pillar to support the neck from the pull of the strings, and seven pedals by means of which it is possible to modulate while playing. During medieval times harps were small both in size and musical span; in the Renaissance, harps of four feet were common but were still tuned diatonically. The tendency toward chromatization again presented instrument makers with a problem. Ingenious solutions were attempted, such as the *arpa doppis* (double harp), used in Monteverdi's *Orfeo,* in which the single row of strings was doubled, thus offering the necessary accidentals but at the expense of facility and technique. A Bavarian named Hochbrucker elaborated the idea of tuning hooks in 1720 by adding pedal control. A Parisian, Cousineau, replaced hooks with metal plates to alter the pitch of each string one or two half-steps. His harp, like the modern one, was tuned to the scale of *C* flat. It was Sébastien Érard (1752-1831) who took significant steps in giving the harp its present form and mechanism, although modifications have occurred since that time. It is interesting to note that a minor battle between the pedal and the "chromatic" harp resulted in the composition of Debussy's *Danse sacrée et danse profane* and Ravel's *Introduction and Allegro for Flute, Clarinet, Harp and Strings.*

SUGGESTIONS FOR FURTHER READING

Bach, C. P. E., *Essay on the True Art of Playing Keyboard Instruments.* New York, Norton, 1949.

Baines, Anthony, ed., *Musical Instruments through the Ages.** Baltimore, Penguin, 1961.

——— *Woodwind Instruments and Their History.** Baltimore, Penguin, n.d.

Boehm, Theobald, *The Flute and Flute-Playing.* New York, Dover, 1922.

Buchner, Alexander, *Musical Instruments through the Ages.* London, Spring, n.d.

Carse, Adam, *The History of Orchestration.* London, Paul, Trench, Trubner, 1925.

Coar, Birchard, *The French Horn.* Ann Arbor, University of Michigan Press, 1947.

Donington, Robert, *The Instruments of Music.** New York, Barnes & Noble, 1962.

Edgerly, Beatrice, *From the Hunter's Bow.* New York, Putnam, 1942.

Geiringer, Karl, *Musical Instruments.* New York, Oxford University Press, 1945.

Goldman, R. Franko, *The Concert Band.* New York, Rinehart, 1946.

Hayes, Gerald R., *Musical Instruments and Their Music, Viols and Violins, 1500-1750.* London, Oxford University Press, 1928.

Landowska, Wanda, *Landowska on Music.* New York, Stein & Day, 1964.

* Available in paperback edition.

Menke, W., *History of the Trumpet of Bach and Handel*. London, Reeves, 1934.
Rendall, F. G., *The Clarinet*. London, Williams & Norgate, 1954.
Russell, Raymond, *The Harpsichord and Clavichord*. London, Faber & Faber, 1959.
Sachs, Curt, *The History of Musical Instruments*. New York, Norton, 1940.
Sharpe, A. P., *Story of the Spanish Guitar*. London, Essex, 1959.
Terry, C. S., *Bach's Orchestra*. New York, Oxford University Press, 1958.

A SAMPLER OF SUPPLEMENTARY RECORDINGS

General Works
The Complete Orchestra   Music Education Record Corp.
Instruments of the Orchestra   Vanguard 1017/1018
Britten, Benjamin, *Young Person's Guide to the Orchestra*
Prokofiev, Sergei, *Peter and the Wolf*
Rimsky-Korsakov, Nikolai, *Scheherezade*
Saint-Saëns, Camille, *Carnival of Animals*
Strauss, Richard, *Don Quixote*
Tchaikovsky, Peter, *Nutcracker Suite*

Works for Single Instrument and Groups
Flute: Griffes, Charles, *Poem for Flute and Orchestra*
Oboe: Barlow, Wayne, *The Winter's Past*
English Horn: Sibelius, Jan, *The Swan of Tuonela*
Clarinet: Hindemith, Paul, *Sonata for Clarinet and Piano*
Bassoon: Dukas, Paul, *The Sorcerer's Apprentice*
Woodwind Ensemble: Ibert, Jacques, *Trois Pièces Brèves*
French Horn: Brahms, Johannes, *Trio for Horn, Violin and Piano, Op.* 40
Trumpet: Copland, Aaron, *The Quiet City*
Trombone: Goeb, Roger, *Concertino for Trombone and Strings*
Tuba: Moussorgsky, Modest, "Bydlo" from *Pictures at an Exhibition,* orchestrated by Ravel
Brass Ensemble: Gabrieli, Giovanni, *Canzon*
Percussion Ensemble: Varèse, Edgard, *Ionisation*
Harp: Ravel, Maurice, *Introduction and Allegro for Harp, Flute, Clarinet and String Quartet*
Violin: Bach, J. S., *Partita No. 2 for Unaccompanied Violin*
Viola: Bloch, Ernst, *Suite for Viola and Piano*
'Cello: Bruch, Max, *Kol Nidre for 'Cello and Orchestra, Op.* 47
Double Bass: Schubert, Franz, *Quintet in A, Op.* 114, "Trout"
String Ensemble: Vaughan Williams, R., *Fantasia on a Theme by Tallis*
Harpsichord: de Falla, Manuel, *Nights in the Gardens of Spain*
Organ: *The Art of the Organ* (Columbia KSL-219)
Atypical Ensemble: Stravinsky, Igor, *L'Histoire du soldat*

OPPORTUNITIES FOR STUDY IN DEPTH

1. Prepare a folio of sketches of standard orchestral instruments with annotations couched in simple language, and, if typed, in capital letters. Donate the finished work to a local elementary school library. As this represents an original compilation, it may be reproduced *ad lib.*

2. Armed with scissors and old magazines, search out and clip musical instruments used in advertisements. Classify them, and analyze on the basis of a random-sample technique, formulating hypotheses as to the reasons why such photographs and drawings aid in selling merchandise.

3. Investigate through reading and visits to instrument dealers musical instruments not included in this chapter. Make an outline of findings and present them in a class report.

4. If a novice, listen to records of the various musical instruments, as noted in "A Sampler of Supplementary Recordings." Then, listen to Béla Bartók's *Concerto for Orchestra,* second movement, identifying the instruments as they appear. Check answers by either consulting the record jacket or a description of the work or an instructor.

5. If possible, visit the shop of a nearby instrument maker, noting everything that can be seen and asking relevant questions. If this is impossible, acquire a free film about instrument-making. Several are available on loan from commercial firms. View the film in class and discuss what is seen.

6. Make a study of instruments of one particular culture or nationality in which one is interested. Note chronology, construction and function in the life of that culture or group.

7. Visit a museum and investigate its collection of old and new instruments, as seen in actuality or reproduction and also in paintings and sculpture. Correlate what was seen with what has been read.

8. Obtain a variety of modern musical instruments of many different kinds. Handle them and try them out. There is no better way to get the feel of an instrument, however superficial the experience may seem, than to touch, blow, beat or bow it. This is a kinetic theory of music education for pre-school children in Australia today, and a very good one it is.

VOCABULARY ENRICHMENT

harpsichord	chest of viols
spinet	*viola da gamba*
virginals	*viola d'amore*
jack action	*legato*
tangent action	*vibrato*
dampers	*pizzicato*
style galant	*tremolo*
Bebung	trill
pianoforte	mute
sostenuto pedal	harmonics
short octave	double stopping
tremulant	*glissando*
stops	*col legno*
register or rank	violin
labial pipes	viola
tongue pipes	violoncello or 'cello
pedal keyboard	contrabass or double bass
diapason	*musette*
mutation stops	oboe

bassoon
flute
chalumeau
embouchure
helican horn
crooks
hand stopping
piston valve
double horn
trumpet
cornett

clarino technique
telescopic slide
trombone
serpent
ophicleide
rotary valve
sousaphone
percussion
kettledrum or tympani
side or snare drum

Chapter 10.

THE DEVELOPMENT
OF AN INSTRUMENTAL REPERTOIRE

The TRUMPET'S loud Clangor
  Excites us to Arms
With shrill Notes of Anger
  And mortal Alarms.
The double double double Beat
  Of the thund'ring DRUM
  Cryes, heark the Foes come;
Charge, Charge, 'tis too late to retreat.

The soft complaining FLUTE
  In dying Notes discovers
  The Woes of hopeless Lovers
Whose Dirge is whisper'd by the warbling LUTE.

  Sharp VIOLINS proclaim
Their jealous Pangs and Desperation,
Fury, frantick Indignation,
Depth of Pains and Heights of Passion
  For the fair, disdainful Dame.

  But oh, what Art can teach,
  What human Voice can reach
    The sacred ORGANS Praise?
  Notes inspiring holy Love,
Notes that wing their heavenly Ways
  To mend the CHOIRES above.

A Song for St. Cecilia's Day—John Dryden (1631-1700)

When vocal polyphony was at its height, new forces of which composers themselves were scarcely aware were at work. Harmony was sensed long before it was systematically established. Secular music had reached an artistic plane before its status was recognized. The experiments that resulted in opera, oratorio and ballet revealed new homophonic paths. Instruments, formerly used as mere accessories to voices, assumed importance and an increasingly independent function. As interest centered in improving keyed, wind and stringed instruments, better instruments in turn produced better performers who demanded of composers (often one and the same) creative ventures that resulted in new musical forms, impregnated with idiomatic writing and exploiting instrumental tone colors.

Before instrumental music became a member in good standing of the European cultural world, it went through the usual processes of crudity and trial and error. Throughout preceding ages, as we have noted, most types of musical instruments had been acknowledged on one occasion or another, but an instrumental art *per se* did not come into being until the peak of the Golden Age of choral polyphony had been reached during the later Renaissance. Then, seeds planted centuries before started germinating in the sixteenth-century soil, favored by a positive social climate. All factors of the season seemed suitable for a rapid, healthy growth which was to yield a rich harvest during succeeding periods. Significant, too, was the cultivation extended to secular music by royalty, nobility and the wealthy middle classes, to whom it became part of gracious living, as our illustrations attest.

Fig. 40. "Music Party"—seventeenth-century French engraving by Abraham Bosse. The lute and *viola da gamba* accompany singers in this popular pastime of the sixteenth and seventeenth centuries. (Courtesy The Metropolitan Museum of Art, Dick Fund, 1926.)

The humanistic temper pervading the Renaissance and Reformation encouraged composers to draw upon both sacred and secular musical sources. To the folk dances they went for greater rhythmic variety (the *suite*); to motet and madrigal for perfection of form and style (the *sonata*); and to the lute for a medium upon which to develop much needed instrumental techniques. The dynamism of seventeenth-century life was reflected in an energetic musical pulsation which punctuated the tonal flow. The principle of contrast which painters found in light and dark (as exemplified by Rembrandt) appeared in music as contrast between independent entities, rather than within them, resulting in multi-sectioned forms and the interplay of large and small sound masses. An outlet for the rationalistic inclination of the times was found in more disciplined forms, notably the monothematic fugue, largely controlled by the composer.

Even as scientists such as Kepler, Harvey, Descartes and Newton were penetrating the mysteries of nature and reformulating our knowledge of the universe and its laws, musicians were forging a brave new musical world. In accompanied monody with its *basso continuo* lay a reservoir of suggestion and potential to be realized in the creation of a comprehensive system of **harmony** and in a redefinition of melody. In fact, melodic variation methods, including that of **sequence,** wherein a tonal-rhythmic pattern is repeated at a different pitch, are as characteristic of Baroque music in general as is the textual polarity between the bass and upper voices.

Composers of the seventeenth and eighteenth centuries eagerly seized the opportunity of contributing to an instrumental repertoire, using formal designs such as the suite, sonata, *sinfonia,* overture, concerto, *ricercar* and fugue, which we shall examine in the following pages. Over the years the instrumental literature attained considerable size, due to the popularity of such works and also to the remarkable productivity of the men involved. The creative output of some of them, as we shall see, staggers the modern imagination, suggesting that there may be an inverse ratio between conscious introspection or subjectivity and degree of fecundity. That certain conventions or stereotypes were employed does not detract from the high quality of this first great age of instrumental composition.

We can discern shades of categorization in the quoted verses of Dryden, where the doctrine of affects, *i.e.,* the use of certain musical colors and devices to achieve certain musical expressions, is outlined, instrument by instrument. In listening to the music we shall now proceed to discuss, we cannot help but be delighted by the freshness, vitality and artistic inventiveness of the Baroque instrumental composers.

BAROQUE INSTRUMENTAL FORMS

One of the oldest forms of instrumental music is the dance. *Estampies,* as we have mentioned, date from the thirteenth century or earlier and may have been derived from the vocal sequence. Jules Combarieu hypothesizes that at first a dance was accompanied by a song; an instrument was added; the song disappeared and the instrument was used alone; disassociated from words and then from active dancing itself, the form became completely stylized and instrumental; traveling musicians carried the tunes from country to country. These, he states, are successive phases in the evolution of the *suite,* an important Baroque instrumental form that developed side by side with the *sonata.* Whatever its ancestry, the instrumental dance retained a symmetrical, sectional structure and relied upon variation to relieve the customary repetitions.

As one of the inherent assets in a work of art is contrast of some sort, musicians had learned early in the development of music that variety of mood and style could be obtained through different rhythms and tempos. The Arabs had accomplished this by combining three or four songs in differing modes and moods. In Europe paired dances were popular. Thomas Morley, for instance, spoke of the desirability of alternating *pavans* and *galliards,* as the *pavan* was "a kind of staid musick ordained for grave dancing," while the *galliard* provided "a lighter and more stirring kind of dancing." In Italy the "varied couples," as Bukofzer calls them, included the *passamezzo* and *saltarello;* in Germany, *Tanz* and *Nachtanz.* The general principle followed was that of a slow dance in duple meter being matched with a livelier version of the same in triple meter. During the seventeenth century the dance group was expanded.

Italy, which led the world in musical composition during the fifteenth and sixteenth centuries, was still supreme when instrumental music entered the lists against vocal music. But international exchanges and closer relations among countries disseminated the knowledge of individual dances and led France, England, Germany, the Netherlands and Spain to group several dances together—some slow, others fast, some in duple, others in triple meter—into a more formal pattern, a **suite.** Early suites consisted of nothing more than selected dances written in the same mode or key. Eventually, however, the *allemande, courante, sarabande* and *gigue* became the principal members. In addition to these, which appeared in almost every suite after 1690, were many other dance forms, used at the discretion of the composer. *Partitas, exercises, lessons, ordres, sonata da camera* and *partien* are some of the names by which suites were known. The following table offers data concerning various dance forms:

Dance	Variant	Nationality	Meter	Tempo	Remarks
Allemande	Almand (Eng.) Almain	German (Swabian)	$\frac{4}{4}$ $\frac{4}{4}$	moderately slow	Written in sixteenth notes.
Courante	Corrente (It.) Corant (Eng.)	French Italian	$\frac{2}{2}\ \frac{3}{2}\ \frac{3}{4}\ \frac{6}{4}\ \frac{6}{8}$	fast	From courir (to run).
Sarabande		Spanish or Moorish	$\frac{3}{2}\ \frac{3}{4}$	slow, stately	
Gigue	Giga (It.) Jig (Eng.)	Italian	$\frac{3}{8}\ \frac{6}{8}\ \frac{9}{8}\ \frac{3}{4}\ \frac{6}{4}\ \frac{12}{8}$ etc.	fast	Named from early fiddle, gigue, geige. Last movement of suite.
Loure		French (Normandy)	$\frac{6}{4}$	moderately fast	Slower than the Gigue, danced probably to a kind of bagpipe. Pastoral or rustic in character.
Gavotte	Gavot	French	$\frac{4}{4}$ ¢	moderately fast	Begins on third beat.
Musette	(Sometimes Gavotte II)	French	$\frac{4}{4}$ ¢	moderately fast	Part of the Gavotte usually with drone bass. From cornemuse (bagpipe).
Bourrée		French (perhaps Spanish)	¢	fast	Begins on fourth beat. Resembles Gavotte.
Rigaudon	Rigadoon (Eng.)	Provence	$\frac{2}{4}$ ¢	fast, lively	Popular in England at end of seventeenth century.
Tambourin		Provence	$\frac{2}{4}$	lively	Drum accompaniment characteristic. Very old.
Minuet	Menuet (Fr.) Menuett (Ger.) Menuetto (It.)	French from Poitou, or perhaps first used by Lully	$\frac{3}{4}$	moderate	Only dance form to survive in Classic sonata and symphony.
Trio	Minuet II		$\frac{3}{4}$		Part of the Minuet replaced 2nd Minuet usually slower or faster than Minuet proper.
Passepied	Paspy (Eng.)	French (sailor-dance from Basse Bretagne)	$\frac{3}{4}\ \frac{3}{8}$	fast	A fast Minuet.
Chaconne	Ciacona (It.) Chacona (Sp.)	Probably Spanish	$\frac{3}{4}$	slow	Written on ground bass of eight measures.
Passacaglia	Passecaille (Fr.)	Early Italian or Spanish	$\frac{3}{4}$	slow	Form used by harpsichord and organ composers. Resembles the Chaconne, also on ground bass.
Pavan	Pavane (Fr.) Pavin (Eng.)	Italian or perhaps Spanish (sixteenth century)	C	solemn, slow	One of the oldest of the dance forms—sung as well as played.
Galliard	Gaillarde (Fr.) Gagliarda (It.)	Italian, from Rome	$\frac{3}{2}$	fast, gay	Also called Romanesca.
Branle	Bransle (Eng.) Brawl	French	$\frac{2}{2}\ \frac{2}{4}$		Round dance from fifteenth century not included in later suites.
Polonaise	Polacca (It.)	Polish	$\frac{3}{4}$	moderate	Court dance originated in 1573 from ancient Christmas carols. Bach and Handel used the form.

Another source of instrumental music lies in the transcription of vocal music. We can perceive this process in the popular French *chanson* as it was transformed into what the Italians termed *canzona francese*. At first the transcriptions of vocal music for keyboard instrument or lute were rather literal and retained the characteristic opening pattern of ♩♩♩ on a repeated tone and also retained most of the musical material. Some attempt at idiomatic arrangement was made, however, in employing scalewise figuration (known variously as *diminution, coloration* or *division*) to provide movement for the longer note values and to dramatize the cadences. Later, the form took on more independence, and in two different aspects served as a forerunner of the *sonata da chiesa* and the fugue.

We have noted the insidious introduction of instruments in the performance of madrigals and motets. William Byrd's directive, "fit for voyces or for viols," as well as Lasso's titles for his German songs, imply an interchangeability of musical resources. As madrigals became more complicated, viols often played along with the voice parts. Soon madrigals were written with instrumental preludes and interludes. As instruments were improved, composers took advantage of their greater technical possibilities to write more ambitious works than those for voices alone. In opera, oratorio and cantata, too, the violin had become the competitor of the finest singers. It was but a short step from these antecedents to a composition for stringed instruments without vocal assistance—namely, the **sonata.**

Although the dance suite reached its format relatively early and hardly survived Johann Sebastian Bach, the sonata was merely in its infancy during Bach's time and has showed its underlying vitality by its continuing development, even now taking place. The earliest sonata is found in the works of Salomone Rossi (1587-*c*. 1630), a violinist at the court of Mantua. The name, from the Italian *suonare* (to sound), was intended to distinguish it from the vocal cantata, from *cantare* (to sing), and cannot be firmly defined in the seventeenth century. Among Rossi's compositions are some that have all the features of the *trio sonata,* an intimate work for two soprano instruments and *basso continuo* (in other words, four performers), that was the result of a compromise between polyphonic and homophonic textures. As a rule early sonatas had several movements but no hard and fast tempo formula. Each movement was based upon one main theme and its second repetition began in the dominant and ended in the tonic key.

In about 1690 sonatas, suites and the *balletto* had become so merged that it was deemed necessary to make some distinction so that frivolous dance music would be kept out of Church services. To that end, compositions were divided into the *sonata da chiesa* (church sonata) and *sonata da camera* (chamber sonata). Those written for sacred performance were supposedly (but not always) dignified and abstract, presaging the Classic sonata of Haydn and Mozart; chamber sonatas, intended for playing in company or at home, were actually suites of dances with initial preludes. Both church and chamber sonatas were composed for strings, lute and organ or other instrumental combinations and, as the use of solo instruments came into vogue, for violin, violoncello or keyboard instruments.

In early usage the term, *sinfonia* (symphony), like *ritornello* and overture, was employed to designate instrumental passages in such works as operas, cantatas and Masses. For example, in 1600 a *sinfonia* for three flutes was performed at the wedding of Marie de' Medici and Henry IV of France. Gradually, however, *sinfonia* came to refer to an instrumental introduction to an air or recitative; and in 1681 Alessandro Scarlatti used it in place of the title, overture (*sinfonia avanti l'opera*). *Ritornello* (from the Italian, to return) at first had meant an interlude provided between stanzas of a song. During the Baroque period, it formed an integral part of *concerto grosso* structure and this, in turn, influenced the *ritornello aria* of Venetian opera. The so-called French and Italian overtures, as we have mentioned, differed from each other both in textures and in tempos. Lully's overture consisted of a slow introduction, a lively movement in fugal style, with perhaps a dance form or two appended for further contrast. The Italian overture or opera *sinfonia,* on the other hand, boasted a three-section pattern of fast—slow—fast. It was influenced by the *sonata da chiesa* in form and modulatory scheme and, in its first portion, foreshadowed the sonata-allegro form of the eighteenth century. Ultimately, overtures and symphonies were to stand as independent instrumental works, not connected with operas or cantatas.

The nomenclature, **concerto,** was first applied to motets for voices and organ which Lodovico Viadana (1564-1645) called *concerti ecclesiastici.* With the addition of other instruments and division into separate instrumental movements these evolved into *concerti da chiesa.* Again we meet with a semantic confusion, for there is lack of agreement about the etymology of the word. Whether derived from the Latin *conserere* (to sound together) or from *concertare* (to strive against), the possible origins of the term help define the form, in which one performance element—solo or group—is opposed by another, yet all share in the musical materials. "It was the baroque spirit, . . ." writes

Paul Henry Lang, ". . . which with its love of virtuosity, display and ornamentation, caused this elemental principle to become the dominating factor in its music."

Many elements contributed to the seventeenth-century concerto, not the least of which were the *opera sinfonia,* the *sonata da chiesa* and the simple *canzona.* Giovanni Gabrieli effectively demonstrated contrast of sonorities. His *Sacrae Symphoniae* (1597) were works for a large body of singers and an orchestra of viols, trombones, trumpets, cornets and organs. In his celebrated *Sonata piano e forte,* Gabrieli used two small orchestras, both antiphonally and together. The first consisted of two alto trombones, one tenor trombone and one cornet, while the second had one *violino,* two tenor trombones and one bass trombone.

Arcangelo Corelli divided his string orchestra into two groups, a *concertino* or solo group (in his case, two violins and a 'cello, plus harpsichord and a *ripieno* or *tutti* (the remainder or all), comprised of the main body of the orchestra or *concerto grosso,* in the literal sense. Although Corelli's *Op.* 6 was a source of inspiration to succeeding composers, it was Antonio Vivaldi who developed an independent concerto structure, in which a *tutti ritornello,* in ternary form and usually homophonic, carried the thematic burden, while the soloists indulged in episodic commentary or in original counterthemes.

In Giuseppe Torelli's (1658-1709) *Op.* 8 we find a new extension of the concerto principle—that of the *solo concerto,* to prove the most stimulating of Baroque concerto structures. Whether or not Torelli's solo violin concertos were the first, they established the form. Cast in three movements—*allegro-adagio-allegro*—they raised the soloist to a position of equality with the orchestra. Moreover, as Bukofzer comments, "For the first time the tutti-solo contrast was also musically defined by means of virtuoso figuration in the solo and a pregnant idea in the tutti"—*i.e.,* thematic differentiation. In 1701 Giuseppe Jacchini wrote the first solo concerto for violoncello and Vivaldi added works for wind instruments. It was Bach who created the first keyboard concertos, to which Handel added concertos for organ.

The most unified form of contrapuntal art, the **fugue,** reached its apex in the works of Johann Sebastian Bach, although its history antedates his age by several centuries. The name comes from the Latin and Italian word, *fuga,* meaning flight. In the use of free imitation we find anticipations in Renaissance motets, madrigals and instrumental *canzone.* But the immediate predecessor of fugue was the *ricercar,* an Italian instrumental style that in the hands of Andrea Gabrieli and Girolamo Frescobaldi assumed a monothematic character, combining intricacies of counterpoint with the vivacity and freedom of the *canzona*. It is important to remember that the fugue is less a form than a set of compositional principles. A cursory survey of Bach fugues, for instance, will readily confirm this premise.

In general, a fugue consists of the following elements: (1) the **exposition,** in which the *subject, answer* (the subject repeated more or less exactly at a transposition "in the fifth") and, possibly, a **countersubject** (a theme contrapuntally fitted to the answer) are imitatively set forth in entries governed by the number of voices, *i.e.,* from two to six or more; (2) the **counter-exposition** (not present in all fugues), in which the subject and answer are stated in reversed order; (3) the **episodes** or digressions, in which parts of the subject and counter-subject are treated canonically and otherwise contrapuntally developed with a variety of modulation; (4) the **stretti,** in which the subject and answer are introduced each time in closer succession, to build up the climax of the composition; and (5) the **organ point,** a stationary tone, usually in the bass voice, around which the other parts move freely, leading to a final cadence.

Among other prominent Baroque forms are **variations** of many sorts, including the *chaconne,* in which a chord progression is the basis for variation (in much the same manner as that of our American "blues"); the *passacaglia,* wherein a short bass melody is repeated many times against variations in the upper voices (a modern counterpart, although not quite identical, is our "boogie-woogie" style); the *chorale-variation,* in which a Lutheran hymn acts somewhat as a *cantus firmus*; and free polyphonic variations, drawing on many sources of technique.

Free forms also occupy a conspicuous place in Baroque instrumental music, due to the popularity of improvisation and virtuoso display. These are variously known as the *toccata* (a "touch" piece), *fancy* (in which the English excelled), *capriccio, voluntary, preludio* and *fantasia,* the latter a favorite with German organists.

*   *   *   *   *

Now that we have a frame of reference of characteristic forms and principles dominating the Baroque instrumental repertoire, we shall examine a bit more closely representative personalities and compositions of composers preceding and contemporary with Bach and Handel, who will be discussed in subsequent chapters. It seems needless to point out that most of these men were also masters of vocal music; equally unnecessary is the qualification that our selection is for the purpose of exposition and is in no way complete. But even a hasty glance at the development of keyboard and string music literature by various composers in various countries during the pre-Classic period will give us insight into the quantity and quality of a wonderful and increasingly popular repertoire.

KEYBOARD MUSIC

The harpsichord had become an imposing instrument by the middle of the seventeenth century. Although a century before it had been used for domestic music, now it took precedence for concert as well as intimate performances. French composers particularly cultivated the *clavecin* and their compositions and virtuosity did much toward building the piano technique of later times. Both clavichord and harpsichord were well adapted to fugues, *toccatas,* suites, *fantasias* and early sonatas, as well as to a dawning type of descriptive music.

Besides Lully, important French *clavecin* players and composers included Jacques-Champion de Chambonnières (*c.* 1602-1672), Jean-Louis Marchand (1669-1732), Jean-Baptiste Loeillet (1680-1730), Louis-Claude Daquin (1694-1772) and Jean Schobert (*c.* 1720-1767). The start was made by Jacques-Champion who blazed a trail for François Couperin (1668-1733) and Jean-Philippe Rameau (1683-1764).

Loeillet came from a family of musicians whose lineage is hopelessly confused. A composer and a splendid virtuoso, he wrote flute music, sonatas for various instruments and six harpsichord suites or "lessons." Claude Daquin, a child prodigy, studied with Marchand and composed a book of *Pièces de clavecin,* including the well-known "Cuckoo" and *Noëls pour l'orgue ou le clavecin.* In 1727 he won the position of organist at St. Paul's, in a competition with Rameau. Born in Silesia, Jean Schobert became organist at Versailles and an active chamber musician in Paris. Among his works are sonatas for *clavecin* and violin, *clavecin* concertos, symphonies for *clavecin,* violin and two horns and solo *clavecin* sonatas. (Mozart's early (K. 39) piano concerto in B flat is based on Schobert's music.)

François Couperin came of a long line of musicians, somewhat analogous to the Bach family. Organist to the King at Versailles, he later was appointed organist of St. Gervais', Paris, where from 1665 to 1826 eight members of his family served in the same post. As clavecinist at court, he rapidly became a favorite and earned the name of *le grand,* as had his predecessor, Lully. Every Sunday evening he played chamber music for the King. Indeed, one of his collections of compositions was entitled *Concerts Royaux,* in the preface of which he inscribed, *"pour les petits concerts du roi"* ("for the little concerts of the King").

Couperin's harpsichord music is graceful and elegant, mirroring the environment in form and spirit. It is miniature rather than broad, expressive rather than profound. In other words, it is perfectly adapted to the instrument, so much so that when it is performed on a sonorous piano, it often seems to be out of its frame. Couperin's charm lies in his exquisite taste; his psychological portraits in music of the court ladies are lightly sketched and always pleasing. His use of ornamentation (*agréments*), necessary to sustain tone in instruments lacking sonority and a feature of the "gallant style," achieves delightful effects. Guided by his delicate sensitivity, his melodic inventiveness and a purity of style which blends French with Italian elements, Couperin is as worthy as any of an honorable niche in the annals of illustrious composers.

His twenty-seven *ordres* (suites) contain little dance pieces, with provocative names, sometimes fashionably pastoral, sometimes daintily tinted with realism, sometimes vivid in feeling but always classically restrained. Among them are *"Les petits moulins à vent"* ("The Little Windmills"), *"Les bergèries"* ("Pastorales") and *"Fureurs bacchiques"* ("Bacchic Passions"). Couperin followed Chambonnières' practice in naming his pieces, a custom anticipating the piano compositions of the nineteenth-century German Romanticists. To Couperin also goes the credit of introducing the trio sonata to France. In *Le Parnasse ou l'Apothéose de Corelli* and *L'Apothéose de l'incomparable Lully,* homages to Corelli's and Lully's works, Couperin revealed his preoccupation with uniting French and Italian musical art. And in his *Méthode: L'Art de toucher le clavecin* (*Method: Art of Playing the Clavecin*), Couperin greatly influenced the theory and practice of *clavecin* performance and composition, even to providing a background for Bach, Haydn, Mozart and Beethoven.

Although Rameau was essentially an opera composer, he too wrote several volumes of harpsichord music in early "programmatic" style, including "The Call of the Birds," "The Hen" and "The Whirlwind." In his three volumes of *Pièces de clavecin,* Rameau showed himself master of French *clavecin* techniques, codifying in his prefaces fingerings and embellishments. Rameau also contributed *clavecin* suites (1741) arranged as ensemble sonatas (*clavecin* with violin, flute and viola). A controversial figure, Rameau was abused by followers of Lully and afiçionados of *opera buffa*; moreover, Louis XVI, debauched and frivolous, extended him little aid. Nevertheless, Rameau persisted and succeeded, although he did not produce his first opera until he was fifty, the year of Couperin's death. Perhaps his most valuable effort lies in his *Traité de l'harmonie* and other theoretical writings which formulated chord construction in thirds, a fundamental bass of root progressions and the identification of a chord and its inversions as one and the same.

In comparison with Couperin, Rameau's work seems more virile, if not quite so polished, and his knowledge of harmony influenced him toward a richer musical texture of chords and modulations and a correspondingly poorer melodic sense. As Couperin was affected by Corelli, Rameau was possibly touched by the artistry of Domenico Scarlatti —both worthy exemplars, yet neither powerful enough to eradicate an inherently French quality common to both composers.

* * * * *

In Italy as elsewhere the practice of writing music to be used interchangeably upon either organ or harpsichord was commonplace during the early Baroque. In the early years of the eighteenth century, however, Italian harpsichord composers appeared in greater numbers. They included Bernardo Pasquini (1637-1710), Azzolino della Ciaia (1671-1755), a Siennese composer and Gaetano Greco (*c*. 1657-*c*. 1728), a Neapolitan who may have been the teacher of the greatest Italian composer of the eighteenth century, Domenico Scarlatti 1685-1757), a son of Alessandro.

Alessandro, his son's first teacher, recognized his precocity and sent him forth from Naples to pursue his musical education. In Venice young Scarlatti met Handel. In 1709, at Rome, they engaged in a harpsichord competition which was refereed a draw but Domenico lost to Handel in an organ contest. The two became fast friends, however, and Scarlatti would cross himself in reverence whenever he spoke of Handel's organ playing. After service at the Vatican and with the Queen of Poland (at her Roman residence), Scarlatti became teacher of the Princess of the Asturias and later her music director at Madrid where she was Queen.

Although the father's operas are still remembered, Domenico's are quite forgotten. But his works for the *gravicembalo* are as vital today as they were in his own time. They number some 600 and are available in many editions. In his influence on the development of keyboard music he can be compared to Chopin and Liszt, and is a founder of piano style, an honor which he shares with Couperin and Rameau. In Scarlatti's case, however, the music seems almost modern, because of its vigor, daring and clarity, while Couperin's and Rameau's compositions are beautifully reminiscent of Gallic snuff boxes and periwigs. Scarlatti forsook the *ordres* and the suites, sending his works nameless into the world, as did Chopin, a spiritual descendant. His sonatas are "sound pieces" in the true Italian sense. They are short, usually in two parts; the harmonic structure and repeats serve to endow them with an attractive balance.

Seven years after Bach and two years before Handel, Scarlatti died in Madrid at the age of seventy-one. Through his creations he had relieved keyboard music of Chambonnières' embellishments and inaugurated new methods of performance, including crossing the hands, passage work in thirds and sixths, wide leaps, arpeggios in contrary motion and rapid repeating notes. In short, he was to the keyboard what Corelli was to the violin.

Fig. 41. Title page of *Parthenia*. "*Parthenia* or *The Maydenhead* of the first musicke that ever was printed for the *Virginalls*. Composed by three famous masters: William Byrd, Dr. John Bull, and Orlando Gibbons. Gentlemen of his Majesties' most illustrious Chappell. Dedicated to all the Masters and Lovers of Musick." *c.* 1611. (Courtesy British Museum.)

At the end of the sixteenth century England recognized the possibilities of the harpsichord, before they were realized in continental Europe. During the following century many harpsichord collections were published, of which the *Parthenia* (1611) and *FitzWilliam Virginal Book* are best known. There was a group of excellent composers, among them Tallis, Byrd, John Bull, Gibbons, John Blow and Purcell, who numbered among their works many for keyboards.

John Bull (*c.* 1562-1628) was particularly adept and seems to have anticipated later pianistic elements. Purcell, of course, showed superior gifts in his suites, "lessons" and dances. But the English school, according to Edward Dickinson, "soon died out in England and had no successor there, and appears to have exerted little influence upon the progress of things on the Continent." This is not difficult to believe, because at the time England was receiving its stimulus from Italy and France through Pelham Humphrey (one of the Children of the Royal Chapel), who, as we have mentioned, went to the Continent and brought back European musical models.

Germany was now climbing to a position of musical ascendancy. One of the most important "pillars of *klavier* music" was Johann Kuhnau (1660-1722), cantor, linguist, lawyer, divine, performer and composer. The work that first proclaimed his gifts was a motet written for the election of the town council. Cantor of St. Thomas' at Leipzig, a post which Bach subsequently filled, Kuhnau wrote delightful, satirical poems in several languages, and was musical director of the University. In his hands the Baroque *sonata* became a sympathetic form for elastic and flexible musical expression. Kuhnau used it devoid of obvious dance elements, not as a *sonata da chiesa* but for secular and general consumption. His version was in several movements, and, although not yet in the Classic form, was a decided harbinger. Seven of these he called *Fresh Fruit for the Clavier* (1696), which suggests that he knew that he was writing in an advanced way. Kuhnau later (1700) launched into what might be called the first real program music, *Biblische Historien . . . in sechs Sonaten (Biblical Stories . . . in Six Sonatas)*. In these, he uses heavy motives for the Giant in the David and Goliath story and in many ways prefigures the devices of tone poets to come.

Up to this time Germany had taken her musical nourishment from Italy and France, but of all the municipalities, Hamburg (always a free city) was the first to break away and develop its own musicians. Among these was Johann Mattheson (1681-1764), organist, singer, composer, writer and conductor. He inaugurated the first musical "Who's Who," with his book, *A German Roll of Honor,* in which he gathered information about German composers. He asked those living to write sketches about themselves, just as we do today for compendiums of biography. He claims to have been of assistance to Handel when he visited Hamburg in 1703. But due to his vanity they had a quarrel, which ended in a duel. Mattheson composed opera, oratorio, violin and *Clavier* pieces, but he is perhaps best remembered as a recorder of the state of music in his own era.

ORGAN MUSIC

Giovanni Gabrieli (1557-1612), nephew and pupil of Andrea, was, like his uncle, organist of St. Mark's. His fame was widespread and he became the teacher of Heinrich Schütz and Michael Praetorius, among many others. Gabrieli was an expert and daring contrapuntalist. His organ works led the way to a new style, as Paul Henry Lang comments, "by transmitting the principles of polychoral writing to the orchestra."

Girolamo Frescobaldi (1583-1643) advanced the organ and its technique, even as Corelli the violin and Scarlatti the piano, by way of the *clavicembalo*. At first Frescobaldi's works were built on vocal lines, but he soon began to develop a daring in composition and technique, based on his belief in the organ's possibilities. His *ricercare* were the first to be treated in modern fashion. Excelling in form, fancy, tonal color and power, they became a foundation upon which Bach built. Among Frescobaldi's compositions are *canzonas, toccatas, ricercare* and pieces in dance form. Although interested in the *camerata,* he freed himself from its influence and went his own unoperatic way. Holding important posts in Antwerp, Florence and Rome (twice at St. Peter's) he became known throughout Europe. Realizing his importance, Froberger, an organist at the court of Vienna, became his pupil in 1637 and was among the first to give South Germany her claim to musical honors.

After Frescobaldi, Italy ceased to be the world's center of organ music, although she was certainly responsible for the rise of the German school. Among Andrea Gabrieli's students in Venice was Hans Leo Hassler who returned to Southern Germany taking with him a love for, and knowledge of, Italian melody which he grafted to the gravity and natural profundity of his German temperament. Although a composer of *Lieder* and polychoral music in the Venetian tradition, it was as an organist that he is best known. He wrote *ricercare, toccatas* and adaptations of *chorales*. Such was his proficiency that he was ennobled by Emperor Rudolf II.

From 1650 to 1675 Germany had been in a repressed artistic condition due to devastating wars. No new impulses were manifested. Italy was supreme; France followed closely on Italy's heels. The Netherlands had been the source of polyphonic composition and had indeed taught the world. England, too, off in her little corner, had her brilliant group of madrigalists. Germany's contribution, through Luther and the fruits of the Protestant Reformation, had been the new church service and the *chorale,* in which lay the germs of much of her supremacy in the eighteenth and nineteenth centuries. The religious inspiration and sincerity of the *chorales* provided an incentive for German organists and for the sublime accomplishments of Johann Sebastian Bach.

As Germany was emerging from crushing warfare, one of her eminent musicians was Johann Jacob Froberger (1616-1667) of Saxony. In 1662 he reputedly left for England, but robbed on his way, accepted a post as organ-blower to ease his destitute condition. A story, probably apocryphal, is told that he enraged Christopher Gibbons (son of Orlando, 1615-1676), the organist of Westminster Abbey, by forgetting to pump the bellows. Froberger published many works for *Clavier* and organ. They are rugged in style. His suites for *Clavier* are among the most important of his era and "prefigure," says Leo Smith, "the highly organized texture of Bach." Among his works are *canzonas, fantasias* and *toccatas* in addition to suites. As a link between the Italian and German schools he is a significant historical figure.

Jan Adam Reinken (1623-1722), an Alsatian organist and pupil of Heinrich Scheidemann (*c.* 1596-1663), became a potent influence in German music. So illustrious was he that Bach walked twice from Lüneberg to Hamburg (thirty miles' distance) to hear him play. Reinken lived to be ninety-nine years old—one of the few contemporaries who appreciated Bach, for, when he heard Bach's improvisation on the *chorale, By the Waters of Babylon,* he remarked "I thought that this art was dead, but I see that it lives in you." Reinken, few of whose works remain, is looked upon as one of the foremost representatives of the North German school of seventeenth-century organists.

A man of Swedish parentage, Dietrich Buxtehude (1637-1707) attracted much attention as organist at Lübeck. The tireless Bach, who must have been a great walker, hiked fifty miles to hear Buxtehude play in a series of concerts, called *Abendmusiken* or Evening Music, which the organist instituted and which continued into the nineteenth century. Buxtehude also helped establish absolute music, that is, music free of a poetic subject or a *chorale* or plainsong basis. His particular genius as an instrumental composer lay in his free organ compositions. Buxtehude's *toccatas* are forceful and his *partitas* are concise. Another significant composer of organ works was Johann Pachelbel (1633-1706), a pupil of Kaspar Kerll (1627-1673), the eminent German composition teacher of the time. During his career, Pachelbel held organ posts at Eisenach, Stuttgart, Gotha, Nuremberg and Erfurt, and taught Bach's elder brother, among others. His elaborations of *chorales* and his *toccatas* raised him to a prominent place among his colleagues.

VIOLIN MUSIC

It is to Italy we look for the first great virtuosos and composers for the violin. In 1617 Biagio Marini of Brescia (*c.* 1595-1665) issued his *Opus* I, the *Affetti musicali,* which included some twenty-seven pieces in various forms arranged, in the composer's words, "so as to be played on violins, cornets or any kind of instrument." As early as 1629 Marini wrote passages of double stopping, even as his less well-known colleagues experimented with *col legno, tremolo* and other string techniques. It is of interest to note that Marini was the first composer to use *Opus* numbering as a means of organizing his works.

The first composer to devote an entire book to sonatas for solo violin and bass was Marco Uccellini (*c.* 1610- ?), who exploited the high register of the violin in such a way that Corelli reacted vigorously. Another early master was Giovanni Vitali (*c.* 1644-1692) who left many works, some of which are said to have influenced Purcell. One of Vitali's pupils was Giuseppe Torelli, whom we have noted as composer of a new kind of violin work, the solo concerto.

In addition to defining elements of the *concerto grosso,* Arcangelo Corelli (1653-1713) is renowned for being one of the first to realize the breadth and scope of the violin. An accomplished performer himself, Corelli helped develop the techniques of bowing and was one of the first composers to use double and triple stopping. Marc Pincherle writes:

> He established a violin technique based on the imitation of the purest form of singing, a technique so rational and so well organized that it has been the basis of teaching in all schools of violin-playing ever since. Corelli was the founder of the first classical school of violin-playing, and thereby made possible the development of an instrumental art without which none of the great classical forms could ever have come into being.

Trained in Bologna, Corelli spent most of his life in Rome. A thoughtful, earnest composer, he left relatively few works: forty-eight *Sonate a tre,* twelve *Sonate a violino e violone o cembalo* (which include the popular set of variations, *La Follia*) and twelve *concerti grossi*—all instrumental works. Yet his influence was widespread, and is found in music of Couperin and of Handel, who had met Corelli in Rome.

An equally influential but much more prolific composer was Antonio Vivaldi (*c.* 1669-1741), the "Red Priest," so nicknamed because of his flaming hair. Although he traveled widely, Vivaldi spent many years teaching in one of the four orphanage-conservatories in Venice, the

Fig. 42. *Grave* from the Second Sonata, *Opus 5*—Arcangelo Corelli, Amsterdam, *c.* 1710. Note the carefully written violin part and the bare indications of the counterlines and figured bass.

Seminario musicale dell' Ospitale della Pietà. This institution, unlikely as it seems, provided the composer with all the facilities of a Juilliard or an Eastman. Its orchestra was famous and its public enthusiastic. An English visitor in 1720 said of it:

> Every Sunday and Holiday there is a performance of music in the chapels of these Hospitals, vocal and instrumental, performed by the young women of the place, who are set in a gallery above, and are hid from any distinct view of those below, by a lattice of ironwork. The organ parts, as well as those of other instruments, are all performed by young women.

Here Vivaldi taught violin, conducted the orchestra and appeared as virtuoso, constantly composing to meet the heavy demand for new music, for in those days a composition was often performed just once. Supplementing these duties, Vivaldi found time to teach privately and produce forty operas, played in Venice and elsewhere. But although he wrote operas and much sacred and secular vocal music, Vivaldi's reputation rests upon his instrumental output which Pincherle estimates as including 454 concertos, two-thirds of which are solo concertos, twenty-three *sinfonia,* seventy-five sonatas or trios and two organ pieces.

Like Corelli, Vivaldi looked to singers for models of tonal perfection and we may be sure he was also completely aware of the dramatic instrumental techniques of theater orchestras, in Pincherle's phrase, the "fierce unisons, muted passages, tremolos and accompaniments lightened by the absence of basses." His concertos are beautifully balanced between *tutti* forces and soloists, replete with thematic materials and vivacious rhythms. In common with other Baroque composers, he uses the mannerism of three "hammerstrokes," built either on tones of the tonic chord or on an emphatic statement of the chords, I—V—I. He exploits the resources of his instruments with high and low arpeggios and extended scale passages, and, by evenly subdividing the beat in the violin part and insisting on running basses, he achieves, in Bukofzer's words, "not only the characteristic breathless drive but also a uniform continuity." His four-concerto-cycle, *Le Stagioni* (*The Seasons*), has remained delightful to this day, its descriptive overtones perhaps obvious and yet freshly rewarding.

Corelli and Vivaldi provided models for the German school of violinists that arose about this time, and Johann Sebastian Bach made transcriptions of Vivaldi's works. But Giuseppe Tartini (1692-1770) was the musical authority of his century, and no violinist felt secure of his place as an artist until he had been heard and approved by Tartini. Among his compositions is the "Devil's Trill," a sonata which challenges the virtuosity of the best player, even today.

Among other men who advanced violin playing and its library were Pietro Locatelli (1695-1764), Gaetano Pugnani (1731-1798), Pietro Nardini (1722-1793) and Francesco Veracini (1690-c. 1750), whose works still possess great interest and are an important adjunct to classical violin training. A much-esteemed composer and authority on the violin and its music was Padre Giambattista Martini (1706-1784) of Bologna, a Franciscan monk, visited for stimulus by Grétry, Gluck, Mozart and Johann Christian Bach. Dr. Burney, the famous eighteenth-century English critic, tells of meeting young Wolfgang with his father, Leopold Mozart, at one of the Philharmonic Society's festivals, through the kind scheming of Padre Martini.

Violin composition got off to a later start in France than in Italy, due to initial resistance to the instrument. But with Corelli's spreading fame, France, too, was conquered and a founder of a national school of violin emerged in the person of Jean-Marie Leclair (1697-1764), who brought out his first book of violin *sonatas* in 1723. Altogether Leclair left forty-eight *sonatas* for violin and *continuo,* as well as trios for two violins without bass, *concerti grossi* and an opera and ballet. Harmonic richness and idiomatic writing for the violin distinguish his creations. Also in France a novel turn was taken by Jean-Joseph Mondonville (1711-1772) who in 1734 published *Pièces de clavecin en sonate avec accompagnement de violin* (*Harpsichord Sonatas with Violin Accompaniment*) that activated a plea of Couperin's (in his *L'Art de toucher le clavecin*) that the harpsichord be used as a solo instrument rather than just an accompaniment to the violin. In Mondonville's sonatas the writing for the two instruments is strikingly *idiomatic, i.e.,* suited to the particular nature of the instrument. With the gradual disappearance of the violin part, the solo keyboard sonata would appear full-blown in the works of Mozart; for the sonatas by Kuhnau and Scarlatti represent isolated examples that were not actively developed at the time.

In Germany, where polyphony stubbornly persisted, violin composers were the first to adapt the older texture to the resources of the violin, utilizing double and triple stopping to an extent undreamed of by the Italians. As a result of this tendency, *scordatura* or alternate tuning, was often used. Outstanding among the early German violin composers was Heinrich von Biber (1644-1704), attached to the court of the Bishop of Salzburg, and composer of *sonatas* for harpsichord and violin, *duos* and works for a single unaccompanied violin, one of which, a *Passacaglia,* dating from 1675, anticipated the masterful *Chaconne* of J. S. Bach.

MUSIC FOR OTHER INSTRUMENTS AND GROUPS

In concluding this chapter, we might mention that the Baroque instrumental repertoire was enriched with solo pieces for the lute, which Bach and Handel still included in their works, and the guitar, for which the most notable composer was Denis Gaultier (1597-1672). Several *ricercare* for violoncello were written in 1689 by Domenico Gabrieli (*c.* 1650-1690), but such compositions were comparatively rare. The oboe, as we mentioned in the last chapter, enjoyed genuine popularity as a solo instrument, but wind instruments in general, both the woodwinds and the embryonic brasses, were still largely confined to out-of-door functions, or used to strengthen or accompany harpsichord or organ selections.

At the sumptuous court of Versailles, presided over by Louis XIV with 6000 retainers and servants, including a large staff of musicians, appeared *Les vingt-quatre violons du roi* ("The Twenty-four Violins of the King"), in reality a string orchestra consisting of six first, four second and four third violins as well as four violas and six basses. Lully, in 1656, created an elite group of sixteen, called *Les petits violons du roi,* used to accompany Court Ballets and for social occasions, of which there were a great number.

During Louis XIV's reign there was also a band called *La musique de la grande écurie de roi* ("Music of the King's Stables"). Among the

Fig. 43. "The Concert"—seventeenth century engraving by Saint Aubin. King Louis XV and his retinue listen to a concert performed on harpsichord, 'cello, violin and flute, an example of *musique de chambre*. (Courtesy The Metropolitan Museum of Art, Dick Fund, 1933.)

instruments were twelve trumpets, eight fifes, drums, the *cromorne* (*krumhorn*—a curved reed instrument), four to six Poitou oboes (probably small oboes), bagpipes, twelve large oboes, violins, sackbuts (akin to trombones) and cornets. The players, being attached to the stables, accompanied royal hunting parties and played wind fanfares which sounded through the forest the calls adopted by each great family.

We shall return to the subject of orchestration and bands in another chapter. Meanwhile, our journey leads us to the fulfillment of many of the Baroque ideals and tendencies that we have been discussing, culminating in the works of two musical giants, Johann Sebastian Bach and George Frederic Handel.

SUGGESTIONS FOR FURTHER READING

Apel, Willi, *Masters of the Keyboard.* Cambridge, Harvard University Press, 1947.

Bedbrook, Gerald S., *Keyboard Music from the Middle Ages to the Beginnings of the Baroque.* London, Macmillan, 1949.

Boyden, David D., *The History of Violin Playing from Its Origins to 1761, and Its Relationship to the Violin and Violin Music.* New York. Oxford University Press, 1965. With demonstration record.

Bukofzer, Manfred F., *Music in the Baroque Era.* New York, Norton, 1947.

Burney, Charles, *A General History of Music.* New York, Dover, 1935 (1776-1789). 2 vols.

Colles, H. C., *The Growth of Music*. London, Oxford University Press, 1956.

Davison, Archibald T., and Apel, Willi, *Historical Anthology of Music,* vol. 2. Cambridge, Harvard University Press, 1949.

Dorian, Frederick, *The History of Music in Performance.** New York, Norton, 1942.

Hayes, Gerald R., *Musical Instruments and Their Music, Viols and Violins, 1500-1750*. Oxford, Oxford University Press, 1928.

Horsley, Imogene, *Fugue*. New York, Free Press, 1966.

Hutchings, Arthur, *The Baroque Concerto.** New York, Norton, 1965.

Kirkpatrick, Ralph, *Domenico Scarlatti*. Princeton, Princeton University Press, 1953.

Mann, Alfred, *The Study of Fugue.** New Brunswick, Rutgers University Press, 1958.

Mellers, Wilfrid, *François Couperin and the French Classical Tradition*. New York, Roy, 1951.

Nettl, Paul, *The Story of Dance Music*. New York, Philosophical Library, 1947.

Newman, William S., *The Sonata in the Baroque Era*. Chapel Hill, University of North Carolina Press, 1959.

Palisca, Claude, *Baroque Music.** Englewood Cliffs, Prentice-Hall, 1967.

Parrish, Carl, *A Treasury of Early Music.** New York, Norton, 1958.

Parrish, Carl and Ohl, John F., *Masterpieces of Music before 1750*. New York, Norton, 1951.

Pincherle, Marc, *Corelli, His Life, His Music*. New York, Norton, 1956.

——— *Vivaldi, Genius of the Baroque.** New York, Norton, 1957.

Sachs, Curt, *World History of the Dance.** New York, Norton, 1937.

Smith, Leo, *Music of the Seventeenth and Eighteenth Centuries*. London, Dent, 1931.

A Sampler of Supplementary Recordings

Collections

Baroque Trumpet	Nonesuch 1002
German String Music of the 17th Century	Oiseau 50175
Heritage of the Baroque	2-Vox 14000
Keyboard Music of the French Court	American Society 1006
Masterpieces of Music before 1750	Haydn 9038/40
Ten Centuries of Music	DGG KL-52/61
Treasury of Early Music	Haydn 9100/3
2000 Years of Music	Folkways 3700
Art of the Harpsichord	Victor LM-2194
Hunting Horn Music	Golden Crest 4014
N. German Baroque Organ Music	3-Vox VBX 34
Clavichord Music	Repertoire 901

Music of Individual Composers

Biber, Heinrich von, *Sonatas*
Buxtehude, Dietrich, *Organ Music*
Corelli, Arcangelo, *Concerti grossi Sinfonias*
Couperin, François, *Concerts royaux*

* Available in paperback edition.

Frescobaldi, Girolamo, *Fiori musicali: Toccatas*
Froberger, Johann Jacob, *Suites de clavecin*
Gabrieli, Giovanni, *Sacrae Symphoniae*
Kuhnau, Johann, *Biblical Sonatas for Harpsichord*
Leclair, Jean-Marie, *Concerti for Violin*
Manfredini, Francesco, *Concerto for 2 Trumpets, Strings, Harpsichord and Organ*
Pachelbel, Johann, *Organ Music*
Purcell, Henry, *Harpsichord and Clavichord Music Fantasias*
Rameau, Jean-Philippe, *Pièces de clavecin*
Scarlatti, Domenico, *Sonatas*
Tartini, Giuseppe, *Sonata in g for Violin,* "Devil's Trill"
Torelli, Giuseppe, *Concerti grossi Sinfonias*
Vitali, Tommaso, *Chaconne for Violin*
Vivaldi, Antonio, *Concerti*

OPPORTUNITIES FOR STUDY IN DEPTH

1. A fugue is a monothematic polyphonic work with two or more voices which proceed in a defined, yet flexible, manner—challenging the composer's ingenuity. Diagram, either from repeated listening or from a score, one fugue, noting details of the exposition and subsequent episodes. A good choice is Bach's "Little" *Fugue in G Minor,* available in its original form and in orchestral transcription.

2. Compare keyboard music of Couperin *le grand* with Maurice Ravel's suite, *Le Tombeau de Couperin.* What stylistic features of the latter are reminiscent of the earlier composer? In what way?

3. If possible, attend a concert of Baroque instrumental music, performed on instruments of the period. (Several professional ensembles use authentic instrumentation.) Note the tone color of these instruments as compared with their modern relations. What are the reasons for performing Baroque music with Baroque instruments? What are the points against such a procedure?

4. On the basis of personal interest, study more intensively any aspect of Baroque instrumental music mentioned in this chapter. Organize the information gained in the form of a magazine article.

5. If practical, learn several early Baroque instrumental pieces, either solos or ensembles. Present a class concert, with oral program notes prefacing each work.

6. Make a study of interpretation of dynamics and tempo in Baroque instrumental music. This topic has been an area of dispute for several hundred years, owing to the lack of precise indications on manuscripts and the loss of Baroque performing traditions. Equipped with as much information as possible, secure an *Urtext*—that is, a facsimile of a composition without added editing—and proceed to edit it on the basis of findings.

7. Compare instrumental improvisation and extemporizing of the Baroque style with that of modern "progressive" jazz. In what way is the performer bound by a composer's intentions? In what way is he free to interpolate his personal resources?

8. During the period, 1650-1750, a prosperous middle class arose in Europe. How

did this group influence composers? painters? architects? performing musicians? public life? Cite examples.

Vocabulary Enrichment

sequence
textural polarity
doctrine of affects
"varied couples"
suite
allemande
courante
saraband
gigue
canzona francese
diminution, coloration or division
sonata
trio sonata
sonata da chiesa
sonata da camera
sinfonia
ritornello
concerto grosso
concertino
ripieno or *tutti*

solo concerto
ricercar
fugue
exposition
counterexposition
episode
stretto
organ point
chaconne
passacaglia
Chorale-variation
toccata
fancy
fantasia
agréments
"gallant style"
ordres
absolute music
scordatura
idiomatic

PART V

The Apogee of the Baroque

Chapter 11.

MUSIC OF THE GERMAN BAROQUE—J. S. BACH

To George Erdmann:
Honoured Sir:
. . . it pleased God to summon me here to this town as *Directore Musices* and cantor at the St. Thomas School . . . The position was described to me in such favourable terms (and especially since my sons seemed disposed to study here) that finally I ventured this step in the name of the Most High and I came to Leipzig, passed my examination, and then made the move. Here, as it pleased God, I have remained to this day. But now I find that:

(1) The position is not nearly so advantageous as I had believed.
(2) Many of the incidental fees have been withdrawn.
(3) This town is very expensive to live in.
(4) The authorities are queer folk . . .

Joh. Seb. Bach
Leipzig, October 28, 1730.

The year 1685, birthdate of Scarlatti, Bach and Handel, may be accepted as ushering in the era of modern music, as most of us know it. The seventeenth century, a period of transition, had witnessed many changes: the breaking down of the Church modes in favor of the diatonic scales and a freer use of the chromatic scale; the recognition of a harmonic system, in addition to the contrapuntal; the rise of opera with its new vocal recitative, *aria* and instrumental accompaniment; the improved manufacture of instruments; the development of instrumental music and the creation of new forms; the establishment of instrumental groups for furthering chamber and orchestral music; the entrance of Germany as a musical power, gradually wresting first place from Italy; and the rise of virtuosos—violinists, opera stars, organists and harpsichordists.

Into this world of tentative revolutions, Johann Sebastian Bach was born. The early experiments and suggested possibilities were welded, through his genius, his profound knowledge of music, his indefatigable study and the power of his personality, into great and noble works, masterpieces that achieve with every generation greater recognition and renewed expressiveness. Johann Sebastian belonged to the fifth of seven generations of musical Bachs. Out of sixty members of the family, dating from 1509, all but seven were organists, cantors or town musicians. The only one who bore the name of Sebastian was born March 21, 1685, at Eisenach, in the shadow of the Wartburg Castle, where Martin Luther had been held prisoner. Behind him lay a large and well-defined heritage of Protestant church music which, in the Lutheran service, exercised a powerful function in projecting exegeses of the all-important Word of God as found in the Scriptures. Many sources had contributed to its emergence.

LUTHER AND THE *Chorale*

Martin Luther, as we have noted, was himself a musical dilettante and very much interested in music as an aid to worship and spiritual improvement. His *Ein' feste Burg ist unser Gott* ("A Mighty Fortress Is Our God") was to become the battle-hymn of the Reformation. In a letter he had stated:

> Music is one of the greatest gifts that God has given us: it is divine and therefore Satan is its enemy. For with its aid many dire temptations are overcome; the devil does not stay where music is.

The **chorale** (German Protestant hymn) is based on an alternation of stressed and weak syllables inherent in the German language itself. Consequently, German folksong provided a storehouse of usable musical material to which vernacular poetry could readily be adapted—a practice known as *contrafacta* or parody. As Catholic hymns followed a similar metric pattern, they too were susceptible of Protestant revision. It is no surprise, therefore, to find Heinrich Isaak's *Lied, Innsbruck, ich muss dich lassen* ("Innsbruck, I Must Leave You") reappearing in the guise of *Nun ruhen alle Wälder* ("Now Rest All the Forests") or St. Ambrose's *Veni redemptor gentium* as *Nun komm der Heiden Heiland* ("Now Comes the Redeemer of the Heathen").

Just seven years after Luther posted his ninety-five theses on the cathedral door (the usual spot for posting notices at that time), no less than four *chorale* books had been published in simple as well as in polyphonic settings by Luther's musical adviser, Johann Walther (1496-1570). The first *Kantoreien* (spiritual singing club) was formed by Walther in 1529 and choral singing became an important part of the *Gymnasium* (secondary school) curriculum, with compositions by des Prés and Lasso highly recommended.

Quite quickly then, a large library of *chorales* was assembled; these were available for both unison singing and in complex polyphonic forms, fashioned from Italian models. Lasso himself, we recall, had written many German songs while he was composer to the Duke of

Fig. 44. Innsbruck, Austria. As part of the practice of *contrafacta*, Isaak's *Lied, "Innsbruck, ich muss dich lassen,"* became the chorale, *"Nun ruhen alle Walder."* (Photograph by the editor.)

Bavaria at Munich. In the next generation, Hans Leo Hassler, born in Nuremberg, educated in Venice and employed at various German courts during his lifetime, brought the Venetian tradition to Germany, writing, in among many other forms, *chorale-motets*.

Chorale ELABORATIONS

No discussion of German Baroque music can fail to acknowledge the importance of the *chorale* in the compositions of Protestant composers, to whom it offered a core of inspiration and a symbol of a universal cultural element. All sorts of variations were possible in using it, from the naïve to the most sophisticated treatments. In the following pages we shall examine some of them, notably the *chorale-prelude* for organ and the unifying role of the *chorale* in such vocal forms as the cantata, oratorio and passion. By analogy the use of a *chorale* appears to be an extension of the Netherlanders' employment of Gregorian *cantus firmi*. But there is at least one difference; that is the poetic implications of the *chorale* texts, which had become inseparable from the melodies, so that, as Einstein comments, we are dealing not only with the liturgical but also with the poetic kernel of sacred music. As he continues, ". . . what had once been meaningless combination was now instinct with poetry."

Chorale-preludes are short organ works which were used in the Lutheran service to introduce the hymn to be sung by the congregation, who, of course, were well acquainted with it. A composer who did much to formalize the form was the Dutch organist, Jan Pieterszoon Sweelinck, whom we have already mentioned. Although he spent most of his life in Amsterdam, among his pupils were many Germans, absorbing from him bits of what was to become the religious style of the eighteenth century. Sweelinck's treatment of the *chorale* featured the principle of *cantus firmus* writing, in which the underlying hymn melody was developed through upper variations that assumed increasingly complex aspects as the piece progressed, in the English variation manner.

Michael Praetorius (1571-1621), composer and historian, was, like Hassler, familiar with Venetian techniques. In his chief collection of compositions, the nine-volume *Musae Sionae* (*Muses of Zion,* 1605-10), Praetorius joined the polychoral tradition with that of German *chorales,* employing a conservative style which almost excluded *continuo.* In copious notes distributed throughout the scores, the composer advises us of three methods of *chorale* arrangement; these he calls the "motet fashion," the "madrigal fashion" and the *"cantus firmus* fashion." In the first a *chorale* appears in fragments pervading a polyphonic texture, rather similar to the use of a tune in a sixteenth-century Mass. "Madrigal fashion" connoted another fragmentary usage, characterized by tossing segments of the melody back and forth among the voices, supported by a *continuo.* In the third method, the *chorale* was presented in its entirety, with other voices providing musical comments by means of imitative or independent counterpoint.

THE THREE S'S

One of Sweelinck's pupils was Samuel Scheidt (1587-1654), who with Johann Hermann Schein (1586-1630) and Heinrich Schütz (1585-1672), made up the "Three S's" of a century before Bach. A master of the organ variation, Scheidt provided a different contrapuntal and harmonic accompaniment for each stanza of a *chorale.* In addition, he developed the *chorale-fantasia,* in which the *chorale-motet* was adapted to the organ. Examples are to be found in his *Tabulatura nova* of 1624. Schein, a cantor at St. Thomas', Leipzig, added to the *chorale* the principle of monody, as illustrated in his *Geistliche Konzerte (Spiritual Concerti)* and his choral motets. He was also a prolific composer of secular works.

The greatest of the three, however, was Heinrich Schütz. A student of both Gabrieli and Monteverdi, Schütz fused Italian and German styles, producing vivid madrigals, large multichoral structures and the first German oratorios, one of which was the *Resurrection History* of 1623. He made relatively little use of *chorales* as such, although he was apt to borrow their texts to set to his own music. He left sixteen volumes of music, none of which contains an instrumental solo.

In Schütz's works can be discerned several general characteristics of German Baroque style. One is the apparent lack of differentiation in writing for violins and voices. Another is the *hemiola,* a distinctive rhythmic treatment of cadences in triple meter—*i.e.,* 𝅗𝅥 𝅘𝅥 | 𝅗𝅥 𝅘𝅥 𝅗𝅥 | 𝅗𝅥. , in which the primary accent is momentarily abandoned in the next to last measure. A third is an extended use of sequence, both melodic and harmonic, as a means of development. Although Schütz accepted new forms with enthusiasm, he was also aware of the temptations of monody and in his old age returned to a conservative *a cappella* style in the *Passions* according to St. Matthew, St. Luke and St. John, in which he reaffirmed strict contrapuntal writing and helped keep the technique alive through Bach.

In his *Psalms of David* (1619), amateur and student choruses will find rewarding works to study, with their freshness, surprising harmonic and rhythmic changes and straightforward projection of the underlying emotions. It is noteworthy, as Henry Raynor states, that Schütz "is the one Protestant composer of his age whose music transcends sectarianism." Einstein adds, "In his urge towards the utmost truth of expression, in his aversion to all surface polish for the sake of mere formal beauty, and at the same time in the instinctive sureness of his construction, Schütz, . . . where he is greatest, is comparable only to a great German painter—Albrecht Dürer."

Dietrich Buxtehude and the Cantata

The Thirty Years' War had drastically disrupted Schütz's career. His enforced isolation may account for the fact that not even Andreas Hammerschmidt (1612-1675), whose *chorale-arias* and *Dialogues* brought a freedom of expression into German church music, came near to matching the master. The city of Lübeck was spared the ravages of war, however, and it was there that Franz Tunder (1614-1667) was organist of the *Marienkirche*. Tunder's compositions united all the accepted forms of *chorale* exploitation, following the conservative tradition to which Buxtehude and Bach were heirs. Each verse was set with special care to reflect nuances of the text's meaning, using instruments and solo voices to produce the desired results. Though stiff in most part, there were moments of vigor in Tunder's work that Buxtehude exploited.

Tunder's successor at the *Marienkirche* was Dietrich Buxtehude, who followed the custom of the time by marrying his predecessor's daughter. (It has been alleged that Handel later refused the Lübeck post because of this stipulation.) Buxtehude's fame as an organist was widespread, as we have noted. His compositions for the instrument fused formal discipline with dramatic elements. The forty *chorale-preludes,* prototypes of the form, were tightly-constructed, featuring elaborate melodic ornamentation which, unlike earlier "coloration," was not abstract but rather a means for interpreting subjectively the mood of the *chorale*. Recently, however, considerable attention has been focused on his cantatas, of which about 124 survive of the many he must have written.

What is a **cantata?** We have previously described the evolution of the form in Italy as a composition in several sections for vocal soloists, chorus and instruments, based upon a poetic libretto that might be either lyric or dramatic, secular or sacred. In 1700, in the course of an official reform of Protestant sacred music, the cantata was moved to a prominent place in the Lutheran service, to be performed each Sunday with a text appropriate to the demands of the church calendar. In addition to utilizing Scriptural excerpts, it could propound subjective dramatizations of Biblical events with a large latitude of freedom on the part of the librettist. From opera were borrowed recitative, *aria* and ensembles. These were synthesized with the grand French overture and the Italian instrumental style, unified by the Reformation German *chorale*.

There is no set pattern to the Buxtehude cantatas, for they may have solo voices or chorus, Latin or German texts drawn from Psalms, *chorale* verses or free poetry. Most of them do commence with an introductory instrumental *sinfonia,* motives from which reappear (in cyclical manner) in the *Amen* or *Alleluia* that concludes the works. In these cantatas is reflected the close union between operatic and religious idioms. Buxtehude's *ariosos* are lyrical and warm, in contrast to those of his contemporaries, and betray evidence of theatrical influence. When we remember the casual ease with which composers, including Bach and Handel, adapted their own secular compositions to sacred texts, we

Fig. 45. Frontispiece, *Musikalisches Lexicon*—J. Walther, Leipzig, 1732. The conductor in this performance of a cantata stands behind the organist, with his back to the string and brass players. Note that he holds a roll of music in each hand. On the organ is inscribed, "All that has had being, praise the Lord."

realize that no hard and fast line existed between secular and sacred styles, as it often does now.

Buxtehude's *chorale* cantata, based on the hymn by Johann Franck (1644-*c.* 1710) and Johann Crüger (1598-1662), *Jesu meine Freude* ("Jesus, My Joy"), is interesting in itself and also in comparison with the celebrated setting of J. S. Bach. Buxtehude's work is scored for two sopranos, one bass, two violins, bassoon and *continuo.* It opens with an overture (called a "sonata" in this case), mingling features of both the Italian and French varieties. The six stanzas of the *chorale* are presented in five different ways, with a repetition of the initial setting and the concluding verse at the end. In Bach's motet version, the hymn of Franck is expanded by the addition of verses from Paul's *Epistle to the Romans,* enlarging the number of sections to eleven. It begins and ends with a four-part setting of the *chorale.* Within are found choruses and trios, sensitively recording the struggle over sin and death implicit in the words. The absence of an accompaniment has been the occasion for dispute among authorities. The motet is usually performed with *continuo,* however, which augments the effectiveness of the music and the stability of the choristers.

OTHER COMPOSERS

No musical giant stands between Buxtehude and Bach and Handel. Yet there were other significant composers contributing to the music of the German Baroque, including Philipp Krieger (1649-1725), who composed cantatas in the new style; Johann Pachelbel; Johann Kuhnau, Bach's predecessor at Leipzig; Johann Joseph Fux (*c.* 1660-1741); Georg Böhm (1661-1733), whose organ works show French influence; Friedrich Zachau (1663-1712), Handel's teacher; and Georg Philipp Telemann (1681-1767).

Of the above, two composers deserve additional comment, although they are not in the direct line of development that we have been discussing. Fux is known to us as the author of a rather academic Latin textbook on counterpoint, *Gradus ad Parnassum (Steps to Parnassus),* published in 1725 and studied by Mozart and Haydn, among others. In this manual, Fux outlines his ideas about sixteenth-century techniques of polyphonic composition, techniques toward which his own music turned, although in his fifty Masses, numerous pieces of Catholic liturgical music and operas, he combined scholastic learning with imagination. For nearly thirty years Fux was *Kapellmeister* of St. Stephen's Cathedral, Vienna, and served with honor under three emperors, whose conservative tastes he amply satisfied.

Telemann, whose music is currently enjoying a popular revival, was an associate of Bach at Leipzig and a friend of Handel. Liberally educated but largely self-taught in music, Telemann was an exceedingly prolific composer whose works outnumber those of Bach and Handel combined—some 6000 items. Of these, the *Paris Quartets* (1733) for flute, violin, gamba or 'cello and *continuo* anticipate Haydn and are historically important as links between Baroque and Classic instrumental conceptions. The three "productions" of *Musique de table*

(1733), although humbly presented as dinner music, are subtly conceived. The second overture is worthy of standing beside Bach's *Brandenburg Concerto No. 1*. As Bernard Jacobson writes, "One could take a more favorable view of the present state of civilization if this were the kind of music one heard at dinners today." Moreover, Telemann ranks after Handel and Keiser as an outstanding German dramatic composer. His *Pimpinone* (1725), an intermezzo with two characters, foreshadows Pergolesi's *La Sèrva padrona*.

By 1740 Telemann's reputation among his contemporaries was a dominating one. Mattheson wrote: "Lully is renowned, Corelli may be praised;/Telemann alone is above plaudits raised." He was considered a far greater composer than Bach. Indeed, he was more "modern," in that he embraced the thinner textures and lively melodies of the "gallant style," inclining away from the pomposity of sacred polyphony and the doubling of the *basso continuo*. Jacobson continues:

> It is not stars of the first magnitude only that light up the night sky, and we should not despise Telemann because the summits and profundities that Bach attains with such ease are beyond his reach. He has sensitivity enough to provide ample contrast for his prevailingly sunny mood; and his cheerfulness and lyricism alike are entirely personal in character and in expression.

But back to Bach!

JOHANN SEBASTIAN BACH—LIFE

Johann Sebastian Bach was the sixth child of J. Ambrosius Bach, who gave his son an early start with lessons on the violin and viola. Bach's parents died when he was ten years old and he went to live with his brother, J. Christoph, who instructed him on the *Clavier* and introduced him to Froberger's organ works. At fifteen Bach joined the choir at Lüneberg, where he became acquainted with a large library of vocal music, which he explored with the avid curiosity he showed throughout his life. There he learned to play the organ and came into contact with Georg Böhm. He went on foot to Hamburg to hear Reinken, and also to Celle, where the court band performed the French music that afterwards influenced his own. After serving as violinist for a few months in the ducal orchestra at Saxe-Weimar, Bach was appointed organist at Arnstadt in 1703.

A year later, he took a leave of absence and journeyed to Lübeck. That Bach had lessons from Buxtehude is generally accepted, although it has been a disputed point. At any rate, the young organist remained away from his post for four months instead of four weeks. On his re-

Fig. 46. Bach's birthplace, Eisenach. The only Bach who bore the name, Sebastian, was born in Eisenach in the shadow of the Wartburg Castle where Martin Luther had been held prisoner. (Photograph courtesy Margret Hofmann.)

turn he was censured not only for the extended vacation and for not rehearsing his choir, but also for *viele wunderliche Variationen* (many strange variations) with which he accompanied the *chorales*. Apparently Arnstadt did not appreciate what he had learned in Lübeck. After unpleasant friction, Bach finally resigned to accept a post at Mühlhausen in 1707. During the same year he married his cousin, Maria Barbara Bach, who was to bear him seven children, four of whom survived her death in 1720. Of these, Wilhelm Friedemann and Carl Philipp Emanuel became famous musicians.

As Bach saw no chance to improve musical conditions in the Mühlhausen church, which was torn between Pietists and orthodox Lutherans, he departed after a year. The rest of his career and the works he composed were influenced by subsequent appointments: at Weimar as court organist, chamber musician and concertmaster to the Grand Duke, Wilhelm Ernst (1708-1717); at Cöthen as *Kapellmeister* to Prince Leopold of Anhalt-Cöthen (1717-1723); and at Leipzig as cantor of St. Thomas' Church (1723-1750). Charles Stanford Terry writes:

> Even had his career stopped at 1717, the work of his Weimer years placed him among the immortals. They announced him to his contemporaries as the foremost organist of his period; they inspired his greatest compositions for the instrument on which he excelled; they contributed some of the finest examples of the Cantata form he developed to its zenith at Leipzig, and no small amount of chamber music. Weimar received from him a reputation for culture which Goethe, Schiller and Liszt prolonged but did not originate.

Bach's years at Weimar were happy, apparently, until the post of *Kapellmeister* was vacated. Disappointed that it was not offered to him, he demanded his release. The six years that Bach passed at Cöthen were also pleasant. Here he had opportunity to write much of his instrumental music. Prince Leopold played in the orchestra that Bach directed and Bach went with the Prince on his travels. During one of these trips, Maria Barbara died.

After a year and a half Bach married Anna Magdalena Wülcken, a singer at one of the small neighboring courts, who was artistically sympathetic and a congenial companion. Bach continued her musical education, as the *Clavierbüchlein von Anna Magdalena Bach* (two books of easy pieces for the *Clavier*) testifies. The couple had thirteen children, most of whom died in infancy; only six outlived the father. These were Gottfried Heinrich, Johann Christoph, Johann Christian, and three daughters. In the meantime, his favorite master, Prince Leopold, had married a frivolous princess and life was less congenial at court. Bach's sons were growing up and needed more advanced schools than Cöthen afforded. So he looked about for a new position.

Bach was appointed cantor of St. Thomas' School in Leipzig to fill the vacancy left by the death of Johann Kuhnau. He was chosen because neither Telemann nor Christoph Graupner (1683-1760), who were offered the post, were free to accept it. Bach was known as an organist, but not as a composer, although he had already written some of his greatest organ works and chamber music as well as some cantatas. The ancient cathedral school, founded in 1212, supplied churches in Leipzig with choirs and in return for services, the choristers were educated. The cantor was obliged to teach singing and instrumental music, Latin and Luther's *Catechism*. He conducted a cantata at St. Thomas' or at St. Nicholas' Church every Sunday, and rehearsed the singers for four churches. In addition, he supplemented his income by officiating with the choir boys at funerals and weddings.

Much of the work must have irked Bach's artist-soul, although he had his compensation in the satisfaction of writing music that was put into use before the ink was dry on the copy. Terry writes, "As the years passed he allowed his pedagogic duties to sit more and more loosely on his shoulders, delegated his task as choirmaster to subordinate though capable hands, and devoted his time and genius to perfecting the musical forms German art had been patiently developing since the Reformation—the Oratorio, Passion and Cantata." The Leipzig services required fifty-nine cantatas a year, and Bach wrote five complete sets, although not all of them have been preserved.

In 1729 Bach was appointed conductor of the *Collegium Musicum.* This society had been formed from various student bodies in Leipzig by Georg Philipp Telemann, while he was organist at one of the four churches, whose choirs were supplied by the students of St. Thomas'. Bach's connection with the Telemann Society gave him better material than he had among his own pupils. In conflict with the council that dictated the policy of running the school and neither an organizer nor a disciplinarian, Bach was subject to severe criticism. Yet with his inadequate choral and instrumental groups, Bach managed to perform his *St. Matthew Passion.* "Nothing is more striking," says Terry, "than the contrast between Bach's pugnacity over the prerogatives of his office, and the buoyancy which floated his creative genius upon a sea of difficulties that must have submerged it, had not the call been irresistible and the inward voice compelling."

Bach dedicated the *Kyrie* and *Gloria* of his masterpiece, the *B Minor Mass,* to the Electoral Prince of Dresden (when he became King of Poland) together with a request that he be given the title of Court Composer. This was granted three years later (1736). Bach had held the honorary title of *Kapellmeister* of the Court at Weissenfels since 1729. Perhaps he thought the honor of being Court Composer might carry weight with the school rector and town council by whom he was regarded merely as a not too proficient cantor.

In 1740, his son, Carl Philipp Emanuel was appointed *Clavier* accompanist to Frederick the Great. Bach's last journey was to Potsdam in 1747, on which occasion Frederick the Great announced his arrival with, "Gentlemen, old Bach has come!" A delightful account is given in Forkel's biography as related to him by Wilhelm Friedemann, who accompanied his father. Bach tried the King's Silbermann "fortepianos." The King, at Bach's request, gave him a fugue subject upon which to extemporize, and then Bach was invited to play all the organs in town. As a result of this visit, Bach used Frederick's fugue subject as the theme of his *Musikalisches Opfer* (*Musical Offering*) which he sent as a gift to the King.

Bach's eyes, always overworked, were failing rapidly when he submitted to an operation by Handel's surgeon in January, 1750, which left him completely blind. At the time he had been finishing his monumental composition, *Die Kunst der Fuge* (*The Art of Fugue*) and revising his eighteen *Chorale-Preludes for Organ*. To his son-in-law, Johann Christoph Altnikol, he dictated the last of these, *Before Thy Throne, My God, I Stand*. It was his last musical word. For a short interval his sight returned and he was able to see the faces of his wife and children. Then he was stricken with apoplexy and died ten days later on July 28, 1750. Bach was buried in the *Johanniskirche* yard with no memorial to mark the spot. In 1894, the old church was demolished and Bach's skeleton was painstakingly identified and placed beneath the altar of the reconstructed church. When the Johann Sebastian Bach Memorial, erected through the assiduity of Mendelssohn, was unveiled in 1843, one grandson, the only living member of Bach's family, was present.

JOHANN SEBASTIAN BACH—MUSIC

Rutland Boughton asserts: "Musicians disagree in most matters concerning music, but regarding the supreme greatness of Bach they are unanimous. Pedants and idealists, antiquarians and realists, futurists and quite ordinary musicians find common ground there." To Bach, music and religion were synonymous; in his own words, "music should have no other aim than the glory of God and the recreation of the soul." He composed as his environment dictated but made little effort to publicize his masterpieces. He drew from the musical literature of the Netherlands, Italy, France, England and Germany for style, form, technique and ideas but infused them all with his genius. Gathering together the experiments of the seventeenth century, he put the stamp of his personality on them for all time. Sacred and secular cantatas, Passions, Masses, preludes, fugues, *toccatas, chorales, chorale-preludes, fantasias,* suites, *partitas,* inventions, *passacaglias, chaconnes* and concertos—all had existed before—yet these titles immediately call forth the name of Bach. His predecessors were the apprentices; he was the master.

His greatest works were left unpublished and he was over forty before the six *Partitas* which constituted Part I of the *Clavierübung* (*Clavier Studies*) were engraved. Parts II, III and IV, containing the *Italian Concerto,* the *B Minor Partita,* the organ preludes on catechismal hymns, four clavichord duets, the *Goldberg Variations,* some hymn tunes in the Schemelli collection, six organ *chorales* and the *Musikalisches Opfer,* complete the list of publications during his lifetime.

Bach's first compositions were for the organ, as his first appointments were as organist. At Weimar, he wrote the *Passacaglia and Fugue in C Minor;* organ preludes, fugues and toccatas; and the *Orgelbüchlein (Little Organ Book)*, containing forty-five *chorale-preludes.* He was promoted to concertmaster with the duty of composing a new work monthly. In all, Bach wrote 150 works for organ based on the German *chorales.*

From the Cöthen period, when Bach was *Kapellmeister,* come the six concertos dedicated to Duke Christian Ludwig of Brandenburg; four orchestral suites or overtures, one of which includes the lovely "Air for G String"; violin concertos, sonatas for violin, violoncello, flute and *viola da gamba,* usually written in sets of six, following the Italian practice. During this time, he also composed for the *Clavier.* His works include the *Chromatic Fantasy and Fugue,* six "English" and six "French" suites, as well as teaching material for his children—*Preludes for Beginners,* two- and three-part *Inventions,* and, in 1722, the first volume of *Das Wohltemperierte Clavier (The Well-tempered Clavichord)*. Later, in 1744, he completed this cycle, which has come to be known as the pianist's Old Testament, for the children of his second marriage.

Although we have implied that Bach created no new forms, he was, nevertheless, an innovator. The old keyboard instruments could not be played in all keys, as the fifths and thirds were tuned absolutely, that is, according to the mathematical divisions of the string. In their own keys the intervals were true, but were out of tune in relation to other tonalities. It was expedient to find a relative tuning, so as to "temper" them sufficiently to be practical for modulating. When the clavichord was built with one string to each note, the problem became more acute. The tuning of the organ also required modification. In 1691 a treatise on *Musical Temperament* had been published by Andreas Werckmeister (1645-1706). His solution was to divide the octave into twelve equal half-steps. Bach was the first composer to demonstrate the method's feasibility in his *Well-tempered Clavichord,* preludes and fugues in twenty-four major and minor keys.

Bach was the inventor of a *lute-Clavier* and the *viola pomposa.* Moreover, he was responsible for a reform of fingering without which keyboard playing could never have reached a virtuoso stage. Carl Philipp Emanuel related that his father, living "in an epoch in which there came about gradually a most remarkable change in musical taste . . . found it necessary to think out for himself a much more thorough use of the fingers, and especially the thumb."

Fig. 47. The Bach organ at St. Thomas' Church, Leipzig. Bach was best known as an organ virtuoso during his lifetime.

As Weimar was the frame for his organ works and Cöthen for the instrumental compositions, so Leipzig and his cantorate at St. Thomas' provided a *raison d'être* for Bach's vast output of cantatas and choral masterpieces. Of the five sets of cantatas, numbering about 295, all but thirty must have been written at Leipzig from 1723 to 1744. About 200 have been preserved, to which may be added some incomplete and doubtful works. They constituted the "Principal Music" of the Lutheran service, and, indeed, were the nearest approach to regular musical performances that the general public had. Bach used texts by the clergyman, Erdmann Neumeister; by Salomo Franck, a colleague at Cöthen; Christian Friedrich Henrici (better known as Picander); and Marianne von Ziegler of Leipzig. Whittacker writes of the cantatas:

> There is a complete absence of stereotyped order of movements, which consists of choruses, *chorales,* plain or elaborated, *arias,* duets, trios, *recitatives,* and instrumental numbers. . . . About one-third of the existing *cantatas* are for solo voices, the number of participants ranging from one to four, and the chorus being either entirely absent, or confined merely to simple concluding of intermediate *chorales.*

The orchestra at Bach's disposal numbered from seventeen to twenty student performers. Instruments included strings, flutes, oboes (also *oboe d'amore,* alto oboe and *oboe da caccia,* tenor oboe), bassoons (also *taille de basson,* a tenor bassoon called *tenoroon*), trumpets (*tromba*), *corno da caccia* (hunting horn) and *clarino. Cornetti* and three trombones are often used to double vocal parts. The *basso continuo* was played by the organ or harpsichord, 'cellos and double basses. Bach used solo instruments, sometimes to support the voice, and at other times as obbligatos. His scores often call for instruments that are now obsolete, such as the *violoncello piccolo, viola pomposa, violino piccolo* and *viola d'amore.*

Grove's Dictionary lists over twenty secular cantatas which Bach composed for academic and civic ceremonies and various other celebrations. Some of these bear the Italian title, *dramma per musica.* He frequently rearranged cantatas to fit different occasions. *Phoebus and Pan* has aroused special interest, as it was evidently written as a rebuttal on the part of Bach to his critics, Mattheson and Scheibe. In this respect it is in the same category as Wagner's *Die Meistersinger* and Strauss' *Ein Heldenleben,* with the difference that Bach defends the old against the new.

Occasionally, Bach shows his sense of humor, as when he made a setting of Picander's poem, *Schweigt stille, plaudert nicht* (*Be Still and Complain Not*), known as the *Coffee Cantata,* in which the new European passion for coffee drinking is amusingly satirized. Many of the cantatas, sacred and secular, were performed by the Telemann Society (*Collegium Musicum*) when Bach was its leader. He also wrote some chamber music for its performances, including concertos for solo *Clavier,* violin, and for two or more *Claviers.*

The *Christmas Oratorio,* one of three works which Bach called "oratorios," is really an assemblage of six cantatas. It was written in 1734 and tells the story of the Nativity as found in the Gospels of Matthew and Luke. Several of the secular cantatas were incorporated into this score. Two other oratorios, now included with the cantatas, celebrate Easter and the Ascension. Two of Bach's most famous choral works, *The Passions of Our Lord,* according to St. Matthew and St. John, were composed in a form which dates back to 1678, when an attempt was made in Hamburg to found a religious opera house. The first "theatrical Passion" (1704) by Keiser was a failure and the form finally found its place in church performances. Barthold Heinrich Brockes had written a rather pedestrian Passion poem which became the standard text, and was set to music by Keiser, Handel, Telemann, Mattheson and Bach. Bach, however, rewrote much of the libretto. The first version of his *St. John Passion,* probably composed in the last year at Cöthen, was presented at an Easter service (1723) in Leipzig and later revised.

The *St. Matthew Passion,* for which Picander wrote the text, is one of the noblest and most inspired masterpieces of choral music. With his limited artistic resources—the students of St. Thomas', a few town musicians, University students and members of the *Collegium Musicum* —Bach conducted it at St. Thomas' Church on Good Friday, 1729. In the *Magnificat,* performed for the first Christmas Bach spent in Leipzig, Rutland Boughton finds the influence of the *chorale* in the Latin setting. Bach's original idea of this work in which Mr. Boughton finds "rapturous music" was almost dramatic in form.

The transcendent *B Minor Mass* is one of five Bach works to bear the title, Mass. The other four were written in accordance with the Lutheran service in which *Kyries* and *Glorias* had been retained. The *B Minor* in its original form, as dedicated to the Elector of Saxony, consisted of a *Kyrie* and *Gloria,* which Bach might have used in his own Lutheran service. The *Credo, Sanctus* and *Osanna* were probably written between 1734 and 1738. Its first complete performance was not until 1834 (Pt. I) and 1835 (Pt. II) when it was given by the Berlin *Singakademie.*

Albert Schweitzer comments:

> The salient quality of the *B minor Mass* is its wonderful sublimity. The first chord of the Kyrie takes us into the world of great and profound emotions; we do not leave it until the final cadence of the *Dona nobis pacem* . . . the *B minor Mass* is at once Catholic and Protestant, and in addition as enigmatic and unfathomable as the religious consciousness of its creator.

After Bach had added sufficiently to sacred literature for use with his choirs (his last cantata was written in 1745), he returned to the educational side of the art and prepared revisions of some of the works which he felt should be published. His last years were devoted to instrumental music—to organ and *Clavier* compositions, to the *Musikalisches Opfer* and to his monumental study, *The Art of Fugue*. Schweitzer explains that *The Art of Fugue* was not left unfinished by Bach, as so often claimed, but that the composer died before the engraving was completed, and it has for this reason come down in a seemingly incomplete form. Bach recorded in this work every type of fugue known to him. It is a colossal feat, a lasting monument to his skill and knowledge. It amply bears out C. S. Terry's statement that "his distinctive achievement was to present in its final shape the fabric of polyphony."

SOME SALIENT FACTORS

It is beyond the scope of our discussion to present more than a skeleton outline of representative compositions from Bach's huge output. It has been said that it would require a lifetime merely to copy what Bach wrote. We hope that the reader will undertake individual research into this rich vein of musical ore, for he will find the results aesthetically satisfying and intellectually astounding. In closing our chapter, however, we should like to suggest several factors that serve the dual purpose of relating Bach to his time and also of accounting for the overwhelming position now accorded him as a master composer—one whom even the egotistical Richard Wagner called "the most stupendous miracle in all music."

(1) Bach's thirst for musical knowledge was unquenchable. Although he had some formal training, he was not content to rest on that alone. He copied, transcribed and imitated the very best examples he could lay his hands on in order to perfect his own powers. For example, we know he copied by hand the entire *Fiori musicali* of Frescobaldi in addition to studying works by other Italian composers such as Giovanni Legrenzi, Tomaso Albinoni (1671-1750), Corelli, Vivaldi, Benedetto Marcello (1686-1739) and Francesco Bonporti (1672-1749). French composers whom he studied included Jean-Henri d'Anglebert (*c.* 1628-1691), Couperin and Marchand; German Catholic musicians were represented by Froberger and Kerll; and German Protestant masters by Reinken, Buxtehude, Pachelbel, Böhm, Ferdinand Fischer (*c.* 1665-1746), Telemann, Graupner, Handel and many others. Ironically, in other fields, Bach was largely uneducated—he knew little of the arts, his German was ungrammatical and his reading largely confined to theology. But in music, he was the pupil (at a distance) of all the leading European composers.

(2) Bach's music drew upon the three leading musical styles of his time: the French, characterized by the overture, dance suite, florid me-

lodic ornamentation, programmatic tendencies and orchestral discipline; the Italian, with its vocal and instrumental concerto style, its tonal harmony and the concerto and sonata forms; and the German, recognized by its solid harmonic-contrapuntal texture. The significant aspect, however, is that, in Bukofzer's words, "The music that finally culminated in Bach attained its universality and distinction through the deliberate fusion of national styles."

(3) Bach was innately an organizer and systematizer. A glance at any of his major works reveals this quality of mind. For instance, in the *Passacaglia in C Minor,* Bach arranged the twenty variations in strictly symmetrical groups, with unifying rhythmic patterns. Midway, in the tenth and eleventh variants, the bass theme is taken to the uppermost voice in double counterpoint and thence makes its way, step by step, back down again. Or consider the twenty-four preludes and fugues in all major and minor keys or the simple to complex order of the *Art of the Fugue.* Bach's was a mentality that not only was cognizant of each and every detail but also in complete control of extensive overall designs.

(4) Bach shared the Baroque predeliction for musical symbolism, an interpenetration of musical and extra-musical ideas. His biographer, Albert Schweitzer, offers a lengthy examination of this aspect of his work. It will suffice here to offer several isolated examples. In the great "St. Anne" *Prelude and Fugue,* the Trinity is represented by the three flats of the key signature (E flat major) and the three themes which are developed in a triple fugue. The title, *Musical Offering,* is actually an acrostic of *ricercar,* the form that opens and concludes the cycle. In the *chorale-prelude, "Durch Adams Fall,"* included in the didactic collection, *Orgelbüchlein,* Adam's fall from grace is depicted by a "falling" diminished seventh in the bass, while an inner voice winds about representing the serpent in the garden of Eden. Such symbolic rising and falling, diatonicism and chromaticism, the simultaneity of dogma and exegesis, the use of strict counterpoint for Old Testament allusions and free polyphony for references to the New Testament—all are essential parts of Bach's art. His distinction lies in the fact that never does he allow the metaphoric content to dominate to the detriment of the music.

(5) Bach was a professional. He did not create as a means of catharsis or just for the fun of it. We have seen that the types of music he wrote coincided with his jobs or the needs of his family and pupils. No one, least of all Bach himself or his sons, thought of him as more than an artisan, turning out music in much the same manner as a cobbler makes shoes. That he never composed an opera is probably explained by the fact that he was never in a position that required one.

(6) Bach was an almost superhuman musical craftsman. Seemingly

without effort, he was able to project the most complex contrapuntal materials in such a way that they supported rather than detracted from the musical purpose, whatever it might be. In the sixth canon of the *Goldberg Variations,* allegedly commissioned as a soporific by an insomniac nobleman, we discern a canon at a distance of but half a step, a very difficult technical problem, yet the music moves along with all the freedom of a dance or sonata. At the end of the *Canonic Variations* on *Vom Himmel hoch,* Bach introduced all four lines of the *chorale-cantus-firmus* simultaneously. In *The Art of the Fugue,* he commences with a simple fugue, followed by a counterfugue, a double fugue, triple fugue, mirror fugue (one constructed so that it can be completely inverted), ending with a quadruple fugue. And the opening *chorale-fantasia* of the *St. Matthew Passion* offers us a complex of double chorus, two orchestras and *continuo,* with a separate chorus of boys singing the *cantus firmus.*

(7) Bach was the right person at the right time. By this, we mean that he lived at the moment when polyphonic resources were fully developed and harmony had just been realized, so that both vertical and horizontal musical forces were at his disposal. Thus, his harmonic writing has linear energy and his polyphonic writing harmonic depth and stability. The result is an unparalleled richness and intensity.

* * * * *

Johann Sebastian Bach ended an epoch, yet in his day he was neither understood nor was the enormity of his accomplishments appreciated. Even his own sons regarded his works as old-fashioned and redolent of the past. One of the few who acknowledged Bach's passing was Telemann, who wrote a sonnet in his honor, not as a composer but as the father of illustrious musicians, notably Carl Philipp Emanuel Bach. Sebastian Bach's compositions were neglected and his name was threatened with oblivion. To Johann Nikolaus Forkel (1749-1818), an early biographer, and Johann Friedrich Rochlitz (1769-1842), who first measured the greatness of Bach's works, we owe a debt of gratitude. Carl Friedrich Zelter introduced Bach's motets at the Berlin *Singakademie* and Felix Mendelssohn, who had studied Bach's scores with his friends, celebrated the centenary of its first performance with a production in Berlin of the *St. Matthew Passion* in 1829. A Bach *Gesellschaft* (Society) was established in 1850. Its purpose was to issue annually a volume of Bach's compositions to subscribers. The first volume appeared in 1851 and the forty-sixth in 1900. Thus, through the indefatigable efforts of a few, one of the greatest musical geniuses the world has known has been immortalized.

SUGGESTIONS FOR FURTHER READING

Bukofzer, Manfred F., *Music in the Baroque Era*. New York, Norton, 1947.

Davison, Archibald T. and Apel, Willi, *Historical Anthology of Music*, vol. 2. Cambridge, Harvard University Press, 1949.

David, Hans T. and Mendel, Arthur, *The Bach Reader.** New York, Norton, 1945.

Day, James, *The Literary Background of Bach's Cantatas*. London, Dobson, 1961.

Forkel, J. N., *J. S. Bach*, New York, Harcourt-Brace & Howe, 1920.

Fuller-Maitland, J. A., *The Keyboard Suites of J. S. Bach*. London, Oxford University Press, 1925.

Fux, Johann Joseph, *The Study of Counterpoint.** New York, Norton, 1966.

Geiringer, Karl, *The Bach Family*. New York, Oxford University Press, 1954.

Grace, Harvey, *The Organ Works of Bach*. New York, Gray, 1922.

Joy, Charles R., *Music in the Life of Albert Schweitzer.** Boston, Beacon Press, 1959.

Liemohn, Edwin, *The Chorale*. Philadelphia, Muhlenberg Press, 1953.

Miles, Russell H., *Johann Sebastian Bach.** Englewood Cliffs, Prentice-Hall, 1962.

Moser, Hans, *Heinrich Schütz*. St. Louis, Concordia, 1959.

Neuman, Werner, *Bach: A Pictorial Biography*. New York, Viking, 1961.

Parrish, Carl, *A Treasury of Early Music.** New York, Norton, 1958.

Parrish, Carl and Ohl, John F., *Masterpieces of Music before 1750*. New York, Norton, 1951.

Rothschild, Fritz, *The Lost Tradition—Rhythm and Tempo in J. S. Bach's Time*. London, Black, 1953.

Schweitzer, Albert, *J. S. Bach*. New York, Macmillan, 1923. 2 vols.

Smallman, Basil, *The Background of Passion Music*. Toronto, Ryerson Press, 1957.

Spitta, J. A. P., *Life of Bach*. New York, Dover, 1951. 2 vols.

Terry, Charles Sanford, *The Passions*. New York, Oxford University Press, 1926. 2 vols.

———— *The Music of Bach.** New York, Dover, 1963.

Whittacker, William G., *The Cantatas of J. S. Bach*. New York, Oxford University Press, 1959. 2 vols.

A SAMPLER OF SUPPLEMENTARY RECORDINGS

Collections

Heritage of the Baroque	Vox 14000
Masterpieces of Music before 1750	Haydn 9038/40
Ten Centuries of Music	DGG KL-52/61
Treasury of Early Music	Haydn 1900/3
2000 Years of Music	Folkways 3700
Music of the Bach Family	4-Boston 1008
Organ Masters from South Germany	DGG ARC-3161
Baroque Organ Music	Period 1022

* Available in paperback edition.

Music of Individual Composers

    Bach, J. S., *Brandenburg Concerti, Nos. 1-6*
            Well-tempered Clavier
            Orgelbüchlein
            Cantata No. 80, Ein' feste Burg
            Cantata No. 211, "Coffee Cantata"
            Violin Partita No. 2
            Motet No. 3, Jesu, meine Freude
            St. Matthew Passion
            B Minor Mass
            Suites for Orchestra
            Concerti for Harpsichord
            Arias
    Buxtehude, Dietrich, *Cantatas*
                 Organ Music
    Hassler, Hans Leo, *Neue teusche Gesäng*
    Praetorius, Michael, *Canticum Trium Puerorum* (Motet)
    Scheidt, Samuel, *Tabulatura Nova:* Selections
    Schütz, Heinrich, *Music of Heinrich Schütz*
               Psalms
               Small Sacred Concerti
               Easter Oratorio
    Sweelinck, Jan, *Organ Music*
              Psalms
    Telemann, Georg Philipp, *Concerti*
                    Cantatas
                    Sonatas

Related Works of Interest

    Bloch, Ernest, *Concerti Grossi Nos. 1 and 2*
    Hindemith, Paul, *Ludis Tonalis*
    Mendelssohn, Felix, *Symphony No. 5 in D, Op.* 107, "Reformation"
    Ormandy Plays Bach, Philadelphia Orchestra (transcriptions)
    Villa-Lobos, Heitor, *Bachianas Brasileiras*
    Walton, William, *The Wise Virgins*

OPPORTUNITIES FOR STUDY IN DEPTH

1. Make a comparison of contemporary Lutheran services with those of eighteenth-century Germany. How are they similar? In which ways does music play a part?

2. Trace the hymn, *Veni redemptor gentium,* from its more or less original Ambrosian form, through its modification to *Nun komm der Heiden Heiland,* and its several uses as a basic *chorale* by various German composers. Copy an initial excerpt from each version collected, and make appropriate annotations.

3. Much has been written about the roles played by numerology and other symbolism in compositions of J. S. Bach. Conduct an investigation of this phenomenon, cite pertinent examples and advance an opinion on the subject.

4. After extensive listening and reading, make note of specific Italianate influ-

ences found in music of the German Baroque. How much truth is there to the statement that music of this period should be designated Italian-international style?

5. Read one of the specialized books listed in "Suggestions for Further Reading" and prepare an oral report of its contents for classroom presentation.

6. Examine carefully one of the Bach cantatas, perhaps No. 140, *Wachet auf ruft uns die Stimme* ("Sleepers Wake, the Watchman Calls") or No. 4, *Christ lag in Todesbanden* ("Christ Lay in the Bonds of Death"), diagramming the various movements, the vocal forces employed, the instrumental accompaniment and the use of the *chorale* in integrating the entire work.

7. Study the role of Felix Mendelssohn in the revival of performances of J. S. Bach's works. Assemble findings in the form of a narrative.

8. Prepare a representative program of compositions by German Baroque composers and present it in a classroom performance prefaced with oral program notes.

VOCABULARY ENRICHMENT

chorale	sequence
contrafacta	*hemiola*
chorale-motet	cantata
motet-fashion	*Kapellmeister*
cantus firmus-fashion	equal temperament
chorale-prelude	Passion
chorale-fantasia	cantor

Chapter 12.

G. F. HANDEL—OPERA AND ORATORIO

For relief of the prisoners in the several Gaols and for the support
of Mercer's Hospital in Stephen's Street and of the Charitable Infirmary
on the Inn Quay, on Monday the 12th of April will be performed at the
Musick Hall in Fishamble Street Mr. Handel's new Grand Oratorio
called the *Messiah,* in which the gentlemen in the Choirs of both Cathedrals will assist, with some Concertos on the organ by Mr. Handel.

Tickets to be had at the Musick Hall and at Mr. Neal's in Christ
Church Yard at Half-a-Guinea each.

Public Notice—*Faulkner's Journal*—March 27, 1742.

George Frederick Handel (1685-1759) and Johann Sebastian Bach
share as many similarities as differences. Basically, they had the same
spiritual and musical heritage; they came into the world one month
apart, in towns an hour from each other, for Halle, the birthplace of
Handel, was close to Eisenach. Furthermore, they were both of Thuringian ancestry, with the same Protestant background and homely philosophy, and were fed by the sentiment of all worthy German families.
Handel outlived Bach by nine years, but both died of apoplexy after
becoming blind. They never met.

Both were organists and masters of polyphony. Bach stayed in his
own country; Handel went to Italy and to England, where he became a
British subject. Bach married and was thoroughly a homebody; Handel
remained a bachelor. Bach's passion was to satisfy his soul's need for
expression; Handel's to please his public. Bach was not successful as
a contender for his rights; while even royalty quaked before Handel's
towering egotism. To Bach, applause meant little; to Handel it was life
itself. Where Handel was dramatic and heroic, Bach was religious;
Handel might be called popular, whereas Bach's inspiration was profound. Bach's achievement was personal; Handel's was worldly. Rock-
stro, an English critic, calls Bach the "Albrecht Dürer of German
music," and then adds, "If the one is a Dürer, the other (Handel) is a
Rubens."

GEORGE FREDERICK HANDEL—LIFE

Handel was born of a second marriage. His father, a barber-surgeon,
was inimical to his becoming anything but a man of business and chose

the law for young George Frederick. Nevertheless, from his seventh year the boy seemed determined to study music, and a story is related that when his father started for Weissenfels to visit a step-brother who was in the service of the Duke, George followed the carriage on foot until his father was forced to take him along. At the Castle, the Duke realized the child's aptitude and Handel, senior, relented and selected Zachau as a teacher (1693). Handel did study law, however, and at seventeen entered the University, where he matriculated in the arts, a course which served him well thereafter.

In 1702 he became assistant organist at the *Domkirche* in Halle, where he met Telemann. In 1703 he joined the orchestra as violinist at Hamburg in Keiser's opera house, where later he became harpsichordist and conductor. Here he met Mattheson, famous as an opera singer and composer. Avoiding the clamors of a gay city, Handel applied himself to composition, which he knew would be a rich field. It was here that Handel and Mattheson had their famous quarrel. Handel was scheduled to lead Mattheson's opera, *Cleopatra,* in order to relieve Mattheson, who sang the part of Antonio. After Antonio was "killed," Mattheson, being free, entered the orchestra pit to take Handel's place. Handel was infuriated. They met later and fought a duel, in which Handel was supposedly saved by a large metal button which snapped Mattheson's rapier. Mattheson's jealousy availed little, however, and Handel's talent triumphed. *Almira* (1705) and three other operas were produced in this period and were imbued with charming melody. Besides the operas, Handel wrote a *Passion of St. John* (1704).

From Hamburg, Handel visited Italy, where he spent the happiest years of his life (1707-1710). There he came under the influence of Cavalli, Cavalieri and Carissimi, oratorio and opera writers, and met the Scarlattis, Lotti, Marcello, Pasquini and Corelli. The Italian style saturated his work. He left Italy to become *Kapellmeister* to George, Elector of Hanover, but, before accepting the post, obtained permission to go to England.

Consequently, in 1710, Handel made his first trip to England, where opera was in a woeful state. Addison, in *The Spectator,* lampooned the state of things with these words, "One would have thought it difficult to have carried on dialogues . . . without interpreters between the persons, who conversed together . . . at length the audience grew tired of understanding half of the opera . . . and the whole opera is performed in an unknown tongue." But it was stimulating to a man like Handel, whose later and celebrated oratorios were created to forestall the righteous criticism of the period. At that time, for example, in English opera the number of singers was prescribed along with the precise type of music they must sing; English was used in the recitatives and Italian for the florid *arias*. In the oratorio, on the other hand, there was a more consistent uniformity.

After traveling back and forth, Handel finally settled in London. *Rinaldo,* written in fourteen days, was given at the Haymarket Theater (1711) and brought the composer great *réclame*. In this occurs the engaging and typical Handelian *aria, "Lascia ch'io piango"* ("Let Me Weep"), taken from a former work of his. Later, Handel became the guest of the Duke of Chandos at Canons. With a splendid organ, good singers and an orchestra at his disposal, he composed twelve anthems for chorus and soloists in the style of Purcell—a style to which he had special affinity and in which are found the roots of English oratorio, to be perfected by Handel himself.

The former Elector of Hanover (Handel's early patron and later George I of England) was supposedly annoyed that Handel had left Hanover, but in 1719 he relented and made Handel director of the new Royal Academy of Music in London. Handel's need of singers gave him ample excuse to travel all over Europe, but he continued composing operas and various other works at an almost maniacal speed. Yet, withal, things were far from pleasant. Jealousies arose between Handel and his associate, G. Battista Bononcini (1670-1747), and the quarrels spread beyond the Academy throughout London. Apropos of this state of affairs, we may quote the contemporary cynical jingle by John Byrom:

> Some say, compared to Bononcini,
> That Mynheer Handel's but a ninny;
> Others aver that he to Handel
> Is scarcely fit to hold a candle.
> Strange, all this difference should be
> 'Twixt Tweedledum and Tweedledee!

After many battles Bononcini left England, but Handel's latest opera failed to make a hit (1729) and the Academy was closed. Immediately, however, another company was started and Handel was appointed director. From Dresden he brought Francesco Senesino (1680-c. 1750), a tenor. But there were incessant disagreements between Handel and his artists and among the artists themselves, particularly between Faustina Bordoni (wife of Johann Adolph Hasse, 1699-1783, opera writer and impresario), and Francesca Cuzzini (c. 1700-1770), another *prima donna*. The warfare was the talk of the town and the meat of the wits. Nicola Antonio Porpora (1686-1768) and Hasse, in another theater under noble patronage, were now the operatic men of the hour. The bankrupt Handel suffered a physical collapse.

Although impoverished and ill, Handel continued writing. Two more operas were unsuccessful, but in 1738 a concert, backed by warm friends, bolstered his finances and not long after, Handel had the satisfaction of seeing a statue erected in his honor at Vauxhall. After his health broke and fatigue oppressed him, Handel had decided that "sacred music was best for a man in failing years." It was in this resolve that the flowering of his genius was manifested in the **oratorio,** the marriage of the musical art of the past to Handelian form and sublimity. In the period between 1739 and 1752, he wrote nineteen oratorios, called by Romain Rolland "artistic summits of the eighteenth century," from which his name is forever inseparable. Although afflicted by failing sight and resting with friends in the country, Handel composed unceasingly until his death. He was buried in Westminster Abbey, the final resting place of England's great.

GEORGE FREDERICK HANDEL—MUSIC

Handel used all forms current in his day for his compositions. His works include approximately forty-two operas, thirteen *pasticcios* (operas written with other composers), two Passions, twenty-one oratorios (including the secular oratorios or epic cantatas), numerous sonatas for violin or flute and for two violins, oboes or flutes and bass, twelve *concerti grossi,* eighteen organ concertos, concertos for strings, for solo winds (and sidedrum), orchestral suites and many *serenatas,* suites, *fantasias* and fugues for organ and for harpsichord.

Deeply affected by the Italians, profiting from English criticism and freedom, influenced by his German ancestry and experiences, Handel possessed an enchanting sense of melody and an intrinsic epic power. Much that he wrote, however, has been somewhat obscured by his fame as an oratorio composer. Yet Handel, with other eighteenth-century composers, is now receiving increasing popular appreciation and we hear his *concerti grossi* and other instrumental works more and more frequently.

Handel was a master of polyphony, but to it he brought rich chording, chromatic interplay and warm, unstilted modulations. He inherited the harmonic style of Monteverdi and the flavor of early English lute and harpsichord composers. A musical opportunist, Handel assimilated ideas from here and there, using his own material over and over again and taking the themes of others. He said that he improved them; posterity says that he gave them immortality.

Although only a few of Handel's many operas remain, these works undoubtedly provided the preparation through which he learned to build the magniloquent choruses, and clear, brilliant orchestral parts of the oratorios. Among the operas that have been revived are *Rinaldo* (1711), with its lovely *bel canto aria, "Cara sposa"; Rodelinda* (1725); *Xerxes* (1738), in which occurs the famous *"Largo,"* originally a *larghetto aria, "Ombre mai fu"* ("Never Was There a Shadow"); and *Giulio Cesare,* which opened the New York City Center Opera season of 1966.

Handel's operas can be divided into three classes of subjects: historical, mythological and romantic. They follow the custom of the time, with recitative telling the story and *arias,* often irrelevant, intruding upon the dramatic action. Yet Handel's work had homogeneity of music and movement, his characterizations showed some independence from stereotypic conventions and his choruses were written with consummate technical skill. Among his librettists were Giacomo Rossi, Nicola Haym, Paoli Roli and Pietro Antonio Trapassi, known by the pseudonym of Metastasio (1698-1782), who alone, of them all, had poetic feeling and a sense of dramatic theater.

Any attempt to revive Handelian opera meets with almost insurmountable difficulties today and we are fortunate indeed when even a rare "concert performance" is offered. Several reasons may be advanced for this. Handel conceived his operas in the basic Neapolitan mold which meant solo opera, in which virtuoso singers of the time were featured, usually to the detriment of plot and action. His melodic gifts were exceptional, to be sure, but Handel did not compose operas at a propitious moment, as the feuds and rivalries we have cited reveal. He was really between developments and a chasm widened which all but swallowed up his large operatic production (he wrote thirty-six operas for London alone).

Acting not only as a composer, but as impresario and director as well, Handel fell prey too often to the imperious whims of his vital *divas,* whose insistence upon "equal time" and their own improvisations and elaborations was legion. As we shall shortly discuss, another intrusive element in the London operatic scene was the support of the public, largely a noble public, but yet a vociferous and demanding one whose will had to be satisfied. Also, the conventions of opera had stiffened to a point where the form was inflexible and is seemingly static to modern listeners.

On the asset side, however, stand the contributions which Handel made to the emergence of later opera. These include the use of dance rhythms and patterns in fashioning *arias; i.e., "Lascia ch'io pianga"* (from *Rinaldo,* the post-Italian-period opera which Handel wrote on a text borrowed from Tasso's *Jerusalem Delivered*), was based upon the *sarabande.* Handel employed rich variety in his accompaniments, occasionally utilizing imitative polyphony as well as an adaptation of the *concerto grosso* principle to offset the monotony of unrelieved *continuo*. His operatic instrumentation was imaginative beyond that of the Italian composers, giving full rein to the use of *timbre* to supplement the "affections" of the moment; *i.e.,* the bird's song of *Rinaldo* is scored for two treble and one sopranino recorders, supported by violas alone.

While his librettos were rather poor, Handel's characterization was more emotionally subjective than that of his colleagues. The textures in his music ranged from homophony through complex polyphony. He added the finishing touches to the French overture which he used exclusively in his operas. Pincherle comments, "Not only did he strengthen

Fig. 48. "A Chorus of Singers"—engraving by William Hogarth. The satire in this picture conveys some idea of the choral conditions prevalent during Handel's time in London. The group is shown performing an oratorio, *Judith,* by W. de Fesch. (Courtesy The Metropolitan Museum of Art, Dick Fund, 1932.)

the chorus and amplify the symphonic episodes in his operas, he also created those great scenes all in one piece in which the airs and *ariosi,* linked by a recitative *sec* or accompanied, are integrated in the action instead of interrupting it."

During the opera season of 1731, when Handel was faring reasonably well, the Children of the Royal Chapel prepared a private performance of *Esther* (with words by Alexander Pope after Racine) on the occasion of Handel's birthday. Such was its success that Handel built up the work and presented six subscription performances at the King's Theater —performances supported by the royal family and the nobility. From such a fortuitous beginning was Handel's career as a composer of oratorio born. *Esther* was followed by a revision of *Acis and Galatea* and an original *Deborah,* the latter defiantly produced (at raised prices) during the opera season of 1732-33. It should be noted parenthetically that these, as well as the later oratorios, were secular, not church works. Whereas modern scores are marked "Part I," Handel actually wrote "Act the first. Scene 1."

Handel's list of oratorios stretches from the *Passion of St. John* (Hamburg, 1704) to *Jeptha* in 1751. Among the greatest are: *Joseph, Heracles, Esther* (the first oratorio given in English), *Athalia* (like a *chorale-*cantata), *Israel in Egypt, Samson* and *Judas Maccabaeus.* Many of the characters were personifications of nations and races. Spontini and Meyerbeer might have written differently had not Handel cut a broad swath for historical music drama. Most of the oratorios drew upon the *Old Testament* or the *Apocalypse* for their inspirations. In all, save *Israel in Egypt* and the *Messiah,* we find essentially dramatic, if non-theatrical, works, in which the forms and fillips of opera were transferred to a concert, that is, theater stage, with the addition of a more prominent place being accorded the chorus who acted as mood-setter, commentator and carrier of the narrative. It is significant that the most popular oratorio of Handel, during his lifetime, was not the *Messiah,* which he tended to reserve for benefit performances, but the rousing *Judas Maccabaeus,* written in 1746 and thrown open to the general public, whose Jewish members helped assure its success.

Of all the oratorios, *Messiah* is best known. In both *Saul* (which contains the somber *Dead March*) and *Messiah,* Handel pushed the choral drama, interspersed with solos, to such a height of grandeur and beauty that it has become one of the most eloquent forms of music. During the summer of 1741, an eccentric friend of Handel's, one Charles Jennens, submitted to the composer a libretto which he claimed he had compiled from the Scriptures. Handel, with unusual facility, even for him, set it in the amazingly short time of twenty-four days, between

August 22nd and September 14th. During the subsequent autumn, Handel was invited to visit Ireland to give some charity concerts; and at this nadir in his career he welcomed the chance to quit London. Toward the end of an enthusiastic season in Dublin, Handel scheduled the first performance of *Messiah,* an announcement of which prefaces this chapter.

The oratorio was received with acclaim at its premiere. Choristers from Christ Church and St. Patrick's Cathedral sang with Signora Avolio, an Italian opera star, Mrs. Colly Cibber, the most popular actress of her day and soloists from the churches. The supporting orchestra consisted of strings and harpsichord, with occasional oboes, bassoons, trumpets and drums. Composers, including Wolfgang Amadeus Mozart, have since attempted to augment the original simple orchestration, but with little success.

Following the opening *sinfonia,* with its chordal dotted-rhythm *grave,* succeeded by an imitative and lively *allegro,* a string group in the major mode introduces a tenor recitative announcing the imminent arrival of a Redeemer. Thus commences the gigantic, three-part work telling of the birth of Christ, the Passion and Resurrection and the promise of immortality to all those who witness for Him. It is of interest to note that concertgoers of that day really got their money's worth, as the program also included several organ concertos "by Mr. Handel." The oratorio was performed once more in Dublin, and, during the following year, in London, where King George II was so impressed, it is said, that he rose at the "Hallelujah Chorus," and the whole audience followed his example, setting a precedent still existing at the present time.

Messiah is a balanced piece of musical architecture. There is a fine contrast between the *arias,* recitatives and choruses, and it proceeds with the inevitability of all good drama. Great religious calm pervades the most emotional parts, only possible to a genius who does not allow emotion to become sentimentality. Einstein writes, *"Messiah* dispenses entirely with action and resolves every event into emotion, and in that way shows how the promises of Christianity are fulfilled."

In 1717 the Duke of Chandos had engaged Handel, who continued to act as the Royal music tutor (at £200 *per annum*), to be chapel music-director at his estate in Canons; there Handel served, interspersed with frequent trips to London, from 1718 to 1721, composing a series of "Chandos Anthems" which foreshadow the oratorio choruses that were to come. These were splended festive verse-anthems for chorus and solo voices, accompanied by orchestra; perhaps their lack of performance today is due to the fact that Handel belies his knowledge of English with faults of accentuation, for the music is powerful and

Fig. 49. Autograph of "I Know That My Redeemer Liveth." Handel's most famous work followed bouts with failure and illness. (Courtesy British Museum.)

varied. There are several brilliant "Hallelujahs" and, in *O Praise the Lord with One Consent,* a setting of the hymn tune known as *St. Anne* ("O God, Our Help in Ages Past"), which is attributed to the Englishman, William Croft (1678-1727). (Bach also used this tune in creating one of his organ fugues.)

From the Chandos period also issued the then-*masque, Esther,* originally entitled *Haman and Mordecai* (1720), and the pastoral music-drama, *Acis and Galatea,* which was probably staged at Canons in 1718. From this period too comes the popular keyboard theme and variations known as "The Harmonious Blacksmith," an appellation that it picked up much later in its journey in music through the ages. In 1727 Handel composed four "Coronation Anthems" (for George II), one of which, *Zadok the Priest,* has been used at such functions ever since. Among his other choral compositions are settings of poet John Dryden's *Alexander's Feast* (1736) and *Ode to St. Cecilia's Day* (1739) as well as *L'Allegro, il Penseroso ed il Moderato* (1740), based on a poem by John Milton. *Semele* (1744), an oratorio-opera, used a libretto of William Congreve. *Hercules* (1745) is yet another work of the same type. Earlier in his English career, Handel had written a *Te Deum* and *Jubilate* (his first with English words) to celebrate the Peace of Utrecht

(1713) and a *Birthday Ode* for Queen Anne (1714). The *Dettingen Te Deum* was composed in 1743.

Although Handel is thought of primarily as a choral-vocal composer, he wrote extensively for keyboard instruments and orchestra. In 1739 he published twelve *concerti grossi* (*Op.* 6) scored for strings and *continuo,* in the form of suites with four to six movements. Among his other well-known compositions is the orchestral suite, *The Water Music* (1717). The reason for its composition is ascribed to the fact that it was ordered for a river party for the King. But this is doubtful, because at that time George I and Handel were reputed to be unfriendly, even though they shortly after were reconciled. In any case, this delightful music is but a revision of pieces Handel had written earlier. His harpsichord music shows a real knowledge of the instrument. In his orchestra Handel often prefers quantity to quality, save in his last works. He made experiments in the use of instruments, having introduced the horn into the opera orchestra, enlarged the expressive scope of the viola and violoncello, exploited the characteristics of the bassoon and of the drum, and employed, early in its history, the double bassoon.

In a list of contemporary musicians of Handel's time, taken from an old source, appear names ranked in order of their supposed importance: Hasse, Handel, Telemann, the two Grauns, Stölzel, Bach, Quantz and Bümler—a curious assessment. Of Handel's music, Gerhart von Westerman remarks:

> . . . all of Handel's music has the . . . recommendation of being marvelously accessible; he deliberately aimed at breadth of effect. His music is addressed to a large public, to the musical layman; there is something artless about the clear simplicity of his forms. His themes are easy to remember and have a strong rhythmic profile; they are quite short. . . . When he writes a fugato it is usually only in two voices, so that even an untrained ear is capable of following the voices. But the music is so rich in ideas and brims with such strength of personality that it would be madness to deny oneself the directness and effectiveness of its content.

BALLAD-OPERAS IN ENGLAND

Handel went to England fifteen years after Purcell had glorified English music and stimulated composers to write along the lines he made popular. At this time, too, **ballad-operas,** descended from *masques,* part-songs and "catches" (separate songs or ballads), were greatly in favor. In England there were many operas made of strings of these same forms, such as the very successful *The Beggar's Opera* (1728) by Gay (akin to Italian *opera buffa, opéra-bouffe* in France and the *Singspiel* in Germany). In fact, John Gay's collaboration with J. C. Pepusch (1667-1752) proved the downfall of Handel's efforts to write popular *opera seria,* even though he was granted the dubious honor of having the march from *Rinaldo* transformed in *The Beggar's Opera* into a song, "Let's Take the Road," and in a sequel, *Polly,* his minuet from the *Water Music* appeared as "Cheer Up, My Lads." Thus did the fickle public turn to an earthy form of entertainment which dared to satirize the government (Lord Walpole) and such topical matters as the hair-pulling scandal between two of Handel's *primae donnae,* Cuzzoni and Bordoni.

Fig. 50. Act III, *The Beggar's Opera*—William Blake after Hogarth. An out-growth of *masques,* ballad-operas were extremely popular both in England and Colonial America. (Courtesy The Metropolitan Museum of Art, Dick Fund, 1932.)

In fifteen years England produced forty-five ballad-operas. Among the arrangers of these very entertaining song-plays were Dr. Pepusch, a German who lived in London; Henry Carey (1692-1743), author of "Sally in our Alley"; and Thomas A. Arne (1710-1778), who wrote the first dated version of "God Save the King," as well as *masques,* ballad-operas and Shakespearean settings that approach the old madrigals in charm and beauty. Samuel Arnold (1740-1802) was a church composer who also contributed to ballad-operas, among which was the *Maid of the Mill* (1765), a *pasticcio* of songs by twenty different musicians. Its success was such that it inspired annual siblings for many years.

Other English composers who wrote ballad-operas and music for the numerous "Catch Clubs," "Glee Clubs" and Madrigal Societies include: William Jackson (1730-1803), Benjamin Cooke (1734-1793), Michael Arne (1741-1786—natural son of Thomas), William Shield (1748-1829), the Samuel Webbs, father and son (1740-1816 and 1770-1843), Stephen Storace (1763-1796), Thomas Attwood (1765-1838) and John Wall Callcott (1766-1821), a pupil of Haydn when the latter visited London.

THE ENGLISH BACH

Most famous in England of all the Bachs was Sebastian's youngest son, Johann Christian (1735-1782), who was the joy of his father's failing years. Talented, brilliant, fascinating and handsome, he struck out on an individual path and was the only member of his family to live outside Germany, to be converted to Catholicism and to write operas. "He belongs to Italy and France as much as to Germany, but to England most of all," writes C. S. Terry in *John Christian Bach: A Biography*.

After his father's death, Christian lived with his brother, Emanuel, in Berlin. There he met many of the leading musicians of Frederick the Great's court and came in contact with opera—German opera sung by foreigners. At twenty-two, young Bach went to Italy and studied, through the generosity of a patron, with the illustrious Padre Martini, preparing to compose church music. The success of his first opera in 1761, however, turned the course of his career, and some authorities today consider his operas comparable to those of Mozart for their melodic fluency and expressive instrumentation.

Invited to London (1762), Bach became affiliated with the King's Theater in the Haymarket. In England, he was known as "John Bach, the Saxon Professor." Famous for his harpsichord playing, he taught in the families of the English aristocracy and was appointed master of music to Queen Charlotte, the German wife of George III, whose flute-playing he accompanied. In 1764, Bach arranged young Mozart's appearances at court. In the same year he associated himself with another German musician, Carl Friedrich Abel (1723-1787), with whom he gave concerts, establishing a series that continued for twenty years.

Among their circle were David Garrick, the theatrical producer; John Brindsley Sheridan, the playwright; and the painters, Joshua Reynolds and Thomas Gainsborough.

By the time Bach married in 1772 he was hailed as a second Handel. He was subsequently commissioned to write two operas in Italian for Mannheim, then the leading German musical center, and an opera in French for Paris, of which Mozart reports in 1778: "Mr. Bach of London has been here a fortnight, having been commissioned to write a French opera . . . Our joy at meeting again you may imagine . . . I love him as you know, with all my heart and have great regard for him." Unfortunately, Bach's opera for Paris was unsuccessful and he was attacked by the Gluckists, Piccinnists, Lullyists and Rameauists! *La Clemenza di Scipione* (1778), was the fifth and last opera which Bach wrote for the Haymarket. It had as great success as his first works had attained. In 1781 the last of the Bach-Abel concerts took place, and after Bach's death, Mozart wrote, "No doubt you know that the English Bach is dead, a sad day for the world of music!"

PUBLIC CONCERTS

The Bach-Abel concerts were among the first musical entertainments to which the public was admitted on paid subscriptions. Public concerts had been established in London in 1673 by John Banister and contined by Thomas Britton, a coal dealer, music lover and friend of Handel. In 1673 Buxtehude had started his annual *Abendmusiken* in Lübeck. These concerts were held on the five Sundays before Christmas. An *Academy of Ancient Music* was founded in London in 1710, "for the study and practice of vocal and instrumental music." Dr. J. C. Pepusch was its director, and a subscription list supported the enterprise, which continued until 1792. The *Madrigal Society,* composed of singers in the cathedral choirs, was organized in 1741 and is still active in London.

Concerts of the *Collegia Musica* were initiated about 1700 in many university towns in Germany, Switzerland and Sweden. In Paris, the *Concerts Spirituels* were inaugurated in 1725 by Anne Danican-Philidor to give music to the people when the *Opéra* was closed for religious holidays. Every year there were about twenty-four concerts that became models for those of the eighteenth century. The *Gewandhaus* concerts at Leipzig grew out of *das grosse Konzert* which occurred during the period of Bach's cantorate at St. Thomas'. Following the Seven Years' War (1756-1763), the concerts were called *Liebhaberconcerte* ("Concerts for Lovers of Music"). After 1778 they were held in the *Gewandhaus,* an ancient market hall of the Saxon linen merchants. Mendelssohn was one of the conductors and after him, Hiller, Gade, Rietz, Reinecke, Arthur Nikisch and Wilhelm Furtwängler. The advent of public concerts did not, however, immediately supplant the patronage system that both supported and bedevilled composers for some years to come, especially in conservative countries such as Austria, as we shall see in the cases of Haydn and Mozart.

Opera Buffa

The Italian opera tradition was strong throughout all Europe at this time, with the possible exception of France, where composers tended to strive for independence. A significant element of the operatic composite, stemming again from Italy, was the emergence of *opera buffa* as a foil to the more grandiose *opera seria*. The prototype of *opera buffa* appeared in a delightful and unpretentious work by Pergolesi, *La Serva padrona* (*The Maid-Mistress,* 1733) which originally figured as an *intermezzo* for his serious opera, *Il Prigionero superbo.*

Born fifteen years before Scarlatti's death, Giovanni Battista Pergolesi (1710-1736), who died when only twenty-six, wrote over a hundred compositions in various forms. He left two immortal works, however, a *Stabat Mater* and the comic opera, *La Serva padrona,* which are models still. In fact, *La Serva padrona,* given in Paris by an Italian company (1752) in Rameau's "reign," caused the renowned musical controversy known as the *"War of the Buffoons."* This merry little work, employing but three characters of whom only two use their voices, a soprano and a bass, proceeds at a swift pace, sparkling with wit and musical lampooning of the first order. In place of complicated *arias,* it featured simple song forms such as the *canzonetta*; in place of static grandeur, it relied upon change of pace. From such a unsophisticated beginning was to come the highly-polished operas of Mozart and Rossini.

Post-Lully Opera

Following the death of Lully, we perceive in French operatic production an interregnum extending to Rameau, but not entirely free of composers of merit, if not genius. Outstanding in this group were such musicians as Marin Marais (1656-1728), known as a composer for viols and a competent orchestrator, who wrote several operas of dramatic power, including *Alcide* (1693), *Alcyone* (1706) and *Sémélé* (1709); André Campra (1660-1744), a gifted melodist, whose talents leaned toward a lighter, more decorative style; André-Cardinal Destouches (1672-1749), a pupil of Campra, whose opera-ballets represented the epitome of Regency taste, as in *Les Éléments* (1721); and

Jean-Joseph Mouret (1682-1738), most removed from Lully in style, who contributed to the development of *opéra-comique* with such works as *Les Festes de Thalie,* which anticipated Rameau.

When Jean-Philippe Rameau (1683-1764) was born in France, Lully's ghost still stalked the land, and Rameau had to struggle against it during most of his life. Little Jean, under the musical training of his father, an organist at Dijon, learned rapidly. In school, music was so much a part of him that he annoyed his classmates by singing out loud, and his teacher by writing music all over his papers, to the neglect of his studies.

At eighteen he went to Italy, but, not liking the music there, the headstrong young man left and never ceased to regret his mistake. He "played" his way during the journey, then became organist for six years at Clermont where he wrote his first *clavecin* works and three cantatas. Tired of his post and not succeeding in getting a discharge, he intentionally played so badly one day, so the story goes, that he achieved his purpose. Later, however, he returned to Clermont as organist and was so honored that until this day his chair is exhibited. After his first Clermont experience, he studied organ with Marchand, theory from Zarlino's works and wrote his treatises on harmony. In 1722 he published the famous work that became the basis of all further harmony studies.

Until he was fifty, Rameau was known only as an organist, teacher of theory and *clavecinist.* After his marriage to a singer, at forty-three, he met wealthy art patrons, diplomats, artists and men of letters, among whom he was appreciated in spite of Lully's ghost. Voltaire and Abbé Pellegrin wrote librettos for his operas and were enthusiastic over his *Hippolyte et Aricie* (1733). Lully's followers, on the other hand, inveighed against his strange chords and declared the opera too difficult to understand. Wits lampooned him and even Rousseau took up "enemy propaganda." In this connection, Voltaire, the seer, stated that it takes a whole generation for the human ear to grow familiar with a new musical style. With his third opera, *Castor et Pollux* (1737), Rameau had his first success. Now he was acclaimed as France's greatest composer.

But the seas were to be riled again, for, at the height of his fame, an Italian troupe, playing *La Serva padrona,* threw him into a maelstrom. Now he and the Lullyists were on the same side; but those favoring Italian comic opera (*opera buffa*) were strongly entrenched on the other side. The "War of the Buffoons" was on. It is difficult for us today to understand the ardor of conflict aroused by such an innocent miniature opera as Pergolesi's which provoked exchanges of diatribes for several years and even ranged France's King and Queen against each other. Actually, *opera buffa* was a natural and needed revolt against the stuffy classical heroes, mythological gods and ballets. It was a recurrence of the veering to *il commedia* when Italy, behind closed doors, alleviated monotony and reveled in amusing and familiar story.

Heretofore, comic *intermezzi* had been placed between the acts of *opera seria* (serious or grand opera), making rather a strange marriage, so that it did not take a great effort to divorce these comedy bits and let them stand alone. The freedom in casting and composition of the *buffa* and its gay and fresh characterization revitalized opera, which had grown into a stiff and worn fabric. Also, its naturalness, vivacity, conciseness and choice of subject corresponded to the ideals of that important group of French philosophers known as the Encyclopaedists, who transferred their previous support of Rameau to the newer *genre*. Despite the bitterness ranged against Rameau, at length he won. It was a Pyrrhic victory, however, for after his death Italian opera flourished in France.

While Rameau was not an operatic innovator, he is studied now by French composers as a milestone in the establishment of a national French style. This is probably due to the facts that (1) he achieved more genuine feeling and color than had Lully, and that (2) he wrote music with more understanding and skill because of his expert knowledge of harmony. Rameau was exceedingly shy and this may have made him seem disagreeable, yet the sheer force of his skills, utterly devoid of royal patronage, won him a secure popularity.

CHRISTOPH WILLIBALD GLUCK—LIFE

When Handel was twenty-nine years old, Christoph Willibald Gluck (1714-1787) was born at Erasbach in the Upper Palatinate. Pratt writes:

> Chronically it [Gluck's life] fell partly within the period of Bach and partly within that of Haydn . . . in spirit and purpose . . . first to the conventional class of Jommelli, Hasse, Piccinni and the rest, while later it escaped into a wholly new class. Gluck is perhaps the most brilliant illustration in music history of a genius that completely outgrew its original ambitions, so that it finally entered upon a creation of which at the start it did not dream. His historic significance lay, not so much in the new ideas . . . for these were not absent from some other minds . . . but in his ability to bring them to tangible embodiment in works so beautiful and powerful as to arrest the attention of the musical world.

Gluck senior was a gamekeeper, but the little son who, like Haydn, Beethoven and others, came from "the people," later became Chevalier von Gluck and gloried in his title. When Gluck's father entered the service of Prince Ferdinand Philipp Lobkowitz, a music lover (as was the Lobkowitz of Beethoven's day), the lad was three. Although the gamekeeper had but a small competence, Christoph was given a good education at Kamnitz and Albertsdorf. A proficient little scholar, he learned to sing and play the organ, violin, violoncello and *Clavier*.

At nineteen he went to Prague where, to support himself, he played at festivals and gave lessons, until Prince Lobkowitz, son of his father's patron, introduced him to the Viennese court (1736), where he met Count Melzi, who took him to Milan. There he studied under Giovanni Battista Sammartini (1701-1775), a prominent organist and contrapuntalist, for four years. In Milan, his first opera, *Artaserse,* on a libretto by the well-known Metastasio, was given successfully. In his five years at Milan Gluck wrote eight operas following the usual Italian prescription. No doubt a revulsion due to his constant immersion in this stultified style accounted for many of his later innovations.

From a number of invitations he had received from European cities, Gluck accepted one from London (1745). At the Haymarket Theater were given *La Caduta dei giganti* (*The Fall of the Giants*), with a patched-up libretto by Vanneschi, and *Artamene,* which Handel helped to produce. Although Handel likened Gluck's skill in counterpoint to that of his cook (who, incidentally, was a trained musician), Gluck gained much from hearing Handel's masterful union of chorus, solo and orchestra in the oratorios.

The failure of his *pasticcio, Pyramus and Thisbe,* due in part to Handel's vogue, and a meeting with Rameau in Paris, from whom Gluck came to realize the value of a well-balanced use of declamation, recitative and music, may have stimulated Gluck to look for new procedures in operatic composition. After visiting Hamburg and Dresden, where he produced an opera and began his study of aesthetics, Gluck settled in Vienna in 1748. There he was commissioned to write an opera, after a poem by Metastasio, *Semiramide riconosciuta* (*Semiramide Recognized*), which was presented successfully. A series of operas with texts by Metastasio followed, including *La Clemenza di Tito* (1752) and *Il Rè pastore* (*The Shepherd King,* 1756), which contained the first glimmer of Gluck's operatic reforms, particularly in its overture. Not long after came his ballet, *Don Giovanni* (1761), notable because it gave Mozart the idea for an immortal opera on the same theme.

In 1761, Gluck was fortunate in meeting a clever librettist, Ranieri Calzabigi (1714-1795), with whom he wrote his epoch-making opera, *Orfeo ed Euridice* (1762). Another masterpiece was *Alceste* (1767). So different was this, so imbued with Gluck's personal style, that the audience heartily disliked it. They had gone to the opera to be amused and instead were confronted with a work as serious as an oratorio. Notwithstanding, *Orfeo* and *Alceste* are cornerstones of modern music drama, further developed by Mozart, Wagner and Debussy. "I seek," wrote Gluck in the preface to *Alceste,* "to put music to the true purpose, that is, to support the poem, and thus to strengthen the expression of the feelings and the interest of the situation without interrupting the action. . . . In short, I have striven to abolish all those bad habits which sound reasoning and good taste have been struggling against in vain for so long."

Earlier Gluck had written some French operas and their success prompted him to go to Paris in 1773, armed with his new ideas about dramatic music. His *Iphigénie en Aulide* (from a text by Racine) was produced in 1774, but his notion of ideal French opera stirred up a hornet's nest of opposition from exponents of Italian-style opera. Although staunchly supported by Marie Antoinette, whom he instructed in singing and harpsichord playing, Gluck found himself beset by enemies. In 1776, the climax came in a figurative battle between him and a rival Italian composer, Niccolò Piccinni (1728-1800). As in the "War of the Buffoons," Paris was again torn between factions representing the two composers. Great men on both sides took part in bitter polemics. (Jean-Jacques Rousseau fortunately was a Gluckist.) Never had there been a more overt struggle for and against new musical ideas. Matters came to a head in 1778 when it was decided that both Gluck and Piccinni should write an opera on the same libretto to see who would excell. The task took Gluck less than a year. (Piccinni required almost three to complete his version.) Gluck's opera, *Iphigénie en Tauride* (1779), was clearly superior to that of his colleague. The overture was superb, the orchestral writing splendid and the characterizations individualized in music and action.

Christoph Willibald Gluck—Contributions

Gluck's contributions to opera were many and varied. In the instrumental area, he utilized an overture made of material drawn from the opera, instead of the usual three-part *sinfonia* of irrelevant music. He introduced cymbals and tympani and conceived of the orchestra not as a tonal filler but as an agent to heighten emotional effect, without stressing the spectacular. Gluck re-introduced the chorus to opera, as it were, employing it as background for situations and as a setting for individual singing. He integrated the function of the chorus as part of the *dramatis personae,* using it at will to accent action and to strengthen climaxes. In line with the thinking of the *camerata,* the text was given primary importance, with music serving to delineate plot, scene and character in which persons were treated as individuals, not stereotypes.

Because of his interest in coordinating the various aspects of operatic production, Gluck dropped the *cadenza,* sometimes written by the singer to show off his vocal prowess. Declamation was toned down and instruments assisted it. Song became part of the story and *arias* became expressive rather than merely decorative. Instead of being singing machines, the characters came alive through the musical material given them. As a result of Gluck's efforts, opera became a dramatic art and not a costumed concert. Instead of a string of hastily-conceived tunes, opera composition became a thoughtful dramatic feat. Singers were required to become interpreters of their roles rather than virtuosos and charlatans. The audiences too were confronted with a demand that they appreciate the total music drama, not just the vocal stunts.

JEAN-JACQUES ROUSSEAU

Interesting among Gluck's contemporaries was the protean philosopher, Jean-Jacques Rousseau (1712-1776), famous for his *Confessions* and *Le Contrât sociale* (*The Social Contract*). At first a Lullyist, later a Gluckist, he composed two numbers for a melodrama, *Pygmalion* (1775) and wrote numerous short musical compositions as well as articles and pamphlets pertaining to music, the latter included in his *Dictionnaire de musique* (1767). Entirely self-taught, Rousseau composed a pastoral opera, *Le Devin du village* (*The Village Seer,* 1752), which challenged Gluck's *Orfeo* in popularity. In 1768 Mozart was to compose his first *Singspiel, Bastien et Bastienne,* on a translation of a parody of Rousseau's libretto.

*   *   *   *   *

Thus, we have moved in our journey in music through the ages from Handel's almost single-handed creation of the English oratorio, to the "English Bach," to the establishment of public subscription concerts, to the shattering reverberations of Pergolesi's *opera buffa* and the English ballad-operas, to Rameau's late but sturdy contributions to French opera, and, finally, to Gluck's monumental efforts toward the molding of modern operatic concepts. We shall now travel into a veritable age of titans, the Classic period, over which tower the great works of Mozart and Haydn, culminating in the colossus himself, Beethoven.

SUGGESTIONS FOR FURTHER READING

Abraham, Gerald, ed., *Handel, A Symposium.* New York, Oxford University Press, 1954.

Bukofzer, Manfred F., *Music in the Baroque Era.* New York, Norton, 1947.

Davison, Archibald T., and Apel, Willi, *Historical Anthology of Music,* vol. 2. Cambridge, Harvard University Press, 1949.

Dean, Winton, *Handel's Dramatic Oratories and Masques.* New York, Oxford University Press, 1954.

Dent, Edward J., *Handel.* London, Duckworth, 1934.

Deutsch, Otto, ed., *Handel: A Documentary Biography.* New York, Norton, 1955.

Dolmetsch, Arnold, *The Interpretation of the Music of the XVIIth and XVIIIth Centuries.* London, Novello, 1915.

Einstein, Alfred, *Gluck.** New York, Dutton, 1936.

Flower, Newman H., *George Frideric Handel.* New York, Scribners-Cassell, 1923.

Gagey, E., *Ballad Opera.* Bronx, Blom, n.d.

Geiringer, Karl, *The Bach Family.* New York, Oxford University Press, 1954.

Lang, Paul Henry, *Handel.* New York, Norton, 1966.

Langley, Hubert, *Doctor Arne.* New York, Macmillan, 1938.

Larsen, Jens Pater, *Handel's Messiah.* Copenhagen, Munksgaard, 1957.

Loewenberg, Alfred, *Annals of Opera.* Cambridge, Heffner, 1955.

McHose, Allen I., *Basic Principles of the Technique of 18th and 19th Century Composition.* New York, Appleton-Century-Crofts, 1951.

Myers, Robert M., *Handel's Messiah.* New York, Macmillan, 1948.

Palisca, Claude, *Baroque Music.** Englewood Cliffs, Prentice-Hall, 1967.

Parrish, Carl, *A Treasury of Early Music.** New York, Norton, 1958.

Parrish, Carl, and Ohl, John F., *Masterpieces of Music before 1750.* New York, Norton, 1951.

Pleasants, Henry, *The Great Singers.* New York, Simon & Schuster, 1967.

Robinson, Michael F., *Opera before Mozart.** London, Hutchinson, 1966.

Sadie, Stanley, *Handel.* London, Calder, 1962.

Schönberger, A., and Soehner, H., *The Rococo Age.** New York, McGraw-Hill, 1960.

A SAMPLER OF SUPPLEMENTARY RECORDINGS

Collections

Masterpieces of Music before 1750	Haydn 9038/40
2000 Years of Music	Folkways 3700
Treasury of Early Music	Haydn 9103
Outlook—1745-1790	3-Victor LM-6137
Ten Centuries of Music	DGG KL-52/61
Heritage of the Baroque	Vox 14000
18th Century Arias	London 5591
French Operatic Airs from Lully to Rameau	Oiseau-Lyre OL-50117
Restoration Ribaldry	Allegro LEG-9007

Music of Individual Composers

Arne, Thomas, *Songs to Shakespeare's Plays*

Bach, Johann Christian, *Sinfonia*

Campra, André, *Fêtes vénitiennes*

Gay, John, *The Beggar's Opera*

Gluck, Christoph W., *Orfeo ed Euridice*
    Iphigénie en Tauride
    Iphigénie en Aulide: Overture

* Available in paperback edition.

Handel, George F., *Acis and Galatea*
　　　　　　　　　Alcina
　　　　　　　　　Alexander's Feast
　　　　　　　　　L'Allegro ed il Penseroso
　　　　　　　　　Anthems for the Coronation of George II
　　　　　　　　　Concerti Grossi (6), *Op.* 3
　　　　　　　　　Concerti (16) *for Organ*
　　　　　　　　　Israel in Egypt
　　　　　　　　　Messiah
　　　　　　　　　Ode for St. Cecilia's Day
　　　　　　　　　Royal Fireworks Music
　　　　　　　　　Suites for Harpsichord
　　　　　　　　　Water Music
　　　　　　　　　Xerxes
　　　　　　　　　Semele
　　　　　　　　　Rodelinda
Marais, Marin, *Pièces à une et à deux violes*
Mouret, Jean J., *Festes de Thalie*
Pergolesi, Giovanni, *La Serva padrona*
Rameau, Jean-Philippe, *Castor et Pollux:* Suite
　　　　　　　　　　　Hippolyte et Aricie (excerpts)
　　　　　　　　　　　Orphée
　　　　　　　　　　　Pièces de clavecin

Related Works of Interest
Brahms, Johannes, *Variations on a Theme by Handel*
Stravinsky, Igor, *Suite Italienne for 'Cello and Piano*
　　　　　　　　　Pulcinella

OPPORTUNITIES FOR STUDY IN DEPTH

1. It has become a truism to state that Handel was a German who wrote Italian music in England. Amplify the facets of this statement, supporting remarks with examples.
2. Check out references to Handel and other operatic figures in contemporary accounts by English writers. Starting points might include Alexander Pope's *Dunciad* and Addison and Steele's *Spectator* and *Tatler*. Record findings in outline form.
3. Make a comparison-study of John Gay's ballad-opera, *The Beggar's Opera* (1728) with Kurt Weill's *Three Penny Opera* (1928). In what ways are they similar? How do they differ? What effect did contemporary society have on the style and outlook of each?
4. Investigate the phenomenon óf the *Rococo,* especially as found in eighteenth-century France. What were possible reasons for its emergence? What forms did it take? How did it foreshadow music to come? Prepare a teaching unit based on findings, complete with audio and visual aids, suitable for correlative use in junior high school.
5. Look further into the "War of the Buffoons." What contributions did Abbé Raguenet, Lecerf de la Viéville and J. J. Rousseau make to this mock battle? What results did the skirmish have on French music?

6. Trace the development of the French *opéra-comique,* including the contributions of François André Danican-Philidor (1726-1795) and Pierre-Alexandre Monsigny (1729-1817).

7. Assemble a collection of English poems set to music during this time. Collate the list with one of recordings. After reading the poetry, listen to as many settings as possible and evaluate the musical products in terms of dramatic power, appropriateness and aesthetic appeal.

8. Examine carefully Handel's great oratorio, the *Messiah,* noting the over-all architectural construction, the sequence of musical forms, the variety of executants and the musical means by which the composer projected the emotional significance of the text. Compare *Messiah* with a Carissimi and a Mendelssohn oratorio score.

VOCABULARY ENRICHMENT

English oratorio
pasticcio
"concert performance"
ballad-operas
Abendmusiken
Collegia Musica

Gewandhaus concerts
opera seria
opera buffa
"War of the Buffoons"
opera-ballets
opera overture

PART VI

Music of the Classic Period

Chapter 13.

THE DEVELOPMENT OF SONATA FORM
—FRANZ JOSEPH HAYDN

He [Haydn] begins with the most insignificant idea but little by little
that idea takes form, is reinforced, grows, stretches, and to our astonished eyes, the dwarf becomes a giant.

—Stendhal (G. Carpani) *Vie de Haydn*

CLASSICISM

The term, **classic**, is an ambiguous one, that requires some clarifica-
tion. It has several general and specific meanings, from which we shall
derive a working definition suitable for our purposes. While "Classic"
is freely employed by authors to cover all the instrumental music of
the seventeenth and eighteenth centuries, including that of Bach and
Handel, in its more restricted meaning, it covers only that period in
which sonata design was the dominating formal principle—an era rather
loosely bounded by the death dates of Bach and Beethoven. Although
its roots rest in the early eighteenth century, its termination is found
in the strivings of Beethoven, Schubert and their colleagues toward a
new aesthetic ideal.

Yet another semantic problem presents itself when we use "classic"
in a sense opposite to "popular," *i.e.,* as enduring, in contrast to tran-
sient, for then all great works are classic. In addition, we must resist
the temptation of leaning too heavily upon "classic" as referring to
the aspirations of ancient Greece and Rome transferred to eighteenth-
century middle Europe; for, while parallels can be found in abundance
and Winckelmann and Lord Elgin were active, the ancients, except in
a few instances, and those not musical, did not provide the direct
stimulation that they had previously exerted. With these qualifications,
therefore, we shall consider the Classic period as a stylistic era of music
history, extending from about 1750 to 1825, with its focus centered on
Vienna, capital of the Hapsburg Empire. Its music is characterized by
logic, restraint and proportion, with the corollaries of moderation,
balance and coherence.

Historical Background

What kind of a world did this short but rich epoch encompass? In general, it was one of alternate war and peace; between 1689 and 1815, for instance, France and Great Britain were at war with each other for some seventy years; the American and French Revolutions were to alter the entire complexion of the future; Napoleon conquered his empire, only to lose it once more. It was a world of improved communications. Roads and canals were extended; regular stage and mail routes established; the first newspapers were started, such as the *London Times* in 1785. It was a world of more intensive urbanization, with displaced agrarians flocking to the cities, which were forced to cope with various social problems, resulting in the formation of the first police force, the *Bow Street Runners* in 1750, among other innovations. It was a world in which intellectuals sought to systematize all knowledge, as in the French *Great Encyclopedia* and the proliferation of textbooks and manuals.

It was a world of scientific adventure, with Lavoisier, Faraday, Jenner, Watt, Franklin, Priestley and the Quaker, John Dalton, widening our knowledge of nature and its forces. It was a world marked by fine craftsmanship; in the porcelain of Limoges, the tapestries of Gobelin, the furniture of Chippendale and Sheraton, beautiful silver, gold and pewter plate, and books bound in full calfskin. It was a world in which absolute monarchy truly existed for the last time in Western Europe and in which the aristocracy, with its protocol, refinement and leisure, set standards in taste and behavior. Finally, it was a world in which there was a great deal of optimism—about mankind's potentials, about the possibility of Utopia and about the benevolence of God. In 1791, for example, Joseph Priestley was able to assert, "The empire of reason will ever be the reign of peace," with the conviction that the empire of reason had indeed arrived.

Musical Characteristics

At the time Bach died, a decided change of taste had taken place in all the arts. In music a new order was working for a more tuneful melodic line, simpler harmonic techniques, more clearly-articulated formal structure, and for an instrumental style that had an enlarged palette of orchestral tone color and dynamic variety. Melody, composed of short fragments or **motives,** was, as our opening quotation implies, spun with unique magic into cogent and surprisingly powerful structures by means of new adaptations of formal techniques that were compatible with the prevailing aura of rationalism, and in reaction against the frequently turgid polyphony of preceding music. Themes modeled on instrumental figures, often triadic in content, were contrasted with eminently singable melodies, cast in graceful stepwise patterns, set forth in short phrases, punctuated with frequent cadences and emphasized by repetition. Tonal harmony had long been firmly established, but now, along with melodic inventiveness, it made the primary scaffolding of Classical structures, so dependent upon key contrast, modulation and cadences for their architecture. Musical texture was lightened to that of **homophony,** that is, a melody with chordal accompaniment, so that elements of harmony, rhythm and counterpoint were exposed with a clarity that revealed the harmonious relationship of all parts. The *timbre* of individual instruments and voices was used lucidly for formal and expressive purposes. An equilibrium of forces was to be achieved in music of the Classic period that has never been equalled, before or since.

The features that characterize Classical music were generated from a variety of sources, including the "gallant style" of the Rococo, the contrasting "bourgeois style," the *Sturm und Drang* (Storm and Stress) literary school of Schiller, Goethe and Rousseau, and *opera buffa.*

Rococo music, epitomized in the compositions of Couperin, consisted, as we have noted, of slight, elegant, spirited, much-embellished, aristocratic works in which many short themes were employed in patterns of repetition, sequence and some contrast. "Bourgeois style," on the other hand, was of the middle class, with simplicity, sincerity and sentimentality dominating considerations. We shall discuss a German modification of these, *empfindsamer Stil,* when we study C. P. E. Bach's music. Reflections of *Sturm und Drang,* very evident in Romantic music, are to be discerned during the Classic period in sudden *fortissimo* passages, in curious dissonances and in eruptive outbursts in the minor key. The *opera buffa* contributed lyric melodies, quick changes of mood and vivacity and spirit to the scene. William Brandt states that in Haydn's music one finds influences of *empfindsamer Stil* combined with folk music; in Mozart's works, a strong influence of Italian comic opera; while in Beethoven's compositional style, is found a blending of *Sturm und Drang* elements, together with "bourgeois style"—in all three cases, uniquely infused with the personality of the individual composer.

What, then, can we say of Classic music in general? It was in many ways a product of its times and environment. Classic music is flavored with the culture of courts and cities. From an intermingling of German, French and Italian streams, it achieved a universality of musical statement. Classic music tends to shun scenic elements in favor of a direct projection of abstract designs in sound. It is a self-contained art in which form is often a façade concealing the composer, who, nevertheless, is somewhat in the spotlight. It is music resulting from an enthusiastic development of amateur music-making in many levels of society. As Hadow writes:

> It is impossible to over-estimate the importance to music of the social and political changes which culminated in the decade of Revolution. They meant that the old *regime* had been tried and found wanting; that the standard of taste was no longer an aristocratic privilege; that the doors of the salon should be thrown open, and that art should emerge into a larger and more liberal atmosphere.

With this overview, let us commence our examination of the music of the Classic period with the accomplishments of Bach's sons, the contributions of the Mannheim symphonists and a survey of the life and works of the first of the Classic giants, Franz Joseph Haydn.

BACH'S SONS

Of Bach's sons, four became accomplished musicians. As Johann Sebastian Bach represented the conservative spirit of the eighteenth century, so did his sons the radical. Bach, the father, closed an era; the sons explored new pathways. The father remained at home, renowned as an organist but comparatively unknown as a composer; the sons spread the fame of the Bach name and won the reputation of having greater talent than the father.

We have already mentioned the "London Bach," John Christian, the maverick of the family, as a significant personality in English musical circles. Reinhard G. Pauly asserts, "To listen to one of Christian Bach's keyboard sonatas, concertos or symphonies is to realize that here is a composer who stands at the doorstep of Classicism, for in his graceful melodies—small in design, elegant, and at times tinged with melancholy—we detect the language, above all, of the young Mozart." In his works we discover the characteristic Classical figurations, the tonic-dominant polarity and the matchless airiness and economy of the coming age.

Wilhelm Friedemann (1710-1784), the oldest son, inherited his father's genius for organ playing, and was organist in churches at Dresden for thirteen years and later at Halle. When Handel returned to Halle from time to time to visit his mother, he must have met young Bach, who had been an unsuccessful messenger sent to arrange meetings between his father and his eminent contemporary. Many of Wilhelm Friedemann's compositions, which reputedly showed extraordinary talent, have been lost, as he was too indolent to write them out and depended on his gifts of improvisation. In 1764 he resigned his position at Halle, where he was director of instrumental music as well as organist. During the last twenty years of his life he drifted about without a permanent post, earning his living by teaching and giving concerts. One of his friends was Johann Nicholaus Forkel, to whom he gave data for his father's biography. C. S. Terry considers that "as a composer, he came nearest among his brothers to his father in the originality and bent of his genius, and in his powers of improvisation." Wilhelm Friedemann Bach wrote cantatas, organ fugues, *chorale-preludes, sinfonias, sonatas, fantasias,* trios, polonaises, *Clavier* concertos and smaller works for flute, violin and viola, many of which are still unpublished.

The "Berlin Bach"—Carl Philipp Emanuel (1714-1788), godson of Telemann and pupil of his father—studied law at the University of Frankfurt and founded among his fellow students a *Collegium Musicum.* In 1740 he was hired as harpsichordist at the court of Frederick the Great, in whose service he remained for twenty-seven years at Berlin and Potsdam. When Telemann died, Emanuel Bach replaced him as musical director and Cantor of the *Johanneum,* at Hamburg, a position he held until his death. Hamburg was no longer the operatic center it had been in Mattheson's and Handel's day. Bach became its leading musician, directing the music of five choirs, and giving concerts at which his works were performed. In 1775 he presented the *Messiah.* He was eulogized after death as "one of the greatest musicians of his generation, both theoretical and practical, the creator of *Clavier* technique, a player unmatched on that instrument and a man of wit and humor whose name will always be held sacred."

Emanuel Bach was a more important innovator of new forms than Sebastian. As such he stands as a predecessor of Haydn, Mozart and Beethoven in the history of the sonata. He regarded his father's work with deep respect, but as counterpoint had become old-fashioned, Emanuel worked for the perfection of a homophonic style, the development of thematic material, clear formal design and refined workmanship.

C. P. E. Bach was a master of the North German Rococo modification known as *empfindsamer Stil* (expressive or sensitive style). The mid-eighteenth century has often been called an age of tears, and in *Empfindsamkeit* we find the musical counterpart, with its emphasis on subtle expression of a variety of sentiments within a single movement of a composition, necessitating short phrases and frequent melodic changes of movement and of volume, as well as such devices as unexpected modulations and chromaticism. The underlying premise of *empfindsamer Stil* was not unlike that of the doctrine of affections but in its application it tended to promote soulful interpretations, short, however, of the maudlin.

In 1742 Bach wrote six *Clavier* sonatas dedicated to Frederick II; in 1744, another six were dedicated to the Duke of Württemburg; six more appeared in 1763; and a fourth set, *Für Kenner und Liebhaber* ("For Connoisseur and Amateur"), was published before his death. Because of these works, Emanuel Bach has sometimes been considered the inventor of the Classic sonata, but it is seldom possible to point to an individual as the inventor of anything musical. Hasse, Galuppi, Dr. Thomas Arne, P. Domenico Paradies (1707-1791), Wilhelm Friedemann and Johann Christian Bach also experimented with sonata-form.

Along with other composers, Emanuel Bach felt a need for contrast in the sonata and he worked toward the idea of using two themes of differing character in the exposition of the first movement and in structuring the first movement in a three-part form that suggests exposition, development and recapitulation. Bach also advanced the cause of the sonata in his choice and development of subjects and in his deliberately expressive use of harmony, modulation and ornaments. Although he composed small pieces in *rondo* form, he did not regard the *rondo* as of sufficient importance to include it in his sonatas. If, however, one compares the first "Prussian" *Sonata in F Minor* with Beethoven's first piano sonata in the same key, it will be apparent that Beethoven must have been familiar with Bach's work.

C. P. E. Bach wrote over 700 works, including concertos, *sinfonias,* flute compositions (Frederick II was an ardent flutist), odes, oratorios, Passions and cantatas. As a solo song composer, he was a pioneer. Discarding the *da capo aria* and obviously under the influence of contemporary German poets, Bach utilized a new approach that caused the historian Riemann to call him the father of the *durchkomponiert* (through-composed) song, that is, a song "the music of which varies with each verse or mood of the poem."

An acclaimed performer on the *Clavier* and an outstanding teacher, Emanuel Bach, having mastered his father's keyboard precepts, expounded them in a book, published in two parts (in 1753 and 1762), entitled *Versuch über die wahre Art, das Clavier zu spielen (An Essay on the True Art of Clavier-Playing)*. In this is included a discourse on the correct interpretation of embellishments, invaluable for authentic performances of mid-eighteenth-century music. Bach's principles laid the basis for modern pianoforte technique, as carried forward by Clementi, Cramer and Hummel.

Johann Cristoph Friedrich Bach (1732-1795) was the first son of Anna Magdalena to grow up. Educated at Leipzig University, he became chamber musician to Count Wilhelm von Schaum-Lippe at Bückeburg. An earnest and thorough composer, he wrote a number of choral works, *Clavier* and chamber music and symphonies "not unworthy to stand by those of Haydn." Although his son, Wilhelm Friedrich Ernst (1759-1845), was the last male of the direct line of Johann Sebastian, it has been claimed that descendants are still living in Silesia, Germany and Poland.

The growth of orchestras, in the modern sense, was coincidental with the development of instrumental music for such ensembles. Still sponsored by aristocratic personalities, these groups, once haphazard collections of palace officials, took on a new order and method. Composers were given a new medium for which to develop new forms. A new system of dynamics was evolved that was to revolutionize musical interpretations, and the concertmaster, no longer an animated metronome, became a controlling force. Under Hasse, the Dresden orchestra had become proficient, and Vienna, Munich, Stuttgart, Rome, Venice, Florence and Milan furthered the progress of orchestral playing and orchestration. Austrian composers, such as Georg Matthias Monn (1717-1750) and Georg Cristoph Wagenseil (1715-1777), stood as transition figures in the evolution of the symphony. While they continued the contrapuntal tradition, they combined it with an extension of the "gallant style," often including minuets in their symphonies as well as contrasting themes.

MANNHEIM SCHOOL

It was at the Electoral court of Mannheim, however, during the sovereignty of Prince Carl Theodor (1724-1799), that happenings of great significance to the full flowering of musical Classicism were occurring. Located at the juncture of the Neckar and Rhine rivers, Mannheim had become the capital of the Palatinate in 1720 and through 1780 was the scene of much scientific and artistic achievement, thanks to the ambitious generosity of its freespending Prince, who is reputed to have expended the incredible sum of 35,000,000 florins as a patron. Dr. Burney writes that in 1772 "the expense and magnificence of the court of this little city are prodigious; the palace and offices extend over almost half the town; and one half of the inhabitants, who are in office, prey on the other, who seem to be in the utmost indigence . . ."—in other words, a miniature Versailles. The orchestra, one of the largest in Europe, in 1756 numbered twenty violins, four violas, four 'cellos and two basses with a wind section that included four horns. Mozart visited Mannheim in 1777 and was highly impressed by what he heard there.

A highly-trained group of musicians—composers, orchestral performers and conductors—gathered at the court of Mannheim and came to be known as the Mannheim school. One of the pioneers was Johann Stamitz (1717-1757), who was the first leader of the orchestra. A skilled string player, Stamitz was responsible for systematically drilling the string section until it achieved a discipline hitherto unknown in the musical world; it was he who introduced uniform bowings and created the position of **concertmaster,** *i.e.,* the principal violinist as conductor. Under Stamitz and later under his successor, Christian Cannabich (1731-1798), the Mannheim orchestra introduced effects that astonished its audience. These included a long *crescendo* (a gradual increase in volume) as a calculated instrumental end, an extended tonic triadic initial-theme known as a "rocket," *tremolos,* sudden contrasts in dynamics and dramatic orchestral rests. The dominance of the violins, the idea of development of initial thematic material, arpeggiated harmonic figuration, a mannerism wherein instruments were gradually added to a repeating phrase—all stemmed from Mannheim and spread throughout Germany, Paris and London. The notion of a symphonic music became almost synonymous with that of German music.

Other members of the Mannheim school included: Karl Stamitz (1746-1801); Franz Richter (1709-1789); Ernst Eichner (1740-1777); Giovanni B. Toëschi (*c.* 1727-1800); and Ignaz Holzbauer (1711-1783). Directly or indirectly influenced by the Mannheim school were François-Joseph Gossec (1734-1829), a Belgian symphonist in Paris; Luigi Boccherini (1743-1805), one of the early composers of string quartets; Giovanni Battista Sammartini of Milan; the sons of Bach; Karl Ditters von Dittersdorf (1739-1799); and Joseph and Michael Haydn.

FRANZ JOSEPH HAYDN—LIFE

Franz Joseph Haydn (1732-1809) was a musical personality in whom all the eighteenth-century trends found an ideal outlet. He was the product of his period, his peasant heritage, his court environment, his natural endowments and his amiable disposition. At the end of the nineteenth century, several critics, including Franz Kuhač and Sir Henry Hadow, put forth the dubious theory that Haydn's forefathers were Croatians and, therefore, that Haydn was a Slav and not a Teuton. Sir Henry pointed out that Haydn's works were profusely sprinkled with Croatian folksongs (a disputed idea) and that his sentiment and humor were not like those of other German composers. In answer, Carl Engel contended that Haydn "is a more typically Viennese composer than are Gluck, Mozart and Beethoven . . ." But, he continued, "Whatever national stock Joseph Haydn came from, we should like to know—though we never shall—whence and by what ancestral indiscretion he derived the drop of indigo that turned the 'peasant' into a genius so thoroughly at home in polite company." The characteristics that Hadow found Slavic, Engel claimed were the effects of "brilliant, gay, frivolous, sentimental Vienna."

Such an exchange may seem merely academic, but it does point up a consideration which is pertinent to our discussion; namely, that Austria, now a colorful but politically insignificant country, was once the seat of an extensive and wealthy empire, including Hungary, Bohemia, Croatia, Lombardy, Venetia and Tuscany, among other territories. Consequently, many ethnic and linguistic differences existed side by side, enriching the Austrian *milieu*. During the "enlightened" reign of Maria Theresa (1740-1780), Vienna achieved increased importance as the heart of a more centralized government. And so closely is Vienna associated with Classical music that the era is often referred to as the *Viennese Period*. Vienna was the place where things were happening and where opportunities offered themselves. It acted as a magnet, luring Beethoven from Bonn, Mozart from Salzburg and Haydn from the bucolic grandeur of Esterház.

Franz Joseph, the second child of Mathias Haydn, master wheelwright, and Anna Maria Koller, daughter of a cook in a nobleman's household, was born at Rohrau, Lower Austria. The sixth child, Johann Michael Haydn (1737-1806), was also destined to become a distinguished musician. Joseph soon showed evidence of unusual talents that attracted the attention of a relative, J. M. Franck. At the age of six, little "Sepperl" was sent to Hainburg, where he attended school and had his first music lessons with Franck, who taught him to sing and to play the *Clavier* and the violin.

In 1740, Haydn was taken to Vienna by Georg Reutter (1708-1772), court composer and *Kapellmeister* at St. Stephen's Cathedral, where the boy remained until his voice changed, when he was replaced by his brother, Michael. "Sepperl" was allegedly expelled for cutting off the pigtail of a fellow chorister. Without funds or food, he was befriended by one Spangler, a poor singer who shared his attic with him. Young Haydn gave lessons, and picked up a living wherever he could. Through acquaintance with a popular actor, Felix Kurz, he was commissioned to write a stage work, *Die neue krumme Teufel* (now lost), which was produced in Vienna and Prague (1752).

Haydn moved into his own attic, purchased a "worm-eaten *Clavier*" and treatises by Fux and Mattheson, as well as the first six sonatas of C. P. E. Bach, which he studied assiduously. Of these he wrote, ". . . I could not tear myself from the *Clavier* until I had played and replayed them, and anyone who knows me well must know how much I owe to Emanuel Bach, because I understood and studied him diligently."

Living in the same house as Haydn was the priest, Metastasio, Gluck's librettist, who taught the young musician Italian and introduced him to a Spanish child, who became his pupil. Through her, Haydn met Nicola Porpora, the illustrious if surly and untidy Neapolitan singing teacher and opera composer. Haydn became his accompanist and valet in exchange for lessons in composition. On one of their trips, he came in contact with Wagenseil, Gluck and Dittersdorf, prominent musicians of the time. Without regular instruction, but by dint of his own hard work and persistence, Haydn developed an individual and promising compositional style.

A musical amateur, Baron von Fürnberg, invited Haydn in 1755 to spend some time at his country home. There Haydn composed a series of works for the Baron's orchestra of strings, oboes and horns. He also wrote his first string quartets, which were played by the steward, the village priest, the violoncellist Albrechtsberger and himself. Haydn was subsequently (1758) appointed music director and court composer to Count Ferdinand Maximilian Morzin, who maintained a small orchestra, for which Haydn composed *divertimenti, cassations* and a symphony, sometimes called his first. In 1760 he secretly married a wigmaker's daughter, Maria Anna Keller, with whom he was thoroughly incompatible throughout his life. Rather ungallantly, he wrote, "She has no virtues and it is entirely indifferent to her whether her husband is a shoemaker or an artist." Their union was without issue.

Due to a decline in Count Morzin's fortunes, Haydn became second *Kapellmeister* to Prince Paul Anton Esterházy at Eisenstadt. His musical resources consisted of an orchestra of three violins, one 'cello and a double bass, with wind instruments doing double duty as a military band. His choir numbered two sopranos, an alto, two tenors and a bass. In 1762 the Prince died and his brother, Nicolaus, an enthusiastic patron of the arts, succeeded him and greatly augmented the musical forces of his establishment. Prince Nicolaus played the **baryton,** an instrument similar to the *viola da gamba,* with six or seven gut strings over a fingerboard and additional sympathetic strings of metal which could be plucked with the left thumb. In all, Haydn composed about 150 *baryton* pieces, combining the instrument in trios with violin, viola, bass and flute accompaniments.

Fig. 51. "Haydn Leading a Concert at Prince Esterházy's"—J. Schmid. Haydn's duties as *Kapellmeister* to the Prince included conducting after-dinner concerts of contemporary music, usually his own.

By 1766, when Haydn was promoted to *Kapellmeister,* his works were widely known and a Viennese journal had called him "our national favorite." The Prince, ever a lover of luxury and display, had built a lavish country palace which he named for himself. "Setting aside Versailles," wrote a visitor in 1784, "there is perhaps in all France no place which can compare in magnificence with Esterház." On the beautifully-landscaped estate, in addition to the castle, were an opera house (seating 400), a coffee house and a marionette theater, whose walls were covered with shells. Haydn had complete charge of musical activities, which included two opera performances a week and two formal concerts in addition to sundry other diversions. He was kept very busy, so much so, that on one of his manuscripts he jotted down the note, "written in my sleep." The Prince encouraged him by constant approval and Haydn was allowed to make experiments "and was thus in a position to improve, alter, make additions or omissions, and be as bold as I pleased; I was cut off from the world, there was no one to confuse or torment me, and I was forced to become original." Despite his demanding schedule, Haydn found time to fulfill commissions such as one from Spain for the *Seven Last Words* (1785), from Paris for six symphonies (1784) and from the King of Naples for concertos (1786). Haydn

might have seconded the remark Bach made in assessing his compositions, "I worked hard."

PATRONAGE SYSTEM

It may be profitable at this point to digress for a moment to consider
the system of musical patronage that prevailed in the eighteenth century.
Hadow comments:

> In every capital from Madrid to St. Petersburg, there were court-ap-
> pointments of varying dignity and position: in most countries aris-
> tocracy followed the royal practice, and established a private orchestra
> as an essential part of its retinue . . . The relation implied in this
> patronage was for the most part, frankly that of master and servant.
> As a rule, genius sat below the salt, and wore a livery like the butler
> or the footman . . . The system in general was not well qualified to
> raise the dignity of art or to increase the self-respect of the artist.

In Haydn's case, the situation was extremely explicit. When he was
engaged by Prince Esterházy as *Vizekapellmeister,* Haydn had of necessity to sign a contract which defined his duties, stated his remuneration
and offered him a possibility of "tenure" after three-years' service. Moreover, there were supplementary clauses. These, unfortunately not unknown to many school teachers and government employees today, included additional duties and sanctions: Haydn was to maintain a reputation of sobriety and respectability; he was to dress in a specific manner;
he was to set a good example to subordinates and avoid familiarity; he
was to compose to the Prince's order; he was to be available at all
times and be responsible for the other musicians' punctuality and conduct; he was to supervise maintenance of all musical equipment; he
was to instruct the female singers and practice his own instruments; he
was to eat at the household officials' table; he was to give six months'
notice if he wished to relinquish his position. In other words, almost
every aspect of his life was circumscribed. That Haydn did not particularly resent such stipulations was testimony to his adaptability and also
to the fact that he really had no choice, other than that of taking the
terms or leaving them. In his time and place, everyone was a subject
of some prince or other, save the princes themselves. In return for
compliance, Haydn gained security.

FRANZ JOSEPH HAYDN—LATER LIFE

With the death of Prince Nicolaus in 1790, Haydn, with an assured
income and the emeritus title of *Kapellmeister,* was set free by the
Prince's successor, Anton, and immediately engaged by Johann Peter

Salomon, the London impresario, for an English tour (1791-2). Marion M. Scott describes the London into which Haydn stepped:

> Music was fashionable because the Royal Family were keen amateurs, and so opera and concert enterprise were well supported by the nobility and gentry. But while there was a strong and lovely English tradition in sacred music, secular music was largely foreign, and continental artists swarmed to London . . . A queer, busy, self-satisfied world, with audiences befrilled and be-hooped . . . and sensibility and taste as the fashionable virtues—a world with scores of clever musicians in it, but none great since the days of Handel.

All doors opened to Haydn. He was an artistic and a social success. Dr. Burney even wrote verses of welcome to him and recommended that he receive a degree of Doctor of Music from Oxford (which, Haydn grumbled, cost him the sum of six guineas altogether!). Haydn was inspired to write some of the greatest compositions of his career—at the age of sixty. He had one English pupil, a Mrs. Schroeter, German widow of the music master to the Queen, of whom, in later years, he said, "I should certainly have married her if I had been single." His concerts under Salomon, for each of which he wrote new works, including six symphonies, were great triumphs. The one cloud on the London horizon was the news of Mozart's death. Haydn and the younger composer had been devoted friends, each giving inspiration and knowledge to the other. "Papa" Haydn, a nickname given him by Mozart, has come down in music through the ages as a term of affection and appreciation for a generous man of noble character.

When Haydn returned to Vienna, Beethoven studied with him briefly until Haydn made a second trip to London (1794-5), which was as rewarding as the first. He added six more "Salomon" or "London" symphonies. The concerts, as before, were conducted by Salomon, a violinist, with Haydn at the pianoforte. Through these he earned enough to free him from financial worry for the rest of his life. "It is England which has made me famous in Germany," he said. Haydn is an exceptional example of a composer who received recognition during his lifetime. On his return from London, he was taken to Rohrau, where a monument and bust of him had been erected.

In 1797, Haydn, fired with enthusiasm by the English *God Save the King,* composed Austria's national anthem, which was adopted and sung until 1918. He used it as a theme for variations in his *"Emperor" Quartet, Op.* 76, no. 3; it is also heard as the hymn, "Glorious Things of Thee Are Spoken." Two of his masterpieces were written in his last years: *The Creation,* on a text drawn partly from Milton's *Paradise Lost* and partly from *Genesis* (1798); and *The Seasons* by James Thomson (1801). These oratorios achieved a popularity only exceeded by Handel's *Messiah*. In 1802-3 he was busy arranging Scottish and Welsh songs.

His last public appearance was at a performance, in his honor, of *The Creation* at the University of Vienna, 1808, where, from his armchair, Haydn acknowledged the heartfelt demonstrations of the public. A contemporary account describes the scene thus:

> To the sound of trumpets and drums, and accompanied by many of Vienna's lovers of the arts, Haydn was carried . . . to a place in front of the orchestra . . . All who could get close to him expressed their veneration, their concern for his feeble state and their joy that he could be present on this happy day . . . Tears were in his eyes when he took leave, and he stretched out his hand in blessing toward the orchestra.

Fig. 52. Haydn's calling card. As he grew older Haydn was aware of increasing physical weakness. His calling card, marked *Molto Adagio* (very slow), reads: "Gone is all my strength; old and weak am I."

Haydn's last years were darkened by increasing physical weakness and inability to accomplish the work that he wanted to do. He catalogued his compositions and enjoyed receiving visitors, who came from near and far. The composer, Weber, recorded his impressions of the old man:

> I went several times to visit Haydn. Apart from the natural weakness of age, he was always in good spirits and lively, choosing to talk of

the events of his life and above all with young artists . . . It is touching to see grown men come in who call Haydn 'Papa' and kiss his hand.

The bombardment of Vienna by the French under Napoleon took place shortly before his death. Haydn consoled himself by playing his national anthem and assuring his household that they would be safe as long as he was by. In fact, an enemy officer visited him expressly to sing an *aria* from *The Creation* for its composer—a deed that moved Haydn very much. In 1820, Haydn's remains were removed from Vienna by Prince Esterházy and reinterred at Eisenstadt, where he had spent so much of his life.

FRANZ JOSEPH HAYDN—MUSIC

"The language I speak is understood by the whole world," said Haydn in reply to Mozart's plea that he refrain from traveling to London. Superficially his idiom seems so simple and inevitable that the fact of his having been an ultramodernist in his day may come as a shock. Through his innovations he shaped what we have come to think of as Classic sonata design and the Classic treatment of the symphony orchestra and the string quartet. A careful and deliberate craftsman, Haydn was never pedantic. In response to Albrechtsberger's accusation of rule-breaking by Mozart, Haydn responded: "What is the good of such rules? Art is free, and should be fettered by no such mechanical regulations. The educated ear is the sole authority on all these questions, and I think I have as much right to lay down the law as anyone." Perhaps the layman has taken "Papa" Haydn so much for granted that a re-evaluation of his contributions to music will not be amiss. A definitive study, however, still awaits the completion of research now going on: a complete edition of his compositions, a project undertaken several times without success; a comprehensive catalogue of his works, now being issued by Antoine van Hoboken; and further documentation of his life.

Apart from his oratorio, *The Creation,* Haydn is best known for his keyboard sonatas, string quartets and symphonies—all instrumental compositions in multiple movements of a certain formal structure. Originally, as we have noted, a "sonata" was just an instrumental work, as distinguished from a vocal one. It further developed in two directions—one leading to the dance suite and the other toward a more abstract conception. Gradually it assumed a more or less characteristic scheme which intrigued composers of the Classic period, who, of course, helped define and extend it. Features of the new style came from the Viennese school (Monn), the Mannheim group (Stamitz *et al.*), the Milanese composers (*i.e.,* Sammartini, whom Haydn called a "scribbler") and such North Germans as C. P. E. Bach and the Grauns. In general, these consisted of a special attitude toward melodic material and its developmental possibilities and a basic modulatory scheme, together with thematic dualism or plurality. Although exceptions can be cited to any diagrammatic presentation, a generalized and simplified description gives us insight into the structure.

Here we must be careful to avoid semantic confusion. In the Classic period the word, *sonata,* refers to a work in several movements for one or two solo instruments. When more instruments are used, the terms, *trio, quartet, sextet, symphony* and *concerto* are employed. Yet all usually contain at least one movement in **sonata-form,** also designated as *sonata-allegro form* or *first movement form.* This is divided into three parts:

1. *Exposition*

   a. First theme in the key of the tonic, followed by a modulating *transition* passage or *bridge* to a
   b. Secondary theme in the key of the dominant or relative major, continuing to a
   c. Closing section with a well-defined cadence.

2. *Development*

   This forms the nucleus of sonata-form, wherein the thematic material, now revealed, is modified, fragmented and varied according to the discretion of the composer, who may even add new musical thoughts. After a free use of modulation, the dominant key is reached, which acts as a preparation for the

3. *Recapitulation*

   The recapitulation presents the original content of the exposition, more or less literally, but deprived of modulation, so that the first theme, transition, secondary theme and closing section are all in the initial tonality.

These three parts which make up a movement in sonata-form may be further modified by the addition of an *introduction* in slow tempo preceding the fast exposition, and a *coda,* attached to the end of the recapitulation. Occasionally, the exposition is monothematic, as in the case of Haydn's *Symphony No. 104.* Often the principal and subordinate themes are similar in quality. In most Classic sonatas, the exposition is marked for repetition, in order that the listener become thoroughly acquainted with the germinal material to be developed. As late as Beethoven, there are also examples of repetition of the development and recapitulation as a unit. With the growing importance of the *coda* as a climax point, however, this practice was discarded.

Other movements of a Classic sonata, quartet or symphony are by no means standardized. The second movement, usually in slow tempo, may be a theme and variations or a ternary song-form (A-B-A) or in sonata-form. The only relic of the dance suite found in the Classic sonata is the Minuet and Trio, often the third movement. Beethoven, who is credited with transforming the minuet into a *scherzo,* was anticipated by Haydn, who first used the term. For the final movement, a jolly *rondo,* derived from the old French *rondeau* or round dance, in which a principal theme alternates with one, two or three secondary themes, often appears, although the use of sonata-form is frequent.

If the invention of the string quartet does not belong to Haydn, he was certainly among the first composers to establish it as a chamber music work for four instruments of a single *timbre,* two violins, viola and violoncello. For him it became a perfect vehicle for music in which newly-discovered possibilities could be explored. In his *divertimenti* and cassations the use of sonata-form took on more importance. Guido Adler points out that in the 1750's, when Haydn was writing his first quartets and symphonies, "the line between these two kinds of music had not been drawn; but, as time went on, the difference between his treatment of them became more and more pronounced." From the eighteen early quartets of *Ops.* 1, 2 and 3 through those of *Op.* 77, one can discern an enormous technical growth. In the early works, the instruments were not equals and the dimensions were small; while in the later works, all four parts are significant, the thematic material is simplified and manipulated more ingeniously and the length of the works has increased substantially. In all, Haydn composed over eighty string quartets. "It was from Haydn," Mozart claimed, "that I first learned the true way to compose quartets."

Haydn might have made a similar acknowledgement to Mozart for the symphonies. When Haydn went to Eisenstadt, he took advantage of every opportunity to study the orchestra, especially the capabilities of wind instruments. In his symphonies, which number over 100, Haydn gradually developed an orchestration less dependent on the strings and more challenging for the winds. Even after he was middle-aged, he was constantly striving to enhance the possibilities of the orchestra. He regretted that he had not become acquainted earlier with the clarinet, then in use at Mannheim and London. In his twelve "London" symphonies, he arrived at a mature mastery of the idiom. The *"Surprise"* Symphony (No. 94 in G), with its emphatic *fortissimo* chord, written according to some to make the ladies jump, was extremely effective. In *Symphony No. 100* (the so-called "Military"), the composer augmented his orchestra with winds and percussion (triangle, cymbals and bass drum) to achieve a grand martial mood. Earlier, in the *"Farewell"* Symphony (No. 45 in F♯ Minor), Haydn had shown a unique personal touch, as he had added a slow *coda* to the end of the last movement, during which the instruments (and performers) are eliminated one by one, until finally only two violinists remain—this as a not so gentle hint to the prince that the musicians wished permission to return to their families (who were not allowed to reside at Esterház).

In addition to the two oratorios, Haydn composed fourteen Masses, musically elaborate in the Austrian manner, of which the "Lord Nelson" (*Missa solemnis in D Minor, No. 9*) is deservedly popular. He also wrote a *Seven Last Words,* designated in the original orchestral version as "Seven Sonatas with an Introduction and at the End an Earthquake." Commissioned by the Cathedral of Cadiz, this was instrumental music to be used following the prostration of the bishop after each of the seven last words was pronounced. It offered Haydn the technical problem of composing seven ten-minute *adagios* "without tiring the listener," no easy task. He subsequently arranged the work for string quartet and only in 1796 did he rework it as a choral composition for Prince Esterházy.

Although Haydn composed many operas and stage works, he did not feel that this form of composition was his *forte* and repeatedly expressed a desire to visit Italy to learn more about opera at firsthand. In answering a request from Prague for an opera, Haydn diffidently replied that he "should run too many risks, for it would be difficult for anyone, no matter who, to equal the great Mozart," whose *Don Giovanni* had recently been produced there. He had written his operas to meet the requirements of Esterház, not those of the public at large.

In Haydn we have a very prolific composer who also wrote many overtures, serenades, dances, concertos, keyboard sonatas, violin sonatas, trios, songs, Church music as well as novelties, such as music for glass harmonica (musical glasses), musical clocks, etc. Of them all he said, "Some of my children are well-bred, some ill-bred, and here and there is a changeling among them." His music is always cheerful and often humorous. Haydn commented that when he thought of all the misery in the world, a small voice said to him, "Perhaps your work may be a source from which those oppressed by care may draw a moment's relief and relaxation."

Goethe's words, in *Kunst und Altertum* (*Art and Antiquity*), provide us with an excellent *finale*.

> . . . I touch on the reproach that is commonly applied to Haydn: that his music lacks passion. To which I reply: the element of passion in music, as in all the arts, is all the less important because it is the most easily perceived. It is not an essential; it is the product of chance. . . . Haydn suits us: child of our own part of the world, he does what he does without over-excitement. Besides, what more does he need: temperament, sensitivity, wit, humor, spontaneity, gentleness, strength, even those two indications of genius itself, naïvety and irony— all these are already his own.

SUGGESTIONS FOR FURTHER READING

Bach, Carl Philipp Emanuel, *Essay on the True Art of Playing Keyboard Instruments*. New York, Norton, 1949.

Barbaud, Pierre, *Haydn*.* New York, Grove, 1959.

Brenet, Michel, *Haydn*. Oxford, Oxford University Press, 1926.

Bukofzer, Manfred F., *Music of the Classic Period*. Berkeley, University of California Press, 1955.

Burney, Charles, *Dr. Burney's Musical Tours in Europe*. New York, Oxford University Press, 1959.

Carse, Adam, *Eighteenth-Century Symphonies*. London, Augener, 1951.

—— *The Orchestra in the XVIIIth Century*. Cambridge, Heffer, 1940.

Dolmetsch, Arnold, *The Interpretation of the Music of the XVIIth and XVIIIth Centuries*. London, Novello, 1915.

Geiringer, Karl, *The Bach Family*. New York, Oxford University Press, 1954.

—— *Joseph Haydn: A Creative Life in Music*. New York, Norton, 1946.

Gotwals, V., ed., *Joseph Haydn, Eighteenth-Century Gentleman and Genius*. Madison, University of Wisconsin Press, 1963.

Hadow, W. H., *Collected Essays*. Oxford, Oxford University Press, 1928.

Haydn, Joseph, *Collected Correspondence and London Notebooks*. London, Oxford University Press, 1959.

Helm, Ernest Eugene, *Music at the Court of Frederick the Great*. Norman, University of Oklahoma Press, 1960.

Landon, H. C. R., *The Symphonies of Joseph Haydn*. London, Universal Edition, 1955.

Mellers, Wilfred H., *The Sonata Principle*. London, Rockliff, 1957.

Newman, William S., *The Sonata in the Classic Era*. Chapel Hill, University of North Carolina Press, 1963.

Pauly, Reinhard G., *Music in the Classic Period*.* Englewood Cliffs, Prentice-Hall, 1965.

Schönberger, A., and Soehner, H., *The Rococo Age*.* New York, McGraw-Hill, 1960.

Starr, William J., and Devine, George F., *Music Scores—Omnibus*,* Part I. Englewood Cliffs, Prentice-Hall, 1964.

* Available in paperback edition.

A SAMPLER OF SUPPLEMENTARY RECORDINGS

Collections

The Mannheim School	Classic Editions 2010
Music of the Bach Family	4-Boston BUA1–402/5
Ten Centuries of Music	DGG KL-52/61
2000 Years of Music	Folkways 3700
Glass Harmonica Music	Vox DL-1110
Musical Clock Music	Lyric 143

Music of Individual Composers

Bach, C. P. E., *Symphonies*
     Sonatas
Bach, Johann Christian, *Sinfonia*
     Sonatas for Clavier
Bach, Johann C. F., *Septet*
Boccherini, Luigi, *Concerto in B flat for 'Cello and Orchestra*
Dittersdorf, Karl Ditters von, *Divertimento in B*
Galuppi, Baldassare, *Twelve Sonatas for Harpsichord*
Haydn, Franz Joseph, *5 Concerti for 2 liras*
     Concerto in E flat for Trumpet and Orchestra
     Divertimento for Baryton, Viola and 'Cello
     Mass No. 7, Missa "in tempore belli"
     The Creation
     Quartet in C, Op. 76, No. 3, "Emperor"
     Sonatas for Piano
     Symphony No. 45 in f sharp — "Farewell"
     Symphony No. 94 in G — "Surprise"
     Symphony No. 101 in D — "Clock"
Haydn, Michael, *Divertimenti*
Richter, Franz Xaver, *Sinfonia con fuga in g*
Sammartini, G. Battista, *Symphonies*
Stamitz, Johann, *Symphonies*
Stamitz, Karl, *Quartets*

OPPORTUNITIES FOR STUDY IN DEPTH

1. At the same time the sonata-form was being developed in German-speaking countries, the literary novel was introduced by Richardson in England. By analogy, is there any relationship between these two phenomena? Present hypotheses.

2. Investigate the aesthetic philosophy of Classicism as compared with Romanticism. What are its tenets? What relationship do they have with human nature, the natural world, the world of society? Are there Classic manifestations in today's American culture? What are they?

3. Make a study of the role and definition of ornaments in eighteenth-century keyboard and violin music. Collate results with examples in poster form and display on bulletin board.

4. Compare a symphony by one of the Mannheim school with one by Haydn

and one by Mozart, using recordings and scores. What differences exist in formal structure? In instrumentation? In integration of movements? In general style?

5. Organize a teaching unit designed for the middle grades concerning Franz Joseph Haydn, the man and his music, including audio-visual aids, and a bibliography of reading matter on the pupils' own level. One suggestion for the latter is Opal Wheeler's and Sybil Deucher's *Haydn, the Merry Little Peasant* (New York, Dutton).

6. Prepare a supplementary report on the eighteenth-century *harmonica* or musical glasses, including the role of Benjamin Franklin in its development. More information about this is presented in a later chapter, "The Beginnings of American Music."

7. We have in this and earlier chapters devoted some space to the position of the musician in eighteenth-century society. Investigate this subject further, amass notes and act as resource person for a classroom discussion.

8. If possible, study music by members of the Bach family and present a class recital devoted to same, prefaced with oral program notes concerning the pieces selected for performance.

VOCABULARY ENRICHMENT

Classicism	exposition
Classic period	transition or bridge
homophony	secondary theme
Rococo music	closing section
empfindsamer Stil	development
durchkomponiert song	recapitulation
Mannheim school	*coda*
uniform bowings	minuet and trio
concertmaster	theme and variations
crescendo	*rondo*
rocket	string quartet
baryton	symphony
Classic sonata	ternary song-form
sonata-form, sonata-allegro form, first movement form	

Chapter 14.

WOLFGANG AMADEUS MOZART

To speak of Mozart is like speaking of a god. When Gretchen asks
Faust, 'Do you believe in God?' he answers 'Who dares name him, who
confess him?' In these profound words of Goethe I would express my
feelings toward Mozart. Where he is greatest he embraces all times . . .
With Mozart even the superficial becomes symbolical, and a deep ethical
spirit pervades the whole work.

—Edvard Grieg

The music lover finds no dearth of encomiums when he approaches
Mozart for, despite chronic financial instability, Mozart has been otherwise "appreciated" by all who heard him from the age of six, well into
the present time. The Danish philosopher, Sören Kierkegaard, for instance, wrote, "Since the hour when my soul was most deeply seized by
Mozart's music and inclined before it in humble admiration it has often
been both a delightful and quickening occupation to reflect upon it as
that joyful Hellenic contemplation of the world . . . , as that gay and
serene way of contemplation repeated in a higher order of things, in
the world of the ideal." No less a personage than Joseph Haydn said to
Mozart's father in an oft-quoted remark: "Before God and as an honest
man, I tell you that your son is the greatest composer known to me,
either in person or in name. He has taste and what is more the most
profound knowledge of composition."

Who was this prodigious Mozart, darling of all European courts as
a child and an embittered drifter as an adult, albeit ever a dedicated
and serious musician? Owing to the many letters Mozart wrote in
which he revealed his kinship with all men, to his well-wishers as well
as his traducers, his character has been either over-eulogized or seriously decried. In his biography, Alfred Einstein states that Mozart's
letters "reveal Mozart so completely a man of the world in all his
warm, childish, human personality, that at least in Germany no one has
even dared to publish them without omissions, and either his widow or
other well-meaning persons made certain passages . . . forever illegi-
ble . . ." And again, the "unity of the man and the creative musician
becomes clearest when we contemplate its two aspects in Mozart, the
uncannily sharp, pitiless and incorruptible judge of human nature and

in Mozart, the great dramatist. His music speaks of secrets of heart that both the man and the artist well understood."

FATHER—LEOPOLD MOZART

Mozart's father, Leopold (1719-1787), an important formative force, came from a family of bookbinders in Augsburg. Possibly under the influence of his godfather, a canon, Leopold departed from the craftsman tradition of the family to become a choirboy and in 1737 a student at the University of Salzburg, a Benedictine institution, where he studied jurisprudence as well as music, excelling in both. In 1740 he took a position as violinist and valet, a common combination in those days, to Count Johann Baptiste of Thurn, Valassina and Taxis, Dean of the Cathedral. In 1743 he became fourth violinist in the court chapel of Archbishop Sigismund, playing, teaching the choirboys violin and composing music for Church services when required.

Leopold married in 1747 and settled in third-floor lodgings in the *Getreidegasse* in Salzburg which were to be homebase for the rest of his life and which today are maintained as a shrine to his famous son, who ironically came to loathe the city. In 1756 Leopold published his *Versuch einer gründlichen Violinschule* (*Essay on a Fundamental Method for the Violin*), an excellent instruction manual which was to establish him as a mentor of musical consequence. During the same year, when Leopold was thirty-seven years old, a son was born on January 27 and christened Joannes Chrysostomus Wolfgang Gottlieb, known to us as Wolfgang Amadeus Mozart (1756-1791).

WOLFGANG AMADEUS MOZART—LIFE

The fabulous ability of the young Mozart is legendary. When the child was three or four, his father began to teach him, only to realize quite quickly that the little fellow was unusually gifted. Leopold decided to train him and his sister, Marianna (Nannerl), who was a few years older than Wolfgang. When Mozart was about six, Leopold became his professional manager, mentor and confidant. "Wolferl" was a supersensitive, loving and spirited boy. He loved games all his life, particularly billiards and skittles, and had a real streak of fun in him.

His first compositions (sonatas) were published when he was seven. He wrote a symphony at eight, listed as No. 16 in Köchel's catalogue of his works. Before that, from his third year on, he had picked out little airs which his father notated. At nine he wrote two Italian *arias* as a test, and at ten an oratorio for two sopranos and tenor; in Paris, when eleven, he composed his first *Kyrie* for four voices. Then followed his precocious efforts at opera (1768-1789) and quantities of instrumental

Fig. 53. "Leopold with Wolfgang and Nannerl Mozart"—engraving by Dela-fosse after a painting by Carmontelle, 1763. Mozart's father acted as impresario for his gifted children on their many tours of Europe. (Courtesy British Museum.)

compositions. In 1770 in Rome, he showed his phenomenal memory by writing down, after he reached home, Gregorio Allegri's (*c.* 1582-1652) nine-part *Miserere,* a twenty-minute work that he had heard but once or twice at the Sistine Chapel.

Mozart is a good example of a man educated by travel, for he had no formal schooling. The years between six and twenty-five were spent in almost constant touring, which took him to Germany, France, England, Italy, Switzerland, Holland and Belgium. After each trip he returned to Salzburg, until he moved permanently to Vienna in 1782. The purposes of Mozart's journeys were several: it was hoped that he would attract patrons to help him earn a livelihood; it was also a deliberate stratagem on Leopold's part to educate the boy in all forms of music and in languages. As a result, Mozart was something of a linguist and an avid mathematician, who often signed himself as a member of the "League of Numbers."

"A crooked destiny," comments Edward Holmes of Mozart's constant bad luck, "was at work to make all his honors fruitless." In spite of manifold experiences, the Mozarts were continually poor, save in honors. Mozart once wrote that he had enough gifts to "set up shop," and again, that he would wear his fourteen watches at the same time, so that no one would dare give him another. Furthermore, the family, not without some reason, was sore beset in its relationship to the Archbishop of Salzburg, who was a temporal as well as spiritual ruler of the church-state. Although Sigismund had been reasonably fair and permitted the Mozarts some latitude, his successor, Hieronymus, was an energetic, punctilious man who paid niggardly salaries and badgered the father and son with indignities. Young Mozart did not have Haydn's docile disposition, and he was of the new revolutionary generation. The Salzburg tie was entirely severed at Vienna in 1781, when Hieronymus, among other things, ordered Mozart to eat with the servants. Invective flashed from both sides and Mozart was literally kicked out of his service. This treatment the composer did not take lightly. He wrote:

> A man is noble by virtue of his character and, if I am not a Count, I have probably more honor within me than many a man who is; and whether anybody is a lackey or a Count, if he insults me he is a cur.

During his various tours, Mozart had heard music continually and was entertained in the glittering world of society. Among those who influenced him were Johann Schobert, Michael Haydn and John Christian Bach, with whom he had fruitful friendships. In Vienna he became acquainted with Gluck's *Alceste*. Padre Martini entered his life at Bologna, where Wolfgang, after a strenuous examination, received a diploma from the Philharmonic Academy at the phenomenal age of fourteen. He also met Niccolò Jommelli (1714-1774) and Hasse, who said of him, "This boy will throw us all into the shade." But of all the composers he knew, Joseph Haydn probably exerted the most magnetism.

In Augsburg Mozart had the opportunity of playing Stein's improved pianoforte. At Mannheim, he met many celebrities. Moreover, he listened to the exceptionally fine orchestra, which revealed to him greater possibilities of instrumentation and introduced him to the clarinet. Here too he began to realize the value of opera in the German language. In Paris, Mozart absorbed French opera, although his letters are not flattering to the singers. But he was diplomatic enough to keep out of the Gluck-Piccinni controversy.

As early as 1770 and through 1782, Mozart had shown himself to be far superior to his contemporaries in quality and mastery. He won every musical competition he entered. He had been awarded the Order of the Golden Spur by Pope Clement XIV, which put him—a fourteen-year-old—in the august company of Lasso and Gluck. Yet no substantial patronage was ever vouchsafed him, although he had been decorated, flattered, admitted into the highest fellowships and had produced some ten musico-dramatic works with professional, if not financial, success. His compositions were considered difficult and he seemed often to be the victim of intrigues so common in the court circles he frequented. His accomplishments were heralded by applause and then overlooked.

In 1781 a turning point appeared to arrive. He had broken with the Archbishop of Salzburg; he was commissioned to write an opera for Munich; he became engaged to Konstanze Weber and took up residence in Vienna. During the following year he was married and produced a significant comic opera, *Die Entführung aus dem Serail* (*The Abduction from the Seraglio*). Due to lack of copyright protection, Mozart made little money from his compositions. Neither his public appearances as a *Clavier* virtuoso nor his teaching were very lucrative. Such money as he did earn was often spent haphazardly, for Mozart had high tastes and little business sense, and his wife was not an able housekeeper. Among his pupils at this time were Johann Nepomuk Hummel and the Englishman, Thomas Attwood.

In 1783 Mozart's wife sang the soprano part in a performance of the incomplete *Mass in C Minor,* K. 427, written for her and presented at St. Peter's in Salzburg while the couple was visiting Leopold. Mozart was working on a set of six string quartets, dedicated in 1785 to Haydn. In addition, he wrote several quintets for piano and wind instruments. In 1784 Mozart was initiated into the secret order of Freemasonry, a society whose membership included Gluck, Haydn and the Austrian Emperor.

Le Nozze di Figaro, presented in Vienna in 1786, was instrumental in securing for Mozart the title of Court Composer, at a stipend of about $400 a year (Gluck had received much more). Ever hopeful of patronage, Mozart was never relieved of monetary anxiety. Sensitive too of the jealousies of fellow musicians, among whom was the Emperor's favorite, Antonio Salieri (1750-1825), a pupil of Gluck, and wasting himself in excessive social diversions, Mozart's health began to deteriorate. In fact, he was never really well after a triumphant visit to Prague in 1787. During his last years, however, he composed his three greatest symphonies, three epochal operas, *Don Giovanni* (1787), *Così fan tutte* (1790) and *Die Zauberflöte* (1791), and the poignant

Requiem, ordered mysteriously by a party unknown to Mozart. At this time his librettist, da Ponte, urged Mozart to go to London with him. The composer refused, writing:

> I wish I could follow your advice—but how can I? I feel stunned, I reason with difficulty and cannot get rid of visions of the unknown man—he presses me and impatiently demands the work. I go on writing, for composition tires me less than resting . . . I am at the point of death; I have come to an end before having had the enjoyment of my talent . . . I must finish my death song. I must not leave it incomplete.

While working on the *Requiem,* Mozart reiterated, "I feel I am not going to last much longer, some one has certainly given me poison." On the afternoon of his death, he and a few friends sang parts of the work; during the *Lacrimosa,* Mozart wept and said to his friend and pupil, Franz Süssmayer (1766-1803), who ultimately finished it, "Did I not say I was writing the *Requiem* for myself?" Later he asked his wife to inform Albrechtsberger that he would be unable to accept the directorship of music at St. Stephen's, the only post ever offered him that would have assured his economic freedom.

At midnight Mozart fell into a coma from which he did not awaken. His wife was so distraught that she was unable to attend his funeral. A few faithful friends followed the rude coffin, but, according to report, had to turn back, as a furious tempest raged and they could not force their way through the driving rain and sleet. Thus passed one of the rarest spirits who ever brought music to earth. He lies in a pauper's grave, unmarked and unknown. In 1859 the city of Vienna erected a monument to his memory at a probable burial site.

WOLFGANG AMADEUS MOZART—MUSIC

"I believe in God, Mozart and Beethoven," stated Richard Wagner. *"Nach Gott kommt Mozart"* (After God comes Mozart"). Discounting the nineteenth-century's tendency toward hyperbole, this creed illustrates the way many great musicians have evaluated Mozart's music. Mozart had the capability of keeping his art within a formal frame and yet giving it spontaneity, verve and an engaging if undefinable quality. His reputation rests on the logical and imaginative uses of thematic material, the essence of his exquisite taste, sensitivity to beauty, felicitous melodic facility, thorough training and a constant immersion and interest in all music, past and present.

Altogether Mozart wrote over 1000 works in his short life span and these in all forms practiced at the time: songs, such as *Das Veilchen* ("The Violet," K. 476), on a text by Goethe; religious music, such as a series of Masses and that tiny gem, *Ave Verum Corpus,* a favorite with all who sing or hear it; sonatas in many forms; concert *arias;* piano and organ pieces; chamber music, including *divertimentos,* string quartets and quintets; concertos for piano, violin, flute, horn and bassoon; forty-nine symphonies and numerous operas and other stage works. In his mature compositions, we encounter a truly formidable musician, in complete command of his technique, and one in whom "the superficial becomes symbolical."

OPERAS

"Mozart's operas," asserts E. J. Dent, "are no more a fit subject for either criticism or enthusiasm than are the epistles of St. Paul." And, indeed, in Mozart, we have the Classic opera composer *par excellence.* During his travels he had, with ecstatic delight, become familiar with the operas of Hasse, Handel, John Christian Bach, Giovanni Paisiello (1740-1816), Pergolesi, Jommelli and Piccinni in Italy and England, and those of Hiller, Dittersdorf, Florian Gassmann (1729-1774) and Holzbauer in Germany and Austria. In his early works, Mozart conformed to Italian conventions, while absorbing Gluckian devices and revivifying the *Singspiel,* a type of comic operetta akin to *vaudeville* in France, that is, assorted tunes and *intermezzi* held together with spoken dialogue.

Mozart's principal operas before 1781 included: a *"Liederspiel," Bastien et Bastienne,* composed when he was twelve (Vienna, 1768); *La finta semplice (The Artful Rogue,* Salzburg, 1769); *Mitridate Rè di Ponto (Mithridate, King of Pontus,* Milan, 1770); *Ascanio in Alba* (Milan, 1771); a "dramatic serenade," *Il sogno di Scipione (The Dream of Scipio,* Salzburg, 1772); *Lucio Silla* (Milan, 1772); *La finta giardiniera* (Munich, 1775); *Il Rè pastore* (Salzburg, 1775); and *Thamos König in Aegyptien (Thamos, King of Egypt,* Salzburg, 1779). These provide an impressive record of apprenticeship, although none altered the history of opera.

After 1781, however, Mozart commenced to show his originality and mastery. He built opera as he would a symphony, on tonal relationships, yet with an outpouring of melody, economy of expression, charming union of color and form and a unique dramatic sagacity. We must remember that Mozart had come into an era of music when the Italian *aria* was in the minds of all composers. Not only was it the crux of opera, but also a dominating influence in most instrumental music. Today we cleave to the instrumental, having lost much of the old vocal-consciousness, but musicians and audiences of the late eighteenth century predicated all forms of music and appreciation on singing. This factor helps account for the predominance of tunefulness during the Classic period and for Mozart's superabundant power of melody, present even in his refreshing contrapuntal passages. If Mozart reformed opera, he did it from within. His keen perception, intuitive grasp, imagination and flair for the dramatic took the place of Gluck's analytical and philosophical bent. He brought to opera a human quality, not found before. His characters were believable, even though his librettos were not what a Gluck or a Beethoven would have even considered. However conventional, he was never routine, as can be heard in his unparalleled ensemble writing.

In 1780 Mozart was offered an opportunity to compose an opera for the Munich carnival. *Idomeneo, Rè di Creta* (1781), on a rather poor libretto by Abbé Varesco, was apparently a conventional *opera seria,* in which French stage effects were blended with the Italian grand style. Yet Mozart's alchemy raised it above its models. Eighteen months elapsed. before he finished *Die Entführung* (1782), which had been ordered by an impresario, Gottlob Stephanie, for Viennese production. Although Mozart called it a *Singspiel,* the work in its continuity of plot and music was far in advance of that form, and marked a new departure for German opera, which Emperor Joseph II envisaged. *Die Entführung* overflows with humor, clever situations and enchanting melody, although it is too seldom performed because of the demands placed upon the singers. "Too fine for our ears, my dear Mozart, and there are too many notes in your score," the Emperor is supposed to have commented; to which Mozart replied, "Just the exact number required, not one more or less, your Majesty." Although it concludes with the customary French *finale* in which each character sings a verse and all join in a refrain, Mozart slips in a personal touch by allowing the harem overseer, Osmin, to burst forth once more with music from the first act.

After *Die Entführung,* four years passed in which were written, among other compositions, the *"Haffner"* (No. 35 in D, K. 385) and *"Prague"* (No. 38 in D, K. 504) symphonies, fourteen piano concertos and the quartets dedicated to Haydn, affirming the composer's unflagging industry. At Baron van Swieten's (librettist of Haydn's oratorios) suggestion, Mozart studied scores by J. S. Bach and Handel, launching upon a frenzy of fugue writing. In 1783 Lorenzo da Ponte (1749-1838), an Italian Jew turned priest and poet, arrived in Vienna as librettist with Salieri's Italian Opera Company. Soon thereafter, Mozart was fortunate enough to engage him as a collaborator.

Le Nozze di Figaro (The Marriage of Figaro, 1787) was the first of three Italian comic operas on which the pair joined forces. Based on a comedy of Beaumarchais, *Le Barbier de Séville, Le Nozze* was in fact a political satire and must have cost Mozart and da Ponte much trouble to get it past the sensitive Austrian censor. Mozart translated the theme, how a gentleman of pleasure treats his domestic servants, into pure art, yet he kept the original flavor of spontaneous gaiety. Italian in design, the opera offered the singers, all but two of whom were Italians, excellent roles. The concerted pieces were superbly contrived and the story and music progressively engaging.

Don Giovanni (Prague, 1787), the result of Mozart's gratitude for his enthusiastic reception by Prague audiences, was written on the old tale of Don Juan, a theme regnant in Europe and suggested by da Ponte with a possible hope of repeating their previous success. Called by the composer a *dramma giocoso,* it skillfully mixes the serious with the humorous. In *Don Giovanni,* Mozart combined Gluckian pathos with an elegance all his own, giving comic opera a new dimension. His grasp of musical characterization is always evident; changes of dramatic mood are carefully reflected in the music. The basic tragedy is set in sparkling and differentiated melodies that tip off sentiment and rollicking wit. It has often been said that Mozart wrote the popular overture the night before the production and the orchestra had to read it at sight. The truth, somewhat less spectacular, seems to be that he scored the overture just before the dress rehearsal. As Mozart worked out all his music mentally before notating it, his was a possible feat, even though it was reported that he commenced by writing the entire flute part, then the oboe, and onward through his instrumentation. Howsoever, *Don Giovanni* remains a fascinating opera, featuring a villain with a sharp sense of humor and challenging theatrical interpretation.

Three years separated *Don Giovanni* from *Così fan tutte,* but they were eventful years during which Mozart wrote his last three symphonies, visited Leipzig at the invitation of Johann Friedrich Doles (1715-1797), a pupil of J. S. Bach, who urged him to give an organ recital at St. Thomas', and journeyed to Berlin. Perhaps on account of his loyalty to the Austrian Emperor, although it might also have been because he loved Vienna's gaiety, Mozart refused an offer to become *Kapellmeister* to the King of Prussia; reputedly he did accept, however, a commission to compose a set of string quartets, of which he finished three. He also composed the *"Stadler" Clarinet Quintet,* K. 581. All the while, Mozart's financial condition and his health were worsening. Konstanze was constantly taking "cures" or bearing children who died in infancy. The family restlessly moved from one lodging to another.

Così fan tutte ossia la scuola degli amanti (They All Do the Same or The School for Lovers, 1790) was written at the request of Emperor Joseph II. In the hands of da Ponte and Mozart, a rather silly story was fashioned into a superb comic opera, frivolous, sparkling, with tripping dialogue and marvelous music. Lord Harewood writes, "The idea is as light as a feather, and yet the music which clothes it suggests not only the comedy which is on the surface and which remains the most important part of the opera, but also the heartbreak which is behind the joke that goes too far . . ." This opera, which Dent refers to as "a last jest at the departing age, to those who understood the humor of it," marked the end of the collaboration between Mozart and da Ponte, who subsequently migrated to America, became a grocer and distiller in Philadelphia and Sunbury, Pennsylvania, and finally filled the first chair of Italian literature at Columbia University.

During his last year of life, Mozart wrote two operas. On a sudden commission from Prague, he hastily composed *La Clemenza di Tito*. Based on an obsolete text by Metastasio and written in the span of two weeks' time (with aid from Süssmayer, who composed the recitatives), it was not an artistic success despite some beauty of detail, for the inflexibility of the old *opera seria* was outdated. *Die Zauberflöte* (*The Magic Flute*), on the other hand, has been called Mozart's finest stage work and the foundation of German opera. Commissioned by a purveyor of popular operetta and a fellow Mason with whom Mozart had worked earlier (when he produced *Der Schauspieldirektor—The Impresario*, 1786), *Die Zauberflöte* is a unique opera defying classification.

Here Mozart used a libretto by Emanuel Schikaneder, that combines fantastic, humorous, religious and allegorical features of bewildering complexity. Much has been written about its symbolic content. Elements of the interdicted Masonic order, such as the *mystique* of the number three, the hero's virile silence and the processes of testing, permeate the work. Nineteenth-century critics have made an analogy of Tamino to Emperor Joseph II, Pamina to the Austrian people, the vengeful Queen of the Night to Empress Maria Theresa and Monostatos to the vested clergy. Yet in the role of Papageno, Schikaneder was provided with gags and stage business in the clown tradition. However interpreted, *Die Zauberflöte* is a masterpiece of spiritual sublimity and human dualism, enjoyable on many levels of appreciation. Beethoven admired it for its great variety of forms, ranging from the simple *Lied* to fugue. In it, Sacher notes:

> Mozart attempted in an ingenious way to characterize different persons musically according to their rank. He symbolized the naive bird-man, *Papageno*, by a light *Singspiel* style; he drew on the style of the *opera seria* for the rich coloraturas of the 'star-flaming' *Queen of the Night*; and for the steps of the initiation he used a chorale melody in the manner of the organ chorales of Bach.

INSTRUMENTAL MUSIC

Mozart's instrumental works are in many forms, including those of **chamber music,** a phrase we have mentioned earlier and that we shall now examine more closely. Chamber music, in general, is music written for a small group of instruments with a single instrument to each part. It had its origins in the Renaissance, and during the Baroque period designated that music not expressly designed for either church or stage, but rather for the Prince's chamber.

With the increasing dominance of sonata-form and **absolute** or **abstract music,** that is, music that has no other than musical connotations, Classic composers began writing for such instrumental ensembles as the string quartet, string trio (two violins and violoncello) and piano trio (violin, violoncello and piano). Distinctions, such as those introduced by Haydn, rested on dual pairs of criteria: (1) a discrimination between music composed purely for entertainment and that with more serious intent; and (2) indoor and outdoor music. Casual music tended to retain the older names, while more ambitious works were designated by form, key and mode, with movements identified by tempo markings, *i.e., allegro, andante, presto.* Indoor music featured the more delicate string and keyboard instruments, while outdoor music was often restricted to members of the wind family.

Among works of both Haydn and Mozart, we find examples of *divertimentos, cassations* and *serenades,* all deriving from the earlier dance suites and written for purposes of entertainment. A *divertimento* was a suite of loosely-designated movements composed for a limited but variable group of instruments and played at social functions; *cassations* were evening affairs, often performed out-of-doors. *Serenades,* in five to seven movements, with the serenade proper flanked by two minuets and begun and ended with marches (presumably for the entrance and exit of performers), were also *al fresco* pieces, written in honor of some celebrity or as was the case of Mozart's *"Haffner" Serenade* (No. 7 in D, K. 250), for a wedding. Street music was very popular in Salzburg and Vienna during the eighteenth century; Mozart's friends once surprised him by playing his *Serenade in E flat,* K. 375, beneath his window on the eve of his name day. It is significant that these forms paved the way for the Classic quartet, soon to replace them. In fact, Mozart later transformed his rather lengthy *"Haffner" Serenade* into a symphony. One of his most famous compositions remains the serenade for strings, *Eine kleine Nachtmusik (A Little Night Music,* K. 525) which in many ways forms a miniature symphony, yet pleasantly reminds us of the "dinner music" of another era. Mozart presented *divertimentos* in both *Così fan tutte* and *Don Giovanni,* enlarging on earlier forms and using more winds and strings. His *Ein musikalischer Spass* (*A Musical Joke,* K. 522), while not one of his best compositions, ridicules musical clichés of his day and is one of the few musical satires.

To Haydn goes the credit for firming up the **string quartet** as a form; a study of his quartets from the earliest to those in his "mature" style reveals a process of delineation in direction and growth—from works designed for amateurs to those requiring the services of extremely skilled players. An account by Michael Kelly, an English singer in Vienna, included in his *Reminiscences* (1826) and quoted by Pauly, describes most entertainingly the informal setting in which quartets were often performed:

> Storace gave a quartet party for his friends. The players were tolerable, not one of them excelled on the instrument he played, but there was a little science among them, which I dare say will be acknowledged when I name them:
>
> | | |
> |---|---|
> | First violin | Haydn |
> | Second violin | Baron Dittersdorf |
> | Violoncello | Vanhall |
> | Tenor [viola] | Mozart |
>
> A greater treat . . . cannot be imagined. . . . After the musical feast was over, we sat down to an excellent supper, and became joyous and lively in the extreme.

Mozart, following the lead of his revered friend Haydn, naturally gave himself to the string quartet as a means of expression. Otto Jahn says that the Emperor likened Mozart's quartets to snuffboxes made in Paris and Haydn's to those made in London. His contemporaries saw something of their grandeur and dignity in clarity and purity of form. The six quartets dedicated to Haydn, however, were considered too highly spiced to be palatable for any length of time. Furthermore, Mozart's Italian publisher sent them back to be corrected because of the unusual, and to his mind, incorrect harmonies. The enigmatic introduction to the *C Major Quartet* (K. 465), "The Dissonant," for example, was a hard pill for his contemporaries to swallow, as the chromaticism was far ahead of its time. If he had lived, Mozart might have anticipated Beethoven's innovations, especially those which deepened the emotional expression and presaged Romanticism.

But, had he written nothing else, these exquisite works would have marked Mozart a master. In his *D Major Quartet* No. 20, K. 499) he made an attempt, without sacrificing form, to meet the public taste. The work is technically beautiful, and a bit of humor akin to Haydn's can be heard. Possibly at the request of Friedrich Wilhelm II of Prussia, Mozart composed his final string quartets (K. 575, 589, 590), in which the violoncello figures prominently. In all his chamber works there is unity; no single instrument extrudes too formidably; there is a perfect sense of proportion, elegance and beauty, together with harmonic richness. In his four great string *Quintets,* K. 515, 516, 593 and 614, a form Haydn did not cultivate, Mozart followed quartet techniques, but loving the viola, he doubled it, resulting in an interesting tonal enrichment.

Of his forty-nine symphonies, the most popular are those of 1788—the *E flat Major* (K. 543), the *"Great" G Minor* (K. 550) and the *C Major "Jupiter"* (K. 551)—all three written in less than two months. Although sick, tired and discouraged, this supernal genius again surmounted himself, leaving a heritage to Haydn, Beethoven and Brahms. In his symphonies Mozart gradually acquired freedom; his melodic gift broadened and his inventiveness increased. Everything serves to strengthen and advance his scheme. Wind instruments gain individuality and contribute their particular nuances and beauty, while the whole of the orchestra is unified.

At first, Mozart took various predecessors as models and used the Italian *sinfonia* as a point of departure. If we follow his symphonies written from the age of nine to that of thirty-two, we discern many signs of growth: contrapuntal treatment is introduced; the rhythmic drive intensifies; the expression becomes more serious and less "gallant"; clarinets are added to the wind family; the overall scope is enlarged; there is more chromaticism and extensive modulation; there is continuous thematic development, often in the recapitulation or the *coda;* there is a variety and multiplicity of themes. At last, Mozart surpassed Haydn himself. The final three symphonies, each different in mood, sum up his achievements. The fugue at the end of the fourth movement of the *"Jupiter"* is a fit memorial to Padre Martini and shows an assimilation of the techniques of J. S. Bach. Robert Schumann speaks of the "swaying Grecian grace" of the *G Minor,* a favorite with the Romantics, while Jahn says of the *E flat,* "It is a veritable triumph of euphony."

Characteristics of Mozart's symphonic music apply to many of his mature works. These include: mastery in the art of counterpoint; enthralling interest in the development of each movement due to his manifold musical resourcefulness; independent movement of parts; imaginative use of wind instruments, both alone and in combination; individuated writing for double bass and other strings; the concept of the orchestra as a living organism expressing in robust and rapturous melody the harmonious relationship of tone to idea; nicety of division of tonal color, blending and balance of *timbres;* unity of idea with its ideal expression; and, finally, Mozart's incomparable spirit of spontaneity, perhaps more apparent than real, for Mozart himself commented, "People make a mistake who think that my art has come easily to me. Nobody has devoted so much time and thought to composition as I."

*   *   *   *   *

Mozart was especially influential in shaping the Classic concerto form, a multi-movement composition for solo instrument(s) and orchestra, built on the sonata principle. Looking backward for a moment, we find the *concerto grosso* with its group of solo instruments evolving into the *sinfonia concertante,* of which Mozart wrote several effective examples, notably K. 364 in E flat for violin and viola. Concertos for solo instruments had originated, as we have noted, with those for violin, developed through the efforts of Torelli, Tartini and Giovanni Battista Viotti (1755-1824), who endeavored to combine virtuosity with structural consistency. Haydn's concertos, although frequently charming, are in pre-Classic style. Mozart in 1775 composed five violin concertos, influenced by the Mannheim composers as well as Italianate features, as exemplified by Luigi Boccherini. It was C. P. E. Bach who contributed to a transition from the old to the new piano concerto, of which Mozart was to become a champion.

An excellent pianist and at the mercy of a public who constantly demanded new works, Mozart created over twenty piano concertos. They fall into two groups: the first are dainty, charming and derivative; while the later Viennese concertos, Grove says, are "perfect in style, melody and balance and often showing a freedom of structural organization . . ." Beethoven is known to have studied them. Westerman comments:

> The duologue between the soloist and the orchestra, the actual 'concertizing' is carefully constructed by Mozart. The orchestra has a significant part to play, and Mozart was very particular about instrumental shading. The ideas and expression of the individual movements are tightened up with the intention of achieving greater unity in the whole.

The Classic concerto follows a modification of sonata-form, in which an orchestral exposition precedes the exposition by a solo instrument with orchestral accompaniment. As there are two expositions, the modulatory scheme is affected. The development section, somewhat foreshortened, features an interplay between the soloist and the orchestra, with brilliant passage work and glittering runs, followed by a double recapitulation dramatically interrupted by a *cadenza,* an opportunity for the eighteenth-century instrumentalist to improvise on the thematic content of the movement and exhibit his virtuosity, after which the opening movement quickly comes to a close. The middle movement is usually a slow song-form (A B A) or a theme with variations, and the final movement either a dance-like, sparkling *rondo* or a *sonata-allegro.* Each movement might include a *cadenza,* created by the performer, not necessarily the composer. In the hands of Mozart, there are always wonderful surprises and interpolations for the listener to enjoy, ornamenting and clothing the bare outline given above. Again, Mozart's innovations exist within the standard form, although he never falls prey to mere schematism.

Mozart also wrote concertos for solo instruments other than the piano: four horn concertos for a Salzburg friend, Leitgeb; concertos for bassoon, 'cello, flute, flute and harp, oboe; and a clarinet concerto, K. 622 in A, for his colleague, Stadler. The latter work is a pillar of the art of clarinet playing.

Mozart held high and definite ideals as a virtuoso of the keyboard. According to Jahn, his aim was "not chord playing or production of mass effects but clearness and transparency, qualities which belonged to the instruments of his day. . . . While the tendency of modern executors is to turn the piano into a sort of independent orchestra, Mozart's endeavor was to reveal the piano in clear and unmixed contrast with the orchestra." In addition, Mozart insisted upon expressiveness, whether in a concerto or a sonata, as abundant dynamic markings prove. His declaration that the admired Muzio Clementi was a mechanical player without feeling tends to affirm this. Clarity and the need for facile execution is part of all his piano works—*fantasias,* sonatas, short pieces and concertos. Today these are basic works for any pianist, despite the rather limited nature of the pianoforte of Mozart's time.

In writing for his favorite instrument, the composer reveals his wit, passion and meditativeness; the best of his sonatas are invaluable possessions. He usually adheres to the standard form of three movements— *allegro, andante, presto*—in which the initial movement is most important and most highly organized. A second, third or fourth theme may emerge logically and in sharp contrast to the first. Song-like melody is often a thematic stamp. New melodies are used for transitional material with unbounded fecundity, bestowing a clear yet curiously kaleidoscopic effect. Left and right hands share equally in much of the thematic development. But Mozart was not afraid of departing from custom, as his *A Major Sonata,* K. 331, illustrates. In this, the first movement is a theme and variations, and the lyric second movement ("Minuet and Trio") is followed by a "Turkish March" *finale,* without any recourse to sonata-form, as such.

CHORAL WORKS

Mozart's choral works are always interesting and sometimes rise to greatness. He wrote seventeen Masses while at Salzburg. These are much shorter than those of Haydn, for a very practical reason. The Archbishop would not tolerate Mass lasting more than forty-five minutes, thus limiting the musical portion to some twenty minutes. As Classic sacred music was essentially conservative, *i.e.*, in a polyphonic old style, we are not surprised to discover that Mozart accepted many of the formal conventions, such as casting the *Laudamus Te: Domine Deus* as a solo or duet, setting the *Credo* syllabically, observing the change of tempo from *adagio* to *allegro* at the words, *Pleni sunt coeli*

Fig. 54. Autograph of "God Is Our Refuge." Mozart composed this motet at the age of 9½ when he visited London. (Courtesy British Museum.)

in the *Sanctus,* and so forth. Yet one finds some relationship in the Masses to Classic instrumental architecture. In the *Eighth Mass* (in F, K. 192), Mozart shows his sure grasp. The *Credo* contains a four-note theme that was to become the subject of the *"Jupiter" Symphony* fugue. Perhaps the finest of the Salzburg Masses is No. 16 in C, "Coronation" (K. 317, 1779). Modern musicologists allege that the popular *"Twelfth*

Mass," with its colorful *"Gloria"* for soprano, is not the work of Mozart, after all.

When Mozart broke with the Archbishop of Salzburg, he had little reason to compose more Masses, as he entered a Vienna in which the Emperor was severely limiting the power and practices of the Catholic Church. Yet Mozart did undertake another Mass, an extended composition for soloists (two sopranos, tenor and bass), double chorus and a full Mozartean orchestra, the incomplete *Mass in C Minor* (K. 427), of which only the *Kyrie, Gloria* and *Sanctus* were finished. This work was of a vision comparable to Bach's *B Minor* or Beethoven's *Missa solemnis*. It has been edited by Alois Schmitt (1901) for liturgical use and a more recent version by Robbins Landon is available for concert performance.

Mozart's last work was a setting of the *Requiem,* also incomplete, as the composer lived to finish only the first two movements, although he had sketched out more of the vocal score. Süssmayer reconstructed the remainder and we do not really know to what extent he was guided by Mozart's ideas. Frequent performances, however, testify to the fact that he obviously did a good job. It is an immensely moving choral-orchestral setting, with but a few incidental solo passages. Its opening bars are among the most eloquent in music through the ages. The "unknown man" who haunted the dying composer's mind turned out to be an agent for Count Franz von Walsegg of Ruppach, who had commissioned the *Requiem* anonymously as a memorial for his wife and who hoped, it is said, to pass it off as his own work.

Ludwig Ritter von Köchel

In concluding our discussion of Mozart's music, we cannot omit mention of the part played in organizing and disseminating this legacy by Ludwig Ritter von Köchel (1800-1877), a Viennese lawyer who made it his lifelong avocation to track down and number chronologically Mozart's widely-dispersed manuscripts. The composer had died in dire circumstances; his works and effects were scattered about and carelessly sold for a pittance by the widow in moments of financial desperation. Köchel conducted a dedicated detective search all over Europe. His catalogue, in a revised edition, is almost invariably used today to identify Mozart's compositions—the Mozart who, bitterly depressed, indeed did not live long enough to have the full enjoyment of his talent. After his death, few operas save his own held the stage until in 1816 appeared *The Barber of Seville* by Rossini, who said, "Mozart is not the greatest musician, he is the only musician!"

SUGGESTIONS FOR FURTHER READING

Anderson, Emily, King, A. Hyatt and Carolan, Monica, eds., *The Letters of Mozart and His Family.* New York, St. Martin's Press, 1966. 2 vols.

Biancolli, Louis, *The Mozart Handbook.* Cleveland, World, 1954.

Blom, Eric, ed., *The Letters of Mozart and His Family.** Annotated by Emily Anderson. Harmondsworth, Penguin, 1956.

Brion, Marcel, *Daily Life in the Vienna of Mozart and Schubert.** New York, Macmillan, 1962.

Broder, Nathan, ed., *The Great Operas of Mozart.** New York, Norton, 1962.

Bukofzer, Manfred F., *Music of the Classic Period.* Berkeley, University of California Press, 1955.

Burk, John N., *Mozart and His Music.* New York, Random House, 1959.

Da Ponte, Lorenzo, *Memoirs of Lorenzo da Ponte.* Philadelphia, Lippincott, 1929.

Dent, Edward J., *Mozart's Operas.* New York, Oxford University Press, 1947.

Einstein, Alfred, *Mozart: His Character, His Work.* New York, Oxford University Press, 1945.

Girdlestone, Cuthbert, *Mozart's Piano Concertos.** London, Cassell, 1948.

Landon, H. C. R., and Mitchell, Donald, eds., *The Mozart Companion.* New York, Oxford University Press, 1956.

Lang, Paul Henry, ed., *The Creative World of Mozart.** New York, Norton, 1963.

Mörike, Eduard, *Mozart on the Way to Prague.* New York, Pantheon, 1947.

Newman, William S., *The Sonata in the Classic Era.* Chapel Hill, University of North Carolina Press, 1963.

Pauly, Reinhard G., *Music in the Classic Period.** Englewood Cliffs, Prentice-Hall, 1965.

Rothschild, Fritz, *The Lost Tradition — Musical Performance in the Times of Mozart and Beethoven.* New York, Oxford University Press, 1961.

Saint-Foix, Georges, *The Symphonies of Mozart.* London, Dobson, 1947.

Starr, William J., and Devine, George F., *Music Scores — Omnibus,** Part I. Englewood Cliffs, Prentice-Hall, 1964.

Turner, W. J., *Mozart: The Man and His Works.** New York, Tudor, 1966.

Valentin, Erich, *Mozart — A Pictorial Biography.* New York, Viking, 1959.

A SAMPLER OF SUPPLEMENTARY RECORDINGS

Collections

Ten Centuries of Music	DGG KL-52/61
2000 Years of Music	Folkways 3700
Mozart Arias (Lehmann)	Eterna 743
Mozart Arias (Vyvyan)	London 5600
Mozart Arias (Slezak)	Eterna 575

Music of Individual Composers

Bach, C. P. E., *Concerti*

Bach, Johann Christian, *Concerti*

Martini, Giambattista, *Concerto in F for Piano and Strings*

Mozart, Leopold, *Cassatio, "Toy" Symphony*
                  Musical Sleigh-Ride

* Available in paperback edition.

Mozart, Wolfgang Amadeus, *Concerto in A for Clarinet,* K. 622
Concerto for Piano and Orchestra, K. 107
Concerto No. 22 in E flat, K. 482
Concerto No. 5 for Violin, K. 219
Divertimenti
Don Giovanni, K. 527
Eine kleine Nachtmusik, K. 525
The Magic Flute, K. 620
Masonic Funeral Music, K. 477
Mass in c, K. 427 — "Great"
Musical Joke, K. 522
Quartet No. 19 in C, K. 465
Quintet No. 5 in g, K. 516
Requiem, K. 626
Serenade No. 7 in D, K. 520 — "Haffner"
Sinfonia Concertante for Violin and Viola, K. 364
Piano Sonatas
Symphony No. 35 in D, K. 385 — "Haffner"
Symphony No. 39 in E flat, K. 543
Symphony No. 40 in g, K. 550
Symphony No. 41 in C, K. 551 — "Jupiter"
Trio in E flat for Clarinet, Viola, Piano, K. 498

Viotti, Giovanni B., *Concerti for Violin*

Opportunities for Study in Depth

1. Mozart is a prime example of the child prodigy whose talents are exploited in the interest of fame and fortune. Make a study of this phenomenon, common among musicians. Evaluate the situation in terms of present-day conditions. Does good come of such precosity? What psychological effects does forcing have upon the personality of a child? Upon Mozart?

2. The theme of Don Juan, utilized in Mozart's opera, *Don Giovanni,* is a recurring one. Study Mozart's interpretation and cite other manifestations, such as those of Molina, Molière, Shadwell, Goldoni, Gluck, Byron, Richard Strauss and Bernard Shaw, as well as Dargomyzhsky's *Stone Guest.* How do the various treatments compare?

3. Mozart was an enthusiastic disciple of the brotherhood of Freemasonry. Make a study of this organization as it existed in the eighteenth century and put forward reasons for its popularity in light of the intellectual atmosphere of the day.

4. If practical, prepare a concert performance of twelve-year-old Mozart's *Singspiel, Bastien and Bastienne.* This miniature opera requires very little technical knowhow and but a small cast, yet affords insight into the musical matter of the Classic period.

5. Prepare in the form of an oral report a history of the serenade before, during and after Mozart's time, including works by Beethoven, Robert Volkmann, Brahms, Tchaikovsky, Dvořák, Hugo Wolf, Max Reger and Vaughan Williams. What essence do these many works in the form of serenades embody to lend charm over so long a period of years?

6. Investigate further any one aspect of Mozart's compositions, discussing specific examples and works.

7. Compare the slow movements of the following, analyzing the forms and essaying the contents of each:

> Mozart. *Symphony in G Minor,* K. 550, second movement
> Haydn. "London" *Symphony in D Major,* second movement
> *"Surprise" Symphony,* second movement

8. Listen, analyze and compare the first movements of piano concertos by C. P. E. Bach, Joseph Haydn and Mozart, noting thematic materials, interplay of solo instrument and orchestra, extent of the development, function of the *cadenza* and overall length. Diagram findings.

VOCABULARY ENRICHMENT

Singspiel	cassation
vaudeville	serenade
characterization	quintet
chamber music	sonata
absolute or abstract music	symphony
string quartet	concerto
string trio	*sinfonia concertante*
piano trio	*cadenza*
divertimento	

Chapter 15.

LUDWIG VAN BEETHOVEN

Sweet sounds, oh, beautiful music, do not cease!
Reject me not into the world again.
With you alone is excellence and peace,
Mankind made plausible, his purpose plain.

. . . .

Reject me not, sweet sounds! oh, let me live,
Till Doom espy my towers and scatter them,
A city spell-bound under the aging sun,
Music my rampart, and my only one.

—Edna St. Vincent Millay, "On Hearing a Symphony of Beethoven"

It was his admirer, Richard Wagner, who called Beethoven "a veritable titan, struggling with the gods." Beethoven himself had said that artists were made of fire. In music through the ages, no composer looms larger than Beethoven, whose personality and music were both products of a raging crucible, boiling with a power, passion, and positive virility that remain unmatched. To the moderate and elegant forms of his predecessors he added elements of drama and magnitude, infusing his compositions at the same time with a subjectivity that was to become the prime stylistic characteristic of the nineteenth century. In Walt Whitman's words, he was "an acme of things accomplish'd, an encloser of things to be."

Ludwig van Beethoven (1770-1827) was born into a world of revolution, when ideas of fraternity, liberty and equality were rife. With the American Revolution, the French Revolution and the Napoleonic wars, the day of the individual had dawned. Beethoven reflected not only a universal point of view, but also the conditioning of his own sordid childhood which had forced him to realize the value of independent thinking and self-reliance. To his friend, Prince Carl von Lichnowsky, he said, "What you are, you are by accident of birth; what I am, I am because of myself. There are and will be thousands of princes; there is only one Beethoven!" In time he won his place among the seers of his age—Goethe, Schiller, Kant, Humboldt, Haydn and Mozart.

LUDWIG VAN BEETHOVEN—LIFE

Ludwig was the second child of Johann van Beethoven, a musician of the Elector of Cologne at Bonn and Maria Magdalena Kewerich, daughter of the chef at Ehrenbreitstein castle. The father was of Flemish descent, which accounts for the *van* before the name (later Germanized to *von*). He was an improvident drunkard; consequently, Ludwig's home was poverty-striken and unhappy. It is still possible to visit Beethoven's birthplace at No. 20 *Bonngasse,* a narrow street adjacent to a market square. There, in a four-story stucco row-house with oversize green shutters, third floor rear, the Beethovens had an apartment, now maintained as a museum dedicated to their son. Among their *Bonngasse* neighbors were the Salomons, one of whom was Haydn's London impresario; the Rieses, of whom the father taught Ludwig violin and the son was his devoted pupil in Vienna; and the Simrocks, destined to be his future publishers.

Ludwig's musical education was initially supervised by his father and Thomas Pfeiffer, a boon companion. His lessons were often accompanied by blows and brutal scoldings as the father had ambitions of making a second Mozart of the boy. He was taught to play both the *Klavier* and the violin and soon composed little pieces; but he was not the prodigy type. Fortunately, before he was eleven, he became the pupil of Christian Gottlob Neefe (1748-1798), a composer and organist, who introduced him to Bach's *Well-tempered Clavichord* and set him on the path toward a philosophy of music that later led him to recreate existing musical forms into revolutionary art works. Of the first drafts of the *Bagatelles, Op.* 33, probably written in 1782, Robert Haven Schauffler notes:

> The lad of eleven actually sounded a new note in the history of piano literature. These little pieces, though not so remarkable in content as was Beethoven's highly original use of the word 'Bagatelle,' were destined to be powerful factors in freeing the piano from its slavery to the larger forms exclusively. The *Bagatelles* founded the family which was to boast such progeny as the Schubert *Impromptus,* the Chopin *Preludes,* the Schumann *Kinderscenen,* the Brahms *Intermezzi,* and Debussy's *Arabesques.*

At thirteen, Ludwig was appointed accompanist, without pay, for rehearsals of the Court operas and second organist to Neefe. At sixteen he made his first trip to Vienna, where he played for Mozart who, thinking he had prepared the improvisation in advance, showed little interest in him. Beethoven begged Mozart for a theme, on which he is said to have improvised so well that Mozart remarked, "Pay attention to this boy; he will make a noise in the world some day!" His Viennese sojourn was abruptly cut short by the death of his mother, to whom he was devoted.

Beethoven had been forced to leave public school in 1783. Four years later he was befriended by the von Breuning family and treated as a son by Frau von Breuning, who encouraged his love of literature and tried to provide him with cultural opportunities. In turn, Beethoven taught the children, Eleanore and Stephan, who became his life-long friends. Two other important figures, Franz Wegeler, who later married Eleanore, and Count Ferdinand von Waldstein, entered his life at this time. Ludwig earned his living as viola player in the Court orchestra. He also gave lessons and had official charge of his father's salary, in order to support his younger brothers and sister.

In 1792 Haydn, returning from London, passed through Bonn, examined a cantata written by the young composer and invited him to become his pupil in Vienna. Count Waldstein obtained a salaried leave of absence from the Elector and sent Beethoven off to Vienna with the following letter:

Dear Beethoven! You are going to Vienna in fulfillment of your long-frustrated wishes. The genius of Mozart is mourning and weeping over the death of her pupil. She found a refuge but no occupation with the inexhaustible Haydn; through him she wishes to form a union with another. With the help of assiduous labor you shall receive Mozart's spirit from Haydn's hands.

At the age of twenty-two, Beethoven arrived in the Austrian capital, small (about five feet five), pock-marked (from a childhood bout with smallpox) and unkempt. Writes Schauffler, "His only assets were a strong personality, a few letters of introduction from Waldstein—and genius." Beethoven studied harmony and counterpoint with Haydn, but, Hadow asserts, "the lessons were not altogether successful. Haydn was a careless teacher, Beethoven a self-willed and refractory pupil." At the same time, he had lessons in secret with Johann Schenck (1753-1836), and, when Haydn returned to London, Beethoven studied with Johann Georg Albrechtsberger (1736-1809), who is reported to have told another student to have nothing to do with Beethoven, saying dourly, "He has learned nothing, and will never do anything in decent style." Beethoven also worked with Antonio Salieri, the opera composer and *Kapellmeister* at the Viennese Court.

The young man quickly made friends with members of the Austrian aristocracy, who recognized and appreciated his talents. He was frequently invited to the home of Prince Carl Lichnowsky. Other friends, among whom were talented musical amateurs, included Prince Lobkowitz, Baron van Swieten, Count von Fries, the Esterházys and Baroness von Ertmann. For the first time, a musician was received on a footing of social equality that had been denied Haydn and Mozart. This was due partly to Beethoven's proud and aggressive personality and partly to the age, in which an individual was more able to demand his rights.

Fig. 55. Portrait of Beethoven—Isidore Neugass. Quick-tempered, oversensitive and abrupt, Beethoven nevertheless became a prince among princes. (Private Collection.)

Beethoven's distinguished and faithful patronage is all the more surprising in view of the fact that he was notoriously quick-tempered and oversensitive, often bad-mannered and abrupt. Although he delighted in practical joking, when leveled against the other fellow, he was at heart a fighter and engaged in open warfare with the musicians of Vienna, who "laughed at his eccentricities, his looks and his Bonn dialect, made game of his music, and even trampled on it, and he retorted with both speech and hands."

Another group of friends acted as unpaid secretaries throughout his life. They played through his string quartets and other works for him and generally took care of his needs. Perhaps they tolerated his irascibility and erratic moods because Beethoven could be amiable and steadfast. When he threw them out of the door, they literally came back through the window. These factotums included Karl Amenda, a divinity student and amateur violinist; Ignaz Schuppanzigh, a violinist whom Beethoven called "Milord Falstaff"; Nikolaus Zmeskall, a Bohemian baron and 'cellist who was Beethoven's "Music Count" and "Baron Greedygut"; Count Ignaz von Gleichenstein; Krumpholz, nicknamed "My Fool"; Ferdinand Ries (1784-1838), a pupil from Bonn; Anton Schindler, his first biographer; and Carl Holz, second violinist in Schuppanzigh's Quartet.

As a pianist, Beethoven quickly won fame, in a period of superficial virtuosity, for his extraordinary depth of feeling, fiery imagination and unsurpassed powers of improvisation. Czerny wrote, "Nobody equalled him in the rapidity of his scales, double trills, skips, etc.—not even Hummel." His first public appearance was at a benefit concert in 1795 for the widows and orphans of the Society of Musicians. During the same year his *Opus* 1, three trios for violin, violoncello and piano, was issued. Haydn advised him against publishing the third trio, possibly because it belonged to a new order that the older composer could not follow. His criticism annoyed Beethoven who, nevertheless, was careful not to break with him. In fact, he dedicated his *Opus* 2, the first three piano sonatas, to Haydn. Also in 1795, after the death of Beethoven's father, his two brothers, Kaspar Anton Karl and Johann Nikolaus, came to live in Vienna. Ludwig's association with them, however, was not particularly close or pleasant.

Just as he was reaching a most enviable position, economically, socially and artistically, Beethoven had the first inkling of the greatest tragedy that could befall a musician—deafness. He hid the truth as long as he could, but due to this impending catastrophe, his personality and style of composing underwent changes. His works deepened in emotional expression and became more tragically poignant, and he produced masterpieces under such a terrific handicap as only a man of his determination, powers of concentration and character could overcome. His deafness may have been an indirect cause of the Romantic movement in music, as it was so calamitous that it drove Beethoven to find solace in expressing his feelings in more personal and emotional music than any composer had ever before attempted. The compositions of his third period, which were not understood by his contemporaries, were criticized as being the work of a deaf man who did not know what he was writing.

There is evidence, from letters to Karl Amenda and Dr. Wegeler, that Beethoven was enormously upset by the prospect of deafness. "Heaven knows what will become of me!" he wrote. In the summer of 1802 he journeyed to the resort of Heiligenstadt and drew up a curious document known as the *"Heiligenstädter Testament,"* a will addressed to his brothers, in which he expressed his despair, although he probably never seriously considered suicide, as some have alleged. Apparently he became reconciled to his condition, however, for he returned from his holiday with the *Second Symphony,* a work characterized by brightness and good humor.

Fig. 56. "Heiligenstadt in Beethoven's Time"—engraving by Joseph Kohl. It was here that Beethoven came to grips with the tragedy of deafness and emerged triumphant.

In the Bonn museum, visitors can find eloquent reminders of Beethoven's deafness, including four ear-trumpets, designed by Nepomuk Maelzel, inventor of the *chronometer,* a forerunner of the *metronome,* that adjunct which helps musicians maintain a consistent tempo. Also in the museum is Beethoven's last piano, built for him by the Viennese pianomaker, Konrad Graf, on which each key is attached to four strings, instead of the customary three. Conversation pads, his final means of communication with friends, remain as mute reminders. In 1808 Beethoven was forced to give up concertizing and at his last conducting appearance, he pathetically continued to gesticulate measures after the music finished, completely oblivious of the applause.

Through dedications of his compositions, Beethoven must have discharged many social and financial obligations. The list reads like a Viennese social register. While these were not always servile attempts to ingratiate himself with powerful allies, and some are meant as greetings to his friends, associates and pupils, dedications often served a useful function in the days before copyright protection. A nobleman might request a work from the composer and pay all expenses relating to it in return for a dedication which allowed him exclusive use of the composition for a specified period of time, perhaps, six months. Then the autograph reverted to the composer, who was free to make his own commercial arrangements with various publishers. Some of the recipients have become better known through Beethoven's dedications than through any personal achievement.

Beethoven's relationship with women has intrigued his biographers. He was apparently both susceptible to, and prudish about, the ladies. Ries wrote that "he was frequently in love, but generally only for a short period." At times he longed for marriage, but on several occasions, social barriers were raised when he became serious, as his teaching often brought him into close contact with women of high position. Wegeler is quoted as saying that Beethoven often "made a conquest which would have been difficult if not impossible for many an Adonis." Among the "mortal beloveds" were Countess Giulietta Guicciardi, to whom the *"Moonlight" Sonata (Op.* 27, No. 2) is dedicated and who was the "dear, fascinating girl who loves me and whom I love" and Bettina Brentano, who as a young girl brought Beethoven to the attention of Goethe, to whom she wrote: "When he [Beethoven] is in such a state of exaltation his spirit begets the incomprehensible and his fingers accomplish the impossible." That there was an "Immortal Beloved" was disclosed after Beethoven's death by the chance discovery, in a secret drawer, of two touchingly-beautiful love letters. Whether they were copies of letters sent to the unknown lady or notes returned after a denouement, no one knows. So speculation continues. Beethoven never married.

In June of 1812 Beethoven spent some days in the company of the illustrious author, Goethe, for whose drama, *Egmont,* the composer had written incidental music. Goethe recorded his impressions of Beethoven as a "self-contained, energetic, sincere artist." His opinion was altered, however, when the two men encountered the Empress and her court one day on a stroll. Goethe bowed and stepped aside, but Beethoven, merely nodding, made his way directly through the group. When Goethe next described him, he called Beethoven an "utterly untamed personality." Beethoven's lack of finesse had prompted Haydn earlier to refer to him as the "Great Mogul."

During the same year, interfering in his brother Johann's affairs, Beethoven urged him into an uncongenial marriage. After the death of his other brother in 1815, he was given joint custody with Kaspar Anton Karl's widow, whom Ludwig referred to as "Queen of the Night," of a nephew, Karl, who became the light and bane of his existence. Beethoven must have been as difficult a guardian as Karl was a charge, although he was exaggeratedly fond of the boy. It has been claimed that Karl "embittered his existence with worry of continued contentions and reiterated disappointments, and at last, directly or indirectly, brought the life of the great composer to an end long before its natural term."

Beethoven's compositions were sought after by publishers, and for most of his mature life he was financially comfortable. To guard against the possibility of his leaving Vienna, Beethoven had been guaranteed an annuity of about $2000 by some Viennese nobles in 1809. When the currency depreciated so much as to reduce his income materially, Beethoven resorted to legal measures to have the full amount paid to him. He often was unscrupulous in driving bargains with his publishers and was known to take advantage of several commissioners, including the London Philharmonic, to which society he gave one of his worst scores instead of composing a new symphony as promised. Beethoven became obsessed with a fear of poverty and the desire to provide for his nephew. Often pleading need, he, nevertheless, refused to touch bank shares and money he had saved, regarding them already as Karl's property.

The London Philharmonic Society, at Beethoven's request, advanced him £ 100 on the proceeds of a benefit concert it had offered him. In return he was to complete a tenth symphony, sketches of which he supposedly had in hand. Death intervened, however, and in 1927, the year of the Beethoven Centenary, the Beethoven Association of New York reimbursed the London Philharmonic Society. The Beethoven Association also was responsible for the publication of Alexander Wheelock Thayer's *Life of Beethoven* in English (1921). Mr. Thayer (1817-1897), an American, devoted years to gathering material for a comprehensive biography that had been published in German in Berlin.

In spite of the fact that his later works were not fully appreciated, Beethoven was considered by his colleagues the greatest living composer of his time. A new composition of his was an event, and he was treated with reverence by both Viennese and outsiders. Especially after total deafness made him a social recluse, Beethoven read widely. Homer, Shakespeare, Ossian, Scott, the contemporary poets and the works of the philosophers were his familiars. "Without pretending to be really learned," he said, "I have always endeavored, from my childhood, to grasp the thoughts of the better and wiser men of every age. Shame to the artist who does not feel obliged to go at least thus far."

His love of nature carried him to extraordinary lengths. Often he left his house while pondering a new work, with sketch book in hand, to walk the woods all day, mumbling, humming, gesturing and shouting, so that he won the title of "the mad musician." In a letter to Therese von Malfatti, Beethoven exclaimed:

> How lucky you are to be in the country so early! . . . I rejoice like a child at the thought of wandering among woods, copse, trees, grass, rocks. No man loves the country more than I do; for woods, trees and rocks echo the thing man yearns for. Every tree seems to speak to me saying, 'Holy! Holy!'

In Beethoven's last days he received a present of Handel's works, and remarked, paraphrasing the *Messiah,* "My day's work is done. If there were a physician who could help me, his name should be called Wonderful." He passed away on March 26, 1827. A flash of lightning and a crash of thunder brought the dying Beethoven to an upright posture; he clenched his fist, a rebel to the last, and then dropped back, dead. He was buried with great pomp; all the musicians of Vienna did him honor. Schubert was one of thirty-six torchbearers. Thousands of people followed the hearse. In 1863, his remains were removed from the *Währing* cemetery to the central *Friedhof* in Vienna. Over him rises an obelisk, significantly marked in bronze by that ancient symbol of divine creativeness, the serpent biting its own tail. This encloses a butterfly—mute witness to the immortality of man's creative genius.

Music—Three Periods

Beethoven had no overt intention of being an innovator. "The new and original is born of itself without one's thinking of it," he had said. Most of his compositions are based on the sonata principle which he had inherited from Haydn and Mozart. As his musical individuality developed, he enlarged the scope of the sonata through his masterful sense of construction, and used the formalism of the eighteenth century as a vehicle moving toward the Romanticism of the nineteenth. Schauffler comments:

> Alternating through the story of the arts run the rhythms of two opposing but complementary impulses: classicism and romanticism. One

is the architectonic, clarifying, and the other is the adventurous, enriching impulse . . . Beethoven embodied in his one person the ideals of both . . . and held the balance true between them. He was at once the eternal sage and the eternal youth. If any artist of any sort can ever be said to have brought one age to a close and inaugurated the next, Beethoven was that artist . . . Indeed, this was so largely his unaided achievement that the younger movement should, perhaps, be called not romanticism, but Beethovenism.

Although he composed an opera, *Fidelio,* a gigantic *Missa solemnis,* an oratorio, *The Mount of Olives,* many songs and a choral symphony, Beethoven's was predominantly an instrumental conception, in which unity and variety, restraint and passion, relaxation and tension reached an ultimate projection during the Classic period. His music cannot be divided into chronological categories characterized by certain types, as was Bach's, but it has become customary to accept Lenz's classification, as set forth in his *Beethoven et ses trois styles* (1852), as a guide for discussion. Lenz states that the work of imaginative creators often falls into three phases: the stage of imitativeness; the development of individuality; and a transcendent period. In Beethoven's case, we might date the early phase from 1782 to 1800; the middle from 1800 to 1815, when he was totally deaf; and the third from 1815 to the time of his death in 1827.

Music of the first period, if not negligible, can hardly be compared to Beethoven's more mature output. In fact, if he had died before 1800 or even at Mozart's age, he would have been remembered primarily as a concert virtuoso, for all performers of his day composed to some extent. Drawn to marches and the key of C minor, Beethoven's first composition may have been a set of nine variations upon a march theme in the key of C minor, probably written in 1781 or '82. He also wrote a set of "Bonn" sonatas and three piano quartets, perhaps antedating Mozart's, but published posthumously. These reveal the composer rather clumsy in his part-writing, as he had not yet studied counterpoint and was barely acquainted with the instrumental form for which he, a fifteen-year-old, was writing. During and immediately after the period of study with Haydn came the piano trios, *Op.* 1, of which the "C Minor" that Haydn had cautioned him against releasing is by far the most interesting. Also stemming from this period are several cantatas composed for state occasions and a few vocal works.

Beethoven's second period began with the *E Flat Major Piano Sonata, Op.* 31, *No.* 3, and two sets of variations, *Op.* 34 and *Op.* 35, of which he wrote to his publishers: "Both are handled in an entirely new manner —usually I hardly realize when my ideas are new, and hear of it first from others; but in this instance I can myself assure you that I have done nothing in the same manner before."

In the summer of 1815, when Beethoven completed the two *Sonatas for Violoncello and Piano, Op.* 102, and the *A Major Sontata, Op.* 101, the third period, which may be said to have started with the *F Minor String Quartet, "Quartett Serioso,"* was fairly launched. In his study of Beethoven in the *Collected Essays,* Hadow offers the following summation:

> It may be observed that the succession corresponds closely to the natural growth and development of Beethoven's character. To the first period belong almost all his experiments in varieties of instrumental combination—experiments which his later judgment modified or discarded—and almost all the works in which either theme or topic recalls, however remotely, his predecessors of the eighteenth century. The second period represents his poetic gift at its full manhood: the three Rasoumoffsky Quartets, the Violin Concerto, the Piano Concertos in G major and E flat, *Fidelio* with its four overtures, the *Mass in C major, Egmont* and *Coriolan* (overtures), the *Kreutzer,* the *Waldstein,* the *Appassionata,* the Symphonies from No. 3 to No. 8—all that amazing wealth of vigor and tenderness and noble beauty which sets upon the stage the whole pageant of man's life as it reveals itself in action, and penetrates to its innermost springs of motive and purpose.

> And so the third period rises from the active life to the contemplative; from the transfiguration of human joys and sorrows to the awe and rapture of the prophetic vision. Sometimes it speaks in parables too hard for our understanding—there is no music in the world so difficult to estimate and appraise; it may be that sometimes the message is too sublime for utterance, and we can only catch faint echoes and intimations of its inner meaning; but where we have ears to hear, it gives us melody the like of which man has never known and will never know again. In the last pianoforte trio, in the last of the sonatas and quartets, in the slow movement of the *Choral* Symphony, there is music which seems to come straight from 'some spiritual world beyond the heavens,' and the thoughts that it arouses in us are too deep for tears.

SYMPHONIES

In the symphony, as he conceived it, Beethoven found a form capable of expressing his epic components of despair, conflict, resolution and triumphant joy. Affirmation, born of his struggle with physical adversity, had led him to exclaim: ". . . I will take Fate by the throat. It shall not overcome me. Oh how lovely it is to be alive—would that I could live a thousand times!" And again, "I am the Bacchus who presses out the glorious wine for mankind. Whoever truly understands my music is freed thereby from the miseries that others carry about in them." The magnitude of such sentiments is projected in Beethoven's nine symphonies, all but two of which stem from his second or middle period. Thanks to the composer's skillful, intensive and often fierce musical emphasis, the power of the music cannot fail to stir the listener, accounting for its popularity. It may be of interest to note that the *Fifth Symphony,* whose terse four-note beginning has gathered so many connotations, is said to have been recorded more often than any other musical composition except Hoagy Carmichael's "Stardust."

The nine symphonies are tabulated below:

No.	Key	Opus No.	Subtitle	Dedication	Publication
1	C	21		Baron van Swieten	1801
2	D	36		Prince Lichnowsky	1804
3	E flat	55	"Eroica"	Prince Lobkowitz	1804
4	B flat	60		Count von Oppersdorf	1809
5	C minor	67		{ Prince Lobkowitz and	1809
6	F	68	"Pastoral"	{ Count Rasoumowsky	1809
7	A	92	"Dance"	Count von Fries	1816
8	F	93		Empress of Russia	1816
9	D minor	125	"Choral"	King of Prussia	1826

We shall not presume to offer the reader more than a hint or two of the wonders of Beethoven's symphonies and refer him to the many excellent studies and analyses available. The *First Symphony* is in many respects derivative, although it is not really an early work. Yet it does offer several characteristically Beethovenian touches. For example, the unconventional introduction, in which secondary seventh chords lead gradually to the tonic, accreting a tension which is released when the brisk first theme of the *Allegro con brio* appears; the writing for woodwinds; the dynamic *Minuet;* and the fitful introduction to the last movement. The instrumentation includes woodwinds (with clarinets), horns and trumpets in pairs, tympani and strings, a scheme retained in the sunny *Second Symphony.*

The "Eroica" is a work surrounded by much myth and fanciful critical interpretations which we may for the most part dismiss. Apparently, it was originally dedicated to Napoleon, whom Beethoven admired as a champion of freedom. But when Napoleon declared himself Emperor and relegated his democratic pretensions to the background, Beethoven is said to have erased his name and substituted the subtitle, "to celebrate the memory of a great man." There is ambiguity about this, but the work is truly heroic in every sense and was a favorite of its composer who admitted that "this symphony is being written at greater length than usual . . ." Its physical scale and spiritual content exceed that of any former symphonies and most subsequent ones. The *coda* to the first movement is 140 measures long and assumes the proportion of a new section. There is a moment before the recapitulation in which the strings sustain a dominant harmony, while a horn sounds the initial theme in the tonic, of which Ries complained that "the damned horn had come in too soon." A "Funeral March" precedes the demonic *Scherzo,* while the last movement is a set of free variations upon Beethoven's *Prometheus Ballet (Op.* 43) theme. Berlioz commented, ". . . it must be allowed that the *Eroica Symphony* possesses such strength of thought and execution, that its style is so emotional and consistently elevated, besides its form being so poetical, that it is entitled to rank as equal with the highest conceptions of its composer."

Beethoven usually wrote in pairs; a serious work was followed by one in a lighter vein. The third, fifth, seventh and ninth symphonies have often been regarded as greater works than the second, fourth, sixth and eighth. Yet this judgment depends on what one is seeking to find in the compositions. The *Fourth Symphony* is a happy work, with a marvellously contented *Adagio.* The *Sixth* has aroused discussion as to whether or not Beethoven intended it as program music, that is, music of a descriptive nature. His own comment—"more an expression of feeling than tone-painting"—would seem to belie his subtitles. Holland states, "The realism resides not in the very slight allusions to natural phenomena (*i.e.,* birdcalls, brooks, thunderstorms) but in the simple acceptance of a common emotional experience." The *Eighth Symphony* is an urbane, good-natured work with an *Allegretto scherzando* in which we may hear the ticking of Maelzel's timekeeper.

If the *Third Symphony* is "Promethean," the terse *Fifth Symphony* is exceptional in its own way as a work in which tension is concentrated in an unparalleled manner, especially in the first movement, where the composer ingeniously employs the four-note "Fate" motif, harmonically, melodically and rhythmically, to build up to an almost hysterical point of climax, broken only briefly by a short oboe solo. The rather formal continuous variations of the second movement are followed by a uniquely planned third movement, upon which bursts the *Finale,* in which Beethoven for the first time in a symphony uses trombones and a double bassoon. The *Seventh Symphony* is controlled by persistent rhythmic ideas and conceived on a large scale. Its *Allegretto,* with its monotonal beginning, is one of the most famous Beethoven movements.

A period of over ten years separates the *Eighth* and *Ninth Symphonies.* There is also a vast psychological difference between the titanic *Ninth* and the previous works. Beethoven called it "Symphony with Final Chorus on Friedrich Schiller's 'Ode to Joy!' " It has moments of transcendent beauty and dramatic power. There are also marks of weakness in the choral plan, the value of which Beethoven came to doubt, but these are more than compensated for by the gigantic plan of the whole. The *Ninth* was the first "choral symphony" to achieve any popularity and it established the *genre*. The melody of the last movement was adapted as a Christian hymn, "Joyful, Joyful, We Adore Thee," and has been chosen for the official hymn of the United Nations. Its initial reception was most favorable, as a review of 1824 reveals:

> The Symphony can boldly measure up to its sister symphonies. Its originality suffices to prove its paternity, but everything in it is new——art and truth celebrate here their absolute triumph, and one can say in all justice *Non plus ultra!*

CHAMBER MUSIC

While Beethoven's symphonies have been considered the foremost focus of his creative energies, they are rivalled by his string quartets. Samuel Laciar writes, "Beethoven wrote his entire creative being into his three groups of quartets, and had we none of his music except the quartets, they would furnish a complete history of his musical life . . ." There are sixteen quartets and a Great Fugue, as follows:

No.	Key	Opus	Subtitle	Dedication	Publication
1	F	18, No. 1	Lobkowitz	Prince Lobkowitz	1801
2	G	No. 2			
3	D	No. 3			
4	C minor	No. 4	"Compliment"		
5	A	No. 5			
6	B flat	No. 6			
7	F	59, No. 1	Rasoumowsky	Count Rasoumowsky	1808
8	E minor	No. 2			
9	C	No. 3	"Hero"		
10	E flat	74	"Harp"	Prince Lobkowitz	1810
11	F minor	95	"Serioso"	Baron Zmeskall	1816
12	E flat	127	"La gaieté"	Prince Galitzin	1826
13	B flat	130	"Scherzoso"		1827
14	C# minor	131		Baron von Stutterheim	1827
15	A minor	132		Prince Galitzin	1827
16	F	135		Johann Wolfmeier	1827
	B flat	133	(*Grosse Fuge*)	Archduke Rudolph	1827

The first quartets, which show the influences of Haydn and Mozart, were written for a group of young men who played regularly with Prince Lichnowsky. So convinced of Beethoven's talents was the Prince, that in addition to contributing to his annuity, he gave the composer a set of Cremona instruments that today are in the Beethoven house at

Bonn. Of all *Op.* 18, perhaps the strongest work is No. 1 in F, that commences, quite unlike either Mozart's or Haydn's quartets with a germ-motive of six tones. As Roger Fiske writes, "Beethoven has found half a dozen dusty-looking notes in an attic and he is going to polish them up until they shine like the gold they are." A slow movement, said to be inspired by the tomb scene of *Romeo and Juliet,* follows, with a *Scherzo* and *Finale,* the latter distinguished by a particularly difficult viola part.

The next three quartets, *Op.* 59, were commissioned by Count Rasoumowsky, Russian ambassador to Austria, who asked the composer to include Russian folksongs in each, a request Beethoven conveniently forgot except in two cases. They belong to one of the richest phases of Beethoven's creative life. From 1804 to 1808 he composed many masterpieces, including these quartets, the "Waldstein" and *Appassionata* piano sonatas, four symphonies, the fourth and fifth piano concertos, the violin concerto, the *"Coriolanus" Overture* and his opera, *Fidelio.* So different were the quartets that some of his friends were shocked and some took them for one of Beethoven's jokes. An Italian violinist said to Beethoven, "You surely do not consider these works to be music?" to which the composer replied, "Oh, they are not for you, but for a later age."

Even more for a later age is the F Minor, *Op.* 95, that Beethoven called *"Serioso."* It is short, concise and due to its cyclical treatment, is unified thematically. *Ops.* 131 and 135 complete the string quartets. In form, these works are entirely emancipated from the past; there are more and shorter movements and frequent changes of tempo, as well as much formal condensation and thematic development. "In these five quartets," says J. W. N. Sullivan, "we have the greatest of Beethoven's music, and much of it is different from any other music that he or anybody else ever wrote. In the last quartets, and particularly in the great three, those in A minor, B Flat Major and C Sharp Minor, Beethoven is exploring new regions of consciousness."

Numerous *opus* numbers are devoted to chamber music in forms other than string quartets, beginning with *Op.* 1, three piano trios, and for the same combination two trios, *Op.* 70 and the famous *Op.* 97 in B flat ("The Archduke"). There are five string trios, *Ops.* 3, 8 and 9, and one for two oboes and English horn, *Op.* 87, as well as two trios for piano, clarinet and 'cello, *Ops.* 11 and 38 and one for piano, flute and bassoon. Moreover, there are three string quintets, *Ops.* 4, 29 and 104, and one for piano and wind instruments, *Op.* 16; two sextets, one for winds, *Op.* 71, and another for string quartet and two French horns, *Op.* 81b; a septet for strings and winds, *Op.* 20 in E flat, one of Beethoven's most popular successes; an octet for winds, *Op.* 130; and several serenades, variations and sonatinas for various instrumental groups.

Beethoven composed five sonatas for violoncello and piano: *Op.* 5, Nos. 1 and 2, dedicated to Friedrich Wilhelm II of Prussia; *Op.* 69, dedicated to Baron von Gleichenstein and *Op.* 102, Nos. 1 and 2, dedicated to Countess von Erdödy, in whose home he had lived for a while. There are ten violin and piano sonatas, beginning with three in *Op.* 12, dedicated to Antonio Salieri; two for Count von Fries, *Ops.* 23 and 24; three (*Op.* 30) for Alexander I, Emperor of Russia; the famous *Sonata in A, Op.* 47, called the "Kreutzer" on account of its dedication to a brilliant French violinist, Rodolphe Kreutzer (1766-1831); and the G major, *Op.* 96, dedicated to the Archduke Rudolph, one of Beethoven's pupils and an influential patron.

CONCERTOS

During the fourteen years from 1795 to 1809, Beethoven wrote seven concertos, including five for piano and orchestra, listed below.

No.	Key	Opus	Subtitle	Dedication	Publication
1	C	15		Princess Odescalchi	1801
2	B flat	19		Edler von Niksberg	1801
3	C minor	37		Prince Louis Ferdinand of Prussia	1804
4	G	58		Archduke Rudolph	1808
5	E flat	73	"Emperor"	Archduke Rudolph	1811

He also composed one concerto for violin, *Op.* 61 in D, dedicated to Stephan von Breuning and performed by Franz Clement in 1806; and a less gratifying triple concerto for piano, violin and violoncello, *Op.* 56, written for Prince Lobkowitz about 1805.

In his concertos, Beethoven took over the forms of Mozart, Viotti and the Mannheim composers, but he enlarged them and gave them a more serious, introspective content. The first and second piano concertos (actually the second and first, as Beethoven's publication dates are not always chronological) bear traces of his illustrious Viennese predecessors. With the third, however, we find subjugation of the solo part to allow the orchestra more equal footing, enhancing the symphonic character as a whole. *Op.* 58, now so popular, was rarely played in Beethoven's time, a fact difficult to explain. Once again, it was Mendelssohn who resurrected it, at a *Gewandhaus* concert (1836), of which Schumann wrote:

> This day Mendelssohn played the G major Concerto of Beethoven with a power and a finish that transported us all. I received a pleasure from it such as I have never enjoyed, and I sat in my place without moving a muscle or even breathing—afraid of making the least noise.

The *Fifth Concerto* for piano and orchestra, *Op.* 73, was the last Beethoven undertook in this form, and was the only one he himself did not premiere. It is now the most often played. Carl Czerny (1791-1857), a Beethoven pupil and later a renowned teacher himself, performed the work (1812) at a benefit concert for the "Charitable Society of Noble Ladies for Fostering the Good and Useful." The program also included an operatic scene and *aria,* another *aria,* a set of violin variations and "living pictures"—hardly the best occasion for presenting a "grand new concerto." The concerto was criticized as being too long, yet it soon managed to assume its rightful lofty place. The *Violin Concerto,* on the other hand, was first presented "at sight," as the composer had not completed it in time for rehearsals. It met with a mixed reception, and the version we hear today is a revised one, the composer implementing his original work with knowledge gained from experience.

PIANO SONATAS

The value of Beethoven's thirty-two piano sonatas in studio, recital hall and drawing room seems to grow greater with time. One hears of pianists whose "Bible" starts with "Genesis" (in F Minor) and ends with "Revelations" (in C Minor). It has often been said that Beethoven supplied a pianist's New Testament to the Old Testament of Bach's preludes and fugues in *The Well-tempered Clavichord.*

While in this heady atmosphere of metaphor and simile, we might pause a moment to comment on the fact that the many subtitles of Beethoven's works, useful and indispensable as they have become, were not Beethoven's, in most cases. He was responsible for calling the *Sonata in E flat, Op.* 81, *"Les Adieux, l'absence et le retour"* ("Farewell, Absence and Return"—referring to the enforced departure from Vienna of Archduke Rudolph, due to Napoleon's invasion), and at least gave tacit consent to naming the early *Sonata in C Minor, Op.* 13, the *"Pathétique."* Other designations, such as "Moonlight," *"Appassionata,"* "Emperor" and "Pastoral" are labels resulting from the tendency of both his publishers and nineteenth-century critics to personalize abstract music, reading into it all sorts of subjective trumpery, for better or worse, as the case may be.

A table of Beethoven's thirty-two piano sonatas reads as follows:

No.	Key	Opus		Subtitle	Dedication	Publication
1	F minor	2,	No. 1		Joseph Haydn	1796
2	A		No. 2			
3	C		No. 3			
4	E flat	7		*Die Verliebte*	Countess von Keglevics	1797
5	C minor	10,	No. 1		Countess von Browne	1798

6	F		No. 2			
7	D		No. 3			
8	C minor	13		*Pathétique*	Prince Lichnowsky	1799
9	E	14, No. 1			Baroness von Braun	1799
10	G		No. 2			
11	B flat	22			Count von Browne	1802
12	A flat	26			Prince Lichnowsky	1802
13	E flat	27, No. 1			Princess von Liechtenstein	1802
14	C# minor		No. 2	"Moonlight"	Countess Guicciardi	1802
15	D	28		"Pastoral"	Edler von Sonnenfels	1802
16	G	31, No. 1				1803
17	D minor		No. 2			1803
18	E flat		No. 3			1804
19	G minor	49, No. 1	Sonatines or			1805
20	G		No. 2	Easy Sonatas		
21	C	53		"Waldstein"	Count von Waldstein	1805
22	F	54				1806
23	F minor	57		*Appassionata*	Count von Brunswick	1807
24	F#	78			Countess von Brunswick	1810
25	G	79		*Sonata facile*		1810
26	E flat	81a		*Les Adieux, l'absence et le retour*	Archduke Rudolph	1811
27	E minor	90			Count M. Lichnowsky	1815
28	A	101			Baroness von Ertmann	1817
29	B flat	106		*Hammerklavier*	Archduke Rudolph	1819
30	E	109			Frl. M. Brentano	1821
31	A flat	110				1822
32	C minor	111			Archduke Rudolph	1822

The early sonatas reflect an expected virtuosity. The slow movement of *Op.* 10, no. 3, marks a turning point, however, as here for the first time, Beethoven sounds an individual emotional depth. The *"Pathétique,"* which brought the composer fame, provides an example of the use of a **cyclical device** that brings thematic unity to the whole. This device, a musical phrase which recurs, somewhat disguised, in different movements of the same composition, is often called a **germ-motive;** it is a Beethoven characteristic and can be discerned in the *"Eroica" Symphony,* the *"Kreutzer" Sonata* and elsewhere. There are also Beethoven autographs known as **source-motives,** that is, musical ideas which occur more or less identically in different works.

What were some of Beethoven's contributions to the modification of Classic sonata? In general, we may cite freely-arranged order of movements and abandonment of the repetition of the exposition, beginning with the *Sonata Op.* 57. Within separate movements we find:

(1) The first movement becomes more dramatic in character; modulations are freer; the secondary subjects are expanded in length and

changed in function; the modulatory bridges connecting themes become an integral part of the movement; episodes and auxiliary themes appear frequently; the development section is enlarged and the *coda* becomes an important developmental adjunct.

(2) The slow movements deepen in emotional character, often becoming intensely personal and expressive.

(3) The *Scherzo,* associated particularly with Beethoven, is "perhaps the most original, individual and epoch-making contribution Beethoven made to the forms of music"; he took it from the minuet class and created a movement "of tumultuous humor and Dionysiac exultation or of elfin wit."

(4) The *Rondo* approaches the dimensions of sonata-form; in Beethoven's hands it grew to provide a brilliant, climactic conclusion; often a monumental fugue is used, as in the *Hammerklavier Sonata, Op.* 106.

We also look to Beethoven for freeing the variation form from its limited application and making of it an elastic medium for his inventive imagination. Beethoven wrote many variations in his sonatas, symphonies and chamber music. Moreover, he used the form for individual compositions as well. Outstanding among these are the "Eroica" *Variations in E Flat, Op.* 35; those in C Minor, *Op.* 91; and the thirty-two variations for piano on a theme by Diabelli, *Op.* 120 in C. Schumann and Brahms built well on the foundations Beethoven left them.

FIDELIO

Beethoven's only attempt at opera has been evaluated "a magnificent failure." *Leonora or Conjugal Love,* an idealistic drama of the late eighteenth century, had been translated from the French of Jean Bouilly by the Sonnleithners, Schubert's friends, and retitled *Fidelio.* The opera was first produced in 1805 by Emanuel Schikaneder, Mozart's collaborator, who in 1803 became director of the *Theater an der Wien.* It had three performances and was withdrawn. With the French occupation of Vienna and the absence of the Austrian Court, the times were hardly auspicious for an opera premiere. Beethoven was persuaded to make cuts in the work, assisted by Stephan von Breuning, and in 1806 *Fidelio* met with slightly more success. The composer, however, in a fit of pique at supposedly being robbed of his royalties by the management, demanded that his opera be dropped from the repertoire. After eight years, the libretto was rewritten by Georg Friedrich Treitschke and Beethoven once again revised the music. In 1814 *Fidelio* entered upon a career that has not yet closed. "This work," opined the composer, "has won me the martyr's crown." He had rewritten one *aria* as many as eighteen times.

There are magnificent pages in *Fidelio,* although Beethoven was at his dramatic best in the abstract instrumental forms. If for no other reason, we are grateful for any work that gave us the *Leonore Overture, No. 3.* (There are three "Leonora" Overtures and one for *Fidelio.*) In this Beethoven brought to fruition the heroic dramatic overture form that he had used in the overtures to *Coriolanus, Op.* 62, *Egmont, Op.* 84, *The Ruins of Athens, Op.* 113 and other works.

CHORAL AND VOCAL WORKS

While Beethoven was not primarily a writer for voices, he has left us several interesting and one supreme choral composition. The *Trauergesang* features the unique combination of four-part male chorus and four trombones. *Christus am Oelberge (Christ on the Mount of Olives, Op.* 85) was a great success during the composer's lifetime but is survived only by its "Hallelujah" Chorus. A reason for this may be the pseudo-operatic mold in which it is cast. Jesus is a tenor virtuoso, while Peter appears as a *basso buffo.* As Westerman comments, "This sort of version of the events in the garden of Gethsemane is hardly palatable to us nowadays." Beethoven's choral masterpiece is the *Missa solemnis in D, Op.* 123, whose inscription reads, *"Von Herzen—möge es zu Herzen gehen"* ("From the heart—may it reach the heart"). The work is symphonic in outline, instrumentally-oriented and totally nonliturgical. Of very large proportions, it requires four soloists, chorus, orchestra and organ, all integrated into a scheme unifying the five sections of the Mass. It is far from a conventional expression of religious belief and often sounds as if one god is addressing another. Written between 1818 and 1823, it may have suggested the possibility of the *Ninth Symphony's* choral *finale.*

Many songs are included among Beethoven's compositions, including seven books of English, Scottish, Welsh, Irish and Italian songs for voice, piano, violin and 'cello. Of special interest is the song cycle, *An die ferne Geliebte (To the Departed Beloved, Op.* 98), which pointed the way for Schubert and other *Lieder* writers to come. Beethoven's setting of *"Ich liebe dich,"* so popular in the Grieg version, is most attractive.

METHOD OF WORKING

Many of Beethoven's sketch books are extant. They reveal to us something of his method of working. Unlike Haydn or Mozart, Beethoven was not blessed with any semblance of effortless facility. Rather, he labored with painstaking care and pitiless self-criticism. No theme was too trivial to be noted, but the difference between the initial idea and the finished product illustrates the intricate processes of a mighty and indomitable mind. Over 300 pages of twelve staves each are devoted to sketches for *Fidelio* alone. We catch a glimpse of the composer struggling with the resistance of his materials, as a sculptor might with granite, hewing, wresting, until the reality approximates the ideal. Beethoven asserted:

> I change and reject much and try again until I am satisfied with it. Then the working out in earnest begins . . . And since I am conscious of what I am trying to do, I never lose sight of the fundamental idea. It rises higher and higher and grows before my eyes until I hear and see the image of it, molded and complete, standing there before my mental vision.

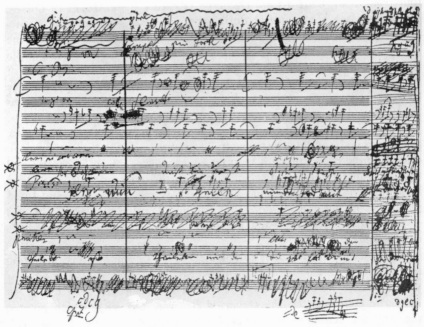

Fig. 57. A page of Beethoven's manuscript. Beethoven's sketch books show the painstaking care and pitiless self-criticism with which he worked. (Courtesy The Bettmann Archive.)

Although arrogant as Napoleon in his relationships with publishers and "the princely rabble," as he called his patrons, Beethoven had the dedicated artist's humility. He is quoted as stating:

The real artist has no pride. Unfortunately he sees that his art has no limits, he feels obscurely how far he is from the goal. And while he is perhaps being admired by others he mourns the fact that he has not yet reached the point to which his better genius like a distant sun ever beckons him.

*   *   *   *   *

Beethoven's music embodied to its ultimate the ideals and aspirations of the Classic period. In turn, it was responsive to the changes that had taken place in the world and, possibly, to the changes that had taken place in Beethoven himself. His masterworks are at once individual and universal, lonely soliloquies and all-encompassing statements. He died full of plans for more music, a tenth symphony and a work based on *Faust*. We cannot imagine what he might have done, had he lived longer. But he left his work as a yardstick against which the coming generations of Romantic composers would measure themselves, and as a timeless legacy to those whose hearts he would reach. As Edward Dannreuther asserts:

> He passes beyond the horizon of a mere singer and poet, and touches upon the domain of the seer and the prophet; where, in unison with all genuine mystics and ethical teachers, he delivers a message of religious love and resignation, identification with the sufferings of all living creatures, deprecation of self, negation of personality, release from the world.

SUGGESTIONS FOR FURTHER READING

Anderson, Emily, ed., *The Letters of Beethoven*. New York, St. Martin's, 1961. 3 vols.

Bukofzer, Manfred F., *Music in the Classic Period*. Berkeley, University of California Press, 1955.

Burk, John N., *The Life and Works of Beethoven*. New York, Modern Library, 1946.

Carse, Adam, *The History of Orchestration*. London, Paul-Trench-Trubner, 1925.

Cockshoot, John V., *The Fugue in Beethoven's Piano Music*. London, Routledge & Paul, 1959.

Hamburger, Michael, ed., *Beethoven—Letters, Journals and Conversations.** New York, Doubleday, 1960.

Kerman, Joseph, *The Beethoven Quartets*. New York, Knopf, 1967.

Nelson, Robert U., *The Technique of Variation*. Berkeley, University of California Press, 1948.

Newman, William S., *The Sonata in the Classic Era*. Chapel Hill, University of North Carolina Press, 1963.

Pauly, Reinhard G., *Music in the Classic Period.** Englewood Cliffs, Prentice-Hall, 1965.

* Available in paperback edition.

Rothschild, Fritz, *The Lost Tradition—Musical Performance in the Times of Mozart and Beethoven*. New York, Oxford University Press, 1961.

Schauffler, Robert Haven, *Beethoven: The Man Who Freed Music*. New York, Tudor, 1947.

Schrade, Leo, *Beethoven in France*. New Haven, Yale University Press, 1942.

Scott, Marion, *Beethoven*. London, Dent, 1947.

Starr, William J., and Devine, George F., *Music Scores—Omnibus,** Part 1. Englewood Cliffs, Prentice-Hall, 1964.

Sullivan, J. W. N., *Beethoven: His Spiritual Development.** New York, Knopf, 1947.

Thayer, Alexander W., *Life of Beethoven*. Princeton, Princeton University Press, 1964. 2 vols.

Tovey, Donald F., *Essays in Musical Analysis*. New York, Oxford University Press, 1935. 2 vols.

Westerby, Herbert, *Beethoven and His Piano Works*. London, Reeves, 1931.

A Sampler of Supplementary Recordings

Collections

The Age of Beethoven	3-Victor 6146
Military Fanfares, Marches and Choruses from the Time of Napoleon	Nonesuch 1075
Ten Centuries of Music	DGG KL-52/61
2000 Years of Music	Folkways 3700

Music of Individual Composers

Beethoven, Ludwig van, *Bagatelles, Op. 33*
Concerti for Piano and Orchestra
Concerto in D for Violin, Op. 61
Egmont: Incidental Music
Missa Solemnis in D, Op. 123
Quartet No. 1 in F, Op. 18
Quartet No. 16 in F, Op. 135
Septet in E flat for Strings and Winds, Op. 20
Piano Sonata No. 8 in c, Op. 13—"Pathétique"
Piano Sonata No. 15 in D, Op. 28—"Pastoral"
Piano Sonata No. 23 in f, Op. 57—"Appassionata"
"Diabelli" Variations, Op. 120
Sonata for Violin and Piano, Op. 47, No. 1
Piano Trio No. 6 in B flat, Op. 97—"Archduke"
"Wellington's Victory," Op. 91
Fidelio, Op. 72
Symphonies (9)

Opportunities for Study in Depth

1. As Cherubini's wife is quoted as saying about the height of the French Revolution, "In the morning the guillotine was busy, and in the evening one could not get a seat in the theatre." What was the immediate effect of the Age of Revolution on the arts, particularly in France?

2. Investigate as far as possible the attachment of Romantic titles to pieces of

absolute music, in order, perhaps, to popularize them. Read some nineteenth-century music criticism and cite examples from it of subjective interpretations, quite foreign to the apparent intent of the composer. Compile research notes in a paper and present it to the class.

3. Make a study of Beethoven's overtures and the works to which they were attached, noting whether or not there is any apparent connection between the musical and dramatic materials and the nature of the literary and tonal themes. Outline findings.

4. Compare, using scores and recordings, first movements of a piano concerto by Mozart and one of the later piano concertos (No. 4 or 5) of Beethoven. In what ways are the movements similar? In what ways different? What are their special points of excellence?

5. There has been a continuing joke in the musical world about Beethoven's "Tenth" symphony. Did the composer write more than nine symphonies?

6. Beethoven is reported to have been shocked by the goings-on in Mozart's opera, *Don Giovanni*. In reaction he wrote *Fidelio*, an opera glorifying conjugal love and self-sacrifice. Study the *libretti* of both operas and then discuss Pauly's statement, "Such a lofty view of the purpose of art does suggest Platonic concepts."

7. Two interesting, if shadowy, personalities dip into the lives of Mozart and Beethoven. They are those of Mesmer, a hypnotist, and Maelzel, an inventor. Who were they? What minor relationships did they have with the composers? What were their contributions to the world?

8. In the preceding chapter we have mentioned the onset and effects of Beethoven's deafness, a malady to all but an especially disastrous one for a professional musician. What are the psychological effects of deafness? Relate them, if possible, to Beethoven's later personality as described in the biographies.

VOCABULARY ENRICHMENT

bagatelles	octet
improvisation	subtitles
metronome	cyclical device
dedication	germ-motive
periods	source-motive
thematic development	sketch books
sextet	*scherzo*
septet	

PART VII

Music of Early Romanticism

Chapter 16.

ROMANTIC LYRICISTS
SCHUBERT AND SCHUMANN

=========================

> Out of my great grief
> I make my little songs . . .

—Heinrich Heine (1799-1856) *Aus meinen grossen Schmerzen*

When we approach music of the Romantic period, that is, the era from approximately 1825 to 1900, we meet with a large repertoire of compositions that the layman considers *his* kind of serious music, with long and expressive melodies, rich orchestrations, subjective insights, picturesque overtones and verbal connotations. It is music full of tunes he can whistle, rhythms he can tap, moods he can recognize and ideas with which he can identify. Gone, at least from the surface of Romantic style, are preciosity, formalism and foolish obeisances; in their places are the broad gesture, bold individuality and enticing glimpses into a spiritual world of the infinite. After all, we say, Heine's great grief is very little different from our own. His "little songs" hit home. Moreover, the stylistic diversity found within Romantic music resembles that of a *smorgasbord* table; it offers something for every taste, readily available to be sampled and savored. And, as many people tend to resist the new until it has become familiar, in art as in edibles, so they still cling to a musical menu of nineteenth-century Romantic favorites.

There are excellent reasons for this state of affairs as we shall see, for, during the Romantic period, music reached an overall popularity that it has rarely enjoyed before or since. The art was accorded respect by the intellectuals and an enthusiastic reception by the hungry middle classes who increasingly flocked to concert halls and opera houses to be amused and nourished. It acquired glamor and a measure of prestige. "Music," wrote Schopenhauer, "is the melody whose text is the world." Indeed, music was to prove the most fecund facet of Romanticism.

ROMANTICISM

Romanticism, the name given to a new stream in literature and the arts, emerged from springs of doubt, revolt and social change that poured forth during the eighteenth and early nineteenth centuries. We have already encountered isolated instances of the Romantic spirit in times past—in the Homeric epics, the medieval *romans* and Shakespearean dramas—and we can readily discern them today in the mid-twentieth century. During the 1800's, however, certain ideas coalesced to create a distinctive attitude which was able to envelop and enclose a great variety of sub-styles and statements. This attitude represented not so much a highly-original view of man and his world, as a sharp swing of emphases and values. These had been building up for some time.

Although Romanticism is seen most dramatically against a backdrop perspective of eighteenth-century Classicism, we should not be misled by the apparent dichotomy posed between Classicism, on the one hand, and Romanticism, on the other. Both derive from a common source, the vital human experience. Each of us, for instance, welcomes a degree of order, control and tradition in his life; yet, at the same time, we yearn to experience the surge of emotion to its depth and height and aspire toward the unknowable and unattainable regions of mystery. We are each Classic and Romantic in our personalities. Throughout history there have been alternations between the Apollonian and Dionysian polarities, as Nietzsche characterized them. This is no less true for the history of art. But the cycles are not and cannot be mutually exclusive. Form and content, if given relative weight, are inseparably combined.

An outstanding characteristic of nineteenth-century Romanticism is its intensely subjective point of view, in contrast to the objectivity of Classicism. When Rousseau asserted: "I am different from all men I have seen. If I am not better, at least I am different"—he heralded the birth of a popular ego and personal creative self-consciousness. No longer was the individual subordinate to his environment; rather, he attempted to surmount and recreate it. He searched his inner being and projected what he found to the eyes, ears and minds of the world. What he felt and what he craved became his subject matter. The pronoun, "I," dominated. As a consequence, emotion was elevated above rationality; sunny matter-of-factness was displaced by what Watts-Dunton calls "the renascence of wonder," with all its implications. The image of an artist swerved from that of a master craftsman to that of a heroic protagonist; from that of a contributor to a stable social order to that of one who stands up against, and often apart from, prevailing circumstances, confidently interpreting them in terms of his own awareness.

Furthermore, as a result of the implementation of democratic and capitalistic systems through military revolutions and the more far-reaching Industrial Revolution, the individual tasted a new kind of freedom. Scores of poets, writers, scientists, philosophers and musicians, both literally and figuratively, embraced the cult of liberation. They included Rousseau, Honoré de Balzac, Victor Hugo, Théophile Gautier, Berlioz, Schumann, Liszt, Byron, Shelley and Keats. It was they and their colleagues who helped define Romanticism through their creative efforts. But all was not as rosy as they might have wished. Although the individual had been released from his former irksome masters, he discovered to his sorrow that freedom could be a mixed blessing and alienation a constant threat. He was free to sink as well as swim, to starve as well as prosper, to lose as well as gain his soul. When Schubert said, "No one feels another's grief; no one understand's another's joy," he was expressing an isolation felt by many.

It was in literature that nineteenth-century Romantic traits first appeared. We have already mentioned the *Sturm und Drang* reaction to the rationalism of the Enlightenment. Although in *Oliver Twist* and *Les Miserables,* we find realism of a particularly vivid kind, we can also discern some very curious manifestations in other popular works, such as *Dr. Jekyll and Mr. Hyde* or *Dracula* or the tales of Edgar Allan Poe —a probing into a mad, violent world of the psyche and the supernatural. Interest in alcohol and drugs stimulated some writers, as in de Quincy's *Confessions of an English Opium Eater;* suicide was made fashionable, at least as a posture, by Goethe's *Werthers Leiden* (*The Sorrows of Werther*). The past was revived by Sir Walter Scott; the exotic was conjured up in books such as *A Thousand and One Nights.* Characters died of love in dank ruin-strewn gardens bathed in flickering moonlight. As one critic puts it, "Whereas the eighteenth century had found its inspiration in ancient Greece, the romantics discovered the so-called Dark Ages." Disease, decay and dismal despair permeate much of the Romantic fabric.

Yet any single definition presents a dangerous oversimplification, for the nineteenth century was an age of contradictions and Romanticism mirrored them. Romantic music was especially receptive to Romantic literary influences, however, as we shall discover in this and the following seven chapters. As all the arts aspired to a glorious unity of forces, they were laced with interactions, in that poetry sought musical values as did painting, while music attempted to describe and depict. This was done with a flamboyancy and ardor which may be ascribed to the fact that many Romantic artists did not reach middle age. There is an aura of youthful excess about much Romantic music, an artistic self-indulgence that in time became the agent of its own destruction. But, at its zenith, as Einstein writes, "Music became a medium through which the ineffable could be made palpable to sense, through which the mysterious, magical and exciting could be created."

Fig. 58. "The *'Hernani'* Battle"—painting by Besnard. A brawl took place at the first performance of Hugo's play, *Hernani*. With this work, a literary revolution began. (Courtesy Musée Victor Hugo, Paris.)

Romanticism did not come to the fore without its battles. On the occasion of the first performance of Victor Hugo's *Hernani*, Paris, as in the "War of the Buffoons," was torn asunder, with conservatives on one side and the fiery Romantics on the other. To read this play today may not reveal the strenuous birth throes of a new era, but it began a literary revolution in 1830. Two years earlier, Franz Schubert, perhaps the first flower of musical Romanticism, had died in Vienna, at the age of thirty-one.

Franz Peter Schubert—Life

Franz Peter Schubert (1797-1828), the son of a schoolmaster, was born in a suburb of Vienna. His father realized, without enthusiasm, that Franz was musically precocious and allowed him to have lessons with the town choirmaster. In addition, through playing chamber music with his father and two brothers, Schubert had an excellent opportunity to learn works by Haydn, Mozart and Beethoven. In 1808 he won a place as soprano in the Vienna court choir and entered the Imperial

Konvikt, the royal chapel and choir school. The ubiquitous Salieri was one of his examiners and in 1812 became his counterpoint instructor. Schubert excelled in his musical studies and profited from playing viola and violin in the school orchestra. He composed steadily and was limited only by the cost of manuscript paper, which such generous friends as Josef von Spaun supplied.

Perhaps the most important thing about Schubert's short school life was the friendships he made, a first sign of a power of personal attraction in this shy, unprepossessing, bespectacled youth. Among the boys at school were von Spaun, Anton Holzapfel, Albert Stadler and Leopold von Sonnleithner. Schubert was always the glowing, fun-making center of a large circle of warm friends. Had it not been for them, he might have passed entirely unheralded, because what slight public recognition he received was a result of their painstaking efforts on his behalf.

In 1813 Schubert left the Konvikt and spent a year at the Normal School of St. Anna, from which he received a teacher's diploma. To avoid a fourteen-year military conscription, he joined the staff of his father's school where he remained until 1817, when he decided to devote himself entirely to music. The dreamy, amiable Schubert was a very poor pedagogue, who hated his work. Composing at cafés after hours was his only solace. In the meantime, he had developed an unquenchable habit of Bohemianism, frequenting beer gardens in company with his friends and spending the furtive florin in soothing diversion. He had tried unsuccessfully to secure the musical directorship of a Normal School at Laibach in 1815. His failure may have been due to Salieri's very cool letter of recommendation. Thus, in 1817, Schubert found himself without a position, a salary or even a home. His friend, Franz von Schober, a singer, took him in and aided him professionally and financially through the remaining eleven years of his life. Schubert never again held a steady job, or enjoyed a regular income, although he composed without abate.

Schubert's first chronicled work was a piano *Fantasy in G,* for four hands, written in 1810, when he was thirteen. His first extant song dates from the following year. During the period from 1815 through 1819, his musical inspiration, always torrential, was as that of one possessed. He composed so easily and swiftly that often he would forget what he had written. Eight songs a day was child's play to him. Asked about his method of working, he replied that he finished one work and started the next. Often music was notated on the back of café menus. It has been said that if his pen sputtered, Schubert, rather than recopy, would incorporate the ink specks into the composition. These years witnessed the composition of six symphonies, Masses, the *"Trout" Quartet,* piano sonatas and hundreds of songs, including *Gretchen am Spinnrade* (1814) and *Der Erlkönig* (1815), among many other works.

It would be a mistake, however, to assume that Schubert was as irresponsible or dissolute as anecdotes suggest. "My work," he explained in his diary, "has been conceived by my understanding and by my sufferings." His friend, the painter Moritz von Schwind, noted that Schubert worked every morning from six or seven o'clock until noon, when he would go to a café, read the papers and if the weather were good, take a stroll in the countryside immediately surrounding Vienna. We know that he occasionally rewrote compositions, until they achieved a form that satisfied him. He was, nevertheless, a spontaneous composer, with a matchless gift of melody.

During this period Schubert was entirely dependent upon his friends, who functioned as a Schubert admiration society and business staff. His circle included Franz Grillparzer, Carl Maria von Weber, Ignaz Moscheles, Julius Benedict, Edward von Bauernfeld and Johann Michael Vogl, a famous baritone. So far no one would publish his work. He lived in abject want, except for a few florins his family sometimes sent him. Therefore, in 1819, he gladly accepted a summer post with Count Esterházy and his music-loving family in Hungary. Although he associated with grooms and chambermaids at the lodge, he was not unhappy. For every lesson he gave the children, he received two gulden. Moreover, he had physical comfort for the first time in his young manhood. His letters to friends show how much he missed them and their lively evenings, "Schubertiads" devoted to literary discussions, music and dancing. When the Count returned to the city, Schubert also went back to Vienna and moved in with the poet, Mayrhofer.

Two years later Schubert eagerly tried his hand at opera, but his productions met with no success. Through the efforts of his staunch friends, the von Sonnleithners, a few songs were finally published on commission by the Diabellis, in 1821. But Schubert, like Stephen Foster, was no business man and often parted with his works for the price of a supper. "The state should support me," he said, "so that I may be untroubled and free to compose." Unfortunately, no such support materialized.

Although living in the same city as Beethoven, Schubert had no opportunity to meet him until Diabelli escorted the young composer, armed with his *Variations on a French Song,* dedicated to Beethoven by "his admirer and worshipper." The master was deaf and handed Schubert a pad to write on so that they might converse. Schubert was so shy that he forthwith bolted out of the house. It is reported that Beethoven liked

Fig. 59. "A Schubertiad"—Moritz von Schwind. Here Schubert is seen at the piano accompanying the singer, Vogl. Although poverty-stricken in this world's goods, Schubert was rich in friends. (Courtesy Schubert Museum, Vienna.)

the *Variations* well enough to play them over and over with his nephew. Schubert saw Beethoven once again, but only during his final illness did Beethoven come to appreciate Schubert's full worth.

In the summer of 1824 Schubert returned to the Esterházy estate, where some biographers claim he endured a silent and hopeless passion for the young Countess Caroline. Upon returning to Vienna he wrote many new works. A trip to the Tyrol with Vogl, in 1825, rested him after his gay Viennese nights. Following a stimulating visit to Graz, Schubert, in 1828, held his first and only concert, realizing the sum of about $160. In the same year, as the result of poor nourishment, late hours and infection with venereal disease, Schubert's constitution, chronically strained for some time, rebelled and he fell prey to depression, delusion and, finally, to typhoid fever. His physical and emotional deterioration was of long standing, however. As early as 1824, he had written:

> I feel I am the most miserable and unfortunate man in the world. Picture to yourself one whose health can never be re-established, who from sheer despair commits fault after fault, instead of amending his life . . . Each night when I go to sleep, I wish that I may never wake again, and each morning recalls the suffering of yesterday.

Schubert died at the home of his brother, Ferdinand. "Schubert is dead and with him all the brightest and the most beautiful we had in life," wrote von Schwind and von Schober. "I now view life as some dreary path, which I must walk alone," said Franz Lachner. In accordance with his desire, Schubert's father buried him close to Beethoven's grave. Schubert left personal effects amounting to less than twenty dollars, but an invaluable musical legacy that was to make him immortal. As Grillparzer had eulogized Beethoven, one year before, "The last master of Song has passed away."

Franz Peter Schubert—Music

Schubert, like Beethoven, stands as a transitional figure between Classicism and Romanticism. In the many compositions of his short life he created no new forms or techniques. Yet there is no doubt that in his music Schubert sounds a new note of expressiveness. Perhaps this is best described as the introduction of lyricism, poetry and inwardness to the content of music, especially in the intimate short forms of the piano piece and the German Romantic song or *Lied,* which Schubert developed so fully that, in Edar Istel's words, "he is and remains the uncontested king of song, whose crown no successor has been able to tear from his brow." One of the world's greatest melodists, Schubert composed in terms of the "long line." His melodies, whether in symphony, chamber music, piano solo, song or chorus, have the inevitable continuity and emotional rightness that we associate with Romantic music and which distinguishes it from the thematic fragmentation frequently found in the music of Classic composers, whose thinking and methods rested on quite different premises.

German Art Song

German art song did not begin with Schubert. Rather, its roots lay in folksong from the distant past; in the compositions of *Minnesingers* and *Meistersingers;* in the *arias* of Heinrich Albert (1604-1651), a cousin of Heinrich Schütz; in the airs of Adam Krieger (1634-1666); in settings of C. P. E. Bach; and in *Lieder* by Johann Friedrich Reichardt (1752-1814), Carl Friedrich Zelter (1758-1832) and the Swabian composer, Johann Rudolf Zumsteeg (1760-1802), whose ballads, featuring a programmatic piano part, were early models for Schubert. Modified forms had been introduced into the *Singspiel* by composers such as Johann Adam Hiller (1728-1804). Haydn, Mozart, Beethoven and Weber were influenced by these. In Schubert's hands, however, the German art song reached a high point. Schumann asserted that in his songs, Schubert made the first noteworthy contribution to music since Beethoven. Many of the *Lieder* are in a form that foreshadowed the tone-poem and modern music drama, in that the music so perfectly fits the mood and action of the verse. Marcel Schneider points out:

> . . . in order that the lied as we know it might be brought to birth, it was necessary to await romanticism's return to source, its revival of national consciousness, and taste for folklore and local tradition. The world had to await Schubert, the most poetic, as Liszt said, of all composers . . . Schubert, by his adoption of the rhythm of the spoken word, was the first to transmute poetry and the natural tones of the voice into song, and to enshrine in poetry and music the common spirit of humanity.

SCHUBERT'S *Lieder*

We cannot distinguish a gradual development of mastery in Schubert's 603 solo songs, for those written at the age of seventeen and eighteen are as daring, as satisfying and as mature as those composed at the end of his life. Nor can we point to any one song and say that it is typical. All we can do is to agree with Edward Dickinson, when he writes that Schubert "raised a musical form from comparative obscurity to a rank among the historic styles." Rudolf Stephan adds, "Schubert's songs combine an inexhaustible wealth of melodic inspiration with an extraordinary sensitivity to subtleties of mood and of transitions, thus producing the expression of the deepest feelings." At best, however, words cannot do justice to these miniature masterpieces; they must be heard as performed by master interpreters, some of whom have devoted a lifetime to their study.

Schubert used three forms in his songs: the **strict strophic form,** in which each verse is sung to the same melody and accompaniment, as in *Das Heidenröslein* ("The Meadow Rose"), which was actually included in Herder's collection of folksongs; the **varied strophic form,** in which there is repetition but also some change, perhaps in the last verse, as in *Die Forelle* ("The Trout"); and the **through-composed form,** in which the music alters with the meaning of the text, as in *Der Erlkönig* ("The Erlking"). His piano accompaniments are unique in their collaboration with the voice. The simple, broken chords of "The Meadow Rose" convey the innocence and serenity of the poem. With a measure or two, we can "hear" the babbling brook in which the trout swim. And in the agitated, reiterated triplets, against which sounds a foreboding bass figure, the eerie atmosphere of Goethe's Erlking narrative is firmly established.

Schubert amplifies his setting of this hair-raising tale of an hallucinating child who is being chased by Death in a wild horseback ride through the dark forest by using an imaginative, colorful and wholly effective modulatory scheme, in which the child's rising terror is accompanied by rises in pitch. The character of the vocal lines is fashioned after the character who is singing; the child almost gasps, the father reassures in a more-rounded way and the Erlking wheedles and threatens. The terrific tension of the pursuit is abruptly broken by silence, by which we instantly know Death has triumphed. That this compact drama was written at all is remarkable; that it was the work of an eighteen-year-old is quite fantastic.

Among the many poets to whom Schubert turned for his lyrics were some great men and others whom he rescued from oblivion. Ravenously, Schubert would seize a collection of poems, wherever he might be, in his own poor room or in a tavern, and instead of writing a single song, he would compose quantities. His favorite author was Goethe, over seventy of whose poems he set to music, including "The Meadow Rose"; "The Erlking"; and "Gretchen at the Spinning Wheel" (from *Faust*), an epochal early work, written at the age of seventeen. With its unity of mood, freedom of tonality, logical musical movement and distinctive piano accompaniment, "Gretchen" serves as a prototype of Schubert's best songs and a model of the art song style.

Other poets include Ossian, Heine, Klopstock and his friend Mayrhofer, who said that Schubert's music made him understand his own verses better (for example, *Einsamkeit*—"Loneliness"). Shakespeare contributed "Hark! Hark! the Lark" and "Who is Sylvia?" Sir Walter Scott provided words for seven songs from *The Lady of the Lake* (1825), of which "Ellen and the Huntsmen" is one. Schiller tendered over forty texts. Wilhelm Müller gave the composer material for two song cycles, *Die schöne Müllerin* ("The Miller's Beautiful Daughter," 1823) and *Der Winterreise* ("The Winter Journey," 1827). *Der Schwanengesang* ("The Swan Song," 1828), Schubert's last cycle of songs, was drawn from poems by Rellstab and Heine, with one by Seidl.

As Schubert grew older, more unhappy and increasingly depressed, his songs became more personal, more tragic and more economical in musical means. We notice the differences in such songs as *Der Doppelgänger* ("The Shadow"), *Die junge Nonne* ("The Young Nun") and songs from "The Winter Journey."

CHORAL WORKS

Schubert was also an impressive choral composer. While in his 'teens, he wrote four Masses for his parish church. Of these the first, composed when he was seventeen, can compare, say some authorities, with Mendelssohn's *Overture to A Midsummer Night's Dream,* written at the same age. The second, *Mass in G,* has become a favorite with choirs both abroad and in the United States. It is short, non-virtuosic and has a tuneful simplicity that captures singers and listeners alike. As Schubert was fully aware of the potentials of the voice, his sacred music is of a beautiful *timbre.* The *Mass in E Flat,* written in the year of his death, is less popular than the *Mass in A Flat,* dated 1822. Fiske considers the latter composition "one of his golden dreams, ravishing the senses with its melody and its endearing harmonic twists." Schubert's sacred music also includes beautiful hymns, Offertories and two cantatas, of which *Miriams Siegesgesang (Miriam's Song of Triumph),* composed in 1828 on a text by Grillparzer, is exceptional.

Other choral works are highly interesting. Several were compositions for German *Liedertafeln* ("Table Singers"), groups of amateur male singers, similar to the *Orphéons* of France and Glee Clubs of England and America. Goethe's *Gesang der Geister über den Wassern* ("Song of the Spirits over the Water," 1821) is scored for male voices, two violas, two 'cellos and a double bass. *Nachtgesang im Walde* ("Nocturne in the Woods," 1827) is arranged for male voices and four horns, suggesting the magic spell of the forest by night. Schubert also wrote part-songs and a work for female voices, *Ständchen* ("Serenade," 1827), for contralto, chorus and piano.

Although Schubert's "Erlking" and other ballads and even the more pictorial songs are suffused with a sense of drama, the composer, because of his insufficient knowledge of theater and an erratic choice of librettos, never succeeded in opera, that remunerative form of composition which he dearly loved. Of all his dramatic attempts, only two operas, *Alfonse und Estrella* (1822) and *Fierrabras* (1823), and the incidental music to *Rosamunde von Cypern* (1823) saw stage light— dimly and inconsequentially. Liszt produced *Alfonse und Estrella* posthumously at Weimar, but it was not successful. Today we occasionally hear the overture, *entr'acte* and ballet music from *Rosamunde* on concert programs.

SYMPHONIES

Schubert succeeded in fusing the power of pain and sorrow with his meager shreds of happiness, particularly in his later instrumental and vocal works. His orchestral music includes seven complete and two incomplete symphonies. A problematical *"Gastein" Symphony* (1825), supposed to have been written in honor of the Austrian *Musikverein* in

Gastein, apparently was lost in transit. The first six symphonies date from the years 1813 to 1816 and despite moments of beauty reveal the composer seeking his way with the aid of Mozart and Beethoven, whose *"Eroica"* provided inspiration for Schubert's *Symphony No. 4 in C Minor* (the "Tragic"). Schubert piled melody on melody, often with less development than was wise. An English critic asserts, "Lovely melodies follow each other but nothing comes of them." In the *Symphony No. 8 in B Minor* (the "Unfinished," 1822) and the *Symphony No. 9 in C Major* (the "Great," 1828), however, Schubert combines Classic form with Romantic spirit in a uniquely Viennese manner.

The *"Unfinished" Symphony,* so designated because it contains but two completed movements, shows a tremendous advance over Schubert's preceding works, as great as that between Beethoven's second and third symphonies. It is *sui generis,* resisting classification. Intended for the Graz Philharmonic, it is more richly scored than previous symphonies, requiring in addition to the usual Classic orchestral complement, two horns, two trumpets, three trombones and two drums, the same instrumentation used in his last symphonic marvel. A wealth of story has grown up regarding the *"Unfinished" Symphony's* composition. Why was it left incomplete, with only nine measures of a third movement sketched? Why did Anselm Hüttenbrenner keep the manuscript in his desk drawer for forty years before showing it to the conductor Johann Herbeck (1831-1877), who performed it for the first time in 1865? Of all Schubert's works, the *"Unfinished"* is best-known to today's concert goers. Its tragically sweet melodies have been presented in popular versions, notably in Sigmund Romberg's operetta, *Blossom Time* (1924).

Schubert's last symphony, composed in the year of his death, was rejected as too difficult by the *Musikverein* of Vienna. It lay undisturbed for ten years, until Schumann discovered it and gave it to Mendelssohn, who performed it at Leipzig. It is a large work, recalling Beethoven's *Ninth,* with which Schubert certainly was familiar. Daniel Gregory Mason writes:

> There is a grandeur of scale and intention, a deliberation and solidity, a sustained power, large touch, and freedom of execution . . . that place it above all his works. The long climaxes bespeak a reserve power not associated with Schubert the song-writer; . . . the harmony is firmer, plainer and stronger; the scoring is done as it were with a larger brush, the colors laid on in wider spaces and free patterns; and in the last movement, the romantic note is for once drowned in a deeper cry of tragic heroism.

CHAMBER MUSIC

It has been astutely stated by Marcel Schneider that although Schubert's greatness "is rooted in the lied, it is not contained by it." As a chamber music composer, Schubert shows himself well-trained in Classicism. In comparison with Beethoven, if such a comparison has any meaning, Schubert has been placed as a peer of Beethoven's second period. His melodic gifts equaled those of Mozart. Posed with Haydn, Schubert is the more personal of the two.

In spite of admitted unevenness, Schubert's chamber music provides us with a delightful collection of some thirty works in various forms. William Mann comments that "they are music to be loved, and they inspire an affection that in human affairs we accord to our closest relations and to those friends from whose company we are never long absent." He continues, "Whether in the breezy holiday atmosphere of the B flat Piano Trio and the 'Trout' Quintet and the Octet, or in the inward contemplation of the C Major Quintet, or in the pathos of the three great string quartets and the C Minor Quartet movement, there is a naturalness that recalls Jean-Paul's phrase about miracles in broad daylight."

Schubert often incorporated his songs into works for instrumental media, usually in slow movements where the melodies serve as points of departure for variations. The celebrated *Quintet in A* (1819), for piano, violin, viola, 'cello and double bass, acquires its subtitle, "The Trout," from the fourth movement variations based on the song of that name. All four movements of the *"Wanderer" Fantasy for Piano* (1822) are derived from the central theme of *Der Wanderer*. The eighteenth song of *Die schöne Müllerin* cycle is paraphrased in the *Introduction and Variations on Trock'ne Blumen* for flute and piano (1824). And in the *Quartet in D Minor, No. 14* (1826) the second movement is a set of variations upon the song, *Tod und das Mädchen* ("Death and the Maiden").

PIANO COMPOSITIONS

Schubert's twenty-one piano sonatas, inspired as they sometimes are, are overshadowed by his compositions in shorter forms for the instrument. The eight *Impromptus* (1827) and six *Moments Musicaux* (1824-27), together with *Ländler* (Austrian country dances), *Écossaises,* Waltzes, *Fantasias, Polonaises* and Marches, including the stirring little "Military March in D," created an artistic vogue and a *modus scribendi* for Schumann, Mendelssohn, Chopin and other Romantic composers for the piano. These small, epigrammatic forms enabled the composer to explore a mood without being bound by formal requirements or the demands of more pretentious structures.

OTHER GERMAN SONG COMPOSERS

The *Lied* tradition of Schubert was to be carried on by Schumann, Brahms, Wolf and Richard Strauss. Lesser composers of the nineteenth century also brought gifts to the world of song. One of these was Karl Löwe (1796-1869), who did for the ballad what others had done for the *Lied*. He gave an almost Wagnerian treatment to motive and action and was particularly skilled in depicting the ghostly, heroic and wild. Among his ballads are settings of *Der Erlkönig* and *Edward*. Robert Franz (1815-1892), one of the finest song writers of the Romantic period, was warmly praised by Mendelssohn, Schumann and Liszt. A man of broad musicianship, Franz composed hundreds of songs, delightful for their finish, melodiousness and taste. They include *Widmung* ("Dedication") and *Die Lotosblume* ("The Lotus Blossom"). Franz Abt (1819-1885) was a prolific composer of songs with more popular appeal. An example of his work is "Over the Stars There Is Rest."

FRANZ SCHUBERT AND ROBERT SCHUMANN

The differences separating Schubert from Robert Schumann are many. Schubert had been briefly trained in a choir school; Schumann was a University graduate, coming to music relatively late. Schubert was a citizen of jovial, pleasure-loving Vienna, while Schumann was a German from the North. Schubert gloried in his friends and in conviviality, whereas Schumann was given to introspection and a quiet family life. Each man came from a different social background—an elementary schoolmaster of the time could hardly be equated with a bookseller and anthologist.

On the other hand, both men were bound by similarities of character and of musical style. They were both shy and inclined to "nerves"; they were both inept at coping with everyday practicalities; they were both weak in the area of theatrical music; and they were both products and molders of the German Romantic tradition of lyricism being implanted in music through the ages.

ROBERT ALEXANDER SCHUMANN—LIFE

The most literary of composers, Robert Schumann (1810-1856) was a Romanticist of the first order. Literature and music were his artistic handmaidens. His early acquaintance with German Romantic literature influenced his compositions. This resulted in using descriptive titles for his piano pieces; in trying to re-create literary moods; and in making musical characterizations of his friends. The short piano piece, as introduced by Beethoven, Schubert, Mendelssohn and the many minor composers of *salon* music, became a perfect medium for Schumann's lyric genius. "Mozart and Haydn were musicians" says Hadow: "Schumann was, in the fullest sense of the word, a tone-poet."

Robert Alexander Schumann, born at Zwickau, Saxony, was the youngest of five children. His father, Friedrich August Schumann, a cultured man, encouraged his son in his love of music and literature. The boy extemporized at the piano when he was so small that he had to stand up to reach the keyboard. His first teacher, a local organist, Johann Gottfried Kuntzsch, prophesied that he would accomplish great things. Schumann senior tried to arrange lessons for Robert with Carl Maria von Weber in Dresden, but the project came to nought. In the meantime, the "little, round-headed, lazy, good-natured boy was left to his own devices, and went on 'picking out tunes' for himself, or portraying on the piano the characters of his school-fellows," comments Hadow.

The death of his father in 1826 was a tragic loss, as Schumann's mother was unsympathetic to his artistic tendencies and wanted him to study law. Before his University years, however, Robert had become familiar with the string quartets of Haydn, Mozart and Beethoven at the home of Carl Carus, an amateur musician. And through the wife of Carl's nephew, Schumann discovered the songs of Franz Schubert. At this time, too, he developed an inordinate love for the writings of Jean-Paul Richter (1763-1825), and tried to imitate his literary style in several unfinished novels. Schumann matriculated at Leipzig University in 1828 but before he settled down to work, he met Gisbert Rosen, who was also a Richter enthusiast. They travelled together, meeting *en route* the poet Heinrich Heine, and Jean-Paul's widow. Leipzig offered little pleasure to Robert outside of visits to Dr. Carus, at whose home he heard music and met famous musicians. Among these were Heinrich Marschner, an opera composer, and Friedrich Wieck, who became his piano teacher, and at whose home Robert met Wieck's young daughter, Clara, a piano prodigy.

Schumann read law at Heidelberg (1829) with Anton Thibaut (1774-1840), who was also the author of a treatise, *On Purity in Musical Art*. Thibaut recognized that it was worth spoiling a bad lawyer to make a great musician. Frau Schumann finally permitted Robert to study music, and the conflict between prose and poetry, law and music, reached an end in 1830. Schumann lived at the Wieck home in Leipzig and worked diligently. Impatient because he was not advancing rapidly enough, Schumann invented a device to strengthen his fourth finger and, as a result, permanently injured his right hand, thus robbing the world of a pianist and giving it a composer. Heinrich Dorn (1804-1892), conductor of the Leipzig Opera, was his composition teacher. Unpublished works of this period include a symphony and a concerto movement.

1832 marks the first published appearance of Schumann, the composer, with *Opus* 1, the *"A-B-E-G-G" Variations,* quickly followed by other piano works. On April 3, 1834, the first issue of a new bi-weekly music journal, the *Neue Zeitschrift für Musik* appeared, devoted to musical criticism and the ideals and aims of the *avant-garde* Romantic school. From 1835 to 1844, Schumann was its editor-in-chief. His first sally into criticism, however, antedated this publication by three years, with an article in the conservative *Allgemeine musikalische Zeitung.* Here for the first time we meet the impassioned *Florestan* and the poetic *Eusebius,* representatives of Schumann's own schizoid nature. In the article, *Eusebius* comes upon the scene with the historic phrase, "Hats off, gentlemen, a genius!" and the composition he has discovered is *Là, ci darem la mano, Op.* 2, variations on a theme from Mozart's *Don Giovanni,* by a then unknown composer, Frédéric Chopin. Schumann brought to life the children of his fancy, and peopled his magazine with members of an imaginary *Davidsbund,* who were fighting against the musical Philistines. It was a struggle of a new order against the old; of an ultra-modern Romanticism against a decadent Classicism; of the youthful, subjective and emotional against the artificial and pedantic.

Between *Eusebius* and *Florestan* stood *Master Raro,* as philosopher and mediator. *Felix Meritis* was Mendelssohn; *Chiara* was Clara Wieck; *Estrella* was Ernestine von Fricken, to whom Schumann had been engaged at one time; *Jeanquirit* was Stephen Heller (1813-1888). Several other characters appear, *noms de plume* of contributors to the journal. Schumann used his personifications not only in his magazine but also in his music. When the *Sonata in F Sharp Minor, Op.* 11 first appeared in print, it was allegedly composed by *"Florestan* and *Eusebius."* The different numbers that make up the *Davidsbündlertänze (Dances of the Band of Davidites, Op.* 6) are signed *F, E,* or *F* and *E.* Many of the twenty-one pieces of *Carnaval, Op.* 9 are named for these characters. *Pierrot, Arlequin, Pantalon* and *Columbine* greet us. Tributes are also paid to Chopin and Paganini.

In 1835, when Felix Mendelssohn arrived in Leipzig as conductor of the *Gewandhaus* concerts, he made the acquaintance of Schumann. "Mendelssohn is the most distinguished man I have ever met," Schumann wrote to Clara Wieck. In 1836, Clara, then a girl of seventeen and an extraordinary pianist, became a serious part of his life. For four years Clara and Robert struggled against the selfish prejudice of a father who could not see his brilliant and famous daughter married to an unstable, unrecognized composer. Wieck even put legal obstacles in their way, but finally, when Clara came of age, Schumann obtained a court order which permitted them to marry. The compositions of these years were written to her as most lovers would write letters; and, sometimes, Schumann felt that they were so revelatory that they should not be played publicly.

To improve his financial condition, Schumann decided to publish his *Neue Zeitschrift* in Vienna, which he regarded as a city of musical progress. He was doomed to disappointment, however, and returned to Leipzig in 1839. His *Faschingsschwank aus Wien (Viennese Carnival Pranks, Op.* 26), in which he concealed the forbidden *Marseillaise,* was a memoir of this sojourn. He had also discovered the score of Schubert's "Great" *C Major Symphony,* at the home of Ferdinand Schubert. After Mendelssohn's first rehearsal, Schumann, in a much-quoted letter to Clara, said of it:

> All the instruments are like human voices, and it is all so intellectual; and then the instrumentation, in spite of Beethoven! And the length of it—such a heavenly length, like a four-volume novel; why, it is longer than the Ninth Symphony!

1840 was a monumental year for Schumann. He received the degree of Doctor of Philosophy from the University of Jena, married Clara Wieck, and literally burst into song. Having previously devoted himself exclusively to piano music, in 1840 he composed a total of 138 songs. His literary proclivities gave him a wide range of texts by many poets, although his favorite was Heine. Among his song cycles are the immortal *Myrthen, Op.* 25, which includes *Die Lotosblume, Du bist wie eine Blume* ("You Are Like a Flower") and *Widmung; Dichterliebe (Poet's Love, Op.* 48), in which is the charming *Im wunderschönen Monat Mai* ("In the Beautiful Month of May"); and *Liederkreis, Op.* 24, on poems of Heine. Schumann's songs, apart from being exceedingly beautiful music, made an invaluable addition to the German art song repertoire as Schubert had left it.

If 1840 was a song year, 1841 was devoted to orchestral music and 1842 to chamber music. Schumann's *Symphony No. 1 in B Flat, Op.* 38 (the "Spring") was presented at the *Gewandhaus* by Mendelssohn in March, 1841. Two other works were performed, with less success, in

December. During this year Schumann also wrote a *Fantasia in A Minor* for piano and orchestra, that he later revised as the first movement of the *Piano Concerto, Op.* 54, completed in 1845.

With a facility we tend to associate with a Mozart or a Schubert, Schumann composed three string quartets (*Op.* 41) in the summer of 1842. He said he had shut himself up with the Beethoven quartets before writing his own. One of the most famous quintets in all chamber music is Schumann's *Quintet in E Flat, Op.* 44, dedicated to his wife. Mendelssohn was the pianist at its first performance in 1842. Berlioz heard the work and carried word of Schumann to Paris. The *Piano Quartet in E Flat, Op.* 47, and a less significant trio, also stem from this year.

In 1843 Schumann was appointed professor of composition and piano at the Leipzig Conservatory, of which Mendelssohn was director. Moreover, he enjoyed one of his few real successes with *Das Paradies und die Peri, Op.* 50, adapted from Thomas Moore's *Lalla Rookh,* and cast in a novel form, that of a dramatic cantata. Schumann entertained the idea of writing an opera to prove, as he remarked, that the Germans did not need to leave the field in possession of the Italians and French. His previous success encouraged him to try Byron's *Corsair,* but he found it unsuitable. His next venture was a choral work from Goethe's *Faust,* intended as a concert oratorio. It was performed in 1847 when Schumann, who had moved to Dresden on account of his health in 1844, was conductor of a new Philharmonic Society. He revised the work and presented it again the next year. When Goethe's Centenary (1849) was celebrated, Dresden, Weimar and Leipzig performed Schumann's *Faust.* The work was finally completed in 1853, with the addition of an overture. Meanwhile, he had written an opera, *Genoveva, Op.* 81 (1848), on a text from Tieck's and Hebbel's legend of St. Genevieve. The first performance in Leipzig (1850) was only a *succes d'estime,* and it achieved but three performances.

During his six years at Dresden, Schumann worked quietly because of a breakdown he had suffered in 1844. Even more reserved and silent than usual, he saw few people but was friendly with Ferdinand Hiller (1811-1885), conductor of a local orchestral society, and became interested in a young opera composer, Richard Wagner. In him, Herbert Bedford writes, Schumann "found a bristling personality in many respects diametrically opposed to his own."

By 1845, Schumann had recovered sufficiently to compose the *Symphony No. 2 in C, Op.* 61. Many choral works also date from this time, and two trios for piano and strings (*Op.* 63 and *Op.* 80), as well as the sketches for *Genoveva.* Among his projects was a new edition of Bach's *Well-tempered Clavichord,* which inspired him to write contrapuntal studies, including six organ fugues on the tones, B-A-C-H. (In German, *B* designates B flat, while *H* indicates B natural.)

That stalwart of piano teachers, *Album für die Jugend* (*Album for the Young, Op.* 68), belongs to one of Schumann's most fruitful years, (1848-49), when Byron's *Manfred* music was composed (*Op.* 115). The overture to *Manfred,* considered one of his best orchestral works, was written first; the other fifteen numbers, with choruses and solos, melodrama and *entr'acte* followed. Schumann conducted the *Manfred Overture* in 1852 at Leipzig when, it is reported, he seemed almost to become the melancholy tortured hero. That same year, Liszt produced two stage performances at Weimar.

J. A. Fuller-Maitland, in an early study of Schumann, writes:

> In this, the latter part of his residence in Dresden, it is curious to notice that, whereas he had always been used to take up one form of musical composition with great energy at one time, and to devote himself exclusively to it while the mood was on him, he now produced works in almost every form; vocal music and instrumental, chamber music and orchestral, works of large and of small caliber, were produced with the greatest possible rapidity . . . The list for 1849 is larger and more varied than that for any other year; but at the same time it contains fewer of those works which have been accepted as his finest.

On hearing a rumor that Julius Rietz (1812-1877), conductor of the *Gewandhaus* Orchestra after Mendelssohn's death, had been called to a post in Berlin, Schumann applied for the position, but Rietz decided to remain. Schumann then accepted a post at Düsseldorf as director of an orchestra and choral society, where he had an opportunity to conduct his own works and to encourage talented young composers by performing theirs. Schumann was not a good conductor; his natural reserve and shyness, coupled with his failing health, doomed any chance of success. His happiness in his work, however, is reflected in the *Symphony No. 3 in E Flat, Op.* 97 (the "Rhenish"). In addition, he wrote many ballads, cantatas, songs and choral works and overtures.

In a Schumann festival held in Leipzig in 1852 the composer was received more respectfully than enthusiastically. Not disturbed, he remarked, "I am quite accustomed to find my deeper and better compositions are not understood at first hearing." Soon, however, Schumann was forced to resign from his position. Withal, he never became bitter or morose; he remained kindly in his attitude toward younger composers and tried to encourage sincerity in art, looking about to find someone to continue his artistic creed.

Little wonder then that he greeted as the awaited musical Messiah, the twenty-year-old Johannes Brahms, who came to him with a letter from Joseph Joachim (1831-1907) and some compositions. After remaining silent for years, Schumann broke into print in the *Neue Zeitschrift* with an article entitled *Neue Bahnen* ("New Paths"). "He has come, the chosen youth, over whose cradle the Graces and the Heroes seem to have kept watch." That the "chosen youth" brought comfort and cheer to the ailing musician as if he had been a son, and, as a faithful friend, stood by Clara Schumann through the rest of her life, records one of the most unique relationships between musicians.

Schumann was able to accompany his wife to Holland, where his music was warmly received. In 1854, he attended a performance of his *Paradise and the Peri* in Hanover, and on his return he set to the task of preparing his literary writings for publication. But mental derangement interrupted all work and he was obsessed by hearing an incessant musical tone. Unable to combat his melancholy, he attempted suicide in the river Rhine.

"Brahms is my dearest, truest support," Clara wrote to a friend. "Since the beginning of Robert's illness he has never left me, but has gone through everything with me and shared my sufferings." Indeed, Brahms and Joachim had rushed to Düsseldorf when the news reached them. Schumann was placed in a private sanatorium near Bonn, and Clara bravely continued her career, caring for the children (she had four girls and a boy) and coping with the tragic condition of her husband with the fortitude of faith. She returned from her first triumphal tour in England to attend Robert on his deathbed. Clara wrote: "He smiled at me and with a great effort clasped me with one of his arms. And I would not give up that embrace for all the treasures on earth." Schumann died on the afternoon of July 29, 1856.

Robert Haven Schauffler concludes his biography of the composer with the following paragraphs:

> Those things that Robert Schumann had all his life feared and hoped had come to pass. He had finally encountered the dreaded heart of darkness, and it had laid his too-young body to molder beneath the young plane trees of Bonn.
>
> On the other hand, as he had wistfully hoped it would, his music was taking on a manifold life. It had now begun reaching out towards all humanity in ever widening circles—like those rings made in the waters of the Rhine by the fall of a golden circlet, or the death-plunge of a desperate sufferer. And young composers in Germany and Scandinavia, France and Russia were falling more and more under the spell of its influence.

Another event was taking place which he had neither hoped nor feared. One of his chief creations had been the taste and artistic intelligence of the loved woman who had inspired his noblest works. And from now on, as long as she should live, this woman with the Schumann-given taste and intelligence was to be the most potent of all the forces that furthered her husband's work, and was to pass on the torch by inspiring the best music of Robert Schumann's greatest successor [Brahms].

PIANO COMPOSITIONS

Robert Schumann left us a wonderful legacy of feeling, expressed in music of the most intimate and delicate nuances. In his *Lieder,* exuberant, yet tender, he refined the piano accompaniment to a point where the voice often is auxiliary to the instrument, which assumes responsibility for the emotional delineation of textual details and provides epilogues. Schumann's mastery of the poetic piano piece is beyond question; some authorities feel that he is at his best in this form, where structural problems are at a minimum and fancies of the moment can be securely captured. Among Schumann's contributions to Romantic form are the collections of diverse short pieces which together form larger works, such as *Papillons* and *Carnaval.*

The following incomplete list of Schumann's piano compositions offers an amazing record of achievement: *Op.* 1, *Variations on the Name Abegg; Op.* 2, *Papillons* ("Butterflies," twelve pieces); *Ops.* 3 and 10, *Twelve Studies after the Paganini Caprices; Op.* 4, *Intermezzi* (six pieces); *Op.* 6, *Davidsbündlertänze* (eighteen characteristic pieces); *Op.* 7, *Toccata; Op.* 9, *Carnaval* (twenty-one pieces); *Op.* 11, *Sonata No. 1 in F Sharp Minor; Op.* 12, *Fantasiestücke* (eight pieces); *Op.* 13, *Études Symphoniques* ("Studies in the form of Variations"); *Op.* 14, *Sonata No. 2 in F Minor; Op.* 15, *Kinderscenen* ("Scenes from Childhood," thirteen pieces); *Op.* 16, *Kreisleriana* (eight pieces); *Op.* 17, *Fantasia in C; Op.* 18, *Arabeske; Op.* 19, *Blumenstück* ("Flower Piece"); *Op.* 20, *Humoreske; Op.* 21, *Novelletten* (four books); *Op.* 22, *Sonata No. 3 in G Minor; Op.* 23, *Nachtstücke* (four "Night Pieces"); *Op.* 26, *Faschingsschwank aus Wien; Op.* 28, three *Romanzen;* and *Op.* 68, *Album für die Jugend* (forty pieces).

Although the *Opus* numbers exceed 100, Schumann's frequently-performed works are far fewer. In addition to the piano compositions and the songs, they include the piano quintet and quartet, the four symphonies, an unsurpassed piano concerto, the *Manfred Overture,* three string quartets, the *D Minor Trio* and a *'Cello Concerto in A Minor, Op.* 129.

Larger Works

Schumann's larger works are often marred by lack of control over the formal structure and, in some cases, over the instrumentation. But we must see him in the light of a composer who has something new to say and who has only old ways available in which to say it. In the *Symphony No. 4 in D Minor, Op.* 120, we realize that he is probing Beethoven's model for a solution. He directs the five movements of the work to be played without pause, and he seeks inner unity by deriving the themes of all movements from sources introduced at the beginning, essaying other irregular devices as well, to create a new species of Romantic symphony. In his *Piano Concerto in A Minor, Op. 54,* he also is forced to cast aside the tried and true Classic formula and combine piano and orchestra in a fashion suitable to his unique requirements.

Perhaps, as A. E. F. Dickinson states, Schumann "was always going off in a huff; as conductor and teacher he was incapable of 'tackling' anybody; his critical work scarcely routed the Philistines; even as a composer he could only feel himself a fore-runner, quite apart from the fact that in reputation he was chiefly Clara Schumann's musical husband." Harsh words these, yet in the distance, we may still hear Schumann invoke his beloved Jean-Paul's words:

> O Music, echo of another world, manifestation of a divine being within ourselves, when speech is impotent and our hearts are numb, yours alone is the voice with which men cry out to one another from the depths of their prison, you it is who end their desolation, in whom are resolved the lonely outpourings of their grief.

Suggestions for Further Reading

Abraham, Gerald, ed., *The Music of Schubert*. New York, Norton, 1947.
Boucourechliev, André, *Schumann.** New York, Grove, 1959.
Brion, Marcel, *Daily Life in the Vienna of Mozart and Schubert.** New York, Macmillan, 1962.
———— *Schumann and the Romantic Age*. New York, Macmillan, 1956.
Brown, Maurice J. E., *Schubert: A Critical Biography*. New York, St. Martin's, 1958.
Capell, Richard, *Schubert's Songs*. New York, Macmillan, 1957.
Carse, Adam, *The Orchestra from Beethoven to Berlioz*. Cambridge, Heffer, 1948.
Chissell, Joan, *Schumann*. New York, Dutton, 1948.
Deutsch, Otto E., ed., *Franz Schubert's Letters and Other Writings*. New York, Knopf, 1928.
———— *The Schubert Reader*. New York, Norton, 1947.
Einstein, Alfred, *Music in the Romantic Era*. New York, Norton, 1947.

* Available in paperback edition.

———— *Schubert, A Musical Portrait*. New York, Oxford University Press, 1951.

Flower, Norman H., *Franz Schubert, The Man and His Circle*. New York, Tudor, 1949.

Gleckner, Robert G., and Enscoe, Gerald E., *Romanticism: Points of View*.* Englewood Cliffs, Prentice-Hall, 1962.

Schauffler, Robert Haven, *Florestan: The Life and Work of Robert Schumann*.* New York, Holt, 1946.

Schneider, Marcel, *Schubert*.* New York, Grove, 1959.

Schumann, Robert, *On Music and Musicians*.* New York, Pantheon, 1946.

Starr, William J., and Devine, George F., *Music Scores—Omnibus*, Part 2.* Englewood Cliffs, Prentice-Hall, 1964.

A SAMPLER OF SUPPLEMENTARY RECORDINGS

Collections

Choral Songs of the Romantic Era	Nonesuch 1081
Romanticism	2- Victor LM-6153
Ten Centuries of Music	DGG KL-52/61
2000 Years of Music	Folkways 3700

Music of Individual Composers

Löwe Karl, *Ballads*

Schubert, Franz, *Gesang der Geister über den Wassern*
    Mass No. 2 in G, D. 167
    Mass No. 6 in E flat, D. 950
    Moments Musicaux, Op. 94, D. 780
    Quartet No. 12 in c, "Quartettsatz", D. 703
    Quartet No. 14 in d, "Death and the Maiden," D. 810
    Quintet in A, Op. 114—"Trout"
    Die schöne Müllerin, Op. 25, D. 795
    Piano Music
    Songs
    Symphony No. 8 in b, "Unfinished," D. 759
    Symphony No. 9 in C, "The Great," D. 944
    Trio No. 1 in B flat, Op. 99, D. 898
    Winterreise, Op. 89, D. 911

Schumann, Robert, *Carnaval, Op.* 9
    Concerto in a for Piano and Orchestra, Op. 54
    Dichterliebe, Op. 48
    Fantasiestücke, Op. 12
    Kinderscenen, Op. 15
    Piano Music
    Quintet in E flat for Piano and Strings, Op. 44
    Requiem for Mignon, Op. 98b
    Symphonic Etudes, Op. 13
    Symphony No. 1 in B flat, Op. 38, "Spring"
    Symphony No. 4 in d, Op. 120

Opportunities for Study in Depth

1. We have frequently encountered Wolfgang von Goethe in this and preceding chapters. This influential personality, so well-known in Europe, is an almost obscure figure to many American students. Read a biography of Goethe and compare his brand of Romanticism to his essentially Classical bias.

2. One characteristic of German *Lieder* is that it fitted poetry to music in an absolute bond, with each supplementing the other. Prepare digests of the poets mentioned in this chapter, giving brief biographical sketches, examples of significant works and résumés of their philosophies.

3. Schumann suffered quite dramatically from the mental disorder known as schizophrenia. Investigate this phenomenon and apply what is learned to manifestations exhibited by this composer throughout his life.

4. Schumann was one of the earliest music critics and performed yeoman duty in hailing new composers and publicizing their works. Read some of Schumann's music criticism and compare it with that of another composer-journalist, Hector Berlioz (see Hector Berlioz, *Evenings in the Orchestra,* Baltimore: Penguin Books, 1963).

5. A feature of German Romanticism was a renewed and rather different interest in the child as both an innocent and a sort of "noble savage." Schumann's *Album for the Young* was one of the first volumes of music created for children, in his case, his own. Cite other composers of music for children, including Stephen Heller.

6. Choose a *Lied* by Schubert and one by Schumann. Study each with score and recording, endeavoring to find similarities and differences in manner of treatment—of the text, the piano accompaniment and the prevailing mood.

7. In this chapter we have devoted far too little space to the subject of Schumann's symphonies. Make a study of the four symphonies and prepare a report for presentation to the class.

8. It has been stated that Schubert often used his songs in instrumental works. Through study of scores and recordings make a comparison between his song, "The Trout," as it is presented originally, and the version found in the fourth movement of his *Quintet in A.*

Vocabulary Enrichment

Apollonian and Dionysian polarities
Romanticism
subjectivity
artistic self-consciousness
"Schubertiads"
Lied (pl., *Lieder*)
"long line"
strophic song
varied strophic song
through-composed song

song cycle
modulation
entr'acte
Musikverein
Ländler
Liedertafeln
ballad
Eusebius and Florestan
dramatic cantata
lyricism

Chapter 17.

ROMANTIC VIRTUOSOS
CHOPIN AND LISZT

Here is a whole fortnight that my mind and fingers have been working like two lost spirits—Homer, the Bible, Plato, Locke, Byron, Hugo, Lamartine, Chateaubriand, Beethoven, Bach, Hummel, Mozart, Weber, are all around me. I study them, meditate on them, devour them with fury; besides this I practise from four to five hours of exercises (thirds, sixths, octaves, trills, repeated notes and cadenzas). Ah! provided I don't go mad, you will find an artist in me! Yes, an artist such as you desire, and such as is required nowadays!

—Franz Liszt, Excerpt from a letter

Liszt's phrase, "an artist such as is required nowadays," is a significant one, in that the Romantic movement projected a unique image of the artist as a person above and beyond ordinary restraints and sensibilities. Einstein, in his authoritative study of the Romantic era, notes what he calls the "contradictions," which include an ever-widening cleavage between the artist and his public and the appeals of both virtuosity and intimacy. He writes, "Among the contradictions of the Romantic movement is the fact that, at the same time that it was reviving the past and manifesting its own tendencies toward extreme intimacy and absorption, it raised virtuosity to unprecedented heights." We observe this in the quiet *salon* favorite, Chopin, and in the flashy, popular idol Liszt. It was the latter who coined the phrase, "play to the gallery," who was a deliberate "longhair" and who established the solo piano recital, introduced by J. C. Bach in London, as a fact, supplanting the hodge-podge type of concert-programming we have already mentioned, in which the performer was but part of a "bill" featuring orchestras, choruses, trained dog acts and master jugglers.

Piano Virtuosos

With the improvement of the pianoforte came players whose virtuosity and compositions were influenced by the instrument. Their music enjoyed a vogue, and because the piano quickly became a favorite home instrument, amateurs demanded attractive works, not too scholarly or difficult. So called *"salon"* pieces flooded the music market. The virtuoso reigned supreme and musical taste, as developed by the Bachs, Haydn, Mozart and Beethoven, was threatened with annihilation. "Technic was an end in itself," says Dickinson, "and not a means. In many circles music reached the lowest stage of levity that it has known in modern times, and the agent of this travesty upon art was the piano." This popular style actually broke down the dynasty of the sonata, and the short piece which was to dominate the Romantic period was represented by the *étude* and other free forms. At first the *étude* was a mechanical drill but in the hands of Chopin and Liszt it attained the rank of an art form. Fortunately for music, the *étude* has had many competent champions.

One school of piano virtuosos had its center in Vienna, with Mozart regarded as progenitor; another, in London, was founded by Clementi. Johann Nepomuk Hummel (1778-1837), a pupil of Mozart and *Kapellmeister* to Prince Esterházy, was put up as a rival of Beethoven. Hummel was a brilliant pianist and wrote concertos, which enjoyed extreme popularity at the time, as well as sonatas and *études*. Carl Czerny (1791-1857), whose multitudinous studies are known to every piano student, was a pupil of Beethoven, and a kindly, generous person who was a famous pianist and respected teacher. Jan Ladislav Dussek (1761-1812), a foremost pianist of his day, traveled widely and wrote piano concertos, sonatas, rondos, chamber music and orchestral overtures. He is claimed to be the first to place the piano sideways on the stage, and to compose finger exercises. Ignaz Moscheles (1794-1870), a follower of Hummel, was Mendelssohn's teacher and a friend of Chopin. He toured Germany, France, England and Holland, and composed many brilliant *études,* concertos and a quantity of *salon* pieces.

Muzio Clementi (1752-1832), sometimes called the father of the pianoforte, was the composer of over 100 sonatas and sonatinas as well as symphonies and the *Gradus ad Parnassum,* a monumental set of 100 studies for the development of technique. Although Italian by birth, Clementi spent most of his life in England as pianist, performer and composer. He made many successful concert tours on the continent, in one of which he entered a contest with Mozart. He also was interested in piano manufacture and music publishing. Grove states, "He is the first completely equipped writer of sonatas . . . He played and imitated Scarlatti's harpsichord sonatas in his youth; he knew Haydn's and Mozart's in his manhood, and he was aware of Beethoven's in his old age."

John B. Cramer (1771-1858) won a reputation among leading pianists for his expressive touch and his ability to read at sight. A pupil of Clementi, and a follower in his footsteps, Cramer wrote some attractive and valuable studies. His concertos, sonatas and chamber music are forgotten, but he is remembered as a music publisher who brought out works of Dussek, Clementi, Haydn, Herz, Hummel, Mozart, Daniel Steibelt (1765-1823), Beethoven and Moscheles in addition to operas by Weber, Meyerbeer and Rossini.

John Field (1782-1837), an Irish pianist, brings us into Romanticism with his nocturnes, to which Chopin was especially indebted. As a boy, Field had been apprenticed to Clementi. Traveling with his master, he went to France, Germany and Russia, demonstrating the Clementi pianos. Field elected to remain in St. Petersburg, where he enjoyed honor as a teacher and performer. He composed several piano concertos which won him a temporary fame. In 1832 he played one of them in London, but returned to Russia to die.

Friedrich Kalkbrenner (1785-1849), Henri Herz (1803-1888), Alexander Dreyschock (1818-1869) and Sigismund Thalberg (1821-1871), whose technical skill was fabulous, are only a few of the long list of early piano virtuosos. Carl Maria von Weber (1786-1826) was a precursor of Franz Liszt in his piano compositions; he is more significant, however, for his contributions to German opera, which we shall discuss in a subsequent chapter.

VIOLIN VIRTUOSOS

The growing interest in instrumental music also stimulated violin virtuosos and composers. Unlike the piano, the violin itself had not changed radically, save, as noted earlier, in the modern bow, perfected by Tourte, assisted by Giovanni Battista Viotti, Gaetano Pugnani's (1731-1798) greatest pupil, who was court composer to Marie Antoinette. Viotti was probably the first composer of a violin concerto in sonata form and was a bridge between Corelli and the nineteenth-century school. In all, he wrote twenty-nine violin concertos, of which *No. 22 in A Minor* is often heard. As with pianists, bravura playing was a dominant concern of the violinists. Renowned virtuosos of this early period include Rodolphe Kreutzer, to whom Beethoven dedicated his "Kreutzer" *Sonata,* and Andreas Romberg (1767-1821), who knew Haydn and Beethoven and succeeded Spohr as concertmaster at Gotha.

Nicolo Paganini (1782-1840), whose wizardry and fame are attested to by the wealth of legend surrounding him, was an entity in himself and above any school—one of the violin geniuses of all time. Born in Genoa, he made his first public appearance in 1795. Thereafter, he played to all Europe. In his hands celerity never became calisthenics, for his profound musical feeling and skill flowered in exceptional depth and brilliancy of tone. As far as can be known, Paganini has never been surpassed in technical accomplishments, such as double stopping, chromatic work and *pizzicato*. His compositions were brilliant and remain a backbone of violin technique, revealing new possibilities in writing for the instrument. Schumann, Liszt, Brahms and others used Paganini's compositions as bases of important piano works, while many composers for the violin became his followers.

Ludwig Louis Spohr (1784-1859), a violinist of great fame, took Pierre Rode (1774-1830) as his model, studied violin and composition, and at fourteen won royal recognition. He toured in Germany and Russia and played with young Meyerbeer in Berlin. Concertmaster in Gotha, he also conducted at festivals, at the Vienna Opera House and performed with Paganini. Weber nominated him for choirmaster at Cassel and for thirty-five years Spohr exerted much influence there and achieved a great reputation. He was a friend of Mendelssohn, Beethoven and Rossini, an early appreciator of Wagner, a frequent visitor to England and conductor of many performances in Germany. More interested in a solid violin technique than in the firework methods of his colleagues, he was a fine quartet player. Although a competent contrapuntalist, Spohr was equally a Romantic. Of his 200 compositions, fifty works are for the violin.

Ferdinand David (1810-1873), Mendelssohn's concertmaster, was a pupil of Spohr and Moritz Hauptmann (1792-1868). David became a renowned virtuoso and amazing interpreter, as well as a composer for violin and orchestra. He performed much contemporary music, particularly Schumann's chamber music.

FRÉDÉRIC FRANÇOIS CHOPIN—LIFE

In Chopin (1810-1849) we find the epitome of a Romantic style of composition—a combination of the school of virtuosity which had held the boards for a generation; of a flowering of lyricism; and of a genius of the "boldest, proudest, poet-soul of his time," as Schumann called him. The virtuosity was a result of his own extraordinary piano-playing, to which he added a depth of sentiment that sounded a new chord in music through the ages. At one end of the ladder, Chopin mounted a rung which was perilously close to the vapid *salon* music of the day; but he scaled heights which are possible only through supersensitive, refined creativity and dedication. He opened new doors in tonal variety, dynamics, touch, imagination and feeling. He struck the fancy of nineteenth-century audiences and he still holds it firmly today.

In 1714 a Pole, Nicolas Szop (pronounced Chop), migrated to Nancy, France. In 1787 his grandson, Nicholas Chopin, returned to the land of his forefathers and married a Polish woman. Their only son was Frédéric François Chopin, born February 22, 1810, at Zelazowa Wola near Warsaw. Chopin's father suffered reverses due to the country's political vicissitudes and its numerous partitionings. For a few years, Napoleon gave a small portion of the country independence, but in 1815 the duchy of Warsaw, where the Chopins lived, again became part of Russia. His employment gone, Nicholas Chopin became a teacher of French to the Polish nobility. Frédéric passed a happy childhood, although surrounded by political unrest. He was brought up in his father's school, with his three sisters. Young nobles were his intimates.

His first music teacher was a Bohemian, Adalbert Zywny, who taught Chopin to play Bach. At eight Chopin performed in public and began to compose. After four years, he had learned all that Zywny could teach him. Next he studied with Joseph Elsner (1768-1854), a respected composer, who wisely encouraged Chopin's creative gifts. Young Chopin spent his summers in the country where he heard the music of the peasants and danced the national *Kujawiak*. He was full of fun, a clever mimic, an amateur actor and gifted in improvisation.

Fig. 60. Chopin's Variations, *Opus* 2. The variations on a theme of Mozart's helped establish Chopin's reputation as a composer. (Courtesy Pleyel Collection, Paris.)

His first composition, the *C Minor Rondo,* dates from 1825. *Op.* 2, the set of variations on the Mozart air, *Là, ci darem la mano,* a *Trio for Piano and Strings, Op.* 8, several works published posthumously, such as the *Rondo for Two Pianos, Op.* 73, and the *Sonata, Op.* 4, the *E Minor Nocturne,* and three *Polonaises,* were written before 1828. In 1828 Chopin visited Berlin, and in 1829 he went to Vienna, where he played a concert with success and was hailed as "a young Mozart." By 1830 he already was launched on the career of a traveling virtuoso and left Poland after three concerts, which had brought praise and some financial return.

Chopin departed from Poland, a land he loved with an almost fanatical devotion, with the premonition that he would never return. He arrived in Paris in 1831, after touring the German musical centers, armed with the *F Minor* and the *E Minor Piano Concertos, Ops.* 21 and 11, some *études, nocturnes, valses, polonaises* and *mazurkas.* He was disappointed that Haslinger, the Viennese publisher, who claimed that it was too expensive to publish good music, accepted only the waltzes. At Stuttgart he heard that Warsaw had been taken by the Russians, and he poured out his heartbreak in the tempestuous *Étude, Op.* 10, No. 12, known as the "Revolutionary." In his notebook Chopin exclaimed:

> The faubourgs fired! Titus and Matuszynski (two friends) killed, no doubt! Paskewitsch and that dog from Mohilew seizing the town . . . Oh God, where art Thou? Art Thou there and dost Thou not avenge Thyself? Art Thou not sated with murder? Or art Thou indeed a Muscovite? . . . Maybe I no longer have a mother, maybe a Muscovite has killed her, while I, empty handed here, sigh from time to time, and soothe despair on the piano.

He was welcomed in Paris by the Polish colony and its sympathizers, and soon wrote to a friend: "I am part of the highest society . . . without knowing myself how I arrived there! At any rate, it is there that I find a condition practically indispensable to my existence." Cordially received by the artists, Chopin numbered among his friends, Kalkbrenner, whose piano playing he admired, Cherubini, Bellini, Berlioz, Meyerbeer, Liszt, Hiller, Herz, Moscheles and Auguste-Joseph Franchomme, a 'cellist. "Artists of consummate merit demand lessons from me," he continued, "and attribute to me a place, at least, equal to that which Field occupies."

Kalkbrenner offered to teach him and Chopin seriously considered accepting, but finally, and no doubt, fortunately, refused. "So much is clear to me," he wrote to his old master, Elsner. "I shall never become a copy of Kalkbrenner; he will not be able to break my perhaps bold but noble resolve—*to create a new art-era.*" Chopin gave his first concert in Paris in 1832, at which he played his *E Minor Concerto* and the *Variations, Op.* 2. Of him, Fétis, a French critic, said: "Here is a young man who, abandoning himself to his natural impressions and taking no models, produces, if not a complete renewal of piano music, at least . . . an abundance of original ideas the type of which is found nowhere else."

"I have to give five lessons every morning," Chopin exclaimed. "Do you believe that I am making a fortune? Wrong! My cab and my white gloves, without which I could not be *de bon ton,* cost me more than I earn." During the winter of 1832-33, Chopin played often in Paris, but after 1835, he was seldom heard in public. Every year from 1833 to 1847, publishers brought out his compositions, and he became known in Germany, thanks to Schumann's notice.

His name was constantly coupled with that of John Field, who also had arrived in Paris in 1832. Field's playing and compositions, particularly his nocturnes, stimulated comparisons and Chopin was undoubtedly indebted to him. Despite Chopin's unquestioned position in the most cultivated circles, he was occasionally the butt of disagreeable criticism. H. F. L. Rellstab, a vitriolic Berlin journalist, wrote:

> The author satisfies his taste (to write abnormally and with affectation) with an odious exaggeration. He is indefatigable and I can say insatiable in his searching for discords to the ear, his forced transitions, his cutting modulations, his horrible deformations of melody and of rhythm. Particularly is it a searching for *bizarrérie,* especially for strange sounds, the most abnormal position of chords and the most contrary combinations of fingering. If Mr. Chopin had shown this composition to a master, one may well believe that he would have torn it to pieces and stepped on them, as we have done. Where Field smiles, Chopin grimaces; where Field shrugs his shoulders, Chopin twists his body; where Field puts seasoning in his food, Chopin empties a handful of Cayenne pepper. In brief, if one were to hold the charming works of Field before a deforming concave mirror so that all delicate expression becomes vulgar, one would obtain a work of Mr. Chopin.

Chopin's romance with Mme. Aurore Dudevant, better known as the French novelist, "George Sand," lasted about ten years, (1836 to 1847). Chopin was delicate, of small stature and a few years her junior. George Sand, while not a large woman, was beautiful, dark, often wore male attire and was called an "Amazon" by Liszt, who claimed to have introduced her to Chopin. Her first impression of Chopin was not favorable but they frequently met in a circle that included Liszt and Countess d'Agoult ("Daniel Stern," the novelist). During the winter of 1838-39, Chopin went to Majorca with Sand and her children, Maurice and Solange Dudevant. Chopin had been ill and Sand urged Majorca for convalescence. There she had the opportunity to show what she called *une sorte d'affection maternelle* ("a sort of maternal affection"). The trip was a failure due to bad weather, Chopin's poor health and the hostile attitude of the peasants. The "Raindrop" *Prelude in D flat,* may have been composed at this time.

The visits to Mme. Sand's château at Nohant seem to have been pleasanter. She encouraged Chopin in his composing, took care of him when he was ill and at the same time wrote books and educated her daughter. It must be admitted that Chopin was not an easy person to get along with. He was sensitive, easily depressed, suffering from tuberculosis and extremely nervous and capricious. Differences in opinion on political problems and discord concerning the children led to a break.

In the meantime, Sand's novel, *Lucrezia Floriani,* was looked upon as a revelation of his character in no flattering terms. In the history of her life, however, she denied any such intention. Chopin left Nohant in the spring of 1847 and never went back. George Sand, it is said, tried to bring about a reconciliation but unsuccessfully. Even at the time of his death, she went to his door but one of his friends, afraid of the emotional effect on Chopin, turned her away.

In 1848 Chopin gave his last concert in Paris. He had played in *salons* occasionally, earning enough to live and to help his Polish friends. During the spring and summer of that year, he went to London, where he hoped to meet with artistic and financial reward. He played in the homes of the English aristocracy and gave lessons, but his social obligations proved too strenuous for his failing health. He spent some time in Scotland at the home of a pupil, Jane Stirling, but autumn in London proved disastrous. Chopin was seized by nostalgia and longed to return to Poland, but his earlier premonition of never returning to his native land was to prove true.

His last public appearance was in London at a ball, where he played the piano between dances. He returned to Paris and continued to compose, although he was too weak to teach. His funds were now exhausted, but he was assisted anonymously by the devoted Jane Stirling. His sister went to him, but on October 17, 1849 he died. Two weeks later he was buried at *Père-Lachaise* cemetery in Paris. His heart, at his request, was sent to Warsaw, where it reposes in the Church of the Holy Cross. Chopin, in spite of spending half his life in Paris, remained essentially Polish, a "lonely soul." As Louis Enault, a biographer, said: "The Slavs lend themselves gladly but never give themselves; Chopin is more Polish than Poland."

Frédéric François Chopin—Music

In discussing Chopin's works, we must consider the patriot, who was imbued with the folk music of Poland and its national dances; the favorite of Paris' most distinguished *salons;* the impressionable artist who had arrived in France when the Romantic movement was in full ferment; the virtuoso pianist, contemporary of Kalkbrenner, Liszt, Hiller, Moscheles and Field; the composer who was the greatest innovator of his day in piano technique; and the inventive artist who was a supercraftsman and scrupulous technician. Influenced by Bach, Mozart, Hummel and Field, Chopin's work was carefully wrought; he went over phrases again and again, avoiding the commonplace and showing the same impeccable taste and fastidiousness in his art as in his personal life. He helped to establish the short piano piece as an art form, and, with Liszt and Schumann, created a new type of piano playing, characteristic of Romanticism.

Chopin made many experiments in the use of the damper pedal, of the singing tone and of *tempo rubato,* that has since suffered so much abuse. Of his *rubato* Chopin said, "Fancy a tree with its branches swayed by the wind—the stem is the steady time, the moving leaves are the melodic inflections." He studied the possibilities and limitations of his instrument as no one had before him. "He adjusted all his technical resources, both as a composer and a pianist," says Daniel Gregory Mason, "in the interests of the greatest possible transfusion and intermixture of impressions. This is the secret of his harmonic scheme, so chromatic and full of dissonance; of his lavish embroidery; of his *tempo rubato,* by which the outline of meter itself, so arithmetical and inexorable, is gently relaxed; of his curious soft, light touch, which seemed to glide over rather than strike the keys . . ." Chopin's embroidery was not applied from the outside, but was a result of an inner urge—it has inevitability. Of his pedaling, a contemporary remarked that "the crudest and most chromatic harmonies floated away under his hand, indistinct yet not unpleasing."

Chopin's meager orchestral efforts, including the two piano concertos, belong to his early years. Although he wrote some Polish songs, *Op.* 74, and is credited with the ballet music, *Les Sylphides* (actually a later arrangement), it is his music for piano that most interests the modern listener.

"Like the fugues of Bach, the symphonies of Beethoven, the songs of Schubert and the music dramas of Wagner, Chopin's piano pieces touch the high-water mark of their kind," writes Edward Dickinson. Unlike Schumann, Chopin used no literary titles, but employed terms describing the type of composition—*polonaise, mazurka, ballade* and *nocturne.* In addition to these, he also composed a *Berceuse* ("Cradle Song") *Op.* 57; a *Barcarolle* ("Boating Song") *Op.* 60; four *Rondos* (*Ops.* 1, 5, 16, and a posthumous work for two pianos, published as *Op.* 73); a *Tarantelle, Op.* 43; a *Bolero, Op.* 19; three sonatas for piano, and one for 'cello and piano; a *Krakowiak, Op.* 14; the *Variations on a Mozart Theme, Op.* 2; three *Écossaises, Op.* 72; and the two concertos for piano and orchestra.

POLONAISES AND MAZURKAS

Chopin's first works were **Polonaises,** the form and rhythm of which were familiar to him from childhood. The **polonaise** was a court dance, originating in 1574 after Henry III of Anjou became King of Poland and received the nobility who marched in procession past the throne to stately music. It became a popular national dance in the eighteenth century. Under Chopin's hands it was transformed into a highly-developed stylized dance form. One of Chopin's biographers, Karasowski, divides the polonaises into two groups: those characterized by strong martial rhythms, representing the feudal court of old Poland, of which the A flat, *Op*. 53, is a brilliant example; and those, dreamy and melancholy, picturing Poland in her adversity. The *Fantaisie-Polonaise, Op*. 61, is said to represent the national struggles ending with a song of triumph.

Of quite another variety is the **Mazurka,** a national dance of the people. Chopin loved the folksongs and dances he heard when he was vacationing, and their mark is found in his mazurkas, in which he introduced Polish airs and extended the form in new and individual fashion. Many Slavic folk pieces are in Church modes, that lend a distinct flavor to the mazurkas. In 3/4 meter, often slower than waltzes and with melodic accent withdrawn from the first beat, Chopin's version falls into a sectional A-B-A pattern (mazurka, contrasting trio, and mazurka repeated), not unlike that of the minuet.

VALSES AND NOCTURNES

In his fifteen **Valses,** Chopin is the composer of aristocratic *salon* music. Nieck says: "In them the composer mixes with the world— looks without him rather than within—and as a man of the world, conceals his sorrow and discontents under smiles and graceful manners—— they are, indeed, dance-poems whose content is the poetry of waltz-rhythm and movement, and the feelings these indicate and call forth." The waltzes are among his most popular compositions, especially with amateurs. They are found in *Ops*. 18, 34, 42, 64, 69, 70, and two are without *opus* numbers. It is said that Chopin found only eight of them worthy of publication; the rest were brought out after his death. The Chopin *Valse* resembles a combination of Schubert's *Ländler* with Strauss' Viennese waltz.

Zdislas Jachimecki compares the first **Nocturnes,** *i.e.,* night pieces, written when Chopin was nineteen or twenty, to the youthful creations of Raphael and Mozart. "Of an ideal precision in its ternary structure," he says of the *Nocturne in B Flat Minor,* "it is the pure incarnation of the artist's individuality and breathes out the real charm of sublime poetry." Some of them have been heard so often that they have become bromidic, but in others, the composer achieved his own aspiration to "create tone-poems having individuality."

Études AND *Préludes*

For the student pianist, Chopin's twenty-four *Études* (*Op.* 10 and and *Op.* 25) find their place beside Bach's "forty-eight" (*Well-tempered Clavichord*), and Beethoven's "thirty-two" (*Sonatas*). During his years of practicing, Chopin conceived the idea of writing studies to conquer the technical problems of piano playing, studies that would be more pleasing than those that had annoyed him. He worked with untiring zeal on his *Op.* 10, the first twelve *études*. But Chopin, the sensitive artist, joined forces with Chopin, the inspired pedagogue, in creating the most beautiful and yet thoroughly useful studies in all musical literature. He began them when he was eighteen. In these and the second series, *Op.* 25, Chopin established a technique for the piano, distinct from that of any other instrument. In 1840 he wrote three more *études* for Fétis and Moscheles, to be included in their *Méthode des Méthodes pour le piano*.

The **Préludes** (*Op.* 28) represent a collection of twenty-four short pieces written over a space of seven years (1831-1838). They run through the circle of major and minor keys. Chopin is believed to have finished them during his sojourn at Majorca. Every style and mood is found in the *Préludes:* some of them approach the nocturnes in type; others are heroic, mystic, subtle, and some bravura. One of the most poetic is *Prélude, Op. 45, in C Sharp Minor*. Since Chopin's time, many composers have borrowed both title and style, including Debussy and Shostakovitch.

Ballades, SCHERZOS AND IMPROMPTUS

In the four **Ballades,** Jachimecki sees "the influence of the Romantic literary culture which fashioned the spirit of Chopin's adolescence. . . . The new poetic forms, the new verbal creations of the works of Mickiewicz (Polish poet and friend of Chopin) produced at this epoch, encouraged, even forced the young composer to open new paths for musical expression." The title, *ballade,* for a piano piece, originated with Chopin. He probably took the idea from the vocal ballads of Schubert and Löwe, and was a free agent in its structure—loosely based on sonata-form. In the *Ballades,* Chopin was an innovator. He anticipated the orchestral tone-poem and the twentieth-century sonata. In the fourth Chopin borrowed not only from sonata-form but also from *rondo* and variation. It is one of his transcendent works.

No.	Opus	Key	Literary Source	Dedication	Publication
1	23	G minor	Konrad Wallenrod and	Baron von Stockhausen	1836 (written before 1831)
2	38	F	Ondine by Mickiewicz	Robert Schumann	1840
3	47	A flat	Die Lorelei by Heine	Mlle. de Noailles	1842
4	52	F minor		Baroness C. de Rothschild	1843

The four **Scherzos,** too, are Chopin originals. Despite the name, the form has no direct relationship to that of Beethoven nor the eighteenth-century minuet; neither is it related to the initial meaning of the word, a "jest." "How is 'gravity' to clothe itself," Schumann asked, "if 'jest' goes about in dark veils?" Broadly speaking, the minuet form is retained in Chopin's use of a trio, as a contrast to the first part, which is repeated after the trio. But sonata-allegro form is strongly suggested in the development of the themes. In the *B Minor Scherzo, Op.* 20, Chopin made use of a Polish Christmas cradle song. Of the four, the *B Flat Minor* has enjoyed for years the greatest popularity.

No.	Opus	Key	Dedication	Publication
1	20	B minor	T. Albrecht	1835
2	31	B♭ minor	Countess Adele de Fürstenstein	1838
3	39	C# minor	A. Gutmann (a favorite pupil)	1840
4	54	E major	Mlle. J. de Caraman	1843

Building on Schubert's title, Chopin wrote four **Impromptus:** *A Flat, Op.* 29; *F Sharp, Op.* 36; *G Flat Op.* 51; and the posthumous *Fantaisie-Impromptu in C Sharp Minor, Op.* 66. The *F Minor Fantaisie, Op.* 49, published in 1842, is one of the greatest works in all piano literature, a tone-poem for piano which might well be considered a prototype of the Liszt symphonic poem, Jachimecki says: "This composition radiates a spirit completely modern and is a source of many of the means employed by the music produced from that day to this."

CONCERTOS AND SONATAS

In Chopin's two concertos (C minor, *Op.* 11, and F minor, *Op.* 21) and his Sonatas, we find Romantic sonata-form, a modification and dissolution of the Classic and the Beethovenian, in accord with Romantic content. The concertos, written before Chopin was twenty, are significant examples of the fecundity of his genius, and gave rich promise of the high place he was to fill. The first was dedicated· to Kalkbrenner, the second to the Countess Delphine Potocka. Two of his three sonatas for piano, the *B Flat Minor, Op.* 35, and the *D Minor, Op.* 58, are heard often. The first, in C minor, is *Op.* 4 and was published after his death. Particularly popular is the *B Flat Minor's* "Funeral March" movement, often parodied. The *B Minor,* however, has a maturity and depth which makes it a masterpiece among all Romantic sonatas. These works have often been criticized as being weak in form. Hugo Leichtentritt, the German critic, contends that no one has yet measured the extreme subtlety of the structure to realize that Chopin had made an intensive study of Beethoven's last works. He says that the last word has not yet been said about the sonatas.

FRANZ LISZT—LIFE

Chopin had written to Franz Liszt (1811-1886), one of the most interesting men of music, that he was not suited to giving concerts. In eighteen years in Paris, Chopin had performed publicly only nineteen times. "The public intimidates me," he wrote, "I feel asphyxiated by their breathing, paralyzed by their curious looks, dumb before their strange faces. But you, you are meant for that, because when you don't win the public over, you have got something you can overwhelm them with." Liszt was indeed a master at overwhelming audiences. Theatrical by nature, he encouraged an orgiastic hero-worship (to the point of ladies collecting his cigar butts) that enveloped him during his adolescent and early adult years. He went so far as to engage in a musical duel with Thalberg, a rival performer, to establish, once and for all, his pianistic supremacy. Liszt furthered the cult by dressing in a most extravagant manner, for instance, wearing green gloves and featuring a different necktie for each day of the year. He is said to have reproved Czar Nicholas I for daring to talk while he, Liszt, was playing.

Liszt was born in Raiding, Hungary, a year after Chopin. His father, a steward employed by Prince Esterházy, was a musical amateur who yearned to have his son become a musician. Liszt's birth, occurring during a comet's advent, assured the parents that their child would be outstanding. Again we meet a father to whom Mozart was an ideal. Adam Liszt was Franz's first teacher, and when the boy was six years old, he was launched on a musical career. At nine Liszt started tours under his father's management, played successfully in Vienna and studied with Salieri and Carl Czerny, who charged little at first, and nothing later, because, he said, "The progress of the small boy in so short a time pays me amply." At twelve Liszt set Paris "on fire." In his own words, he was thrown into the midst of a brilliant society that applauded the *tours de force* of a child to whom it gave the glorious and withering stigma of a little prodigy. The experience helped to create a complex that made him in turn loathe and crave adulation.

Liszt's improvisations and technical skill were prodigious. He easily attracted wealthy patrons, and a six-year subsidy was arranged for him.

London was as kind to him as were Vienna and Paris. George IV remarked, caressing the little boy's curls, "I have never heard his equal, not only for his perfection in playing, but for the richness of his ideas." In 1823 his father brought Liszt to Cherubini to be entered in the Paris Conservatory, but the stern old Italian looked the awe-inspired little boy in the eye and said, "impossible . . . you are not French." So, he studied under Ferdinand Paer (1771-1839) and Antonin Reicha (1770-1836). Paer suggested that Franz write an opera, and, to a mediocre libretto, he composed *Don Sanche ou le Château d'Amour* (*Don Sanche or The Castle of Love*). In 1825 it was produced successfully in Paris.

After Liszt's father died in 1827, the young man gave up his tours and, as his subsidy had reached its end, he started teaching. Furthermore, he gave his mother all the money he had earned during his remunerative years because, he said, she had always sacrificed for his benefit. Thus, he early showed the generous nature that contributed so largely to his future reputation. For eight years he continued giving lessons in Paris. During this time he plodded along, but inwardly he was maturing in a *milieu* that formed his character for better and for worse. In his personality were mysticism and pragmaticism, vanity and humility. But Paris, emerging from the Revolution, was just as complex. License in ethical and moral matters challenged past standards of behavior.

As a center of art life, Paris attracted all varieties of intellectuality and froth, side by side. Social life was gay and frivolous. Composers of tinsel and coruscation were popular—Kalkbrenner, Pleyel and others were *salon* favorites. Solid musical fare had to be served with decorative garnishes for popular assimilation, the more arabesque the better. It was in such an environment that the youthful Liszt grew up, and with all his desires for greatness, he was seriously affected by his worldly surroundings, causing him to turn constantly to religion and philosophy in search of an adjustment between life and art as he experienced them.

Liszt was a student and possessed a fine mind. His manner was artistry personified. He was in the center of post-Revolution and nascent freedoms, when the watchword of Paris, "to fight for liberty," was heard in the brilliant *salons* as well as in the streets. Saturated in Romanticism, he lived in the time of George Sand, Chateaubriand, Balzac, Flaubert, Victor Hugo, Delacroix and Lamartine. He showed a marked interest in Saint-Simon's socialistic program, yet he was an aristocrat at heart. "Nobility was innate," writes Felix von Weingartner. ". . . He possessed a certain aloofness. He was not everyone's familiar, and was particular in his choice of associates. But he admired only intellectual distinctions, and paid no heed to caste."

In 1834 Liszt's intimacy with the Countess D'Agoult began, and although he was "too keen-minded to be really deceived by the current fallacies, but at the same time not austere or independent enough to reject what was so universally accepted, he let himself go with the current, and half-blindedly, half-ironically, played the game he saw others playing," chronicles Daniel Gregory Mason. At any rate, he became involved with this beautiful married woman, and although he sporadically tried to end the relationship, it lasted for ten years, spent in Switzerland and Italy. The couple had three children, one of whom was Cosima, later to be the wife of von Bülow and later still of Richard Wagner. It is an undecided point whether Liszt offered marriage and was denied it on the ground of his inferior social rank, but it is well known that the Countess and Liszt experienced an accumulating distaste for each other.

Liszt took refuge in religious study for surcease from amorous experiences. Not for long, however, for, as Mason says, "If paganism had . . . summed itself for him in . . . Countess d'Agoult, . . . monastic Christianity to which he now reacted found its . . . priestess in the Princess of Sayn-Wittgenstein," who lived with him platonically from 1847 on. Theirs was a sad affair in many ways. She had tried to divorce her husband, the divorce was retracted, and even at her husband's death, the couple did not marry. Nevertheless, she was a tremendous power in leading Liszt to broader paths and things greater than mere instrumental virtuosity.

Liszt's most brilliant period of virtuosity was in the years between 1839 and 1847, during which he composed many piano transcriptions and made incessant international tours, including one to London. His amazing technique, brilliant improvisations and magnetic personality made him a dominating power among pianists, probably the greatest that ever lived—a Paganini of the piano.

His *largesse* was unfailing. For some reason, the London tour was not as successful financially as his agent had hoped, so Liszt, characteristically, made up the loss. When Pesth, later Budapest, was inundated by flood in 1837, he personally supplied the victims with money. He established a poor fund for Raiding. After he had passed his youthful period, he never again accepted payment for teaching and thus became a one-man philanthropic institution for hundreds of students. Moreover, in 1839, when the funds were insufficient for the Beethoven Memorial at Bonn, it was Liszt who supplied the deficit of $10,000.

With his appointments at Weimar, a second phase of Liszt's career commenced. From 1843, he was visiting court artist, and from 1849 musical director, with every resource at his command. Weimar was captivated by his breadth of view, his virtuosity and his personality. It

Fig. 61. "An Afternoon at Liszt's"—lithograph by Josef Kriehuber. Liszt, the virtuoso's virtuoso, is seen here (from left to right) with the artist, Berlioz, Czerny and Ernst. (Courtesy New York Public Library.)

was at Weimar that Liszt became the great *Meister* and where he seized every opportunity to bring out so-called "radical" works. At the Princess' urging, Liszt labored with an avowed purpose of helping living composers, even to his own undoing (as when he produced Cornelius' *Barbier*). In collaboration with the Princess Caroline, he also prepared some not very dependable brochures on Chopin and the young Wagner.

During his Weimar tenure, Liszt gave, among other lasting encouragements to musicians, Wagner's *Tannhäuser* (1849) and *Lohengrin* (1850); Joseph Joachim Raff's (1822-1882) *König Alfred* (1851); Anton Rubenstein's (1829-1894) *Das verlorene Paradies* (*The Lost Paradise*, 1851); Berlioz's *Benevenuto Cellini* (1852); Wagner's *Der fliegende Holländer* (*The Flying Dutchman*, 1853); Schubert's *Alfonso und Estrella* (1854); Schumann's *Genoveva* (1857); Edouard Lassen's (1830-1904) *Landgraf Ludwigs Brautfahrt* (*Count Ludwig's Wedding Journey*, 1857); and Peter Cornelius' (1824-1874) *Der Barbier von Bagdad* (1858).

Had Liszt only helped Wagner, in whom his interest was steadily manifested, he would have done a great deal. Wagner commented:

When ill, broken down and despairing, I sat brooding over my fate, my eye fell on the score of *Lohengrin*, totally forgotten by me. Suddenly I grieved that this music would never sound from off the death-pale paper. I wrote two lines to Liszt; his answer was the news that preparations for the performance were being made on the largest scale the limited means of Weimar would permit.

Weimar become a Mecca; musicians of all nations gathered at this spot to investigate the *Zukunftsmusik* ("Music of the Future"), a rather mystical concept of the synthesis of the arts as envisaged by Liszt, Wagner and Berlioz. Amy Fay, an American attending Liszt's master classes at Weimar, offers us a description of the stimulating atmosphere in her book, *Music Study in Germany*:

> Liszt is the most interesting and striking looking man imaginable—tall and slight, with deep-set eyes, shaggy eyebrows, and long, iron-gray hair, which he wears parted in the middle. His hands are very narrow with long and slender fingers that look as if they had twice as many joints as other people's. All Weimar adores him, and people say that women still go perfectly crazy over him. When he walks out he bows to everybody just like a king! The Grand Duke has presented him with a house beautifully situated on the park, and here he lives elegantly, free of expense, whenever he chooses to come to it.

Liszt's mode of life at Weimar was quite rigidly scheduled. He arose at four in the morning and composed until seven. After a second breakfast he attended early Mass. Following an hour's rest he would return to work or pay some visits. His noon meal was taken regularly with the Princess. Returning to his quarters, he received pupils every other day in the late afternoon. It was not unusual to have a "lesson" last four hours. Afterwards, he might play cards for an hour. About eight in the evening he would join the Princess for supper, a repast consisting of ham and Hungarian red wine, with cigars enjoyed by both. At nine he retired.

His teaching was concerned less with matters of technique than with interpretation, and all was governed by the strictest protocol. Everyone would stand when he entered a room, and no one dared speak to him unless he were first addressed. While a student was playing, Liszt would walk about, smoking and occasionally interrupting to illustrate at the piano how a passage should be performed. Even Liszt was not without his problems, however, as the following anecdote from Weingartner's *Memoirs* indicates:

> Once, when a pretty young lady played a Chopin ballade in execrable fashion, Liszt could not contain ejaculations of disgust as he walked excitedly about the room. At the end, however, he went to her kindly, laid his hand gently on her hair, kissed her forehead, and murmured, 'Marry soon, dear child—adieu!'

Liszt's life at Weimar was almost too full, with teaching, conducting and performing. A final concert for his own benefit was held in 1847, but he continued to donate his services to others. Moreover, during this period Liszt managed to compose some of his most outstanding works, including symphonic poems, symphonies and other compositions that projected the ideals of the "Music of the Future." But an end comes to everything. Considerable consternation had been aroused by his sympathy for Berlioz and Wagner. In 1859, because of unmerited criticism for presenting Cornelius' opera and complications about his relationship with the Princess, Liszt found his Weimar post untenable and soon relinquished it, thereafter dividing his time between Weimar, Rome and Budapest, where he was publicly feted and received all he could desire of acclaim, having his oratorio, *Christus,* performed (1873) and being made president of the new Hungarian Academy of Music (1875).

Pope Pius IX was fond of Liszt, who spent much of his time in Rome after leaving Weimar. In 1866 the Pope conferred on this ertswhile Saint-Simonite and free-thinker the title of Abbé, with four minor Franciscan orders. Liszt's religious yearnings and his fatigue led him to seek a rather egoistic solace in Catholicism and to aspire to write great music for the Church, including *Christus, The Legend of St. Elizabeth* and the *"Gran" Mass.* Other significant works are a *Fantasia and Fugue* on the *chorale, Ad nos ad salutarem undam,* from Meyerbeer's opera, *Le Prophète;* a *Fantasia and Fugue on B-A-C-H;* and an *Evocation in the Sistine Chapel,* based on Mozart's *Ave Verum Corpus.*

Although he had had a glorious life, save, perhaps, for his self-inflicted love affairs, Liszt had failed to make much of an impression in Great Britain. In 1886, however, he received his ultimate English triumph, when his oratorio, *St. Elizabeth,* was given at St. James' Hall, with an ovation such as no man had ever before enjoyed. After more successes in Paris, London and in Luxembourg, where Liszt presented his last concert in July, 1886, he visited his widowed daughter, Cosima, at the Wagner Festival in Bayreuth, where he attended performances of *Parsifal* and *Tristan und Isolde.* He was so weakened by bronchitis that upon reaching home he was confined to bed and passed away on the last day of the month. Liszt, as he wished, was buried in Bayreuth. The Princess Wittgenstein, his heir and executrix, died six weeks later.

Franz Liszt—Music

Paul Henry Lang writes: ". . . as a composer, Liszt occupies a unique position in the history of modern music: almost all of our accomplishments in the field of harmony, orchestration, and construction of form originated in his inspired and inquisitive mind." Like Schumann,

Liszt was very much influenced by Romantic literature. He, too, was confronted with the problem of finding a new way of stating his musical message. In his twelve symphonic poems, which we shall discuss in the next chapter, he hit upon a solution that other composers recognized as congenial. Moods and movement suggested by scenes and feelings in verbal form were organized in terms of program and through **thematic transformation,** in which a musical idea, often associated with a non-musical image, undergoes extensive alterations, metric, rhythmic, inter-vallic, etc., but always serves the musical purpose of its creator, which Liszt asserted was the "renewal of music through its inner connection with poetry." Unlike Schumann, Liszt dared to throw off the restraints of Classicism and fuse intellectuality with ecstasy, through boldly rhap-sodic writing.

PIANO COMPOSITIONS

Although capable of nuance and delicacy, Liszt, we must admit, often reveled in effect rather than in substance. Albeit a "learned" man of vision, he was also a practical virtuoso who too frequently gave his pub-lic "what it wanted." He stretched the possibilities of the piano far be-yond what should be expected of it. Were it not for the fact that few musicians had his amazing technique, the instrument might have lost its inherent beauties and rightful function. Yet, his transcriptions for the piano have sweep, freedom and freshness. They also served to bring symphonic and other works to those who were unable to attend orches-tral and opera performances. Among Liszt's transcriptions are the Beethoven symphonies, several compositions by Berlioz, many opera selections, paraphrases of songs by Schubert, Schumann, Franz and Chopin and assorted miscellany, now quite neglected. Despite Liszt's virtuosity and love of applause, he conscientiously interpreted every work he performed in the style intended by its composer.

Liszt's piano compositions range from the sentimental lyricism of the popular *Liebestraum* ("Love's Dream," one of three nocturnes originally conceived as songs), to the powerful rhetoric of the one-movement *Sonata in B Minor* (1854), written at Weimar and dedicated to Schu-mann. Flashing moments are to be found in the *Études d'execution transcendante,* the two concert studies, *Waldesrauschen und Gnomen-reigen* ("Forest Rustlings" and "Gnomes' Dance"), and the *Paganini Studies.* The three series of *Années de pèlerinage* (*Pilgrim Years*) con-tain some lovely things, such as *Les Jeux d'eau à la Villa d'Este* ("The Fountains at the Villa d'Este," inspired by his Cardinal friend's fabulous water displays outside Rome). In the nineteen published *Hungarian Rhapsodies* is captured the picturesque vigor of Gypsy music. Liszt's legend, *St. François d'Assise prédicant aux oiseaux* ("St. Francis of Assisi Preaching to the Birds") is a moving lyric.

Liszt wrote one of the first cyclic piano concertos in his *Concerto No. 1 in E Flat* for piano and orchestra (1849). In this, the piano roars along with a large orchestra and its virtuosic idiom seems built in. The second and third movements are melded together with a review of initial thematic materials at the end. Other works for piano and orchestra, conceived in a *fantasia*-like free form, are the *Totentanz* ("Dance of Death," 1849, a paraphrase of the *Dies Irae,* inspired by an Orcagna fresco) and a second piano concerto (1848, revised 1856-61).

A composer of some excellent songs, Liszt set *Du bist wie eine Blume, Der König von Thule, Die Lorelei* and *Kennst du das Land* ("Knowest Thou the Land"), among other poems. Moreover, Liszt was a prolific creator of secular choral works.

Der Meister

As a teacher Liszt probably influenced more musicians than any other, unless it be Cherubini. Some men coming under Liszt's tutelage and stimulus, in addition to the opera composers already mentioned, were Leopold Damrosch, the German-American conductor; Alexander Ritter (1833-1896), a composer who married Wagner's niece; Emil Sauer, an eminent pianist and teacher; Carl Lachmund, an American who established his own conservatory in New York City; Edvard Grieg; Alexander Borodin; Isaac Albéniz; Rimsky-Korsakov; Camille Saint-Saëns; Bedřich Smetana; Franz Scharwenka (1850-1924) and the American composer, Edward MacDowell.

One of Liszt's most far-reaching contributions was the inestimable effect he had on men such as Grieg and Dvořák, whom he encouraged to emphasize inherent nationalistic elements in their music, thus establishing national schools. Liszt himself was far from being a nationalist. Although Hungarian by birth, he did not speak the language, conversed in broken German and was fluent only in French. His thoughts, as we have seen, were saturated in Italian themes and sentiment; his province was universal. Although a man of the world, he foresaw a larger role for himself and his colleagues. "We believe," he wrote, "as unshakably in art as in God and mankind, both of which find in it a means of noble expression."

* * * * *

In both Chopin and Liszt, the virtuosos, we find similarities and differences that characterize musical Romanticism. Both, in their private lives, flaunted convention and indulged themselves as others secretly wished to. Both, in common with many Romantic innovators, neglected chamber music and opera in favor of other concerns. Both, in individual ways, enlarged the possibilities of writing for the piano; Liszt often attempted to "orchestrate" the instrument, while Chopin emphasized the lyricism of the voice—"Everything must be made to sing," he said. Both espoused a fashionable if egoistic Catholicism, a Romantic aspect particularly prominent among the poets. Both met the public taste. Both were influenced by French Romanticism. Both contributed to modifications of Classic sonata form and the repertoire of short lyric works. Both apparently found artistic sustenance in their grand passions.

Yet Chopin was an introvert, while Liszt was an extrovert; Chopin was abstract, while Liszt was literary; Chopin was essentially self-centered, while Liszt was extremely generous; Chopin limited his art to a particular idiom, while Liszt spread himself too thin, in pursuit of his grandiose ambitions.

Again and again in the following pages we shall encounter the rich variety that characterizes Romanticism, both in its music and in its colorful personalities. A unifying thread, linking Schubert and Schumann, Chopin and Liszt, Berlioz and Mendelssohn with other composers of the early Romantic period, exists in their wholehearted dedication to what they were doing, despite the odds for or against them. As Schubert wrote:

> To thee 'tis given, holy Art and great,
> To figure forth an age when deeds can flourish,
> To still the pain, the dying hope to nourish . . .

SUGGESTIONS FOR FURTHER READING

Abraham, Gerald, *A Hundred Years of Music*. London, Duckworth, 1949.
Beckett, Walter, *Liszt*. New York, Farrar-Straus-Cudahy, 1956.
Boucourechliev, André, *Chopin: A Pictorial Biography*. New York, Viking, 1963.
Bourniquel, Camille, *Chopin*.* New York, Grove, 1960.
Day, Lillian, *Paganini of Genoa*. New York, Macaulay, 1929.
Einstein, Alfred, *Music in the Romantic Era*. New York, Norton, 1947.
Gide, André, *Notes on Chopin*. New York, Philosophical Library, 1949.
Hedley, Arthur, *Chopin*.* New York: Collier, 1962.
Huneker, James, *Franz Liszt*. New York, Scribner, 1911.
Jonson, G. C. Ashton, *A Handbook to Chopin's Works*. London, Reeves, n.d.
Lahee, Henry C., *Famous Violinists of To-day and Yesterday*. Boston, Page, 1899.
Liszt, Franz, *Frederic Chopin*. Glencoe, Free Press, 1963.
Lucas, Veronica, *Letters of George Sand*. London, Routledge, 1930.
Mason, Daniel Gregory, *The Romantic Composers*. New York, Macmillan, 1930.

* Available in paperback edition.

Schonberg, Harold C., *The Great Pianists from Mozart to the Present.** New York, Simon & Schuster, 1963.

Searle, Humphrey, *The Music of Franz Liszt.* London, Dent, 1954.

Sitwell, Sacheverell, *Liszt.* New York, Philosophical Library, 1956.

Starr, William J. and Devine, George F., *Music Scores—Omnibus,* Part 2.* Englewood Cliffs, Prentice-Hall, 1964.

Weinstock, Herbert, *Chopin: The Man and His Music.* New York, Knopf, 1949.

Wierzynski, Casimir, *The Life and Death of Chopin.* New York, Simon & Schuster, 1949.

A SAMPLER OF SUPPLEMENTARY RECORDINGS

Collections

Romanticism	Victor LM-6153
Ten Centuries of Music	DGG KL-52/61
2000 Years of Music	Folkways 3700

Music of Individual Composers

Boccherini, Luigi, *Quartet in A, Op. 33, No. 6*

Chopin, Frédéric, *Ballades*
  Concerto No. 1 in e for Piano, Op. 11
  Études
  Krakowiak, Rondo, Op. 14, for Piano and Orchestra
  Mazurkas
  Nocturnes
  Polonaises
  Préludes
  Scherzos
  Sonata No. 3 in b, Op. 58
  Waltzes

Clementi, Muzio, *Concerto in C for Piano and Orchestra*

Dussek, Johann Ladislaus, *Piano Music*

Hummel, Johann Nepomuk, *Concerto in b for Piano and Orchestra, Op. 89*

Liszt, Franz, *Années de pèlerinage*—2nd Year, "Italy"
  Concerto No. 1 in E flat for Piano and Orchestra
  Consolations
  Hungarian Rhapsodies for Piano
  Mephisto Waltz
  Missa solemnis (Gran Festival Mass)
  Prelude and Fugue on B-A-C-H for Organ
  Réminiscences de Don Juan (after Mozart)
  Sonata in b for Piano
  Transcendental Études (6) after Paganini
  Wanderer Fantasie, Piano and Orchestra (after Schubert)

Paganini, Nicolo, *Virtuoso Violin Music*

Spohr, Ludwig, *Concerto No. 8 for Violin, "Gesangscene"*

N.B. It is very interesting, especially in Chopin's case, to compare the interpretations of different pianists as they perform the same works.

OPPORTUNITIES FOR STUDY IN DEPTH

1. Compare an *impromptu* of Schubert with one by Chopin. What, if any, features do they have in common? What are the formal and stylistic differences? What is an *impromptu*?

2. Make a study of Chopin and Liszt as teachers, citing their individual points of view, their methods, their unique pedagogical contributions.

3. We have mentioned that Liszt in his youth was very much impressed with the social philosophy of Saint-Simon. Prepare a paper on Saint-Simon and his doctrines, striving to show how they relate to other Utopian ideas of the time.

4. Read George Sand's novel, *Lucretia Floriani,* of which Heine remarked, "She has outrageously ill-used my friend Chopin in a detestable novel divinely well written." Are Chopin and Prince Karol similar? In what ways?

5. In this chapter we have noted in some detail the rise of a cult of musical virtuosity during the nineteenth century. What has become of the star performer of yesteryear? Have we continued this tradition? In what ways is musical virtuosity manifest today? Cite examples.

6. Paganini was not only an outstanding violinist but a composer whose themes have been used again and again by others. Investigate versions of Paganini themes found in works by Schumann, Liszt, Brahms and Rachmaninov. Present a digest of conclusions to the class.

7. Chopin originated the Romantic piano form known as a *prélude,* although in reality it does not necessarily preface anything but rather stands as an independent short work. Debussy and Shostakovitch have also written sets of preludes. With the aid of recordings and scores, compare the preludes of these three composers, noting similarities and stylistic differences.

8. Investigate more fully the career of John Field and write a report on the subject in the form of a magazine article. Periodical references will be of help here as well as volumes included in "Suggestions for Further Reading."

VOCABULARY ENRICHMENT

virtuosity	*ballade*
salon piece	*berceuse*
piano recital	*barcarolle*
technique	*tarantella*
étude	*scherzo*
nocturne	"Music of the Future"
valse	master class
polonaise	rhapsody
mazurka	transcription
prélude	posthumous
tempo rubato	thematic transformation
damper pedal	

Chapter 18.

PROGRAM MUSIC—BERLIOZ AND MENDELSSOHN

If the composer's tone is grave,
He puts us all to sleep;
If the composer's tone is gay,
He isn't one bit deep.

. . . .

No matter how he turns his phrase,
Nobody's content;
Therefore the composer must
Follow his own bent.

—Felix Mendelssohn, March 15, 1826, "Verses for his mother's birthday"

To "follow his own bent" was certainly a credo of the Romantic musician who, starting with materials and forms of the past, felt a destiny which beckoned him into previously unexplored territory and teased him with tantalizing possibilities of new combinations and functions of tone. Each composer's bent, being personally oriented, leaned in an individual direction, creating for us the many paradoxes of Romanticism, that in turn were responsible for the movement's wealth of expression. Berlioz and Mendelssohn, for example, differed in many ways, as we shall discover. They were temperamentally, aesthetically, nationally and vitally dissimilar; yet both Berlioz and Mendelssohn contributed to, and were tempered by, the prevailing aura.

Each new era in music attests to its validity as a living thing. Vital art adapts itself to new necessities and new erasures, with the advent of new conditions and the birth of new ideas, heralding new eras. Whether or not the new direction men give to an art satisfies majorities is beside the point; expansion is its life-blood and without it music would have died before it had even established itself. In the nineteenth century, Classicism and Romanticism played their foundational and characteristic parts. The best composers built on both, but music, closely allied to heart and mind, was now prepared for a further expansion. It was, as it were, magnetically-drawn to the increased possibilities of the orchestra, and its collusion with it resulted in program music, a salient factor of this period.

PROGRAM MUSIC

Program music is instrumental music with extra-musical connotations, in which a composer introduces a poetic idea into the context of sound, or by tonal means suggests a scene or deliberately reflects a mood through his use of the various elements of music. As the poets of Romanticism became more individual, so did poetry fire the imagination of composers, impelling them toward suggestion and symbolism in music. The composer could now choose any subject he desired, compatible with his ability to clothe it aright. He was held to no set form, to no one procedure or method of handling his material. Indeed, another renaissance had dawned with all the advantages and pitfalls of a new freedom.

Program music, of course, was not radically new. All songs are programmatic in the sense that the texts condition the listener's response to the wedding of words and music. We have noted the concern of early opera composers with this problem. The germs of instrumental program music have been glimpsed in Janequin's *Battle of Marignan*, Daquin's *Cuckoo*, Rameau's *The Hen*, Kuhnau's *Bible Sonatas,* Schumann's *Carnaval* and Beethoven's *"Pastoral"* *Symphony*. Two distinctly different types of program obtain here. For instance, Kuhnau's *Bible Sonatas* tell, as far as the music of his day could, a concrete story, whereas Mendelssohn's *Hebrides Overture* depicts in onomatopoetic music the emotional effect of the marine cave on the senses of the composer. Therefore, program music may mirror the psychological as well as the literal.

The questions arise—Is program music a step down? Is absolute (unprogrammed) music a higher type? We are inclined to the belief that music without a program, unfettered with concrete picturing, can rise to greater heights and deeper profundities. But, as Rolland comments, "Do not let us say Music can . . . or Music cannot express such and such a thing. Let us say rather, if genius pleases, everything is possible . . ." Whatever one's opinion, it cannot be gainsaid that program music further developed the orchestra's potential and provided a valuable connection between literature and music. Besides being a keynote of advance in nineteenth-century art, it was also a final answer to the strivings of musicians in the distant past to weld poetry and music together. Moreover, the Classic sonata, as a form, seemed to have worn itself out with the ultimate expansion of Beethoven, and composers began to examine poetry, history, science, fiction and legend, to treat their materials with freer transfusion of thought, in a welcomed capitulation to whatever scheme the subject dictated.

Before proceeding to a discussion of the various types of Romantic program music, we shall pause a moment to consider several pertinent tenets of musical perception, that are expanded in L. B. Meyer's admirable study, *Emotion and Meaning in Music*. The author asserts that musical meaning is a product of expectation. "If, on the basis of past experience, a present stimulus leads us to expect a more or less definite consequent musical event, then that stimulus has meaning." Conversely, a stimulus that does not arouse expectations is meaningless. Music may activate tendencies or instincts, that is, pattern reactions which are automatic within the cultural conditioning; *i.e.,* music in slow tempo, minor mode and low register can evoke a dolorous response in mood communication.

In connection with program music, Meyer continues:

> The difficulty with an aesthetic of music based upon connotative and mood responses is not that the associations between music and referential experience are fortuitous or that there is no causal connection between music and feelings. The difficulty is that in the absence of a specific referential framework, there is no causal nexus between successive connotations or moods . . . What the program does is to provide the causal connection between the successive moods or connotations presented in the music . . . The great disadvantage of a program lies in the fact that it is a powerful temptation toward extra musical diversion.

During the Romantic era program music evinced itself in five forms: (1) incidental music to plays; (2) the concert overture; (3) the program symphony; (4) the programmatic orchestral suite; and (5) the symphonic or tone-poem. An early Romantic example of incidental music is that written by Mendelssohn for Shakespeare's play, *A Midsummer Night's Dream*. Mendelssohn also wrote a seascape in the form of a concert overture, *Hebrides, Op.* 26 ("Fingal's Cave"). Berlioz's *Symphonie fantastique* is the prototype of a program symphony. Programmatic suites, derived from incidental music or ballet scores, abound in the works of Romantic composers. But perhaps the most original and the most significant form of Romantic program music is the **symphonic poem** or the **tone-poem,** pioneered by Franz Liszt. This is a self-contained orchestral work in a single movement structured in a series of contrasting sections, integrated by non-musical as well as musical means.

LISZT'S SYMPHONIC POEMS

Liszt developed the symphonic poem to subjective lengths and freed composers to write to the limit of their skill and imagination. Classic forms were left so far behind in this "expansion," as Bekker calls it, that it needed a Brahms to intensify musical ideas and keep the forms of Haydn and Beethoven from vanishing altogether. It was Beethoven and Mendelssohn in their overtures and Berlioz in his *Symphonie fantastique,* however, who opened a way for the tone-poem. Liszt's greatest contribution to the music of the nineteenth century.

He took his ideas from poetic sources and sometimes wrote extraordinary music. His *"Faust" Symphony* (1857) is the consummation of his musical and literary experience. Wagner was influenced by it, for some of the themes evidently made unforgettable impressions on him. Although entitled a symphony, the work is actually a combination of three symphonic or tone-poems: "Faust," "Marguerite" and "Mephistopheles," major figures in the Goethe drama. There is a companion work, *Symphony after Dante's Divine Comedy* (1867), originally with three movements, "Inferno," "Purgatory" and "Vision of Paradise." (*Faust* was dedicated to Berlioz, *Dante* to Wagner.) Whether or not these works are indeed program symphonies or tone-poem cycles is a moot point. They amply illustrate Liszt's dependence upon, and use of, literary inspirations.

If, on the one hand, Liszt's chromaticism, which Wagner borrowed and employed with skill, his cannonading octaves, and the over-sentimentality of his quieter moments presage the extravagance of post-Romanticism, his effective use of thematic transformation and musical logic, on the other, are milestones in Romantic music, as exemplified by the twelve symphonic poems. In them, Liszt arrives at a fine coherence and excellence that, for instance, makes the third *Les Préludes* (1854), based on verses of Alphonse Lamartine, one of the most interesting works of the era. Liszt's is an essentially subjective interpretation of the poetic theme—"What is life but a series of preludes to that unknown song whose initial solemn note is tolled by Death?" Subdivided into six sections, *Les Préludes* blends two leading motives (*Leitmotifs*), subjecting them to many kinds of expressive thematic transformation. In such a work we find freedom from formulae—a gift from Liszt to his contemporaries and to his twentieth-century musical heirs. Others of the symphonic poems that are occasionally performed include *Tasso, Lament and Triumph* (*Symphonic Poem No. 2,* 1849), initially intended as an overture to Goethe's work of that name and dominated by a triplet theme; *Orpheus* (*Symphonic Poem No. 4,* 1854), a hymn to music with the mythical Orpheus as its protagonist; and *Mazeppa* (*Symphonic Poem No. 6,* 1854), adapted from an earlier concert study with the same title, drawn from a poem by Victor Hugo, who celebrates the fortitude and apotheosis of the Cossack hero, Hetman Mazeppa.

HECTOR BERLIOZ—LIFE

A French critic writes of Hector Berlioz (1803-1869):

> From the first he strove to free French music from the oppression of the foreign tradition that was suffocating it . . . He was fitted in every way for the part . . . His classical education was incomplete. M. Saint-Saëns tells us that 'the past did exist for him' . . . He did not know Bach. Happy ignorance! He was able to write oratorios like *L'Enfance du Christ,* without being worried by memories and traditions . . . Berlioz never sought to be anything but himself . . . By the extraordinary complexity of his genius, he . . . showed us . . . a great popular art, and that of music made free.

To which Cecil Gray adds:

> To his admirers he is . . . one of the very greatest composers . . . to his adversaries he is less than a second-rate figure, a mere scene-painter in sounds, with nothing save a gift for orchestration . . . Either you receive at once from the very first work of his that you hear, a thrill akin to an electric shock, or else you are completely insulated and rendered forever immune by a pachydermatous rubber hide of indifference or distaste.

Hector Berlioz was born near Lyons, France, the son of a physician who insisted upon Hector studying medicine. As he was peculiarly unfitted to do this, Berlioz broke with his father after attempting to accede to his demand and thereby cut himself off from parental patronage. In 1822 he began his musical studies, supporting himself by ushering in a theater, singing in choruses and teaching. Unlike Mozart, Mendelssohn and Liszt, who in boyhood were accomplished technicians, Berlioz had very little background, except the will to compose and some knowledge of the guitar and flute. Had he not been endowed with an imagination comparable to a steam roller, he never could have overridden his deficiencies.

After entering the Paris Conservatory, he was taught by Jean-François Lesueur (1760-1837) and made rapid progress, soon writing the *St. Roche Mass.* But for the next seven years Berlioz was in alternate conflict and disgrace, and at sword's point with everyone except Lesueur. Beethoven, Gluck and Shakespeare were his idols. Cherubini, the director of the Conservatory, was anathema to the young man. Despite everything, however, he forged ahead. After the *St. Roche Mass,* Berlioz composed *8 scènes de Faust Op.* 1, the overtures, *Les Francs-Juges* and *Waverley,* the *Symphonie fantastique Op.* 14 and a *fantasia* on Shakespeare's *The Tempest.*

In 1830 Berlioz at last achieved his soul's desire, the coveted *Prix de Rome,* only to petition the government, after two years in Italy, to be allowed to return to his beloved but unsympathetic Paris. Permission granted, he returned to France in 1832 with *La Captive,* a work delineating the anguish of an alien in a foreign land; *Lélio, Op.* 14b, intended as a sequel to his revised *Symphonie fantastique*; and the overtures, *King Lear, Rob Roy* and *La Corsaire.*

During the same year he met and married an Irish actress, Henrietta Smithson, whom he had long admired from afar. Their life together was unhappy, but Berlioz never ceased to support Henrietta, even though he left her and engaged in other affairs, making himself and everyone else miserable. At the end of his life, he laments in his *Memoirs,* "I am a poor little child worn out by a love that was beyond me." It was this love of love, a Romantic characteristic, that he put into his opera, *Les Troyens (The Trojans)* and in the *"Nuit serene"* ("Serene Night") movement of *Roméo et Juliette.*

Berlioz joined the staff of the *Revue et Gazette Musicale* in 1837 and proved to be an outstanding, if begrudging, music critic. The first edition of his valuable work on orchestration, *Traité de l'instrumentation et d'orchestration modernes avec supplement, Le Chef d'orchestra,* was published in 1844. In 1852 Berlioz joined the Paris Conservatory as librarian, thereby having ample opportunity to study scores, which seem to have been from boyhood his main source of instruction.

In the meantime, Berlioz composed steadily. From 1834 to 1840 he wrote *Harold en Italie, Op.* 16, a work for orchestra with viola *obbligato,* commissioned by none other than Paganini himself, who paid the creator the munificent sum of 20,000 francs; a huge and unconventional *Messe des Morts, Op.* 5 (*Requiem*); a grand opera, *Benvenuto Cellini,* which aroused little enthusiasm; a "symphony with choruses," *Roméo et Juliette, Op.* 17; *Symphonie funèbre et triomphale, Op.* 15; and some songs and cantatas. His later compositions include a "concert opera" and "dramatic legend," *La Damnation de Faust, Op.* 24, from which we occasionally hear selections, such as the irrelevant but stirring "Rakoczy March" and the "Dance of the Sylphs"; a *Te Deum, Op.* 22, for tenor, three choirs, orchestra, brass band and organ; the appealing sacred trilogy, *L'Enfance du Christ, Op.* 25; an *opéra-comique, Béatrice et Bénédict* based on Shakespeare's *Much Ado about Nothing* and premiered by Liszt in 1862, and a gigantic grand opera in two parts, *Les Troyens,* not performed in its entirety until 1920.

Berlioz's commitments did not prevent him from traveling extensively. In 1842-43, he made a tour through Germany, where, for the first time, he met appreciation—oxygen for such a one as he. He was acclaimed by Liszt and the Weimar circle, and reverberations of his success reached Paris, his cold mistress. Another tour of Germany and France enhanced his reputation; a trip to Russia in 1847 was also triumphal. Berlioz conducted the New Philharmonic concerts in London (1853) and directed performances in Baden-Baden and elsewhere. Paris esteemed him enough by 1856 to make him an Academician, although to Berlioz the honor, with its stipend, only meant "fifteen less reviews a year." He wrote to the Princess Wittgenstein that he had not yet become pompous, for his uniform had not arrived!

In 1855 Berlioz remarried, but his relationship with Mlle. Martin Recio, a singer, was as unfulfilling as his first marriage had been. When she died, however, Berlioz found life an agony of loneliness. Moreover, his only son, Louis, died at sea, and his *Les Troyens à Carthage* was dropped from the repertoire of the *Théâtre Lyrique*. This was the final straw. In 1864 he exclaimed, "I have no more hopes or illusions or aspirations. I am alone. Every hour I say to Death, 'When you like!' " But consistent with his temperament, he feared that which he beckoned. After *Les Troyens,* Berlioz never composed again. In 1868, following a trip to Russia, his health failed and he died at the age of sixty-six. Paris, which had killed him with her indifference, honored him with a great public funeral, and, ten years later, a memorial concert. Supersensitive, impetuous, quick-tempered, brilliant to the point of burning up his own strength and courageous in holding firmly to his musical philosophy, Berlioz was another in the long precession of art martyrs.

Hadow, in a typically effusive Romantic vein, states of Berlioz:

> That he possessed genius is beyond all question . . . No composer has ever been more original, in the true sense of the term; none has ever written with more spontaneous force . . . His imagination seems always at white heat; his eloquence pours forth in a turbid, impetuous torrent which . . . overpowers all restraint.

HECTOR BERLIOZ—MUSIC

Although Berlioz was a contemporary of Schumann, Chopin, Liszt, Mendelssohn and the young Wagner, he was nonetheless an independent and, in comparison with the North German Romanticists, out-romanced Romanticism, in a uniquely Latin way. Superficially his *forte* was violent effect and bizarre combinations, which resulted in people criticizing his music as deafeningly noisy, as our illustration attests. It is certainly true that he had a tendency to subordinate beauty to accent, and charm to conglomerate sonority. Nevertheless, Berlioz shows an extraordinary sense of rhythm and a gift for strong melodic lines that often penetrate his turbulences. Heine called Berlioz "a gigantic nightingale, a lark the size of an eagle, such as existed in the primitive world." Schumann tagged him a "raging bacchant."

Fig. 62. "Hector Berlioz Conducting"—German satirical engraving. Berlioz was a skilled conductor as well as composer, but as we see here his orchestration was considered deafening by some of his listeners.

Berlioz wrote effective sound pictures, tinted with local color, often of an Italian nature, as in his popular *Le Carnaval romain, Op.* 9. As representative of the Romantic movement in French music as was Victor Hugo in French literature, Berlioz felt that music must excite the imagination. But he was far too French to sacrifice form and clarity altogether. As one critic puts it, he was "cooly impetuous," and his daring rests on different premises than that of his Teutonic colleagues. Berlioz is *the* French Romantic composer and the only outstanding one to his time, save Rameau, who was French-born and unfettered by foreign trappings. If a musical megalomaniac, Berlioz's nice skill in orchestration often leads him to fine discriminations. For his studies and accomplishments in orchestration alone, he has been placed with the greatest masters.

"He does not command his familiar spirit, he is its slave," writes Rolland. "Those who know his writings know how he was simply possessed and exhausted by his musical emotions." Berlioz wrote so quickly that he was forced to invent a shorthand to notate the *Messe des Morts* rapidly enough to encompass inspiration. His style of writing for voices illustrates his ability to utilize every means to heighten emotional effects. We recognize in *Tristan* how definitely Wagner was influenced by the score of *Roméo et Juliette*.

Not for Berlioz was the short lyric piano piece. His thoughts were couched in larger terms. Of *Les Troyens,* Cecil Gray writes that "in sheer grandeur and vastness of conception there is nothing in the whole range of opera to be compared with it, with the exception of the very different *Ring*." The remarkable *Messe des Morts* is scored for sixteen trombones, sixteen trumpets, five *ophicleides* (keyed brass instruments invented at the end of the eighteenth century), twelve horns, eight kettledrums, two bass drums and a gong, together with the usual nucleus. When asked if he weren't the man who wrote for orchestras of 500, Berlioz replied, "Not always, Monseigneur, I sometimes write for 450." Love of the largest certainly had its birth in Europe and not in America! In his autobiography, Richard Wagner speaks highly of performances of Berlioz's *Symphonie funèbre et triomphale* that he had heard in Paris, performed originally by a wind band of 200 instruments and subsequently by combined military band (120) with symphony orchestra (130).

BERLIOZ—CONTRIBUTIONS

Berlioz's contributions to music through the ages include: (1) the formulation of the **program symphony;** (2) the creation of *l'idée fixe* as a dramatic and structural unifying device; and (3) many unique innovations in the field of orchestration. Examples of each of these are found in the *Symphonie fantastique.* Written but three years after the death of Beethoven, this symphony departed from all previous models to create a symphonic (or anti-symphonic) form consistent with the composer's Romantic ideals, and one which, in sheer sound, overwhelms us to this day.

An *episode de la vie d'un artiste* (*An Episode in the Life of an Artist*), the *Symphonie fantastique* projects a detailed autobiographical program, written by the young composer as a result of his infatuation with Henrietta Smithson. It describes the drug-laden amorous dreams of a young musician who muses with alternate hope and despair upon the thought of his beloved. The five movements are entitled: I. *Rêverie, Existence passionnée* ("Reveries, Passions"), a free-form movement, discontinuous in motion, in which the lover examines his "weariness of soul" and "volcanic love"; II. *Un Bal* ("A Ball"), in the form of an elegant French waltz, wherein the lover visualizes his beloved at a brilliant fête; III. *Scène au champs* ("Scene in the Country"), a bucolic idyll of variations in 6/8 meter, in which the artist broods and wonders about her, as shepherds pipe and thunder rumbles in the distance; IV. *Marche au supplice* ("March to the Gallows"), in which the lover dreams he has killed his loved one and is condemned to death by guillotine (depicted with extreme realism); V. *Songe d'une nuit de sabbat* ("Dream of a Witches' Sabbath"), an orgiastic fantasy and double fugue, full of "unearthly sounds, groans, shrieks of laughter, distant cries," carried into satire with a parody of the Gregorian *Dies Irae* theme, interwoven in a complex tonal tapestry. This type of musical satire, we believe, prefigures Strauss' *Till Eulenspiegel* and other black-humor compositions.

Berlioz does not rely solely on his overwrought "program," however. Rather, he employs a musical device to draw together the various hysterical aspects of the work, an *idée fixe* (a recurrent theme), through which, as the composer explains, "the beloved one herself becomes for him a melody . . . that haunts him everywhere." Stated simply in the first movement, Berlioz's basic musical idea of forty measures is subsequently subjected to all sorts of transformations by the composer, but, in contrast to variations of Classic writers, it retains a literary significance as well as a musical one. Mason notes:

> By discerning that . . . a composition might be unified rather by the interplay of characters and events, or in other words, of dramatic motives, of which the music was merely representative, he opened the way for Liszt and the modern program composers.

By the time he was forty-five years old (when Mendelssohn died), Berlioz had completed the bulk of his work; yet it would require a book in itself to detail his orchestral innovations. As Carse writes, Berlioz "delved deeper and with more success into the art of orchestration than did any one before him."

The instrumentation of the *Symphonie fantastique* is enlightening in its size and variety. The score calls for the usual strings and double woodwinds, with the addition of four horns, two cornets, two trumpets, three trombones, two tubas, two more bassoons, bells, bass drum, four tympani, piccolo, clarinet in E flat, English horn and harp. Many individual touches appear. The harp makes one of its first entrances in a symphonic composition in the second movement; the pastoral affinity of the English horn colors the third movement; the little clarinet shrieks effectively in the diabolical fifth movement; and trombones are allowed to carry important themes. Moreover, we encounter new methods of using instruments, such as muting the horns, striking the cymbals with sticks, tipping drumsticks with sponges, employing *divisi* writing for double basses and tympani—all commonplace practices today, but extremely radical in Berlioz's time.

According to Carse, Berlioz's "knowledge of the instruments and his thorough investigation of their techniques, capabilities, and the possible uses to which they might be put, are set forth in his well-known textbook and are put into practical form in his own works"—all this in tribute to a musician who was unable to play any instrument well enough to perform in public.

DEVELOPMENT OF THE ORCHESTRA

A short digression seems appropriate here in order to review the development of the Romantic orchestra, which, with the piano, was the Romantic composers' favorite "instrument." The large symphony orchestra was a product of the nineteenth century, an outgrowth of chamber orchestras of the eighteenth-century courts, of the first opera orchestras and of movements in Germany, such as the Viennese and Mannheim schools. Court bands of the fourteenth and fifteenth centuries antedate the innovations of the *camerata* and of Monteverdi, who shocked the forty musicians accompaniying *Orfeo* by demanding such string techniques as *tremolo* and *pizzicato*. Alessandro Scarlatti had employed the string section as the nucleus of his orchestra, using it to accompany voices. Bach and Handel, in some of their *concerto grossos,* accompanied the *concertante* with a *ripieno* consisting of the string section. Lully used harpsichord, string, trumpets, flutes, oboes and tympani, then new to the orchestra. Handel wrote for the instrumentation of the standard chamber orchestra (excluding the clarinet), although he did not concern himself with the blending of various *timbres.*

Between Bach and Handel and Haydn and Mozart lay a transition in methods of orchestration. The same evolution that turned composers from polyphonic forms to those of the sonata and symphony necessitated a different type of instrumentation. While Rameau worked in Paris, others were laboring in Germany. In Gluck, we find that the transition is no longer in progress, but actually completed. "Instruments ought to be employed not according to the dexterity of the players, but according to the dramatic propriety of their tone," he said. Carse explains, "To the viola, the Cinderella of the string orchestra, Gluck was the fairy-god-mother who rescued the instrument from a mean position and made it not only independent and indispensable, but discovered in it an individuality which was quite its own . . ." Although Gluck used the clarinet charily, he amplified trombone harmonies in *mezzo-piano* passages.

Orchestration of the Classic period was no longer improvised. The choice of instruments was carefully indicated in the score. Many instruments became obsolete, as we have noted earlier, and others were standardized. The Classic symphony orchestra was largely a German creation. In the schools "poor scholars" were given a free education with the understanding that they were to follow the "musician's trade" and to play in concerts organized by the cities and the courts. Thus, orchestras were instituted in Munich, Stuttgart, Dresden, Darmstadt, Hamburg, Leipzig, Berlin and Mannheim.

Haydn's orchestra at Esterház consisted of strings, one flute, two oboes, two bassoons, horns, trumpets, kettledrums and after 1776, a clarinet. Mozart learned the possibilities of color effects from the Electoral orchestra at Mannheim. Gossec, a pioneer symphonist in Paris, established an orchestra in the *Concerts des amateurs* (1770) and laid a foundation of symphonic music that was continued by François-Antoine Habeneck (1781-1849), founder of the *Société des concerts du Conservatoire*. The London Philharmonic Society was founded in 1813 and The New York Philharmonic Society in 1842.

Beethoven picked up the orchestra as it was at the end of the eighteenth century, and soon made changes in the treatment of the winds, particularly the clarinet and horns, as well as the percussion instruments. Although the trumpets and trombones did not make much headway, the string section was much changed from Haydn's arrangement of parts. Carse notes, "The viola seems to transfer its allegiance, and becomes, so to speak, a large violin rather than a small violoncello." The *"Eroica"* marks the emancipation of Beethoven's orchestra. In the *tutti* of the first movement of the *Ninth Symphony,* Carse continues, ". . . Beethoven touched a type of orchestration well ahead of his time." Through use of sudden dynamic changes, from *fortissimo* to *pianissimo,* strongly-accented beats and long, well-constructed climaxes, often achieved by means of orchestral scoring, Beethoven augmented the dramatic intensity of his works.

Beginning with Weber, the Romanticists further developed the orchestra's emotional possibilities, Weber produced according to Carse, "a type of orchestration more highly colored, more showy, and generally more transparently effective than that of the greater master of symphonic development." Spontini furthered dramatic orchestration by his practical and effective solution of problems of balance and power. Rossini contributed variety and colorful use of the woodwinds in solo. Extraordinary progress was made from 1820 to 1830, a decade that witnessed Beethoven's *Ninth Symphony,* Weber's *Der Freischütz, Euryanthe* and *Oberon,* Schubert's *"Unfinished" Symphony,* Rossini's *Semiramide* and *William Tell,* Mendelssohn's *Midsummer Night's Dream Overture* and Berlioz's *Symphonie fantastique.*

The four-family instrumental complement was enlarged and standardized. More attention was given to the brass as solo instruments and to the use of woodwinds to balance the strings. The natural horn was gradually discarded in favor of the valve horn, and more daring innovators wrote melodies for solo trumpet. With the introduction of the trombones, the brass choir completed its four-part harmony. Giacomo Meyerbeer made use of many accessory instruments, such as the piccolo, English horn, bass clarinet, four trumpets besides the usual brass, extra stage windbands, bells, organs, three tympani and two harps. Although his orchestration was often more interesting than were his musical ideas, Meyerbeer was "a keen colorist, and one who loved rich and showy effects . . . He handled his orchestra with more independence and enterprise than any of his Parisian or German contemporaries, Berlioz alone excepted," Carse comments.

FELIX MENDELSSOHN—LIFE

If the gods wilfully denied Schubert, taunted Schumann and bedevilled Berlioz, they smiled on and even embraced Felix Mendelssohn-Bartholdy (1809-1847), who came of a well-to-do, cultivated Jewish family, who had adopted Christianity. His grandfather, Moses, had been an erudite philosopher and historian, and his father was a prosperous banker. From childhood Felix was surrounded by loving care and the most stimulating people. His parents were versed in music; his beloved sister, Fanny, was a fine pianist and is said to have written some of the *Songs without Words*; his brother, Paul, was a violoncellist and baby Rebecca sang.

We have already noted that Mendelssohn's "bent" or path diverged almost completely from that of Berlioz. Where the latter pushed into new, dense and lonely ways, Mendelssohn strolled along the middle of a stylish avenue, an attractive kindly person and a polished, facile artist. As D. G. Mason writes:

> That Mendelssohn should have been a romanticist at all is a proof of the strength of the romantic tendency in his day; he seemed born rather for the severest, purest, most uncompromising Classicism; and if he did, as a matter of fact, come to share the ideals of his age, it

was in his own way and for his own ends. The crudities, the exaggerations, the morbid self-involution of the extreme phases of the movement, certainly never infected him. For this happy immunity he was indebted largely to the fortunate conditions of his life, both personal and artistic.

His home life was idyllic. The family moved from Hamburg, where he was born, to his grandfather's house in Berlin (1812). They soon outgrew this home and moved to *Leipzigerstrasse* No. 3, where they had a large hall in the garden in which they held Sunday afternoon concerts. In Berlin the Mendelssohns became the center of a large international group, among whom were Heine, Wilhelm von Humboldt, Paganini, G. W. F. Hegel (who always played cards), Raehel and Karl August Varnhagen, W. Müller, Rietz, Ferdinand David, Mendelssohn's favorite violinist and later concertmaster of the *Gewandhaus* Orchestra; Bettina Brentano von Arnim, friend of Goethe and Beethoven; Carl Friedrich Zelter (1758-1832), Moscheles and hundreds of others. Felix composed for these Sunday afternoon concerts and conducted them, while Paul and Fanny played, and Rebecca and Edward Devrient, a baritone, sang.

By the age of twelve Mendelssohn had written many works and was barely second to Mozart in style, grace, taste, spontaneity and prolific production. Moreover, he was familiar with the great masters, of whom Bach and Beethoven were his favorites, while Weber fascinated him. In addition, he issued from his own presses, two "garden" newspapers.

Although living in a happy environment, he had inherited a delicate constitution and was high-strung and nervous. He was baffled by defeat and hated Berlin when the Italian producer. Spontini, withdrew his opera, *Die Hochzeit des Camacho* (*The Wedding of Comacho,* 1825), after its first performance. Mason notes:

> His affection for his relatives was of passionate intensity; a slight misunderstanding or coolness would reduce him to tears; he could not work when his brother or sister was ill; and the death of his sister Fanny was a shock from which he never recovered. His friendships were romantic in their ardor and in their exacting demands; he showed in them, indeed, the childish egotism of the over-sensitive.

Between the ages of seventeen and eighteen, Mendelssohn composed *Die Hochzeit,* a surprisingly mature *Octet for Strings, Op.* 20, and his magical *Midsummer Night's Dream Overture, Op.* 21, worthy of the play itself, which is praise enough. A Romantic spirit manfests itself in the lyricism of these early works. It was Mendelssohn's good taste, however, that disciplined all his undertakings, whether in landscape drawing which he loved, or in his studies from the ancients, that he began by translating Terence's *Andria* (the first Latin poem to be translated in its original meter) for entrance into the University of Berlin (1826).

Fig. 63. Thomaskirche, Leipzig—Felix Mendelssohn. Mendelssohn's affinity for Leipzig was heightened by his discovery of, and high regard for, Bach, whose church he sketched. (Courtesy The Bettmann Archive.)

In 1828 Mendelssohn started his campaign Bach-ward. He sparked a performance of the *St. Matthew Passion,* with a few amateurs, which fired the *Singakademie* to present it under his baton in 1829, one hundred years after its premiere in Leipzig. But whether it was due to his youth, his Jewish background or the high position of his family, Felix received little appreciation from the musicians of Berlin.

Accordingly the young man set out on an extended tour, visiting London and Scotland (1829), Munich (1830), Vienna, Rome, Naples and other Italian towns, Düsseldorf, Switzerland, Paris and once again, London (1832). In London he made his debut in 1829 with the Philharmonic Society in the Argyll Rooms, where he presented his *Symphony No. 1 in C Minor, Op.* 1, composed in 1824. He wrote to his mother, "I was received with immense applause . . ." Before his second London sojourn he had written the *Symphony No. 5 in D Minor, Op.* 107 (the "Reformation"), the *Hebrides Overture, Op.* 26, a *String Quartet in E flat, Op.* 12, the *Concerto No. 1 in G Minor* for piano, *Op.* 25, vocal music and an organ piece to celebrate Fanny's marriage to William Hensel, an artist. Although Mendelssohn loved London, where he was always popular, he loathed Paris. One visit there was sufficient.

Throughout the tour, Mendelssohn composed every morning and was a social lion the rest of the day. But he made spiritual and intellectual grist of all he experienced. When he first saw the sea at Dobberan on the Baltic, he was inspired to compose *Die Meerstille und glückliche Fahrt, Op.* 27 ("Calm Seas and Prosperous Voyage"). His first ideas for the "Scottish" *Symphony No. 3 in A Minor, Op.* 56, and the *Hebrides Overture ("Fingal's Cave," Op.* 26), came from his visit to Scotland. Like many North Germans, he fell in love with the sunny climes of Italy, which he later drew upon for his *Symphony No. 4 in A, Op.* 90 (the "Italian"). Everywhere he met the world's great and made brilliant appearances as a conductor, performing his own compositions as well as masterworks of the past. As an able conductor, he raised the standard of orchestral performance and was one of the first to abandon an instrument and give himself wholly to the baton.

On the death of his teacher, Zelter, who was director of the Berlin *Singakademie,* Mendelssohn applied unsuccessfully for the vacant position. Again, Berlin had defeated him. Shortly thereafter, he conducted for the first time the Lower-Rhine Festival, and then accepted the management of musical affairs in Düsseldorf, only to relinquish the post because it was not congenial, although he was immensely appreciated. After another appearance as conductor at the Lower-Rhine Festival in Cologne (1835), Mendelssohn eagerly accepted directorship of the *Gewandhaus* Orchestra in Leipzig, which he developed, with the aid of Ferdinand David, into a virtuoso outfit. Busy as he was, he still had time for sports and society. At the home of Clara Wieck, he was introduced to his warm and enthusiastic friend, Robert Schumann.

At the *Cäcilienverein* at Frankfurt, Mendelssohn not only enjoyed professional success, but also met the daughter of a French Reformed Church clergyman, Cécile Jeanrenaud, whom he married in 1837. The union proved a happy one, from which were born five children. Moreover, in 1837, Mendelssohn had the opportunity of listening to his oratorio, *St. Paul, Op.* 36, as a member of the audience at Exeter Hall (he had previously conducted it in 1836 at Düsseldorf). He said he found it "very interesting." Before leaving for Birmingham, where *St. Paul* was repeated, Mendelssohn played a recital of Bach's organ works at Christ Church, London. His skill was so captivating that the verger finally withdrew the organ blowers, in order to empty the church.

All the while, Mendelssohn was ceaselessly busy. He showed his interest in the obscure genius of Schubert by introducing the "Great"

Symphony No. 9 in C, which Schumann had unearthed. His concerts were made even more memorable by performances of all four Beethoven overtures to *Fidelio.* He and his wife also attended the unveiling of a statue to Bach, in front of the St. Thomas' School. While in Leipzig, Mendelssohn persuaded the town council to raise the salaries of the men in the *Gewandhaus* Orchestra, a characteristically generous gesture.

After the completion of other festival work in Birmingham, Mendelssohn accepted, after eleven years' entreaty by King Friedrich Wilhelm IV, the directorship of music at a proposed Academy of Arts in Berlin (1841). As *Kapellmeister* of Saxony and Prussia, he was now unhappy in hapless Berlin and often sought comfort in Leipzig, Düsseldorf, London and Switzerland. Within a year the Berlin Academy was doomed, but the King appointed Mendelssohn director of the *Domchor* (Cathedral choir), with the privilege of living where he pleased. So off he went to Leipzig in 1843, and, with a monetary grant from the King, opened a conservatory.

After nine years' work on the score, Mendelssohn presented his oratorio, *Elijah,* at Birmingham, on his ninth visit to England (Aug. 26, 1846). This performance brought him the greatest ovation of his career. Not satisfied, the composer immediately began to rewrite the sprawling work, which, despite moments of unevenness, is a Romantic and exciting adaptation of the Bachian and Handelian form. Pressed for compositions by the King, working on a *Christus* (unfinished), seeking a suitable opera libretto—not so easily pleased as Mozart—teaching, conducting, ceaselessly active in outside affairs, Mendelssohn, already tired from his labyrinthine life, was prostrated by the shock of his sister Fanny's death. He became so depressed and ill, that after a few months, he succumbed at Leipzig on November 4, 1847, with his wife, David, Moscheles and Conrad Schleinitz (1802-1881), who succeeded him as director of the Conservatory, at his side. The excitement caused by his short illness and death was as if royalty had passed—not only in Leipzig, but all over Europe and America. An elaborate church funeral was given this "darling of the gods," appropriately ending with portions of Bach's *St. Matthew Passion.* Numerous Mendelssohn Societies were formed in his honor.

Felix Mendelssohn had aided the cause of music and musicians, including Chopin, Schubert, Liszt, Bach, Schumann, Beethoven and countless others. He was quick to assess the genius of Paganini, Moscheles and other virtuosos, and gave himself to their advancement. Everyone, including Goethe, had loved this well-adjusted, erudite, kindly man, who was in everything he did, punctilious, high-minded, affectionate and generous.

FELIX MENDELSSOHN—MUSIC

Mendelssohn's music is characterized by its grace and attention to detail. Far from the bombast of Berlioz, it is delicately-conceived, relatively unimpassioned, approximating the contours of traditional German melody, imbued with lyricism and controlled through musical logic. Always harmonious in its symmetry and craftsmanship, Mendelssohn's music elevates clarity over richness, and, above all, exalts a refinement that precludes robustness and vulgarity. His use of differentiated orchestral colors, clean and undimmed, is a marvelous achievement. And while this most Classic of Romanticists adhered to old forms and old precepts, he garbed them in new raiment, with a tendency toward darker instrumental colors and an evolution stemming from Beethoven's *Sixth,* in that impressions, rather than concrete images, are evoked. Mendelssohn was in his own way a poet of nature, a subjective interpretor, so well illustrated in his drawings as well as in his musical seascapes. As a Classically-oriented composer, however, Mendelssohn added to the chamber-music repertoire and produced the most interesting oratorios since Bach and Handel.

His contributions include additions to the repertoire of short lyric piano pieces, an original and very popular violin concerto, *Op.* 64, wherein certain formal changes occur, as evinced in the functional integrated *cadenza* and the elimination of the orchestral exposition, works on the Weber-modeled form of **concert overture** (an independent, single-movement composition for orchestra based on a program but developed in terms of symphonic technique), the increment of six sonatas to the literature for the organ and the composition of **incidental music** (numbers to be performed during important scenes and between acts of a play). Indeed, Mendelssohn, if overestimated in his day, is a much larger musical figure than that suggested by the composer of a too-familiar saccharine *"Spring Song,"* the exit march for the bride and groom (first used in 1858 at the wedding of the English Princess Royal) or an inflated graduation processional (the "March of the Priests" from incidental music to Racine's *Athalie, Op.* 74).

As well known as anything Mendelssohn composed are the eight volumes of *Lieder ohne Worte* (*Songs without Words*), a very apt title for the short lyric piano pieces. A partial survey of his many compositions includes five symphonies, of which a symphony-cantata, the *Lobgesang* (*Hymn of Praise*), is counted No. 2; seven concert overtures; two piano concertos; two, two-piano concertos; a *Violin Concerto in E Minor, Op.* 64; seven string quartets; two string quintets; two piano trios; three piano quartets; a sextet for piano and strings; several violin and violoncello sonatas; numerous piano works—three piano sonatas and a *Rondo Capriccioso in E, Op.* 14; variations, among which are the *Variations Sérieuses in D Minor, Op.* 54; six organ sonatas, *Op.* 65; a *Liederspiel, Die Heimkehr aus der Fremde (Homecoming)*, composed for his parents' silver wedding anniversary; two *Festgesänge* for male voices, one written to commemorate the 400th anniversary of the invention of printing; incidental music to works by Shakespeare (*i.e., The Midsummer Night's Dream, Ops.* 21 and 61), Goethe (*i.e., Die erste Walpurgisnacht-The First Walpurgis Night, Op.* 60) and Sophocles (*Antigone, Op.* 55 and *Oedipus in Colonos, Op.* 93); many vocal quartets for male and mixed voices; eighty songs; the two great oratorios; eight *Psalms* for various media; a cantata, *Lauda Sion, Op.* 73; and unpublished material, now in the Berlin State Library.

Until Berlioz's, Liszt's and Wagnerian methods were assimilated, Mendelssohn's orchestration was considered exemplary. He used the strings to good advantage, somewhat audaciously dividing the violoncellos and exploiting the lower registers for effect. Yet he was master enough to keep the strings graceful, light and brilliant. His handling of the woodwinds was discriminating. Toward the brasses, however, he remained conservative. Carse comments:

> The lack of trombones in most of the symphonies and concert overtures certainly left his brass section harmonically more or less helpless, and although the horns are often allowed expressive melody, and the trumpet parts do occasionally include notes other than the open notes of its natural instrument, he seems to shrink from allowing the brass group to develop the fuller use of its melodies and harmonic capabilities . . . Love of refinement, and dread of anything approaching vulgarity, no doubt proved the drag . . . in this particular respect. In making frequent use of brass tone played very softly, Mendelssohn helped considerably to diffuse knowledge of that valuable effect.

ROLE OF THE CONDUCTOR

Only second to his creative efforts came Mendelssohn's role as a conductor, that figure who was to emerge as yet another virtuoso, until he assumed the stature of such prominent personalities of the twentieth century as Arturo Toscanini, Leopold Stokowski or Leonard Bernstein. Conducting, as an art, had developed gradually over hundreds of years. The leader of an ancient Egyptian orchestra kept time by clapping his hands. Heinrich von Meissen, the *Minnesinger,* conducted a choir of singers and players early in the fourteenth century with a long baton in his left hand. In the fifteenth century, time was beaten by a roll of paper called a *sol-fa*. The conductor was a time-beater when the intricacies of polyphonic music demanded his aid. When the contrapuntal style declined, the baton disappeared, and in early Italian opera, the director sat at a harpsichord, accompanying recitatives and leading the players. (Purcell, Handel and Schütz conducted this way.) In succeeding opera, too, it became customary for the harpsichordist to lead the singers, while another conductor, playing the violin, looked after the instrumentalists.

An account from 1719 states that "one man conducts with the foot, another with the head, a third with the hand, some with both hands, some again take a roll of paper, and others a stick." As a rule, the baton was used in churches and for choral singing. But when Bach went to the St. Thomas' School, he asked to have a harpsichord in order to conduct the orchestra and choir.

Gluck conducted in Vienna with violin in hand, and Rousseau stated in his *Dictionnaire de musique* that "audible time-beating with a big wooden stick prevailed at the Paris *Opéra*." (Lully died as the result of dropping his baton on his foot!) When Haydn was in London, he sat at the harpsichord and Salomon played first violin, and together they conducted the orchestra—a customary method, planned, perhaps, to pay the composer the compliment of seeming to direct his own work. Later, the violin-conductor or leader, as he was called in the early nineteenth century, became the concertmaster.

In his *Autobiography,* Spohr tells how he conducted the Philharmonic in London for the first time without the aid of a piano (1820). Standing at a desk in front of the orchestra, he drew a baton from his pocket and gave the signal to begin. "Quite alarmed at such a novel procedure, some of the directors would have protested against it; but when I besought them to grant me at least one trial, they became pacified." Spohr indicated not only the tempo, "in a decisive manner," but also the entries, thus assuring a confidence the players had not known before. He also politely but firmly made suggestions and corrections. "Surprised and inspired by this result, the orchestra immediately after the first part of the symphony, expressed aloud its collective assent to the new mode of conducting . . ."

A "sensational" conductor and colleague of Berlioz in London, Louis Jullien (1812-1860), displayed many eccentricities that dramatize the new status of the conductor. He wore elaborate clothes and pantomimed the music he was leading, seizing a violin or piccolo at the point of climax and sinking exhausted into a velvet chair. An article in *Punch* stated, "All pieces of Beethoven's were conducted with a jewelled baton, and in a pair of clean kid gloves, handed him at the moment on a silver salver." Jullien even went so far as to face the audience, rather than the orchestra, so that no one would miss his grimacing!

Mendelssohn was one of the first to whom the term, interpreting-conductor, can be applied. As director of the *Gewandhaus* concerts, he used a baton (although at his London debut he sat at the piano) and the orchestra became an immense instrument upon which he played. His enemies called the Mendelssohn tradition the "elegant school" of conductors. Berlioz too was an effective conductor, as was Liszt.

MENDELSSOHN'S INFLUENCE

Mendelssohn also exerted influence as an educator and example. In establishing the Leipzig Conservatory, he assembled about him colleagues and associates who are worthy of mention.

Moritz Hauptmann was educated in science and architecture as well as in music. He became Cantor of the St. Thomas' School on the recommendations of Spohr and Mendelssohn in 1842. For the next twenty-five years he was a most successful teacher of counterpoint. His theoretical writings are important, as are his exposition of Bach's *Art of the Fugue* and his essays.

Ignaz Moscheles, the virtuoso pianist, taught Mendelssohn and competed with Meyerbeer, Hummel and Beethoven. He was one of the ablest instructors at the Leipzig Conservatory, but was more conservative than Hauptmann. His piano works issue from a sound technique and are still occasionally played by advanced students.

Ernst Friedrich Richter (1808-1879) was Hauptmann's assistant, an outstanding organist and leader of the *Singakademie*. He succeeded Hauptmann as Cantor of St. Thomas' in 1868. An excellent teacher, Richter authored books on harmony and counterpoint that have been translated into many languages and are still instructive.

Karl Reinecke (1824-1910) adhered to Mendelssohnian standards. He made many tours as a pianist, composed over 250 works and for fifty years was a professor at the Leipzig Conservatory, of which he became director in 1897. As a composer, he was versatile and technically-proficient. With Jadassohn he taught many nineteenth-century Americans.

Salomon Jadassohn (1831-1902), a pupil of Hauptmann and Liszt, was a conductor and professor of composition and orchestration at the Conservatory. His valuable textbooks are still consulted. Composer of about 130 works, in nearly all forms except opera, he revealed a facile contrapuntal skill.

Composers who worked in Mendelssohn's style include William Sterndale Bennett (1816-1875), who founded a Bach Society in England and who composed piano and sacred music. The latter exerted influence over Samuel S. Wesley (1810-1876), writer of church music and Joseph Barnby (1838-1896), whose works include 246 hymn tunes. Others number Ferdinand Hiller, a popular conductor and composer in the Romantic vein and Niels Wilhelm Gade (1817-1890), a Dane, who became Mendelssohn's successor as director of the *Gewandhaus* Orchestra.

* * * * *

Thus, in our discussion of program music and the compositions of Liszt, Berlioz and Mendelssohn, we have uncovered additional components of the early nineteenth-century Romantic aesthetic. Although, as we have pointed out, differences of all kinds appear, it is interesting to observe the shadow of Beethoven, exercising an influence over both French and German composers. Berlioz, neglected in his lifetime, has arisen to popularity, through the efforts of Charles Münch, French conductor of the Boston Symphony Orchestra and Colin Davis, the promising British conductor. Mendelssohn, on the other hand, has suffered a posthumous downgrading by the critics, consistent, perhaps, with our dismissal of the Victorian period in general. A reevaluation of both Mendelssohn and Liszt seem in order. Berlioz has at last found his place.

Berlioz's preoccupation with opera was not an isolated one by any means, as the musical stage was in many ways an ideal outlet for Romantic strivings. In the following chapters, we shall take a look at Romantic opera in its various aspects.

SUGGESTIONS FOR FURTHER READING

Abraham, Gerald, *A Hundred Years of Music. London,* Duckworth, 1949.

Barzun, Jacques, *Berlioz and His Century: An Introduction to the Age of Romanticism.** New York, Meridan Bks., 1956.

Berlioz, Hector, *Evenings in the Orchestra.** Baltimore, Penguin, 1963.

———— *Memoirs.* New York, Tudor, 1935.

———— *Treatise on Instrumentation.** New York, Kalmus, 1948.

Carse, Adam, *The Orchestra from Beethoven to Berlioz.* Cambridge, Heffer, 1948.

Einstein, Alfred, *Music in the Romantic Era.* New York, Norton, 1947.

Jacob, Heinrich E., *Felix Mendelssohn and His Times.* Englewood Cliffs, Prentice-Hall, 1963.

Mason, Daniel Gregory, *The Romantic Composers.* New York, Macmillan, 1930.

Meyer, Leonard B., *Emotion and Meaning in Music.** Chicago, University of Chicago Press, 1956.

Pratt, Carroll C., *The Meaning of Music.* New York: McGraw-Hill, 1931.

* Available in paperback edition.

Radcliffe, Philip, *Mendelssohn*. New York, Dutton, 1954.

Revitt, Paul, *Nineteenth-Century Romanticism in Music.** Englewood Cliffs, Prentice-Hall, 1967.

Searle, Humphrey, ed., *Hector Berlioz: A Selection from His Letters*. New York, Harcourt-Brace-World, 1966.

Starr, William J. and Devine, George F., *Music Scores—Omnibus,** Part 2. Englewood Cliffs, Prentice-Hall, 1964.

Swalin, Benjamin F., *The Violin Concerto—A Study in German Romanticism*. Chapel Hill, University of North Carolina Press, 1941.

Turner, W. J., *Berlioz, The Man and His Music*. London, Dent, 1935.

Werner, Eric, *Mendelssohn: A New Image of the Composer and His Age*. London, Macmillan, 1963.

A Sampler of Supplementary Recordings

Collections

Romanticism	Victor LM-6153
Ten Centuries of Music	DGG KL-52/61
2000 Years of Music	Folkways 3700

Music of Individual Composers

Berlioz, Hector, *Damnation of Faust, Op.* 24
               L'Enfance du Christ, Op. 25
               Harold in Italy, Viola and Orchestra, Op. 16
               Overtures
               Requiem, Op. 5
               Roméo et Juliette, Op. 17
               Symphonie fantastique, Op. 14
               Symphonie funèbre et triomphale, Op. 15
               Te Deum, Op. 22
               Les Troyens: Royal Hunt and Storm

Liszt, Franz, *Faust Symphony*
               Dante Symphony
               Les Préludes, Symphonic Poem No. 3
               Tasso, Lament and Triumph, Symphonic Poem No. 2
               Orpheus, Symphonic Poem No. 4
               Mazeppa, Symphonic Poem No. 6

Mendelssohn, Felix, *Concerto No. 1 in g, Op.* 25 (piano)
               Concerto in e for Violin, Op. 64
               Elijah, Op. 70
               Midsummer Night's Dream Music, Ops. 21, 61
               Octet in E flat for Strings, Op. 20
               Overtures
               Piano Music
               Symphony No. 3 in a, Op. 56, "Scotch"
               Symphony No. 4 in A, Op. 90, "Italian"
               Symphony No. 5 in d, Op. 107, "Reformation"
               Variations sérieuses, Op. 54
               Sonata No. 1 in f for Organ, Op. 65, *No. 1*

Reinecke, Karl, *Concerto in e for Harp, Op.* 182

OPPORTUNITIES FOR STUDY IN DEPTH

1. Prepare a book report of Leonard B. Meyer's *Emotion and Meaning in Music* (see "Suggestions for Further Reading"), recounting his main points and the evidence he gives to support them.

2. Program music has been used extensively in teaching children to listen intelligently, as it can be supported by verbal and visual materials. Examine one of the filmstrips-in-color-with-recordings series, such as those put out by Jam Handy Organization, Inc. (Detroit, Michigan), called *Music Stories* and *Stories of Music Classics*. Present it in class, followed by a discussion of its good and weak features.

3. Experiments have frequently been devised, such as one at Columbia University some years ago, to validate the communication of meanings and images through music. Within practical limits, plan and carry out an experiment with the aid of the class, endeavoring to discover whether indeed a heterogeneous group of people can react to musical stimuli in the same general ways. Write up findings.

4. Liszt is said to have carried a Bible and a volume of Goethe with him wherever he went. We have noted the literary references in many of his compositions. Make a further study of these referents as they are operative in Liszt's program music.

5. Shakespeare, often in translation, was a fertile source of inspiration to Romantic composers, as we have seen in the cases of Berlioz and Mendelssohn. Compile a list of Romantic compositions by other composers who found in the works of Shakespeare a point of departure.

6. We have quoted a French critic as saying, in effect, that ignorance was bliss in the case of Berlioz. What freedoms did Berlioz's inadequate training and background afford him? What disadvantages did they provide? Evaluate the situation.

7. The ubiquitous Goethe's and others' interpretations of the Faust legend have been encountered again and again. Collect and describe five musical expositions of Faustian elements. Why did this particular subject appeal to Romantic composers?

8. Investigate more fully any one aspect of special interest that has been noted in this chapter. Outline the supplementary data together with a bibliography, including periodical references.

VOCABULARY ENRICHMENT

program music	music critic
incidental music	Academician
concert overture	*ophicleide*
program symphony	*mezzo-piano*
programmatic suite	songs without words
symphonic or tone-poem	baton
Leitmotif	divided strings
l'idée fixe	interpreting-conductor
theme transformation	

Chapter 19.

ROMANTIC OPERA

Even the best, most sensitive, . . . attends the opera only to feed upon the striking scenery, the luscious hips of the ballerina, or the pretty voice of a singer . . . Everything is sympathetically observed but the music . . . Second to them are those theatre-goers who attend the opera only to observe Society, fashions and the latest coiffures, all of which are best visible during the prelude and certain well-lighted scenes . . . The ultimate in the whole category of the species is achieved by those who attend the opera for no other reason than to let themselves be seen. They come regularly only after the last notes of the overture fade away, as noisy in their entrance as poorly mannered children, slamming their seats and snapping their inevitable opera-glass cases open with as much noise as possible before beginning to talk. . . .

—Hugo Wolf, "Audiences in Vienna" (1884)

Wolf's plaint of the apparent lack of interest in music by Viennese opera audiences of his day is one that has been applied to other opera-goers, before and since. **Opera** or drama set to music, either wholly or in part, seems to encourage observance of certain extraneous customs that militate against musical purposes and understanding. The plush surroundings, the air of its being an "event," the artificiality heightened by elaborate costumes, *corps de ballet* and the personalities of star performers all contribute to his outcry: "Is it any less music if it is played in a theater instead of a concert hall?" What is significant about Wolf's wails is that the nineteenth-century composer was concerned with opera as an art form, worthy to stand beside a symphony or tone-poem. Unlike his eighteenth-century colleagues, he did not consider musical theater (or instrumental composition) a matter of mere entertainment, but rather a most serious business indeed. In fact, Romantic opera became the province of specialists. In this spirit, Wolf, as a music critic covering a performance of Beethoven's *Fidelio,* expressed his dismay.

During the late eighteenth century, features of opera had gradually been changing. After 1750, for instance, a "Turkish" element had entered the picture with its unique instrumental colors, its half-comic, half-exotic, highly unreal situations, that Mozart had utilized in *Die Entführung,* and Gluck, Grétry and others had tackled. Folk and fantasy subject matter were blended with patriotic emphases, retiring classical motifs to limbo. In addition to modifications in *opera buffa, opéra-comique* and *Singspiel,* the defunct *opera seria* was being transformed into **grand opera,** which, like American cinematic spectaculars, presented grandiose scenes, lavishly staged, with an enlarged and vigorous cast of participants. Often, too, a spirit of mystery pervaded the story and the natural world was infused with animism, so that, as Pincherle puts it, "forces of nature, water and woodland sprites . . . had a part to play, and invisible and omnipresent spirits governed the thoughts and acts of the characters." In this chapter we shall discuss facets of German, Italian and French opera and operetta as they manifested themselves during the nineteenth century, and examine their relationship to Romanticism.

Romantic composers found in opera an ideal vehicle for one of their basic tenets, the **union of the arts,** in contradistinction to previous pigeonholing of music as music, painting as painting and drama as drama. In opera, music, drama, visual effects, dancing, miming and message were as one. The serious, self-conscious Romantic opera composer would rarely consider taking his task lightly. He often took longer to write his works and, in turn, expected much more of them than had his predecessors. He rejected the interpolation of unrelated materials and resisted relegating responsibility to assistants. His, on the whole, was a total conception. The lyric stage provided German Romanticism with one of its primary expressive platforms. It was the composer Carl Maria von Weber, "the most German of German composers," as Richard Wagner inaccurately calls him, who was to continue the development of German opera, taking up where Mozart had left off and paving a way for the works of Wagner. Weber, however, did not emerge from an artistic vacuum; he was heir to many earlier influences.

Before Weber, Domenico Cimarosa (1749-1801), a prolific composer of seventy operas, as well as oratorios and cantatas, wrote in a manner similar to Mozart, with strong *buffa* leanings. He was invited to St. Petersburg in 1787 by Catherine II and subsequently filled Salieri's place in Vienna. We have already met Gasparo Spontini (whom, with Cimarosa, we shall discuss more fully later) as the villain who withdrew from the boards Mendelssohn's sole attempt in the form. Nor can we except Beethoven as precursor of Romantic opera. *Fidelio* was a "rescue opera," in which the subjects of man's freedom and his struggle against injustice are developed. Although there have been times when the principal characters of *Fidelio* have impressed us as both wooden and unbelievably noble, the wicked Pizarro, the idealistic Leonore and Florestan appear real enough to us now, after our recent wholesale initiation into the way of tyrants.

GERMAN OPERA—CARL MARIA VON WEBER

Mozart must have been a bugbear in the lives of young musicians in the eighteenth and nineteenth centuries, for, like Weber's father, many parents tried to make Mozarts of their sons. Nevertheless, Carl Maria von Weber (1786-1826), born in Eutin near Lübeck, showed decided musical gifts when a lad, and, as his father was Konstanze Mozart's uncle, it is understandable that Weber senior held Mozart up to his youngest son as a model. Born of a second marriage, Carl was a sickly child, never free of a limp, due to congenital hipbone disease. Because of the wastrel nature of his father, the boy was yanked from pillar to post. Not until some time after his mother's death did father and son settle down long enough for Carl to have six months' tuition with Michael Haydn in Salzburg. His first published composition appeared in 1798, when the boy was twelve.

Following the Salzburg sojourn, Weber studied in Munich, and completed his first opera, *Die Macht der Liebe und des Weins* (*The Power of Love and Wine*). A second opera, *Das Waldmädchen* (*The Forest Maiden*), was a failure at its public performance in 1800; a third was no more successful. Realizing that he needed more training, although he was certainly gaining valuable experience, Carl began work with a distinguished Viennese theorist, Abbé Vogler (1749-1814), and, after a year's intensive study, was awarded the post of conductor of the Breslau Opera.

Unlike Mozart, the eighteen-year-old Weber was a confident and able organizer, although given to extravagance in his productions. All did not go smoothly at Breslau, however, for veteran members of the company resented the authority of a youth and, moreover, an unfortunate accident took place. In 1799 the Webers had met the erratic Aloys Senefelder, who was the inventor of lithography. Both were attracted to the new process, the father actually engaging in it for a short while. Mistaking nitric acid for wine, Carl Maria swallowed some in 1806, permanently damaging his vocal cords. Later that year, Weber and Breslau parted company by mutual agreement.

Carl then became secretary to the playboy Duke Ludwig of Württemberg, under whose aegis he fell into bad company and drifted into money difficulties. But he found time to read and, encouraged by his friend, Franz Danzi (1763-1826), a conductor, to try his hand once again at composition. Two years later, Weber got into a scrape trying to extricate his father from a financial impasse, and was banished by the King. Cleared of guilt, but remaining in exile for a time, he settled down to work and wrote his first mature opera, *Silvana* (1810), a Romantic work replete with hunting horns, a thunderstorm, lively dances and simulated folksong.

During the year 1810 Weber traveled to Mannheim and Darmstadt and composed a one-act "Turkish" opera, *Abu Hassan,* introduced at Munich in 1811. He concertized as a pianist and planned new ventures, finally becoming in 1813 director of the National Theater in Prague, where he charmed with his versions of national songs and acquired renown as a conductor. While there, he went to Vienna to recruit singers and renewed acquaintance with his future wife, Caroline Brandt, who had sung in *Silvana.* In the meantime, through friendship with a clarinetist, Heinrich Bärmann, he had written several works for clarinet, had met Goethe at Weimar, Spohr at Gotha and befriended another Vogler pupil, Jakob Liebmann Beer, to whom he dedicated his *Momento Capriccioso* for piano.

Throughout his three-year tenure at Prague, Weber was far too busy staging other composers' works to create much of his own. In 1814 he produced *Silvana* in Berlin, and, after the Battle of Waterloo, he did compose a chauvinistic cantata, *Kampf und Sieg (Struggle and Victory),* a great success when performed in 1815. This led to his appointment as director of German opera at Dresden. In 1817, his appointment was confirmed to him for life and thus the "enchanted wanderer" at last put down roots. He married and subsequently composed the three operas for which he is famous.

Shortly after settling in Dresden, Weber made the acquaintance of Friedrich Kind, a lawyer-writer. Weber suggested that Kind write a libretto on a supernatural tale he had read some seven years before, *Der Freischütz (The Sharpshooter),* in which a gamekeeper must win a shooting match in order to claim the hand of his betrothed. Being an indifferent shot, the young man is persuaded to use magic bullets, six of which will hit the mark but the seventh of which will be directed by the will of the Devil. This diabolical bullet strikes Max's fiancée but is deflected by a consecrated wreath of roses that she wears, hitting the villain instead. A monk, the *deus ex machina* (a providential character who straightens everything out), resolves all in this story of the forests of Bohemia. It was a typical Gothic tale and somewhat puerile, but very much in tune with the spirit of German Romanticism. *Der Freischütz* stunned the world in 1821, snatching laurels from Rossini, Spontini and their followers. Five hundred performances were given in Berlin alone; elsewhere, too, Weber became the rage.

Der Freischütz was a new departure, though it retained the spoken dialogue of *Singspiel.* For the first time a serious opera was based on burgher and peasant subjects, and some of the music was in a German folk style. Like Mozart, Weber combined the real and supernatural with imagination and a thorough command of his materials. Quiet and brilliant moments are balanced to produce powerful drama. The overture is one of the first in which an operatic composer uses complete melodies from the opera. The vocal writing is masterful, the ensembles and choruses inventive. In the Wolf's Glen scene (Act II), the music is "the most expressive rendering of the gruesome that is to be found in a musical score," Kobbé asserts.

As a result of the success of *Der Freischütz,* Weber was commissioned by the Opera at Vienna to compose a grand opera. For this, he chose a libretto by a nineteenth-century version of the modern beatnik, Helmina von Chezy, who is described by Weber's pupil and biographer, Julius Benedict (1804-1885), as "a stout elderly lady, with all the qualities of a real blue-stocking, careless and slovenly in her appearance, not blessed with any earthly goods, but with a great deal of self-sufficiency." *Euryanthe* was first produced in 1823, but because of its poor libretto, was not well received, although it contained some lovely music. Schubert was to discover Frau von Chezy's inadequacies in writing incidental music to her *Rosamunde.*

After this failure, Weber became depressed and ill, but was encouraged by a commission from England, offering him £1000—a sum he needed to provide for his family. He selected the subject of *Oberon,* took English lessons and completed the opera in 1826, personally directing the first performances in London, and engaging in other concert activities as well. The music of *Oberon* shimmers and glows in an elfin atmosphere; the introduction to the *Overture* is a marvelous feat of orchestration (comparable to Mendelssohn's *A Midsummer Night's Dream* music and Berlioz's *"Queen Mab" Scherzo*). In form, *Oberon* is a *Singspiel,* concocted from materials by Wieland, arranged by J. R. Planché, and full of Romantic color and effect. The tragic epilogue to this work was that Weber died shortly thereafter, far from family and home, of a recurrence of tuberculosis.

Weber, as much as anyone, established German Romantic opera. Closely related to the current Romantic literature, opera used Teutonic folklore, fantasy and the supernatural, realistically and symbolically. The quality of artlessness was sought; realism and the uncanny in physical nature were dramatized. Imagination outweighed the Italian passion for vocal display. Yet Weber was certainly influenced by his fellow German composers, as well as by Cherubini and Rossini. He shows the German predilection toward the orchestra and, like Wagner, often turns to it in moments of climax. Between Weber and Wagner, however, German

Fig. 64. Von Weber conducting an opera at Covent Garden—lithograph by Hullmann, after J. Hayter. Weber established German opera and paved the way for its full flowering.

opera lapsed into the moralistic and oversentimental. This led to Wagnerian diatribe, disgust and, finally, to Wagnerian "cures."

Although Weber is a composer more written about than listened to, he wrote attractive music in many forms other than those of opera. His works include incidental music for several dramas, such as the Gozzi-Schiller *Turandot*; nine cantatas; piano sonatas; sets of variations; a *Rondo Brilliant in E Flat, Op.* 62; dances, of which the best known is *Aufforderung zum Tanz* ("Invitation to the Dance," orchestrated by Berlioz); two piano concertos; the famous *Konzertstück in F, Op.* 79; violin sonatas; concertos for clarinet, bassoon and horn; two symphonies; over 100 songs; and two Masses. As J. W. Dent concludes, "Without Weber, there could never have been a Chopin or Liszt, and the best parts of Mendelssohn owe their inspiration to memories of Weber"—not to mention Wagner.

OTHER GERMAN OPERA COMPOSERS

Predating Weber's *Der Freischütz* was an opera by the author-composer, E. T. A. Hoffmann (1776-1822), (the "Kreisler" of Schumann's *Kreisleriana*), whose *Undine* was produced in 1816. Within the same year, Spohr offered his *Faust*. Neither of these works had that combination of technique and talent that Weber possessed, but each added ingredients to the Romantic pot. Among Weber's fellow composers were Ludwig Louis Spohr, Heinrich Marschner and Gustav Albert Lortzing. In many of their works are reflected either the folk idiom of *Der Frei-schütz* or the medieval spirit-world aura of *Euryanthe*.

We have already met Spohr as a violin virtuoso. He also wrote some excellent Romantic operas, although he never wholly accepted Beethoven or Weber, leaning more toward Mozart. His *Faust* and *Jessonda* (1823) were conventional, but in his *Kreuzfahrer* (*The Crusader,* 1845), he blazed a new trail by through-composing the entire work. Marschner (1795-1861), whom Weber admired, dove deep in the Romantic pool with such operas as *Der Vampyr* (1828), derived from Lord Byron's "Lord Ruthwen," *Der Templer und die Jüdin* (*The Templar and the Jewess,* 1829), based on Sir Walter Scott's *Ivanhoe,* and *Hans Heiling* (1833), which Einstein calls a " 'Lohengrin' theme in a more folklike garb." Albert Lortzing (1801-1851) composed operas in the *Singspiel* style, rather pedestrian but effective works, such as an *Undine* (that popular water nymph), *Zar und Zimmermann* (*Czar and Carpenter,* 1837) and *Hans Sachs* (1840), a forerunner of *Die Meistersinger*.

Continuing our chronicle of German Romantic opera (excluding Wagner for the moment) we come to Otto Nicholai (1810-1849), a North German educated in Italy, who created a delightful German *opera buffa* in *The Merry Wives of Windsor* (1849); Friedrich von Flotow (1812-1883), a diplomat from Mecklenburg, who fitted nicely with his German sentimentality into the *opéra-comique* situation in Paris, and who bequeathed us two clever, if insipid, operas, *Alessandro Stradella* (1844) and *Martha or The Fair at Richmond* (1847); and Franz von Suppé (1819-1895), influenced by the diverting works of Offenbach, and composer of *Das Mädchen vom Lande* (*The Country Girl,* 1848) and *Fatinitza* (1876), as well as the *Poet and Peasant Overture,* a "must" for Sunday band concerts and television potpourris.

ITALIAN OPERA

Italian opera, as we have seen, had proliferated over the face of Europe, establishing its dominance in many and distant places. Paris, Vienna, Berlin and St. Petersburg all boasted their Italian opera companies. It was against such dominance that German composers were struggling. In Paris, Luigi Cherubini (1760-1842), a Florentine like Lully, had risen to great power during the years in which Germany was experiencing her extraordinary musical flowering. Cherubini had been trained in modal counterpoint, as were Haydn, Mozart and Beethoven. Although aloof and erudite, he was able, because of his long life and his position as director of the Paris Conservatory, with which he was associated from 1795 to 1841, to get a full view of musical activities in Europe. And, if he was authoritarian, he did not deter the French composers, whom he guided, from expressing native characteristics.

At first Cherubini devoted himself to sacred music, of which an outstanding example is his *Requiem in C Minor*. After a visit to London, however, he disclosed a new dramatic style that became a backbone of Parisian opera. His operas include *Démophon* (1788), pompous rather than trivially "canary-birdish," as Schumann characterized Italian opera; *Lodoiska* (1791); *Médée* (1797); and the most popular, *Les deux journées* (*The Water Carrier,* 1800). It was Cherubini's opera, *Faniska* (1807), that competed, to Beethoven's disadvantage, with *Fidelio* in Vienna. Cherubini brought to opera enhanced drama, supported by rich orchestrations and inventive ensemble numbers—features that were adopted by many French composers. A weakness of his operas is the drag of dramatic action through excessive musical prolongation.

Domenico Cimarosa, an older contemporary of Cherubini, captured the fancy of the people and moved from one triumph to another. Among his many operas are *La Ballerina amante* (*The Amorous Ballerina,* 1782) and *Il Matrimonio segreto* (*The Secret Marriage,* 1792). Cimarosa wrote with great facility; in one year (1781), for instance, he produced two operas for Naples, two for Turin and one for Rome. A master of melody and form, he was particularly gifted in writing comedy opera. In 1920, Diaghilev, the Parisian impresario, produced his *Le astúzie femminíli* (*Feminine Cunning,* 1794), reviving some interest in his operas and overtures. Cimarosa, in 1799, joined the Neapolitan revolutionists in demonstrating against the entrance of the French army and was imprisoned. Through the intercession of Ferdinand, he was released, but his spirit was broken and he died suddenly and somewhat mysteriously two years later.

Gasparo Spontini (1774-1851), an admirer of Mozart, carried forward Gluck's ideals and was a decided influence on German opera as court composer to Wilhelm Friedrich III at Berlin. He held the stage until Weber's *Freischütz* supplanted everything else for a time, even in France. Spontini, much admired by Berlioz, was one of the first composers of historic opera, which Meyerbeer and others espoused later. Doubtless, Handel's large canvases, based on past events and personages, provided some inspiration to both Spontini and Meyerbeer. Unpopular when he first went to Paris in 1803, Spontini made a study of Mozart and Gluck and soon, with the assistance of an able librettist, Étienne de Jouy, produced the ambitious *Milton* (1804). Next came his masterpiece, *La Vestale* (1807), winning a prize in a contest for the best dramatic work, judged by Méhul, Gossec and Grétry, and bestowed by Napoleon. In *La Vestale,* Spontini used great masses of sound and vivid, rich effects, unusual at the time, which is probably why modern audiences, accustomed to orchestral turbulence, still enjoy its far-flung scenic breadth. Other works by Spontini include the grand opera, *Fernand Cortez* (1809) and *Nurmahal (Lalla Rookh,* 1822).

GIOACCHINO ROSSINI

Gioacchino Rossini (1792-1868) has been called the most forceful Italian genius since Scarlatti. We might add that he was a pioneer of the star system and the spoiled child of Europe. Rossini built on public taste. A versatile, resourceful musician and a master of embellishment, Rossini was yet wise enough to take cognizance of German composers. He never capitulated to ugliness or vulgarity. As master of the trivial, he made the trivial masterful.

By the time Rossini was thirty-seven years old, he had completed almost all his compositions, including six string quartets and thirty-eight operas. Although he was at the summit of his powers and much-performed and acclaimed (in 1823, for example, twenty-three of his operas were staged in Europe—the composer was but thirty-two), hard work and a certain amount of dissipation had taken their toll. Rossini was to spend the remaining thirty-nine years of his life creating very little, but enjoying his fame and leading the existence of a *bon vivant.* (A *gourmet* steak dish bears his name, *Tournedos Rossini.*) Although legend has it that he was notoriously indolent, to the point of composing in bed and neglecting to bend over should a page of manuscript fall to the floor, Rossini, during his active period, regularly turned out four or five operas a year, no mean production schedule.

Born the son of a town trumpeter and ardent Francophile, who subsequently was relieved of his municipal duties, Gioacchino experienced only a rudimentary general and musical education until he was twelve, although he had a naturally attractive voice and had managed to pick up knowledge of the *cembalo,* horn and viola. His parents established a permanent domicile in 1804 in Bologna and Rossini was enrolled as a student at the *Liceo Musicale,* where he studied, sometimes tempestuously, with Padre Mattei, a pupil of Padre Martini and a fanatical contrapuntalist.

Because of family financial problems, Rossini left the *Liceo* in 1810 and composed a one-act opera at the behest of Venice, *La Cambiale de matrimonio (The Marriage Contract).* This he wrote in three days' time and promptly collected forty dollars for the effort. Other operas followed, but his first real success was *La Pietra del paragone* (*The Stone of Comparison*), produced at La Scala, Milan, in 1812, which, among other things, secured him exemption from military duty. The following year saw the production of his first serious opera, *Tancredi* (1813), based on a libretto from Voltaire, in which appeared the only tender love music Rossini ever composed. Venice loved it and *"Di tanti palpiti"* ("So Many Palpitations"), an amorous *aria,* was hummed by one and all. Less than three months later, *L'Italiana in Algeri* (*The Italian Girl in Algiers,* 1813) was introduced and its mischievous, high-spirited music made it another hit. Only three years out of the Conservatory, Rossini had already become the most famous opera composer in Italy.

In the spring of 1815, Rossini accepted a contract to go to Naples where, it was supposed, he would have a hard time, for provincial and personal reasons. It was at Naples, however, that he substituted orchestral accompaniment for that of the *cembalo* and where he alone controlled the singers' every note, thereby curbing *cadenzas* and extraneous interpolations. In the winter of the same year, the composer journeyed to Rome to produce two operas, one of which, written in two weeks and based on a Beaumarchais play, was finally entitled *Il Barbiere di Siviglia* (*The Barber of Seville,* 1816). Its first performance was a fiasco, due to a rival *claque,* but the audiences grew to like it and its all-conquering career was begun.

During the next six years, Rossini completed sixteen operas, among which were *Otello* (1816); *La Cenerentola* (*Cinderella,* 1817); *La Gazza ladra* (*The Thieving Magpie,* 1817), perhaps an ancestor of *verismo;* and *La Donna del lago* (*The Lady of the Lake,* 1819). In 1822 Rossini married his mistress, the *prima donna* Isabella Colbran, formerly of Naples, and the couple went to Vienna. Rossini's four-month stay there was one continuing triumph and, despite Weber's initial hostility, Rossini collected accolades from such as Beethoven and the philosopher, Hegel. During the following year, Rossini produced another success in Venice, *Semiramide* (1823), and visited England with remunerative results (some £7000 in five months).

In 1824 Rossini became director of the *Théâtre Italien* in Paris, a tenure he held two years; after that he was appointed "Composer to His Majesty and Inspector General of Singing," a post abruptly abolished by the July Revolution (1830). In the end, however, the composer was granted a pension for life and spent many of his later years in France. His only Parisian operatic achievement was probably his greatest, *Guillaume Tell* (*William Tell,* 1829), based on Schiller's play of the same name. Francis Toye writes:

For originality, for carefulness of workmanship, for elaboration of scoring, it stands in a class apart. Verdi, Wagner, and Meyerbeer were all influenced by it. Even to-day the overture, which is in reality a symphonic poem in miniature, remains an acknowledged masterpiece.

Rossini succumbed to violent attacks of neurasthenia and lingered for some time on the edge of a nervous collapse. He did, however, acquire a mistress, Olympe Pélissier, whom he married fifteen years later and who ministered to him with the utmost devotion. His later years were spent in reorganizing the *Liceo Musicale* in Bologna, composing two sacred compositions—*Stabat Mater* (1842), a florid but vital choral work, and a *Petite Messe solennelle* (1864)—and indulging in hosting his fabulous Saturday evening parties, which were the *ne plus ultra* of Paris and Passy. It was to these that all aspired to be invited, to rub elbows with the famous and to savor Rossini's wit. A sample of the latter is found in the following anecdote. A young composer stopped by at Rossini's apartment in Paris to play two selections for the master. After listening to the first, Rossini quickly quipped, "I like the other one better."

Rossini died in 1868 and was buried in *Père-Lachaise* cemetery in Paris. Later, however, at the urging of the Italian government, his remains were transferred to the "Italian Westminster Abbey," the church of St. Croce, in Florence. Rossini, like his Italian colleagues, did not succumb to the spell of Romanticism in the manner that the Germans had. His music retained a wryness and verve, punctuated by humor, that was essentially opposed to the somberness of the Teuton. Blessed with facility, Rossini endlessly plagiarized himself and occasionally others. He was not above writing to order and is quoted as having said, "Give me a laundry list and I will set it to music."

Yet he produced an unblemished masterpiece in *The Barber of Seville*. He paid careful attention to the orchestra and developed the extended *crescendo* as a device. He did much to curb the swamping and foolish *cadenza*. His skill was extraordinary in concerted pieces and his work, although ornate, showed vitality and grasp. He had a sense of "good theater" and gave Meyerbeer and others encouragement and productions. Strange to say in a man so volatile and free, technique was of vast importance to him; and if his methods may have retarded the advance of grand opera, there is a tendency today to return to the Rossini spirit of *opera buffa*.

GAETANO DONIZETTI AND VINCENZO BELLINI

Born at Bergamo, Gaetano Donizetti (1797-1848) was a devoted Rossini-ite; so much so, in fact, that only after Rossini had stopped writing operas (1829), was Donizetti able to develop his own gifts. His father apprenticed him to an architect and urged him to study law, only reluctantly permitting him to pursue music, first at Bergamo and later at the *Liceo* of Bologna, where he was instructed by Rossini's teacher, Padre Mattei. Determined to compose for the theater, contrary to his father's church preference, Donizetti suddenly joined the Austrian army and used all his leisure time to write. In 1822, with *Zoraïde di Granata,* he achieved enough success to be relieved of military service. Thereafter he wrote opera after opera—twenty-three in seven years—all derivative. With *Anna Bolena* (1830), however, he came into his own and subsequently composed the works for which he is now known.

Donizetti had a gift for the Romantic love song. Moreover, he had a penchant for dramatic effect, such as is found in *Lucia di Lammermoor* (1835), based on Sir Walter Scott's novel. In addition, the composer made lasting contributions to lighter opera in his amusing *L'Elisir d'amore* (*The Elixir of Love,* 1832), *La Fille du régiment* (*The Daughter of the Regiment,* 1840) and the glittering *Don Pasquale* (1843), the latter written in only eight days. Seventy-one operas, many songs, cantatas, sacred music and string quartets are included in Donizetti's output. He was on the staff of the Naples Conservatory, traveled considerably and labored so incessantly that he incurred a serious brain disorder that brought on his death.

Vincenzo Bellini (1801-1835), who died when he was thirty-four, was probably more gifted than Donizetti, although Bellini wrote solely in the grand style. Verdi and Wagner thought of him as a master of the long vocal melody, which often necessitated a slow *coloratura,* so difficult to sing. The most familiar of his works are *La Sonnambula* (*The Sleep Walker,* 1831), *Norma* (1831) and *I Puritani* (1835). Judging from the fine dramatic sense of *Norma,* an opera written under the influences of his era, it is difficult to imagine what Bellini might have done had he lived longer.

FRENCH OPERA—GIACOMO MEYERBEER

The French had had Romantic opera before the Revolution; they even had their "village opera." Grétry and Nicolas Dalayrac (1753-1809) widened the field with medieval and chivalric subjects, with fantasies that vied with sentimental tales and horror stories. After the Revolution, opera became more exciting and intense. It gloried in the crashing storm and reveled in the "rescue opera" theme, in which the hero or heroine is saved, just in the nick of time, from a villain. The French were lucky (as were the Italians) in having skillful librettists. From their brews came the *melodrama,* originally spoken drama to a musical background, and a greater development of the *aria* at the expense of recitative. It was in this period, however, that conventions crystallized and became hampering operatic traditions, some of which had to wait for Wagner for reform. Others are still awaiting another genius!

"In Paris," wrote Richard Wagner in 1865, "Italians and Germans immediately become French; and the French, though with less aptitude for music, have always imposed their own taste so emphatically on the production of foreigners that even far beyond our frontiers this taste has left its mark on every work." In Giacomo Meyerbeer (1791-1864), we find a man born in Germany and trained in Italy, performing a chameleon-like transformation in becoming the foremost composer of French grand opera. Whether charlatan or genius, Meyerbeer, originally named Jakob Liebmann Beer, was certainly an opportunist. The son of a wealthy Berlin banker, Meyerbeer spent several years as a musical prodigy, making his concert debut when seven years old. He studied with Clementi and later with Abbé Vogler, Weber's teacher. During 1810-12, he composed his first opera and a cantata, of which a critic in Berlin wrote admiringly, describing its "glowing life, genuine loveliness and above all the perfect power of burning genius." The critic was Carl Maria von Weber, invited to Berlin for the occasion. The subsequent failure of several operas convinced young Meyerbeer, with the advice of Salieri, that he should study the form in Italy.

Once in Italy, Meyerbeer acclimated himself all too well. "All my feelings became Italian," he wrote. "All my thoughts became Italian. After I had lived a year there, it seemed to me that I was an Italian born." So *Jakob* became *Giacomo* and Meyerbeer became one of the most popular composers of opera in Italy. This "knack," as one authority calls it, "of representing at peak intensity the nation in which he happened to be living for the time being" disturbed Weber. "My heart bleeds," he said, "to see a German composer of creative power stoop to become an imitator to win favor with the crowd." Meyerbeer's Italian operas, of which he himself was not proud later, had a healthy air of Rossini about them.

The next stop was Paris, where once again he studied what the people wanted, as he had done in Germany and Italy, making success his goal. In 1831, with Augustin-Eugène Scribe (1791-1861) as librettist, Meyerbeer presented his first French *grande opéra, Robert le Diable.* It was an immediate and permanent popular success, earning over 4,000,000 francs during a period of twenty-five years. A Romanticized historical work mixing German, Italian and French methods, *Robert le Diable* featured a ballet of nuns rising from their graves to dance in the ruins of a monastery at midnight, antics which created quite a sensation among the Parisians. Twenty-year-old Mendelssohn, no lover of Paris anyway, was thoroughly shocked by the eroticism that was evident in all Meyerbeer's French operas. "If that is the sort of thing that spells success," he wrote to his father, "I prefer to write church music . . ."

Robert le Diable was followed by *Les Huguenots* (1836), an opera that aroused admiration in Berlioz and young Richard Wagner. A third triumph occurred in 1849 with *Le Prophète,* which had been preceded by the moderately successful *Ein Feldlager in Schlesien (A Camp in Silesia,* 1844), written for Prussia. Regardless of the fact that he was anathema to Mendelssohn and Schumann, Meyerbeer had achieved fame and fortune, including an impressive collection of appointments and medals. His last years were spent on *L'Africana* (1865), begun in 1838, but first performed posthumously, for the composer died in 1864. After a hero's funeral, Meyerbeer was buried in a humble Jewish cemetery in Germany.

However pretentious his operas, the man himself was frugal, ascetic and unassuming. However meretricious and superficial his work, it was at the same time marked by originality and an unerring theatrical sense. Despite his pandering, Meyerbeer contributed to the constructive side of opera, built great climaxes, advanced orchestration and had often written big tunes even if not distinguished ones. He influenced French opera greatly in establishing the grand manner.

Opéra-Comique

Among the first representatives of native French *opéra-comique* were Pierre-Alexandre Monsigny (1729-1817) and Grétry. Later, when extensive amalgamation of contrasting styles occurred, Cherubini, Méhul and Jean-François Lesueur expanded the field. Gluck had changed the face of French opera and rescued it from florid Italian influences. Under Grétry, the *buffa* was refined to **opéra-comique,** which in time approached grand opera in seriousness, and only differed from it because of its spoken dialogue.

André-Ernest Grétry (1741-1813), of Belgian birth, was the first important composer in France since Rameau. Educated in Liège and Rome, he went to Paris on Voltaire's advice. There, where the Italians had introduced *opera buffa* in 1752, he transformed its wit and intimacy, its naturalness and directness, with the usual Gallic adaptability, into *opéra-comique,* which, because it could be performed in a small theater, was both practical and popular. Grétry composed fifty operas, in addition to church music and instrumental works. He was known as the "Molière of music." On account of his opera, *Richard Coeur-de-Lion* (1784), full of nobles and peasants, medieval chivalry and dangers, he is often considered a transition figure between Classic and Romantic opera styles. Honored and respected during his life, Grétry retired to Rousseau's former home at Montmorency.

François-Joseph Gossec (1734-1829), another Belgian, was influential in the development of the symphony, as we have mentioned. He also composed some excellent light operas, such as *Les Pêcheurs* (*The Fishermen,* 1766). An able organizer, Gossec directed the *École Royale de Chant* which, in 1795, became the Paris Conservatory. An enthusiastic Revolutionist, Gossec may have anticipated Berlioz in the enormity of musical forces required by some of his works. A *Te Deum* calls for 1200 singers and 300 wind instruments.

Étienne-Nicolas Méhul (1763-1817), who was urged by Gluck to compose operas, wrote thirty of them, of which the best known is *Joseph* (1807), wherein he attained unusual effects in harmony and melody. Influences of Méhul's *Joseph* are to be found in Weber's *Der Freischütz*; as a conductor, Weber was thoroughly acquainted with the popular French work. Méhul's scholarly taste and judgment, as well as his position as an inspector of the Paris Conservatory, made an impression on men of the next generation.

Other composers of *opéra-comique* include François-Adrien Boïeldieu (1775-1834), remembered for the charming *La dame blanche* (*The White Lady,* 1825); Daniel-François-Esprit Auber (1782-1871), often called the "Prince of *opéra-comique*," a director of the Paris Conservatory and Chapelmaster to Napoleon, whose operas *Fra Diavolo* (1830), *Le Domino noir* (*The Black Domino,* 1837) and *La Muette de Portici* (1828) are still heard in France; Louis-Joseph Hérold (1791-1833), referred to as the "French Weber," and represented by his operas, *Zampa* (1831) and *Le Pré aux clercs* (*The Field of Honor,* 1832); and Jacques-François Halévy (1799-1862), who wrote *opéra-comique,* although he is best known for a grand opera, *La Juive* (*The Jewess,* 1836), conceived on the Spontini-Meyerbeer historical recipe.

LYRIC OPERA

In **lyric opera,** we find a combination of the melody, vitality and sparkling vivacity of *opéra-comique,* and the technique, color and, at times, the grandeur of grand opera, although without its elaborate settings. The men writing lyric opera were well-grounded in Romanticism and in Mozart. For these works, a special theater, the *Théâtre Lyrique,* was founded in Paris. Among the first composers of lyric opera was Félicien David (1810-1876), with his *Lalla Roukh* (1862). He is also known for a symphonic ode, *Le Désert* (1844), and many other operas, among which are *La Perle du Brésil* (1851) and *Herculaneum* (1859), for which he was awarded a prize of 20,000 francs.

Ambroise Thomas (1811-1896), a director of the Paris Conservatory, was a composer who went to great writers for librettos. His *Mignon* (1866) was derived from Goethe's *Wilhelm Meister* and *Hamlet* (1868) from Shakespeare. *Mignon,* with its catchy music, has immortalized Thomas, who possessed the sensuous charm of his compatriot, Gounod. Another composer known for a single opera, chiefly because of one melody, the *Berceuse* from *Jocelyn* (1888), was Benjamin Godard (1849-1895), who also wrote three programmatic symphonies and many *salon* pieces for amateur pianists.

Charles-François Gounod (1818-1893) is a composer whose fame is inextricably connected with his opera, *Faust* (1859), based upon the love story of Marguerite and Faust, from Goethe's celebrated drama. Standing midway between grand opera and *opéra-comique, Faust* introduced no new elements *per se,* but ". . . the dreamy languor of the love music, the cloying sweetness of the harmonies, the melting beauty of the orchestration, all combine to produce an effect at that time entirely new to opera," states W. S. Pratt. *Faust* is among the first sentimental operas and, despite elements of the maudlin and the obvious, remains one of today's most popular works.

A Parisian, Gounod was trained at the Paris Conservatory and won the *Prix de Rome* in 1839. At one time he considered entering the priesthood and actually studied theology for two years; this accounts for Emile Zola's reference to *Faust* as being "the music of a voluptuous priest." Gounod was familiar with the compositions of Palestrina, who had been rediscovered by the Romantics, as well as with those of Bach, Mozart, Rossini and Weber. Two years after he had written the familiar *Ave Maria,* based on the first prelude of Bach's *Well-tempered Clavichord,* he completed a *Messe solennelle* (1861). During the Franco-Prussian War, the composer moved to England and established a Gounod Choir, which introduced his two sacred trilogies—*La Rédemption* (1882) and *Mors et Vita* (1885). As might be expected, Gounod fell heir to the crowns of Handel and Mendelssohn with the chorally conscious British. Among Gounod's other compositions are the operas, *Le Reine de Saba* (*The Queen of Sheba,* 1862) and *Roméo et Juliette* (1867), whose brilliant "Waltz Song" keeps it alive; and the whimsical *Marche funèbre d'une Marionette* for orchestra (1873). Gounod is still dear to those who wish to recapture a beautiful melodic line.

Georges Bizet (1838-1875) was another Conservatory graduate and *Prix de Rome* winner. This young man, who died prematurely, possessed an uncommon talent. His masterpiece is *Carmen* (1875), held by many to be a perfect opera. Originally an *opéra-comique,* it is realistic, exotic, rhythmic, teeming with melody—a work that wins both professional musicians and the public. Bizet's orchestral tone painting is exceptional; his power of captivating with scenic and musical color, unmatched. In *Carmen,* drawn from Prosper Merimée's novel of Spanish bullfighters, alluring cigarette girls, smugglers, soldiers and primal passion, Bizet found a subject well suited to his gifts. Nothing is omitted to make the opera gripping, dramatic and suspenseful. In its realism, *Carmen* marks a step toward the *verismo* school, as does Verdi's *La Traviata.* It also

Fig. 65. Scene from l'Opera de Paris production of Georges Bizet's *Carmen,* Act 1. The nineteenth-century composer was concerned with opera as an art form, worthy to stand beside a symphony.

takes its place in the long list of French compositions conceived in a Spanish idiom.

Among Bizet's other works are the operas, *Les Pêcheurs de perles* (*The Pearl Fishers,* 1863) and *La jolie Fille de Perth* (*The Pretty Girl of Perth,* 1867); a youthful but pleasingly contrived *Symphony No. 1 in C*; and two picturesque *L'Arlésienne Suites,* written in 1872 as incidental music to Daudet's play of that name and often used as ballet music for *Carmen.*

LIGHT OPERA

Our story of the development of opera in the nineteenth century cannot overlook **operetta** or **light opera,** which, in Einstein's words, "belongs to Romantic opera as the satyr play belonged to Attic drama." A foremost master of this form was Jacques Offenbach (1819-1880), whose operas flourished when neither Wagner nor Berlioz could obtain hearings in Paris. A German from Cologne, Offenbach, like Meyerbeer, became more Parisian than the natives. His clothes were more *coloratura* than Italian opera and many a tale is told of his costumes and gaudy umbrellas. Nevertheless, he wrote light opera of the most engaging and graceful variety, with fine melody, becoming dignity and amusing librettos, mirroring the atmosphere of gaiety during the Second Empire. In a statement written in 1856, Offenbach left no doubt as to his intentions as a composer. He felt that the current French operas were mongrels, whereas those of the eighteenth-century masters, like Grétry, pointed a way to purification of the line. Offenbach aspired to revive the earlier *opéra-comique, "le genre primitif et gai"* ("the primitive and merry kind"), whose virtues consisted of brevity, simplicity and genuine tunefulness, coupled with social parody.

Offenbach's most successful operas were *Orphée aux enfers* (*Orpheus in Hades,* 1858), *La belle Hélène* (1864), *Barbe-Bleue* (*Bluebeard,* 1866), *La Vie Parisienne* (*Parisian Life,* 1866), *La grande Duchesse de Gérolstein* (1867) and a grand opera, *Les Contes d'Hoffmann* (*The Tales of Hoffmann*), which was left unfinished, but produced in 1881, soon after his death. This work alone gives Offenbach an unqualified right to his reputation as a highly skilled composer.

Among Offenbach's followers in France were Jean-Robert Planquette (1848-1903), composer of *Les Cloches de Corneville* (*The Chimes of Normandy,* 1877); and Alexandre-Charles Lecocq (1832-1918), writer of *La Fille de Mme. Angot* (1872). Lecocq shared, with Bizet, a prize offered by Offenbach in 1857.

A distinguished Viennese violinist, composer and conductor, Johann Strauss, Jr. (1825-1899) came of a musical family. His father, Johann, and his brothers, Joseph and Edouard, also composed, conducted and played the violin. Had Johann Jr. obeyed his father, the world would never have known his music. Instead, he became the toast of Vienna, indeed of a world swept off its feet by a dancing craze, in which couples whirled and twirled themselves to breathless exhaustion in immense pleasure palaces especially constructed for that purpose. Brahms is said to have claimed Strauss as the one composer with whom he would trade places. On a lady's fan, Brahms quoted the opening measures of "The Beautiful Blue Danube" waltz, with the comment, *"Leider nicht von Brahms"*—"Alas, not by Brahms." In 1872, at the invitation of the city of Boston, Strauss visited the United States, conducting 20,000 singers and a huge orchestra (with the aid of 100 assistants). In fourteen Boston performances and four in New York City Strauss earned a net $100,-000 for his efforts.

Among his brilliant operettas are *Die Fledermaus* (*The Bat,* 1874), recently revived as *Rosalinda*; *Der Zigeunerbaron* (*The Gypsy Baron,* 1885); and *Eine Nacht in Venedig* (*A Night in Venice,* 1883). Strauss acquired the name, "Waltz King," because of his rhythmically scintillant, piquant, tuneful and well-orchestrated dances, numbering almost 500. Among the favorites are "The Beautiful Blue Danube" (1867), "Wine, Women and Song" (1869), "Tales from the Vienna Woods" (1868) and "Roses from the South" (1878).

Although England had relinquished its indigenous expression to Handelian and Mendelssohnian influences, it developed a delightful light opera of its own, from Balfe through Noel Coward's musical comedies. Michael William Balfe (1808-1870), born in Ireland, early showed signs of precocity. He became a conductor and singer, as well as a composer, spending some time in Italy, after which he wrote his first English work, *The Siege of Rochelle,* produced in 1835. Its success was such that the celebrated singer, Malibran, took a part in his next Drury Lane production, *The Maid of Artois* (1836). *The Maid of Honour* was presented at the same theater in 1847 under the baton of no less a personage than Hector Berlioz. Of Balfe's thirty operas, only *The Bohemian Girl* (1843) survives obscurity. The English musical stage during the nineteenth century was not a distinguished one, in general, and when we recall that England's vocal contributions to Romantic music literature included " 'Twas the Last Rose of Summer" and "Home, Sweet Home," we can better understand the contemporary stature of Balfe, and his Irish compatriot, William Vincent Wallace (1812-1865).

Following the lead of Offenbach in Paris and Strauss in Vienna, was Arthur Seymour Sullivan (1842-1900), the widest known and best loved of English light opera composers. With W. S. Gilbert as librettist

Fig. 66. "Johann Strauss in Heaven"—caricature by Th. Zasche. Here Strauss is displayed surrounded by an audience of famous listeners, including (from left to right): Haydn, Mozart, Lanner, Beethoven, Strauss the elder, Offenbach, Schubert, Brahms, Verdi, Wagner and Bruckner.

par excellence, Sullivan composed twenty sparkling light operas, including *Trial by Jury* (1875), *H.M.S. Pinafore* (1878), *The Pirates of Penzance* (1879), *Patience* (1881), *Iolanthe* (1882), *Princess Ida* (1884), *The Mikado* (1885), *Ruddigore* (1887) and *The Gondoliers* (1889), all topically witty when they were first presented and still good fun today.

Son of a clarinetist, Sullivan had been a choirboy before he entered the Royal Academy of Music on a Mendelssohn Scholarship, established after Mendelssohn's death and in his honor. Sullivan continued his studies at the Leipzig Conservatory, again associated with Mendelssohn. And he attained his first notice in England with incidental music to Shakespeare's *The Tempest*—shades of Mendelssohn once more. In 1867, he and George Grove made a trip to Vienna, where they uncovered Schubert's long neglected score of the *Rosamunde* music. Here any close association with Mendelssohn ends, however. The historic collaboration between Gilbert and Sullivan began in 1871 with *Thespis*. In addition

MUSIC OF EARLY ROMANTICISM

to light operas, Sullivan composed cantatas, such as *The Golden Legend* (on words by Henry Wadsworth Longfellow, 1886); and a grand opera, *Ivanhoe* (1891), that, while temporarily popular, adds nothing to his reputation. How many realize that Sullivan also composed the stirring hymn, "Onward Christian Soldiers" and that Victorian relic, "The Lost Chord"?

* * * * *

In summary, we have noted that German, French and, to a lesser extent, Italian opera composers participated in the Romantic movement. We have seen how Shakespeare, Scott, Goethe, Beaumarchais, Schiller, Moore, Hoffmann and other authors inspired their musical dramas. Weber set an example with *Der Freischütz*; Rossini brought *opera buffa* to its culmination; and Meyerbeer provided a prototype for epic grand opera, with its five acts, its pageantry and its stereotypes.

We have yet to discuss the two towering operatic specialists, Richard Wagner and Giuseppe Verdi, the most significant composers of opera in the nineteenth century. We may gain an intimation of their stature from Einstein, who writes: "Wagner and Verdi, each in his way surmounted *'grande opéra:'* Wagner through opposition, exploitation and virtuosity; Verdi through sincerity, simplicity and the honesty of his feeling and musicianship."

SUGGESTIONS FOR FURTHER READING

Abraham, Gerald, *A Hundred Years of Music*. London, Duckworth, 1949.

Barzun, Jacques, *Berlioz and the Romantic Century*.* New York, Columbia University Press, 1950.

Blom, Eric, *Music in England*.* New York, Penguin, 1947.

Cooper, Martin, *French Music from the Death of Berlioz to the Death of Fauré*. London, Oxford University Press, 1951.

Curtiss, Mina, *Bizet and His World*. New York, Knopf, 1958.

Dean, Winton, *Bizet*. London, Dent, 1948.

Einstein, Alfred, *Music in the Romantic Era*. New York, Norton, 1947.

Hughes, Gervase, *The Music of Arthur Sullivan*. New York, St. Martin's Press, 1956.

Jacob, Heinrich E., *Strauss, Father and Son*. New York, Greystone, 1940.

Kracauer, Siegfried, *Orpheus in Paris*. New York, Knopf, 1938.

Loewenberg, Alfred, *Annals of Opera*. Cambridge, Heffer, 1955.

Mayer, Dorothy Moulton, *The Forgotten Master: Life and Times of Louis Spohr*. London, Weidenfeld & Nicolson, 1959.

Offenbach, Jacques, *Orpheus in America*. Bloomington: University of Indiana Press, 1957.

Pastene, Jerome, *Three-Quarter Time: The Life and Music of the Strauss Family*. New York, Abelard-Schuman, 1951.

Pleasants, Henry, *The Great Singers*. New York, Simon & Schuster, 1967.

Poutales, Guy de, *Weber*. New York, Harper, 1932.

* Available in paperback edition.

Revitt, Paul, *Nineteenth-Century Romanticism in Music.** Englewood Cliffs, Prentice-Hall, 1967.

Starr, William J. and Devine, George F., *Music Scores—Omnibus, Part 2.** Englewood Cliffs, Prentice-Hall, 1964.

Stebbins, L. and R. P., *Enchanted Wanderer, Life of Carl Maria von Weber.* New York, Putnam, 1940.

Toye, Francis, *Rossini: A Study in Tragi-Comedy.* New York, Knopf, 1947.

Williamson, Audrey, *Gilbert and Sullivan Opera — A New Assessment.* New York, Macmillan, 1953.

A SAMPLER OF SUPPLEMENTARY RECORDINGS

Collections

Romanticism	Victor 6153
2000 Years of Music	Folkways 3700
Ten Centuries of Music	DGG KL-52/61
Viennese Operettas (Gueden)	London 5360
Art of the Prima Donna (Sutherland)	London 4241
Fabulous Vienna	Scala 841/858
German Opera	London 5807
French Opera Arias (Callas)	Angel 35882
Operatic Arias (Caruso)	Victor LCT-1007
Operatic Arias (Siepi)	London 5255
Mad Scenes	Angel 35764

Music of Individual Composers

Beethoven, Ludwig, *Fidelio*
Bellini, Vincenzo, *Norma*
Bizet, Georges, *L'Arlésienne Suites*
    Carmen
Cherubini, Luigi, *Overtures*
Cimarosa, Domenico, *Overtures*
Donizetti, Gaetano, *Lucia di Lammermoor*
    Don Pasquale
Flotow, Friedrich von, *Martha*
Gounod, Charles, *Faust*
    Messe solennelle ("St. Cecilia")
Lortzing, Albert, *Ballet Music: Undine* and *Zar und Zimmermann*
Meyerbeer, Giacomo, *L'Africaine*
    Les Huguenots
    Le Prophète
Nicholai, Otto, *Merry Wives of Windsor*
Offenbach, Jacques, *Orpheus in Hades*
    Tales of Hoffmann
Rossini, Gioacchino, *The Barber of Seville*
    Stabat Mater
    William Tell
    L'Italiana in Algeri
Strauss, Johann Jr., *Fledermaus*
    Waltzes

Sullivan, Arthur, *Mikado*
Suppé, Franz von, *Overtures*
Thomas, Ambroise, *Mignon*
Weber, Carl M. von, *Abu Hassan*
Der Freischütz
Kampf und Sieg
Oberon
Overtures

OPPORTUNITIES FOR STUDY IN DEPTH

1. If possible, attend a performance of one of the operas mentioned in this chapter. Secure a libretto beforehand in order to become familiar with the dramatic action. Take notice of the Romantic features, as indicated here.

2. Life in nineteenth-century Vienna has often been called the "Biedermeyer Age." What is meant by this? Who was Biedermeyer? What manifestations appear in Viennese music?

3. The Salzburg Marionette Theater is known for its presentations of Mozart operas. As a class project, design puppets and "produce" a scene from an opera by Weber, Rossini or one of the French composers. If practical, present a performance for children, with an explanation couched in terms they can understand.

4. The name of the nineteenth-century novelist, Sir Walter Scott, has been mentioned frequently in the foregoing account of Romantic opera. Make a study of the use of his works by Romantic composers, and comment on his popularity as a source of inspiration.

5. With the aid of scores and recordings, analyze and compare three *arias* drawn from the Baroque, Classic and Romantic periods. A suitable selection could include: *"Gioite al canto mio"* ("Rejoice to See the World!") from Peri's *Eurydice; "Là, ci darem la mano"* ("Pledge Now Thy Hand") from Mozart's *Don Giovanni;* and *"Connais tu le pays?"* ("Know You the Land?") from Thomas' *Mignon.*

6. Investigate further the similarities and differences between German, French and Italian opera during the Romantic period. In what ways has the "universalism" of Classic opera been modified?

7. Explore more carefully any one aspect of, or composer of, Romantic opera. An interesting topic for consideration would be the part played by ballet in the Romantic musical theater, together with some of the music used.

8. We have mentioned the production dates of most of the operas discussed within the chapter. When were they introduced to America? Where? By whom? With what effect?

VOCABULARY ENRICHMENT

union of the arts	*opéra-comique*
corps de ballet	*prima donna*
"rescue opera"	*coloratura*
lithography	lyric opera
deus ex machina	operetta or light opera
blue-stocking	Viennese waltz

PART VIII

Music of Later Romanticism

Chapter 20.
TWO OPERATIC COLOSSI
— WAGNER AND VERDI

I know perfectly well that success is impossible for me if I cannot write as my heart dictates, free of any outside influence whatsoever, without having to keep in mind that I'm writing for Paris and not for the inhabitants of, say, the moon. Furthermore, the singers would have to sing as I wish, not as they wish, and the chorus . . . would have to show the same goodwill. A single will would have to rule throughout: my own. That may seem rather tyrannical to you, and perhaps it is. But if my work is an organic whole, it is built on a single idea and everything must contribute to the achievement of this unity.

—Giuseppe Verdi, Genoa, December 7, 1869.

One of the few things two such different composers as Wagner and Verdi had in common was a total dedication to the operatic stage. Each man composed for performance, although Verdi was luckier than Wagner in this respect. Each was thoroughly acquainted with, and personally active in, all phases of production, from the largest aspect to the smallest detail. Each was adamant in his vision of opera and in belief in his own powers of creation. Although Verdi wrote as his heart dictated and unblushingly used the word, inspiration, we may dismiss any thought of a sentimental approach and rather remember that Verdi was a simpler human being than the sophisticated and articulate Wagner. What, after all, is the definition of "heart"? Yet each man played a large role in the later phases of Romanticism, and it is strange that, in what often appears to have been one big European musical social club, Wagner and Verdi never met, although Verdi is said to have been saddened by news of the death of his German nemesis.

RICHARD WAGNER—LIFE

Richard Wagner (1813-1883), perhaps the greatest Romanticist of all, was born in Leipzig, the youngest of nine children. His father died shortly after his birth and his mother married Ludwig Geyer, an artist and actor, who made him an excellent stepfather. It was he who introduced Richard to the theater, the institution that was to dominate his life. Wagner attended the Kreuz School in Dresden and mastered the classics, language, poetry and drama with avidity. He seemed to care more for poetry, especially Shakespeare, than for music. Although music became the cornerstone of his life, he always preferred to be called a poet.

When he returned to Leipzig in 1827, Wagner's interest centered in the *Gewandhaus* concerts and in the orchestral music of Beethoven, much of which he laboriously transcribed for the piano. A performance of *Fidelio* made a lasting impression on him. At the University, where he enrolled as a music student, he was rather dilatory and disinclined toward arid formal instruction, much preferring his independent investigations. He wrote an overture, mysteriously notated in three colors of ink, which was given a public (but anonymous) performance in 1830 at the Leipzig Theater, where his quixotic drumbeat, coming at every fourth bar, convulsed the audience and convinced the composer he needed the discipline he had been avoiding. For about six months, he studied with the responsive Theodor Weinlig (1780-1842), then Cantor of St. Thomas', and was introduced to counterpoint and the practices of Palestrina, Bach and Beethoven. Among his youthful works are a *Sonata in B flat* (published, thanks to Weinlig, by Breitkopf and Härtel), a *Polonaise in D* for four hands and a symphony that was submitted to Mendelssohn and lost. Wagner's first attempt at opera was the abandoned *Die Hochzeit (The Wedding,* 1832) and his second, written after he was appointed chorusmaster at Würzburg, was an equally bloody work, *Die Feen (The Fairies,* 1834), never performed during his lifetime, although we occasionally hear its overture now.

At Leipzig, Wagner met Wilhelmina Schröder-Devrient, a celebrated soprano, whose interest and friendship influenced him deeply. Under her enchantment, *Das Liebesverbot (Forbidden Love),* a rather sensual version of Shakespeare's *Measure for Measure,* was produced in 1836. Its failure and the resulting bankruptcy of his non-subsidized company were his first fiascos, compounded by his marriage to a small-time actress, Minna Planer. Wagner spent a year in Königsberg, after which he secured a post in Riga. From 1836 to 1839 he composed two acts of *Rienzi.*

With the Riga contract at an end, Wagner, characteristically very much in debt, fled to Paris. En route he heard a sailor's tale that planted the seed for *Der fliegende Holländer (The Flying Dutchman).* When he reached Paris, he sought to ingratiate himself with Meyerbeer, who gave him letters of introduction to the *Opéra* directors but from whom he received no commissions. Starving by now, Wagner did hack work for publishers and wrote essays. Early in 1840 he composed *A Faust*

Overture, his first composition to be regarded as distinctive, and completed *Rienzi, Last of the Tribunes.* He constantly tried to stimulate interest in his works but everywhere met with flattering comments and nothing else. Liszt, who later became his advocate, snubbed him and Meyerbeer, although well disposed, did nothing more for him. Wagner took his libretto of *The Flying Dutchman* to the *Opéra* management who, ironically, bought it for Pierre Dietsch (1808-1865), a conductor, to set to music. Nothing daunted and grateful for the 500 francs, Wagner composed his own score during a seven-week stretch in 1841. *Tannhäuser* was now occupying his mind and while researching the story, Wagner conceived the idea of *Lohengrin.*

Borrowing his carfare, Wagner returned to Dresden in 1842 to conduct a production of *Rienzi,* with Madame Devrient in the cast. It was such a success that Wagner was assured of a performance of *The Flying Dutchman,* with Devrient as Senta, in the following year. If the Meyerbeer craze aided *Rienzi,* it doomed *The Flying Dutchman* in frivolous Dresden, although the work enjoyed a favorable reception at Cassel, when Spohr presented it. For a short time, Wagner's music was in some demand. Moreover, he was appointed Royal *Kapellmeister* in Dresden, where he worked hard to raise musical standards. His first official act was to assist Berlioz with his rehearsals. He also spearheaded a campaign to have Weber reinterred in the town that he had served for ten years.

Tannhäuser had its premiere in 1845 and met with hostility, due to a poor performance and to the fact that Wagner would not make concessions to his audience. The opera triumphed, however, in Weimar, Munich, Berlin and Vienna. Both Schumann and Mendelssohn saw it. Schumann felt that it definitely advanced German opera, but Mendelssohn thought only the canon in the second *finale* worthy of mention. Lack of appreciation did not discourage Wagner from completing *Lohengrin.* But it may have precipitated his subsequent rash actions.

Although he was given a raise and his debts were paid by the Dresden authorities, Wagner was increasingly unhappy with the state of affairs in general and with his demanding routine in particular. Always a free thinker, he came to feel that the theater was corrupt because society and the government were likewise corrupt. He was drawn to the socialist *Vaterlandsverein* and became involved in local politics that definitely threatened the conservative court. Typically, he threw restraint to the winds. Revolution did indeed come and Wagner was lucky to escape dire consequences by fleeing in 1849, first to Weimar and then to Switzerland, where he felt "free at last."

From 1849 through 1852 Wagner wrote no music but instead concentrated on clarifying his ideas and expounding his beliefs in a series of tracts that include *Art and Revolution* (1849), *The Art Work of the Future* (1850) and the important *Opera and Drama* (1851), as well as a scurrilous unsigned diatribe, *Das Judenthum in der Musik* (*Judaism in Music*). In Zürich, where he and a bewildered Minna had settled, Wagner made more enemies than friends because of his outspoken and fiery views. He kept in contact with opera through Franz Abt, the song composer who was director of the Zürich Theater until 1852 and through the kind offices of Hans von Bülow (1830-1894), a devoted follower. Wagner's music was infrequently included in subscription concerts; for instance, *Tannhäuser* was presented in 1855. But there were very few men like Franz Liszt who had the courage to espouse a radical's cause by presenting *Lohengrin* at Weimar—an opera that took nine years to reach Dresden and Berlin and did not cross the English Channel until 1875.

During this period Wagner had time for the investigations that eventuated in *The Ring* cycle and his last three operas. Before he left Dresden he had formulated the basis of *Siegfried's Death,* under the influence of the Russian anarchist, Sakunin. After completing *Opera and Drama,* he proceeded to put his theories in effect by writing the libretto of *Siegfried's Death,* only to realize that a full exposition required three more music dramas. He commenced writing *Das Rheingold* while on a trip to Italy in 1853. In 1854 he undertook *Die Walküre.* And in the following year Wagner conducted a series of concerts in London and again met Berlioz. But his zeal for Beethoven in a thoroughly Mendelssohnian area, combined with his unorthodox opinions, did not endear Wagner to London, where he was considered little more than his *prima donna* niece's uncle. He discarded *The Ring* for *Tristan und Isolde.*

In the meantime, two influences shaped his decision. One was that the composer had made the acquaintance of a wealthy Zürich merchant, Otto Wesendonck, who, in Wagner's words "had amassed a not inconsiderable fortune through his connection with a big New York silk business." Following his usual custom, Wagner began to impose on the friendship, dwelling in a house Wesendonck purchased for him, borrowing money he had no intention of repaying and having an affair with his friend's wife, Mathilde. "Curiously enough," he commented, "this neighborly intimacy coincided with the beginning of my poem of 'Tristan und Isolde.' " The other influence was exerted by the dour philosopher, Arthur Schopenhauer, whose *The World As Will and Idea* Wagner is said to have read through four times in a span of nine months. "It was probably partly the serious mood that Schopenhauer had induced in me, and that now demanded ecstatic expression, which suggested the conception of 'Tristan und Isolde,' " he explained. In any case, alone and depressed, Wagner set to work on *Tristan* in Venice during 1858.

Wagner decided to revisit Paris. Through the good graces of Madame de Metternich, a production of *Tannhäuser* was arranged in 1861. "Its failure was as great as the opera," write Stanford and Forsyth. Intrigue and cabal did their worst. When ordered to put in a ballet (the "New Venusberg Music"—probably the most brilliant thing he had written), Wagner interpolated it in the first act. This offense against Parisian taste became the excuse for bitter demonstrations and jeering; the *débâcle* was complete.

A silver lining to the cloud presented itself in Wagner's renewed popularity in Germany and expedited his return, through Minna's interceding petitions for pardon, after thirteen years' exile. Moreover, he was called to Vienna in 1861 to rehearse *Lohengrin,* which he had never heard, and for some seventy-seven rehearsals of *Tristan,* which was finally shelved, leaving the composer understandably disconsolate. On his way back from exile, however, Wagner received an ovation at Weimar and at Mannheim he found an interest in *Die Meistersinger,* on which he had worked in Paris. From 1862 to 1864 he engaged in what he called "a long series of absurd undertakings," conducting concerts in Russia and elsewhere.

In 1864 Wagner arrived in Stuttgart, as usual, with waning funds. As a consequence of serendipitous circumstances, he was invited to Munich by young Ludwig II of Bavaria, to complete *The Ring.* Furthermore, in 1865, von Bülow presented *Tristan und Isolde* in Munich. But Wagner's lack of diplomacy soon incurred enmity again and he returned to Switzerland. There he stayed for seven years, during which he finished most of *The Ring* operas and exasperated musicians by his vituperative attacks on all rivals.

Previous to this, however, Wagner had become emotionally embroiled once more, this time with the wife of von Bülow, Liszt's daughter, Cosima. When Wagner had established himself in Munich, he quickly secured a post there for von Bülow, so that Cosima would be near. She became Wagner's amanuensis and mistress. After much scandal and the birth of two daughters, one brazenly named Isolde, the couple left Munich and settled in Lucerne in 1865. There Cosima bore Wagner a son, Siegfried. Richard and Cosima were finally married, after Minna's death and Cosima's divorce, in 1870 at *Triebschen,* their Swiss retreat. As a result of his behavior, Wagner's relations with Liszt and the King became strained. But at *Triebschen* he completed *Die Meistersinger* (1867), presented by the ever devoted and much wronged von Bülow at Munich in 1868, and *Siegfried* (1869), conducted by Hans Richter at Bayreuth in 1876.

King Ludwig, in the meantime, abandoned his idea of building a theater in Munich for Wagner's *Ring* cycle. So Wagner, his star in the ascendant and his popularity as a composer mounting, turned his attention to the town of Bayreuth. He moved there in 1872 and with money from the King and funds collected in Europe and America, he commenced the construction of a theater built to his own exacting specifications, a big barn of a place with a huge stage and a recessed orchestra pit, the *Festspielhaus* (Festival Theater), whose cornerstone was laid in 1872 and which has ever since been a Mecca for Wagner devotees. In 1874 *The Ring* was completed and in 1876 it was presented in its entirety. Although a financial failure, its debut was a glittering affair, attended by musicians such as Tchaikovsky, Gounod, Grieg, Liszt and Saint-Saëns as well as the German Emperor, the Emperor of Brazil, princes and dukes galore, together with the working press, including correspondents from New York. It brought such *réclame* that later success was assured.

Fig. 67. The Festival Opera House at Bayreuth. Wagner devoted much time and energy to obtain funds to build his own opera house which is still operated today by members of his family. (Photograph of the editor.)

Thanks to the interest and generosity of innumerable persons, the *Festspielhaus* had become a reality and Wagner had his permanent monument. A Lucerne friend, who had worked zealously in behalf of the scheme, was the philosopher, Friedrich Nietzsche, then professor of philology at the University of Basle. The aggressive self-satisfaction of the new Imperial Germany with its "beer-mug patriotism" disgusted Nietzsche, however, and his increasing disillusionment with Wagner is a story in itself.

Had Wagner been less anxious to spread his dogma and theories in vitriol, he might have avoided the initial difficulties he encountered; but he was ever irascible. Faced with an appalling deficit of some $40,000, Wagner journeyed to London in 1878 to raise money by concert-giving. From 1877 to 1882 he was also writing *Parsifal,* his last music drama, which was presented at Bayreuth in 1882, a year before his death. Except for a period of ten years during World War I, the *Festspielhaus* has been open and operated by members of the Wagner family, first Cosima, from 1886 until her death, then Siegfried (until 1930) and now by the composer's grandsons, of whom Wieland Wagner, who died in 1966, created a wholly new staging for his grandfather's works.

With failing health a problem, Wagner and Cosima moved to Venice and lived in the *Palazzo Vendramini* on the Grand Canal. There Wagner enjoyed his surroundings and happily explored the jeweled city. Liszt visited the Wagners for a month but declined an offer to live with them permanently. In addition to a *dermatitis* which had always troubled Wagner, it was discovered that he had heart disease as well. He died quite suddenly on Feb. 13, 1883. His remains lie in an ivy-covered vault he had built at Bayreuth at the rear of his home, the villa, *Wahnfried.*

RICHARD WAGNER—CONTRIBUTIONS

As a man, Wagner was despicable by most standards; he was arrogant, self-centered, ruthless and opportunistic. "The world owes me what I need," he once said proudly. He slandered his colleagues, rejoiced in their defeats, constantly proclaimed his own supremacy and indulged himself in every luxury, including silk underclothes, fur-lined trousers and a wardrobe of twenty-four dressing gowns of different colors. Whenever possible he lived in palatial homes, betraying one friend after another but denying himself nothing. His aims never faltered; no one, nothing impeded him. He was rapacious in acquiring his due, for he was convinced that he was indeed creating the "Music of the Future."

Fig. 68. Richard Wagner with wife Cosima, and father-in-law Franz Liszt—painting by W. Beckman. A complex man, Wagner composed his music dramas amid the luxurious surroundings he demanded for his work. (Courtesy The Bettmann Archive.)

No man did more to revolutionize opera than Wagner. Thomas Mann makes the interesting statement that Wagner was "the complete expression" of the nineteenth century. The composer's talents developed gradually. Successively he solved his self-imposed problems, until he reached exalted heights in the music dramas of *The Ring, Tristan und Isolde* and *Parsifal*. No estimate of Wagner's work can preclude his theories, although he did not always practice what he preached. What he achieved, however, was enough for any man, and has enriched music through the ages, so much so that today we are tempted to speak of "before Wagner" and "after Wagner."

In terms of orchestral development, Wagner was an important innovator. He knew few instruments unknown to Beethoven, yet by dividing the orchestra into separate choirs, subdividing the choirs themselves, doubling and adding instruments, when he required them, Wagner made over the Beethovenian orchestra into a Wagnerian orchestra. His *divisi* violin writing in the *Overture to Lohengrin* lends a silvery shimmer to the music. When the gods cross over to Valhalla in *Das Rheingold,* Wagner uses not one, but six harps, each with its own part. Brasses become as necessary as the strings. Often Wagner adds a third oboe or a third bassoon or a third trumpet. By adroit manipulation, he attains in each set of instruments complete chords of a uniform *timbre.* In order to capture an effect that standard instruments could not produce, Wagner designed his own—*i.e.,* the "Wagner tuba." The orchestra became an active protagonist in the drama.

Wagner's concept of music drama was symphonic, in contrast to the vocal orientation of Italian composers. To coordinate vocal and instrumental forces, Wagner turned to the device of *Leitmotif* (or *Grundthema,* as he called it), similar to Berlioz's *l'idée fixe* in function and used somewhat in the manner of Liszt's thematic transformation in the symphonic poems. A **Leitmotif** is a brief motto theme, intimately associated with either a character, an object, an idea or a place. It parallels in sound the dramatic action and the psychological values of a situation at any given moment, weaving through the music as a means of identification, reminiscence and thought projection, instantly recognizable by the listener, although constantly altered. As Machlis writes, "Through a process of continual transformation the leitmotifs trace the course of the drama, the changes in the characters, their experiences and memories, their thoughts and hidden desires."

To accomplish his lofty purpose, Wagner exhausted every resource at his command, utilizing counterpoint and harmony, rhythm and *timbre* to augment emotional expression when required, but never for mere superficial effect. Unstable harmonies and curious dissonances abound in his later works. Especially in *Tristan und Isolde,* he pushed chromatic harmony to its extreme limit, so that the harmony transcends both melody and rhythm as an agent portraying "states of soul." His scores are minutely marked, leaving nothing to the whims of performers or conductors.

"Every bar of dramatic music is justified only by the fact that it explains something in the action or in the character of the actor," Wagner had written. In implementing his ideas, he found that the traditional pace of opera, with its recitatives, *arias* and choruses, was not satisfactory. Although *Rienzi, Tannhäuser* and *Lohengrin* adhere in many respects to convention, the later music dramas depart from it. Wagner omitted the "set pieces" in favor of an *arioso* style, a "continuous melody," less dry than recitative and more elastic than the *aria.* He abandoned folksong for ecstatic and epic declamation. Following in the footsteps of Weber and Gluck, he treated soloists and chorus only as part of the whole. His demands upon singers are tremendous. Even his friend, Madame Devrient, said, "You are a man of genius, but you write such eccentric stuff, it is hardly possible to sing it."

Not satisfied with librettos that reduced musical forms to absurdities, Wagner wrote his own, based on the idea of "shorter and more plastic germ themes . . . to cast no obstacle in the musician's way," as Newman states it. With the greatest stretch of imagination, Wagner's verse often falls short of the poetic. Newman calls it "telegraphic style." For example, in Act II of *Tristan und Isolde,* Wagner carries brevity to almost ludicrous lengths:

> Tristan: *Isolde Geliebte* (Isolde beloved).
> Isolde: *Tristan Geliebter* (Tristan beloved).
> Tristan: *Hab' ich dich wieder?* (Have I you again?)
> Isolde: *Darf ich dich fassen?* (Dare I embrace you?)

If indeed Wagner failed to scale the summits to which he aspired, it may have been because he was a better musician than poet, although in writing his own librettos, he gained a unity of subject, language, action and music necessary to drama in music. Gluck and Weber had held similar ideas, but neither had the orchestral resources nor the imagination to create an autoprogressive tale in the way Wagner did. His subjects were equal in grandeur to those of the ancient Greek dramatists who, like Wagner, made grist of the breadth and scope of their lofty ideas.

OPERAS

Wagner's significant operas begin with *Der fliegende Holländer,* in which he vaulted ahead and introduced one of his favorite themes, redemption through love. Newman comments, "There is no mistaking the intensity and certainty of his vision now. He no longer describes his characters from the outside, they are *within him,* making their own language and using him as their unconscious instrument."

In *Lohengrin,* a Germanic story of intrigue and love, Wagner comes nearer to the ideal of continuity, although he continues to employ the *aria*—chorus—ensemble pattern, but transfused with a richness and inventiveness peculiarly his. Newman writes:

> . . . the text still retains a number of nonemotional moments for which no really lyrical equivalent can be found, but what would have been recitative naked and unashamed in *Rienzi* is now almost fully clothed song . . . The choral writing attains an unaccustomed breadth and sonority . . . becomes a more psychological instrument . . . In *Lohengrin* the voice is still the statue, and the orchestra the pedestal.

After extricating himself from the vortex of a philosophical and political maelstrom, Wagner again took up work on *The Ring* cycle, projecting a three-act drama, *Siegfried's Death,* which later developed into *Die Götterdämmerung* (*The Twilight of the Gods*), the fourth and last of the prologue and trilogy that constitute *Der Ring des Nibelungen,* "a stage-festival play for three days and a preliminary evening." *Das Rheingold* (*The Rhine Gold*) serves as a gate to Wagner's new realm of gods, humans and supernatural creatures, drawn from an ancient epic, the *Nibelungenlied.* It is followed by *Die Walküre, Siegfried* and *Die Götterdämmerung.* In essence, the theme of *The Ring* is that greed destroys and only by unselfishness and immolation is there salvation. Freedom, desire and redemption by love all play parts in the rather complicated narrative. In these four music dramas, Wagner reaches musical maturity. His resources are marshalled and controlled. The music has been concentrated. An end comes to the *aria.* Music drama emerges as a pictorial symphony, program music *in excelsis.* Occasionally, repetition and over-long speeches threaten Wagner's desired continuity. Nevertheless, he succeeds, to a large degree, in synthesizing the arts into a single expressive entity.

Although *Tristan und Isolde* is based on an Irish legend, it was considered by its composer "as an accessory to the *Nibelungen* inasmuch as it presents certain aspects of the mythical matter for which in the main work there is no room." Of all love dramas in music, this is the most ecstatic and sublime. The music, telling the story far better than the words, expresses love and thwarted love with a passionately-mounting power such as had never been heard before. If the long explanation in the first act had not been necessary, and had there not been other minor discrepancies, Wagner would have composed the perfect music drama.

Die Meistersinger von Nürnberg, Wagner's only comic opera, depicts colorful doings during a song contest in Renaissance Germany. The clash of rival musicians, the old tale of Walther and Eva, the carping Beckmesser (patterned after Wagner's bitter critic, Eduard Hanslick), the noble Hans Sachs and the trade guilds are bathed in luminous beauty. In this opera, Wagner took an opportunity to flay, by means of music, entrenched ideas. It was his answer to his detractors, to the struggle between old and new and a plea for spontaneity instead of prescribed artificialities. He shows his skill by not only delivering his doctrines humorously, but also by joining the jocose with deeper human sentiments. Whereas Fate plays the greater part in *The Ring,* human beings play their parts in *Die Meistersinger,* and the music is significant of the difference. Wagner demonstrated that he could portray the naïve, simple, charming and witty as well as the noble, idealized and sublime.

Wagner's last music drama was *Parsifal,* based on medieval legends, of which one was by the *Minnesinger,* Wolfram von Eschenbach. In this work, Wagner created an Arthurian mythology of his own, with the Holy Grail as a subject. Occasionally the music reaches a peak equaled only by Bach's *B Minor Mass.* Nevertheless, there is a static quality about much of *Parsifal,* which may be due to the prominence of the orchestra, to Wagner's failing health or to the poem itself. Furthermore, in *Parsifal,* the character of Gurnemanz is but an empty shell, a verbal libretto, detailing the antecedents of the story. Newman says, "As far as his music is concerned, he has neither mental characteristics nor bodily form." Although the entire opera is seldom performed, the "Good Friday Spell" is a popular mood painting.

"As Beethoven fertilized not the symphony but the music-drama, so Wagner fertilized not the music-drama but poetic instrumental music," states Wagner's biographer, Ernest Newman. It is ironic that Wagner bequeathed his orchestra to his followers but that no one ventured further with his cherished idea of a "universal art work." Newman continues:

> The towering greatness of Wagner is nowhere more strikingly shown than in the failure of all his successors to handle his form—or, indeed, any other—with anything like the same power, freedom and consistency; both the opera and symphonic music are waiting for some one big enough to build afresh from the foundations Wagner has laid and with the material he has left. At present . . . his successors . . . fit a few of the more manageable stones together, with a deplorable quantity of waste and confusion all around and in between. *Salome* and *Elektra* (R. Strauss) may be taken as instructive examples. Like Bach and Beethoven, Wagner closes a period . . .

Followers

After Wagner, German opera trod a difficult road, as far as works approaching the Wagnerian ideal were concerned. Peter Cornelius composed *Der Cid* (1865), following the *Lohengrin* pattern. August Bungert (1845-1915), with his opera cycles, *Homerische Welt* (*Homeric World*), tried unsuccessfully to emulate the seer of Bayreuth. Alexander Ritter (1833-1896), who influenced Richard Strauss, wrote *Der faule Hans* (*Naughty Hans,* 1885) and *Wem die Krone?* (*To Whom the Crown?* 1890), but lacked the inspiration of Wagnerian style.

Among the more successful Wagnerians were Max von Schillings (1868-1933), whose opera, *Mona Lisa* (1915) was given in America and who visited our shores several times as a conductor; Hans Pfitzner (1869-1949), who wrote *Der arme Heinrich* (*Poor Henry,* 1895) and the sometimes revived *Palestrina* (1917); Edmund Kretschmer (1830-1908), whose best work was *Die Volkunger* (1874); and Carl Goldmark (1830-1915), with a decided flair for the stage that the others lacked, who composed *The Queen of Sheba* (1875), *The Cricket on the Hearth* (1896) and a popular overture, *Sakuntala* (1865).

Engelbert Humperdinck (1854-1921), second only to Strauss in late-Romantic Germany, was born in Bonn. His *Hänsel und Gretel* (1893), a fantasy opera, was not originally written as an opera but composed for his sister, who asked him for songs to please some children. Later, he incorporated them in opera form, but had difficulty in getting the work produced. Once heard, however, it was beloved by all the world. *Hänsel und Gretel* is Wagnerian in method, not in vein. The most engaging songs and dances, in folk style, do not break its continuity. In it, Humperdinck unwittingly exceeds all the intentional Wagnerians in his results. Simplicity, tunefulness, humor and imagination are mixed in an enchanting decoction of voices and instruments. Humperdinck's work with Wagner on the score of *Parsifal* and his familiarity with the theater should have netted more than one highly-successful opera, but such was not the judgment of history.

GIUSEPPE VERDI—LIFE AND WORKS

While Germany was pressing toward unification and Wagner was establishing a new order of German opera, Italy, too, was struggling to be born as a free nation, under the leadership of the King of Sardinia, of Giuseppe Mazzini and of Garibaldi. To these patriots, we must add a musical man of the hour, Giuseppe Verdi (1813-1901), who became identified with the passion for liberty that resulted in Italian independence. He arrived on an operatic scene still wedded to weak librettos, the star system, pyrotechnics and other stagnating traditions. Despite these disadvantages, he produced good, better and incomparable operas. He drew upon the resources of Donizetti, Bellini and Rossini, but wove a magnificent fabric all his own. Paul Henry Lang goes so far as to say that Verdi was the last great hero of Italian opera. In any case, he towered above his compatriots.

Giuseppe Verdi, born a few months after Wagner, spent his early years in Le Roncole, near Parma, Italy. His father, an inn-keeper, was of peasant extraction, a fact which may account for a certain streak of toughness in his son's character as well as for his common sense and integrity. Not particularly precocious, Verdi did, however, show signs of musical proclivity and at the age of ten was sent to live in Busseto with a grocer-friend of his father, Antonio Barezzi, so that he might gain from the larger musical facilities of the town. There he studied with a local organist, Ferdinando Provesi, who was also director of the Philharmonic Society. So impressed with young Verdi were the Busseto citizens that they made up a purse and sent him to Milan to further his education. In 1892, Verdi applied for admission to the Milan Conservatory, only to be rejected because he was too old (at eighteen) and considered not sufficiently talented to waive the rules.

After studying privately and conducting a Milanese choral group, Verdi returned to Busseto when Provesi died (1833) and became leader of the Philharmonic Society. In 1836 he married the young daughter of his benefactor and in 1839 moved his wife and family and a manuscript of his first opera back to the metropolis of Milan. On November 17, 1839, *Oberto, Conte di San Bonifacio* was performed at La Scala Opera House and well enough received that the youthful composer was offered publication by Ricordi and a contract to write three new operas. It appeared that the small town boy had made good in the big city.

It was not long, however, before tragedy struck. While at work on a comic opera, *Un Giorno di regno (A Day of the Kingdom,* 1840), Verdi fell ill, his two children sickened and died within two days of each other, and several months later his wife also expired. To complete the sequence of disaster, his opera was a total failure. Distraught from these incredible blows, Verdi forswore music of any kind. It was only through the patient efforts of the manager of La Scala who forced upon the griefstricken man a libretto on the subject of Nebuchadnezzar that the opera, *Nabucco,* was written. Premiered in 1842, it was an instant success.

We sometimes find it difficult to realize the enormous enthusiasm of the Italian public for opera. In this case, on the strength of one opera, Verdi was able to command the highest fee possible for an Italian composer. In addition, he became the fashion, with ties, toys, hats and sauces named in his honor. Of *Nabucco,* Verdi himself wrote:

> With this score my musical career really began . . . It was a group of carpenters that gave me my first assurance of success. The artists were singing as badly as they knew how and the orchestra seemed bent only on drowning out the noise made by the workmen who were doing some alterations in the building. Presently, the chorus began to sing, as carelessly as before, the '*Va, pensiero,*' but before they had got through half a dozen bars the theater was as still as a church. The men had left off their work one by one and there they were, sitting about on the ladders and scaffolding, listening. When the number was finished, they broke out into the noisiest applause I have ever heard, crying, '*Bravo, bravo, viva il maestro!*' and pounding on the woodwork with their tools.

Verdi's next opera, *I Lombardi* (1843), was another triumph and provided the first instance of many tussles Verdi was to have with the Austrian authorities, who were very sensitive to any political implications against the prevailing order. *Ernani* (1844), derived from Victor Hugo's play and commissioned by the Fenice Theater of Venice, also involved Verdi with the Censor, although it established his European reputation. It was at Venice that Verdi met Francesco Piave, who was to be librettist of many of his best-known operas.

Between the years 1844-1851, Verdi wrote ten operas, of which *Macbeth* (1847) is interesting because it evidenced Verdi's life-long attachment to Shakespeare, and *Luisa Miller* (1849), derived from Schiller's *Kabale und Liebe* (*Intrigue and Love*), is significant in that it revealed the composer as a master of the intimate and personal as well as the grand and heroic. The best works were yet to come, however. In 1851 *Rigoletto* was introduced at Venice, after much dissension with the Censors who objected to just about everything in the story, adapted from Victor Hugo's *Le Roi S'amuse*. *Il Trovatore* (*The Troubadur*), composed in four weeks, was first performed in Rome in 1853 and, even though the Tiber had overflowed and the audience had to wade through mud to reach the theater, the house was full and wildly enthusiastic.

La Traviata (*The Lost Lady,* 1853) did not achieve immediate popularity due to a complex of factors. Some thought the plot, which Piave took from Dumas' novel, *La Dame aux camelias,* was immoral. Others took exception to the contemporary costumes. Some failed to understand the simple nature of the music. Others were nonplussed by the plump *prima donna,* who played the role of a dying consumptive. It was only after Verdi, practical as usual, changed the setting (which was of little importance to him) to the time of Louis XIII and supervised a competent production, that the opera gained its following. Verdi had written of it, "Time will tell," and it certainly did.

Other memorable operas flowed from Verdi's pen: *Les Vêpres Sicilennes* (*Sicilian Vespers,* written for Paris 1855); *Simon Boccanegra* (1857); *Un Ballo in maschera* (*The Masked Ball,* 1859), in which the Austrians compelled the composer to transfer the scene of action from Sweden to Boston, of all places; *La Forza del destino* (*The Force of Destiny,* 1862); and *Don Carlos* (1867), Verdi's second and last French opera. These works exemplify Verdi's command of his resources, abounding in a healthy gusto, rich melody, vivid color and an uncommon sense of good theater.

Much had happened to the composer during this period. He had purchased a farm at Sant' Agata, near Busseto, where he spent many happy hours actively engaging in agriculture. While in Paris, he had renewed his acquaintance with a singer who had appeared in *Nabucco,* many years before. Much to the dismay of the good citizens of Busseto, Verdi brought Giuseppina Strepponi to his estate. He later married her.

Because of the political implications of his operas, and the fact that *"Evviva Verdi"* had come to be interpreted as a seditious acrostic, *"Evviva Vittorio Emmanuele, Re D'Italia,"* Verdi had acquired the reputation of a national patriot. When Cavour convened the first Italian parliament in 1860, he asked Verdi to stand for election as deputy, and Verdi felt he could not refuse. He remained a deputy until 1865, but contributed little save his name to legislative deliberations, as he was a thorough independent, yet blindly followed Cavour's policies. In 1874 Verdi was appointed a Senator by the King, but, as it was an honorary title, it required nothing of the composer.

Up to this point in his career, Verdi had been reaching for a finer unity and giving an increasing emphasis to instrumentation. He did not imitate Wagner. In fact, while conversant with his ideas, Verdi felt that they were both inappropriate and alien to Italy. With increasing maturity and experience, however, Verdi's music gained depth and insight, perhaps in a path parallel but not similar to Wagner's. Always a supreme lyricist, with an unfaltering command of melody and a directness of emotional impact, the later Verdi was developing into a superb musical dramatist as well.

In 1869 Verdi was asked to write an opera for the Khedive of Egypt to celebrate two openings—those of his new opera house and of the Suez Canal. Verdi twice refused, but became interested in a *précis* submitted to him by a Mariette Bey. With his wife and Antonio Ghislanzoni, Verdi fashioned a libretto and composed *Aïda,* which was produced in a dazzling manner at the Cairo Opera House in 1871. Verdi, who did not attend, was disgusted by what he heard of the opening, which was somewhat of a circus. But when the work was performed in Milan, six weeks later, its success was assured. A few critical voices were raised, exclaiming that Verdi had become Wagnerian and too complex. Clara Schumann noted in her diary:

> . . . it is curious to see the old composer venturing along new paths. Many parts of it pleased me very much, but many others I did not like. But I must say it fills me with respect for Verdi.

The only significant work that Verdi composed in the fifteen years after *Aïda* was a *Requiem Mass,* which some wits have called "Verdi's finest opera." In 1873 Alessandro Manzoni, author of the classic novel, *I Promessi Sposi (The Promised Spouse),* died and Verdi offered to write a *Requiem* to be sponsored by the city of Milan. Already the composer had parts of it completed, for he had engaged in an abortive attempt to collaborate in a *pastiche*-memorial to Rossini who had died in 1868. The *Requiem* was introduced at Milan (1874) and then taken on tour throughout Europe. In view of Verdi's orientation it is not surprising that elements of the theatrical are present. Toye comments:

> Its genius was obvious at once to no less a person than Brahms, but the famous pianist and conductor, von Bülow . . . found nothing good to say of it in the first instance. Beyond question the Mass must be regarded essentially as a dramatic work . . . But this in no way detracts from the emotional sincerity that is in fact one of its outstanding characteristics; while its general vitality, the skill of choral writing, the vivid colours of the orchestral score, remain as striking today as ever.

After the *Requiem,* Verdi settled down at Sant' Agata, tired, politically-pessimistic and written-out. He became the complete farmer, introducing threshing machines to the countryside instead of operas and attending weekly breeding stock sales at Cremona. Through the connivance of certain friends, however, he again started thinking of music in 1879, when he reluctantly accepted Arrigo Boito (1842-1918) as librettist for what was to be one of the masterpieces of his old age, an opera based on Shakespeare's *Othello.* Boito had written several operas himself, of which *Mefistofele* (1868) is occasionally given today. In 1862 he had supplied words for a cantata which Verdi set, but after that had deserted to the Wagnerian camp. Now Verdi tested him with a revision of *Simon Boccanegra,* before commencing the new opera.

Otello was presented at La Scala in 1887, and Blanche Tucker Roosevelt, who was present, reported the total success which Verdi met, including all sorts of personal tributes by his fellow Milanese. Amazing for a man of seventy-four was the vitality of the work, the refined but melodic recitatives and the blending of music and words. Aging and weakening, Verdi was ready to call it quits but again a Shakespearean theme, this time a comedy, drew him into activity. Boito, basing his libretto on parts of *The Merry Wives of Windsor* and *Henry IV,* created *Falstaff,* probably commenced in 1889 and introduced at Milan in 1893—another incredible work, into which Verdi poured the total experience of his eighty years. *Falstaff* and the *Quatro Pezzi Sacri* (*Four Sacred Pieces*) were his final compositions.

Massenet visited the elderly Verdi in 1895 and wrote:

> He opened the door himself. I stood nonplussed. His sincerity, graciousness, and the nobility which his tall stature gave his whole person soon drew us together, I passed unutterably charming moments in his presence, as we talked with the most delightful simplicity in his bed-

room and then on the terrace of his sitting room from which we looked over the port of Genoa and beyond on the deep sea as far as the eye could reach. I had the illusion that he was one of the Dorias proudly showing me his victorious fleets. As I was leaving, I was drawn to remark that 'now I had visited him, I was in Italy.'

Fig. 69. Verdi statue before the Rest Home for Musicians, Milan. In 1896 Verdi established a Home for Aged Musicians, endowing it in his will. He is buried in its chapel. (Photograph by the editor.)

Verdi was responsible for establishing in Milan (1896) a *Home for Aged Musicians,* endowing it in his will. In 1897 his beloved Giuseppina died and Verdi fled from Sant' Agata, so closely associated with her. He became increasingly feeble and finally succumbed to a paralytic stroke on January 27, 1901. Hundreds of thousands of Milanese lined the streets as his funeral cortège proceeded to the Oratory of the Musicians' Home, where he was buried. Toye concludes:

> It was fitting that this should be so, for Guiseppe Verdi was one of the greatest Italians, in his character, in his patriotism and in his music . . . Of all composers he must be reckoned one of the sanest, the strongest and the most sincere.

LIBRETTOS

Beethoven could find but one libretto he thought worth using; Wagner would not use any but his own; Brahms claimed that he never wrote an opera because he could not find a suitable libretto; and Verdi watched his librettists as a cat a mouse. No one knew better than Verdi the value of a libretto imaginatively written, with a good story and action. Many a good tale and interesting he turned down because it had no action.

In Europe, as we suggested earlier, one-man libretto factories were rampant. Best known among these were Metastasio and Eugène Scribe. While these men lived (and they spanned the eighteenth century through the middle of the nineteenth), many composers made use of them and the librettos becames lusterless. Verdi employed Scribe for his *Sicilian Vespers,* but the work was dull and he was uninterested, until Duveyrier assisted in giving it some life. The French librettists used many plots, often trite, in their bags of tricks, but they fitted ideas to words skillfully. German librettists, on the other hand, did not think much about fitting ideas to words nor about how they might sound when sung. They veered to sentimentality, and worst of all, to moralizing. This is well-illustrated by *Fidelio* and the creations of that arch-librettist and opera-doctor, Richard Wagner.

The Italian librettists, on the other hand, thought of the singer and of display. Since Roman times "good theater" and decoration, often deteriorating into tawdriness, had dominated the Italian stage. With constant guidance and meticulous alteration, Verdi naturally had best results with Italian librettists, among whom were Piave, with *Ernani, Rigoletto, La Traviata, Simon Boccanegra* and *La Forza del destino;* Boito with *Otello* and *Falstaff;* and himself and his second wife in the best version of *Aïda's* libretto, although it is credited to Ghislanzoni.

Nevertheless, Verdi's librettos were more or less routine, nor did they far depart from conventional Italian opera forms. As Einstein comments:

> The long history of Verdi's operas, extending from 1838 to 1893, or almost as long as the reign of Queen Victoria, is the story of an ever greater refinement of musical means within the traditional frame . . . As a rule, Verdi's operas are in four acts, or have three acts and a prologue . . . The stressed portions of Verdi's works, too, almost always come at the same places: the grand finales at the end of the second and third acts, the great duet in the middle of the third, the heroine's prayer at the beginning of the fourth, usually a prayer with chorus, etc. Everything seems to be a matter of . . . highly conventional machinery.

Verdi did not express himself in bizarre rhythms, strange harmonies or tormenting effects produced by overwhelming dynamics, yet he was fully aware, as was Wagner, of the need of change and renewal in opera. He contributed to the improvement of the art, not as a reformer but as a transformer, using his unfailing melodic gift, his inventiveness and his taste to enrich the repertoire. Unfortunately, he was in constant comparison with his highly self-publicized contemporary in Germany. It has taken many years to cede Verdi full credit for his universality and his quality of eternal youth in music.

* * * * *

In discussing Wagner and Verdi, we have noted that each man was sensitive to the emergence of his nation as an independent power in Europe. Although neither employed folksong *per se,* Wagner is thoroughly German while one cannot dispute Verdi's Italian qualities. The development of various schools of nationalistic music is very much a part of musical Romanticism. In the next chapter, we shall explore some manifestations of musical nationalism and representative composers associated with them.

SUGGESTIONS FOR FURTHER READING

Abraham, Gerald, *A Hundred Years of Music.* London, Duckworth, 1949.

Barzun, Jacques, *Darwin, Marx, Wagner.** New York, Doubleday, 1958.

Burk, John, *Letters of Richard Wagner.* New York, Macmillan, 1950.

Donington, Robert, *Wagner's 'Ring' and Its Symbols.* London, Faber & Faber, 1963.

Einstein, Alfred, *Music in the Romantic Era.* New York, Norton, 1947.

Gatti, Carlo, *Verdi: The Man and His Works.* New York, Putnam, 1955.

Hadow, W. H., *Richard Wagner.* London, Butterworth, 1934.

Hussey, Dyneley, *Verdi.* New York, Pellegrini & Cudahy, 1949.

Lavignac, Albert, *Music Dramas of Richard Wagner.* New York, Dodd-Mead, 1942.

Mann, Thomas, *Freud, Goethe, Wagner.* New York, Knopf, 1937.

Mellers, Wilfrid, *Romanticism and the Twentieth Century.* London, Rockliff, 1957.

Newman, Ernest, *The Life of Richard Wagner.* New York, Knopf, 1933–46. 4 vols.

———— *Wagner As Man and Artist.** New York, Tudor, 1948.

Revitt, Paul, *Nineteenth-Century Romanticism in Music.** Englewood Cliffs, Prentice-Hall, 1967.

Shaw, George Bernard, *The Perfect Wagnerite.* New York, Bretano, 1916.

Sheean, Vincent, *Orpheus at Eighty.* New York, Random House, 1958.

Starr, William J., and Devine, George F., *Music Scores—Omnibus,* Part 2.* Englewood Cliffs, Prentice-Hall, 1964.

Stein, Jack M., *Richard Wagner and the Synthesis of the Arts.* Detroit, Wayne State University Press, 1960.

* Available in paperback edition.

Toye, Francis, *Giuseppe Verdi*. New York, Knopf, 1946.
Turner, W. J., *Wagner*. New York, Wyn, 1948.
Wagner, Richard, *Opera and Drama*. New York, Scribner, 1913. 2 vols.
———— *My Life*. New York, Tudor, 1936. 2 vols.
Walker, Frank, *The Man Verdi*. New York, Knopf, 1962.
Werfel, Franz and Stefan, Paul, eds., *Verdi: The Man in His Letters*. New York, Wyn, 1948.

A SAMPLER OF SUPPLEMENTARY RECORDINGS

Collections

Ten Centuries of Music	DGG KL- 52/61
2000 Years of Music	Folkways 3700
Romanticism	Victor LM- 6153
At La Scala (Callas)	Angel 35304
Operatic Duets (Del Monaco/Tebaldi)	London 5175

Music of Individual Composers

Goldmark, Carl, *The Queen of Sheba, Op.* 27
Humperdinck, Engelbert, *Hänsel und Gretel*
Pfitzner, Hans, *Lieder*
Verdi, Giuseppe, *Aïda*
   Arias
   Ernani
   Nabucco
   Overtures and Preludes
   Quatro Pezzi Sacro
   Requiem
   Rigoletto
   La Traviata
   Il Trovatore
   Falstaff
Wagner, Richard, *Overtures*
   Symphony in C (1832)
   Arias
   Der fliegende Holländer
   Götterdämmerung
   Lohengrin
   Meistersinger
   Parsifal: Good Friday Music
   Siegfried Idyll (1870)
   Wesendonck Songs
   Tristan und Isolde: Prelude and Liebestod

OPPORTUNITIES FOR STUDY IN DEPTH

1. An interesting topic for further investigation is that of the Bible in opera. One might start by studying Rossini's *Mosè in Egitto* (1818), Verdi's *Nabucco* (1842) and Saint-Saëns' *Samson et Dalila* (1877), identifying the Biblical sources, noting their relationship to the librettos and searching for any religious or ethnic evidences in the music.

2. Friedrich Nietzsche, a Wagner enthusiast at Lucerne, proved a defector from Bayreuth. In fact, he proposed using Bizet's *Carmen* as an antidote for the poison of Wagner. Prepare an oral report on Nietzsche's attitudes toward Wagner, citing relevant statements and suggesting reasons.

3. Examine Verdi's Shakespeare operas, comparing the librettos with the plays and the characterizations of both men. We know that Verdi toyed with the idea of composing an opera based on *King Lear,* a project never carried out. Would *King Lear* be a good subject for an opera? Defend a negative and positive answer.

4. Make a harmonic analysis of the first bars of the famed "Prelude" to *Tristan und Isolde.* Justify the oft-made statement that with these sequences of sound the standard tonal world of harmonic relationships was shattered, paving the way for atonality.

5. Compare an aria of Verdi, perhaps Alfredo's *"Libiamo"* in *La Traviata,* with one of Wagner, perhaps "Elsa's Dream" from *Lohengrin.* Note treatment of the voices, relevance to dramatic action, style, participation of the accompaniment and any other differences perceived.

6. Richard Wagner was Hitler's favorite composer and achieved a tawdry posthumous place in annals of National Socialism in the Germany of the 1930's. After reading and deliberation, write a paper concerning Wagner and National Socialism, citing evidence of the political usefulness of his music and his prose.

7. Make a complete list of Verdi's operas with dates of composition and derivation of subject matter, attaching a short *précis* to each. What generalizations can be drawn *in re* Verdi's subject matter as it relates to the Romantic movement as a whole? Amplify.

8. Einstein states that *Parsifal* is "one of the concluding documents of the Romantic era." What does he mean by this? See pp. 245–46 of *Music in the Romantic Era* and proceed from there.

VOCABULARY ENRICHMENT

music drama	*arioso* style
opera cycle	autoprogressive
Bayreuth festival	symphonically-developed opera
"Music of the Future"	censorship
Leitmotif or *Grundthema*	*"Evviva Verdi"* acrostic

Chapter 21.

NATIONALISM IN MUSIC

Do you see the fjords over there—the lakes and streams, the valleys and forests, and the blue sky over all? They have made my music—not I. Frequently when I am playing, it seems to me as if I merely made mechanical motions and were only a silent listener while the Soul of Norway sings in my soul.

—Ole Bull (1810-1880)

The strong Teutonic and Italianate traditions that had dominated European music for so long were infused, in the nineteenth century, with elements drawn from folk sources. The substrata for these had existed when Europe was made up of Celtic, Frankish, Vandal, Norse, Latin and Tartar tribes. National or ethnic consciousness, however, was nurtured by the particular political and social conditions of the mid-1800's, which provided fertile soil for music of a local as well as a universal persuasion; moreover, music was utilized as a forceful branch of aspiring trees reaching for their places in the sun. Especially true was this of regions whose former climates had stifled any manifestations of native germination, such as Russia, Scandinavia, Bohemia and Spain.

NATIONALISM

Nationalism in music has a dual nature: conscious nationalism is based on folk music and popular song, influenced by the rhythm and *melos* of the language; nescient nationalism is an automatic and ever-present reflection of a people's inherent qualities, a tonal projection of their soul, which mirrors the character, philosophy and social customs of various areas. It makes the ultimate distinction between a Robert Browning and a Walt Whitman; a George Bernard Shaw and a Eugene O'Neill; a Chopin and a Schumann; the Empire State Building and Regent Street.

Weber made use of his patriotic ardor and won a reputation as a nationalist by his settings of Körner's war songs, after viewing the return of the victorious Prussian troops from the Battle of Leipzig. These songs, sung by German singing societies, were *echt Deutsch* (authentically German), as was his cantata, *Kampf und Sieg,* composed after the Battle of Waterloo. He introduced a national spirit into his operas as well and was hailed as the first German opera Romanticist. In another sense, Martin Luther's hymns were sufficiently Germanic to penetrate the musical consciousness of the people and to determine a direction. Chopin's polonaises and mazurkas combined the composer's nostalgia for, and his love of, Polish folk music that he had imbibed as a child. Liszt's exploration of Gypsy music opened another facet.

Indeed, if it were possible to associate the national movement with any one person, that man would be Franz Liszt. He was one of the first to acknowledge the importance of Glinka's strivings toward the creation of a Russian school and the achievements of young Russians, such as Rimsky-Korsakov, Cui, Balakirev and Borodin. He offered to bring the works of César Franck to the attention of publishers; wrote enthusiastic letters to Camille Saint-Saëns and produced his opera, *Samson et Dalila,* at Weimar; examined Giovanni Sgambati's (1841-1914) compositions in Rome; and, after seeing his *Sonata in F for Violin and Piano, Op.* 8, complimented the young Grieg and invited him to Weimar. Smetana and Albéniz also came under Liszt's aegis.

Nationalism in music was encouraged by allied interests of the Romantic movement. German poetry, and to a lesser degree, that of France, was set in the idiom of *Lieder* and *chansons,* clearly reflecting the nuances of each language. Program music in its several forms provided an ideal outlet for paeans to national heroes and events as well as for the tone painting of local musical landscapes. Romantic opera often turned to nationalistic librettos. Political implications were manifest, as we have noted, in Verdi's struggles with the Austrian Censor and Wagner's lofty position as a symbol of the newly-formed German Empire. In turning to the Middle Ages, Romanticists discovered a new world of nationalistic legends and antecedents upon which to draw. All these trends and tendencies aided the emergence of nationalism in music.

Russian Music

The history of Russian art music is unique in that it really begins with the nineteenth century and is a direct result of nationalistic feeling. During the eighteenth century, Russia had imported opera from Italy and concert artists from Germany. Catherine II had invited Galuppi, Tommaso Traetta (1727-1779) and Paisiello to her court. They were followed by Giuseppe Sarti (1729-1802), Martini and Cimarosa. In the early nineteenth century, French opera flourished in Russia and Boïeldieu spent some time there. John Field, the Irish pianist and composer, also won Russian fame, and Berlioz and Wagner made several visits.

The first composer to use Russian folklore and historical subjects for opera was Catterino Cavos (1775-1840), a Venetian, who adopted Russia before the turn of the century. Mikhail Ivanovitch Glinka (1804-1857), whom Liszt called the "prophet-patriarch" of Russian music, followed Cavos' example with his opera, *A Life for the Tsar* (1836), based on the same story used by Cavos in *Ivan Susanin* (1815). Glinka's opera was received as a new departure, although it was derided as "coachmen's music," for the cultivated Russians were avowed Francophiles and spoke their native language only to serfs or cabmen. In his second opera, *Russlan and Ludmilla* (1842), on a poem by Pushkin, Glinka used Russian folk music as its basis.

The Napoleonic invasion awakened nationalistic sentiment in Russia, as elsewhere. Alexander Pushkin (1799-1837), in a revolt against Classicism in literature, reverted to pagan lore, and, with Dostoievsky, Gogol and Turgeniev, established a national school of literature, supplemented by Ostrovsky in drama, Stassov and Mihailovsky in criticism, and, in music, by Glinka, Dargomijsky and "The Mighty Five," with Tchaikovsky on the periphery.

Alexander Dargomijsky (1813-1869) turned from imitating Rossini's style to the use of popular themes and a distinctive treatment of recitative. One of his operas is *The Stone Guest,* after a poem by Pushkin, derived from the Don Juan theme. Another opera composer was Alexander Serov (1820-1871), a Russian Wagnerite, whose *Rogneda* (1865) was extremely popular.

"THE MIGHTY FIVE"

"The desire to be natural, the craving for simplicity and for truth in all things, even in music, was engendered by the great Liberation of 1861," writes Montagu-Nathan. "The spirit of individual liberty which inspired junior characters in Turgeniev's *Virgin Soil* was the impulse from which sprang the energies of the young group of reformers in the musical world." In 1861 the emancipation of the serfs brought an end to feudal Russia. Either it was to join forces with the West or remain bound by its own traditions. Advocates of both points of view were vocal, although in music there could be no such dichotomy, as Russia perforce used Western forms and techniques, for she had none of her own. But a "young group of reformers" in St. Petersburg, "The Mighty Five"—Balakirev, Borodin, Cui, Rimsky-Korsakov and Moussorgsky—were Slavophile in their leanings. "They adored Glinka; regarded Haydn and Mozart as old-fashioned; admired Beethoven's last quartets; thought Bach . . . a mathematician rather than a musician; they were enthusiastic over Berlioz, while, as yet, Liszt had not begun to influence them greatly," states Rosa Newmarch.

Tchaikovsky commented, "The young Petersburg composers are very gifted, but they are all impregnated with the most horrible presumptuousness and a purely amateur conviction of their superiority to all other musicians in the universe." Although the five were not equally mighty by any means, they shared the fact of being amateurs, more or less self-trained and ambitious to start from the top. In addition, they all had vocations other than music. Yet their music has verve, vigor and exuberance.

Mily Balakirev (1837-1910), a mathematics graduate of the University of Kazan, was the leader of "The Mighty Five." After meeting a friend of Glinka, Balakirev became convinced of the necessity for Russia to develop her own music, carrying forward Glinka's ideas, and combating foreign influences. He founded a *Free School of Music,* in which he expounded his principles. "I believe in the subjective, not the objective power of music," he said. ". . . Mediocre or merely talented musicians are eager to produce *effects,* but the ideal of a genius is to reproduce his very self, in unison with the object of his art. There is no doubt that art requires technique, but it must be absolutely unconscious and individual . . ." Balakirev's compositions include a *Fantasia on Russian Themes* (1859); many songs; a symphonic poem, *Tamara* (1883); and *Islamey,* a brilliant Oriental fantasy for piano. In his later years, Balakirev retired from music and pursued mystic studies.

César Cui (1835-1918), whom he met in 1856, was Balakirev's first convert. Cui was the son of a former Napoleonic officer and was himself an authority on military science. Although his operas were performed in Russia, Belgium and Paris, his chief contribution was in the publicity he gave "The Mighty Five," through newspaper articles and a pamphlet, *Music in Russia.* His music is known to us only through a rather anemic piano piece, *Orientale.* He also contributed to a set of variations on "Chopsticks," with Borodin, Anatol Liadov (1855-1914) and Rimsky-Korsakov.

Alexander Borodin (1833-1887), the illegitimate son of a Caucasian prince, was a gifted musician, a surgeon of repute, an experimental chemist, an author of scientific treatises and an educator, regarded by Liszt as one of the best orchestral masters of the nineteenth century. When did he have time to compose two symphonies, a symphonic poem, *In the Steppes of Central Asia* (1880), string quartets, songs, and his unfinished opera, *Prince Igor?* We may get some idea of the hectic pace of Borodin's schedule by quoting Rimsky-Korsakov, who wrote, "Even in the midst of playing or talking, he would jump up all of a sudden and fly to his retorts and burners (his laboratory was in an adjoining room) to make sure that all was well—filling the air, as he went about, with incredible sequences of sevenths and ninths, bellowed at the top of his voice." As with his fellow Russian composers, Borodin's music is pervaded by a colorful Orientalism; his orchestration is colorful and his impressionistic touch often sounds quite modern. The popular American musical, *Kismet,* is based upon Borodin's themes.

Another musical amateur who was a naval officer by profession was Nikolai Rimsky-Korsakov (1844-1908), a pioneer, after Berlioz, of the modern school of orchestration. He was "an exception" to the St. Petersburg "mutual admiration society," according to Tchaikovsky, who wrote to Mme. von Meck, "Rimsky-Korsakov is the only one among them who discovered . . . that the doctrines preached . . . had no sound basis, that their mockery of the schools and the classical masters, their denial of authority and of the masterpieces, was nothing but ignorance."

In 1861 Rimsky-Korsakov met Balakirev and became his pupil. As an officer in the Russian Navy, Rimsky was required to make a three-year cruise, during which he visited America. When he returned home in 1865, he brought with him the first symphony composed by a Russian. His next composition was a symphonic poem, *Sadko, Op.* 5 (1867), from which he later made an opera. A *Serbian Fantasia, Op.* 6 (1867), another symphony, the *Capriccio Espagnole, Op.* 34 (1887), the famous *Scheherazade, Op.* 35 (1888) and *The Russian Easter Overture, Op.* 36 (1888) are among his best-known orchestral works. In addition he composed a piano concerto, songs and arrangements of Russian folk-songs. To librettos from Gogol, Ostrovsky, Pushkin and others, Rimsky-Korsakov wrote fifteen operas, including *A Night in May* (1880), *The Snow-Maiden* (1882), *Sadko* (1898), *The Tsar's Bride* (1899) and *The Golden Cockerel* (*Le Coq d'or,* 1909). Many short works, such as "The Flight of the Bumblebee," "Dance of the Buffoons" and "A Song of India," are extracted from his operas.

Equally significant as his compositions was Rimsky-Korsakov's contribution as an educator in a country that had been without a conservatory or trained music teachers. In 1871 the composer was asked to serve as professor of composition and instrumentation at the new St. Petersburg Conservatory of Music, established by the pianist-composer, Anton Rubenstein (1830-1894). Of this opportunity, Rimsky-Korsakov wrote:

At the time, I could not harmonize a chorale properly, had never written a single contrapuntal exercise in my life, and had only the haziest understanding of strict fugue. I didn't even know the names of the augmented and diminished intervals or the chords . . . My grasp of the musical forms . . . was equally hazy. Although I scored my own compositions colorfully enough, I had no adequate knowledge of the technique of the strings, or of the practical possibilities of horns, trumpets and trombones.

Through a combination of intensive study and bluff, Rimsky-Korsakov managed to stay one lesson ahead of his students until he had mastered the rudiments of theory. He became director of Balakirev's *Free School* in 1874 and there taught many younger composers and evolved his own course of orchestration, still a reliable source of instruction.

The most original and mightiest of "The Mighty Five" was Modeste Moussorgsky (1839-1881). Perhaps he was more in tune with their avowed aims than any of the others, although this was not acknowledged during his lifetime. His early years were spent in the country where, as the son of a well-to-do landowner, he studied the peasantry and learned the music of the Orthodox Church from a local priest. Although evincing musical talent as a child, Moussorgsky entered upon a military career in a smart regiment, where his charm made him a favorite of society. In 1856 he met an army doctor, Borodin, who reported that Moussorgsky was a splendid type of young officer, aristocratic, refined and well educated. From this time also dates his friendship with Dargomijsky, whose opera, *Russalka* (1856), had failed to impress a hostile public.

After study with Balakirev, Moussorgsky relinquished his military commission in 1859 to compose. As a result of the Imperial Ukase freeing the serfs and his brother's poor management of their estate, Moussorgsky, at twenty-two, began his never ending struggle with poverty. In order to live, he had to seek subordinate government positions, which were constant hindrances to his studies. Unfortunately, his health could not tolerate the irregularity of his mode of life and his high-strung nervous system broke under the strain.

While living in St. Petersburg with five comrades, in what they called a "community," Moussorgsky had composed his songs, "Night," "Kallistrate" and "The Peasant's Cradle Song." It was here that Nicolsky had suggested to him the idea of *Boris Goudonov,* a Pushkin historical tale, and here that he had commenced an opera on Flaubert's *Salammbô,* a project he later abandoned. He also collected and arranged many Russian folksongs and interested the other four in undertaking collections.

After three years in the country, where he regained his health, Moussorgsky returned to St. Petersburg in 1868, with the unfinished score of *Boris Goudonov*. During this interval he had also written the orchestral tone-poem, *A Night on Bald Mountain* (1860-1866), the *"Hopak"* (1866), the first act of *The Marriage-Broker* (on a play by Gogol, 1864) and the first of his song cycle, *In the Nursery* (1872).

Boris absorbed Moussorgsky's attention for several years, although in its original version it was completed in 1869 and orchestrated the next winter. When the composer submitted *Boris* to the theater directors, he met with refusal "because," said they, "it contained too many choruses and too many ensembles, and because the scanty nature of the principal roles gave them insufficient importance." Moussorgsky spent the entire year of 1871 revising the opera, adding more formal *arias* and a love scene with a soprano-tenor duet, as well as removing some episodes that might have displeased the state Censor. Again, the work was turned down. From this time on, Moussorgsky indulged more and more in excessive drinking and his working schedule became erratic, although

Fig. 70. Coronation scene from Mussourgsky's *Boris Goudonov*. Boris, played by Ezio Pinza, portrays most movingly a tragic, historic figure from Russia's past. (Courtesy The Bettmann Archive.)

he retained his creative powers. His life became a miserable struggle against hardship and ill health.

The premiere of *Boris* finally took place at the Marinsky Theater on January 24, 1874. The performance marked a triumph for Moussorgsky in spite of, or because of, the attitude of outraged critics and the elation of the younger generation. Stassov, a sympathetic critic, proclaimed, "The younger generation cared nothing for all this banality, rudeness, stupidity, scholasticism, these rooted customs, the envy and the malice . . . they realized that a great artistic power had created and was presenting to our people a wonderful national work, and they exulted and rejoiced and triumphed." Moussorgsky's moment was short, however. *Boris* was presented in the next season in a severely cut form and then dropped from the repertoire.

During the last six years of his by now sordid life, Moussorgsky wrote two great song cycles: *Sunless* (1874) and *Songs and Dances of Death* (1875-1877)—dramatically-powerful works—and "The Song of the Flea" (1879), on a text from Goethe's *Faust*. As a tribute to a painter friend, Victor Hartmann, who died in 1873, and whose posthumous exhibit the composer visited, Moussorgsky wrote one of the most important Russian piano works of the nineteenth century, *Pictures at an Exhibition,* later orchestrated by Maurice Ravel.

In 1879 Moussorgsky lost his government clerkship and attempted to augment his paltry income by accompanying a singer in a tour of southern Russia, which he apparently enjoyed. In 1880 some friends intervened, making him an allowance so that he might finish the two operas on which he was working: *Khovanshchina* (completed by Rimsky-Korsakov) and *The Fair of Sorotchinsk* (completed by Cui and later re-worked by Nikolai Tcherepnin [1873-1945]). Shortly thereafter, Moussorgsky collapsed with epilepsy and was hospitalized. A portrait, painted by Repin, shows him just before his death, a debauched prey to alcohol and disease, with no trace remaining of that "true little dandy" Borodin had described in 1856.

In 1871 Moussorgsky had shared an apartment with Rimsky-Korsakov, working on the same table and at the same piano. After Moussorgsky died, Rimsky revised *Khovanshchina* for publication, and made many changes in the score and orchestration of *Boris*. He, with more knowledge and less genius than its composer, corrected and refined points which he regarded as mistakes. Today we look upon Moussorgsky's "crudities" as signs of his originality and fearlessness. It is a step forward in the development of music that twentieth-century publishers have had the perspicacity to venture editions in their original forms.

In only a few respects can Rimsky's solicitous changes be considered improvements.

With *Boris Goudonov,* Moussorgsky gave Russia its greatest national opera. Of its tardy climb to appreciation, Olin Downes says:

> The career of this work in its own land has a curious and inescapable analogy to the course of Russian history. It slept on shelves for about fifty years in the form in which Moussorgsky conceived it. In this form it did not see the light of day until the consummation of the revolution. Until then it existed for the public only in an emasculated form acceptable to the imperial theaters of 1874, and after that in a conventionalized and still incomplete version of Rimsky-Korsakov.

Moussorgsky was a Romanticist and yet he felt impelled to push beyond the conventional limits of the movement, ever seeking truth in art—"truth no matter how bitter . . ." Like Melville's Ahab, he was an uncompromising and realistic pursuer of the profound imponderables. He was uninterested in the merely pretty and decorative; rather he proposed to "look life boldly in the eye" and address mankind. In *Boris Goudonov* Moussorgsky achieved his purposes by the simplicity and directness of his idiom; by means that were audacious and free; by adapting folksong and characterization to his needs with stark realism; and by molding his music, as in his songs, to the prose rhythms of the Russian language.

SCANDINAVIAN MUSIC

In Edvard Grieg (1843-1907) we meet a composer who did more to establish a Norwegian national style than any man who preceded or followed him. As in the cases of Mendelssohn and MacDowell, Grieg's interest in nature and the Norwegian landscape almost led him to become a painter. But Ole Bull, the famous violinist, prevailed on the Grieg family to send the lad to the Leipzig Conservatory. There he drank at the Mendelssohn-Schumann fountain and became acquainted with a fellow student, Arthur Sullivan. Grieg continued his studies in Copenhagen where, under Niels Gade's guidance, he composed some of his earliest works.

It was in Copenhagen that he met his future wife, Nina Hagerup, an intelligent musician and singer, for whom he composed his celebrated song, *"Ich liebe dich"* ("I Love You"), on a text by Hans Christian Andersen. There too he encountered Rikard Nordraak (1842-1866), an ardent musical nationalist, who introduced him to native folksongs. Of his reaction, Grieg said, "It was as though scales fell from my eyes, for the first time I learned . . . to understand my own nature. We adjured the Gade-Mendelssohn insipid and diluted Scandinavianism and bound ourselves with enthusiasm to the new path which the Northern School is now following." With Nordraak, Grieg founded a Euterpe Society for the purpose of promoting Scandinavian music. He served as its conductor until 1880.

Grieg was a poetic Romanticist, a master of the miniature, who added a new dialect to the musical speech of the late Romantic period. He never composed better than in his youth. As early as the *Poetic Tone-Pictures, Op.* 3 (1864), he showed his musical characteristics: a peasant-like harshness in intervals of fifths; a pervading lyricism; short, stepwise motives, immediately repeated in higher sequences; and a harmony that was warm, despite a Northland detachment. Mason comments:

> His most characteristic works . . . were composed between his graduation from the Conservatory and the early seventies—between his twentieth and thirtieth years . . . Two inimitable *Sonatas for Violin and Piano, ops.* 8 and 13; the *Piano Sonata, opus* 7; the incidental music to Ibsen's *Peer Gynt;* some of the most charming of the *Lyric Pieces* for piano and of the Songs, and the *Piano Concerto, opus* 16, the best certainly of his entire musical product.

Grieg met Liszt and Henrik Ibsen, the dramatist, in Rome in 1870. In 1879 he performed his *Piano Concerto in A Minor* at a *Gewandhaus* concert at Leipzig, greatly enhancing his reputation. He made his first English appearance in 1888 with the same work. In 1874 the Norwegian government granted Grieg a life pension of approximately $500 a year so that he might devote himself to composition. Shortly thereafter he composed the incidental music to *Peer Gynt,* which immortalized Ibsen's play. With this one work, his nation was amply compensated, for no country has been better publicized than by the two *Peer Gynt* suites. At this time, too, Grieg built his "gingerbread" villa, *Troldhaugen* ("Hill of the Trolls"), a few miles from his birthplace, Bergen. There, apart from his tours, he and his wife lived quietly and welcomed a constant stream of visitors. The villa is now maintained as a Grieg museum.

At times, Grieg arrived at a beautiful exoticism in his music, but it was irrefutably Scandinavian tone color, with the flavor of pine woods and fjords, suggestive of elf and troll and of the moods of peasants in celebration and quietude. A disadvantage to Grieg's music is that it has been played so often that the mannerisms have become tiresome. Yet, as Mason writes:

> It [is] a hopeless as well as a useless task to describe in words the qualities of these compositions. What shall we say in words of the flavor of

Fig. 71. Aurland Fjord, Norway. Grieg almost singlehandedly created a Norwegian national music colored by the characteristic feeling of the Norseman for his country. (Photograph by the editor.)

an orange? Is it sweet? Yes. And acid? Yes, a little. And it has a delicate aroma, and is juicy and cool. But how much idea of an orange has one conveyed then? And similarly with this indescribable delicate music of Grieg . . . It is like the poetry of Henley in its exclusive concern with moods, with personal emotions of the noblest, most elusive sort. It is intimate, suggestive and intangible . . . The phrases are polished like gems, the melodies charm us with their perfect proportions, the cadences are as consummate as they are novel.

Grieg has been looked down on by musicians, but there is no reason to belittle Anacreon because Sophocles was more profound. As a human being, Grieg was an unassuming person, thoroughly middle class, yet such an egalitarian that to his own detriment he decried the injustices of the Dreyfus affair in France and refused to appear there. He identified in music, if not in fact, with the common people. In his music "is the untrammeled outpouring of the inner lives of the Norwegian people; an expression of their character, their indomitable will, the dauntless energy, the deep feeling that are the natural characteristics of the Norseman," according to an anonymous critic. Hans von Bülow called

Grieg "the Chopin of the North." His melodies provided the material for a recent piece of musical theater, *Song of Norway*.

While Grieg almost singlehandedly created a Norwegian national music, other composers also contributed to the movement. Another Norwegian composer, older than Grieg, was Halfdan Kjerulf (1815-1868). Henrietta Sontag and Jenny Lind (1820-1887), the "Swedish nightingale," gave his songs international fame. Among his works are an attractive "Lullaby" and "Album Leaf" for piano and the song, "Last Night." Johan Severin Svendsen (1840-1911) was a Wagnerite, but absorbed some of Grieg's local coloring. Christian Sinding (1856-1941), the greatest national composer since Grieg, also donned Scandinavian garments, although influenced by Liszt and Schumann. His *Frühlingsrauschen* ("Rustle of Spring") remains a very popular piano piece; in it we note a decided Wagnerian flavor, particularly of *Die Walküre,* but then that too is a Norse myth. Sinding spent a year teaching at the Eastman School of Music in Rochester, N.Y.

Among Swedish and Danish composers are Emil Sjögren (1853-1918), "the Schumann of the North," who wrote songs, *Erotikon* for the piano and other instrumental works; Andreas Hallen (1846-1925); Niels Gade, associated with the *Gewandhaus* concerts, who composed with a mixture of Romantic, Classic and Danish elements; Johan Peder Hartmann (1805-1900), "the father of Danish music" and Gade's father-in-law; Asger Hamerik (1843-1923), a pupil of von Bülow and Berlioz, who became director of the Peabody Conservatory in Baltimore; Otto Malling (1848-1915) director of the Copenhagen Conservatory; and Ludvig Schytte (1848-1909), a student of Liszt and Gade and prolific composer in miniature forms.

BOHEMIAN MUSIC

Bedřich Smetana (1824-1884), son of a brewer, was a founder of the national school of Czech or Bohemian music. A splendid pianist, he was known for his interpretations of Chopin. As a young man, he lived in a time of political upheaval, when Bohemia was trying to throw off the Hapsburg yoke. During these troubled days his only pleasure was in meetings with Liszt, Clara Schumann and other distinguished visitors to Prague. Smetana was openly on the side of liberty and was a sincere patriot, at a time when suspicion of such sentiments made life miserable.

He finally left the country in 1856 and became conductor of the *Harmoniske Sallskept* in Göteborg, Sweden, where he found the musical outlet denied him in Bohemia. In Sweden Smetana composed symphonic poems inspired by Bohemian traditions and structured on Liszt's procedures. "Liszt's *Symphonic Poems* seem a bold solution," says Nejedly, "showing that music ought also be brought into touch with the intellectual movement of the time . . . ." Czech interest in music up to this time had existed privately, but someone with power and vision was needed to transcend the nation's difficulties. Above all, more freedom of action and opinion was necessary.

In 1860 an Imperial Diploma was suddenly issued that granted the Czechs more liberty. Resigning his post in Sweden, Smetana returned to Bohemia and declared his intention of stressing nationalistic elements in music. According to Hadow:

> The first need [Smetana] said, was to cut her cornerstone from her own quarries, and build her art on the peasant tunes in which the whole of her musical tradition was comprised. He had no sympathy with the more classical forms; in any case, he found them unsuitable to a music of which the very foundations were still to be laid . . .

Smetana's first works after his return to Prague were operas, which made an appeal to the masses of people, and offered the composer an opportunity to embrace a group of arts rather than music alone. Whereas it has been considered that many of these works were "artless and immature . . . some day we shall learn," writes Hadow, "that we are in error. The *Bartered Bride* is an achievement that would do credit to any nation in Europe; . . . it claims our interest as the turning point of an artistic revolution." Smetana was lionized by his countrymen as the first truly-Bohemian composer, and although Dvořák is the greater man, his country owes Smetana a deep debt of appreciation.

Among Smetana's works were eight operas, of which the last was not completed; five symphonic works in tone-poem form, among which is *My Country,* in six parts, with *Vltava* (1874) the second; a number of piano selections, including characteristic pieces and polkas; vocal and choral works; and chamber music, including a *Piano Trio in G Minor* (1855) and a *String Quartet in E Minor,* entitled *Aus Meinem Leben* (*From My Life,* 1876).

The second of the tone-poem cycle, *My Country,* which, incidentally, Smetana composed after he became deaf, is better known by its German name, *Die Moldau.* A program attached to the score specifically details the course of Bohemia's chief river as it emerges from twin springs, flows through the countryside, dashes in the rapids of St. John and flows majestically past Prague, aurally disappearing in a kind of fade-out, reminiscent of film techniques. Its lyric theme is variously ascribed to Czech folk sources, to Swedish origin and to the Jewish melody, *Yigdal.* In this work the composer withdrew as far as he ever did from

Lisztian inspiration and model, although the brass apotheosis at the end reminds the listener of the *Meister* of Weimar. Its variety and naïveté make *The Moldau* a cherished work for those who claim a dislike for serious music. Parenthetically, we may note that much of it has a quality that might be described as resembling movie mood-music—a rather understandable analogy, as most twentieth-century background music for films is the product of central European composers with much the same background as Smetana.

Although his works were typically Czech, Smetana reached beyond mere imitation of folksong. His thinking was Czech. Like many of the nationalist composers, Smetana left his country to find it; he struggled against the indifference of the very folk whom he immortalized. In his inimitable merry opera, *The Bartered Bride* (1866), Smetana does not use a single folksong, but the work is so drenched in nationalistic idioms as to be unmistakable. The characters are simple human beings and the writing highly individualistic. Hadow asserts:

> Smetana's position in his own country is unique among musicians. Neither Chopin nor Grieg have quite the same powerful material significance . . . he made his art a wonderful stimulus to the national rebirth . . . His works . . . are the best medium for a Czech to become conscious of his national character.

Antonin Dvořák (1841-1904) was born in Nelahozeves (Muhlhausen) on the Vltava near Prague, the son of a butcher and innkeeper. He became a composer who devoted himself to the further development of a national movement in music.

Most of us are familiar with Bohemia only as the home of a famous glass industry, the scene of Shakespeare's *A Winter's Tale* and the country of John Huss and "Good King Wenceslas." Bohemia, however, has had a turbulent history (through the present day) and one filled with legend and persistent turmoil, including the martyrdom of the great Reformer in the fifteenth century and intermittent bids for independence, usually severely suppressed. This heritage, along with Smetana's musical pictures, was passed on to Dvořák and influenced him, consciously and unconsciously, in his compositions.

Coming from the people, Dvořák was familiar with folksongs and folk tales, and, although his father wanted him to follow in his footsteps, the son showed a decided talent and preference for music. He learned to sing, to play the violin and the organ, and studied harmony. Later he went to Prague to continue his studies. Smetana befriended him, and five years after he entered school Dvořák composed his first string quartet. Thirteen years afterward he became an organist at a salary of sixty dollars a year. Liszt helped him by performing his works and finding publishers for them. Dvořák became known to the world through his fascinating *Slavonic Dances, Op.* 46 and was invited to London to conduct his *Stabat Mater, Op.* 58 in 1884. It was so well received that he was commissioned to write a cantata, *The Specter's Bride, Op.* 69, for the Birmingham Festival in 1885, which was followed by his oratorio, *St. Ludmila, Op.* 71, for the Leeds' Festival in 1886. The University of Cambridge made him a Doctor of Music in 1891. Before that, he had been appointed professor of music at the Prague Conservatory.

Success and security had come slowly to Dvořák. In 1892, he was lured to New York City to become director of the short-lived National Conservatory of Music, with the bait of $15,000 a year and summers off. This was ten-times the sum he was accustomed to in Prague. He and his wife were met at the dock by a chorus of 300 and an orchestra of eighty, with speeches, wreaths and a rendition of "America." The composer settled in a brownstone on East Seventieth Street and devoted himself to his new duties. Being particularly interested in nationalistic music, Dvořák acquainted himself with Negro and Indian melodies. H. T. Burleigh, the Negro composer, was a student at the Conservatory, and he and the Bohemian musician had an intimate and fruitful friendship.

Life was made more endurable in the New World by summers spent in Spillville, Iowa, a town populated by persons of Bohemian stock, where Dvořák could relax and live among people of his own background. It was there that he orchestrated a new work, the *Symphony in E Minor, No. 5, Op.* 95, popularly known as the "New World" Symphony. While in America, he also composed the *Quartet No. 6 in F, Op.* 96 (the "American") and the string *Quintet in E flat, Op.* 97, neither actually containing Indian melodies, but employing, as the composer himself explained, "original themes embodying the peculiarities of Indian music."

Homesickness prevailed over the offer of renewal of his Conservatory contract and Dvořák returned to Prague in 1895. His remaining years were filled with honors, although only one more work, the opera *Armida, Op.* 115, was presented before he died of Bright's disease, in 1904.

Dvořák was a sound if eclectic musician. He had studied Mozart, Beethoven and Schubert as well as Brahms, but was dedicated to his own folklore and the harmonies that appealed to his nation. At his best when unbound by program, he achieved lofty effects with original ideas. His slow movements have spiritual power and beauty. Dvořák wrote many operas, symphonic poems, seven published symphonies and other compositions. Although he was conventional in the use of form, his music is free-flowing, full of emotion and imagination. It is distinguished by warm color, pronounced rhythms, flaming melody, daring modulation and naturalness.

A master of orchestration, Dvořák used simple means for startling effect. Although his operas have not been as popular outside Czechoslovakia as are *St. Ludmila* (celebrating Bohemia's conversion to Christianity) and the *Stabat Mater* (written in grief after the death of a daughter), his songs, such as "Songs My Mother Taught Me" (which is said to have reduced the composer himself to tears), the oft-parodied "Humoresque" (written in America), the *"New World" Symphony* (with its famous *"Largo"* theme set to the words, "Going Home") and his *Concerto for 'Cello and Orchestra in B Minor, Op.* 104, (a standard number in a violoncellist's repertoire) are well-known and often performed.

Fig. 72. "Violin and Pipe"—Georges Braque. Bohemia, struggling to be free from an alien yoke, found a distinguished nationalistic expression in music. (Courtesy Philadelphia Museum of Art, Louise and Walter Arensberg Collection.)

Smetana had revived Bohemian music; Dvořák, his disciple, was more cosmopolitan and his international fame tempted him to swerve from provincialism. Whereas Smetana's polkas are to Bohemia what the mazurka is to Poland, Dvořák's *Slavonic Dances* lie more in the realm of sophisticated art. Smetana preserved the youthful freshness of a folk-based style. Dvořák, however, was a richly-endowed musician, who, according to Hiram Moderwell, was "a veritable Schubert in fertility . . . It is pleasant to add that he got universal love in response to this more than Midas-like transmuting power of his, and that the poor Bohemian boy, after becoming rich and famous, died full of honors, but as simple at heart as ever."

SPANISH MUSIC

In point of time, Spain was among the last of the European nations to cultivate a national school. In so doing Spain found that she had infinite resources and her renaissance was a brilliant light of the early twentieth century. Probably no other country has dealt so lovingly and yet so casually with her folk and national music. It is only comparatively recently that it has been incorporated in works of her trained composers. Due to the efforts of Francisco Asenjo Barbieri (1823-1894), Felipe Pedrell (1841-1922), Federico Olmeda (1865-1909), Isaac Albéniz (1860-1909) and Enrique Granados (1867-1916), in reviving the vast Spanish heritage, a veritable new look appeared.

Barbieri, a composer of *zarzuelas,* was interested in folklore and his valuable collection, *Cancionero musical de los siglos XV y XVI,* attest to research in native music of the fifteenth and sixteenth centuries, which gave Spain a glimpse of what her music of the future could be.

Pedrell's musico-archeological gift was a happy thing for his nation's musical development. The most learned musician of Spain, Pedrell was practically self-taught, although he was impelled by his first teacher, Juan Antonio Nin y Serra, to use themes from the songs his mother sang for his compositions. He published his first works in 1871 (before Albéniz or Granados). His pamphlet, *Por nuestra música (For Our Music,* 1891), brought him to the attention of European musicians as a composer pleading for a national lyric drama based on folksong. His ambitious trilogy, *Los Pirineos (The Pyrenees,* 1891), marked him a leader of the Spanish nationalist movement.

Pedrell met with problems, however, as Wagnerians did not appreciate his music, nor did the larger public, who were unacquainted with the traditional background of his compositions. Although his operas contain pages of fine workmanship, they are outranked by Pedrell's other contributions, including the publication of the complete works of Tomás Luis de Victoria, the sixteenth-century Spanish composer, the cataloguing of music in the Barcelona Library and the issuance of old Spanish theater music and madrigals. Pedrell opened the eyes of the world to Spanish music, but in his own land, he was unknown—like the proverbial prophet.

Federico Olmeda was an organist, composer and musicologist. His greatest contributions to Spanish music were his writings on early polyphony; his booklet describing the music of the twelfth-century *Codex of Calixtus II* (Santiago Cathedral Ms., 1895); a study of the folklore of Castile (1902); and treatises on the performance of liturgical music.

His compositions include four symphonies, *Rimas* for piano and Church music.

Isaac Albéniz was another infant prodigy who fulfilled his initial promise. From early life Albéniz loved travel and was an adventurer. At the age of nine he started earning his way by his excellent piano playing. He studied at the Madrid Conservatory and later came under Gavaert and Brassin in Brussels, and Jadassohn and Reinecke in Leipzig. After 1880 he set about teaching in Barcelona and Madrid, but did not like the role of pedagogue. In 1893 Albéniz left Spain and spent the rest of his life in Paris and London.

While in Paris and London, Albéniz composed many operas on Spanish themes and an unfinished trilogy, *King Arthur,* of which only *Merlin* was completed. He was a prolific composer of piano music, but considered his earlier works of little importance. His meeting with Debussy brought him into the *avant-garde* school of composition. *Iberia,* the best known of his piano works, *Catalonia, Navarra* and *Azulejos* (finished by Granados) stamped Albéniz as a Spanish nationalist of high merit.

Iberia (1906-1909), a suite of twelve pieces, records scenes in many parts of Spain, using varied rhythms, colorful harmonies and other nationalistic earmarks. Although Albéniz used Spanish material with less penetration than Falla, he nevertheless laid a solid substructure, according to J. B. Trend, because he "realized that its determining features were the combination of strong, conflicting rhythms; the harmonic effects naturally obtained from instruments tuned in fourths; and the wavering, profusely ornamental melodies of the native *cante hondo*." Perhaps because of his Impressionistic orientation, Albéniz suggested national traits rather than reproduced them. He was an evoker of Spanish popular music in all the provinces, without whom the researches of his predecessors might have been in vain and the advent of the Spanish renascence postponed. His *Tango in D* has achieved widespread recognition.

Enrique Granados, like Albéniz, was an excellent pianist. He did not aspire to modern innovations, however, but retained the older, accustomed harmonies. Yet with the publication of the two books of *Goyescas,* he may be said to have created the *genre* of Spanish piano music. These works, in precise Spanish rhythms and authentic color, were named after canvases and tapestries of the great Spanish painter, Goya (1746-1828). Later, the music was developed into an opera, the first opera by a Spaniard to be presented at the Metropolitan Opera House (1916). Granados also wrote four books of Spanish dances, suites and *Dante*—a symphonic poem for orchestra. The composer died during World War I, when his ship was torpedoed by a submarine while Granados was on the way home from a visit to New York.

* * * * *

Nationalism in music was not confined to the Romantic period. It is still very much with us, especially in such musically underdeveloped nations as the United States and such politically conscious countries as the Soviet Union. As G. Jean-Aubry writes:

> The Russian school spread throughout Europe the magic of its rhythms and colors, introduced new sonorities, communicated to aged Europe the singular ingenuity and splendor of Asia through the art of Rimsky, Balakirev, Borodin, Moussorgsky, Stravinsky, Prokofiev; then it was the Scandinavia of Grieg and of Sjögren; the Bohemia of Smetana and Dvořák, and then the sudden Spanish blossoming of Albéniz and of Pedrell, of Manuel de Falla, of Turina; today it is the Italy of Pizzetti, Casella and Malipiero which is forcing them to rediscover the national road, it is the England of Vaughan Williams, of Lord Berners and of Eugene Goosens, the young Hungary of Béla Bartók and Kodály, who rival each other in the same effort.

SUGGESTIONS FOR FURTHER READING

Abraham, Gerald, *Eight Russian Composers.* New York, Oxford University Press, 1943.

————, ed., *Grieg: A Symposium.* Norman, University of Oklahoma Press, 1950.

———— *A Hundred Years of Music.* London, Duckworth, 1949.

Calvocoressi, M. D., *Modeste Moussorsky.* Fair Lawn, Essential Books, 1956.

Chase, Gilbert, *The Music of Spain.* New York, Norton, 1941.

Einstein, Alfred, *Music in the Romantic Era.* New York, Norton, 1947.

Fischl, Viktor, ed., *Antonin Dvořák: His Achievement.* London, Drummond, 1942.

Hadow, W. H., *Studies in Modern Music.* London, Seeley, 1926.

Leonard, Richard A., *A History of Russian Music.* New York, Macmillan, 1957.

Leyda, J., and Bertensson, S., eds., *The Moussorgsky Reader.* New York, Norton, 1947.

Newmarch, Rosa, *The Music of Czechoslovakia.* New York, Oxford University Press, 1942.

———— *The Russian Opera.* New York, Dutton, 1912.

Rimsky-Korsakov, Nikolai, *My Musical Life.* New York, Knopf, 1942.

———— *Principles of Orchestration.** (Digest—Adolf Schmid) New York, Boosey & Hawkes, 1950.

Robertson, Alec, *Dvořák.* New York, Dutton, 1945.

Seroff, Victor, *The Mighty Five.* New York, Allen, Towne & Heath, 1956.

Starr, William J., and Devine, George F., *Music Scores—Omnibus,** Part 2. Englewood Cliffs, Prentice-Hall, 1964.

Stephan, Paul, *Anton Dvorak.* New York, Greystone, 1941.

Trend, J. B., *Manuel de Falla and Spanish Music.* New York, Knopf, 1934.

* Available in paperback edition.

A Sampler of Supplementary Recordings

Collections

Ten Centuries of Music	DGG KL-52/61
2000 Years of Music	Folkways 3700
Romanticism	Victor LM-6153
Russian Musical Masterworks	Family 142
Norwegian Musical Masterworks	Family 143
Slavonic Dances	Colosseum 008
Moussorgsky, Glinka, etc. (Chaliapin)	Angel COLH 100
Songs of Norway (Flagstad)	London 5525
Reizen Sings Rimsky-Korsakov	Bruno 23044L
Russian Operatic Arias	Monitor 2046

Music of Individual Composers

Albéniz, Isaac, *Cantos de España, Op.* 232

Balakirev, Mily, *Russia*

Borodin, Alexander, *In the Steppes of Central Asia*
          Prince Igor

Dargomyzsky, Alexander, *Russalka*

Dvořák, Antonin, *Concerto in b for 'Cello, Op.* 104
          Slavonic Dances
          Stabat Mater, Op. 58
          Symphony No. 9 in e, Op. 95 ("New World")
          Quartet No. 6 in F, Op. 96 ("American")

Glinka, Mikhail, *A Life for the Czar*

Granados, Enrique, *Goyescas*
          Escenas Romanticas
          Spanish Dances

Grieg, Edvard, *Concerto in a for Piano, Op.* 16
          Holberg Suite, Op. 40
          Peer Gynt Suites, Ops. 46, 55

Moussorgsky, Modest, *Boris Godounov*
          Night on Bald Mountain
          Pictures at an Exhibition
          Songs

Rimsky-Korsakov, Nikolai, *Fantasy on Russian Themes for Violin, Op.* 33
          Russian Easter Overture, Op. 36
          Scheherazade, Op. 35
          Sadko

Smetana, Bedřich, *Bartered Bride*
          The Moldau

Related Works of Interest

  Kismet

  Song of Norway

Opportunities for Study in Depth

1. We have noted in this chapter an instance of a grateful government in effect subsidizing a creative artist, so that he might work free of financial pressures.

Today, in the United States, a legislative bill awaits action by the Congress. It concerns federal subsidy of American arts and artists. Study this matter and formulate an opinion about it.

2. Paintings and prints have often served as inspiration for musicians. Write a paper about Goya's contribution to Granados' *Goyescas,* Victor Hartmann's to Moussorgsky's *Pictures at an Exhibition* and Hogarth's to Stravinsky's *Rake's Progress.*

3. Prepare a teaching unit on one of the major composers mentioned in this chapter, including visual and audio aids. Adapt the material to the learning level and experience of the group for which it is intended.

4. We have already noted that Rimsky-Korsakov's good intentions in "improving" Moussorgsky's score of *Boris Goudonov* are not appreciated by modern critics. Ravel prepared a masterful orchestration of the same composer's *Pictures at an Exhibition.* Listen to a recording of this and one of the original piano version. How do they compare? What differences are there in the aural impressions received?

5. Grieg is often accused of leaning rather heavily upon certain mannerisms in his compositions. Analyze several of his piano pieces and list with examples the various devices uncovered.

6. In discussing Bizet we stated that French composers were often drawn to Spanish themes and, in many cases, wrote music more "Spanish" than that of the native composers. Make a comparison of Glinka's *Jota Aragonesa* (or Rimsky-Korsakov's *Capriccio espagnol, Op.* 34) with Albéniz's *Rapsodia española, Op.* 70 or an orchestral work of Granados. What "Spanish" features did the Russian composer borrow? What explanation is there for this sort of thing?

7. Although we know very little of Moussorgsky's early years, we do have ample source material concerning his later life. Read Leyda and Bertensson's *Moussorgsky Reader* and act as resource leader for a class discussion of what is revealed of the man and of the Russia in which he lived.

8. In politically deprived countries, such as Bohemia, we have found that music served as a form of social protest. Investigate this phenomenon further and draw analogies with a similar situation in our world today.

Vocabulary Enrichment

musical nationalism	"The Mighty Five"
conscious nationalism	dilettantism
nescient nationalism	polka
echt Deutsch	codex

Chapter 22.

ROMANTIC ABSOLUTISTS

The 'cellos, setting forth apart,
Grumbled and sang, and so the day
From the low beaches of my heart
Turned in tranquillity away.

And over weariness and doubt
Rose up the horns like bellied sails,
Like canvas of the soul flung out
To rising and orchestral gales;

Passed on the left irresolute
The ebony, the silver throat . . .
Low over clarinet and flute
Hung heaven upon a single note.

—Robert Nathan, *At the Symphony* (Franck's D Minor)

The mantle of Beethoven ultimately fell upon the Herculean shoulders of Johannes Brahms, the outstanding, if "posthumous," Romantic composer of absolute music. Although born only six years after Beethoven's death, Brahms was a legatee of Schubert, Mendelssohn and Schumann, as well as of Beethoven and the earlier masters. Quite unwittingly he cleft the rock of Romanticism: one half forming a base on which Liszt, Berlioz and Wagner stood; the other becoming a pedestal for Beethoven. Again we encounter the old struggle between Romanticism and Classicism, masquerading this time as program music and absolute music. Brahms was not active in the controversy that occurred between partisans of the two polarities. Wagner, like Handel, had found his best medium in the lyric drama. Brahms, like Bach, found a personal means of expression in instrumental music, although he was by no means limited to that sphere, as his *Lieder* and choral works attest. "The emotional romantic conception of music is common to both Brahms and Wagner," says Paul Bekker, "but they develop it in entirely different ways, the one through a process of expansion, the other through a process of concentration."

JOHANNES BRAHMS—LIFE

The second of three children, Johannes Brahms (1833-1897) was born in a poor district of Hamburg. His father, Johann Jakob, organized a group of itinerant musicians, such as we know as the "little German band." Jakob married Johanna Nissen, a woman of sensitive nature and kind heart, seventeen years his senior. She augmented the family income by running a little notions shop and by taking in a boarder. The father picked up musical odd jobs, and eventually became a double-bass player in a theater orchestra.

Little "Hannes" had profound affection for his curiously mated parents. Johannes' father was his first teacher, but soon Otto Cossel, a pupil of Eduard Marxsen (1806-1887) taught him, and lamented the fact that the very gifted and lovable little boy wasted so much time at his "everlasting composing." Hannes, eager to learn, practiced with superlative enthusiasm and covered every available scrap of music paper with notes. He was a rabid reader and formed a habit of haunting second-hand bookstalls. In time, he accumulated a valuable library.

At the age of twelve Brahms went to Marxsen, an extraordinary teacher. He memorized much Bach and Beethoven, at that time not a common accomplishment, as even composers themselves used scores when performing their own works. In fact, when Brahms became accompanist for the violinists, Reményi and Joachim, he played his part "by heart." As a boy he earned money by performing in waterfront dives and dance halls, spending his poverty-stricken childhood amidst sordid surroundings and with unsavory characters, although his home was a haven of rectitude. He early developed a love for German folksongs, which he retained throughout his life.

Brahms' passion for nature was first indulged when he spent a summer in the country with the Giesemanns. The boy was sent daily into the woods with books, a little mute piano, a lunch box and his Beethoven-like notebook, in which he registered musical and poetic ideas. Lieschen Giesemann was his devoted comrade and his first and none-too-talented piano pupil. Although only fourteen, Brahms was asked to conduct an amateur choral society, for which he also arranged folksongs.

When he returned to Hamburg, in fine physical condition, he appeared in a concert, making so favorable an impression that he was fairly well launched on a pianistic career. During this early period, Brahms made transcriptions and arrangements, under the pseudonym of G. W. Marks, and as "Karl Wurth," he wrote some pieces in popular style.

In 1849 a Hungarian refugee, Eduard Reményi (1830-1898), gave a concert in Hamburg, with Brahms as accompanist. Later they toured Germany together and Brahms had an opportunity to learn something about Gypsy music, of which he made good use in his *Hungarian Dances* (1869-1880). The greatest benefit from the association, however, was meeting Joseph Joachim (1831-1907), a Hungarian who had been

Reményi's classmate at the Vienna Conservatory. Brahms showed him some compositions, and a life-long friendship of mutual benefit sprang up. Joachim, the greatest violin master of his age, was then (1853) concertmaster to the King of Hanover. When the King heard the twenty-year-old Brahms, he prophetically called him a "young Beethoven."

Brahms continued his travels, armed with letters from Joachim to Liszt at Weimar and Schumann at Düsseldorf. Liszt saw in Brahms a possible recruit to the cause of "Music of the Future." But Brahms, with characteristic caution, resisted the charm and enthusiastic praise of the older man, for he had already set his feet on the path which Beethoven had blazed. His meeting with the Schumanns has already been related and the article, *Neue Bahnen,* quoted. In a letter, Schumann spoke of "the young eagle who has so suddenly and unexpectedly flown down from the Alps to Düsseldorf." He wrote to Dr. Härtel of the publishing firm in Leipzig, recommending Brahms' compositions, resulting in the publication of three piano sonatas. Schumann's interest also led to Brahms' first appearance as a pianist in Leipzig.

Fig. 73. Autograph of Second Movement, *Piano Sonata, Opus 5*—Brahms. Sternau's prefacing verse reads:

> *Der Abend dammert, das Mondlicht scheint,*
> *Da sind zwei Herzen in Liebe vereint*
> *Und halten sich selig umfangen.*
>
> (Evening darkens, the moonlight shines,
> Two hearts are joined in love,
> Held in a blissful embrace.)

(Private Collection.)

To Clara Schumann fell the privilege of making known Brahms' music, as she had Schumann's. What a compensative friendship theirs was. This young man, brusque, loving a joke but ashamed of showing tenderness and sentiment, must have found in the mature, richly endowed pianist an ideal that became a dynamic incentive. Women came and women went but Clara Schumann remained Brahms' friend to the end of her life. The boy lost his heart and loved the woman, but the experience ripened into a platonic affair which was as much a part of his better self as was his devotion to his mother. Their summers were spent in the same places and Johannes was looked upon by the Schumann children as a second father, or, perhaps, an older brother.

In 1857 Brahms was offered a post at the Court of Lippe-Detmold by Princess Friederike, a pupil of Frau Schumann. There he gave piano lessons to the royal children, directed the court choir and performed at concerts. He also composed two orchestral serenades (*Ops.* 11 and 16), his first string sextet (*Op.* 18), choral works and the *Concerto No. 1 in D Minor for Piano, Op.* 15. In 1859 he played the concerto at Hanover, with Joachim directing the orchestra, and immediately thereafter at Leipzig where, as the composer wrote to Joachim, it was "a brilliant and decided failure."

Leipzig at the time was a hotbed of two factions—the adherents of Beethoven and Mendelssohn and those aligned with the progressive school of Weimarites. In 1860 Brahms, with Julius Otto Grimm (1827-1903), Joachim and others, antagonized the Lisztian party by drawing up a manifesto against the "Music of the Future" movement, objecting to its statements that the most prominent musicians were in full accord with its aims and that only compositions by leaders of the new school were to be recognized as of artistic value. In a short span, "Johannes Kreisler, Junior," as he signed some early works, borrowing the name of E. T. A. Hoffmann's hero, disappeared and the neo-Classic master, Johannes Brahms, emerged.

There are many interesting parallels between Brahms and his idol, Beethoven. One obvious fact is that both, although of German birth, spent the greater part of their lives in Vienna. Both were Classicists; both were bachelors; both made staunch friends; both loved nature; and both could be extremely disagreeable, gruff and ill-tempered. Brahms enjoyed practical jokes, even when he was the butt; Beethoven loved to play jokes on others, but would not stand having the tables turned.

The second half of Brahms' life began in 1862, with his first visit to Vienna. A successful appearance in a chamber-music concert, playing the piano part of his *G Minor Quartet, Op.* 25, had been his introduction, followed by a solo concert in which he performed Bach, Schumann, his *"Handel" Variations and Fugue, Op.* 24, and participated in the *A Major Piano Quartet, Op.* 26. A year later he was made conductor of the choir of the *Singakademie,* for which he wrote many choral works. Brahms resigned the following July, as he wished independence to work and travel. As in Leipzig he had met with antagonism from the Liszt faction, so in Vienna the Wagner enthusiasts, headed by Anton Bruckner, were pitted against him.

The *Gesellschaft der Musikfreunde* (Society of Friends of Music) presented three sections of *Ein Deutsches Requiem* (*A German Requiem,*

Op. 45) in December, 1867, at a memorial concert. The first complete performance was at Bremen on Good Friday, 1868. It was a great event for Brahms, particularly as Clara and her daughter, Marie, surprised him by appearing at the church door. The work was composed on Biblical excerpts which Brahms chose, and to which he purposely gave the name of *German Requiem* to distinguish it from Roman ritual. The seven parts are arranged to present the ideas of sorrow consoled, doubt overcome and death vanquished. Brahms composed the *Requiem* in memory of Schumann; all, that is, except Part V, "Ye That Now Are Sorrowful," that was written after his mother's death in 1865.

In 1872, after his father's death, Brahms moved to *Carlsgasse* 4 in Vienna, which was to be his home for twenty-five years. He was appointed director of the chorus of the *Gesellschaft der Musikfreunde* and presented programs that included his choral works, *Rhapsodie, Op.* 53, for alto (sung by Frau Joachim), male chorus and orchestra; *Schicksalslied (Song of Destiny, Op.* 54) and the *Triumphlied (Song of Triumph, Op.* 55), written in commemoration of the Franco-Prussian War. Brahms relinquished his post in 1875, but continued to serve as a valued member of the Society's committee. After his death, Brahms' library became the property of the Society.

Brahms was by now an acclaimed composer, although much of his contribution thus far had been in the field of chamber music. He had, however, been at work for ten years on a symphony, the *Symphony No. 1 in C Minor, Op.* 68, that was finally performed at Carlsruhe, in 1876, under the baton of Otto Dessoff (1835-1892). Brahms himself conducted it in various German cities and Joachim directed it in Cambridge. Although there was some outcry against its opening astringency, Hans von Bülow considered it the "Tenth Symphony," linking it to Beethoven's Nine. Moreover, it was he who coined the phrase, the "Three B's"— Bach, Beethoven and Brahms. With customary modesty, Brahms had waited until he was past forty to present his first symphony.

Cambridge University offered him an honorary degree of Doctor of Music, but, reluctant to go to England, Brahms declined. He did accept the title of Doctor of Philosophy from the University of Breslau, however, conferred, as it was worded, "upon the most illustrious Johannes Brahms of Holstein, now master of the stricter style of the art of music in Germany." In acknowledgment of the honor, Brahms composed an *Akademische Festouvertüre (Academic Festival Overture, Op.* 80), a wonderful *potpourri* using German student songs as themes, concluding with the universal *Gaudeamus igitur*. In 1889 Hamburg extended to its gifted son the freedom of the city, a gesture that Brahms especially cherished.

In addition to Clara Schumann and Joachim, Brahms had a wide circle of friends, who called themselves the "Brahmins," including: Eduard Hanslick (1825-1904), the critic; von Bülow, the conductor; Julius Stockhausen (1826-1906), a singer; Julius Otto Grimm, a composer; Albert Dietrich (1829-1906); Theodor Kirchner (1823-1903); Franz Wüllner (1832-1902); Herman Deiters (1833-1907); Antonin Dvořák; Carl Goldmark; Theodor Billroth (1829-1894); Eusebius Mandyczewski (1857-1929); Julius Epstein (1832-1926); Johann Strauss, Jr.; and Max Friedländer (1852-1934)—all eminent personalities in German music.

Elisabet von Herzogenberg, whom Brahms had taught when she was Fräulein von Stockhausen, was the third woman to exert a strong influence over the composer. With her husband, an amateur composer and enthusiastic champion of the "Three B's," she did much to make Brahms' music known in Leipzig. In 1874 the von Herzogenbergs arranged a Brahms Week. Max Kalbeck states that "Brahms was the hero of the hour, his social success being hardly less marked than his public triumphs." Elisabet noted that the composer had not "suffered shipwreck on that rock called Fame; but we all felt that it had mellowed him, and made him kinder and more tolerant. He does not wear a halo of infallibility à la Richard Wagner, but has a quiet air of having achieved what he set out to accomplish, and is content to live and let live."

Joseph Joachim premiered Brahms' only violin concerto (*Concerto in D for Violin, Op.* 77) in Leipzig at a *Gewandhaus* concert. It soon took its place beside those of Beethoven and Mendelssohn. A contemporary critic wrote, "As to the reception, the first movement was too new to be distinctly appreciated by the audience, the second made considerable way, the last aroused great enthusiasm." Yet others agreed that "Joachim played with a love and devotion that brought home to us in every bar the direct or indirect share he has had in the work." Not particularly felicific in the violin writing, the concerto is, nonetheless, in its fiery independence, a priceless enrichment to the repertoire.

After years of composing chamber music, choral works and orchestral compositions, Brahms returned to the piano and wrote some of his masterpieces for that instrument, among which are *Ops.* 76 and 79 and the *Concerto No. 2 in B flat for Piano, Op.* 83, dedicated to his teacher, Marxsen. The latter is a reflective work, conceived under the sunny skies of Italy. The composer introduced it at Budapest in 1881, characterizing it as a "tiny, tiny piano concerto, with a tiny, tiny wisp of a scherzo." Actually, it is a tremendous and unique contribution to piano literature.

Thanks to von Bülow, Brahms visited the court of the Duke of Saxe-Meiningen. With complete freedom of the castle, Brahms "did not abate one jot . . . of his usual independent expression of opinion, and would defend his own point of view with characteristic bluntness and tenacity," writes Florence May. His last symphony, the *Symphony No. 4 in E Minor, Op*. 98, was first performed in 1885 by the Meiningen orchestra under the composer's baton. A great ovation greeted it at its Viennese premiere the following year. The *Finale,* a *passacaglia* or set of variations on a ground bass derived from Bach's Cantata No. 150, *Nach dir, Herr, verlanget mich* ("For Thee, Lord, I Long"), brought forth the opinion that Brahms was a modern Bach, as perhaps he was. "Power, passion, depth of thought, exalted nobility of melody and form, are the qualities which make the artistic manual of his creations," concluded a Hamburg critic of Brahms.

From 1886 to 1889, Brahms passed his summers at Thun, where he composed the *Sonata in A for Violin and Piano, Op*. 100, a work that is sometimes referred to as the *"Preislied" Sonata,* as its opening theme closely resembles Walther's song in Wagner's *Die Meistersinger.* During these years Brahms was showered with honors—from Prussia, Austria and France. He was made honorary president of the Vienna *Tonkünstlerverein* (Musicians' Club); on his sixtieth birthday, he was presented with a gold medal from the *Gesellschaft der Musikfreunde,* to which award he replied, "It is too late!"

When Clara Schumann died in 1896, Brahms hurried to Frankfurt. The excitement aggravated a malady from which he had begun to suffer. After he had seen Frau Schumann buried next to her husband, he went with a group of friends to a nearby town for a few days' rest. He wished to show them the manuscripts of two new works—the last he was to write: *Vier Ernste Gesänge (Four Serious Songs, Op*. 121); and an obvious tribute to Bach, the organ *Chorale-Preludes, Op*. 122. The texts of the *Four Serious Songs* were Biblical, dealing with the thought of death, but ending with St. Paul's glorification, from I Corinthians xiii: 13: "Now remain faith, hope, love; but the greatest of these is love."

The disease (cancer) made rapid progress, although Brahms fought against it with all his power. The city of Vienna gave the master a public funeral, attended by Vienna's greatest musicians and other celebrated men and women. Tributes were sent from courts, music societies and friends from all over Europe. Brahms was buried close to the graves of Beethoven and Schubert in the Central *Friedhof,* where, in an unidentified grave, Mozart also lies.

JOHANNES BRAHMS—MUSIC

The music of Brahms does not fall into distinct periods, as did Beethoven's. Walter Niemann, however, suggests four groupings: (1) that of the youthful works, chiefly for piano, through *Opus* 10; (2) that from 1856 to 1867, filled mainly with chamber music written in Detmold, Hamburg, Vienna and Switzerland; (3) that from 1868 to 1884, the period of great choral and orchestral compositions; and finally (4) that from 1884 until his death, marked by a return to chamber music.

Brahms, the neo-Classicist, used the sonata-form as consistently as did Beethoven. He contributed to every branch of music except opera. As a song writer, he stands with the supreme masters of German *Lieder*. His short piano pieces are Romantic in content, but Brahms satisfied his Classic convictions by general titles, such as *Intermezzo, Capriccio, Rhapsody* and *Ballade*. His four symphonies place him beside Beethoven. His two piano concertos and one violin concerto are among the greatest of their kind. As a chamber-music composer, he is incomparable. Brahms favored different combinations of instruments, so we have three violin sonatas, two violoncello sonatas, two clarinet sonatas, three piano trios, one horn trio, one clarinet trio, three string quartets, three piano quartets, two string quintets, a clarinet and string quintet and the famous *F Minor Piano Quintet, Op.* 34.

Einstein has written that "Brahms is the greatest representative of the musical Romantic movement, which sought to come to terms creatively with the past." He did not do this in the guise of program music, but rather in a return to, and striving after, strict forms and economy of expression. For while his music is certainly Romantic in content, with rich harmony, long melodic lines, contrasts of introspective brooding with outbursts of spirit, along with innovations of rhythmic complexity and asymmetric phrasing, it is Classic in its neatness and self-contained-ness, attributes of former times. Brahms was an extremely competent contrapuntalist, employing devices of fugue and other techniques with unquestioned skill.

The composer is particularly gifted in utilizing variation form, a standby of the eighteenth century. Among his variations are those on a theme of Schumann, *Op.* 9, on an Hungarian air, *Op.* 21, on a theme of Handel, *Op.* 24 and two volumes on a theme by Paganini, *Op.* 35. Per-haps the most famous of all is his *Variations on a Theme by Haydn, Op.* 56a, actually based on the "St. Anthony Chorale," found in Haydn's *Di-vertimento in B Flat*. Originally written for two pianos and so performed by Brahms and Clara Schumann, the variations were orchestrated by the composer in 1874. In Brahms' hands the staid, dotted-rhythmed, five-bar phrases undergo sweeping changes, concluding with a *passacaglia,* in which a variant of the theme is repeated seventeen times with seventeen short variations riding above it.

Brahms wrote over twenty chamber-music works, a large collection in view of the fact that he destroyed many others to prevent posthumous publication. He was conscious of Beethoven's stature in the field. "You don't know what it means to the likes of us when we hear *his* footsteps behind us," he is quoted as saying. In reality, however, Brahms became recognized as Beethoven's successor. Traces of his influence and that of Schubert do not prevent Brahms' unique qualities from shining through. Peter Latham writes:

> Let us enjoy tunes, kindle to his rhythms, rejoice with him, grieve with him, dream with him. But let us also remember that he was a very reserved man. He tells us his thoughts, but leaves us to guess at his feelings, though the feelings are surely there. In speech he was often obscure, saying things that were susceptible of more than one meaning, and his music often presents the same ambiguity.

In writing for voices, Brahms excelled Beethoven. In the smaller choral works, the influence of folksong is evident. There are unaccompanied and accompanied choruses for mixed voices, for men's and for women's voices; religious motets, derived from Bach's example; quartets for solo voices; including two series of *Liebeslieder Waltzer, Ops.* 52 and 65 and the *Gypsy Songs, Op.* 103; and *Op.* 113, a group of canons, charmingly unpedantic, some of which are based on nursery rhymes and folksongs.

An entire chapter might advantageously be devoted to Brahms' songs. If Schubert shaped the Romantic art song, Brahms perfected it. "Let it (the song) rest and keep going back to it and working on it," he advised a composer, "until it is completed as a finished work of art, until there is not a note too much or too little, not a bar you could improve upon." Brahms wrote songs throughout his life. They began with his lovely *Liebestreu (True Love)* from *Op.* 3, No. 1, which, at the age of twenty-one, he dedicated to Bettina Brentano von Arnim. More than fifty poets supplied texts for over 200 solo songs and duets. Brahms also published fourteen *Folksongs for Children* (for the Schumanns) and in 1894, six books of German folksongs, which, he said, were "the only work whose publication has given me any amusement."

It was for years the custom to call Brahms' orchestration thick and muddy, but as modern conductors have studied the composer's intentions more carefully, they have come to understand its individual character. Brahms built on Beethoven and Schumann. "Impervious to contemporary movements in the arts," *Grove's Dictionary* states, "he went on in his own sturdy fashion, tethered to the past, and hammering out imperishable themes. He had a sense of orchestral color which was quite as personal as Wagner's was . . ." Anyone who has listened attentively to his orchestral works finds that Brahms has a sound all his own, distinguished by the *chalumeau* writing for clarinets, extensive use of horns, brass-choir treatment and textural viscosity. Limitations of space prevent more than mere mention of the four magnificent symphonies that issued from Brahms' imagination: *Op.* 69, which Niemann calls his *"Pathetic";* *Op.* 73, which Specht describes as "suffused with sunshine"; *Op.* 90, which Hans Richter referred to as Brahms' *"Eroica";* and *Op.* 98, filled with an autumnal melancholy so characteristic of the composer's music.

ANTON BRUCKNER

Brahms wrote to a friend:

> Nietzsche once alleged that I became famous only by accident: that the anti-Wagner party made use of me as the anti-pope whom they required. That is naturally nonsense, I am not at all a suitable person to place at the head of any party . . . But in Bruckner's case it does not apply. For since Wagner's death his party naturally required a pope, and they could find nobody better than Bruckner.

Anton Bruckner (1824-1896), an Upper Austrian by birth, was a Classicist and a Wagnerite. His aim was to graft the Wagner melodic-harmonic system and orchestration onto Classic forms in symphony and church music. By the Viennese he was regarded as direct descendant of Schubert, with Brahms an interloper. Bruckner's nine symphonies, the last unfinished, were developed to unusual length, and show a distinct musical personality. They reflect his religious nature and his love of German folk music, as well as his homage to Wagner. Bekker says, ". . . he created a number of symphonies and religious works which incline towards a new cult music with a universal appeal. . . . Through the simplicity of his feeling Bruckner is the first to return to the expression of an impersonal, a universal attitude."

With Bruckner the opening theme of the first movement reappeared as the *finale* of a symphony, often as a *chorale*. Wagnerian effect was heightened by his use of the brasses. Other mannerisms include the notorious *lunga pausa*—a period of silence following a pyramid of climaxes; an overattention to details, often resulting in overall structural weakness; a certain longwindedness in efforts to reach transcendency; and the introduction of brief motives, only gradually developed into themes which in turn are extensively cultivated. As Westerman remarks, Bruckner's music is superdimensional in form and infinite in content. It requires much staying power of the listener. Because of length and the large forces necessary for performance, Bruckner's music has not received the hearing it deserves, although he has always had a coterie of admirers, among whom was his pupil and successor, Gustav Mahler.

Bruckner spent much of his life in relative obscurity, serving as a schoolmaster and organist at Linz. In 1868 he was appointed to teach theory and organ at the Vienna Conservatory, possibly as a tactical maneuver in the Wagner-Brahms war. This was a decisive step for Bruckner, who wrote all but one of his symphonies in Vienna. A simple human being, of peasant stock and child-like piety, Bruckner was as unlike Wagner as he was dissimilar to Brahms. Besides the symphonies, he composed a string quartet, three Masses, a *Te Deum* and much sacred music for the Roman liturgy. Einstein concludes that "the religious element and the feeling for nature converge into the mystical, thus making it possible for one to set Bruckner upon the throne of musical theosophy."

César Franck

A possible counterpart to Brahms and Bruckner in Vienna was César Franck (1822-1890) in Paris. A French school of instrumental music in absolute forms was the product of him and his followers. This quiet unassuming master, little understood or appreciated, undisturbed by the lack of interest shown him by the other composers and the public, went his way perseveringly, simple in faith, rich in knowledge and not questioning the results of his achievements.

His life was unglamorous and secluded. He was organist at Ste. Clothilde for almost half his years. Not only did he give his pupils a thorough theoretical foundation, but his home was a center where they heard each other's compositions, discussed musical problems and received his constructive criticism. He spent his days going from house to house to give piano lessons. After his marriage, he reserved but two hours every morning for his composing, arising at five-thirty A.M. to have "time for thought."

César Franck was born at Liége, of Flemish stock. His father, a stern and autocratic banker, encouraged his musical career. At eleven, the boy, a pupil at the Liége Conservatory, made a concert tour of Belgium as a pianist. In 1836, the family moved to Paris, so that César might attend the Conservatory. There he received a *grand prix d'honneur* from Cherubini but was refused the opportunity of competing for the *Prix de Rome* in 1842, on the grounds that he was not a Frenchman. Franck then returned to Belgium but remained there only two years.

"From this time (1844) began that life of regular and unceasing industry lasting nearly half a century," writes his devoted disciple, composer Vincent d'Indy (1851-1932), "without break or pause, during which the musician's sole diversion was a concert—at rare intervals—at which one of his own works was given." Franck's father, disappointed by his son's decision to be a composer rather than a virtuoso, was alienated completely, when César married the daughter of an actor during the Revolution of 1848.

In 1858, Franck became organist of Ste. Clothilde in Paris. D'Indy states that he "had or rather *was* the genius of improvisation." When Liszt visited the church, he compared Franck to Bach. Yet no one was more surprised than Franck himself when he was appointed professor of organ at the Paris Conservatory in 1872.

Although acclaimed as an organist, Franck fared less well as a composer. His first rebuff from the critics came when the Biblical eclogue or pastoral, *Ruth,* was performed in 1846. It was considered but a "poor imitation" of David's *Le Désert.* The first performance of his oratorio, *La Rédemption,* presented by Édouard Colonne (1838-1910) at a *Concert spirituel* in 1873, was also unsatisfactory and a private hearing of *Les Béatitudes,* on which Franck had been at work for ten years, was a fiasco in 1879. The latter was not performed in its entirety until Colonne conducted it in 1893, three years after Franck's death, when, ironically, it was an overwhelming success. As a protest against the Conservatory giving the vacant chair of composition to Léo Délibes (1836-1891), composer of the popular ballet, *Coppelia,* and the opera, *Lakmé,* instead of to Franck, pupils and friends organized a Franck Festival in 1887. D'Indy reports that Franck, who was radiantly happy to hear his works and to be so honored, "was the only person who did not regret the wretched performance."

Even the *Symphony in D Minor,* introduced in 1889 by the *Société des concerts du Conservatoire,* shared the fate of his other "first performances." Gounod caustically called the work "the affirmation of incompetence pushed to dogmatic lengths." In reply to his asking a factotum of the Conservatory how he liked the work, d'Indy was told: "That, a symphony? . . . But my dear sir, who ever heard of writing for the *cor anglais* in a symphony? Just mention a single symphony by Haydn or Beethoven introducing the *cor anglais.* There, well, you see—your Franck's music may be whatever you please, but it will certainly never be a symphony!" Franck himself mildly commented, "It sounded well, just as I thought it would."

Franck's *Sonata in A for Violin and Piano* (1886) was made famous by the Belgian violinist, Eugène Ysaÿe (1858-1931), to whom it was dedicated as a wedding gift. Ysaÿe also introduced the *Quartet in D* (1889), which was received with such enthusiasm that Franck remarked, somewhat naïvely, "There, you see, the public is beginning to understand me."

One month later the composer was struck by an omnibus. While apparently only superficially injured, he suffered complications that led to his death.

Like Verdi, "the grand old man of Italy," Franck wrote his best compositions at an age when creative power is supposed to be depleted. The popular setting of *Panis Angelicus,* first conceived for tenor, organ, harp, 'cello and double bass; the organ *Pièce héroique;* the *Variations symphoniques* for piano and orchestra; the *Prélude, choral et fugue* for piano; the symphony and the violin sonata—all were composed after 1872.

César Franck has been called the "French Brahms," although, apart from his defense of absolute music, there seems little reason for the comparison. Brahms was a spiritual descendant of Beethoven, while Franck was closer to Bach, as his titles and forms reveal. He used the sonata principle, but treated it cyclically and with wide latitude. Franckian melodies are often long, perhaps as a protest against the short two- and four-measure phrases that had become a mannerism of much Romantic music. In his chromatic harmony and his orchestration we find traces of Liszt and Wagner. Yet Franck evolved a truly personal style, that was imitated by many of his followers.

"At his death César Franck left a legacy to his country in the form of a vigorous symphonic school, such as France had never before produced," states d'Indy. Alexis-Emmanuel Chabrier (1841-1894) delivered Franck's funeral oration, in the name of the *Société nationale de musique.* He eulogized:

> In you we salute one of the greatest artists of the century, and also the incomparable teacher whose wonderful work produced a whole generation of forceful musicians, believers, thinkers, armed at all points for hard-fought and prolonged conflicts. We salute, also, the upright and just man, so humane, so distinguished, whose counsels were sure, as his words were kind.

THE *Société national de musique*

Franck, with Edouard Lalo (1823-1892) and Saint-Saëns, worked against disheartening odds to develop French instrumental music, for, as we have noted, a musical apathy pervaded the Second Empire and only opera enjoyed real popularity. Jules Pasdeloup (1819-1887) offered only German works at his *Concerts populaires* and, as Saint-Saëns commented:

> The few chamber-music societies that existed were also closed to all newcomers . . . In those times one had really to be devoid of all common sense to write music.

Fig. 74. "Round the Piano"—painting by Fantin Latour, 1855. Emmanuel Chabrier is shown at the piano while Vincent d'Indy appears standing at the right, holding a cigarette. (Courtesy Louvre Museum, Paris.)

"A new generation was growing up, however," writes Romain Rolland, "a generation that was serious and thoughtful, that was more attracted by pure music than by the theater, that was filled with a burning desire to found a national art." Incited by the Franco-Prussian War, which awoke national consciousness, and led them to declare for musical freedom, these young composers founded the *Société nationale de musique* (National Music Society), "the cradle and sanctuary of French art." The musical chauvinism for which the French are known had its incipiency then and there, and, without the *Société,* it is questionable whether or not French music would have made the advances that have placed it in its present front rank.

The founders of the *Société* were Camille Saint-Saëns and Henri Bussine, a professor of singing at the Conservatory. With them were César Franck; Ernest Guiraud (1837-1892), who was born in New Orleans but lived most of his life in Paris as an opera composer and Conservatory teacher; Jules Massenet; Jules-Auguste Garcin, violinist and conductor; Gabriel Fauré; Henri Duparc (1848-1933); Théodore Dubois (1837-1924), famous organist, professor and composer of the lachrymose *Seven Last Words of Christ*; and Claude-Paul Taffanel (1844-1908), flutist and composer.

On November 25, 1871, the *Société* presented its first concert. Since that time, all representative French music has been performed under the *Société*'s auspices. And, as Rolland says, the group "possessed the rare merit of being able to anticipate public opinion by ten or eleven years, and in some ways it has formed the public mind and obliged it to honor those whom the Society had already recognized as great musicians." Saint-Saëns resigned in 1886 and the Franckian forces took over.

CHARLES-CAMILLE SAINT-SAËNS

Charles-Camille Saint-Saëns (1835-1921) occupies a peculiar place in French music. He was perhaps damned by his own versatility. In addition to being a prolific composer, he was, to quote Philip Hale, "an organist, pianist, caricaturist, dabbler in science, enamored of mathematics and astronomy, amateur comedian, *feuilletonist,* critic, traveler and archeologist." Berlioz hailed him as "one of the greatest musicians of our epoch," and Hanslick asserted, "Since Berlioz, Camille Saint-Saëns is the first musician who, not being a German, has written pure instrumental music, and created in that line, original and valuable works, the reputation of which have passed beyond the limits of France . . ."

Of Saint-Saëns' many compositions, numbering 169 opuses, only a few have found their places in the standard repertoire. They include the *Introduction et Rondo capriccioso* for violin and orchestra (1863); the *Piano Concerto No. 2 in G Minor* (1868); a symphonic poem, *Danse Macabre* (*Dance of Death,* 1875); the opera, *Samson et Dalila* (1877); the *Symphony No. 3 in C Minor,* featuring the organ (1886); and *Le Carnaval des animaux* (*The Carnival of Animals*), for two pianos and orchestra. The last-named work was first presented privately at a Mardi Gras concert in 1886, but was withheld from the public until after the composer's death, perhaps because he feared that some of the "animals" he lampooned would be recognizable. Only one section, *Le Cygne* (*The Swan*), escaped the performance prohibition and it quickly became a favorite 'cello solo. In *The Carnival,* Saint-Saëns enjoyed employing musical satire. He also interpolated a number of quotations from his own and others' compositions, including bits of Berlioz, Mendelssohn, Offenbach and Rossini, that provide the curious listener with an opportunity for musical sleuthing. Of special interest to some of us is *Hail California,* for chorus and orchestra, written for the Panama Exposition of 1915.

GABRIEL FAURÉ

The French regard Gabriel Fauré (1845-1924) as holding a key to the secret of a new idiom. Fauré was interested in absolute music and deliberately avoided "descriptive inventions, imitative harmonies and metaphysical aims," according to André Coeuroy. Born in the south of France, Fauré was reared in an atmosphere of education, as his father was an inspector of schools. From the age of nine he attended the Niedermeyer School of Religious Music in Paris, where he studied with Saint-Saëns. Subsequently he was an organist at Rennes in Brittany from 1866 to 1870; served in the Franco-Prussian War; taught at the Niedermeyer School; replaced Saint-Saëns as organist at the *Madeleine;* and was a charter member of the *Société nationale*. Fauré succeeded Jules Massenet as professor of composition at the Paris Conservatory in 1896 and served as its director from 1905 to 1920.

Among his piano works are impromptus, barcarolles, *valse-caprices* and nocturnes, written in a graceful Romantic vein, with subtle modulations and refined pianistic style that influenced French composers of this century. Fauré's *Messe de Requiem* (1887) is a favorite work and many of his ninety-six songs are in the finest tradition of French *chansons*. Hill asserts:

> Fauré's distinctive melodic invention and his highly original harmonic sense constitute his chief gifts as a composer. He is a born lyricist, and herein lie both the strength and the weakness of his artistic personality. In the large forms, his constructive faculty is not always on a par with the preeminent qualities mentioned above . . .

PETER ILYITCH TCHAIKOVSKY—LIFE

Peter Ilyitch Tchaikovsky's place as a Romantic absolutist can be both justified and challenged, for much of his music is programmatic and intensely nationalistic. He openly disdained Brahms' aims and accomplishments, yet he was an heir of German traditions and a Mozart enthusiast. He stands apart from "The Mighty Five" in that he was a professionally-trained composer and did not consciously build his art on native folk music, although he used Russian folk tunes and contributed to the music of the Orthodox Church. In his six symphonies and his concertos, Tchaikovsky worked in the great abstract forms; in his tone-poems, he tended to speak Liszt's language, but with a decided Russian accent.

Tchaikovsky (1840-1893) grew up in St. Petersburg, attended a school of jurisprudence and for a short time held a post in the Ministry of Justice. But when he was twenty-one, he started a serious study of music, first with Nikolai Zaremba (1821-1879) and then with Rubenstein at the St. Petersburg Conservatory. "Do not imagine I dream of being a great artist," he wrote to his favorite sister. "I only feel that I must do the work for which I have a calling. Whether I become a celebrated composer, or only a struggling teacher—'tis all the same . . . Of course,

I shall not resign my present position until I am sure that I am no longer a clerk, but a musician." In 1863, he made his decision. When Nicholas Rubenstein (1835-1881), Anton's brother, established the Moscow Conservatory, he appointed Tchaikovsky professor of harmony and became a strong influence in the composer's life.

Tchaikovsky had decided likes and dislikes. The school of "young Russians" known as "The Mighty Five," who were "modern" in their views and opposed to Anton Rubenstein, aroused his hostility, as we have already mentioned. Although Tchaikovsky benefited from acquaintance with Balakirev, who actually suggested and outlined his overture-fantasy, *Romeo and Juliet,* Tchaikovsky was not enthusiastic about the others and especially abhorred Moussorgsky. The "Five," on the other hand, felt that Tchaikovsky was too Europeanized and too little nationalistic for their tastes.

Tchaikovsky's personality was a complex and undoubtedly neurotic one. "The story of Tchaikovsky," writes Rollo Myers, "is, in fact, a study in morbid psychology, but it is also the story of a great artist and of a man of singular charm." In composition, the man found a catharsis for his personal bewilderment and confusion, one that kept him sane and provided a reason for living. Tchaikovsky was constitutionally shy and professed a dread of society which he avoided, whenever possible. Yet in 1866 he wrote to his sister of his success as a teacher with something like boyish enthusiasm.

> Much to my surprise, my course is very successful. My nervousness has completely vanished, and I am gradually acquiring the proper professional demeanor. My hypochondria is also disappearing. But Moscow is still a strange town for me . . .

Evidence seems to support the belief that Tchaikovsky was a sexual deviate, much to his own dismay and alarm. It has been alleged that his knowledge of this fact forced him, through some kind of mistaken gallantry, into a disastrous marriage with one of his students, who had fallen madly in love with him, in a reverse situation to the plot of the opera on which he was then working, *Eugen Onegin.* Whatever the motivation, the marriage lasted but a miserable nine weeks and was an utter failure. The experience cost Tchaikovsky a year to surmount his emotional scars. His wife continued to be a constant source of embarrassment, until she was finally confined to an asylum.

At the same time that he had composed his first three symphonies—*Op.* 13, "Winter Dreams"; *Op.* 17, "Little Russian"; and *Op.* 29, the "Polish"—and had had his brief fling at domesticity, Tchaikovsky attracted the attention of another woman, a widowed mother of eleven, his senior and extremely wealthy. She was Mme. Nadejda von Meck, a recluse with a compelling love of music, especially that of Tchaikovsky. With this "beloved friend," the composer entered into a unique relationship, made even more dramatic by the fact that they never formally met during the thirteen years of their increasingly intimate acquaintance. In addition to affording Tchaikovsky an outlet for verbal soul-searching and discussion of his work in almost daily letters, the affair had its practical side, as Mme. von Meck subsidized Tchaikovsky with an annual stipend of some $3000, which allowed him to devote himself entirely to the joy of composition and the refreshment of travel. The *Symphony No. 4 in F Minor, Op.* 36 was dedicated to his influential patroness. "How glad I am," Tchaikovsky wrote, "that it is *our* work, and you will know when you hear it how much I thought about you in every measure."

The remainder of Tchaikovsky's life was spent in composing and making tours. In 1891, he came to America, where he conducted the inaugural concerts at Carnegie Hall, presenting four concerts in New York, one in Baltimore and one in Philadelphia, all featuring his bombastic *Ouverture solennelle "1812,"* a noisy work originally written for outdoor performance, celebrating the Russian victory at the Battle of Borodino. Although homesick for Russia during his short visit to the United States, he liked our country. "American customs, American manners, and habits are generally attractive to me," he noted in his diary.

In 1893, with Saint-Saëns, Boito, Max Bruch and Grieg, Tchaikovsky was honored by a Doctor of Music degree from Cambridge University. During this year, he also completed his sixth and last symphony, the *"Pathétique," Op.* 74, for which he apparently had a vague program in mind, although he stated, "Let them guess it who can." In this work he obscurely included an excerpt from the Russian Requiem service (in the trombones), as if to indicate that his days were numbered, which indeed they were. Thoughtlessly drinking unboiled water at a café, Tchaikovsky contracted cholera and died. Three months later, Mme. von Meck passed away.

PETER ILYITCH TCHAIKOVSKY—MUSIC

Tchaikovsky's music is characterized by what might be called emotional exhibitionism and lugubrious self-pity. A certain musical snobbery deplores his "unbearable vulgarities" as well as his great popularity with the masses of untutored music lovers. His creative output is uneven in quality and his grasp of form far from perfect, as he himself admitted. Yet, at his best, Tchaikovsky wrote music full of brooding and religious feeling, with glimpses of humor and charm, keen orchestral coloring, and, above all, a genius for sentimental melody that is unparalleled. It is a standing joke that our Tin Pan Alley would have been out of business in the 1930's were it not for pirating so many of his tunes and supplying them with rather nauseating lyrics. Regardless of such adulterations, the melodies remain magical. Too little attention has been paid to his direct emotional appeal and his marvelous sense of orchestration, while too much has been focused on obvious banalities. To the listener goes the final judgment. It is no accident that his most popular song is "None But the Lonely Heart."

Of the symphonies, the last three, tinged as they are with melancholy, are best known. The *Symphony No. 4 in F Minor* was a favorite of its composer, who wrote a detailed analysis of its content, concluding with "Rejoice in the happiness of others—and you can still live." The *Symphony No. 5 in E Minor,* perhaps his greatest, filled the composer with self-doubt. "Am I really played out, as they say?" he despaired. In the *Symphony No. 6 in B Minor,* Tchaikovsky reveals himself most clearly. Streatfield comments, "It must stand as a very interesting and complete picture of a certain frame of mind, probably the completest expression in music of the *fin de siècle* that has ever been written."

Among other characteristic works are the tone-poems, *Romeo and Juliet,* in which elements of Shakespeare's drama are projected, and *Francesca da Rimini,* a "whirlwind" of a work inspired by part of Dante's *Inferno;* the lilting ballets, *Swan Lake* (1877), *The Sleeping Beauty* (1890) and *The Nutcracker* (1892), in which trifling material is brilliantly orchestrated; the operas, *Eugen Onegin* (1879) and *Pique Dame* (*The Queen of Spades,* 1890); the *Quartet No. 1 in D, Op.* 11, from which comes the familiar *Andante cantabile* theme, based on a folk tune; the *Piano Concerto No. 1 in B Flat Minor, Op.* 23, with its booming opening chords and brilliant instrumental writing, introduced in Boston by von Bülow in 1875; and the *Concerto in D for Violin and Orchestra, Op.* 35, of which Hanslick wrote, "The violin is no longer played . . . it is beaten black and blue." This reminds us that a contemporary critic, after hearing Brahms' *Violin Concerto,* exclaimed that it was not written *for* the violin but *against* it.

*   *   *   *   *

In this and previous chapters, we have followed the course of musical Romanticism along direct and indirect byways of experimentation, innovation, recrystallization and intensification to a point where it hovers on the brink of a chasm of reaction. Various phases have seemingly been explored to their utmost potential. New tendencies are about to burst from the matrix of the late nineteenth century.

Yet as cultural forms do not appear full-blown, neither do they suddenly fall into oblivion. Perhaps due to what sociologists call "cultural lag," the weight of any phenomenon tends to linger on, filtering through various strata of appreciation and evaluation. After Wagner, after Brahms, after Berlioz, after Tchaikovsky, what more could be expressed in terms of the Romantic vocabulary? A partial answer awaits us in the next chapter.

SUGGESTIONS FOR FURTHER READING

Abraham, Gerald, *The Music of Tchaikovsky.* New York, Norton, 1946.

Bowen, Catherine D., *Beloved Friend.* New York, Random House, 1937.

————, *Free Artist: The Story of Anton Rubenstein and His Brother.* New York, Random House, 1939.

Cooper, Martin, *French Music from the Death of Berlioz to the Death of Fauré.* London, Oxford University Press, 1951.

Demuth, Norman, *César Franck.* New York, Philosophical Library, 1949.

D'Indy, Vincent, *César Franck.** New York, Dover, 1965.

Einstein, Alfred, *Music in the Romantic Era.* New York, Norton, 1947.

Evans, Edwin, *Tchaikovsky.** New York, Avon Bks., 1960.

Geiringer, Karl, *Brahms.** New York, Oxford University Press, 1947.

Hanslick, Edward, *The Beautiful in Music.* New York, Liberal Arts Press, 1957.

Harvey, Arthur, *Saint-Saëns.* New York, Dodd Mead, 1922.

Hill, Edward B., *Modern French Music.* Boston, Houghton-Mifflin, 1924.

Lakond, Wladimir, ed., *Diaries of Tchaikovsky.* New York, Norton, 1945.

Latham, Peter, *Brahms.** New York, Collier Bks., 1962.

May, Florence, *The Life of Brahms.* London, Reeves, 1948. 2 vols.

Newlin, Dika, *Bruckner, Mahler and Schönberg.* New York, King's Crown, 1947.

Redlich, Hans F., *Bruckner and Mahler.* New York, Farrar-Straus-Cudahy, 1963.

Revitt, Paul, *Nineteenth-Century Romanticism in Music.** Englewood Cliffs, Prentice-Hall, 1967.

Schauffler, Robert Haven, *The Unknown Brahms.* New York, Dodd Mead, 1933.

Shostakovitch, Dimitri, *et al., Russian Symphony: Thoughts about Tchaikovsky.* New York, Philosophical Library, 1947.

Starr, William J., and Devine, George F., *Music Scores—Omnibus,** Part 2. Englewood Cliffs, Prentice-Hall, 1964.

Suckling, Norman, *Fauré.* New York, Pellegrini & Cudahy, 1951.

Wolff, Werner, *Anton Bruckner: Rustic Genius.* New York, Dutton, 1942.

A SAMPLER OF SUPPLEMENTARY RECORDINGS

Collections

Ten Centuries of Music	DGG KL-52/61
2000 Years of Music	Folkways 3700
Romanticism	Victor LM-6153

Music of Individual Composers
    Brahms, Johannes, *Academic Festival Overture, Op.* 80
                Concerto No. 2 in B Flat for Piano, Op. 83

* Available in paperback edition.

Concerto in D for Violin, Op. 77
"German" Requiem, Op. 45
Liebeslieder Waltzes, Ops. 52, 65
Songs
Symphony No. 1 in c, Op. 68
Symphony No. 3 in F, Op. 90
Variations on a Theme by Haydn, Op. 56a
Quintet in b for Clarinet and Strings, Op. 115
Piano Works

Bruckner, Anton, Mass No. 3 in F, "Great"
Fauré, Gabriel, Requiem, Op. 48
Franck, César, Pièce Héroique
Sonata in A for Violin and Piano
Symphonic Variations for Piano and Orchestra
Saint-Saëns, Camille, Carnival of the Animals
Concerto No. 2 in g for Piano, Op. 22
Danse Macabre, Op. 40
Tchaikovsky, Peter, Concerto No. 1 in b Flat for Piano, Op. 23
Concerto in D for Violin, Op. 35
The Nutcracker, Op. 71
Romeo and Juliet
Swan Lake
Symphony No. 6 in b, Op. 74, "Pathétique"
Piano Trio in a, Op. 50

OPPORTUNITIES FOR STUDY IN DEPTH

1. Paul Landormy has written that Saint-Saëns is important historically because he is the French Mendelssohn. After reading and listening to music of Saint-Saëns, comment on this statement.

2. Make a comparison of the popular settings of Psalm 150 by Bruckner, Franck and Stravinsky (Third Movement, Symphony of Psalms), specifically citing the musical means each composer employs to project the exultation of the text, and noting similarities and differences of style.

3. Compile a list of so-called "popular songs" whose melodies have been adapted from works of serious composers. Check the original with the arrangement and prepare an oral report for the class. (Tchaikovsky alone will supply a formidable start.)

4. Make a study of Broadway musicals which have tapped Romantic sources for their materials. We have already noted several in this text. In addition, there are two recent ones with scores devised by Robert Wright and George Forrest: Anya (with music by Rachmaninov) and Dumas and Son (with music by Camille Saint-Saëns).

5. Eduard Hanslick played an interesting role in the later Romantic musical scene, in which, to quote Verdi, the "flagellation of the critics" became a factor. Wagner's attitude toward Hanslick is memorialized in his character, Beckmesser (Die Meistersinger), who was originally called "Hans Lick." Write a paper concerning Hanslick's part in the Wagner-Brahms dispute.

6. Prepare an outline-guide to the various musical quotations used by Saint-Saëns

in *The Carnival of Animals* and lead a class listening-hour devoted to this work, inserting any informative material to assist the understanding of the group.

7. Analyze, with particular emphasis on harmonic materials, a piano composition of Brahms and formulate an assessment of his harmonic resources as compared with those of Franck and Wagner. What similarities and what differences are perceived?

8. Investigate the symphonies of either Brahms, Bruckner or Tchaikovsky, with the aim of identifying outstanding features of construction, instrumentation and emotional content. What distinguishes these symphonies and accounts for their stature in music through the ages?

VOCABULARY ENRICHMENT

neo-Classic	*ballade*
absolute music	*lunga pausa*
Wagner-Brahms war	musical theosophy
"German" Requiem	cyclical symphony
"Three B's"	eclogue
"Brahmins"	asymmetric phrases
intermezzo	rhythmic counterpoint
capriccio	*Société nationale*
rhapsody	

Chapter 23.

EXTENSIONS OF ROMANTICISM

A linking up with the Beethoven of *Coriolan, Egmont,* the *Leonore III Overture,* of *Les Adieux,* above all with late Beethoven, whose complete *oeuvre,* in my opinion, could never have been created without a poetic subject, seems to me the only course for the time being by which an *independent further* development of our instrumental music is yet possible . . . Of course, purely formalistic, Hanslickian music-making will no longer be possible, and we cannot have any more random patterns . . . and no symphonies (Brahms excepted, of course) . . .

—Richard Strauss, *Letter to von Bülow,* Munich, 1888

During the final decades of the nineteenth century, it was apparent that Romanticism had reached the end of its tether and that composers must either out-romanticize Romanticism, which some of them attempted, or find new avenues of expression with new means and different goals. Writing to von Bülow, young Richard Strauss was addressing himself to submitting a symphony for performance by the Meiningen Orchestra. In the process he unburdened himself of a few ideas about the future of instrumental music. As it turned out, Strauss was not destined to add to the "nine and four" of Beethoven and Brahms. What is significant about his letter is his reference to continuing the implications of the music of Beethoven, pushing even farther along paths already cleared in the jungle of musical creation.

In this chapter we shall survey some of the contributions of the composers of post-Romanticism, that is, the last phases of the movement, the *Götterdämmerung,* as it were, of an overblown epoch that flourished at the same time that other forces were gathering strength which was to burst forth at the turn of the century. We shall follow the opera production in Italy, festooned by the wonderful musical theater of Puccini; opera and instrumental expansion in France, as seen in the music of Massenet, Charpentier and the followers of Franck; the music of the last great German composers, Mahler, Wolf and Strauss; and the nationalistically-oriented music of Vaughan Williams, Sibelius, Janáček and Rachmaninov—the extensions of Romanticism.

What distinguished the music of post-Romanticism, in reality a conglomerate, was a consciousness of the past as it affected the present and a desire for continuity that in effect provided a transition. Each composer felt he was creating in the only way he could and, to a degree, he was. But lurking just behind him were specters of Berlioz, Liszt, Verdi or Wagner. It is this awareness of, and relevance to, the Romantic legacy, especially as it influences selection of subjects and materials, that tends to separate a Strauss from a Debussy and a Sibelius from a Bartók, although the lines of demarcation are necessarily fuzzy.

Verismo

In Italy, opera remained the natural outlet of composers, with Verdi reigning supreme and his successors a little less lustrous, although venturing on byways of their own. Up to the time Pietro Mascagni (1863-1945) won the Sonzogno competition for one-act operas with *Cavalleria Rusticana* (*Rustic Chivalry,* 1890), there had been little new offered. To be sure, Puccini had written a harbinger of his future success in *Le Villi* (1884); Spiro Samara (1861-1917) with *Flora Mirabiles* (1886) and Alfredo Catalani (1854-1893), whose most interesting opera was *La Wally* (1892), had sounded new notes. It was Mascagni, however, who "started a school . . . of compressed emotionalism, commonplace brutality converted into dramatic force," states *The Art of Music*— i.e., verismo. In *Cavalleria* we find "the realism of *Carmen,* a dash of French opera banality, the typical melodramatic sensations—love, jealously, murder, and Italian melody; the sharply cut, incisive tunes of young Italy . . . There is . . . brutal strength and insidious charm, with a blood-red spontaneity . . . ," *The Art of Music* continues. The opera deals with primitive passions in a realistic setting of Italian peasant culture.

Ruggiero Leoncavallo (1858-1919) did not succeed so flamingly as did Mascagni. He had composed many operas before *I Pagliacci* (*The Strolling Players,* 1892). In this, he conceived a dramatic libretto so well adapted to the Italian singer that it will probably outlive many greater works. The *Prologue* ("By Your Leave, Ladies and Gentlemen") and *"Vesti la giubba"* ("Now don the motley"), the *Ballatella* ("Bird Song") and *"Din, don, suona vespero"* ("Ding Dong, the Vesper's Bell") are fine moments, when singers may grimace and sob to the audience's satisfaction.

GIORDANO, WOLF-FERRARI AND MONTEMEZZI

Umberto Giordano (1867-1948), of the Neapolitan group with Nicola Spinelli (1865-1909) and Leoncavallo, strayed into distant regions for his opera librettos. Of Giordano, Bie says, "He was too intellectual for Italy and too musical for the intellect"—a difficult position for an opera composer. Local political intrigue fascinated him. If his music does not always hold the listener, even when his story does, it often rises to fine lyric heights, as in *Andrea Chénier* (1896) and *Fedora* (1898).

A musical descendant of Mozart, Ermanno Wolf-Ferrari (1876-1948) was the son of a German father and an Italian mother. His *Il Segreto di Susanna* (*The Secret of Suzanne,* 1909), based on the story of a young bride who surreptitiously smokes, unknown to her adoring and jealous husband, is a delightful one-act *opera buffa. I Giojielli della Madonna* (*The Jewels of the Madonna,* 1911) is a mixture of the sensuous, lyric and flamboyant, a boiling tale of love, cabal and religious sentiment. Wolf-Ferrari was both realist and idealist. When accused of having relinquished the charming archaisms of *The Secret of Suzanne* in his later operas, the composer replied, "When I deal with puppets of the eighteenth century, I am graceful; and passionate when it is a question of the sensuality and religion of modern Naples."

Another Italian who abandoned the *verismo* school was Italo Montemezzi (1875-1952), whose best-known work is *L'Amore dei tre re* (*The Love of Three Kings,* 1913). The music is stylistically Wagnerian. While not radical, it is always convincing and never dressed in Italian pyrotechnics. *Arias* and recitative (*musica parlanti*) appear as the drama requires.

GIACOMO PUCCINI

It was Giacomo Puccini (1858-1924), who nearest approached Verdi in popularity and mastery among the post-Romantic opera composers. Although his operas are often suffused with the elements of *verismo,* they are displayed in a poetic and stylized guise. Puccini came from a family of musicians in Lucca. If not for the event of hearing Verdi's *Aïda* (to which he walked to Pisa), Puccini may have been content to follow the footsteps of his father, an organist and teacher. In 1880, the young man enrolled in the Milan Conservatory, where he studied with Amilcare Ponchielli (1834-1886), composer of *La Gioconda* (1878), from which comes the familiar "Dance of the Hours." Ponchielli urged Puccini to enter a Sonzogno competition, for which he hastily wrote *Le Villi* (*The Vampires*), an opera concerning the ethereal spirits of jilted damsels. Puccini did not even receive mention in the prize-giving, but Boito, Verdi's librettist, was so impressed that he subsidized a Milanese production, that was quite successful.

On the promise of this triumph, the publishing house of Ricordi advanced Puccini a small allowance for another opera. After five years, *Edgar* (1889) appeared and was a signal failure. During this period the composer often knew the pangs of hunger and the privations of penury. With *Manon Lescaut* (1893), however, Puccini's personal tide turned, and for this work, based on the same story as Massenet's *Manon,* composed some ten years earlier, Puccini was acclaimed a master of his art. The incomparable *La Bohème* (1896), taken from Murger's *Vie de Bohème,* followed, a near-perfect opera score, transforming realism into a fabric of humor, pathos and drama, and deliberately dooming Leoncavallo's opera on the same subject, which appeared a year later and was lost in Puccini's wake.

Through various machinations, some of an allegedly dubious nature, Puccini secured the libretto of *La Tosca* (1900), a histrionic play of love and hate, suicide and murder, taken from a sensational drama by Sardou, in which Sarah Bernhardt had starred on the stage. By now, Puccini had acquired recognition in both Europe and America. He was able to indulge in snappy clothes and fine foods, in a magnificent villa at Torre del Lago (maintained at present as a Puccini museum) and in fancy

Fig. 75. Tablet on Puccini's villa. "The people of Torre del Lago placed this stone as a token of devotion on the house where were born the innumerable creations of imagination that Giacomo Puccini extracted from his immortal spirit and brought to life with the mastery of his art in order that they would say to the universe—ITALY." (Photograph by the editor.)

sports cars. Nevertheless, he did not claim to measure up to Verdi and said of Wagner, "Beside him we are all mandolin players." Puccini's gifts were lyric in nature and beautifully expressed in his next opera.

Madame Butterfly (1904), written while the composer was in a wheelchair convalescing from an auto accident, was one opera in which Puccini had complete faith, although audiences were slow to react favorably to it. Its pseudo-Oriental matter and manner, its evocations of cherry blossoms and geisha girls, its experimental harmonies, in which a trace of Debussy is apparent, initially baffled listeners. Through the encouragement of Arturo Toscanini (1867-1957), however, a few changes were made and *Madame Butterfly* joined her sisters in popularity.

While supervising rehearsals at the Metropolitan Opera House in New York, Puccini, in his enthusiasm for America, offered to compose an opera on a "Western" theme. He found his libretto in a Broadway play, adapted by David Belasco from a Bret Harte story. The Metropolitan commissioned Puccini to write *La Fanciulla del West* (*The Girl of the Golden West,* 1910), premiered in a gala performance. Despite the efforts of Toscanini, Enrico Caruso, Emmy Destinn and other brilliant artists, it failed to find a permanent place in the repertoire, and is only sporadically revived.

During the years of World War I, Puccini wrote *La Rondine* (*The Swallow,* 1917) and a trilogy of one-act operas, of which *Gianni Schicchi* (1918) is acknowledged a masterpiece of comic opera. After this, the composer started work upon *Turandot,* a fairy tale of a cruel Chinese princess. He succumbed to cancer of the throat before completing the opera, which was finished by Franco Alfano (1876-1954). Although it is exotic and guided by Puccini's unfailing feeling for the theater, *Turandot* is not as rewarding in musical ideas as in musical technique and scenic grandeur.

Puccini's music has been characterized as "theater, pure and simple." In his own way, he uses *Leitmotifs* for character and atmosphere, sketching them in again and again with spontaneity and freshness. His operas have a continuity that only applause interrupts. In short, Puccini attains a close connection between story and music. As long as people have a sense of the dramatic and demand melody and gripping scene, Puccini's operas will live. We again quote *The Art of Music*:

> (His) is the music of modern Italy, the *veristio* school softened with a now luscious, now gallant lyricism, rising now and then to passionate melodic climaxes whose emphasis is due to underlying rather than to an anterior strengthening of the matter. Harmonically, there is no remarkable advance; Wagnerian freedom in key relations and the use of

dissonance has found its way into this idiom, biting major sevenths in passing notes or appoggiaturas, radical juxtapositions of unrelated triads, altered chords, a rather mannered use of consecutive octaves and fifths (often very telling in coloristic effects) and a refreshing chromatic variety are its distinguishing characteristics. To this is to be added a very spontaneous, often sparkling, rhythmic animation akin to the *opéra comique* school and an effective if not highly ingenious orchestration.

Opera in France

The tradition of French Romantic opera continued in the works of Massenet and Charpentier, although neither was totally unaffected by the influences of Wagner and *verismo*. Yet with true Gallic tenacity, their operas are thoroughly French.

Jules Massenet (1842-1912) used the Wagnerian concept of continuous melody and something of *Leitmotif,* although he built more directly on Gounod and Thomas, Meyerbeer and Offenbach. At their best, Massenet's operas contain a lyric originality. The composer was well aware of what would please the public, and, although his orchestration is somewhat thin, it has a decided cleverness and charm. Of his fifteen operas, the most memorable are *Manon* (1884); *Le Jongleur de Notre Dame* (1902), on a story by Anatole France; and *Thaïs* (1894), whose "Meditation" (for violin and orchestra) keeps it alive.

We have already mentioned the *Société nationale de musique* which did so much to give French composers audience exposure. It is noteworthy that the *Société's* endeavors were seriously menaced by Charles Lamoureux (1834-1899), who established a series of concerts in 1881 that, while they included compositions by Lalo, d'Indy and Chabrier, were largely devoted to presentations of Wagnerian music dramas in concert (*i.e.,* non-staged) form. The Lamoureux Concerts "had forced Wagner on Paris, and Paris, as always, had overshot the mark, and could swear by no one but Wagner. French musicians translated Gounod's or Massenet's ideas into Wagner's style; Parisian critics repeated Wagner's theories at random, whether they understood them or not—generally when they did not understand them," comments Rolland.

Into this musical climate came Gustave Charpentier (1860-1956), who succeeded Massenet at the Institute in 1912. In early life Charpentier, who was something of a musical social worker, had been a factory accountant at Tourcoing, where he organized an orchestra. The town later gave him a subsidy to study at the Paris Conservatory. In 1900, *Louise,* his only opera of consequence, was introduced at the *Opéra Comique* and was an immediate success. The opera reflects Charpentier's own life and that of Bohemian Paris. He aptly called it a musical novel.

A realist, Charpentier had unhesitating command of his ideas, musical and sociological. As Hill says, "If Charpentier often betrays himself as a pupil of Massenet by his procedure in thematic development or in the manipulation of orchestral timbres, he nevertheless gives evidence of a positive individuality . . ."

EXTENSIONS OF FRANCKIAN IDEALS

Not far in distance from the Paris *Opéra* but vastly separated in terms of points of view were the students, colleagues and successors of César Franck, several of whom we have already mentioned. A far-reaching product of their endeavors was the founding in 1894 of the Schola Cantorum, by Charles Bordes (1863-1909), Vincent d'Indy and Alexandre Guilmant. The Schola Cantorum, in several ways, provided a Franckian answer to what was considered reaction and favoritism in the Paris Conservatory. The Schola's professed aims were to teach theory on the basis of Gregorian chant, to revive an interest in sacred music based on ancient models, to raise the standards of performance in Paris' churches and to extend César Franck's teachings, which, founded on Bach and Beethoven, admitted imagination and all liberal ideas and drew to Franck, according to d'Indy, "all the sincere and artistic talent that was scattered about the different classes of the *Conservatoire,* as well as that of his outside pupils."

Franck's influence on the Schola was both aesthetic and moral, as it attempted to reflect the master's profound faith, which "shone round him like a glory." In 1900, d'Indy became its president. In addition to instruction, the Schola Cantorum offered concerts of orchestral, choral organ and chamber music, and revived, among others, Monteverdi and Rameau operas. It also published anthologies of fifteenth- to eighteenth-century choral and organ music as well as folksong collections.

In addition to establishing the Schola, Franckian sympathizers were active in perpetuating and stimulating organ virtuosity in France. Organ playing had always been a part of French musical life, beginning with Léonin and Pérotin in twelfth-century Paris, ancestors of a long and brilliant line. Franck, who restored the soul of Sebastian Bach in all its richness and depth, was the teacher of Auguste Chapuis (1858-1933), Paul Vidal (1863-1931) and Georges Marty (1860-1908), and a friend of Alexandre Guilmant.

Guilmant (1837-1911), organist of *La Trinité,* composed organ works that are much played, taught at the Schola and Conservatory and numbered among his pupils Marcel Dupré (1886-   ), Joseph Bonnet (1884-1944) and, in America, William Carl (1865-1936). Charles-Marie Widor (1844-1937) followed César Franck as professor of organ at the

Conservatory (1890) and taught hundreds of organists, including the eminent Albert Schweitzer (1875-1965). Widor was appointed organist of St. Sulpice while he was serving in the Franco-Prussian War, and remained there sixty-two years. His many compositions are considered models for composers for the instrument.

Perhaps most closely associated with Franckian ideals was Vincent d'Indy (1851-1932), who was trained as a pianist and, after serving in the French Army, studied composition and organ with Franck. D'Indy was Colonne's second drummer and directed rehearsals for Lamoureux, afterward conducting the Schola Cantorum concerts.

In character and point of view, d'Indy seems like a reincarnation from the Middle Ages. His interests as a writer and teacher were rooted in the achievements of early centuries, and his *Cours de composition musicale* has been described as a work in which a living science and a Gothic spirit are closely intermingled. He wrote a biography of César Franck and a book on Beethoven, as well as many short articles; he edited Rameau's works and reconstructed Monteverdi's operas. His many compositions include chamber music, orchestral works and operas. "So vast an erudition has seldom been united in the person of a composer," writes Hill.

D'Indy's musical influences were Franckian on the one hand and Wagnerian on the other. He made slavish use of the cyclical idea in sonata form and also wrote in fugue, variation and canonic forms. In his early years, he authored his own librettos, including *Fervaal* (1897), a character called by Hill "a Gallicized compound of Siegfried and Parsifal." Among his orchestral works are a trilogy of symphonic poems after Schiller's *Wallenstein, Op.* 12; and the *Symphonie Cévenole* (*Symphony on a Mountain Air* for orchestra and piano, 1887), based upon folksong.

Ernest Chausson (1855-1899) was yet another gifted Franck pupil, whose life was cut off unfortunately early by a bicycle accident. A man of comfortable means, Chausson acted as secretary of the *Société*. He composed relatively little music, but his works are of fine quality. Among Chausson's compositions are chamber music; some fine songs; a *Hymne védique* (*Vedic Hymn* for chorus and orchestra); two operas; and the popular *Poème* for violin and orchestra (1897). Paul Landormy comments that Chausson's music "is charming, very tender and warm in tone, and most refined and delicate in feeling." Like d'Indy, Chausson reflected both Franck and Wagner. E. B. Hill reminds us that his career "closed just as he was acquiring self-confidence and a mastery over technical problems that justified ardent hopes for the future."

Other Franck colleagues and pupils include: Alexis-Emmanuel Chabrier who, although a Wagner enthusiast, is best known for his exotic *España* (1883); Henri Duparc, whose promising song-writing career was prematurely halted by mental illness; Alexis de Castillon (1838-1873); Guillaume Lekeu (1870-1894); Guy Ropartz (1864-1955), composer of works based on Breton folk tunes and of many organ compositions; and Gabriel Fauré, whose music Aaron Copland characterizes as "almost a kind of neo-romanticism—delicate, reserved and aristocratic."

VIENNESE AND GERMAN DEVELOPMENTS

"Dunkel ist das Leben, ist der Tod" ("Dark Is Life and Dark Is Death") is a refrain from the opening song of Mahler's *Das Lied von der Erde* (*The Song of the Earth,* 1908). In many ways its philosophy may serve as comment on both the composer and his music. Gustav Mahler (1860-1911), the last of the great line of Viennese symphonists, remains to this day a controversial composer, renowned as an opera conductor and tireless in composing monumental orchestral and vocal works, uncompromisingly Romantic in content and individual in form. He enlarged the symphony until it lost its basic balance and, according to *Grove's Dictionary,* "became something which though still structurally sound and self-sufficient yet differed in feeling and idea from the classical model."

Mahler once remarked that he was thrice homeless—"As a Bohemian born in Austria. As an Austrian among Germans. And as a Jew throughout the world." Educated at the Vienna Conservatory, where he studied with Julius Epstein and Robert Fuchs (1847-1927), Mahler was so impressed by meeting Bruckner that he undertook working out some of the older composer's symphonic problems. Except for externals, however, Mahler's solutions are quite his own. After conducting assignments in Prague, Leipzig, Budapest and Hamburg, the composer was engaged by the Vienna Opera, on Brahms' recommendation. In the decade that followed, Vienna became the world's opera center, thanks to Mahler's organizing ability and his efficient and painstaking rehearsals. In 1908 he made his debut at the Metropolitan Opera House, offering fine versions of *Tristan und Isolde, Don Giovanni* and a revival of *Fidelio.* During the next two years he was musical director of the New York Philharmonic Society. When he left America in 1911, this complex personality was broken in health and spirit. He died of pneumonia shortly after his return to Vienna.

Although he never completed an opera of his own, his close association with the form is evident in his song cycles and symphonies, especially in the wayward freedom of structure and the intense emotionalism.

Mahler tended to expand the ideas of his songs in symphonic form; thus, we find references from *Des Knaben Wunderhorn* (*The Youth's Magic Horn,* 1888), *Lieder eines fahrenden Gesellen* (*Songs of a Wayfarer,* 1883-85) and *Kindertotenlieder* (*Songs of Infants' Death,* 1901-4) in several of the symphonies. Mahler pursued Beethoven's use of voices, either solo or chorus, in four of his ten symphonies. The other six, Nos. 1, 5, 6, 7, 9, and 10 (the latter unfinished by the composer, although completed by Ernst Křenek and Deryck Cooke) are entirely instrumental and disclose Wagnerian traits.

Mahler, like Bruckner, has his enthusiastic admirers, who regard him as an unappreciated genius. Other listeners are wearied by the length, breadth and thickness of the works. For instance, the *Symphony No. 8 in E flat* (1907), called the "Symphony of a Thousand," is scored for two large mixed choruses, a boys' chorus, eight soloists and an orchestra of 120, and lasts almost two hours. The musical requirements alone limit the hearings most of his works receive. Yet there are many moments of beauty, of almost naïve folk-like melodies and dances, of brilliant orchestral lyric polyphony and matchless instrumentation. Through all Mahler's compositions, we are aware of a brilliant and profound mind, seeking to bend music to its will in solving the loftiest problems of the universe—those of life and death, faith and love, the wonders of nature. *Das Lied von der Erde,* settings of six poems from Hans Bethe's *Chinese Flute,* for contralto, tenor and orchestra, is Mahler's most accessible large work and has a dignity, self-restraint and condensation absent from many of the others. It is magical in its evocation of both joy and despair. Although Mahler's place in music through the ages has not yet been settled, he was a unique individual whose aspirations toward perfection remain unquestioned.

Often called the "Wagner of the *Lied,*" Hugo Wolf (1860-1903) is, with Strauss, one of the great German art-song composers. He was born in Lower Styria and his life, most of which was spent in Vienna, was one of tragedy, unhappiness and a chronic inability to conform— whether in school, conservatory, as a teacher, conductor or human being. Impatient and high-tempered, Wolf, in spite of several excellent opportunities, became more or less of a vagabond, struggling with poverty and ill health. His mind began to fail early, and, apparently aware of the living death ahead, he worked with incredible speed and energy during his periods of lucidity.

Wolf did not compose seriously until he was twenty-eight and his creative moments covered only four or five years. At fifteen he had heard *Tannhäuser* and *Lohengrin* and met Wagner. These were decisive experiences. "Although he got nothing . . . but a more or less kindly snub, he became from this moment, and remained all his life, an ardent disciple," notes *Grove's Dictionary*. This was so much so, that when he was a music critic, he wrote with unnecessary bitterness against Brahms.

Almost self-educated musically, Wolf often studied scores while sitting on a park bench. He read much poetry and showed exceptional literary taste in choosing song texts. His aim was to reinterpret in music the poet's intention. This voluntary submergence of self to the poetic idea he had gained from Wagner. Wolf used music to intensify the emotional value of the word. His piano accompaniments are works of art in themselves and demand excellent musicianship to perform them effectively.

Wolf claimed to compose under the influence of an external force. He would sit down to a volume of poems and work at white heat, flinging off songs day after day, hardly stopping to eat or sleep until the fit of inspiration had passed, when he would relapse into a siege of despondency and lethargy that lasted until the next furious outburst. His acknowledged musical gods were Gluck, Mozart and Wagner, "which Holy Three become One in Beethoven," he wrote.

Wolf's songs can be grouped according to his choice of poets. There are fifty-three settings of poems by Edouard Mörike, forty-three of which were composed in four months in 1888. He set a group of twenty Eichendorff poems and during six months in 1889 composed fifty-one Goethe songs. There are forty-four songs in the *Spanisches Liederbuch* (*Spanish Songbook,* after Paul Heyse and Geibel, 1890) and forty-six in the two parts of the *Italienisches Liederbuch* (*Italian Songbook,* 1891, 1896, after Heyse), twenty of which Wolf himself orchestrated; others were orchestrated by Reger. In all a total of over 300 songs. In addition, Wolf composed a comic opera, *Der Corregidor* (1896), whose dismissal by Mahler, then at the Vienna Opera, supposedly precipitated a nervous breakdown; an *Italienische Serenade* (for string quartet, 1887, and string orchestra, 1892); *Christnacht* for solo voices, chorus and orchestra (1886-89); and assorted instrumental works.

The neo-Classicism of the nineteenth and twentieth centuries is spanned by Max Reger (1873-1916), a pupil of Hugo Riemann (1849-1919), who trained him along strict lines of absolute music. Reger's *opus* numbers extended to 147 and there are many unnumbered works. His music is interesting chiefly because of its revival of polyphonic technique, colored by Wagnerian chromaticism and Brahmsian propensities, and the rediscovery of Bachian forms, such as prelude and fugue, *chorale-prelude,* etc. His great scholarly knowledge led him to write works of a certain complexity, bristling with difficulties. Toward the end of his short life, he turned toward a lighter texture. He also enriched the organ literature, paralleling the magnificent development which orchestral music had undergone in the nineteenth century. A most pleasant introduction to Reger's music is the *Variationen und Fuge über ein Thema von Mozart, Op. 132.*

RICHARD STRAUSS

Perhaps the greatest post-Romantic German composer was Richard Strauss (1864-1949), "an authentic lord of tone, amazing in the range and richness and expressiveness of his art," as Lawrence Gilman comments. Westerman adds: "His style became the general musical language of his time, and went on to dominate the music of the first twenty years of this century; Mahler's influence was small in comparison, and the effect of Schönberg, for example, made itself felt only much later."

The son of a leading opera hornist, who had played under Wagner's baton, Strauss was given a thorough musical education. James Huneker quotes Strauss as saying:

> My father kept me very strictly to the old masters, in whose compositions I had a thorough grounding. You cannot appreciate Wagner and the moderns unless you pass through this grounding in the classics. Young composers bring me voluminous manuscripts for my opinion on their productions. In looking at them I find that they generally want to begin where Wagner left off. I say to all such, "My good young man, go home and study the works of Bach, the symphonies of Haydn, of Mozart, of Beethoven, and when you have mastered these art works come to me again." Without thoroughly understanding the significance of the development from Haydn, via Mozart and Beethoven to Wagner, these youngsters cannot appreciate at their proper worth either the music of Wagner or of his predecessors. "What an extraordinary thing for Richard Strauss to say," these young men remark, but I only give them the advice gained by my own experience.

This acquaintance with Classic forms and techniques gave Strauss a sure footing, when he chose to wander in those Romantic regions previously explored by Berlioz, Liszt and Wagner. In his treatment of program, he was the epitome of musical realism. In this respect Berlioz is more logically his progenitor than is Liszt. Liszt, however, ceded him the symphonic-poem structure, which Strauss augmented and modified to suit his personal needs and intentions. His orchestral palette was inherited from Wagner, Brahms and Berlioz, as his study of orchestration (1905) attests. Where Liszt suggested a program, the young Richard Strauss carried it to the nth power of realism. Where Wagner proclaimed the doctrine that the symphonic poem as program music was unable to make itself understood without the aid of the stage, "Richard II" upheld the form as a means of expressing practically any narrative. One critic explains:

> Although Strauss fell heir to the romantic heritage as regards orchestral technique, harmonic vocabulary, and idiom generally, he applied them to wholly different ends. His avowed object of bringing music into direct relation with daily life, and of developing its descriptive scope to such a pitch that it would be possible to depict a teaspoon in music, is at the opposite pole from the aim of the romantic composers, who sought to depict vague intangible moods and ideas rather than concrete realities, and are more attracted to the exotic, the strange, and the remote than to the commonplace actualities of everyday existence.

Strauss began composing at the age of six and continued through his school and university years. In fact, some of his loveliest *Lieder*, such as *Zueignung* ("Dedication," 1882) and *Allerseelen* ("All Souls," 1883), were written before he was twenty. These are of sufficient quality to place Strauss in the company of Schubert, Schumann, Brahms and Wolf. All of his twenty-six albums of songs, beginning with *Op.* 10 and ending with *Op.* 56, were composed before 1907, with the exception of *Op.* 77, *Gesänge des Orients* (*Songs of the Orient,* 1929).

After leaving the University of Munich in 1884, Strauss met Hans von Bülow, who played his *Serenade for Thirteen Wind Instruments, Op.* 7 (1881), on tour and who invited the young man to conduct one of his own compositions at Meiningen. (Strauss had already enjoyed a U.S. premiere, when Theodore Thomas presented his *Symphony in F Minor, Op.* 12, with the New York Philharmonic, 1884.) He became von Bülow's assistant and succeeded him as conductor of the Meiningen orchestra in 1885. This started Strauss on a career in which he was eminent, with positions in Munich, Berlin and Vienna, and frequent appearances as visiting conductor.

Due to meeting Alexander Ritter, poet, composer and husband of Wagner's niece, Strauss turned his back to absolute music. Ritter may have seen in Strauss a possible knight of the "Music of the Future." Wagner was dead and Liszt close to the end. Strauss said of Ritter: "He urged me on to the development of the poetic, the expressive in music, as exemplified in the works of Liszt, Wagner and Berlioz. My symphonic fantasia, *Aus Italien,* is the connecting link between the old and new methods."

Aus Italien (1887) a programmatic symphony in four movements resulting from the composer's first trip to Italy, marked the beginning of a remarkable procession of tone-poems, including: *Macbeth, Op.* 23 (1886-87); *Don Juan, Op.* 20 (1888); *Tod und Verklärung* (*Death and Transfiguration, Op.* 24, 1890); *Till Eulenspiegels lustige Streiche*

(*Till Eulenspiegel's Merry Pranks, Op.* 28, 1895); *Als*
thustra (*Thus Spake Zarathustra, Op.* 30, 1896); *Don*
(1897); *Ein Heldenleben* (*A Hero's Life, Op.* 40, 189ⁱ
Domestica, Op. 53 (1903). In 1915 Strauss completeⁱ
fonie, Op. 64, his largest orchestral work.

Lack of space precludes anything but the most cursory comments
upon these popular compositions, which took the musical world by
storm. In them, Strauss reveals his preoccupation with long and vivid
melodies, his brilliant orchestral scoring, his brash egoism and his concern for program, in which the basic poetic idea dictates the structure.
In *Don Juan,* after Lenau's poem, two virile themes represent the hero,
while three subordinate tunes symbolize the feminine elements, put together as a free rondo. *Death and Transfiguration* uses Liszt's *Tasso* as a
model. Its two sections describe the struggles of living and the joy of
release or transfiguration. It is significant that the rather emotional program was written by Ritter *after* the music was composed. *Till Eulen-*
spiegel, "Set in the Old-Time Roguish Manner in Rondo Form," portrays the antics of a fourteenth-century German folk hero. From the
opening phrase, it plainly says in music, "Once upon a time . . ."

Of *Zarathustra,* a ponderous score built from the book by Friedrich
Nietzsche, Strauss declared: "I did not intend to write philosophical music or portray Nietzsche's great work musically. I meant to convey
musically an idea of the development of the human race from its origin
through the various phases of evolution, religious as well as scientific,
up to Nietzsche's idea of the Superman." Titles from Nietzsche are employed as suggestive subheads for the very free and extended variations.
Don Quixote, an "Introduction, Theme with Variations, and Finale
. . . on a Theme of Knightly Character," is a musical illustration of
Cervantes' famous personality, as heard in the solo 'cello, with Sancho
Panza represented by a solo viola.

Strauss himself is the hero of *A Hero's Life.* He had said: "There is
no need of a program. It is enough to know there is a hero fighting his
enemies." He betrays himself, however, by quoting bits of *Don Juan,*
Death and Transfiguration and *Zarathustra,* in the section entitled "The
Hero's Achievement." In the *Sinfonia Domestica,* which was first performed in New York City, Henry T. Finck says, "Strauss gave to the
world another tone poem which again caused the critics of two continents to spill gallons of ink." The listener is admitted into the most intimate happenings of a day in the composer's life, with the *dramatis per-*
sonae featuring Papa, Mama and Baby. After a twelve-year lapse, Strauss
returned to nature for *An Alpine Symphony.* Here he boldly wrote his
program into the score, describing his mountain climbing experiences.

ınd machine and a device to increase the lung power of the wind ayers—an aerophone—are included in the orchestration.

During these productive years of composing tone-poems and conducting, Strauss began writing operas, the best to emanate from Germany since Wagner's. Strauss' dramas hold the stage because of their subject matter, their lack of triteness, their good theatrical sense and their sensuous melodic power. His first, *Guntram* (1894), was completely Wagnerian in cast, medieval in setting and less than a great success. With *Feuersnot* (*Need for Fire,* 1901), Strauss produced a joyous, folk-spirited work that attracted little attention. In *Salome* (1905), however, the composer became a stark realist, building on a lurid libretto taken from Oscar Wilde's play. Dissonance and original musical ideas flash through this almost brutal opera. It has a score of superb musicianship and rare beauty, with melodic lines and rhythms focused upon the raw and often repelling incidents. Baker comments, "In this score he went

Fig. 76. Lisa della Casa as Salome in the "Dance of the Seven Veils" from *Salome.* Strauss' dramas hold the stage because of their subject matter, their lack of triteness, their good theatrical sense and their sensuous melodic power. (Courtesy Bavarian State Opera, Munich, photograph by Rudolf Betz.)

far beyond the limits of Wagnerian music drama, and created a psychological tragedy of shattering impact; the erotic subject was illustrated by sensuous music." The "Dance of the Seven Veils" is a popular and unexcelled concert excerpt.

With *Elektra* (1908), Strauss began his happy collaboration with librettist, Hugo von Hofmannsthal. This opera also revolves about a dour theme, matricide. It is a rich work, perhaps overly rich in harmonic texture, painting in dark colors a dark story, and wavering toward being a powerful tone-poem with vocal *obbligato*.

As if to demonstrate his versatility, Strauss next composed the charming *Der Rosenkavalier* (1911), a masterful comedy laid in the Vienna of Marie Theresa. *Der Rosenkavalier* is Mozartean in its simple exuberance, Wagnerian in scope and Straussian in the matter of melody. With continuously effulgent orchestration, the music centers on the Viennese waltz, embroidered with daring and entirely individual harmonies.

Other operas by Strauss include *Die Frau ohne Schatten* (*The Childless Woman,* 1919), which one critic has compared to Wagner's *Ring*; *Intermezzo* (1924); *Arabella* (1933), the last with von Hofmannsthal; *Die schweigsame Frau* (1935), with a libretto by Stephan Zweig, based on Ben Jonson's *The Silent Woman;* and *Die Liebe der Danae,* performed posthumously at the Salzburg Festival in 1952. Of all the later operas, perhaps the most interesting is *Ariadne auf Naxos* (1912), a *tour de force,* in which Strauss actually offers two operas at once—a morsel of Italy's old *commedia dell'arte* and a quasi-Greek piece in the classic order. Taken from Molière's *Le Bourgeois Gentilhomme, Ariadne* is a relatively short work, in which "Mozart dances a minuet with Mascagni and Handel with Offenbach," to quote Cecil Gray.

Although it has often been said that his creative career as an instrumental composer ended in 1899 and as an opera composer in 1911, Strauss had indeed become the leading musical figure in Germany during the early decades of the twentieth century. Devotees made pilgrimages to his villa at Garmisch and his honorary home in the park of the Belvedere Palace at Vienna. When the Nazis came to power, Strauss loyally accepted Hitler and became President of the Third Reich Music Chamber. Unfortunately, he did nothing to keep Bruno Walter at Leipzig, and, when Toscanini refused to conduct at Bayreuth, Strauss filled in for him. The honeymoon was of short duration, however, and Strauss resigned his official position in 1935 and went into seclusion. After World War II, he was exonerated by an American military court. A partial explanation of his National Socialist sympathies may lie in the fact that Strauss the musician was far superior to Strauss the man. Henpecked by a wife who kept him on a strict allowance and ran most details of his life,

Strauss was vain, jealous of rivals and parsimonious to the degree that he victimized his orchestral players when winning at cards, at which he was adept.

His music, nevertheless, remains glorious in its honeyed phrases and almost raucous melodies fitted, one to the other, with telling significance. Not the least of his virtues is orchestral virtuosity. Richard Strauss asked for more instruments in an orchestra than any composer except Berlioz. In addition, less familiar members of different families were added. For instance, Strauss scored the *Sinfonia Domestica* for piccolo, three flutes, two oboes and *oboe d'amore,* English horn, one clarinet in D, one in A, two in B flat, a bass clarinet, four saxophones (*"ad libitum* only in extreme necessity"), four bassoons, three trombones, a bass tuba, four tympani, a triangle, a tambourine, a *glockenspiel,* cymbals, bass drum, two harps, sixteen first, sixteen second violins, twelve violas, ten 'cellos and eight double basses. William Wallace makes the wry comment, "One missed two instruments in the orchestra which would have added color to this charming picture of homeliness, namely a sewing-machine, and a vacuum cleaner in B flat *alt."*

ENGLISH COMPOSERS

Most of us have at least a nodding acquaintance with the British scholars, critics and lesser composers who contributed to music and literature about music through the turn of the century: Charles H. H. Parry (1848-1918), director of the Royal College of Music, composed prolifically for church, stage and orchestra, and was the author of numerous articles; Charles Villiers Stanford (1852-1924), of Irish birth, studied with Reinecke in Leipzig and was a professor at Cambridge University; John Stainer (1840-1901) was professor at Oxford and composed the popular cantata, *The Crucifixion* (1887); Edward German (1862-1936) is best known for his rollicking incidental music to *Henry VIII* (1890); and Samuel Coleridge-Taylor (1875-1912), an English Negro, rapidly became a favorite composer, frequently using African or American Indian themes, such as in his trilogy, fashioned from Longfellow, *Hiawatha* (1898-1900).

Most popular among the English of his generation was Edward Elgar (1857-1934), who, perhaps because he had little formal training, developed comparatively late, as he did not write in large forms until after 1889. From then through 1904 he composed the works upon which his reputation is based. These include an oratorio, *The Dream of Gerontius, Op.* 38 (1900); *Variations on an Original Theme, Op.* 36 (the "Enigma" Variations, 1899), in which each of the fourteen variations is designated by initials associated with Elgar's friends but never revealed, causing a flurry of speculation that still exists; and the familiar *Pomp and Circumstance* military marches, *Op.* 39 (1901-7, 1930), of which the first has become a workhorse for graduations and other formal events. Elgar had remarkable skill in instrumental and choral writing, although his procedures, characterized as "functional romanticism," were essentially conservative. His music is highly thought of by his countrymen, and his *'Cello Concerto in E Minor, Op.* 85, first performed in 1919, is increasingly appreciated.

ENGLISH NATIONALISTS

Musical nationalism continued to exert a strong influence upon the production of many post-Romantic composers, among whom were Gustav Holst (1874-1934) and Ralph Vaughan Williams (1872-1958) in England; Jan Sibelius (1865-1957) in Finland; Leoš Janáček (1854-1928) in Czechoslovakia; and Sergei Rachmaninov (1873-1943), born in Russia. Each of these composers in their music extended the Romantic tradition, while lending it a special nationalistic coloring.

Significant among Englishmen and largely responsible for that country's musical renaissance in the twentieth century were Gustav Holst and Vaughan Williams. Holst, the issue of a musical family, studied with Stanford in London and thereafter became associated with St. Paul's Girls' School and Morley College, positions he retained until his death. He was an enthusiastic propagandist for Tudor music and that of Henry Purcell. In his own works, he reflects equal interest in English folklore and exotic subject matter. His compositions include: *The Mystic Trumpeter* for soprano and orchestra, *Op.* 18 (1904); two suites for military band, *Op.* 28 (1909-1911); *St. Paul's Suite* for string orchestra (1913), an evocation of eighteenth-century style; *The Planets, Op.* 32 (1916), a large orchestral suite that is his best known work; *Hymn of Jesus, Op.* 37 (1917), for two choruses, orchestra, piano and organ; and operas, such as *At the Boar's Head, Op.* 42 (1925).

In 1898 the Folk-Song Society of England was organized, reviving old tunes and dances and enriching English life and composition. In 1904 Ralph Vaughan Williams joined the Society and participated in its activities. His early works are impregnated with English folksong. Gradually his interests widened to include Elizabethan music and more advanced harmonic and polyphonic techniques. Of his music, Peter Warlock, also known as "Philip Heseltine" (1894-1930), writes that it is "characterized by a strong melodic invention (often traceable to folksong music), and a most original fund of contrapuntal resource in which there is nothing even faintly reminiscent of scholasticism." There is a quality of rhapsody about much of Vaughan Williams' music that is comparable to that of one of his favorite poets, Walt Whitman, whose verses inspired Williams' *Symphony No. 1, "A Sea Symphony"* (1910), which had been preceded by a cantata based on Whitman, *Towards the Unknown Region* (1905).

A random sampling of Vaughan Williams' compositions reveal his exploring mind, trained by Parry and Stanford at the Royal College and by Max Bruch (1838-1920) in Berlin. We find, in addition to many folksong arrangements, a ballad opera, *Hugh the Drover* (1911-14); a song cycle for tenor, string quartet and piano, *On Wenlock Edge* (1909); the beautiful *Fantasia on a Theme by Tallis* for strings (1910); a *Mass in G Minor* (1923); *The Pilgrim's Progress,* a "morality" (1929); *Job* (1931), "a masque for dancing" inspired by William Blake; a *Concerto for Bass Tuba and Orchestra* (1954); and nine distinctive symphonies extending from 1910 to 1958. With his *Folk Song Suite* for military band and *Fantasia* on "Greensleeves," Vaughan Williams has had the honor of appearing on American jukeboxes.

JAN SIBELIUS

In many ways, the ideas of Vaughan Williams and his Scandinavian contemporary, Jan Sibelius, were similar. (Williams dedicated his *Symphony No. 5 in D* (1943) to the Finnish composer.) Trained for the law but gifted as a violinist, Sibelius turned to music as a vocation. At the Helsingfors Conservatory, his teacher was Martin Wegelius (1846-1906), leader of the national movement, who stood between Fredrik Pacius (1809-1891), founder of the Finnish school, and Robert Kajanus (1856-1933), the first interpreter of Finnish folklore in instrumental music. Subsequently, Sibelius studied in Berlin and Vienna with Carl Goldmark and Robert Fuchs, among others.

Sibelius has been likened to the three heroes of the Finnish national epic, the *Kalevala*—Wainamoinen, the great harper; Ilmarinen, a cunning artificer and smith; and Lemminkainen, a Northern Don Juan. Cecil Gray writes:

> In the symphonies it is the great harper, the inspired singer of his race who speaks; in many works such as the *Nightride and Sunrise,* we find only the skillful and accomplished craftsman following timidly and without originality of outlook in the footsteps of Wagner, Tchaikovsky, Grieg and even Brahms; finally there is the composer of the *Valse Triste,* the *Romance in D flat,* and many similar works of popular and frequently even vulgar character. Probably no composer of such high distinction has ever written such a large quantity of thoroughly bad works . . .

At his best, however, Sibelius incorporates a rugged atavism, that is unconscious and instinctive. This primitiveness constitutes a subtlety of utterance which connotes breadth, vigor and sincerity. Because many of us are not familiar with Finnish attributes, we have thought Sibelius' music to be severe, bare, dour, bleak and so on, whereas, to quote Hiram Moderwell, Sibelius "is at once the most national and most personal composer in the whole history of Scandinavian music."

The *Symphony No. 4 in A Minor, Op.* 63 (1911) brought Sibelius to serious critical appreciation outside his native land, where previously he had been represented by slighter, if more popular, works. In this symphony, Sibelius turns to nature for inspiration. He stated, "It stands out as a protest against the compositions of today. Nothing, *absolutely nothing,* of the circus about it." To whom could he be referring? Here was music of deep meaning—dramatic, thoughtful and animated. Its brilliance resembles jet rather than diamond. An extremely individual work, it exhibits Sibelius' method of dealing with symphonic form. As Julian Herbage remarks, it has the "asymmetrical growth of nature," yet clings to inner logic in its architecture.

Among Sibelius' works are many of nationalistic expression, including *En Saga, Op.* 9 (1892); the *Four Legends from the Kalevala, Op.* 22, including *The Swan of Tuonela* (1893); and *Finlandia, Op.* 26 (1900), so stirring that the Czarist oppressors prohibited its performance. Sibelius composed much incidental music: for example, the castigated *Valse Triste, Op.* 44 (1903) was conceived for a Järnefelt play; the "Dance of Death" for Adolph Paul's play, *King Christian II.* Sibelius' symphonic suites include *Karelia, Op.* 11 (1893). He composed almost 100 songs, covering a wide range of subjects, often with Swedish lyrics. It is upon his seven symphonies and single violin concerto, however, that Sibelius' future rests. The *Concerto in D Minor for Violin, Op.* 47 (1903), written when the composer was thirty-eight, is akin in freedom and originality to his symphonies, being a closely-knit work in a unique form, which, while not ostensibly virtuosic, is difficult to perform. The seven symphonies span the years from *Op.* 39 (1898-99) to *Op.* 105 (1924). The first two are wonderfully Romantic, the third (which followed the *Violin Concerto*) prepares the way for the strength of the fourth. The fifth is less introspective than its predecessor, the sixth is pastoral in mood, and the seventh is a coherent, one-movement work, removed from the influences of Grieg, Liszt and Tchaikovsky, that we notice in his earlier work.

To the Finns Sibelius is more than a composer; he is a national hero. Arriving as he did at a time when Finland was under the Russian heel, and infusing his early works with elements of his native heritage, Sibelius became a symbol in the struggle for freedom. In 1897 a grateful government granted him an annual pension so that he might compose without financial worries. After 1904, he lived with his family outside Helsingfors in the "Villa Ainola," more and more withdrawing from the chaotic world around him but never relinquishing his fierce pride of country, nor, incidentally, his love of fine cognacs and cigars.

CZECH COMPOSERS

The further development of a school of composers in Czechoslovakia is illuminating. Smetana had uncovered a Bohemian idiom that was continued by Dvořák; Zdenko Fibich (1850-1900), who applied Wagnerian methods to Bohemian subjects and who is known to us for his short *Poème, Op.* 41, No. 6 for piano; and Josef Suk (1874-1935), a follower and son-in-law of Dvořák, whose music is thoroughly Romantic in character.

Fig. 77. "Hommage à Janáček"—Karel Svolinsky. A contemporary Czech artist expresses the color and rhythms projected in Janáček's music.

In Leoš Janáček (1854-1928) a more modern vein appears, especially in his later works which are indebted to French Impressionism. Janáček studied at the Prague and Leipzig Conservatories, but spent most of his life in the Moravian capitol of Brunn (or Brno), where he taught, conducted an orchestra, made researches into Bohemian folk music and composed, all in relative obscurity. There is a similarity between Moussorgsky's and Janáček's musical prosody, but although the Czech was an ardent student of Russian music and literature, he did not succumb to imitation.

Among his works are the operas *Jenufa* (*Her Foster Daughter*, 1903), an immediate success; *Kata Kabanová*, after Ostrovsky's play (1921); *The Cunning Little Vixen* (1924), a symbolic tale in which some of the characters are animals; *The Makropulos Affair* (1925), in which a singer born in 1576 is placed in a modern setting of hotels and telephones; and *Memoirs from a House of the Dead* (1928), based on Dostoievsky's story of Siberian prison life. Janáček also wrote a comic opera with the provocative and timely title, *Mr. Broucek's Excursion to the Moon*, 1920. Other compositions include the piano trio, subtitled "From Tolstoi's Kreutzer Sonata" (1908); a song cycle, *The Diary of One Who Vanished* (1916); a rhapsody after Gogol, *Taras Bulba* (1918); the *Glagolitic* or *Festival Mass* (1927); and many attractive piano pieces. Fame came late to Janáček, but he was an inspiration and model to younger men.

RUSSIAN COMPOSERS

The spirits of Tchaikovsky and Rimsky-Korsakov prevailed in Russia during the post-Romantic period. Alexander Gretchaninov (1864-1956) composed in a variety of forms; Alexander Glazunov (1865-1936), a pupil of Rimsky-Korsakov, wrote most of his music, including eight symphonies, before 1906; Vladimir Rebikov (1866-1920) graduated from Tchaikovsky's shadow to the *avant-garde,* experimenting with new tonalities, old modes and free forms; Nikolai Medtner (1880-1951), less of a nationalist than his compatriots, is known for his delicate sets of fairy tales in sonata form for piano; Nikolai Tcherepnin (1873-1945), another pupil of Rimsky-Korsakov, composed in the nationalistic tradition.

Of all late Romantic Russian music, perhaps the most popular is that of Sergei Rachmaninov, who successfully combined the careers of concert pianist, conductor and composer. As a youth, Rachmaninov had met Tchaikovsky, who gave him friendly advice and encouraged his talent. At the age of nineteen Rachmaninov composed his very popular *Prelude in C♯ Minor, Op. 3, No. 2.* Unaffected by radical musical doctrines, the composer remained true to his premise of working simply and directly. "I intend," he stated, "to 'sing' a melody on the piano as singers do, and to find a suitable accompaniment which would not drown out the theme." Among his famous creations are the *Concerto No. 2 in C Minor, Op.* 18 for piano and orchestra (1901), reputedly written with the aid of a psychoanalyst (Rachmaninov was recovering from a nervous breakdown at the time); *The Isle of the Dead, Op.* 29 (1907), a tone-poem inspired by Arnold Böcklin's painting; a choral symphony, *The Bells, Op.* 35 (1913), on a text by Edgar Allan Poe; and *Rhapsody on a Theme of Paganini, Op.* 43 (1934). An "individual" composer like Rachmaninov provides a link between the earlier Russian Romanticists and the more "original" composers, such as Prokofiev. In its melancholy mood Rachmaninov's music is analogous to Chekhov's plays. Whether or not it will be able to survive its popularity is another matter.

*   *   *   *   *

Throughout this chapter we have seen that various components of Romanticism continued to persist in the music of composers whose later years were spent in the twentieth century, yet whose orientation was basically that of the nineteenth. Later we shall take the opportunity of discussing the music of the same and later generations who rejected nine-teenth-century Romanticism as decadent and sought out other means of musical projection, with results that still confront and influence us today. Before moving into the fresh air of the twentieth century, however, we shall pause to recount what had happened and what was happening to American music up to this time.

SUGGESTIONS FOR FURTHER READING

Abraham, Gerald, *The Music of Sibelius.* New York, Norton, 1947.

Carner, Mosco, *Puccini.* New York, Knopf, 1959.

Demuth, Norman, *Vincent d'Indy.* London, Rockliff, 1951.

Fiorentino, Dante del, *Puccini, Immortal Bohemian.* New York, Prentice-Hall, 1952.

Foss, Hubert, *Ralph Vaughan Williams.* London, Harrap, 1950.

Gray, Cecil, *Sibelius.* London, Oxford University Press, 1945.

Hans von Bülow-Richard Strauss Correspondence. London, Hawkes, 1955.

Holst, Imogen, *Gustav Holst.* London, Oxford University Press, 1938.

Johnson, Harold E., *Jean Sibelius.* New York, Knopf, 1959.

Mahler, Alma, *Gustav Mahler: Memories and Letters.* New York, Viking, 1946.

Marek, George R., *Puccini: A Biography.* New York, Simon & Schuster, 1951.

————, *Richard Strauss: The Life of a Non-Hero.* New York, Simon & Schuster, 1967.

Massenet, Jules, *My Recollections.* Boston, Small-Maynard, 1919.

Mellers, Wilfred H., *Romanticism and the Twentieth Century.* London, Rockliff, 1957.

Newlin, Dika, *Bruckner, Mahler and Schönberg.* New York, Columbia University Press, 1947.

Newmarch, Rosa, *The Music of Czechoslovakia.* London, Oxford University Press, 1943.

Redlich, Hans F., *Bruckner and Mahler.* New York, Farrar-Straus-Cudahy, 1963.

Reed, W. H., *Elgar.* New York, Pellegrini & Cudahy, 1949.

Salazar, Adolfo, *Music in Our Time.* New York, Norton, 1946.

Seroff, Victor, *Rachmaninoff.* New York, Simon & Schuster, 1950.

Starr, William J., and Devine, George F., *Music Scores—Omnibus,** Part 2. Englewood Cliffs, Prentice-Hall, 1964.

Strauss, Richard, *Recollections and Reflections.* London, Boosey & Hawkes, 1953.

Vaughn Williams, Ralph, *The Making of Music.* Ithaca, Cornell University Press, 1955.

Walker, Frank, *Hugo Wolf.* New York, Knopf, 1952.

Walter, Bruno, *Gustav Mahler.* New York, Greystone, 1941.

A Sampler of Supplementary Recordings

Collections

2000 Years of Music	Folkways 3700
Ten Centuries of Music	DGG KL-52/61
Romanticism	Victor LM-6153
French Organ Music	Columbia ML-5707

Music of Individual Composers

Chausson, Ernest, *Poème for Violin and Orchestra, Op.* 25
Charpentier, Gustave, *Louise*
Coleridge-Taylor, Samuel, *Song of Hiawatha, Op.* 30
D'Indy, Vincent, *Symphony on a French Mountain Air, Op.* 25
Elgar, Edward, *Enigma Variations, Op.* 36
German, Edward, *Henry VIII: Dances*
Giordano, Umberto, *Andrea Chénier*
Glazounov, Alexander, *Concerto in A for Violin, Op.* 82
Holst, Gustav, *The Planets, Op.* 32
Janáček, Leoš, *Taras Bulba* (1918)
Leoncavallo, Ruggiero, *Pagliacci*
Mahler, Gustav, *Das Lied von der Erde*
        Symphony No. 2 in C, "Resurrection"
Mascagni, Pietro, *Cavalleria Rusticana*
Puccini, Giacomo, *Arias*
        La Bohème
        Gianni Schicchi
        Turandot
Rachmaninov, Sergei, *Isle of the Dead, Op.* 29
        Piano Music
Reger, Max, *Organ Works*
Sibelius, Jan, *Symphony No. 1 in E, Op.* 39
Stainer, John, *Crucifixion*
Strauss, Richard, *Don Juan*
        Der Rosenkavalier

* Available in paperback edition.

Songs
Serenade in E flat for 13 Winds, Op. 7
Widor, Charles Marie, *Symphony No. 5 in F for Organ, Op.* 42, No. 1
Wolf, Hugo, *Songs*
Wolf-Ferrari, Ermanno, *Music*

OPPORTUNITIES FOR STUDY IN DEPTH

1. Both Massenet and Puccini wrote operas based on a novel of Abbé Prevost, *Manon* and *Manon Lescaut.* Compare the two operas, noting similarities and differences in musical style and in the librettos. Are there French elements in Massenet that are counterbalanced by Italian features in Puccini? Comment.

2. We have mentioned the idea of *verismo* without going into elaborate detail about its definition and significance. Make a thorough study of Mascagni's *Cavalleria Rusticana,* noting what differentiates it from Verdi's *Otello,* produced one year earlier. Is *verismo* a factor in modern opera? How?

3. Compare selected *Lieder* of Hugo Wolf with songs by Gabriel Fauré. What are the differences between the French and German approaches to art song? What are the excellences of each?

4. In *National Music* (London, 1934) Ralph Vaughan Williams wrote: "If the roots of your art are firmly planted in your own soil and that soil has anything individual to give you, you may still gain the whole world and not lose your own soul." How did the composer carry out his conviction? With what results?

5. Many of Sibelius' works are based upon subject matter drawn from the *Kalevala.* Read a translation of this saga and write a paper concerning Sibelius' choice of material and its meaning to his fellow Finns.

6. Richard Strauss makes use of certain characteristic harmonic patterns in many of his compositions. They are immensely effective, yet tend to become mannerisms associated with him alone. Analyze a waltz from *Der Rosenkavalier* and compare any patterns discerned with portions of his other works. Compile a digest of findings.

7. Poland contributed a musician to the world who, in addition to being a concert pianist and composer, became premier of his country. He was Ignace Paderewski (1860-1941). Prepare an oral report on this fascinating personality for class presentation.

8. Explore in detail the functions and achievements of the Schola Cantorum in Paris as a rival of the Conservatory during the years before and after the turn of the century.

VOCABULARY ENRICHMENT

post-Romanticism	Viennese waltz
verismo	wind machine
Lamoureux Concerts	Tudor music
Schola Cantorum	*Kalevala*
cyclical symphony	concert form

PART IX

Music of the United States

Chapter 24.

THE BEGINNINGS OF AMERICAN MUSIC

I must study politics and war that my sons may have the liberty to study mathematics and philosophy . . . in order to give their children a right to study painting, poetry and music.

—John Adams (1735-1826)

While fully aware of the stern realities to be dealt with before sufficient leisure and prosperity would encourage the arts in the United States, John Adams did not mean that three generations would pass before music-making itself became part of the American scene, for the settlers brought their musical heritage with them to the New World. By the advent of the nineteenth century, although some were still slaughtering Indians and continuing to conquer the vagaries of our large and varied land, those in the Eastern and Southern coastal cities, thanks to their remoteness from the frontier, had established a community of musical interest with their peers in Europe, as we shall see.

Adams was conservative, however, in his estimate of our musical creativity. Although music, either in the art or folk form, flourished, it was largely bound to the patterns of European thought. Its emancipation has been a long and difficult one. Throughout the nineteenth century, we were prepared and eager to dip into the Romantic stream and ready to pay handsomely for the privilege. But not until the turn of the century did most composers make an effort to write music competitive in quality and quantity with that of the Old World but individual in its content. Whether or not we are yet entirely free of European domination is a moot point, but an examination of our musical beginnings may provide us with a background against which to evaluate the current situation.

To this day no one has defined just how old a set of conditions must be to constitute a tradition. We in the United States have not only stimulating antecedents but a country so full of variations in climate, topography and population that we presumably have all that is needed to create an American music. Still the search for a definition persists, because of our comparative youth and our polynational origin. We have been painfully aware of our status as a cultural conglomerate, a phenomenon that never bothered England, whose people are almost as diverse in origin. When, for example, a musician is spoken of as English, it makes little difference that his name is (von) Holst, Delius, Williams or Beauchamp (Beecham). With us, however, we hesitate, with some reason, to claim Rachmaninov, Stravinsky or Schönberg as American composers, although each spent many years of his productive life here and each was a naturalized American citizen.

Who then is an American composer? "Try this definition," answers John Tasker Howard. "A composer is an American, if by birth, or choice of permanent residence, he becomes identified with American life and institutions before his talents have had their greatest outlet; and through his associations and sympathies he makes a genuine contribution to our cultural development."

What has the United States contributed to music through the ages? In this and the following chapters we shall try to provide some indications. Fortunately, we no longer must be either defensive or chauvinistic, as was formerly the case.

COLONIAL PERIOD

Excluding that of the Indians and the Spanish, American music dates from 1620, when Plymouth Rock became the cornerstone of our land. This preliminary or Colonial period continued until about 1800, when we were established as an independent country. Naturally, most of our music was imported as were many other commodities. One factor, however, tended to preselect and prescribe our musical fare. That was the Puritan attitude that any form of music other than the ascetically religious was improper. The first song book printed in America was the *Bay Psalm Book* (1640), whose complete title gives us a clue—*The Psalms in Meter: Faithfully translated for the Use, Edification, and Comfort of the Saints in publick and private, especially in New England.* At first "spiritual songs" other than psalms were not sanctioned, but somewhat later fifty English hymn tunes were published and went into many editions, some even finding their way back to England and Scotland. Instrumental music was taboo. One colony went so far as to pass a law in 1675 allowing only a drum, trumpet and Jew's harp to be played. An organ arrived from England in 1713, but remained unpacked for seven months, lest it should profane the church services. Music as a vocation was forbidden in New England and it is recorded that a dancing master was fined for attempting to pursue his profession. Only gradually did the musical atmosphere become more liberal. Oscar G. Sonneck, an authority on the history of American music, comments:

> The Puritans, the Pilgrims, the Irish, the Dutch, the Germans, the Swedes, the Cavaliers of Maryland and Virginia and the Huguenots of

the South may have been zealots, adventurers, beggars, spendthrifts, fugitives from justice, convicts, but barbarians they certainly were not . . . Possibly, or even probably, music was at an extremely low ebb, but this would neither prove that the early settlers were hopelessly un-musical nor that they lacked interest in the art of "sweet conchord" . . . What inducements had a handful of people, spread over so vast an area, struggling for an existence, surrounded by virgin-forests, fighting the Red-man, and quarreling amongst themselves, to offer to musicians? We may rest assured that even Geoffrey Stafford, "lute and fiddle maker" by trade and ruffian by instinct, would have preferred more lucrative climes and gracefully declined the patronage of musical Governor Fletcher had he not been deported in 1691 to Massachusetts by order of his Majesty King William, along with other Anglo-Saxon convicts.

There were no musicians by trade . . . and as the early settlers were not unlike other human beings in having voices, we may take it for granted that they used them not only in church, but at home, in the fields, in the taverns, exactly as they would have done in Europe and for the same kind of music as far as their memory or their supply of books carried them. That the latter, generally speaking, cannot have been very large, goes without saying . . . Instruments were to be found in the homes of the wealthy merchants of the North and in the homes of the still more pleasure-seeking planters of the South. Indeed, there can be little doubt that the nearest approach to a musical atmosphere . . . was to be found in the South rather than in the North. Still, we might call the period until about 1720 the primitive period in our mu-sical history.

After 1720 we notice a steadily growing number of musicians who sought their fortunes in the Colonies, an increasing desire for organs, flutes, guitars, violins, harpsichords, the establishment of "singing-schools," an improvement in church music, the signs of a budding music trade from ruled music paper to sonatas and concertos, the advent of music engravers, publishers and manufacturers of instruments, the ten-tative efforts to give English opera a home in America, the introduction of public concerts, in short, the beginnings of what may properly be termed the formative period in our musical history, running from 1720 until about 1800.

Between 1712 and 1744 there were many editions of a book on *The Art of Singing* by John Tufts (1689-1750), a minister in Newburyport. It was our first instruction book and contained thirty-seven tunes very much like those in John Playford's *Whole Book of Psalms* (1677). Then came books by Thomas Walter of Roxbury, Massachusetts; a version of *A Complete Melody in Three Parts* by William Tans'ur (1706-1783), an Englishman of German extraction; and *A Collection of the Best Psalm*

Tunes, written in 1764 by Josiah Flagg (1737-*c*.1795), and engraved by Paul Revere.

To Boston goes the honor of having the first public concert. In 1731 Peter Pelham, a dancing master, engraver and tobacconist, as well as master of other odd trades and a music lover, produced a concert in his own home, just four months before a concert of secular music was given in Charleston, South Carolina. Protestations were rife about both concerts and theaters, although in 1750 Otway's *Orphan* was presented in a Boston coffeehouse, and led to the prohibition of public perform-ances, as, a contemporary account alleges, "tending to discourage in-dustry and frugality, and greatly increase impiety."

Although there are few early records of musical events among the Pennsylvania Germans, the New Amsterdam Dutch, the Swedes and the Moravians, the paucity does not indicate that these groups lagged behind but rather we can be reasonably sure that they were far ahead of the New England contingent. It is reported, for example, that Johann Kel-pius installed an organ in 1694 in his church near Philadelphia. *The Beggar's Opera* was performed in New York (1750) and in Philadel-phia (1759). *Flora or Hob in the Wall,* another ballad-opera, had been produced in Charleston in 1735. A troupe was performing excerpts from *vaudeville* and an occasional Grétry and Boïeldieu opera in 1791 in New Orleans. George Washington himself attended a puppet opera in 1787. And performances of Handel's *Messiah* and Haydn's *Creation* were presented during the late eighteenth and early nineteenth centu-ries. Considering that these were the years of Haydn and Mozart, how-ever, the infant United States was no match for Europe.

EARLY AMERICAN COMPOSERS

Yet composers arose. The identity of the first American composer has long been a matter of speculation. Some authorities say that he was Conrad Beissel, a member of the Ephrata Cloister, who was responsible for the *Ephrata Hymnal,* that contained hymns in four to seven parts, an unusual feature, as unison singing was the rule in other sections of the country. Perhaps it is safer to select Francis Hopkinson (1737-1791), born in Philadelphia a few years before William Billings (1746-1800) and two years after James Lyon (1735-1794).

An intimate friend of Franklin, Washington, Jefferson and Joseph Bonaparte, a member of the Continental Congress and a signer of the Declaration of Independence, Francis Hopkinson had enviable social and cultural advantages. He was a college graduate, lawyer, poet, essay-ist, harpsichordist, organist and inventor as well as a composer. His best-known work is a song, somewhat in the style of Carey and Arne,

"My Days Have Been So Wondrous Free." Although his works lack striking originality and professional polish, they have a certain charm and quaintness. Moreover, they indicate that America was beginning to show signs of musical growth.

In 1749 one John Beals, a "musick-master" from London, arrived in the Quaker City to teach "violin, hautboy, flute, and dulcimer" and advertised that he was available for parties and entertainments. Not only Philadelphia but other parts of Pennsylvania also were advancing in the "art of musick." Fine music was to be found in Bethlehem, probably because of the German background of the Moravians who settled there. Both Franklin and Washington appreciated it. Today Bethlehem is no less musical, for people from all over the country flock to the annual Bach Festival, presented by the Bethlehem Bach Choir, established by J. Frederick Wolle (1863-1933) and since 1939 directed by Ifor Jones.

William Billings, born in Boston, was of humbler estate than Hopkinson, and was considered peculiar, as he notated his music on pieces of leather in his tannery. Nevertheless, he published *The New England Psalm Singer or American Chorister* in 1770 (the year of Beethoven's birth). While knowing next to nothing about contrapuntal composition, he determined to write original songs in counterpoint, calling them *fuguing tunes*. Of this form he exclaimed:

> It has more than twenty times the power of the old slow tunes, each part straining for mastery and victory, the audience entertained and delighted . . . sometimes declaring for one part, and sometimes for another. Now the solemn bass demands their attention, next the manly tenor; now the lofty counter, now the volatile treble. Now there; now here again, O ecstatic! Rush on, you sons of harmony!

In the preface of a subsequent collection, *Billings' Best,* the composer expressed his own musical declaration of independence—"Nature and not Knowledge must inspire thought" and "It is best for every composer to be his own carver." Later, however, he showed an amusing streak of humility:

> Kind Reader, no doubt you [do or ought to] remember that about eight years ago I published a Book . . . and truly a most masterly and inimitable performance I then thought it to be . . . How lavish was I of encomiums on this infant production of my own Numb Skull? . . . After impartial examination, I have discovered that many of the pieces in that Book were never worth my printing or your inspection . . .

A fiery patriot, Billings must have been delighted that the Continental Fifers played his tunes and that the Army sang his songs. "Chester," Billings' most popular song, was sung from Maine to Georgia. In fact,

Elie Siegmeister calls it the *Marseillaise* of the American Revolution. In 1774 Billings founded a singing society in Stoughton, Massachusetts, to study and perform psalms and oratorios. It was the second oldest musical organization in the Colonies, the first being the St. Cecilia Society of Charleston (1740).

Chester

William Billings

Fig. 78. *Chester*—William Billings. Billings' *Chester* was sung from Maine to Georgia during the American Revolution. Originally a hymn, the composer republished it with stirring martial words.

In 1761, *Urania,* an album of psalms, anthems and hymns, was published by the Reverend James Lyon of Princeton University. He included several of his own compositions, in addition to instructions for his singing school in Philadelphia. Lyon also established the Musical Fund Society, as important to that city as the Handel and Haydn Society was to become to Boston.

In the latter half of the eighteenth century, many other men were composing and undertaking musical ventures. In New England were Andrew Law (1748-1821); Oliver Holden (1765-1844), who in 1793 composed the hymn tune, *Coronation,* sung to the words "All Hail the Power of Jesus' Name"; Samuel Holyoke (1762-1820); and William Libby (1738-1798), an English organist active in Boston. From other locales came John L. Birkenhead of Trinity Church, New York City, that had formed the first boys' choir school; Peter Albrecht van Hagen who pushed Charleston ahead in his teaching and concerts; and Alexander Reinagle (1756-1809), a friend of C. P. E. Bach, who settled in Philadelphia where he composed in an Haydnesque style. James Hewitt (1770-1827) wrote an opera, *Tammany,* based on an Indian story that also lends its name to a political organization; Victor Pelissier was a composer, French hornist and member of the Old American Company, formed by Reinagle. There was also Benjamin Carr (1768-1831) who, as Howard states, "bridged the turn of the century, arriving in this country in the post-revolutionary days, when concert activities were re-awakening. . . ."

To this list we might add the name of John Antes (1740-1811), although it is difficult to classify him as an American composer, in terms of Howard's definition. Antes left this country while in his 'teens and spent the remainder of his life abroad as a missionary for the Moravian Church. His musical technique was sure and his ideas ambitious, but his idiom was essentially that of Haydn. The music of Antes and several other obscure composers is being made available to us through the efforts of the Moravian Music Foundation and such men as the organist and composer, Robert Elmore (1913-   ).

THE FOUNDING FATHERS

The Founding Fathers were not indifferent to music, as many accounts attest. Boston had secret singing clubs organized by Governor Samuel Adams "to stir up enthusiasm for independence." Thomas Paine wrote "The Liberty Tree" and "Bunker Hill." Paul Revere engraved the first volume of original hymns and anthems published in this country. George Washington, although he neither played nor sang, was a frequent concert-goer and provided musical educations for his stepchildren and their progeny. Several volumes of music can be seen today at Mt. Vernon.

That Thomas Jefferson played the violin and arranged string-quartet readings at Monticello is a known fact. He also invented an ingenious music stand for quartet players. Siegmeister quotes a letter written by Jefferson in 1778, in which he was considering having a private orchestra, such as existed in Europe:

> I retain among my domestic servants a gardener, a weaver, a cabinet-maker, and a stone-cutter, to which I would add a *vigneron.* In a country where music is cultivated and practised by every class of men, I suppose there might be found persons of those trades who could perform on the French horn, clarinet, or hautboy, and bassoon so that one might have a band . . . without enlarging their domestic expenses.

Perhaps Benjamin Franklin was most active in several phases of music. He had printed the *Ephrata Hymnal* and in 1741 he published

Dr. Watts' hymns. Later he invented or at least modified an instrument called the *harmonica*—a set of thirty-five circular glasses arranged on a central rod, tuned to play three octaves and enclosed in a spinet-like case. A similar novelty had enjoyed a vogue in Europe where Franklin became acquainted with it. Mozart had first encountered "musical glasses" at the home of Dr. Mesmer. Gluck performed a concerto on twenty-six drinking glasses, accompanied by "the whole band." He claimed that he could play anything on them that could be executed on a violin or harpsichord. The amazingly versatile Franklin also composed a string quartet, discovered in 1941 among documents in the Paris Conservatory Library. Written for three violins and a violoncello, the work is actually in suite form—an untitled opening movement is followed by a minuet, a *capriccio,* another minuet and a *siciliano.* The music has a London Bach flavor about it.

Fig. 79. *Quartetto a 2 Violini con Violoncello—Del Sig^{re} Benjamin Francklin* (*sic*). The first page of the alleged Franklin *Quartet.* (Courtesy Bibliothèque du Conservatoire, Paris.)

TRADITIONAL SONGS

It is of interest to note that many of our traditional American songs date from the period we have been discussing and often were introduced in the popular ballad-operas of the time. For instance, the nursery tune, "Old King Cole," made its initial appearance in John Gay's *Achilles* (1733), while "Girls and Boys Come Out to Play" was taken from Gay's *Polly* (1729), a sequel to *The Beggar's Opera.* "The Girl I Left Behind Me" stems from about 1758, and "Oh Dear, What Can the Matter Be?" was first published in Shaw's *Gentleman's Amusement* in 1795.

The marching song of the Revolution, "Yankee Doodle," probably appeared during the days of the French and Indian Wars, when crack British troops used it to poke fun at the ragged Colonials. "God Save the King" may have been composed in England in 1740, although Lully, Handel and Henry Carey have all been given credit for it. During the late eighteenth century, the melody was treated to a variety of texts, but it did not come by "My Country, 'Tis of Thee" until 1832. The song, "Hail Columbia," was an emotional outcome of a near-war with France, who had been heaping ignominy on our diplomats over an international disagreement in 1798. The lyrics were written by Joseph Hopkinson, son of Francis, and the tune was originally that of the "President's March," possibly composed during Washington's administration.

Below is reproduced a program from a concert subscription series offered in 1792 in Philadelphia, the national capitol. It offers us a graphic idea of the scope of American musical activities at the turn of the century.

Act I

Grand Overture of Haydn, called la Reine de France

(The first movements of symphonies were sometimes offered as "overtures." No doubt, this was the first movement of Haydn's *"Paris" Symphony No. 4, "La Reine,"* composed in 1786.)

Song   Mrs. Hodgkinson

Quartetto composed by Mr. Gehot (Jean or Joseph Gehot [1756-*c.* 1820] was a Belgian violinist who emigrated to the U.S. in 1792.)

Concerto Violoncello (composed by the celebrated Duport) (The celebrated Duport was Jean-Louis [1749-1819], considered the foremost French 'cellist of his day.)

Sinfonia   Bach (Johann Christian)

Act II

Quartetto   Messrs. Reinagle, Gehot,
                                          Moller and Capron

(While the name of the composer is not given, this may have been a quartet by Ignaz Joseph Pleyel [1757-1831], a pupil of Haydn and a noted piano manufacturer.)

Song	Mrs. Hodgkinson
Sonata Piano Forte	Mr. Moller
Double Concerto, Clarinet and Bassoon	Messrs. Wolf and Youngblut
Overture	Reinagle

1800-1860—MUSICAL ACTIVITIES

During the Colonial period we have seen that our country participated vicariously in Classicism and produced a few interesting, if not important, composers whose music, however humble, represents a beginning and, in the case of Billings, a bit of originality. We had been held back by the exigencies of colonization and by a cultural dependence on Europe which was to continue while we established our own institutions. If we had achieved any homogeneity by the turn of the century, we were to lose it after 1800 because of the extension of the frontier and the influx of political refugees from France and central Europe, who brought with them their superior musical training and experience. A positive aspect of this was that the regional theocratic prejudices, especially against instrumental music and the theater, were weakened. The new Western settlements demanded music and were not bound by religious fanaticism, so that concerts, operas and musical shows, performed by professional as well as amateur musicians, gave American music a new impetus in the period between 1800 and 1860. Several examples suffice to support this statement.

Operatic performances became more frequent. After 1800, French opera was presented regularly in New Orleans. Moreover, as Louis Elson asserts, "At the beginning of the nineteenth century Charleston and Baltimore entered the operatic field, and traveling troupes came into existence, making short circuits from New York through the three large cities, but avoiding Boston, which was wholly given over to Handel, Haydn and psalms." The first grand opera heard in New York was Weber's *Der Freischütz*. It was probably a very crude performance, as many changes were made to conform to public taste, but it was a great success. In 1825, Manuel Garcia (1805-1906), a Spanish tenor, arrived in New York with his family, which included a daughter, the famous Mme. Malibran. Garcia introduced *The Barber of Seville* and other Italian operas—a revelation to New York audiences. In fact, Garcia earned the name, "Musical Columbus."

In the meantime, Spanish soldiers had come up the coast of California in 1769 and discovered San Francisco Bay. A settlement was established seven years later, where, within a mission and a fort, Spanish padres taught the Indians hymns of the Church and *alabados,* that is, religious songs of simple character. In 1846 the territory came under North American control and, two years afterward, gold was discovered, precipitating the great "Gold Rush." Musicians were not long to appear. In 1850 the brilliant pianist, Henri Herz, with his concert grand, sailed in with a boatload of prospectors. Gilbert Chase records that at his first concert Herz was given a pan full of gold worth 10,000 francs. In the early 1850's, Ole Bull; Carlotta Patti, Adelina's sister; Anna Bishop, a singer and pianist; and an Italian opera company appeared in mining camps. The first orchestra was established.

During and immediately after the War of 1812 two significant if separate events occurred. The first was the composition of our national anthem, written by Francis Scott Key as he watched the bombardment of Fort McHenry on Chesapeake Bay. His text was set to the tune of an old English drinking-song, "Anacreon in Heaven," and, of course, was "The Star-Spangled Banner." Shortly afterwards, the choir and fifty members of the Park Street Church in Boston formed the Handel and Haydn Society, for the purpose of "cultivating and improving a correct taste in performance of sacred music." The group is still active. So anxious was the Society for good music that it asked Beethoven to compose a work for it. He was pleased with the recognition and in one of his notebooks had written, "The Oratorio for Boston."

ESTABLISHMENT OF ORCHESTRAS

During the early 1800's our first orchestras were established. In 1799, Gottlieb Graupner (1767-1836) came to Boston. He had earlier played in an orchestra directed by Haydn in London. In 1810 he organized the Philharmonic Society, the first American orchestra. About the same time the Euterpean Society was launched in New York City and for thirty years gave an annual concert. From 1820 to 1857 Philadelphia's Musical Fund Society flourished, improving musical taste and assisting needy musicians. Beethoven's *Symphony No.* 1 and some of his choral works were presented by this group. In 1824 Graupner's orchestra was disbanded, to be supplanted in 1837 by the Harvard Musical Association, controlled by those devoted to Handel, Haydn and Beethoven. In this group, however, were dissenters who seceded and banded together as The Philharmonic Society (1857-1863) to present music by the "anarchists," Berlioz and Wagner. The Boston Music Hall was constructed in 1852, to accommodate Jenny Lind.

Through the efforts of Ureli Hill (*c.* 1802-1875), a student of Spohr, The New York Philharmonic Society was founded in 1842. As its first conductor, Hill set a pace for the best in music. In 1855, Carl Bergmann (1821-1876), in association with Theodor Eisfeld (1816-1882), served as conductor. A friend told Bergmann that people did not like Wagner's music and remonstrated with him for playing it. "What! They don't like Wagner?" Bergmann exclaimed. "Well, I'll have to play it oftener until they do like it!"

Theodore Thomas (1835-1905) came to this country at the age of ten from Germany. It was he who gave us our first taste of chamber music, and with William Mason presented Schumann and Brahms to American audiences. Thomas also pioneered the music of Wagner, at a time when Europe itself was torn by differing opinions about its quality. In fact, thanks to Franz Liszt, parts of Wagnerian scores were performed here by the young conductor before they were played abroad. Thomas was a musical missionary. He formed his own orchestra in 1864 and took it on tour to other cities. Between 1877 and 1879 he conducted The New York Philharmonic. After 1890, Thomas was active in Chicago, where he remained until his death.

REPRESENTATIVE AMERICAN COMPOSERS

Amid the growing array of opera troupes, choral societies and orchestras were American composers and executants, working diligently and with some distinction. William Fry (1813-1864) was one of the first Americans to compose an opera, *Leonora* (1845). In the Balfe-Donizetti tradition, it was performed in Philadelphia and thirteen years later in New York. Fry was also an active propagandist for American music, writing articles for the *New York Tribune*. In 1855 George Bristow (1825-1898) contributed another American opera, *Rip van Winkle*. With Fry, Bristow spearheaded a crusade against foreign, notably German, influences in American musical life, fearing they would extinguish the feeble flame of national composition. When Ole Bull, however, took over the Academy of Music in New York, where operas were performed until the Metropolitan was built in 1882, he actually offered prizes for American compositions.

Several significant musical personalities and a distinguished musical family were active during this period. One of the most fascinating was Louis Moreau Gottschalk (1829-1869). His teacher, Berlioz, said of him, "Gottschalk is one of the very small number who possess all the different elements of a consummate pianist—all the faculties which surround him with an irresistible prestige, and give him a sovereign power." Victor Hugo characterized Gottschalk as "a poet, a man of gay imagination, an eloquent orator who can move his audience." Yet we today may ask, Who was he?

Gottschalk was born in New Orleans, the son of an English father and a Creole mother. An infant prodigy, he left the United States at the age of thirteen to study in Paris. As he was regarded by the majority of Americans as a foreigner, he was most successful here in his many concert appearances. He was the first of our musical matinée idols, combining the attractiveness of a pianist-composer with that of a *beau ideal*. Through his aunt, the Countess de Lagrange, he became a favorite with the European aristocracy. Chopin prophesied that he would become a "king of pianists." After touring France and Spain, Gottschalk gave a concert in New York at Niblo's Theater (1853), where his reception was comparable to that of Jenny Lind the year before. He did, however, have the good sense to refuse P. T. Barnum's offer of $20,000 a year and toured independently, presenting some eighty concerts in New York City alone, and almost a thousand in Cuba and South America. He died at age forty in Rio de Janiero, too delicate to stand the strains of constant travel and numerous social obligations.

Recently Jean Behrend has edited lively selections from Gottschalk's *Journals,* which chronicle the musical scene of his time in the West Indies, North, Central and South America. Gottschalk's charm, intelligence and sense of humor is readily apparent from these pages. At his death he was internationally mourned as a great pianist, a popular composer, a pioneer of music therapy and an American good-will ambassador. Although most of his compositions are forgotten today, save, perhaps, for "Banjo" or "The Last Hope," Howard remarks that Gottschalk was "a forerunner of Ethelbert Nevin—at heart, and by necessity a sentimentalist—he was a composer of *salon* music *par excellence.*"

In contrast to the highly trained Gottschalk, Stephen Foster, our native bard, may seem something of a country bumpkin. With no musical education to speak of, Foster knew very little about harmony and less of counterpoint. His is "music that has come into existence without the influence of conscious art, as a spontaneous utterance, filled with characteristic expression of the feelings of a people," writes H. E. Krehbiel.

Stephen Foster (1826-1864) was born in a small village near Pittsburgh, Pennsylvania. At seven he showed musical tendencies and taught himself to play the flute. His first performed composition was a "Tioga Waltz" for four flutes, played at school with the composer on the podium. For several years five boys met at Foster's home. There he taught them part-songs and composed tunes for the sessions. From his Southern parents and their servants he learned something of Negro folk music.

Foster's name is almost inseparable from that form of popular entertainment, known as the minstrel show. About 1830, an actor, Thomas

(Daddy) Rice, conceived the idea of dressing like a Negro porter, from whom he borrowed clothes, and singing and dancing to the song of a stage driver. His act took the audience by storm, especially when the porter appeared on stage, half-dressed and demanded his clothing, as the whistle of a steamboat summoned him back to work. Thus Rice became the father of minstrels, a dance-song and patter format, and traveled all over the United States and England. Six years after his first song, "Open Thy Lattice, Love," was published, Foster in 1848 submitted "Oh! Susanna" to an itinerant minstrel company. Its immediate popularity persuaded the composer to devote himself to song writing as a profession, in spite of objections from his family that he was wasting his time.

Foster, because of his disposition and his lack of business acumen, was notoriously unsuccessful. He was estranged from his family, he failed as a husband and he spent his last years on the Bowery, narrowly escaping a grave in potter's field. He seemed never to realize the value of his songs and even suggested that Christy, of the original Christy's Minstrels, should sign his own name as composer of "Old Folks at Home." Foster sold out his royalty rights and in 1860 engaged himself to write twelve songs a year for $800. Too unreliable to fulfill this obligation, he drew his money in advance and accepted pittances for his songs. "He would write one in the morning . . . sell it in the afternoon and have the money spent by evening," comments Howard.

Yet Foster's songs are probably the most typically American expression that any composer had yet achieved. They express mood, spirit and event so perfectly and are so simple and direct in appeal that they have come to be considered as folksongs. Harold Milligan, in his biography of the composer, states, "Every folk-song is first born in the heart and brain of some one person whose spirit is so finely attuned to the voice of that inward struggle, which is the history of the soul of man, that when he seeks for his own self-expression, he at the same time gives a voice to that vast multitude who die and give no sign."

One of the most influential musical families in America has been the Masons. Lowell Mason (1792-1872), Massachusetts born, founded a musical dynasty, continuing into the twentieth century. Because of his popular hymn-tune collections, he has often been called the father of American Church music. Among his many hymns, still included in most denominational hymnals, are *Work Song* ("Work, for the Night Is Coming") and *Missionary Hymn* ("From Greenland's Icy Mountains"). Equally important, however, were Mason's other musical roles. He served as president of the Handel and Haydn Society and traveled extensively, training choruses and encouraging musical activities. It was he who established classes based on Pestalozzi's pedagogical principles and introduced music to the public school curriculum in Boston (1838).

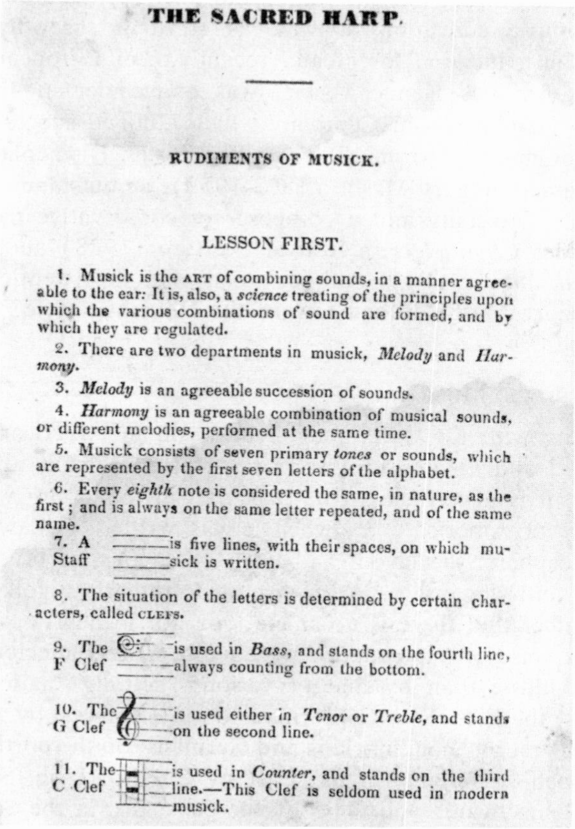

THE SACRED HARP.

RUDIMENTS OF MUSICK.

LESSON FIRST.

1. Musick is the ART of combining sounds, in a manner agreeable to the ear: It is, also, a *science* treating of the principles upon which the various combinations of sound are formed, and by which they are regulated.

2. There are two departments in musick, *Melody* and *Harmony.*

3. *Melody* is an agreeable succession of sounds.

4. *Harmony* is an agreeable combination of musical sounds, or different melodies, performed at the same time.

5. Musick consists of seven primary *tones* or sounds, which are represented by the first seven letters of the alphabet.

6. Every *eighth* note is considered the same, in nature, as the first; and is always on the same letter repeated, and of the same name.

7. A _____ is five lines, with their spaces, on which mu-
Staff _____ sick is written.

8. The situation of the letters is determined by certain characters, called CLEFS.

9. The ⌯ is used in *Bass*, and stands on the fourth line,
F Clef —— always counting from the bottom.

10. The 𝄞 is used either in *Tenor* or *Treble*, and stands
G Clef —— on the second line.

11. The 𝄡 is used in *Counter*, and stands on the third
C Clef —— line.—This Clef is seldom used in modern
—— musick.

Fig. 80. "Lesson First," *The Sacred Harp*—J. H. Hickok, 1832. Collections of church tunes, such as this, offered musical instruction to the American public.

Lowell Mason's son, William (1829-1908), was born in the same year as Gottschalk. He studied abroad with Moscheles, Hauptmann, Richter and Liszt and was acquainted with Wagner, Brahms, Schumann, Meyerbeer, Anton Rubenstein, von Bülow and Grieg. During his lifetime he witnessed the growth of American music from a primitive state to one that was distinguished by choruses and orchestras comparable in quality to those in Europe. As we have noted, he and Theodore Thomas presented a significant chamber-music series in New York City, introducing European works to American audiences. With William S. B.

Mathews (1837-1912), Mason wrote a piano method (1876) that gained many adherents. He also composed numerous piano selections of the *salon* variety, including "Silver Spring" and *"Rêverie poétique."* While William Mason, like his father and uncle before him, supported American music education, it was, as Einstein shrewdly observes, ". . . only an education for greater receptivity of European imports."

William's brother, Henry Mason, was co-founder in 1854 of the Mason and Hamlin Organ Company which attained success as manufacturer of organs and (from 1882) of pianofortes. His nephew, Henry's son, was Daniel Gregory Mason (1873-1953), an outstanding professor at Columbia University and a composer of conservative tastes, whose music includes *Chanticleer,* a festival overture (1928) and *Suite after English Folksongs* (1934). Although active in the twentieth century, Daniel Gregory Mason leaned toward the Romantic style of which he wrote so well.

AMERICAN FOLK MUSIC

Co-existing with the developing hybrids of an American art music was a varied and vigorous folksong repertoire. Difficult to classify or systematize, it is nevertheless true that, as Carl Sandburg writes, "The song history of America . . . when it gets written . . . will give the feel to atmosphere, the layout and lingo of regions, of breeds of men, of customs and slogans . . ." In discussing American folk music, we must remember that there is no single type, for in nearly every part of the great expanse of our country, we have been less affected by primitive Indian music than by that of various "settling" nationalities: in Louisiana by the French; in California and the Southwest by the Spanish; in the Northwest by Scandinavians and Germans; on the northern border by the French-Canadians; in the East by English, Irish, Scottish and Welsh; in Pennsylvania and Ohio by the Germans; in the South by the West African Negro; and in the Plains by the cowboys.

Moreover, we have songs of the dock and wharf, chanties, railroad songs, lumberjack and mining songs as well as love songs, quaint, earthy and sentimental, full of beauty and of bawdy suggestion. Our folksongs reflect the life of the desperado and the gambler, the romance of New Orleans and stringencies of the frontiers. They reveal American life, history and legend in music. In the period we are discussing, for example, we find numerous musical documents regarding what was actually happening: the lengthy voyages of the Baltimore clipper ships; the 1812, Florida and Mexican wars; the religious revivals; the development of canals and railroads; life on the Southern plantation; and the pressures of Abolition. All these, whether coming from known or unknown sources, have a simplicity and a spontaneity of invention that is inescapable. As Burl Ives writes, "What one immediately recognizes in a folksong is this basic immediacy of personal experience, which gives the song its strength."

Throughout history every nation has, unheeded, gone through an amalgamating process. The difference between the United States and other countries lies in the fact that for three centuries we have been conscious of the "melting pot." We know folk-tune origins and we are contemporaries of many of the folksong authors, as the process is a continuing one, which we see in the so-called "protest" songs of today. Our intimacy has robbed our songs, according to some commentators, of their folksong rating. Yet Louisiana Creole songs, a mixture of French and Negroid elements, are certainly as much American as Breton songs, combining Greek modes with Celtic traits, are French.

BRITISH INFLUENCES

American folksong has probably been most influenced by that of Great Britain. We accept as American those tunes that we have either adopted or adapted, originally stemming from the early settlers of our first frontier, the Eastern seacoast. Cecil Sharp (1859-1924), the English folksong expert, made exhaustive collections from the southern Appalachian Mountain dwellers. It is interesting to note that he found English folksongs existing in a variety of mutations. Some, from the more isolated regions, were almost as they had been in eighteenth-century England, while others either had variants in the music or different texts, related to the new life. To his delight he discovered English folksongs preserved here which had been completely lost in the mother country.

Sharp's experiences suggest several generalizations about American folk music that we venture to offer the reader for verification or qualification. (1) Because of the oral tradition associated with folk music, derivations from national or ethnic sources may depart from the original in many ways, as individuals make alterations to suit their expressive needs, abilities and resources. Such an obvious factor as a poor memory may result in a definite formal or melodic change. (2) The degree of geographical and social isolation tends to modify the degree of change. (3) As opposed to primitive Indian music, our folk repertoire is largely indebted to the Western cultural tradition. (4) As new songs appear, old songs are lost. (5) Much of our folk music is monodic or assumes the arrangement of a melody, simply accompanied by banjo, guitar, dulcimer or harmonium. (6) Our folk melodies are usually strophic in form. (7) As yet we know very little about the way music is composed by non-literate groups.

SPANISH AND NEGRO INFLUENCES

Limitations of space restrict us to a very abbreviated discussion of the varieties of American folksong and dance but we would be remiss to omit mention of Spanish and Negroid influences that later proved to be such potent factors in both American art and popular music. "Flowers of our lost romance," is what Charles Lummis says of the Spanish-American folk tunes. They come as an utterance of transplanted Spanish people, as heart's ease in a strange world. Emotional and colorful, they possess all the sound and sense revealing essences of Spanish folk music. Added to the Old World Spanish is a characteristic New World wit, "quaintness, charm of phrase, peculiarity of construction . . . which . . . elevate them to the rank of classics of folksong." Among those that are well known are the languorous "Juanita," the lively *La Cucaracha* ("The Mexican Cockroach Song") and *Cielito Lindo*. In these and many others we find music influenced by the American scene attached spontaneously to a Spanish stem. Spanish-American folksong exhibits a wealth of Hispanic-African features: a leaning toward fast and slow triple meters; diatonicism; rhythmic syncopation; a certain assymetry of phrasing; and a modification of Spanish Gypsy dance patterns, so prominent in Mexican music.

Many of us, if asked to name a typical American folk music, would point to that of the Negro in the South. The fact that the American Negro has taken his themes, his subjects of sorrow and happiness, often his melodies, from his experience among white Americans permits us to call his "unpremeditated lays" American instead of African folksongs. His music, like that of the ancient Hebrews, is often an outcome of religious impulse and an escape from the unwarranted circumstances in which he found himself. Therefore, his songs are imbued with dignity and sublimity vividly illustrated by such spirituals as "The Blood Came Twinkling Down," "Let the Church Roll On" and hundreds as vibrantly and sincerely worded. In the spirituals we discern the groping of an uprooted African people among alien words, alien customs and heartbreaking readjustments. H. E. Krehbiel records, "They contain idioms which were transplanted hither from Africa, but as song they are the product of American institutions; of the social, political and geographical environment within which their creators were placed in America, of the influences . . . and experiences which fell to their lot in America."

This statement raises the question of how much African influence there is in Negro folksong. Authorities agree that while West African features remain, they are diffused through environmental factors. There are several reasons for this. One is that West Africa, from which most American Negroes came, had a heterogeneous culture of many tribes, many languages and many rituals. Another is that conscious efforts were made to separate the Negroes from their African background when they were brought to America. Yet another is that in the United States, in contrast with parts of South America, the Negroes lived closely with white culture and were unable to retain the distinctive features of their background. In addition, they were exposed to Protestant Christianity, to which they became attached. It seems fair to say that while much of the material of Negro folksong is derived from Southern white rural culture, the style is often African.

James Weldon Johnson asserts:

> . . . the spirituals are not merely melodies. The melodies of many of them so sweet or strong or even weird, are wonderful, but hardly more wonderful than the harmonies. One has never experienced the full effect of these songs until he has heard their harmonies in part singing of large numbers of Negro voices . . . What led to this advance . . . beyond primitive music? It was by sheer spiritual forces that the African chants were metamorphosed into the Spirituals; that upon the fundamental throb of African rhythms were reared those reaches of melody that rise above earth and soar into the pure ethereal blue. And this is the miracle of the Spirituals . . . In form spirituals often run strictly parallel with African songs, incremental leading lines and choral iteration.

The Bantu song, "The Story of Tangalimlibo," illustrates a primitive African procedure of response and refrain:

It is crying, it is crying
Sihamba Ngenyango
The child of the walker by moonlight
Sihamba Ngenyango.

In terms of a spiritual, this antiphonal method is carried over into:

Leader: Swing low, sweet chariot
Group: Coming for to carry me home
Leader: Swing low, sweet chariot
Group: Coming for to carry me home
Leader: I look over Jordan, what do I see?
Group: Coming for to carry me home
Etc.

In addition to antiphonal group singing, other African features permeate Negro folksong. One is the strict adherence to metric patterns, made interesting through the use of syncopation. Innumerable combinations are possible and it is this variety that is fascinating. In the place of African drums, the American Negro used anything available to supply and enhance the rhythms—washboards and tubs, frying pans, clapping and stamping. As in Africa there is a close relationship between song and dance, between music and ritual, between voices and instruments. Work songs, such as "Pick a Bale of Cotton," seem African in origin, if not in style. There is a refreshing tendency toward improvisation and a dependence on the pentatonic scale. Lastly, in contrast to the pinched, nasal sounds of neighboring Southern white singers, there is among Negro folksingers a distinctive relaxed, throaty and slightly harsh vocal quality.

Negro folksong includes secular as well as spiritual forms. In his comic songs, the Negro created counting-out rimes, game songs and parodies on Biblical stories. His laments or "blues," often in the first person, express the sad and lonely and desolate, in a unique way. A curious element of fantasy and humor is present, too, as in "The Grey Goose." Furthermore, there is no lack of love songs, children's songs, songs about heroes and cabin life and injustice, and other matters of immediate concern.

The whole subject of American folk music has only recently become a serious area of scholarly investigation. We are indebted to the Lomaxes, John Jacob Niles, Bruno Nettl and other individuals, as well as to various universities and the Library of Congress for their research. Much more remains to be uncovered and evaluated before definitive pronouncements can be made. The factor of population mobility enters and complicates the picture. For instance, in the so-called "Pennsylvania Spirituals" we find English Methodist hymns infused with Negro style and practiced in a relatively secluded German-American community. Nevertheless, American folksong was to have its effect upon art music of a later period and to lead to what some Europeans feel is the only American musical contribution, jazz.

* * * * *

In 1820, the Rev. Sydney Smith had written in the *Edinburgh Review* the following scathing words:

> During the thirty or forty years of their independence they (Americans) have done absolutely nothing for the Sciences, for the Arts, for Literature, or even for the statesman-like studies of Politics or Political Economy . . . In the four quarters of the globe, who reads an American book? or goes to an American play? or looks at an American

picture or statue? What does the world yet owe to American physicians or surgeons? What new substances have their chemists discovered? or what old ones have they analyzed? What new constellations have they discovered by the telescopes of Americans?—what have they done in mathematics? . . . Finally, under which of the tyrannical governments of Europe is every sixth man a Slave, whom his fellow-creatures may buy and sell and torture?

As Irving Lowens replies, "The charges were then just about unanswerable, and they consoled themselves with the strong conviction that America must eventually shake off its cultural dependence on Europe, that it must eventually achieve uniquely American glories in the arts, the sciences, and letters." By 1850, American men of literature had begun to produce works of high quality which left their marks on Europe, but musicians, despite the best intentions, lagged woefully in the rear, at best striving to imitate European models and at worst abandoning themselves to the crassest entertainments. After the Civil War and over the turn of the century, composers struggled through musical adolescence toward the goal of cultural maturity.

SUGGESTIONS FOR FURTHER READING

Barbour, James M., *The Church Music of William Billings*. Ann Arbor, University of Michigan Press, 1960.

Breslin, Howard, *Concert Grand*. New York, Dodd-Mead, 1963.

Chase, Gilbert, *America's Music from the Pilgrims to the Present*. New York, McGraw-Hill, 1955.

Chase, Richard, ed., *American Folk Tales and Songs*.* New York, New American Library, 1956.

Courlander, Harold, *Negro Folk Music U. S. A.* New York, Columbia University Press, 1963.

Elson, Louis C., *The History of American Music*. New York, Macmillan, 1925.

Gerson, Robert A., *Music in Philadelphia*. Philadelphia, Presser, 1940.

Goldman, Richard F., and Smith, R., *Landmarks of Early American Music*. New York, Schirmer, 1943.

Gottschalk, Louis M., *Notes of a Pianist*. New York, Knopf, 1964.

Haywood, Charles, *A Bibliography of North American Folklore and Folksong*. New York, Dover, 1961. 2 vols.

Hitchcock, H. Wiley, *Music in the United States: A Historical Introduction*.* Englewood Cliffs, Prentice-Hall, 1967.

Howard, John Tasker, *Our American Music*. New York, Crowell, 1965.

Johnson, H. Earle, *Hallelujah, Amen*. Boston, Bruce Humphries, 1965.

Kmen, Henry A., *Music in New Orleans: The Formative Years, 1791-1841*. Baton Rouge, Louisiana State University Press, 1967.

Lang, Paul Henry, ed., *One Hundred Years of Music in America*. New York, Schirmer, 1961.

* Available in paperback edition.

Ives, Burl, *et al., The Burl Ives Song Book: American Song in Historical Perspective.** New York, Ballantine, 1953.

Lowens, Irving, *Music and Musicians in Early America.* New York, Norton, 1964.

Marrocco, W. Thomas, and Gleason, Harold, eds., *Music in America: An Anthology 1620-1865.* New York, Norton, 1964.

Mellers, Wilfrid, *Music in a New Found Land: Themes and Developments in the History of American Music.* New York, Knopf, 1965.

Metcalf, Frank J., *American Writers and Compilers of Sacred Music.* New York, Abington Press, 1925.

Nettl, Bruno, *Folk and Traditional Music of the Western Continents.** Englewood Cliffs, Prentice-Hall, 1965.

Rich, A. L., *Lowell Mason: The Father of Singing among the Children.* Chapel Hill, University of North Carolina Press, 1946.

Stevenson, Robert, *Protestant Church Music in America: A Short Survey of Men and Movements from 1564 to the Present.* New York, Norton, 1966.

A Sampler of Supplementary Recordings

Collections

Early American Psalmody	Folkways 5108
Moravian Festival	Columbia ML-5427
America the Beautiful	Victor LM-2662
Anthology of American Folk Music	6-Folkways 2951/3
Library of Congress Recordings	3-Elektra 271/2
Ballads (Niles)	2-Tradition 1046
Spirituals and Blues (Josh White)	Elektra 193
The Organ in America (Biggs)	Columbia ML-5496
The American Harmony	Washington WLP-9418
The American Revolution through Its Songs and Ballads	Heirloom HL-502
The New England Harmony	Folkways FA-2377

Music of Individual Composers

Antes, John, *Anthems*
    Trios
Billings, William, *Hymns and Anthems*
Foster, Stephen, *Music of Stephen Foster*
    Songs of Stephen Foster
Gottschalk, Louis Moreau, *Nuit des Tropiques*
    Piano Music
Mason, Daniel Gregory, *Chanticleer: A Festival Overture*

Related Works of Interest

Bennett, Robert Russell, *Commemoration Symphony* "Stephen Foster"
Copland, Aaron, *Old American Songs*
Cowell, Henry, *Hymn and Fuguing Tune*
Schuman, William, *Overture for Band: Chester*
Thomson, Virgil, *Louisiana Story: Acadian Songs and Dances*

OPPORTUNITIES FOR STUDY IN DEPTH

1. We have recently been enjoying a renaissance of American folk music, some authentic, some quasi-authentic and some frankly bogus in origin. Make a study of one aspect of the current folk repertoire, including the role of protest songs.

2. Compile a bibliography of periodical literature concerning the beginnings of American music. Sources might include the *Journal of the American Musicological Society*, the *Journal of Research in Music Education*, the *Bulletin of the New York Public Library* and *The Musical Quarterly*. Annotate several of the articles.

3. We have mentioned the role of P. T. Barnum as impresario for the "Swedish Nightingale," Jenny Lind, on her American tour. Read a biography of this colorful figure and assess his contributions to the American society in which he dwelled.

4. William Henry Fry, American composer and critic, became increasingly outspoken about the reactions of audiences to serious American music. He said in a lecture (1853): ". . . it is time we had a Declaration of Independence in Art . . . Until this Declaration of Independence in Art shall be made—until American composers shall discard their foreign liveries and found an American school—and until the American public shall learn to support American artists, Art will not become indigenous to this country . . ." Comment on Fry's statement in view of the present artistic situation.

5. Utilizing the aid and cooperation of local historical societies and libraries, conduct research into the musical development and resources of a particular community, one of interest to the reader. How do the results compare with the general picture we have presented here?

6. If possible, visit the Foster Hall Collection, housed at the University of Pittsburgh, Pennsylvania. If this is not feasible, request from the director materials relevant to our native singer, Stephen Foster.

7. After reading and examination, prepare a teaching unit for the middle grades on the subject of our national songs. The report of O. G. Sonneck on "The Star-Spangled Banner," "Hail Columbia," "America," and "Yankee Doodle," issued in 1909 by the U. S. Government Printing Office, will provide an excellent start.

8. Write a detailed history of a nearby symphony orchestra, complete with items of its beginnings, a list of conductors and their tenures and, if possible, sample programs through the years.

VOCABULARY ENRICHMENT

Bay Psalm Book	Handel and Haydn Society
Moravians	The New York Philharmonic Society
fuguing tunes	spirituals
harmonica	"blues"
Musical Fund Society	syncopation

Chapter 25.

THE ADOLESCENCE OF AMERICAN MUSIC

. . . When I think of these older men, and especially of the most important among them—John Knowles Paine, George Chadwick, Arthur Foote, Horatio Parker—who made up the Boston school of composers at the turn of the century, I am aware of a fundamental difference between their attitude and our own . . . They loved the masterworks of Europe's mature culture not like creative personalities but like the schoolmasters that many of them became . . . It may not be gracious to say so, but I fear that the New England group of composers of that time were in all their instinct overgentlemanly, too well-mannered, and their culture reflected a certain museumlike propriety and bourgeois solidity.

—Aaron Copland, *Music and Imagination*

In general, American music in the later nineteenth century belatedly followed the lines of European Romanticism and, with but two possible exceptions, we look in vain for manifestations of true originality or pioneer efforts. This situation was perfectly natural, as one must pass through adolescence before reaching maturity. And that is just what happened. The United States needed its well-trained schoolmasters. These in turn fostered an enormous expansion of musical activity and interest. Among the music of representative composers we shall find the programmatic forms, the short lyric piano pieces, works based on Indian and Negro idioms, operas and oratorios, well-written, acclaimed at the time and now lost in oblivion, because we insist on judging them against the masterworks of Europe, instead of in their own context. The philosophy of Transcendentalism had lent them dignity. Emerson, although he admittedly had a tin ear, noted in his *Journal* of 1838, "Music takes us out of the actual and whispers to us dim secrets that startle our wonder as to who we are . . . All the great interrogatories, like questioning angels, float in on its waves of sound." This same Emerson was given a complimentary ticket to a concert by Chopin. The Sage of Concord wrote to his wife, "Could he only lend me ears!" His position, however, was quite in accord with the mystique of European Romanticism.

In this chapter we shall discuss the New England quartet mentioned by Copland, the nucleus of our first native school of composers. We shall mention others who were working to develop an American music. We shall note the development of operetta and the symphonic band. And we shall notice, entering through the back door, as it were, an earthy, untutored, vital and original music of the people—ragtime, blues and jazz. Rather like Smetana's hot and cold springs that combine to form the river Moldau, Bostonian academicism and the emanations of Bourbon Street gradually come together to suggest a direction for American music to follow.

SIX NEW ENGLAND COMPOSERS

After the Civil War, Boston became the musical capital of the United States. Although only one-third the size of New York, it already had its Handel and Haydn Society, orchestras and teachers like Benjamin James Lang (1837-1909). In 1866-67 the Harvard Musical Association inaugurated a new series of concerts that prospered until, in 1881, the Boston Symphony Orchestra was founded by Henry Lee Higginson (1834-1919), who engaged George Henschel, a German, as conductor. These surroundings constituted a *milieu* for our first school of composers who, as Copland continues, "within the framework of the German musical tradition in which most of them had been trained, . . . composed industriously, . . . set up professional standards of workmanship, and encouraged a seriousness of purpose in their students that long outlasted their own activities."

Some consider that with John Knowles Paine (1839-1906) American art music begins. He first brought music into Harvard in 1862, lecturing without compensation. With the advent of Charles Norton Eliot as president, music became an integral part of the curriculum and Paine was appointed director of the new department, a post he held from 1875 until his death. Among his pupils are numbered John Alden Carpenter, Arthur Foote, E. B. Hill, Frederick S. Converse and Daniel Gregory Mason.

In addition, Paine composed the first oratorio by an American. It was *St. Peter, Op.* 20, performed in Portland, Maine, in 1873. His *Mass in D, Op.* 10, was presented at the Berlin *Singakademie.* A composer of instrumental and choral music in both small and large forms, Paine wrote a *Centennial Hymn, Op.* 27 (1876) that opened the Philadelphia Exposition and met with more approval than Wagner's *Grosser Festmarsch,* commissioned for the same occasion. Paine also composed a *Columbus March and Hymn* for the Chicago Exposition (1893), a

Hymn of the West for the St. Louis Exposition (1904) and an opera on his own libretto, *Azara* (1901). He was a pioneer in many fields and inspired younger American composers to pursue his ideals.

George Whitefield Chadwick (1854-1931) was born in Lowell, Massachusetts and trained in Europe by Reinecke, Josef Gabriel Rheinberger (1839-1901) and Jadassohn, who told Louis Elson that Chadwick was the most brilliant student in his class. Previously he had studied at the New England Conservatory of Music (founded in 1867), where, on his return to Boston, Chadwick became an instructor and, in 1897, its director. Some of his distinguished pupils were Horatio Parker, Arthur Whiting (1861-1936), J. Wallace Goodrich (1871-1952) and Henry K. Hadley.

Chadwick's music is ardently Romantic, Wagnerian in harmony and lush in sound. A prolific composer, he wrote three symphonies; five string quartets; about 100 songs of which "Allah" is the best known; several operas; incidental music; overtures; and secular and sacred choral music, an example of which is the Christmas pastoral, *Noël* (1908). John Tasker Howard says, ". . . our recent composers make our earlier writers seem tame by comparison. Yet there is a steadiness in Chadwick's music . . . a freshness that is a matter of spirit rather than of style or idiom."

Arthur Foote (1853-1937) was an exception to the rule, as his training bears the label, "made in America," for he never studied abroad. Born in Salem, Massachusetts, he studied with a local teacher and then at Harvard, where he was a member of Paine's department. After organ study with B. J. Lang, he commenced his long career as teacher, organist (he was a founder of the American Guild of Organists), pianist (often with the Kneisel Quartet) and composer. His music is of a lyrical Romantic nature and includes chamber and orchestral music, of which his *Suite for Strings in E, Op.* 63 (1909) enjoys a certain popularity. Perhaps best known are some of his more than 100 songs, among which are "The Night Has a Thousand Eyes" and "Constancy." He was also the author of several instruction manuals.

One of the most unusual of the New England group was Horatio William Parker (1863-1919). His works, particularly his choral writings, stand with some of the best. A student of Chadwick in America and Rheinberger in Germany, Parker held posts in several churches and was made professor of music at Yale in 1894, where he remained until his death. The year 1893 was significant for the premiere of his most popular work, the oratorio, *Hora Novissima* (*The Last Hour, Op.* 30), taken from a medieval poem by Bernard de Morlaix, with an English translation by Parker's mother, who also prepared texts for two other oratorios. *Hora Novissima* enjoyed the distinction of being the first American work presented at the English Worcester Festival. Of it, Theodore Finney writes:

> The music was composed by a man who approached his work with no doubts concerning the expressive efficacy of the musical conventions of his own time. Within these conventions he created a minor masterpiece, deeply felt and completely realized. It has qualities of genuine sincerity, even eloquence, which may carry it through the cult of prejudice against works of its form, time and place.

Parker in his day enjoyed renown both at home and abroad. He was commissioned to write *A Wanderer's Psalm, Op.* 50 for the Festival at Hereford, England and another oratorio, *Morven and the Grail, Op.* 79, for the Handel and Haydn Society. In 1902 he received an honorary Doctor of Music degree from Cambridge University. With Brian Hooker, he won two $10,000 prizes, one offered by the Metropolitan Opera Company in 1911 for the best opera by an American (*Mona*, a tale of the Druids) and another offered by the National Federation of Music Clubs in 1915 (for the opera, *Fairyland*). Yet today his thick scores gather dust.

A most interesting member of the New England group of composers was Mrs. H. H. A. Beach (1867-1944), if only for the fact that she represents the distaff side with some distinction. Born Amy Marcy Cheney of New Hampshire, she early evidenced signs of musical talent and made her debut as a pianist while in her teens. In 1885 she married a Boston doctor and became actively associated with the musical life of that city. Like Arthur Foote, she was educated solely in America, and her music tends to be rather academic and conservative. Her first large work was a *Mass in E flat,* performed by the Handel and Haydn Society in 1892. She next composed a *scena* and *aria* for contralto and orchestra, the first work by an American woman presented by the New York Symphony Society. Yet another first is her *Gaelic Symphony* (1896). A prolific composer of piano, chamber and choral works, she is now known chiefly for her songs, among which are "The Year's at the Spring" and "Ah, Love, But a Day."

We might pause here for a moment to interpolate mention of several European women composers who were contemporaries of Mrs. Beach and achieved some reputation. Perhaps best known is Cécile Chaminade (1857-1944), a French composer who wrote, in addition to larger works and songs, the popular *salon* piano pieces, "The Flatterer" and "The Scarf Dance," still included in many collections. An Englishwoman, Dame Ethel Smythe (1858-1944), managed to dent the double

Fig. 81. "Harmony in Green and Rose: The Music Room"—James Macneill Whistler, 1860. This Massachusetts-born, European-trained painter often used musical analogies to characterize his subtle impressions. (Courtesy The Smithsonian Institution, Freer Gallery of Art, Washington, D.C.)

standard with her operas, which were presented in Weimar, Berlin, London, Leipzig and New York. The most successful was *The Wreckers,* originally written to a French libretto, first produced in German form (1906) and three years later in an English translation by the composer. Another Englishwoman, Liza Lehmann (1862-1918), was the first to be commissioned to write a musical comedy, *Sergeant Brue* (1904), although she is known to us for her song cycle, *In a Persian Garden,* to words from Fitzgerald's version of the *Rubaiyát* of Omar Khayyám.

Yet another distinguished student of Harvard, Chadwick and Rheinberger was the American composer Frederick Shepherd Converse (1871-1940), who was the first American to have an opera produced at the Metropolitan (*The Pipe of Desire,* 1909). He returned from Germany in 1898 with a symphony completed. From 1900 to 1907 he taught at Harvard and later became dean of the New England Conservatory in Boston. His setting of *Job,* for soloists, chorus and orchestra, was the first American oratorio heard in Germany (1908). Although his early works have a strongly Teutonic flavor, his later compositions reflect a more modern approach, as seen in *Flivver Ten Million* (1927), composed in response to Honegger's locomotive *tour de force, Pacific No. 231.* Among his works are *The Mystic Trumpeter,* an orchestral fantasy after Walt Whitman (1905); six symphonies; and a symphonic suite, *American Sketches,* after Carl Sandburg (1935).

OTHER AMERICAN COMPOSERS

At the same time that the New England school, with its German and English overtones, prospered, composers of equal stature were to be found in other parts of the land. A highly-respected composer was Edgar Stillman Kelley (1857-1944), who was born in Wisconsin of a family whose forefathers dated from 1650. After study in Chicago and Stuttgart, Kelley went to California, where he was an organist, teacher, composer and music critic. Later he taught at Yale, in Berlin and finally served as dean of composition at the Cincinnati Conservatory, at the same time holding a fellowship at Western College (Oxford, Ohio), which gave him leisure and economic freedom to compose. Among his popular works were songs; a comic opera, *Puritania* (1892); incidental music to *Ben Hur* (1900); two symphonies—"Gulliver" (1900-1936) and "New England" (1913); and a suite for orchestra, *Alice in Wonderland* (1919).

Ethelbert Woodbridge Nevin (1862-1901) was what Walt Whitman would have called a "Sweet Singer." He was born in a little town near Pittsburgh, to which his mother had brought the first grand piano to cross the Allegheny Mountains into Edgeworth. Far more cosmopolitan than his music suggests, Nevin studied in Pittsburgh, Boston, New York, Dresden and Berlin, under such famous instructors as Lang and von Bülow. Nevertheless, the composer was a Romanticist who found his best medium of expression in short songs and piano pieces. He had a gift for sentimental melody surpassed by few and he reached the heart as perhaps no other American except Stephen Foster. His "Narcissus" and "The Rosary" swept the country, selling in the millions. The song, "Mighty Lak' a Rose," published after his death, was a close third in popularity.

Many other composers and musicians were active during this period, although most of them were victims of the tone-poem, Brahms-Wagner syndrome, finding that, to quote novelist Henry James, "It's a complex

fate, being an American. . . ." Among those who merit mention are
Frank van der Stucken (1858-1929), a pupil of Reinecke and acquaint-
ance of Grieg and Liszt, whose most noteworthy contribution was in-
troducing works of Chadwick, Foote, Huss, MacDowell and others to
European audiences; James H. Rogers (1857-1940), a student of
Guilmant and Widor, who wrote many piano pieces, songs and cantatas;
Mary Turner Salter (1856-1938) of New England, who composed a
number of song cycles; Henry Holden Huss (1862-1953), a pupil of
Rheinberger, known for his symphonic poems, piano and choral works;
Henry Kimball Hadley (1871-1937), a Boston-Vienna trained programmatic composer whose opera, *Cleopatra's Night,* was performed
at the Metropolitan in 1920; Ruben Goldmark (1872-1936), student
of Fuchs and Dvořák and composer of a popular *Negro Rhapsody*
(1923), who will probably be remembered most as a teacher of Frederick
Jacobi (1891-1952), George Gershwin, Aaron Copland, Vittorio Giannini (1903-1966) and Abram Chasins (1903-   ); and Ernest Schelling
(1876-1939), whose most successful work was *A Victory Ball* (1923),
an orchestral fantasy after Alfred Noyes' anti-war poem.

THE DAMROSCH FAMILY

As American music progressed through the nineteenth century, the
focus of activity moved gradually from Boston to New York City. It
is there we meet another influential family associated with music
making—the Damrosches. Leopold Damrosch (1832-1885) was a most
interesting man. Educated as a medical doctor, he turned to music as
a career and became an intimate of Liszt and von Bülow. He arrived
in New York from Germany in 1871 and soon revealed his many musical talents, as conductor, organizer and composer. Not long afterward,
he was joined by his family, including sons, Frank (1859-1937) and
Walter (1862-1950), who also became important figures in American
musical life.

To Leopold's credit goes the establishment of the Oratorio Society
of New York in 1873 and the New York Symphony Society in 1877.
In addition, he vied with Theodore Thomas in presenting the newest
European music. Among his American premieres were performances
of Berlioz's *Damnation of Faust* and Brahms' *First Symphony*. As conductor of German opera at the Metropolitan in 1884, he introduced
us to Wagner's *Ring, Tristan* and *Die Meistersinger,* engaging skilled
Wagnerian singers, like Mmes. Materna, Brandt and Seidl-Kraus and
Anton Schott, who secured Wagner's reputation in the United States.

Leopold's sons followed in their father's footsteps. Frank became an
eminent music educator, forming various choral groups and serving as

supervisor of music in the public schools of Denver, Colorado and New York City. In 1905 he established the Institute of Musical Art which affiliated with the Juilliard Foundation in 1926. The Institute became a foster parent of chamber music in America, with the aid of the disbanded musicians of the Kneisel Quartet. In 1898 he began the "Symphony Concerts for Young People," which he conducted for many years.

Walter Damrosch, after study with his father and von Bülow, played in the orchestra of the Metropolitan and was made assistant director of German opera at the age of twenty-three. It was he who introduced to our stage Lillian Nordica, one of the first American grand-opera singers at the Metropolitan. His life was filled with a dizzying amount of musical activity. As conductor of the New York Symphony from 1903 until 1927, when it combined with the Philharmonic Society, Damrosch presented interesting programs with many first American performances of contemporary composers. He was the first conductor to give a radio concert with a symphony orchestra (1926). After 1927 he joined the newly-formed National Broadcasting Company as a music consultant and arranged music appreciation courses articulated with classroom scheduling. Moreover, he was a prolific composer. Among his works are operas, such as *The Scarlet Letter* (1896) and *Cyrano de Bergerac* (1913); choral pieces; incidental music; and songs, including a popular setting of "Danny Deever."

EDWARD ALEXANDER MACDOWELL

Our greatest late nineteenth-century composer was Edward Alexander MacDowell (1861-1908). Some of the Romanticism of the early nineteenth century had become mere imitation of a style that arose as protest against the trivia of Classicism. But the true spirit of wonder never turns artificial and such spirit had MacDowell. Always a poet, always himself, in spite of his Irish-Scotch background, his French and German training and his attraction to Norse legends, MacDowell was a composer of integrity who expressed his individuality in every note.

Born in New York City, MacDowell began study of the piano at the age of eight. His first teacher was Jean Buitrago and he also had a few lessons with the brilliant South American Gottschalk pupil, Teresa Carreño (1853-1917), who later played her pupil's concerto with many world orchestras. At fifteen, MacDowell entered the Paris Conservatory where he worked with Marie-Gabriel Savard (1814-1881) in composition and Antoine-François Marmontel (1816-1898) in pianoforte. While there he showed an aptitude for drawing and was actually offered free lessons from a master of *L'École des Beaux Arts* but the budding musician refused. A classmate at the Conservatory was a young fellow with strange musical ideas—Claude Debussy—whose path was to take a very different direction from that of MacDowell. Soon MacDowell left Paris for Stuttgart, where Joachim Raff (1822-1882) befriended him and introduced him to his master, Liszt. Through Liszt, MacDowell was invited to perform his *First Modern Suite, Op.* 10, at Zürich.

In 1884 MacDowell married a former pupil, Marian Nevins of New York. The couple settled in Wiesbaden, Germany, and remained there until 1887, when they sailed for Boston. There MacDowell appeared as a pianist with the Kneisel Quartet. During the next few years he established his reputation, teaching, touring and playing his piano concertos with the Boston Symphony and the Theodore Thomas Orchestras. His renown was so great that Columbia University called him in 1896 to be the first incumbent of the Center Chair of Music, citing the composer as "the greatest musical genius America has produced."

Through a series of unkind onslaughts of the fates following the death of President Seth Low, reports of which are too complicated and unverified to analyze here, MacDowell resigned his professorship in 1904. His health broke and for the last few years of his life he was hopelessly invalided. All the attentions of physicians, devoted wife and friends could not restore his mental capacities and he died four years later and was buried at Peterborough, New Hampshire. A natural boulder from which he often watched the sunset marks the spot—fitting for one who was an intense reflector of the moods of nature or, as Rollo W. Brown calls him, "a watcher of the winds."

Some illustrious men have statues erected to them but MacDowell, who frequently had said he wished other artists could share the infinite loveliness of his home in Peterborough, has the MacDowell Colony as tribute to his memory. There creative artists are privileged to visit in summer and winter to work in peace and beauty, unannoyed by other concerns. This paradise is due to the efforts of his wife, who raised funds for the Colony's maintenance and, with a group of friends, formed the MacDowell Memorial Association to perpetuate the project. Shortly before the composer died, the MacDowell Club of New York was founded to promote "a sympathetic understanding of the correlation of all the arts, and of contributing to the broadening of their influence, thus carrying forward the *life purpose of Edward MacDowell*."

"Edward MacDowell," writes Brown, "meant to prove that there was a place for a serious musician in the United States of America. He meant to come home and occupy himself and reveal its possibilities to others." And there is no question that MacDowell did give music in

Fig. 82. MacDowell's composing cabin at Peterborough, N.H. MacDowell gave music in America a new impetus, not an easy thing in 1888. His country home is now an artists' colony. (Photograph courtesy Bernice B. Perry.)

America a new impetus, not an easy thing in 1888. His works were immensely popular and were usually performed as soon as written. His very recognition was a significant phenomenon in American music.

The frequent comparisons of MacDowell to Grieg and Schumann are probably justified. All three were thorough Romanticists and masters of the miniature, particularly of the short lyric piano piece, with its rather dark coloring, its rhythmic flow and its poetic quality. Grieg and Mac-Dowell share what one perceptive critic calls a "rugged northern quality," somewhat impersonal, as if they were describing, instead of experiencing, feelings. In this aspect, MacDowell may be said to have foreshadowed Impressionism. Yet there are many moments in MacDowell's music, as Olin Downes notes, "such as those of the sonatas, of the second piano concerto, and certain of the short piano pieces, which remain unique, eloquent, articulate of one of the most gifted and sincere of American composers." MacDowell was a master craftsman and may have surpassed his European colleagues in thematic clarity, proportion and logic.

Among his works we find symphonic poems, such as *Hamlet and Ophelia, Op.* 22 and *Lancelot and Elaine, Op.* 25; orchestral suites, of which the *Suite No. 2,* "Indian," *Op.* 48, is exceptional; songs, often with original words; four piano sonatas, all effectively dramatic—No. 1, *"Tragica," Op.* 45, No. 2, *"Eroica," Op.* 50, No. 3, *"Norse," Op.* 57 and No. 4, the *"Keltic," Op.* 59; two piano concertos, of which the *Concerto No. 2 in D Minor, Op.* 23 is a favorite; and the piano suites, *Six Poems after Heine, Op.* 31 (which includes the "Scotch Poem"), *Twelve Virtuoso Studies, Op.* 46, *Woodland Sketches, Op.* 51 (in which are "To a Wild Rose," rescued from a wastepaper basket by his wife, "To a Water Lily" and "From an Indian Lodge"), the *Sea Pieces, Op.* 55 and *Fireside Tales, Op.* 61.

Of MacDowell, Copland says:

> In some strange way Edward MacDowell . . . managed to escape some of the pitfalls of the New Englanders . . . Nowadays, although his music is played less often than it once was, one can appreciate more justly what MacDowell had; a sensitive and individual poetic gift, and a special turn of harmony of his own . . . It seems likely that for a long time MacDowell's name will be secure in the annals of American music. . . .

NATIONALISTIC COMPOSERS

Even though he occasionally used native themes in his works, Mac-Dowell envisioned American music as an expression of "the youthful optimistic vitality and the undaunted tenacity of spirit that characterizes the American man." For the most part, the composers we have been discussing were extending European culture, composing largely in terms of more Brahms, more Grieg and more Liszt and Wagner. But there were others in the late nineteenth and early twentieth centuries who were looking more closely to home for materials, if not techniques, with which to advance an individual American art. While American music need not be defined as Negro folksong or Indian war whoops with a tomahawk vocabulary, valiant attempts were made to use Indian, Negro and folk elements as the bases of a nationalistic composition. An examination of some of them gives us an idea of the scope of such endeavors, whatever their ultimate destiny.

It was Harvey Worthington Loomis (1865-1930) who stated a position concerning the use of Indian themes. "If we would picture the music of the wigwam and the war path," he said, "we must aim by means of the imagination to create an art work that will project, not by *imitation* but by *suggestion,* the impression we have ourselves received in listening to this weird savage symphony in its pastoral *entourage* which, above all, makes the Indian's music sweet to him." In other words, he was acknowledging the fact that complete identification was impossible but that a potential existed for exploiting this particular form of exoticism. A pupil of Dvořák, as were many of our nationalistic composers, Loomis, in addition to works in other idioms, published arrangements and compositions patterned after Indian melodies, including a collection of Omaha tunes called *Lyrics of the Redman,* issued in 1904.

Charles Sanford Skilton (1868-1941) also accepted the challenge of integrating Indian material with sophisticated techniques. A New Englander by birth, Skilton, after study with Harry Rowe Shelley (1858-1947) and Dudley Buck (1839-1909), continued his musical education in Germany. He became interested in Indian music "when an Indian pupil," reports Howard, "offered to trade tribal songs for harmony lessons," while the composer was a professor at the University of Kansas. Skilton conducted intensive research into primitive American music and used Indian motives in many of his compositions, striving to invest them with a genuine feeling of authority, although he employed traditional forms. Among his efforts were three Indian operas; a *Suite Primeval* (1915-1921); and *Sioux Flute Serenade* for small orchestra (1920).

Arthur Finley Nevin (1871-1943), brother of Ethelbert, based his chief works upon the music of the Blackfeet Indians, with whom he had lived for a time. His opera, *Poia* (1910), was performed in Germany, with Humperdinck assisting in making the German libretto.

More influential was the pioneer work of Arthur Farwell (1872-1952), a graduate of the Massachusetts Institute of Technology who turned to music, studying with Homer Norris (1860-1920) in Boston, Humperdinck in Berlin and Guilmant in Paris. Tireless in promoting national ideas in art, Farwell established the Wa-Wan Press in 1901, because he felt that publishers were not inclined to accept American works. This gave creative impulse and practical assistance to many American composers, among whom were Loomis, Kelley and Henry F. B. Gilbert. His music for Percy MacKaye's pageants, such as *Caliban by the Yellow Sands* (1916), opened up a new field. To authenticate his collections of Indian and folk melodies, he lived with the people and made hundreds of phonograph recordings. From this source material he composed works on American subjects, including *Symbolistic Study*

No. 3 after Walt Whitman (1905); a *Symphonic Song on "Old Black Joe"* (1923) and *Dawn,* a fantasy on Indian themes (1901-1926).

Many of us know Charles Wakefield Cadman (1881-1946) through his songs, "From the Land of the Sky-Blue Water" and "At Dawning." He was immensely interested in American Indian music, as reflected in his *Thunderbird Suite* for orchestra (1917); an opera, *Shanewis (The Robin Woman,* 1918); and a cantata, *Father of Waters* (1928).

Another recruit to Indian lore was Thurlow Lieurance (1878-1963), well known for the song, "By the Waters of Minnetonka." He engaged in considerable Indian research, living on various reservations and absorbing the tribal culture. Its influence is felt in his many publications, including *Songs of the North American Indian* (1921) and symphonic pieces such as *Medicine Dance.*

Despite earnest attempts to create a national music using Indian themes and subject matter, the results have been disappointing and not to be compared with the successes in Mexico and parts of South America, perhaps because our composers were not courageous enough to strip the Amerindian down to his figurative loincloth, preferring instead to keep him in collar and tie. Whatever the case, the exploration of Negro music was somewhat more rewarding. Although the Jubilee Singers had toured Europe and America in the Victorian era, it was not until Dvořák visited our shores in 1892 that we realized we had a native song in the music of the Negro. Since then, spirituals and other forms of Negro music have become more familiar to us than the tunes of any of the nations which have been grafted to our song tree.

A bit of a changeling and a complete non-conformist among the New England composers was Henry Franklin Belknap Gilbert (1868-1928), who avoided academicism and went his own way, not seeking to out-Europe Europe but rather to find stimulation in our own musical past. He was one of the first to take Dvořák's advice to use American folk themes. After studying with Edward MacDowell, Gilbert became one of the Wa-Wan Press circle and turned his creative attention to a thorough investigation of Negro music. From this came some attractive, if not polished, music, including piano pieces; songs; and orchestral works like *Humoresque on Negro Minstrel Tunes* (1903), *Comedy Overture on Negro Themes* (1905), *The Dance in Place Congo*—a symphonic poem based on five Louisiana Creole songs—and *Negro Rhapsody* (1913). If Gilbert was not entirely successful in achieving his artistic ideals, he at least contributed fresh air to a stuffy artistic atmosphere.

Several eminent Negro musicians turned to their own music for inspiration. One of these was Harry Thacker Burleigh (1866-1949), a pupil of Dvořák and a songwriter and arranger of distinction. Another was Clarence Cameron White (1880-1960), a violin virtuoso who had studied with Samuel Coleridge-Taylor. His arrangement of the spiritual, "Nobody Knows the Trouble I've Seen," has been used by many great violinists. Among his works are a book, *American Negro Folk Songs* (1928); an opera, *Ouanga,* based on a Haitian incident; and violin and orchestral compositions. R. Nathaniel Dett (1882-1943) was long associated with outstanding musical activities at Hampton Institute. In addition to many arrangements and collections of Negro folksongs, his corpus embraces *In the Bottoms Suite* for piano (1913, in which is the lively "Juba Dance"); and two oratorios, *The Chariot Jubilee* (1921) and *The Ordering of Moses* (1937).

John Powell (1882-1963), a Virginian and Harold Morris (1890-1964), a Texan, represent composers who were influenced by Southern folk music because it was part of their environment. Thoroughly trained in America and in Europe, Powell won renown for his *Rapsodie Nègre* for piano and orchestra, introduced in 1918. In most of his many compositions he freely used Negro and Anglo-Saxon folk tunes, as in the overture, *In Old Virginia* (1921); a suite for piano, *At the Fair* (1925); and *Natchez on the Hill* (1932), three dances for orchestra. Morris was a neo-Romanticist, who instinctively created in terms of the melodic line of the spiritual and the easy-flowing syncopation of Negro music. Among his compositions is *Dum-a-Lum,* variations on a Negro spiritual for chamber orchestra (1925).

Two contemporary composers who use Negro and folk melodies in their works are David Guion and William Grant Still, both born in 1895. Of the two Guion, a Texan, is the more conservative, retaining his melodic outlines in connection with folk flavors. His transcription for piano of *Turkey in the Straw* is as characteristic as any of Dett's work, while his *Alley Tunes,* which includes the popular "The Harmonica Player," are excellent bits of Americana. Still, at the outset of his career, was determined to develop a symphonic type of Negro music. His background includes study with Chadwick and with Varèse as well as experience as an arranger of music for W. C. Handy and Paul Whiteman. With his *Afro-American Symphony* (1931) he earned the honor of being the first Negro composer to produce such a work. He was also the first Negro to conduct a major American symphony orchestra. In his music he has used both Negro and pseudo-Negro themes, expertly orchestrated.

Two composers who utilized mountain and cowboy melodies in their larger works were Howard A. Brockway (1870-1951) and Arthur Shepherd (1880-1958). Among Brockway's arrangements are *Lonesome*

Tunes (1916) and *20 Kentucky Mountain Songs* (1920). Shepherd's *Horizons* (1927) is a symphony with a decided Western flair, drawing upon the cowboy ballads, "The Dying Cowboy" and "The Old Chisholm Trail."

Our list of composers who have sought inspiration in American folk sources could go on and on. We have mentioned a very few, as representative of the many omitted. One other facet of the application of native folk material must be noted, however; that is its place in the drama and the musical theater. Negro folk material occupies a prominent position, for example, in Dubose and Dorothy Heyward's *Porgy,* which became the libretto of Gershwin's folk opera, *Porgy and Bess* (1935). Cowboy songs were featured in Lynn Riggs' *Green Grow the Lilacs* (1931), out of which evolved *Oklahoma!* (1943) by Richard Rodgers and Oscar Hammerstein II.

AMERICAN OPERETTA COMPOSERS

Musical theater has long been popular in the United States, beginning with ballad-operas and extending through minstrel shows to operetta. The sparkling works of Offenbach, Strauss and Gilbert and Sullivan found as enthusiastic a reception in America as they did in Europe, and still enjoy a certain favor, even as our own musical theater has expanded to include wonderful productions by Jerome Kern (1885-1945), composer of *Show Boat* (1927); Sigmund Romberg (1887-1951), whose *Student Prince* (1924) is a nostalgic masterpiece; and Vincent Youmans (1898-1946), responsible for the song, "Tea for Two" in *No, No, Nanette* (1925).

Predating these composers as a creator of American operetta was Victor Herbert (1859-1924), a grandson of the Irish novelist and composer, Samuel Lover (1797-1868). Herbert was born in Dublin, but upon his mother's remarriage, moved to Germany where he was educated as a violoncellist and occupied many musical posts, including membership in the Eduard Strauss (1835-1916) Waltz Orchestra, conducted by Johann Strauss' brother. His early compositions were for 'cello and orchestra: a *Suite in F* (1883) and a *'Cello Concerto in D* (1885).

After his marriage to a *prima donna* of the Court Opera in Vienna (1886), Herbert came to New York as a member of the Metropolitan Opera House Orchestra, and played his 'cello concerto with the New York Philharmonic during the next year. Although overshadowed by his wife's celebrity, Herbert managed to keep very busy, performing in and with various orchestras, including that which Tchaikovsky conducted in Philadelphia. From 1889 to 1891 he was associate conductor of the Worcester (Mass.) Festival, for which he composed an oratorio,

The Captive (1891). In 1893 he replaced P. S. Gilmore as bandmaster of the Twenty-Second Regiment Band.

At this time William MacDonald, manager of the Boston Ideal Opera Co., asked Herbert for an operetta, which turned out to be *Prince Ananias* (1894), the first of forty which were to come from his pen during the next thirty years. Meanwhile, Herbert continued composing and from 1898 to 1904 was conductor of the Pittsburgh Symphony Orchestra. All his previous experiences served him in good stead. He had a gift for captivating melody, a command of the Viennese waltz tradition, together with a freshness and vitality that communicated itself to audiences. Because of his performing and conducting education, he invested his operettas with far more substance than those of his colleagues. Among his many successes were *The Fortune Teller* (1898); *Babes in Toyland* (1903); *Mademoiselle Modiste* (1905); *The Red Mill* (1906); *Naughty Marietta* (1910); *Sweethearts* (1913); and *Eileen* (1917).

Another prominent composer of American light opera was Reginald De Koven (1859-1920), an exact contemporary of Herbert's who, although born in Connecticut, was educated abroad, studying with Leo Délibes, among others. Returning to America, he became an orchestral conductor and music critic, as well as the writer of the very successful *Robin Hood* (1890-91), in which is his celebrated song, "O Promise Me." Like Herbert, De Koven tried his hand at grand opera but found his true metier in operetta, songs and incidental pieces. He was essentially a melodist with a keen sense of orchestration and a marked dignity in his compositions.

AMERICAN BANDMASTERS

In another area of popular music, the United States made an unique contribution in the creation of stirring marches scored for symphonic band. If, as a visitor related, Hindus were whistling "Oh Susanna" on the streets of New Delhi, they may also have been tapping their feet to strains of Sousa marches which quickly became known worldwide. The father of the concert band was Patrick Sarsfield Gilmore (1829-1892), who came to Canada from his native Ireland, but soon settled in Massachusetts, where he organized his own group. He served as a Federal bandmaster during the Civil War and wrote "When Johnny Comes Marching Home Again" (1863), which remained a favorite tune long after hostilities were ended.

It was John Philip Sousa (1854-1932), however, who carried further the virtuoso band and created a standard that is still bearing splendid fruit. The son of a Portuguese father and a Bavarian mother, Sousa was born in Washington, D.C. and entered the U.S. Marine Band when he was thirteen. At eighteen he was directing an orchestra at a Washington variety theater. In 1876 Sousa played under Offenbach when that composer visited Philadelphia. And in 1880 he was appointed conductor of the Marine Band, a position he retained until he resigned in 1892 to form his own band, with which he toured annually until his death. By all accounts Sousa was a delightful personality and a witty and fascinating *raconteur*.

As a musician, Sousa had an intimate knowledge of his instrument. He encouraged beauty of tone, invented novel instrumental combinations and enabled the wind band to reproduce the nuances of a symphony orchestra. Although he composed comic operas, dances and songs, above all he was the "March King," even as Johann Strauss was the "Waltz King." Sousa had the knack of creating sharply-etched melodies and infectious rhythms, scored brilliantly and convincingly. Among his marches are *El Capitan; Semper Fidelis; The Washington Post;* and, of course, *The Stars and Stripes Forever*.

Continuing the line of creative bandmasters was Edwin Franko Goldman (1878-1956), who came from a musical family. He studied with Dvořák at the National Conservatory in New York and subsequently was appointed solo cornetist with the orchestra of the Metropolitan Opera. His ideal, however, was to form a symphonic band and this he achieved in 1911. Advancing the goals of Sousa, he endowed his group with the elasticity and scope of an orchestra. He arranged masterworks from Bach to Raval with a masterly grasp of instrumentation and also commissioned compositions specifically written for the medium. His open-air concerts became a fixture of New York's musical life, whether on the Columbia campus, in Prospect Park, Brooklyn or in Central Park. His most famous march is entitled *On the Mall,* where so many of his concerts took place. It has an irresistible lilt that sets audiences humming whenever it is performed.

JAZZ AND ITS ANTECEDENTS

The late "Fats" Waller (1904-1943) once said of jazz, "If you gotta ask what it is, you'll never know." Perhaps he was right. But its influence has been so great that we cannot dismiss it quite that abruptly. To most of the world jazz represents the typical American idiom and our only important contribution to music through the ages, showing an American spirit of adventure and daring that had been absent from the music of our academic composers. Actually, jazz is a synthesis of several elements: African, European and American. From Afro-Americans comes the most prominent feature—percussive rhythm. From Europe comes the harmony, polyphony and form. And from American folk sources come the components of brass instruments, Cuban dance patterns and "blues."

Ragtime preceded jazz, appearing on the musical scene about 1895. It consisted of an essentially regular duple accompaniment, often of the "um-pah" variety and strongly accented on primary beats, combined with one or more melodies that fight against the fundamental accents, either through stress on the offbeats (false accentuation) or by a re-arrangement of movement within the barlines. A characteristic of rag-time was the so-called "Scottish Snap" which we have mentioned earlier, and which we meet in Debussy's "Golliwog's Cakewalk," *i.e.,* ♪♩ ♪♩♩. The syncopation of such works as "The Maple Leaf Rag," composed in St. Louis by Scott Joplin (1869-1917), is a relatively simple af-fair. "Jelly Roll" Morton (1885-1941), composer of "Tiger Rag" and Irving Berlin (1888-   ), who wrote "Alexander's Ragtime Band" (1912) are two composers who aided the transition from ragtime to jazz.

An extension of the Negro folk **blues** augmented the scalar and stylistic resources of jazz. Most conspicuous was the persistent use of "blue" notes; that is, the flatting, in a major scale, of the third and seventh degrees, resulting in a polymodal situation not unlike that practiced by the Impressionists during the early 1900's. Erik Satie is quoted as saying, "What I love about jazz is that it's 'blue' and you don't care." "Blues" developed after the Civil War, probably from field work songs. The earliest published works were those of William Christopher Handy (1873-1958), a schoolteacher and minstrel man, who composed the "Memphis Blues" (1911) and the famous "St. Louis Blues" (1914). Dorothy Scarborough reports an interview with Handy, in which he stated that each of his "blues" was "based on some old Negro song of the South, some folk song I heard from my mammy when I was a child . . . I can tell you the exact song I used as a basis for any one of my blues." Huddie ("Leadbelly") Ledbetter (1888-1949), twice jailed for murder, also forwarded the cause of the "blues" through his genuine talent as a folksinger.

No one is sure about the origin of **jazz.** Even the name is somewhat of a mystery. O. S. Osgood ruminates about "Razz's Band" in New Orleans, but discards the etymology and goes on to speak of Chas. or *Chaz* Wash-ington in Vicksburg. Vincent Lopez suggests that the word comes from *jazzbo,* a corruption of Jasper, a circus roustabout, while Kingsley says it is "a form of the word common in the varieties, meaning the same as *hokum* or low comedy verging on vulgarity." Clay Smith adds the il-luminating insight that "If the truth were known about the origin of the word jazz, it would never be mentioned in polite society!" Despite its

Fig. 83. "Composition with Clarinets and Tin Horn"—Ben Shahn. The "blues" is an original American contribution to music through the ages. In them is mirrored the despair of the displaced. (Courtesy The Detroit Institute of Arts.)

hazy ancestry, we do know that the term was used early in the twentieth century on San Francisco's Barbary Coast and in the South.

If ragtime issued initially from St. Louis, jazz is a product of New Orleans—from the shanties, the dram shops and the brothels. Brass bands had mushroomed after the Civil War and came to be used among the *demi-monde* for ceremonial occasions, such as parades and funeral processions. Gradually they also functioned as accompaniments for dances. In the years preceding World War I New Orleans jazz slowly traveled northward along the Mississippi River to Chicago. The ensembles were still small and consisted of a bi-division of forces between rhythm and melodic instruments: on the one hand, tuba, banjo and drums; on the other, trumpets and trombones. In Chicago the bands grew larger in size; the piano and double bass supplanted the tuba and banjo; and reed instruments were added. Eventually the movement shifted its center to New York and the "Dixieland" style was diffused.

The British critic, Ernest Newman, has made an interesting analogy between jazz and the procedures of composers of fourteenth-century England.

> In that epoch men were just beginning to realize dimly what a jolly effect could be made by a number of people singing different things at the same time. As yet they did not know how to combine different melodic strands, so they indulged experimentally in a sort of catch-as-catch-can descant . . . The singers, amateurs like the early jazzers, used to decide upon a given *canto firmo* and then all improvise upon it simultaneously . . .

Copland qualifies this idea by noting a basic difference, when he writes, "Our polyrhythms are more characteristically the deliberate setting, one against the other, of a steady pulse with a free pulse." In other words, the "jolly effect" is unified by a common metric scheme, "around which the melody instruments can freely invent rhythms of their own." In any case, the factor of improvisation added to the excitement and dynamism of jazz in its early history.

We might define jazz as ragtime to which was applied an improvisational orchestration, derived from the New Orleans brass bands, becoming ever more elaborate, more colorful and dissonant, until it achieved a *timbre* all its own. Because it was a spontaneous expression, jazz resisted exact notation. In spite of the markings that appeared in published scores, players took great liberties in the use of *rubato, agitato* and other devices. Its techniques have become so highly developed that ramifications have reached into the field of art music, and, in fact, have become art music. Jazz as such has revealed limitations as well as opportunities to the serious composer, but as Gershwin declared:

> Jazz is the result of the energy stored up in America. It is a very energetic kind of music, noisy, boisterous and even vulgar. One thing is certain. Jazz has contributed an enduring value to America in the sense that it has expressed ourselves. It is an original American achievement which will endure, not as jazz perhaps, but which will leave its mark on future music in one form or another.

Men like Paul Whiteman (1890-   ) and Ferde Grofé (1892-   ), at one time an arranger and pianist for Whiteman, helped make jazz "respectable." Although it is anticipating our chronology, we will cite one significant event in which these gentlemen took part. In New York's now-vanished Aeolian Hall, on February 12, 1924, Whiteman changed the face of jazz by revamping it from a "rah-rah" noisemaker to a combination of beautiful new tone colors and original effects. Says Osgood, Whiteman "made an honest woman" of jazz. It was on this evening that George Gershwin introduced his *Rhapsody in Blue,* commissioned by Whiteman and orchestrated by Grofé. In many ways it represented an amalgamation of the commercial, the folk and the serious aspects of American music in a new guise—symphonic jazz.

Richard Wright makes an eloquent statement of the appeal of "blues" and jazz in his book, *Twelve Million Black Voices,* a folk history of the Negro in the United States, when he explains:

> Why is our music so contagious? Why is it that those who deny us are willing to sing our songs? Perhaps it is because so many of those who live in cities feel deep down just as we feel. Our big brass horns, our huge noisy drums and whirring violins make a flood of melodies whose poignancy is heightened by our latent fear and uneasiness, by our love of the sensual, and by our feverish hunger for life . . . Our blues, jazz, swing, and boogie-woogie are our "spirituals" of the city pavements, our longing for freedom and opportunity, an expression of our bewilderment and despair in a world whose meaning eludes us. The ridiculousness and sublimity of love are captured in our blues, those sad-happy songs that laugh and weep all in one breath, those mockingly tender utterances of a folk imprisoned in steel and stone. Our thirst for the sensual is poured out in jazz; the tension of our brittle lives is given forth in swing; and our nervousness and exhaustion are pounded out in the swift tempo of boogie-woogie . . . We are able to play in this fashion because we have been excluded, left behind; we play in this manner because all excluded folk play.

*   *   *   *   *

During the adolescence of American music, extending irregularly through 1920, at least three lines of endeavor guided composers: one which trudged in the shadow of European Romanticism; another that, while using the same techniques and forms, sought a native subject matter in the folk resources of the nation; and, finally, that which synthesized African, European and American commercial elements, resulting in the birth of jazz. Where now? We shall return across the Atlantic once again to discover the new tendencies that had entered the musical scene, potent harbingers of twentieth-century music. And we shall join with MacDowell in his courageous avowal:

> Americans should not strive with one another for ascendancy. Far better would be the comparison of American with foreign art. This gives us a standard for criticism and does no harm.

SUGGESTIONS FOR FURTHER READING

Blesh, Rudi, and Janis, Harriet, *They All Played Ragtime.* New York, Knopf, 1950.

Chase, Gilbert, *America's Music.* New York, McGraw-Hill, 1955.

Copland, Aaron, *Music and Imagination.** Cambridge, Harvard University Press, 1953.

Damrosch, Walter, *My Musical Life*. New York, Scribner, 1930.

Davis, Ronald L., *A History of Opera in the American West*. Englewood Cliffs, Prentice-Hall, 1965.

Feather, Leonard G., *The Book of Jazz*. New York, Horizon, 1957.

Franko, Sam, *Chords and Discords*. New York, Viking, 1938.

Goldman, Richard Franko, *The Wind Band*. Boston, Allyn & Bacon, 1961.

Hitchcock, H. Wiley, *Music in the United States: A Historical Introduction*.* Englewood Cliffs, Prentice-Hall, 1967.

Howard, John Tasker, *Our American Music*. New York, Crowell, 1946.

Lang, Paul Henry, ed., *One Hundred Years of Music in America*. New York, Schirmer, 1961.

MacDowell, Edward, *Critical and Historical Essays*. Boston, Schmidt, 1912.

Mellers, Wilfrid, *Music in a New Found Land*. New York, Knopf, 1965.

Osgood, Henry O., *So This Is Jazz*. Boston, Little-Brown, 1926.

Sargeant, Winthrop, *Jazz: Hot and Hybrid*. New York, Dutton, 1946.

Semler, Isabel P., *Horatio Parker*. New York, Putnam, 1922.

Smith, Cecil, *Musical Comedy in America*. New York, Theatre Arts, 1950.

St. John, Christopher, *Ethel Smythe*. London, Longmans, 1959.

Tanner, P. O. W., and Gerow, Maurice, *A Study of Jazz*. Dubuque, W. C. Brown, 1964.

Upton, William Treat, *Art-Song in America*. Boston, Ditson, 1930.

A SAMPLER OF SUPPLEMENTARY RECORDINGS

Collections

Jazz	11-Folkways 2801/2811
Best of the Blues	Imperial 9557
Jazz, Dixieland and Chicago Style	Grand Award 33-313
Outstanding Jazz Compositions	2-Columbia C2L-31
Sousa Favorites	Mercury 50291
Sousa-Fillmore Marches	WFB 1404
What is Jazz	Columbia CL-919
Here Comes the Band (Goldman)	Decca 8185
Stout-Hearted Men (Eddy)	Harmony 7142

Music of Individual Composers

Beach, Mrs. H. H. A., *Trio for Violin, 'Cello, Piano, Op*. 150

Cadman, Charles Wakefield, *American Suite* (1937)

Chadwick, George, *Tam O'Shanter* (Sym. Ballad—1915)

Chaminade, Cécile, *Concertino for Flute, Op*. 107

Converse, Frederick, *Mystic Trumpeter* (1905)

Foote, Arthur, *Night Piece for Flute and Strings* (1917)

Gilbert, Henry F., *Dance in the Place Congo* (1906)

Kern, Jerome, *Music of Jerome Kern*

MacDowell, Edward, *Concerto No. 2 in d for Piano, Op*. 23
    Sonata Eroica, Op. 50
    Suite No. 2, Op. 48 ("Indian")
    Woodland Sketches

Morris, Harold, *Passacaglia, Adagio and Finale* (1955)

Parker, Horatio, *Hora Novissima*

Powell, John, *Rapsodie Nègre, for Piano and Orchestra* (1918)

* Available in paperback edition.

OPPORTUNITIES FOR STUDY IN DEPTH

1. As many compositions, especially piano pieces and songs, are available by composers mentioned in this chapter, but relatively few are recorded, if practical, develop a program for classroom performance of selected works, devoting a period of time afterwards to discussion of the strengths and weaknesses, affinities and individualities of the works heard.

2. Because of their relatively minor positions in the larger canvas of music through the ages, we have omitted many composers who are occasionally represented in recitals or in church music. Investigate and compile a capsule vignette for one or all of the following: Dudley Buck (1839-1909); William Wallace Gilchrist (1846-1916); Harry Rowe Shelley (1858-1947); Oley Speaks (1874-1948); Felix Borowski (1872-1956); Constantin Sternberg (1852-1924).

3. We have briefly noted the position of the female composer, more obvious for her absence than presence in music history. Prepare a paper devoted to women composers and formulate hypotheses for their relative lack of distinction in the field of composition. Selections might include: Margaret Ruthven Lang (b. 1867); Mary Turner Salter (1856-1939); Mana Zucca (1887-   ); Carrie Jacobs Bond (1862-1946); Mary Howe (1886-1964); Marion Bauer (1887-1955); Louise Talma (1906-   ).

4. John Philip Sousa earned the title of "March King" deservedly, as he contributed a typically American spirit to the military march, widely copied but never surpassed. Prepare a teaching unit about this colorful composer, utilizing excerpts from his works, for presentation to a class of slow-learner teenage boys in junior high school. Allow time for guided group discussion.

5. Make a detailed study of MacDowell's four piano sonatas, using devices of harmonic and formal analysis as well as over-all exploration of style, mood and depth of expression. On the basis of this, relate his work to that of European contemporaries.

6. Write a paper about New England composers we have discussed as they compare to their literary colleagues. Van Wyck Brooks' *Flowering of New England* provides a frame of reference.

7. Many of the conservatories and departments of music in America were founded during the period we have just surveyed. Select one for intensive study, and assemble an outline of data concerning it and its contributions to the American musical scene.

8. Examine music of any one of the early schools of jazz, and act as resource leader for a class discussion of findings.

VOCABULARY ENRICHMENT

academicism	"blues"
concert band	ragtime
MacDowell Colony	jazz
"tomahawk vocabulary"	schools of jazz
spirituals	improvisational orchestration

PART X

Music of the Twentieth Century

Chapter 26.

NEW TENDENCIES—IMPRESSIONISM

Car nous voulons la Nuance encor
Pas La Couleur, rien que la Nuance!
Ah! La Nuance seul fiance
Le rêve au rêve et la flûte au cor.

(For we wish above all—nuance,
No color, nothing but half-shades!
Ah! Nuance alone joins
Dream to dream and flute to horn).

—Paul Verlaine, (1844-1896)

In the kaleidoscopic rise and fall of structural forms, schools, eras; the musical dominance of first one nation and then another; the appearance of towering geniuses whose achievements have summed up their era—we are confronted with a single irrefutable principle—the inevitability of change. If we could confine art within definition and standardization, its death knell would be sounded. Its dynamic essence and its power to escape from limitations, have made it possible for one civilization to produce a Palestrina, a Bach, a Beethoven, a Chopin, a Wagner, a Brahms, a Debussy, a Stravinsky and a Hindemith.

The Old and the New

There is constant battle between the static and the dynamic in art; the Romantic and the Classic; absolute and programmatic; substantial and formal; secular and sacred; simple and sophisticated; popular and esoteric; natural and artificial; vocal and instrumental. Every epoch thinks it has to meet a situation which has never risen before; but if it were only realized, people of every age have had the same problems.

Art cannot be separated from its social and political background. And the several arts reflect more or less the same tendencies, eccentricities and boundaries. If one does not like the phases art expresses today, one must examine outside conditions. Shafts of unrest, of speed, of technological change, have driven deep into the marrow of the universe and left their marks as "signs of the times" on dance, drama, poetry, sculpture, painting, architecture and music.

What did the nineteenth century know of *whole-tone scales,* of *mystic chords,* of *polytonality,* of *atonality* or of *oscillators?* This new terminology is token of transformations that have taken place. If one were to be plunged without preparation into a concert of contemporary music, one's ears would probably rebel and the brain register incoherent, disagreeable impressions. The road must be taken step by step and the new country reached by comfortable stages. No one can promise that the scenery will be appreciated along the way. Traveling is neither in a stagecoach, a victoria, nor by bicycle, but by automobile or jet aircraft. An airplane-consciousness is an indispensable adjunct for the appreciation and understanding of the twentieth-century art.

Liking or not liking contemporary music is largely a matter of temperament and experience. Some find in it fascination, color, vividness of rhythm, originality and a relation to the spirit of the times; others come to it with preconceived prejudices, hating it because they cannot fit it to the principles and rules which applied to the masterpieces of the past. Many treat it with derision because it is human nature to decry and laugh at what is not understood.

Every new work is not a masterpiece; neither are many innovations more than new twists to old ideas. But out of these may come grist for another's imagination and creative gifts, and the next generation will choose what it wants and needs from the musical repertory of the present age. George Dyson warns us of the danger in assuming "that even the most convincing of the immediate products of reform have more than temporary significance," and he says further, "It is the natural privilege of each succeeding generation to point out how blindly its fathers have erred, and in the historical perspective of criticism there is no feature more striking than the high confidence with which men have uttered prophetic blunders."

The dynamic line of the arts is not always a *crescendo.* Not every age is a great creative age. In looking back through history we see which periods were fruitful and which were barren. As a rule, however, transitions are not as radical as they may seem at the time.

*   *   *   *   *

The twentieth century opened with Strauss at the height of his power; Debussy was just coming into prominence; Schönberg was turning away from the influences of Wagner, Strauss and Mahler, and beginning his experiments in tonality; Alexandre Scriabin, who had paid tribute to Chopin and the Russian nationalists, was forging his own musical mysticism; Stravinsky had hardly made up his mind to follow music and had not yet met Diaghilev, a director of Russian ballet. To these divergent personalities may be traced many of the characteristics of present-day music. While they are directly responsible for much of the music of the twentieth century, causes for the changes lay deeper than individuals, who merely reflected them.

World thought was in revolt against Classicism before Romanticism was effected. And similarly, Romanticism in literature, painting and music was to be cast aside or reshaped as Symbolism, Impressionism, post-Impressionism, Expressionism and numerous other -isms. The future will separate the chaff from the wheat. Meanwhile, we can but acquaint ourselves with some of the ideas and means underlying twentieth-century music which, after all, is our music and has something to say of our age.

IMPRESSIONISM

To define **Impressionism,** we must turn to painting and literature. The term was first applied in derision to a maverick school of French painters, who, rejected by the official Academy, mounted an exhibition that included Claude Monet's picture, *Impression: Soleil levant* (*Rising Sun,* 1867). In this and other of his works, Monet succeeded in fixing the fugitive changes of nature, thus accentuating the meaning of the term, Impressionism. A colleague, Edouard Manet (1832-1883), in drawing away from the "true to nature" idea, one that had ruled art since the Renaissance, made a study of the effects of light and atmosphere on color, resulting in a *plein-air* or fresh air movement from the studio to the out-of-doors. The painter became intensely interested in the emotional reaction to what the eye beheld. He began to speculate and evolve new techniques. A choice had to be made between "reality as the eye sees it and the world of action as the mind perceives it," to quote Stephen Bourgeois. In other words, in place of photographic realism is substituted an emotional reaction, and this to more or less commonplace scenes and objects and human beings. A parallel movement occurred in French poetry under the aegis of a group designated as the Symbolists, who exploited words in their most sensuous capacity, striving to create a verbal music unbound from precise meaning—as Verlaine writes—suggestive of halfshades and nuance.

Musical Impressionism followed the lead of her sister arts in throwing off the grandiose and the intellectual logic of development in favor of suggesting images—a thought, an emotion, a poem, a scene, an object—used not to reproduce tangible or concrete things but to suggest the feelings aroused by the image, with Gallic clarity revealing subjective impressions translated into mystic, exotic, shimmering sound masses. As Debussy wrote, "The music I desire must be supple enough to adapt itself to the lyrical effusions of the soul and the fantasy of dreams." Just as poets employed the rhythms and sounds of language, and painters the

Fig. 84. "Mlle. Gachet at the Piano"—Vincent van Gogh, 1890. In attempts to convey the impression of emotions aroused by an image, new techniques and a new aesthetic were developed. (Courtesy Kunstmuseum, Basle.)

rhythms of line and color, so musicians searched for new concepts of rhythm, harmony and melody to delineate sentiments that often defy verbal analysis. Although Impressionism can be thought of as a species of French post-Romanticism, for it retained many elements of the Romantic aesthetic, it reworked the musical vocabulary and syntax and assumed international proportions.

CLAUDE-ACHILLE DEBUSSY

In many ways the extension of French literary and artistic Impressionism to music was the achievement of one man, Claude-Achille Debussy (1862-1918). He was first brought to music by Mme. de Sivry-Mauté, a pupil of Chopin and mother-in-law of Paul Verlaine. At eleven Debussy entered the Paris Conservatory where his career was stormy, because of his disrespect for the sacred rules of traditional composition and his disturbing originality, but successful, because of his undeniable talents. At the Conservatory he studied with César Franck (improvisation) and Ernest Guiraud (composition), and received prizes for piano and accompanying and, finally, the coveted *Prix de Rome* (1884) with a cantata, *L'Enfant prodigue* (*The Prodigal Son*). During several summers before this, the young man had been employed as house pianist by Mme. von Meck, Tchaikovsky's patroness. With her he visited Switzerland, Italy, Austria and in 1881 and '82 he visited Russia, where he became acquainted with the works of Balakirev, Borodin and Rimsky-Korsakov. He was attracted by the peculiar modulations of the folksongs. The effect of these experiences was to create a new and original color in his own composing. Moussorgsky's influence on his music, which is strongly apparent in the score of the opera, *Pelléas et Mélisande,* is of a later date.

Debussy's first period of creativity closed when he joined the group of Symbolists and Impressionists after his return from Rome. His songs of 1876-1890 attest to an extreme individuality and sensitivity and include, among others: *"Beau soir"* (*"Lovely Evening"*); *Fêtes galantes,* of which *"Mandoline"* and *"Fantoches"* are the most famous; and *Ariettes oubliées* ("Forgotten Songs"), six of his loveliest early songs, on poems by Verlaine: *"C'est l'extase"* ("Ecstasy"), *"Il pleure dans mon coeur"* ("My heart is weeping"), *"L'ombre des arbres"* ("In the shade of the Trees"), *"Chevaus de bois"* "(Merry-go-round"), "Spleen" and "Green." The *Deux Arabesques* (1888) and the *Suite Bergamasque* (1890-1905), from which comes *"Clair de lune,"* and six other piano pieces, also belong to this early phase. Works written at Rome include *Le Printemps* (*Spring*) for orchestra and *La Damoiselle élue* (to Rossetti's *The Blessed Damozel*) for orchestra and chorus.

His first major composition was the well-known *Prélude à l'après-midi d'un faune* (*Prelude to the Afternoon of a Faun,* 1894), an eclogue for orchestra, after Mallarmé's poem. From the first notes of the hauntingly chromatic flute solo that opens the work, we enter a magic world of sensuality and wonder and we encounter musical innovations which were to become mannerisms of Impressionism: a continuity of theme and fluidity of rhythm; a delicate dynamic scheme; gliding parallel chords; the whole-tone scale; and a sensitive, limpid instrumentation.

Debussy's next compositions for orchestra were three *Nocturnes* (1899), including *Nuages* (*Clouds*), *Fêtes* (*Festivals*) and *Sirènes* (*Sirens*). The first two are heard more often than *Sirènes,* in which Debussy introduced a chorus of women's voices without words. In 1905

La Mer (The Sea) appeared, and it is considered by many Debussy's most beautiful score. His works for orchestra close with three *Images* (1906-12)—*Gigues tristes, Iberia* and *Rondes de printemps.*

Among his vocal works, composed between 1890 and 1913, are some thirty songs on texts by Baudelaire, Verlaine, Pierre Louÿs, Charles d'Orléans, Tristan L'Hermitte, François Villon and Mallarmé and *Trois Chansons de Charles d'Orléans* for unaccompanied mixed chorus (1908).

Debussy's only string quartet was written in 1893 and has been a source work for twentieth-century composers. Of it César Franck said, *"C'est de la musique sur les points d'aiguilles,"* meaning it is "split-hair" music. Lockspeiser comments, "The quartet is unique among Debussy's works in that it shows him at the beginning of his career with one foot in the camp of Franck and his followers and the other in the revolutionary world he was about to enter . . ." According to Hill, Debussy's desire to create a style similar to the methods of Impressionist painters was achieved by avoiding academic development of musical ideas; by relaxing some of the conventional indications of tonality; and by using harmony largely as a means of *coloristic* effect. In the quartet Debussy demonstrated his ideas in absolute music. He created a highly-original work in cyclical form and exhibited an unparalleled example of economy in the use of material and detail. Other chamber music includes a work for chromatic harp, *Danse sacrée et Danse profane,* with string-orchestra accompaniment (1904) and a *Rhapsodie* for clarinet and piano (1910).

No work since *Tristan und Isolde* had shaken the traditional foundations of opera as did Debussy's *Pelléas et Mélisande,* based on Maeterlinck's drama and produced at the *Opéra Comique* in 1902, with Jean Perier and Scottish-American Mary Garden in the title roles. It "exhibited not simply a new manner of writing opera," says Lawrence Gilman, "but a new kind of music—a new way of evolving and combining tones, a new order of harmonic, melodic and rhythmic structure . . . The thing had never been done before, save in a lesser degree by Debussy himself in his then little known earlier work."

Debussy worked for almost ten years on the score. It was "revolutionary" in the extreme, if one remembered Wagner and Strauss. And yet, Debussy succeeded in doing what Wagner had tried to do—writing an opera in which text, action, and music should be a blended perfection; in orchestrating so that the word should not be covered by the music; in eliminating all vocal melody in the set forms of *arias,* duets or concerted numbers; and avoiding orchestral thematic development. The sincerity with which Debussy sought to engulf his individuality in that of the personalities of the drama, and his intense desire to separate himself from the artificialities of the theater relate him to Gluck as an operatic innovator.

Lawrence Gilman in 1907 described *Pelléas et Mélisande* as:

> . . . written for the voices, from beginning to the end, in a kind of recitative which is virtually a chant . . . in which an enigmatic and wholly eccentric system of harmony is exploited; in which there are scarcely more than a dozen *fortissimo* passages in the course of five acts; in which, for the greater part of the time, the orchestra employed is the orchestra of Mozart—surely, this is something new in modern musico-dramatic art; it requires some courage, or an indifference amounting to courage, to write thus in a day when the plangent and complex orchestra of the *Ring* is considered inadequate, and the 113 instruments of *Salome,* like the trumpeters of an elder time, are storming the operatic ramparts of two continents.

With *Pelléas et Mélisande,* Debussy's style was at its meridian; it is the first work in which he completely achieved his aims. Obviously he had digested Wagner, although disapproving of his musical methods; also Chabrier, Franck, Fauré, Duparc and even Massenet. He departed from their chromaticism, however, and the despotism of the major and minor modes, deliberately reviving medieval Church modes which he used with new freedom, imagination and effective charm. (He knew his plainsong well!)

Debussy broke down slavish adherence to harmonic principles such as one learns in student days, recognizing no rules save those of taste. Instead of resolving each chord according to method, he allowed them to progress with smooth fluidic grace. His highly receptive nature and the subtlety of his dynamic and harmonic sense place Debussy in the same relation to the early twentieth century as Chopin was to the nineteenth. Debussy's ears were extremely sensitive and he heard overtones unnoticed by the average listener. Musicians trained to hear along conventional lines had difficulty in believing that Debussy was not perversely combining sounds merely to create bizarre effects.

During the Paris Exposition of 1889, Debussy was a frequenter of the Javanese concerts. The results of the concentrated attention he gave to the *gamelan* (Javanese and Balinese orchestras) is reported to have suggested many Impressionistic and colorful *timbres,* including the whole-tone scale. The **whole-tone scale** was not original with Debussy but on account of his characteristic and expert use of it, it has been completely identified with his work. He may have heard it in the Javanese harmonies, or in the compositions of Rimsky-Korsakov and the other Russians; he may have deduced it through his study of the old modes. Yet it may be that in the functional evolution of the overtone series, the day of the whole-tone scale had arrived and Debussy was its chosen prophet.

Debussy was striving to establish a French music that should free itself from the influence of Teutonic Romanticism. He believed that the

German school of the nineteenth century was foreign to the French temperament, and he engaged in a study of French *clavecin* compositions of the eighteenth century to recapture the lost speech, a native tongue that would express the soul of the French people. He continued the propaganda begun by the *Société nationale de musique*.

Practically all Debussy's piano music belongs to his second period. Replete with the resources that make up Impressionism, it created a new literature for the instrument, demanding a new style of touch, a new technique and a new use of dynamics. Alfred Cortot points out that two of the earlier works, *Danse* and the *Suite Bergamasque,* "are descriptive in type, creating *sensations* rather than *sentiments*. Here I have touched on one of the secrets of Debussy's incisive and penetrating genius," Cortot continues:

> He had so perfect a faculty for crystallizing in sound visual impressions, whether direct or suggested, by the imagination, by the plastic arts or by literature, that he could turn the full force of his art into a channel of sensations hitherto hardly ever opened to music at all . . . And rather than work on our feelings by the poignancy of personal emotion, rather than create a tone-architecture of lovely line and form . . . he contrives, in a hidden sensuousness of linked chords, in the sinewy throb of a rhythm or the sudden mystery of a silence, to let fly this secret arrow whose delicious, subtle poison drugs us, almost without our realizing it, into the sensation which he deliberately intended; and we experience it as intensely as in actual reality.

Among the piano works coming from Debussy's pen in the years between 1901 and 1913 are *Pour le Piano* (*Prélude, Sarabande, Toccata*), *Estampes* (*Engravings*), *D'un cahier d'esquisses* (*From a Sketch Book*), *Masques, L'Isle joyeuse* (*The Island of Joy*) and *Images,* Bk. 1 in 1905 and Bk. 11 in 1907, including *Reflets dans l'eau* (*Reflections in the Water*) and *Poisson d'or* (*Goldfish,* suggested by a Chinese lacquer panel). In 1908 the delightful children's album, *Le Coin des enfants* (*The Children's Corner*) appeared, dedicated to Debussy's little daughter, "Chouchou," who used to draw the manuscript around in a toy wagon and tell anyone who would listen, "This is my music, my father wrote it for me." Cortot places *The Children's Corner* with Schumann's *Kinderscenen,* Moussorgsky's *Chambre d'enfant* (*The Nursery*) and Gabriel Fauré's *Dolly.*

Hommage à Haydn followed in 1909, one of six pieces by Debussy, Dukas, Reynaldo Hahn (1875-1947), d'Indy, Ravel and Widor, to be succeeded in 1910 by the significant *Douze Préludes* (*Twelve Preludes*), in which are found *Danseuses de Delphes* (*Delphic Dancers*), an excellent example of Debussy's modal harmony; *Voiles* (*Sails,* written almost entirely in the whole-tone scale); the deceptively simple *La Fille aux cheveux de lin* (*The Girl with the Flaxen Hair*); *La Cathédrale engloutie* (*The Engulfed Cathedral*), based on a Breton tale of a Cathedral in the inundated isle of Ys, supposed to be seen occasionally by peasants who hear the chimes and chanting of priests; *La Danse de Puck,* in which Shakespeare's Puck is represented with humor and charm; and *Minstrels,* a delightful music-hall picture in which Debussy shows his knowledge of American ragtime.

A second book of *Douze Préludes* was published in 1913. Although these works bear a date which carries Debussy into his later period, some of them may have been written earlier, as their style and intention relate them definitely to the outright Impressionism of the first group of *Préludes.* Indications of a changing technique are visible, however. Among them is *La Puerto del Vino,* the famous gate at Granada, of which Manuel de Falla had sent Debussy a picture postcard; *General Lavine-Eccentric,* a portrait of an American entertainer dancing in Debussy's version of ragtime rhythms; and *Hommage à S. Pickwick, Esq., P.P.M.P.C.,* an ironic bow to Dickens' hero, in which Debussy's humor was never more delightfully displayed.

The theater again claimed Debussy's attention in 1911 when he wrote *Le Martyre de Saint Sébastien* (*The Martyrdom of St. Sebastian*) for chorus and orchestra to Gabrielle d'Annunzio's play. It has not yet made its way successfully, although the music is profound and beautiful. Debussy also composed three ballets for Diaghilev: *La Boite a joujoux* (*The Box of Toys,* 1913) which was written for piano, *Khamma* (1912), an Egyptian story, and *Jeux* (1913).

When the First World War began, Debussy showed signs of the incurable carcinoma which led to his death six months before the Armistice. During this harrowing period he wrote a *Berceuse héroique,* dedicated to Albert I of Belgium and a song, *Noël pour les enfants qui n'ont pas de maisons* (*Christmas Song for the Homeless Children*). He also composed a group of *Six Épigraphs antiques,* which reflect his studies of old music. Asked to edit Chopin's works for a French publisher, Debussy, as a result, wrote twelve *Études* (1915), dedicated to the memory of the Polish composer. The same year he composed a work for two pianos, *En blanche et noir,* showing signs of new ideas which later were developed by younger men. His last works were chamber music in which Debussy obviously attempted simplification and disclosed a neo-Classic spirit which again presaged the future. These included a sonata for flute, viola and harp (1915), one for 'cello and piano (1915) and another for violin and piano (1917).

For several years, Debussy had contributed articles and reviews to journals, such as *La Revue blanche, Gil Blas, Le Mercure de France, Figaro, Comoedia* and the *S. I. M.,* the journal of the Paris section of the *International Society for Contemporary Music.* Some of his critical writings have been published in book form as *Monsieur Croche anté-dilettante (Monsieur Croche, the Dilettante Hater),* in which Debussy airs his opinions on a variety of musical subjects, presenting an excellent picture of his environment.

Debussy ushered in and, perhaps, closed, a new musical era and his influence upon twentieth-century composers has been extensive, both directly and indirectly. Others adapted his ideas to their needs and a wave of Impressionism threatened to inundate the musical world. Yet it was Debussy himself who was, in biographer Oscar Thompson's words, "the poet of mists and fountains, clouds and rain; of dusk and of glints of sunlight through the leaves; he was moonstruck and seastruck and a lost soul under a sky bespent with stars." As Monsieur Croche asserts:

> Discipline must be sought in freedom, and not within the formulas of an outworn philosophy only fit for the feebleminded. Give ear to no man's counsel; but listen to the wind which tells in passing the history of the world.

Erik Satie

In 1891 Debussy had met the curious musical personality, Erik Satie (1866-1925), who was then playing the piano in one of the Parisian cabarets Debussy loved to frequent. Their conversations helped Debussy clarify his own musical thinking. In fact, it was Satie who suggested the subject of Debussy's controversial opera. The son of a French father and a Scottish mother, Satie might be called the father of humor in modern music. Was he a caricaturist gone wrong or was he trying to teach by means of ridicule and satire? Teach he did, not by precept, however, nor even by example, but by conveying his musical creed to Debussy, Ravel, *Les Six* (whom we shall discuss in a later chapter), to Virgil Thomson, the American composer, and to a group of four, *L'École d'Arceuil,* named for the Parisian suburb where Satie lived.

His first works were for piano: three groups of dance forms with three pieces in each: *Sarabandes* (1887), in which we find ninth chords freely linked in intervals of fifths; *Gymnopédies* (1888), in which beautifully-drawn melodies float above simple seventh chords in the accompaniment; and *Gnossiennes* (1890), in which Gregorian and exotic modes appear. All are deceptively simple works containing materials that antedated Debussy's Impressionistic techniques.

About 1890 Satie was drawn to the mystical Order of the Rose Cross, founded by Sar Péladan, and aimed at reviving the Greek spirit in art.

Works induced by this connection exhibit a mystical preoccupation. In the three preludes for *Le Fils des Étoiles* (*The Son of the Stars,* 1891) Satie broke new ground by using chords built in fourths, anticipating Schönberg and others. Eaglefield Hull comments, "In his aspirings towards a new kind of mysticism, Satie hit upon the theory of harmonic formations by superimposed 'fourths,' thus foreshadowing Scriabin and leaving a rich harmonic heritage of which Ravel has given a good account in many of his piano pieces."

At the age of forty, Satie resumed his erratic musical education at the Schola Cantorum, working with d'Indy and Roussel. He had previously spent one miserable year at the Conservatory and studied with Guilmant. Later Satie compositions show the fruits of this self-imposed discipline in terms of contrapuntal texture and an increasing concern for form. Often they bear ridiculous titles: for instance, *Trois Morceaux en forme de poire,* which may be translated as "Three Pieces in the Shape of a Pear" (*poire* is also a French slang term, used as we use "lemon"); and *Véritables préludes flasques pour un chien* ("True Flabby Preludes for a Dog"). As Collaer notes in comparing Satie with Charlie Chaplin, "Satie's little pieces drop the comic touch into an atmosphere of delicacy, balance, and charm which endows them with incontestable poetic value."

Fig. 85. Curtain for *Parade*—Pablo Picasso. With *Parade* at the Russian Ballet in 1917 Satie planted his flag of victory.

Satie reached his zenith as a composer with the ballet, *Parade,* written in collaboration with Diaghilev, Picasso and Jean Cocteau. André Coeuroy writes: "With *Parade* at the Russian Ballet in 1917, Satie planted his flag of victory. With *Mercure* at the *Soirées de Paris* in 1924 he began his retreat. With *Relâche* at the Swedish Ballet in 1925, it was a complete rout." Satie's most serious composition was *Socrate,* a symphonic drama with female voice, adapted for the stage from dialogues of Plato and performed at a *Société nationale* concert in 1920, where, to "the velvet gentleman's" dismay, it called forth guffaws.

Perhaps the most important influence Satie exerted was that he taught musicians by means of his music to laugh and to break through the sanctimonious attitude which had grown up about traditions. As Virgil Thomson states, "He had the firmest conviction that the only healthy thing music can do in our century is to stop trying to be impressive."

PAUL DUKAS AND ALBERT ROUSSEL

Two other Frenchmen adapted features of Impressionism in individualistic fashion. One was the composer, Paul Dukas (1865-1935), who is now known outside France for but a few works. Surrounded by a group of pupils and friends in Paris, where he lived quietly, he wrote music criticism and revised operas by early French masters. A Classicist by nature, he nevertheless was an independent and employed a variety of styles which, according to Hill, "are the product of reflection, of a severe artistic conscience . . . He is to be considered as an evolutionary composer whose assimilative processes have produced a perfectly definite personality." His symphonic poem, *L'Apprenti sorcier* (*The Sorcerer's Apprentice,* 1897), based on Goethe's ballad, reminds us of Debussy's harmonic scheme and Impressionistic color, as does an opera on a Maeterlinck drama, *Ariane et Barbe-bleue* (*Ariane and Bluebeard,* 1907), which has been ranked with Debussy's *Pelléas et Mélisande,* Guy Ropartz's (1864-1955) *Le Pays* (*The Country,* 1912), Ravel's *L'Heure espagnole,* Fauré's *Pénélope* (1913) and Déodat de Séverac's (1873-1921) *Le Coeur du moulin* (*The Heart of the Mill,* 1909), as leading stage works by French composers.

An officer in the French Navy and a Schola Cantorum graduate who developed a personal musical idiom was Albert Roussel (1869-1937). Roussel's early works combine Impressionism with an exoticism that was probably the result of his travels in the Far East. *Évocations* (1912), three symphonic sketches of India, reveal this mixture. In 1913 his ballet, *Le Festin de l'araignée* (*The Spider's Feast*) was produced, taking the listener to a crystalline world of entomological fantasy which, like much Impressionistic poetry, exploits atmosphere and intimacy. An opera-ballet followed, *Pâdmâvatî* (1914-1918). With his *Suite en fa* (1927) Roussel completed the transition from post-Impressionism to neo-Classicism, best exemplified in his four symphonies. But with his use of medieval modes and Oriental scales, his tetrachordal tonality and his interest in the unifying potentials of rhythm, Roussel is clearly indebted to his Impressionistic forebears.

DEBUSSY AND MAURICE RAVEL

The soil that produced Debussy also nurtured his celebrated colleague, Maurice Ravel (1875-1937), whose talents developed in the same *milieu,* but followed a different pattern. Dukas once remarked, "One should know a great deal and make music with what one does not know," that is, be free from either dogmatism or schematization. It is hard to believe that Ravel would subscribe wholeheartedly to such a dictum. Despite claims that Ravel imitated Debussy, even a cursory examination of their styles and methods of working makes apparent fundamental divergences.

Ravel might be compared to the post-Impressionist painters in the sharp contour of his melodic outlines, in contra-distinction to Debussy's misty melting of one tone-mass into another and the formal precision of construction, in contra-distinction to Debussy's rather amorphous meanderings. Ravel is more rhythmically incisive than Debussy. With an experimenter's curiosity, Ravel shifted his style and technique to fit the individual problem of each composition—and he loved problems. In matters of form, Debussy created his own, deliberately avoiding those of either Classicism or Romanticism, while Ravel's work is based on more traditional musical architecture. Harmonically, the two differ greatly. Debussy's dissonance stems in large part from his use of chords made possible by the whole-tone scale. Ravel extended the concept of dissonance by using two or more tonalities simultaneously, a device known as **polytonality.** In the seventh of his *Valses nobles et sentimentales,* for example, Ravel combines the keys of F major and C sharp minor in an effective polyharmonic way.

MAURICE RAVEL

Maurice Ravel (1875-1937) was born in a town near the Spanish border but spent much of his life in Paris. He attended the Conservatory, where he was a student of André Gedalge (1856-1926) and Gabriel Fauré. Gedalge once recommended Mozart's quartets to Ravel as models for a chamber-music work; Ravel frankly stated that Mozart was old-fashioned and not for him. But the wise master, one of the greatest teachers France has had, gave the impetuous young composer an ultimatum—a quartet based on Mozart or he was to leave the class. Gedalge proudly stated that the lovely *F Major String Quartet* (1902-3) was the result.

An influence as strong as Debussy's was that of Erik Satie, who opened the eyes of many of the younger men. Alexis Roland-Manuel (1891-), critic, cómposer, friend, pupil and biographer, tells that when Ravel played Satie's *Sarabandes* and *Gymnopédies* for his fellow students, he completely scandalized them. Moreover, Ravel studied the works and styles of Chabrier and Liszt. If one compares Debussy to Chopin, one might compare Ravel to Liszt in the technical brilliance of his piano compositions. Ravel received the second *Prix de Rome* in 1901 but was never awarded the first, due to prejudice on the part of the judges, a factor that led to Theodore Dubois' resignation as director of the Conservatory.

As a composer for piano, Ravel is one of the most important of the twentieth century. Some of his familiar works are among his earliest, such as *Habanera* (1895), *Pavanne pour une Infante défunte* (*Pavan for a Dead Infanta*, 1899), *Jeux d'eau* (*The Fountain*, 1901) and the *Sonatine* (1903-05). Later Ravel composed *Miroirs* (1905), *Gaspard de la Nuit* (1908), *Valses nobles et sentimentales* (1911, subsequently orchestrated in part to form the ballet, *Adélaïde*) and *Le Tombeau de Couperin* (1917), a suite of six pieces based on old dance forms (each dedicated to a friend killed at the war front). *Ma Mère l'Oye* (*Mother Goose*, but no relation to our American counterpart) was originally composed as a piano duet in 1908, and afterwards orchestrated for production as a ballet.

Stage works include a short *opéra-comique*, *L'Heure espagnole* (*The Spanish Hour*, 1907) and *L'Enfant et ses sortileges* (*The Child and Its Sorceries*, 1924-25), a most interesting two-part lyric fantasy, composed on a text by Colette, in which a spoiled child vents his rage on all the inanimate things in his room only to be reproached by them when he falls asleep. The work reveals Ravel's love for children and his predilection for animism and *automata,* of which he was very fond. He once said of a mechanical chaffinch, "I can feel his heart beating."

Among his last compositions were two piano concertos (1931), one for the left hand alone, composed for, and played by, an Austrian pianist, Paul Wittgenstein, whose right hand had been amputated in World War I.

As master of the modern orchestra, Ravel stands almost without rival. We have mentioned that several of his orchestrated works were originally composed for piano. For orchestra he wrote a *Rhapsodie espagnole* (*Prélude, Malaguena, Habanera, Feria,* 1907) and *La Valse, poème chorégraphique* (1920), of which he said, "I conceived the work as a sort of apotheosis of the Viennese waltz, mixed in my mind with an impression of fantastic and fatal swirling." Ravel pictured it as being danced in an Imperial court about 1855.

Ravel came under the sway of the influential ballet producer, Diaghilev, whose *Ballet Russe* had held its first Parisian season in 1909. In 1912, Diaghilev produced Ravel's *Daphnis et Chloë*. "My intention in writing *Daphnis et Chloë* was to compose a vast musical fresco," wrote Ravel, "less concerned with archaism than with fidelity to the Greece of my dreams, which is very similar to that imagined and depicted by the French artists at the end of the eighteenth century." After the ballet appeared, Ravel arranged two concert suites ("symphonic fragments") from the score. In Suite I are *Nocturne, Interlude* and *Danse guerriere* (*Warrior Dance*) and in the second suite are *Lever du jour* (*Daybreak*), *Pantomime* and *Danse générale*.

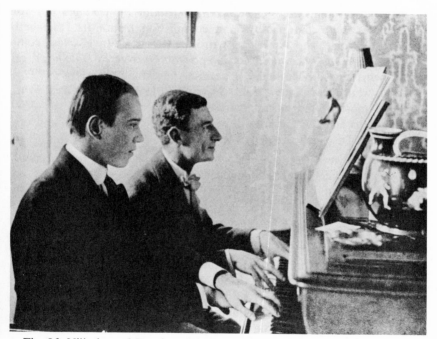

Fig. 86. Nijinsky and Ravel at the piano, 1912. Ravel composed music for the ballet, *"Daphnis et Chloë"*, at the request of the celebrated Russian dancer, Nijinsky. The score is on the music stand.

Boléro, frequently played as a concert piece, was originally written as a ballet (1928), produced at the *Opéra* by Ida Rubinstein. It created a sensation on account of the hypnotic effect produced by its obstinate rhythm and repetitious melody, fashioned after a Spanish dance (*Cachucha*). Ravel's problem here was one of orchestration; he achieved exciting variety through the *timbre* of individual instruments, and built up to a colossal climax by gradually adding more instruments, instead of the usual method of demanding greater volume from each instrument. It is one of the few musical masterworks to make a virtue of monotony.

The Ravel songs are individual and beautiful. Among them are *Sainte; Deux Epigrammes* (*Two Epigrams*) on texts by Clément Marot of the sixteenth century; *Shéhérazade,* consisting of *"Asie," "La Flûte enchantée"* (*"The Enchanted Flute"*) and *"L'Indifferent"* (*"The Indifferent One"*); five Greek melodies; four folksongs—Spanish, French, Italian and Hebrew; two Hebrew melodies; and the amusingly ironic *Histoires naturelles,* celebrating the Peacock, the Cricket, the Guinea Hen, the Swan and the Kingfisher. In 1913 Ravel composed *Three Poems by Mallarmé* for voice and chamber-music accompaniment, and in 1926 he wrote *Chansons Madécasses* (*Songs of Madagascar*) for voice, flute, 'cello and piano, on a commission from Mrs. Elizabeth Sprague Coolidge, the American patroness of arts. Ravel's last composition was *Don Quichotte à Dulcinée* (*Don Quixote to Dulcinea*), on three poems by Paul Morand, for baritone and small orchestra (1932).

Ravel, whose works stem from after as well as before the Great War, exploited most of the harmonic resources revealed by Debussy. Virtuosity, color and the picturesque vie with formality, terseness and objectivity. M. D. Calvocoressi says of him:

> In all his works Ravel stands as a typical product of French culture, essentially intelligent, versatile, although he deliberately restricts his field, purposeful, and uniformly keen in investigating the possibilities of music . . . In his musical humor the sympathetic quality is as striking as the wit.

SLAVIC IMPRESSIONISTS

The influence of Impressionism and post-Impressionism was not restricted to France but spread through continental Europe, to England and across the Atlantic to America. In its travels its features became both diffused and enriched, assuming forms sometimes far removed from those of the French. Two Slavic composers whose music discloses Impressionistic features are Alexander Nikolai Scriabin (1872-1915) and Karol Szymanowski (1882-1937). Both were interested in mysticism.

Scriabin might be described as a mystic Impressionist. His attempt at the esoteric correlation of life and art carried him almost to fanaticism. Bach's music had reflected his fervent religious nature, as did César

Franck's. Beethoven's spiritual struggles are mirrored in his works. Wagner's music dramas are the apotheosis of his philosophy of life expressed in art. Scriabin used his music as a means of producing religious ecstasy. He was the musical prophet of the Russian Symbolists, as Debussy was of the French. Their interests centered in the mysterious, the unknown, in occult practices. Scriabin conceived art as an agent for transforming life into joy.

Although at first a conservative composer, Scriabin became increasingly original, dispensing with tonality in favor of a complex chromaticism and building new chord structures, such as the **mystic chord** we mentioned earlier. Composed of the eighth, ninth, tenth, eleventh, thirteenth and fourteenth overtones, the six-tone (*i.e.,* C, F sharp, B flat, E, A and D) chord formed the harmonic basis of his ambitious *Prometheus* (*The Poem of Fire, Op.* 60, 1911), an orchestral-choral composition with a prominent piano part. This work also called for a color-organ (*clavier à lumières*), intended to project changing colors according to the scale of the spectrum. The composer desired that *Prometheus* should be regarded as a liturgical work, and "wanted to see the hall submerged in changing lights, operated by his color-organ, and to have the chorus-singers in white robes, carrying out prearranged movements," writes Eaglefield Hull.

Scriabin freed himself from traditional shackles in some ways, notably harmonically, but not in all, as his phrases are prone to squareness, being, as a rule, four measures long. His orchestration, too, was founded on Wagner's and many critics think his greatest contribution lies in his piano works, which include ten sonatas and many shorter pieces. At the time of his death, Scriabin was at work on an oratorio-opera, a *Mystery,* in which "music, gesture, scent and color" were to combine as the means of expressing his religious belief in tangible terms. This ambitious project was never completed.

The Polish composer, Karol Szymanowski (1882-1937), was influenced by a variety of styles before forming his own. Early in his career his music reminds us somewhat of Richard Strauss; later, he turned toward the ideas of Scriabin; after the First World War, he leaned toward French Impressionism. From all these he managed to synthesize a personal style which places him as the most significant Polish composer after Chopin.

Latin Impressionists

From sunnier climes comes the music of Manuel de Falla (1876-1946) and Ottorino Respighi (1879-1936), both of whom were influenced by Impressionism to some degree. De Falla, born in Cadiz, went to Paris in 1907 after winning a prize in Spain for his opera, *La Vida breve* (*Life Is Short,* 1905). He was befriended by Debussy, Ravel and Dukas and took on aspects of their styles without, however, relinquishing his interest in Spanish music. Although he reproduced the spirit of folk music in many of his compositions, he did not use genuine folksong except in a group of *Seven Popular Spanish Songs,* for which he supplied accompaniments in exquisite taste and appropriate idiom. His principal works include: *El Amor brujo* (*The Ghostly Lover,* 1915), a ballet with voice that concentrates the essence of Andalusian Gypsy music into what one authority calls a "magical vertigo"; *Noches en los jardines de España* (*Nights in the Gardens of Spain,* 1916), which expresses what the composer feels about Andalusia in a symphonic impression for orchestra and piano; *El Sombrero de tres picos* (*The Three-Cornered Hat,* 1919), a ballet on the same story as Hugo Wolf's *Der Corregidor; El Retablo de Maese Pedro* (*Master Peter's Puppet Show,* 1919), based on an incident from Cervantes' *Don Quixote,* and written for marionettes, singers and chamber orchestra; and *Concerto for Harpsichord and Five Instruments* (1926, flute, oboe, clarinet, violin and 'cello), commissioned by the late Wanda Landowska and revealing an ever more economical and stark style. In addition, de Falla composed a series of four *Homenajes* (*Homages*)—*Pour le Tombeau de Debussy* (1920), *Fanfare pour Arbós* (1933, in honor of Enrique Arbós, 1863-1939), *Pour le Tombeau de Paul Dukas* (1935) and *Pedrelliana* (1938).

A student of Rimsky-Korsakov and Max Bruch, Ottorino Respighi had a special talent for evoking the Italian scene, as evidenced in his popular symphonic poems, *Le Fontane di Roma* (*The Fountains of Rome,* 1917) and *I Pini di Roma* (*The Pines of Rome,* 1924), where his brilliant orchestral technique shines forth. Like other leaders of the Italian musical renaissance that occurred in the 1920's, Respighi studied earlier Italian and French music, resulting in several charming suites for small orchestra: *Tritico Botticelliano* (*Botticelli Tryptik,* 1927), inspired by Botticelli's paintings; *Gli Uccelli* (*The Birds,* 1927), on themes by Rameau; and *Antiche arie e danze per liuto* (1931).

ENGLISH IMPRESSIONISTS

Of the English composers influenced by Impressionism, the first was Frederick Delius (1862-1934). Of German parentage, Delius studied in Leipzig, where he was encouraged by Grieg; spent several years managing an orange grove in Florida; and lived most of his mature life in France. His works have a flavor of Impressionistic Romanticism, which he seemed to develop without attachment to any particular school. According to Streatfield, "It is the blending of the psychological with the pictorial element that gives to his music its peculiarly characteristic quality."

Delius compiled a musical biography in such orchestral works as *Over the Hills and Far Away* (1895), inspired by his native Yorkshire; *Paris, the Song of a Great City* (1899); *Appalachia* (1902), named for our Southern mountains; *Brigg Fair* (1908), an English rhapsody; *On Hearing the First Cuckoo in Spring* (1913); and *North Country Sketches* (1914). His operas include *Koanga* (1904), in which the Florida Negro plays a part and *A Village Romeo and Juliette* (1910), in which is the familiar "The Walk to Paradise Garden." Impressionistic influence is to be found in Delius' use of the whole-tone scale, in his harmonic progressions and in his treatment of orchestral color.

In Cyril Scott (1879-   ) we find another mystic Impressionist who was trained in Germany. Scott confessed to having been deeply influenced by the German poet, Stefan Georg. Hull notes that critics have spoken of Scott's kinship with Debussy but says that he owes as much to Richard Strauss as to the French composer. And "like Scriabin," Hull continues, "Scott looks to music as a means to carry further the spiritual evolution of the race . . ." His harmonic equipment is definitely Impressionistic and much of his work is infused with an exoticism, a poetical vagueness and power of evocation that discloses his affinity with the movement. Although his star is on the wane, Scott is represented to us by his piano piece, "Lotus Land" (1905).

Other English Impressionists include Frank Bridge (1879-1941), a teacher of Benjamin Britten; John Ireland (1879-1962), whose music often has a modal cast; and Eugene Goosens (1893-1962), whose prolific and frequently exotic music has been eclipsed by his activities as a conductor.

AMERICAN IMPRESSIONISTS

Charles Martin Loeffler (1861-1935) was the bridge between French and American Impressionism. He was not a mere imitator of Debussy, as has been charged, but rather he reacted to the same factors that resulted in Debussy's Impressionism. Each man, after all, is the sum of his experiences. To Loeffler's early life can be traced definite trends in his music: his French birth in Alsace; his early childhood in Russia; later years in Hungary, where he heard Gypsy music; his violin study with Joachim in Berlin; and his return to France, before coming to the United States.

Settling in Boston in 1882, Loeffler found himself among German musicians. His was a new voice and as such his music was subject to misunderstanding as was that of late nineteenth-century France. Although foreign-born, Loeffler did all his composing on this side of the Atlantic, where for twenty years he was a member of the Boston Symphony Orchestra. Philip Hale wrote in 1895 that Loeffler "believes in tonal impression rather than in thematic development," and that he "has the delicate sentiment, the curiosity of the hunter after nuances, the love of the macabre, the cool fire that consumes and is more deadly than fierce, panting flame."

Loeffler was a fastidious and self-critical worker. His compositions are those of a born Impressionist, as his earliest songs demonstrate. Whether paralleling in music the Symbolist values or reflecting his knowledge of Gregorian plainsong, he was a unique composer whose inspirations ranged from Virgil to Keats. Among his many works are the symphonic poem, *La Mort de Tintagiles* (*The Death of Tintagiles,* 1900), based on Maeterlinck's play of youth and death; *A Pagan Poem* (1901), after an eclogue of Virgil, imaginative and richly Impressionistic; a song cycle, *La Bonne Chanson* (*The Good Song,* 1902), with words by Verlaine; *Hora Mystica* (*Mystic Hour,* 1917), a choral symphony for orchestra and men's voices which evokes a mood of religious meditation; *Beat! Beat! Drums!,* after Whitman (1917), uniquely scored for unison male chorus, six piccolos, three saxophones, brass, drums and two pianos; and *Memories of My Childhood* (*Life in a Russian Village,* 1924), replete with the modality of Slavic folksong.

Our first native-born Impressionist was John Alden Carpenter (1876-1951). A student of Paine at Harvard and Edward Elgar in Rome, Carpenter's tendencies were certainly Impressionistic and he well understood the charm of rich and unusual harmonies, the use of contemporary melodic and orchestral effects and the value of humor in music. Yet as John Tasker Howard points out, when Carpenter first began experimenting with whole-tone progressions and ninth chords, he had not heard any of Debussy's music. In many of his compositions he succeeded in melding the materials of Impressionism with American urban subjects, as in amusing *Adventures in a Perambulator* (1915), which describes the sensations and emotions of a baby wheeled about by its nurse, or in the jazz-pantomime, *Krazy Kat* (1921), inspired by the comic-strip character, wherein Carpenter employs what might be called an Impressionistic jazz.

Carpenter passed through metamorphoses out of which a phase of American composition gradually evolved with its own accent and grammar. No one has better clothed Tagore's *Gitanjali* (1913) than Carpenter in such songs as "The Sleep that Flits on Baby's Eyes" and "When I Bring You Colored Toys." In his *Concertino* (1916), a lighthearted conversation between piano and orchestra, the composer introduces complex cross rhythms, ⅝ measures and a waltz with a setting more of this country than of France. Fine suggestion rather than a realistic Orientalism is apparent in the Chinese song-tone-poems, *Watercolors* (1918). With *Skyscrapers,* a ballet mounted at the Metropolitan in 1926, Carpenter achieved a high point in his career, if only for the fact that Europe saw in this work a typical expression of American urbanization.

The early death of Charles Tomlinson Griffes (1884-1920) robbed us of one of our most promising men of music. In less than forty compositions, he left an indelible mark on American music. Fundamentally a serious student, Griffes was reticent, modest and determined, a man to whom public opinion meant little. As Norman Peterkin states: "Like many of the young composers the world over, he was influenced by and temperamentally attracted to the methods and innovations of Debussy and Ravel and later to some of the advanced Russians. However, he was never enslaved by these elements he needed to set free his own personality."

Born in Elmira, New York, Griffes commenced his musical studies with Mary Broughton who, recognizing her young pupil's unusual talent, took him to Germany. There he worked with Humperdinck and Philippe Rüfer (1844-1919), eking out a living by teaching and playing. In 1907 he returned to the United States and until his death taught music at the Hackley School in Tarrytown.

German Romanticism colored his first songs, including "We'll to the Woods and Gather May" and "By a Lonely Forest Pathway." His sensitivity to stimuli, however, is glimpsed in an event that marked a turning point in his life. In his lodging house, Griffes heard some unfamiliar music emanating from a near-by apartment. He was so intrigued that he went to the pianist's door and found Rudolph Ganz playing Ravel's *Jeux d'eau.* Thereafter a new Griffes emerged in two Oscar Wilde songs, *La Fuite de la lune* ("The Flight of the Moon") and "Symphony in Yellow."

His next three compositions heralded the first important American piano composer since MacDowell. *Three Tone Pictures (The Lake at Evening, The Night Wind* and *The Vale of Dreams,* 1915) were products of an Impressionist-Romanticist. Although French in atmosphere and delicacy, they are far from imitative, coming from the hand of a creator seeking "the new, the great unfound." With *Roman Sketches* (1917), suggested by poems of William Sharpe and including "The White Peacock," Griffes showed his mastery of pure Impressionism with an individual sweep and power. The composer's love for the tenuous beauty and imagery of Fiona MacLeod's poems is reflected in his songs, as is his lifelong preoccupation with Oriental folklore.

Other works by Griffes include music for a dance-drama, *The Kairn of Koridwen* (1917), written for five woodwinds, *celesta,* harp and piano; a *Poem* for flute and orchestra (1919); a tone-poem, *The Pleasure Dome of Kubla Khan* (1919); and a *Sonata in F* for piano (1921), his last work, in which the composer reached an almost austere musical idiom.

Lawrence Gilman says of Griffes:

> He was a poet with a sense of comedy . . . Griffes had never learned how to pose—he never would have learned how if he had lived to be as triumphantly old and famous as Monsieur Saint-Saëns or Herr Bruch or Signor Verdi . . . It was only a short while before his death that the Boston Symphony Orchestra played for the first time (in Boston) his *Pleasure Dome of Kubla Khan* . . . and the general concert-going public turned aside . . . to bestow an approving hand upon this producer of a sensitive and imaginative tone-poem who was by some mysterious accident, an American! . . . He was a fastidious craftsman, a scrupulous artist. He was neither smug nor pretentious nor accomodating. He went his own way—modestly, quietly, unswervingly . . . having the vision of the few . . .

* * * * *

During the early years of the twentieth century, Impressionism had become an international style, epitomized in the music of Debussy. Just what niche the movement will occupy in the future is a matter of speculation. Aaron Copland wonders aloud concerning the durability of much of its music, so ultra-refined and "cushioned." Ernest Newman was openly hostile to it, while Paul Collaer cites Debussy, especially his *Pelléas et Mélisande,* as the point of departure for such composers as Stravinsky, Bartók and Schönberg, whom we shall discuss in the following chapter.

In concluding our discussion, we feel obliged to append some warning words *in re* labeling music as belonging to one -ism or another. We have been speaking of Impressionism and its ramifications as a new tendency in twentieth-century music, as indeed it was. Let us not forget, however, that Debussy himself was the first anti-Debussyite; that is, he would not rest content with formulae and actually disliked the word, Impressionism, intensely. Satie, Roussel and Ravel were, as was late Debussy, post-Impressionists, if by that we mean that they realized the weaknesses of full-blown discipline through freedom and listening to the winds and reached toward simplification and more solid structure. All were united in being heirs of the French cultural tradition but each followed his own artistic conscience.

Even before 1914, Impressionism had spent itself. As Collaer states:

The *fauves* began to speak their more turbulent and anguished language, and the thunderclap of *Le Sacre du Printemps* resounded. The world realized that a new era had begun in which moral values, and consequently artistic values, were undergoing a change.

SUGGESTIONS FOR FURTHER READING

Austin, William W., *Music in the 20th Century*. New York, Norton, 1966.

Bauer, Marion, *Twentieth-Century Music*. New York, 1947.

Beecham, Thomas, *Frederick Delius*. New York, Knopf, 1960.

Collaer, Paul, *A History of Modern Music*.* New York, Grosset & Dunlap, 1961.

Copland, Aaron, *Our New Music*. New York, Whittlesey House, 1941.

Cortot, Alfred, *French Piano Music*. London, Oxford University Press, 1932.

Deane, Basil, *Albert Roussel*. London, Barrie & Rockliff, 1961.

Debussy, Claude, *Monsieur Croche, the Dilettante Hater*. (*Three Classics in the Aesthetic of Music*).* New York, Dover, 1962.

Goss, Madeleine, *Bolero: The Life of Maurice Ravel*. New York, Holt, 1940.

Hansen, Peter S., *Twentieth-Century Music*. Boston, Allyn & Bacon, 1961.

Hill, Edward B., *Modern French Music*. Boston, Houghton-Mifflin, 1924.

Howard, John Tasker and Lyons, James, *Modern Music*.* New York, Crowell, 1957.

Hull, A. Eaglefield, *Scriabin*. New York, Dutton, 1916.

Hutchings, Arthur, *Delius*. New York, Macmillan, 1948.

Jankélévitch, Vladimir, *Ravel*.* New York, Grove, 1959.

Lenormand, René, *A Study of Twentieth-Century Harmony*.* Vol. 1. London, J. Williams, 1940.

Lockspeiser, Edward, *Debussy*. New York, Pellegrini & Cudahy, 1951.

Machlis, Joseph, *Introduction to Contemporary Music*. New York, Norton, 1961.

Maisel, Edward M., *Charles T. Griffes: The Life of an American Composer*. New York, Knopf, 1943.

Mellers, Wilfred, *Romanticism and the Twentieth Century*. Fairlawn, Essential Books, 1957.

Myers, Rollo, *Erik Satie*. London, Dobson, 1948.

Roland-Manuel, Alexis, *Maurice Ravel*. London, Dobson, 1947.

Salazar, Adolfo, *Music in Our Time*. New York, Norton, 1946.

Schmitz, Elie R., *The Piano Works of Claude Debussy*. New York, Duell, Sloan & Pearce, 1950.

Seroff, Victor, *Maurice Ravel*. New York, Holt, 1953.

Slonimsky, Nicolas, *Music since 1900*. New York, Coleman-Ross, 1949.

Starr, William J. and Devine, George F., *Music Scores—Omnibus,** Part 2. Englewood Cliffs, Prentice-Hall, 1964.

A SAMPLER OF SUPPLEMENTARY RECORDINGS

Carpenter, John Alden, *Concertino for Piano and Orchestra*
Skyscrapers

* Available in paperback edition.

Debussy, Claude, *Children's Corner Suite*
   La Mer
   Prélude à l'après-midi d'un faune
   Preludes for Piano
   Quartet in g, Op. 10
   Sonata No. 2 for Flute, Viola and Harp
   Songs
Delius, Frederick, *Florida Suite*
   Brigg Fair
De Falla, Manuel, *El amor brujo*
   Nights in the Gardens of Spain
Dukas, Paul, *Sorcerer's Apprentice*
Griffes, Charles T., *Poem for Flute and Orchestra*
   Roman Sketches, *Op.* 7
   Three Poems for Voice, Op. 11
   Pleasure Dome of Kubla Khan
Loeffler, Charles Martin, *Memories of My Childhood*
Ravel, Maurice, *Bolero*
   Concerto in D for the Left Hand
   Daphnis et Chloë, Suite No. 2
   Ma Mère l'Oye: Suite
   Quartet in F
   Le Tombeau de Couperin
Respighi, Ottorino, *Ancient Airs and Dances*
   The Fountains of Rome
Roussel, Albert, *Divertissement for Flute, Oboe, Clarinet, Bassoon, Horn*
   and Piano
   Spider's Feast, Op. 17
   Bacchus et Ariane, Op. 43
Satie, Erik, *Piano Music*
   Mass for the Poor
   Socrate
Scriabin, Alexander, *Piano Music*
   Poem of Ecstasy, Op. 54
Szymanowski, Karol, *Harnasie* (1926)
   Symphony No. 2 in B flat, Op. 19

OPPORTUNITIES FOR STUDY IN DEPTH

1. Due to limitations of space we have been forced to omit from our discussion of Impressionism certain French composers who also contributed to the movement. It might be interesting to find out about Florent Schmitt (1870-1958), Charles Koechlin (1857-1950), Déodat de Séverac (1873-1921) and André Caplet (1878-1925).

2. In *Music in Our Time*, Adolfo Salazar writes: "If Impressionism is the logical continuation of romantic harmony, it follows that, with Debussy and Ravel, there comes to an end a cycle of European music which began in France . . . with Hector Berlioz." Discuss the implications of this statement.

3. Investigate further the history, personalities and contributions of Impressionist

painters in France. There are many volumes available on the subject; an intimate and informative one that is recommended is Jean Renoir's *Renoir, My Father* (Boston: Little-Brown, 1962).

4. Make a critical study, working from originals or translations of one of the Symbolist poets, who include Charles Baudelaire (1821-1867), Stéphane Mallarmé (1842-1898), Paul Verlaine (1844-1896) and Arthur Rimbaud (1856-1891). Was the approach of the Symbolists essentially a musical one?

5. Satie's *Parade* (1917), a ballet based on a text by Jean Cocteau and with scenery and costumes by Pablo Picasso, took the public by storm and injected a new note into the musical scene. What was it all about? Why was it significant? Collaer (see "Suggestions for Further Reading") presents an interesting essay on this subject.

6. Compare the technique of *pointillisme* practiced by Georges Seurat and others with the resources of Debussy, as shown in the *Douze Préludes* of 1910. What importance did the presence or absence of line possess? How was it expressed?

7. Debussy and Ravel each wrote but a single string quartet and that early in their respective careers; yet each work is a masterpiece. By means of scores and recordings, prepare analyses of these compositions noting similarities and differences, instrumental treatment and manneristic devices.

8. Fauré, Debussy and Ravel all composed outstanding suites dedicated to children. Examine selected compositions for children written by master composers. Are they really children's music? Or are they perhaps evocations of memories of childhood? State a personal opinion, supported with as much evidence as possible.

Vocabulary Enrichment

Impressionism	ninth chords
Symbolists	Order of the Rose Cross
parallel chords	superimposed fourths
whole-tone scale	post-Impressionism
gamelan	polytonality
neo-Classicism	mystic chord
L'École d'Arceuil	color-organ

Chapter 27.

NEW TENDENCIES—PATHFINDERS

> The true tradition is not the symbol of a forgotten past; it is a living
> force that inspires and instructs the present . . . One associates oneself
> with a tradition in order to create something new.
>
> —Igor Stravinsky, *Poetics of Music*

If we were to look at the span of several years immediately preceding World War I, at a glance we could discern that vital and violent things were happening on the music front. In 1910 Bartók's strident *Allegro Barbaro* was born, as was Stravinsky's distinctive *The Firebird* while across the Atlantic, Charles Ives' *Sonata No. 2 for Violin and Piano* appeared. Within the next two years Schönberg completed his monumental *Gurre-Lieder* and the provocative *Pierrot Lunaire,* while Stravinsky added another significant ballet, *Petrouchka.* And in 1913, the date of the scandalous premiere of *Le Sacre,* New York was equally outraged by the Armory Show. The first concert of "noise music" took place in the following year at Milan. In 1915 a young string-player, Paul Hindemith, became concertmaster of the Opera Orchestra at Frankfurt. From these varied phenomena emitted forces still felt to this day. We might note once again that these same years witnessed Strauss' *Der Rosenkavalier,* Debussy's *Préludes,* Ravel's *Daphnis et Chloë,* Puccini's *Girl of the Golden West,* Mahler's *Das Lied von der Erde,* Sibelius' *Fourth* and Vaughan Williams' *First* and *Second Symphonies,* as well as "Alexander's Ragtime Band" and the "St. Louis Blues."

Yet however radical the new musical developments appeared, they issued from the "true tradition" to which Stravinsky refers. In the case of each composer we shall discuss in the following pages—composers who stand as pathfinders in twentieth-century music—we encounter a musician of unique artistic personality, of force and originality, who extends the threads of the past into a fabric woven to clothe a contemporary mannequin, albeit in an appropriately individual fashion. Gone but not quite forgotten are echoes of Brahms, Wagner, Mahler, Reger, Debussy, the Russian nationalists, d'Indy and Horatio Parker, as well as features of Renaissance, Baroque and Classic music. In such matters as nonfunctional harmony, contrapuntal techniques, parodistic practices, folk music investigations and the re-evaluation of consonance and dissonance, we find but a new application of old principles, whose inherent vitality is evidenced in their adaptability to a different musical environment.

In another sense, these men—Russian, Viennese, American, Hungarian, French and German in background—were uniquely responsive to life and events surrounding them. Theirs was not exclusively an ivory tower pursuit, as we shall see, although they share a common and immutable artistic integrity. With World War I the comfortable and relatively secure European *milieu* was destroyed. The tempo and rhythms of life quickened, psychological insights deepened, scientific discovery reshaped our conception of, and control over, natural forces. Inventions in communication and in locomotion increasingly enlarged our horizons and new problems as well as new sources of inspiration had to be confronted. All this with a breakneck speed that has left us reeling. The complexities of modern music can only reflect the corresponding complexity of modern life. Perhaps the estrangement between listener and creator also reflects a more profound estrangement, endemic to our time.

IGOR STRAVINSKY—LIFE

While Scriabin was attempting an esoteric correlation of life and art, a gigantic pathfinder of the twentieth century was emerging in the person of Igor Stravinsky (1882-   ). No composer of our era has been more discussed, more praised, more condemned and more imitated than he, who stands as a musical barometer of the 1900's. As Harold C. Schonberg writes:

> The famous episode in F sharp against C major in "Petrouchka," (actually anticipated by Charles Ives five years earlier) started the European polytonal school. The wild rhythms of "Le Sacre du Printemps" were almost immediately echoed by every important Western composer, even such great ones as Bartók and Prokofieff. Stravinsky's shift to neoclassicism carried musical Europe with him; he was, more than anybody, the man who drove the final nail into Wagner's coffin. He has been to music what Picasso has been to painting.

Stravinsky was born in Oranienbaum, a suburb of St. Petersburg or Leningrad, as it is now called. His father, an opera singer, urged him to study law. When he was twenty-two, however, Stravinsky was advised by Rimsky-Korsakov to take up music and for a short time Rimsky gave the young man systematic training. From this period of apprenticeship came a conventional symphony (1907) and the *Scherzo fantastique* (1909). Diaghilev (1872-1929), the Russian impresario, who at that time led a group of painters and writers and who dreamed of producing spectacles combining music, dancing and *décor,* heard the *Scherzo* and asked Stravinsky to write a work for the *Ballet Russe.* This request changed the course of Stravinsky's career and, in consequence, that of twentieth-century music. Stravinsky's collaboration with Diaghilev covered almost twenty years (1909-1928).

A musical descendant of Moussorgsky and Rimsky-Korsakov, Stravinsky's youthful crude fearlessness is more in line with the former than with the polish and refinement of the master of orchestration. Like "The Mighty Five," Stravinsky drew on native folklore and folksong but in addition he introduced to music a kind of primitivism analogous to that of Gauguin and Matisse in painting. He struck an elemental chord throbbing with vital, passionate, exuberant life. His music expresses no spirituality, no eroticism as does Scriabin's. Stravinsky's works are impersonal, without overt sympathy or expression of opinion for what he depicts, with no attempt to preach. They are "sound structures" in the literal sense of the phrase.

MUSIC FOR THE THEATER

Among Stravinsky's compositions for the theater, first performed under Diaghilev's aegis, is *The Firebird* (1910), his initial full-fledged work, based on a fantastic story drawn from Russian sources by its choreographer, Michel Fokine. In its original version it required a very large orchestra, but in arranging the music into concert suites, Stravinsky reduced the instrumentation (1919) and in further revising it (1945) retained the smaller orchestra. *The Firebird* met with an enthusiastic reception. While completing the score, Stravinsky had already, as he recounts, "had a sudden, absolutely unexpected vision . . . of the spectacle of a great pagan religious rite," to become the theme of his third ballet.

This he communicated to Diaghilev, who thereupon commissioned it. When Diaghilev visited the composer in Switzerland, however, he found him at work on a piece for piano and orchestra, which Diaghilev, when he heard the title, immediately asked to make into a ballet. With the opening polyharmonic or bitonal chords, Stravinsky had in mind a dispute between the orchestra and the piano, a protest against the long-haired Romanticist who had outlived his day. The piano solo would be a caricature of the concert style of a past generation—mere clownery. "In this, rather than in the discovery of a new chord system, is the essential newness of *Petrouchka,*" comments André Schaeffner. With the aid of Alexandre and Michel Benois, Petrouchka, the poet-pianist, was turned into a pathetic puppet, who is brought to life by a Magician or

Charlatan by means of his flute. Two other puppets, a Ballerina and a Moor, share this experience. The scene at the fair is an example of Stravinsky's use of Russian peasant life and folk tunes. John Burk comments that *Petrouchka: Scènes burlesque en 4 tableaux,* "adds yet another chapter to the *Commedia dell'Arte . . .*"

Le Sacre du printemps (*The Rite of Spring,* 1913) was arranged by Nicholas Roerich with choreography by Vaslav Nijinsky. It is an evocation of pagan Russia, involving two ideas: the primitive belief in the holiness of spring; and the consecration of the chosen one, a maiden. For this Roerich drew on prehistoric barbaric rituals. With its first performance the storm, which had been brewing against "modernism," broke with a force of antagonism comparable to that which greeted Hugo's *Hernani* in 1830. The uproar was so great that the dancers could no longer hear the orchestra, and the composer forcibly restrained Nijinsky in the wings of the theater.

Fig. 87. Stravinsky rehearsing *Le Sacre du printemps*—drawing by Jean Cocteau. At its premiere, the barbaric music of *Le Sacre* seemed outrageous and profoundly disquieting.

Lawrence Gilman states that when *Le Sacre* was given in concert form in London (1921), the music still seemed outrageous to many.

"One alarmed listener published a letter in which he declared that the *Sacre* was a threat against the foundations of our tonal institutions . . . But he affirmed, 'this music will not live—and that is my only hope.' The gentleman's only hope has been tragically disappointed," Gilman continues. "Not only has *Le Sacre du printemps* lived, but we have come to recognize that its score contained the soil and roots of much postbellum music, as *Pelléas* nourished the music of the decade before the war, and *Tristan* the music of the generation that witnessed the dying glories of the nineteenth century."

Not to be outdone, Boston contributed the following jingle, when the music was first played there.

> Who wrote this fiendish *Rite of Spring*?
> What right had he to write the thing?
> Against our helpless ears to fling
> Its crash, clash, cling; bing, bang, bing?

When it was staged in Philadelphia and New York (1930), however, *Le Sacre* was recognized as a masterpiece. Gilman wrote:

This music is profoundly disquieting,—a thing of despotic power and intensity. It has the impact and something of the mystery of an elemental force . . . This music is essentially a glorification of Spring as the supreme expression of the creative impulse—a Spring stripped bare of sentiment, austere and ruthless, yet with interludes of strange, incalculable tenderness . . . What Stravinsky has made of this conception is one of the subduing things of art . . . a thing of gigantic strength, or irresistible veraciousness . . . It teaches us again the inexhaustible responsiveness of music to new ways of apprehending life, new adventures of the imagination, new conceptions of sensibility and truth and beauty.

Rossignol (The Nightingale), begun in 1909 as an opera on a story of Hans Christian Andersen, was completed in 1914 and performed by the *Ballet Russe* in the spring. A change of style had taken place. In 1917, Stravinsky made an orchestral work of the music of a second version and called it *Le Chant du rossignol (The Song of the Nightingale)*. The music has much in it which reminds one of earlier influences of Debussy and also of Rimsky's *Coq d'or*.

Stravinsky spent the war years in Switzerland and it was there that he composed *Le Renard (The Fox, 1922)*, a chamber-opera pantomime, and *L'Histoire du soldat (The Soldier's Story)*, on a text by C. F. Ramuz, for a narrator and two pantomimists, accompanied by seven instruments. Its first performance was in 1918 at Lausanne. The suite's subtitles—"March," "Tango," "Valse," "Chorale" and "Ragtime"—

show the effect jazz was having on Stravinsky. In some parts it is extremely dissonant, but the composer did not return to his former complex manner, employing instead a severe economy of forces, perhaps dictated by wartime conditions.

Also issuing from this period (in addition to *Four Russian Songs, Three Pieces for Solo Clarinet,* two piano "Ragtimes" and a special *Étude* for pianola, a player-piano refinement) was *Les Noces* (*The Nuptials*), devoted to marriage customs in ancient Russia. Although Stravinsky began it in 1914, it was not finished until 1917 and the composer changed the instrumentation four times until, in 1923, it assumed its final form of ballet with chorus and an accompaniment of four pianos and thirteen percussion instruments. In spite of its folk basis, it is the most abstruse of all Stravinsky's earlier ballets, and marks a turning point toward simplification, the eighteenth-century musical forms and neo-Classicism.

As a consequence of national hostilities, the *Ballet Russe* moved to Italy and Diaghilev created two ballets on music of older Italian masters: *Les Femmes de bonne humeur* (*Good-Humored Matrons*), based on sonatas of Scarlatti, orchestrated by Vincent Tommasini (1878-1950); and *La Boutique fantasque,* drawn from instrumental pieces of Rossini, orchestrated by Ottorino Respighi. When the indefatigable Diaghilev discovered some unpublished music by Pergolesi, he notified Stravinsky who started rewriting and reworking the material. The result was *Pulcinella* (1920), a ballet with chorus, with *décor* by Picasso and choreography by Massine.

Too much importance should not be attached to the fact that Stravinsky had found in the sonatas of Pergolesi a delightful archaism which fitted into his mood. It did not indicate a complete change of heart, although Stravinsky had obviously changed his style after *Les Noces.* In spite of the new usage of harmony and instruments, the melodic freshness and rhythmic vivacity of Pergolesi have not been disturbed. The personnel of the orchestra was Classic but what the instruments did was purely Stravinsky. Audiences were asking themselves, however, what had happened to the once-savage Stravinsky, whose *Le Sacre* had been a high point of violent expression?

Mavra, an *opéra-bouffe* in one act after Pushkin, was performed by Diaghilev's opera company in 1922. It was not as great a success as Stravinsky was accustomed to because the public had not yet realized the transitional stage through which the composer was passing. As Collaer remarks:

> *Mavra* perplexed a great number of listeners, as did the *Octet for Wind Instruments* (1923) and the *Concerto for Piano and Orchestra,* (1924).

What was the significance of this style—this meeting ground for Bach and a certain nineteenth-century quality in which Rossini and Liszt were brought together? . . . Henceforth, and until the performance of his most recent works, critics have not ceased to be confounded . . . So, from piece to piece, *Le Sacre du Printemps* was defended against *Mavra*, *Mavra* against the *Baiser de la Fée*, the *Baiser de la Fée* against *Jeu de Cartes*.

Stravinsky called *Oedipus Rex* (1927) an opera-oratorio. The story, adapted from Sophocles, was made into a text by the composer and Jean Cocteau and was translated into Latin by Father Daniélou. It was performed with giant puppets, in order to carry out Stravinsky's idea that the actors were to be "as immovable as columns and should appear and disappear by means of a mechanical process." Here, Stravinsky was no longer in transition but had found a new style, a new language as gripping and as individual as was his idiom in *Le Sacre*. It was more profound and less cruelly dissonant. He had always a colossal facility which seemed to intoxicate him with its limitless possibilities. The facility was still there but controlled and matured, and Stravinsky remained the impersonal onlooker, retelling in music a story so horrible and tragic, that had he, with his powers of expression, been a Romanticist, it would have been unbearable to hear. For the first time since 1914, Stravinsky used a full orchestra.

In contrast to *Oedipus Rex, Apollon Musagètes* (1928) is a chamber-ballet. Stravinsky set himself a problem—to write a work in which there should be no contrast, no intrigue, even among the instruments themselves. "That *ennui* might result from such a musical asceticism did not frighten Stravinsky," says Schaeffner. Stravinsky intended to make the action choreographic "not by the relation of the rhythm of almost all music and that of the dance, but by the exclusive use of figures borrowed from the technique of the days of the white tarlatan ballet." Adolph Bolm, who created the ballet in Washington, D.C., mounted it in eighteenth-century fashion, dressing Apollo in Greek costume with a disconcerting Roman plumed-helmet, such as Handel's stage people had worn.

After straying into **neo-Romanticism** with *Le Baiser de la Fée* (*The Kiss of the Fairy,* 1928) "inspired by the Muse of Tchaikovsky," Stravinsky returned to the Greek classics for *Perséphone,* a choral ballet commissioned by French dancer Ida Rubenstein, on a poem by André Gide. The score, called a melodrama, was composed for chorus, orchestra, tenor and speaker and premiered in 1934 in Paris. "A ballet in three deals," *Le Jeu de Cartes* (*Card Party*) was written for Stravinsky's visit to America in 1937. It represents a game of poker with dancers dressed as picture cards from a deck. *Orpheus,* a distinguished ballet, was introduced in 1947.

Stravinsky has since returned to the musical theater with an opera, *The Rake's Progress* (1951) on a libretto by poet W. H. Auden and Chester Kallman, dramatizing Hogarth's well-known series of engravings. It is a singers' opera, not particularly effective on the stage, but engaging in its eighteenth-century Mozartean features. *Agon* (1957), an abstract ballet with serial features, completes the stage works of Stravinsky, unless we include a ballet commissioned by Ringling Brothers and Barnum and Bailey Circus, performed in Madison Square Garden in center ring during the spring of 1942, and scored for band, but later revised as the "Circus Polka" for symphony orchestra, and a score for Billy Rose's *Seven Lively Arts,* a Broadway musical.

OTHER COMPOSITIONS

Stravinsky has written many songs with varied accompaniments. In them the composer is humorous, ironic, sometimes tender and often more personal than in other forms of composition. Although Moussorgsky, Borodin, Debussy and Ravel may come to mind, Stravinsky always predominates. Among the more recent are *Three Songs from William Shakespeare* (for mezzo-soprano, flute, clarinet and viola, 1953) and *In Memoriam Dylan Thomas* (for tenor, string quartet and four trombones, 1954).

Masterful, if uncompromising choral works are to be found in Stravinsky's output, including a *Mass* (for mixed chorus and double wind quartet, 1948); a *Cantata* on old English texts (1952); *Canticum Sacrum* for St. Mark's, Venice (1956); *Threni,* a setting of the "Lamentations of Jeremiah" (1958); and most recently the dissonant and somber *Requiem Canticles* (1966). Best known, and perhaps most enduringly profound is the beautiful *Symphony of Psalms,* composed at Serge Koussevitsky's request for the fiftieth anniversary of the Boston Symphony Orchestra in 1930. As its name indicates, it is a choral symphony, based on excerpts from Latin Psalms. The orchestra is unique in that it contains no violins, violas or clarinets, and the choral writing is skillfully integrated into the whole of the composition.

In 1914 Stravinsky had published *Three Pieces for String Quartet,* which, as Eric White points out, tempted Amy Lowell to reproduce the idiom in poetry:

> Bang! Bump! Tong!
> Petticoats,
> Stockings,
> Sabots,
> Delirium flapping its thigh bones . . .

A *Concertino* for the Flonzaley Quartet and a *Symphonie d'instruments à vent,* written in memory of Debussy, followed in 1920. These works, with the *Octuor* for wind instruments of 1923, represent Stravinsky's beginning of activity in the realm of absolute music, after the appearance of *Pulcinella.* Nowhere, however, can we discern a mellowing, but rather we discover a more impersonal abstraction, in which the composer seems definitely and purposely to avoid emotional display of any kind.

The hour had arrived for a new Classicism. It did not originate with Stravinsky (Prokofiev had written his *Classical Symphony* in 1917) but he was sufficiently sensitive to the undercurrents of musical development to be drawn into the stream. In theory, at least, **neo-Classicism** reflected the renewed interest that composers had in the music of the eighteenth century and the late Baroque, as evinced by Hindemith's remark, "One can still learn much from 'Papa' Haydn." This retrospection and search for roots represented a further revolt against Romanticism and Impressionism, which had come to be recognized as a child masquerading in its mother's clothes. Musicians aimed at complete emancipation from the graphic, the literary, the philosophical and the emotional. As Stravinsky said, what they hoped to achieve was "a wholesome return to the formal idea. . . ."

Stravinsky combined his vigorous rhythmic impulse with a study of Bach and Handel and the hybrid result was his *Concerto for Piano and Wind Instruments* (1924), in which an affinity for pandiatonicism and for the key of C, however freely interpreted, is found. Other works in this style include the *Capriccio* for piano and orchestra (1929) and the *Concerto in D* for violin and orchestra (1931), which approached a suite in form, comprising a *Toccata, Aria I, Aria II* and *Capriccio.* According to Stravinsky and others, the difference between the Classicism of the eighteenth and nineteenth centuries, consisted of the elimination of nonessentials and condensation of material. The composer said to Guido Gatti, an Italian critic:

> The duration of a composition nowadays can no longer be measured by those of the past. For a Mozart, the invention of the theme, or of the themes, represented, if one may say so, the maximum effort; all the rest was made up in great part of a certain formalism, or at least technical skill had the upperhand over creative fantasy . . . With the developments of the theme, the repetitions, refrains, and necessary *cadenze,* the half-hour was soon reached.

> But now that in a scholastic sense this development of the theme no longer exists, and still less repetitions . . . proportions have changed, and a concerto of fifteen minutes is already a monumental work. Natu-

rally it would be easy to lengthen the duration, but what would be added would be nothing but padding, inert matter, sound, not music.

Among Stravinsky's other compositions, the following demonstrate the diversity of his instrumental and choral conceptions: *Concerto for Two Pianos* (1935), without orchestral accompaniment; *Concerto in E Flat Major,* subtitled "Dumbarton Oaks" (1938), for sixteen instruments; the cheerful *Symphony in C* (1940), written in neo-Classic style for the fiftieth anniversary celebration of the Chicago Symphony Orchestra; *Tango* (1941); *Ebony Concerto* (1945), written for jazz bandleader, Woody Herman; *Elegy* for Raoul Dufy (1959); and *Monumentum pro Gesualdo di Venosa* (1960). Collaer goes so far as to say of the compositions since 1950, ". . . these works may well represent for our time what Bach's *Musikalisches Opfer* was for the eighteenth century."

In 1934, Stravinsky, who had made Paris his home since the First World War, became a French citizen. In 1939 he came to America, and gave a series of lectures at Harvard University. The composer applied for American citizenship the next year and has since made his home in Beverly Hills, California.

Stylistic Characteristics

What most characterizes Stravinsky's long and brilliant career, analogous with that of Picasso, is his continual development, his refusal to allow audience satisfaction to influence his artistic demands upon himself. He is primarily a craftsman and problem-solver, a composer, as Alexei Haieff (1914-   ) states, "who lives by his music as a shoemaker does by his cobbling or a banker by his strategy with money." As Stravinsky himself remarked, a composer should write music "as a notary draws up a contract." Roland-Manuel adds that "Stravinsky is the most methodical man in the world and the least systematic." Ramuz, friend of his Swiss years, commented that "Stravinsky's writing table resembles the instrument stand of a surgeon . . . Here was an order which did enlighten, by its reflection of an inner clarity."

We have traced Stravinsky's musical development from the association with Diaghilev, when he wrote ballets which shook the foundations of the musical world. He caused a harmonic and orchestral upheaval in a day of revolution. Polytonality, polyharmony, **polyrhythms** (many different rhythms heard simultaneously), **multi-rhythms** (a rapid succession of metric changes), **atonality** (the absence of a central tonality) and serialism—all can be found in his scores.

Stravinsky's individualistic use of rhythm, forward urge and figural repetition is instantly recognizable. His melodies are often short, spasmodic, and usually a resultant of his harmonies, except when he introduces folk tunes. His knowledge of instrumentation is dazzling. And his application of dynamics has been minutely worked out with incredible ingenuity and scientific thought. Each instrument plays according to the nature of its possibilities. Each musician practically plays a solo. Stravinsky often eliminates the strings completely as being too sentimental. He has taught the twentieth century the value and possibilities of diverse small chamber-music groups. All in all he has been an astounding influence on present-day composers.

ARNOLD SCHÖNBERG AND EXPRESSIONISM

Apparently at an opposite polarity to Stravinsky, who candidly wrote that "music is, by its very nature, essentially powerless to express anything at all . . ." stood Arnold Schönberg (1874-1951), who confessed, "If a composer does not write from the heart, he simply cannot produce good music." Schönberg's musical credo, that the primary goal of an artist is to *express himself,* sounds curiously Romantic, but the results, known generally as **Expressionism,** are very different, as we may judge from the music of Schönberg and his disciples, from writings of Franz Kafka, the acting of Conrad Veidt or the paintings of Oscar Kokoschka, Paul Klee and Vasily Kandinsky. Not uninfluenced by the eminent Viennese doctor, Sigmund Freud, these men established the symbols of inner experience as the sole reality, and their work is introspective, highly personal and, in some cases, extremely difficult to communicate to others. The latter is very noticeable in the case of Arnold Schönberg, acknowledged as one of the most vital forces and dominant personalities in contemporary art, yet rarely performed.

Painting had a deep influence on Schönberg. He was a painter himself and a close friend of Kandinsky. To Kandinsky, an artist expresses personality by means of his art. Kandinsky felt the spiritual force of Schönberg's compositions, and claimed that Schönberg was not working from any material standpoint; certainly the martyrdom he has suffered would point to his having the courage, vision and tenacity of a prophet. Kandinsky states the Expressionist viewpoint:

> To those who are not accustomed to it, the inner beauty appears as ugliness, because humanity in general inclines to the outer and knows nothing of the inner. Almost alone from severing himself from conventional beauty is the Austrian composer, Arnold Schönberg . . . The freedom of an unfettered art can never be absolute . . . Schönberg is endeavoring to make complete use of his freedom, and has already discovered gold-mines of new beauty in his search for spiritual harmony. His music leads us into a realm where musical harmony is an

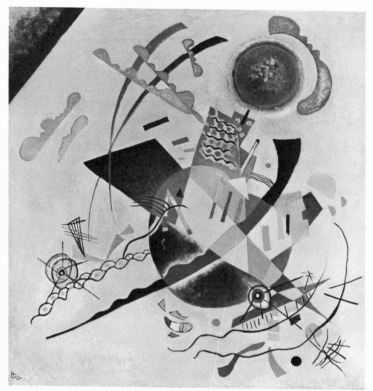

Fig. 88. "Blue Circle, No. 242"—Vasily Kandinsky, 1922. Schönberg himself was a talented artist and a musical counterpart of the Expressionists. (Courtesy The Solomon R. Guggenheim Museum Collection.)

experience of the soul, and not of the ear alone. And from this point of view begins the music of the future.

Schönberg said to a disciple, musicologist and composer Egon Wellesz (1885-   ):

How can we say, That sounds good or bad? Who is judge in this case? The authoritative theorist? He says, even if he does not justify his opinion, what he knows—that is to say, not what he had discovered for himself but what he has learned; or what every one believed because it it every one's experience. I believe that art comes not of ability but of necessity. The practical artist *can* do something. What is innate within him he can develop, and if he *wills* he can. What he *wills*—whether good or bad, shallow or profound, modern or antiquated—he *can*. But, above all, the artist *must*. He cannot influence what he produces; it depends not on his own will. But since necessity drives him, he can produce.

Arnold Schönberg was born in Vienna. Devoted to chamber music from childhood, he was instructed as a violinist and played in amateur fashion with his schoolmates, composing music for them. He did not study composition until he had entered manhood and then he worked for a short time with Alexander von Zemlinsky (1872-1942), who became his brother-in-law. Zemlinsky once pointed to the short, thick-set young man with keen eyes and dark, close-cropped hair, with the remark:

> That is Arnold Schönberg, one of my pupils; he is still under thirty and I have already taught him all I know. He brought me a score recently of a tone-poem (it was *Pelleas und Melisande*) and he had pasted together two sheets of ordinary orchestral score paper to carry his orchestration. He has a phenomenal gift.

IDEAS AND RESOURCES

Not yet thirty, Schönberg had keen intelligence, supersensitive hearing, great physical vitality, a nature bordering on fanaticism, and a searching, restless spirit. His early period was one of initiation. *Opuses* 1 to 3 are extremely beautiful songs which, when sung in 1900, aroused hostile demonstrations although today they seem in direct line with the traditional *Lied*. From this same time came the fulsome sextet for strings, *Verklärte Nacht (Transfigured Night, Op.* 4), *Pelleas und Melisande, Op.* 5, which one critic called "a fifty-minute-long wrong note" and *Gurre-Lieder,* a cantata on poems by Jacobsen for five solo voices, four choruses and a huge orchestra in which he reflects Wagner, Mahler and Strauss. Schönberg built great tone-masses, divided his instruments into many parts and developed his thematic material architecturally according to Romantic traditions. In his remarkable *String Quartet No. 1 in D Minor, Op.* 7 he followed in the footsteps of the last Beethoven quartets, adding Schumannesque and "Viennese" touches.

Next came an experimental period, including six songs with orchestra (*Op.* 8), the *Kammersymphonie, Op.* 9 (*Chamber Symphony*) and the *String Quartet No. 2 in F Sharp Minor* (*Op.* 10) in which, in the third and fourth movements, Schönberg introduces a soprano voice in settings of two poems by Stefan Georg. In this Gray sees ". . . at once the highest point to which Schönberg attains during this period of self-imposed discipline and probation and, in the last movement, his final farewell to it, his triumphant liberation from all restrictions . . . In discarding tonality Schönberg seems to leave the ground for the first time and soar away into the air like a captive bird when it is liberated. With this work he makes an end and a beginning."

After he had come through a transitional labyrinth (about 1909)

Schönberg evolved an atonal style—a new melodic, harmonic, formal and rhythmic order. For consonant tone-masses played by 100 or more instruments, Schönberg substituted tone-masses produced by the juxtaposition of dissonances using less volume but creating an illusion of volume through the unfamiliarity of tonal relationships, decidedly jarring to the ear. Short arabesques replace long phrases; the good old overworked tonic and dominant are lost in a chromatic maze; melody moves by jagged skips and leaps; sonata-form is exchanged for a terse, telegraphic, almost telepathic, style implying much that is not on paper.

Three Pieces for Piano (Op. 11) and *Five Pieces for Orchestra (Op.* 16) which provoked world-wide criticism and dissension, are excellent examples of the new style. Schönberg's setting of Stefan Georg's fifteen poems, *Das Buch der hängenden Gärten (The Book of the Hanging Gardens, Op.* 15); his two dramatic works, *Erwartung, Op.* 17 (*Expectation*), a short opera for one female character on a grisly text by Marie Pappenheim, *Die glückliche Hand, Op.* 18 (*The Lucky Hand*) and *Pierrot Lunaire (Pierrot of the Moon*) belong to this period.

Pierrot Lunaire (Op. 21) had its first performance in Berlin in 1912 with Schönberg conducting. Its text was the "Thrice Seven Poems," translated from the original French of Albert Giraud into German and conceived for a *Sprechstimme,* which is to be "neither sung nor spoken," and a small instrumental group, consisting of a pianist, a violinist (who also plays viola), a 'cellist, a flutist (who also plays piccolo) and a clarinetist (doubling on bass clarinet). The effect of this curious blending of stylized recitation and sparse instrumentation is extraordinary. With great skill, Schönberg bent his command of polyphony to fit a new melodic and tonal mold, using *passacaglia,* crab canon and fugue to carry his thoughts. Although the poems, after a cursory reading, were condemned as "decadent," they are symbolic of the relentless struggle between the ideal and the real, between the spiritual and the material (Moonlight connotes ideality), which intrigued the composer.

Pierrot Lunaire was Schönberg's last composition until after World War I. In it we find a transition from neo-Wagnerian chromaticism to an extended disintegration of tonality, with chords in fourths and a generally lacerating harmony. **Atonality** or **pantonality,** as some prefer to call it, removed the single key center by creating twelve independent centers, one on each semi-tone of the chromatic scale, with liberated relationships. Schönberg realized what such a concept entailed. He wrote:

> Tonality, tending to render harmonic facts perceptible and to correlate them, is therefore not an end but a means . . . Its refinement, it is true, implies a corresponding relinquishment of the structural process founded upon the very principle of tonality.

The terms, consonance and dissonance, once again required a revised definition. Schönberg defined consonance as the closer and simpler relation with a fundamental tone, and dissonance as the more remote and complicated. "Through the removal of the distinction between consonance and dissonance, the esthetic evaluation, which has gradually been losing ground, of consonance as being beautiful and dissonance being ugly, disappears altogether."

When Schönberg wrote his *Harmonielehre* (*Harmony Treatise,* 1911), a subject which he confessed he had learned from his pupils, he said that the laws by which he wrote were largely unknown to him. He used them intuitively and tried to expand the old harmony without destroying it. He questioned, however, the necessity of clinging to a centuries-old system of chord building in thirds. After he had instinctively used chords in fourths in *Pelleas und Melisande* and the *Kammersymphonie,* he studied more deeply the possibilities of new chord formations. Scriabin had used them but not in series of perfect fourths. Schönberg, in searching for a solution to the structural problems created by discarding tonality, finally devised a procedure which he called "Method of Composing with Twelve Tones which are related only with one another," and which is variously known today as **twelve-tone, dodecaphonic** and **serial.**

Twelve-tone Method and Later Works

Although Schönberg did not codify his method into a system, several of his disciples have tried. Essentially, the twelve-tone system starts with a serial pattern derived from an arbitrary arrangement of each of the twelve tones of the chromatic scale. This tone-row is the basis for thematic material which the composer augments by means of rhythmic differentiation and contrapuntal devices, as well as subdivision and transposition. Theoretically, the entire series or tone-row must be invariably utilized, either horizontally or vertically, that is, either simultaneously or in sequence. Although this would seem, at first glance, extremely mechanical, the possibilities are almost endless. It has been calculated, for instance, that there are 479,001,600 different tone-rows available to a composer.

In the period between World War I and Hitler's ascension as Chancellor of Germany, Schönberg received belated recognition in being appointed professor of composition at the Prussian Academy of Fine Arts in Berlin. His compositions during this time included six *Little Piano Pieces, Op.* 19; *Herzgewächse, Op.* 20 (*Hothouses*), a setting of Maeterlinck's poem for soprano (with a range of three octaves) with harmonium, *celesta* and harp; four orchestral songs, *Op.* 22; a *Serenade, Op.* 24; *Suite, Op.* 25, a piano work written in the twelve-tone technique; a

Quintet for woodwinds, *Op.* 26; a third string quartet, *Op.* 30, in which the composer carried the principle of composing on pattern to a musical geometry, with, however, some searchingly poignant effects; and *Variations for Orchestra, Op.* 31, the first extended twelve-tone composition for full orchestra. His one-act opera, *Von Heute auf Morgen* (*From Today until Tomorrow, Op.* 32) is a gay comedy on a text by Max Blonda, which Schönberg wrote to demonstrate that the twelve-tone technique could produce light and cheerful effects.

In 1933 Schönberg lost his teaching post and fled to the United States where, after a brief sojourn in Boston, he taught and worked in California until his death. Compositions from his American period are no less austere than earlier ones but show an increasing interest in utilizing larger forms. These include a *Violin Concerto, Op.* 36; another string quartet and a chamber symphony; a *Kol Nidre* for speaker, chorus and orchestra, *Op.* 39; an *Ode to Napoleon,* a setting of Byron's poem, for speaking voice, piano and string orchestra, *Op.* 41b, which is a gesture against tyranny and dictatorship; a *Piano Concerto, Op.* 42; *Theme and Variations* for band, *Op.* 43a; *A Survivor from Warsaw,* for speaker, men's chorus and orchestra, *Op.* 46, expressing his deep anxiety for European Jews caught in the holocaust of annihilation; a *Psalm CXXX,* for unaccompanied six-part chorus, sung and spoken in Hebrew, *Op.* 50b; and an unfinished opera, *Moses and Aron,* commenced in 1930, and first performed in the United States in 1966 by the Boston Opera Company.

Schönberg never became the Grand Old Master and was openly bitter that his works were so seldom performed. Although he and Stravinksy were near neighbors in California, they were never friends, owing perhaps to the international reputation of the one and the relative obscurity of the other. But as Kurt List writes, "In his search for truth, his life without compromise, and his striving for new musical worlds, (Schönberg) has waged a ceaseless war against hypocrisy, decay and stagnation." Schönberg reintroduced Baroque polyphony to music and at the same time opened wide a whole new avenue of vision.

ALBAN BERG AND ANTON VON WEBERN

The Viennese period of the eighteenth century provided a background to the Classic era and established a tradition of which Austria has been proud. In the nineteenth century, Beethoven's last works gave an incentive to Bruckner and Brahms, although in opposite camps, to carry on the Classic ideals which resulted in nineteenth-century neo-Classicism. Gustav Mahler and Hugo Wolf were apostles of the true Viennese spirit and Mahler's musical descendants were Alexander von Zemlinsky and

Arnold Schönberg. With Schönberg the Classic spirit had another renaissance and he handed down his convictions, discoveries and methods to a group of devoted disciples, among whom were Alban Berg and Anton von Webern.

Alban Berg (1885-1935), a Viennese by birth, met Arnold Schönberg, his only teacher, in 1904. "Through him," says Willi Reich, Berg "gained a thorough knowledge of the composer's craft and that idealistic conception of art which lifts Schönberg's circle above the party conflicts of the modern musical scene." Berg's first works include an extremely chromatic *Piano Sonata* (1908); *Four Songs* (1909), on texts by Mombert and Hebbel; a *String Quartet* (1910), which aroused the attention of progressive musicians; *Five Songs* with orchestral accompaniment (1912), after postcard texts by Peter Altenberg, "real treasures of the art of musical miniature," that caused a riot at their first performance in Vienna; and *Four Pieces for Clarinet and Piano* (1913).

From 1914 to 1920, Berg was occupied with writing the masterpiece for which he is best known and which is undoubtedly one of the great compositions of twentieth-century music. *Wozzeck,* a sordid dramatic fragment of fifteen scenes by the early nineteenth-century Georg Büchner, recounts the trials of a soldier, his mistress, their child, a sadistic physician and a seductive drum major. It proved that the "atonal manner" could be employed for effective grand opera, due largely to the fact that Berg used his musical means to explicate every nuance of the plot, be it emotional or pictorial. Symmetry and proportion are given to the individual scenes and so a well-conceived, balanced drama is evolved from a naturalistic sketch.

Berg's three acts divide into exposition, *dénouement* and catastrophe. As Reich comments:

> The grotesque element in the delineation of the characters, especially of the Physician, finds its echo in modern art. The interpolated folktunes and the opportunities for the use of tone-color in various episodes must have attracted the musician. . . . The method by which the poetic material is developed contains the germ cell of Berg's music.

That Berg combined formal and folk elements with atonality in an extensive work was surprising, but a greater mark of his skill, technical equipment and musicianship was shown in his employment of traditional forms. The scenes of Act I are structured as a suite, a rhapsody, a military march and cradle song, a *passacaglia* with twenty-one variations and an *andante*—quasi rondo. In Act II we find a symphony in five movements: Sonata-*allegro*; *Fantasia* and fugue; *Largo*; *Scherzo and Rondo martiale*. Act III follows the organization of six Inventions—on a theme, a tone, a rhythm, a chord, a key and a persistent rhythm (*perpetuum mobile*).

After *Wozzeck,* Berg entered a period of chamber music, composing a *Chamber Concerto* (1923-25), for piano, violin and thirteen wind instruments, celebrating Schönberg's fiftieth birthday; and the *Lyrische Suite* (1926), a six-movement work for string quartet, in which the composer first uses the twelve-tone procedure, although not mechanically. *Der Wein* (1929), a concert *aria* for soprano and orchestra on a text from Baudelaire, is, according to Reich, "not merely a successful revival of an old form but a promising preparation for Alban Berg's next opera, which will set to music the *Lulu-Tragedy* of Frank Wedekind." Unfortunately, *Lulu* was never completed, as Berg interrupted his labors to write his last composition, a *Violin Concerto* (1935), dedicated as a memorial to Manon Gropius, the young daughter of the widow of Gustav Mahler. This essentially Romantic work is built from a twelve-tone series, arranged almost wholly in thirds together with a folksong and a chorale, so that much of it is strongly tonal in feeling.

Anton von Webern (1883-1945) was one of Schönberg's first pupils, and with Berg, was a leading member of the Expressionist trinity. In 1906 he took his doctorate at the University of Vienna, for research work under Guido Adler (1855-1941), the eminent musicologist. For the rest of his life he composed, conducted choral and instrumental groups and championed new music. His end occurred tragically at the hands of an American MP when the composer idly broke the strict Occupation curfew to light a cigarette. His complete output numbers only thirty-one works and can be performed in less than three hours. Yet von Webern has emerged as an increasingly influential beacon for contemporary composers.

Most of his music falls into the intimate chamber-music category, in which he followed Schönberg's precepts and attempted utmost condensation of form and intensity of expression. Erwin Stein calls him the "composer of the *pianissimo expressive,*" and Schönberg himself said of the short pieces that each was "a whole novel condensed in a single sigh." His early *Opuses,* through No. 11, were conceived before the first World War and are terse, dissonant, audacious and almost fragmentary in quality. For instance, the fourth of his *Five Pieces for Orchestra, Op.* 10, scored for clarinet, trumpet, trombone, mandolin, *celesta,* harp, drum, violin and viola, lasts less than twenty seconds. His later compositions, songs, chamber music, two cantatas and a set of variations for piano, employ twelve-tone techniques, although von Webern's homogeneity of style is not disturbed. His ample use of silence as a foil for sound, his minute dynamic gradations, his division of a melody, note by note, among his musical forces, his preference for wide intervals and contra-puntal texture, his unique tone coloring, his pointillistic manner, his painstaking organization, all remain intact. It is toward von Webern's style of serialism that Stravinsky now leans. Of Berg and von Webern, René Leibowitz (1913-   ), author, conductor and composer, writes:

> While the genius of Berg always strove to establish a connection be-tween the discoveries of Schoenberg and the past—thus profiting by the retroactive elements in Schoenberg's work—the genius of Webern is concerned with the possibilities for the future inherent in his work, and thus succeeds in projecting the particularly novel and radical elements.

OTHER PATHFINDERS—CHARLES IVES

Although in many ways the music of the first half of the twentieth century seems to have been dominated by the compositions and artistic evolution of Stravinsky and Schönberg, we cannot omit from considera-tion as musical pathfinders such pioneer composers as Charles Ives, Béla Bartók, Edgard Varèse or Paul Hindemith, for each of these four men, among many others we might include, was an individualist of the first order. Each from the background of a solid academic training ventured into new regions of musical exploration and each contributed substan-tially to the repertoire and techniques of contemporary music.

Charles Ives (1874-1954), whose music was written between 1900 and 1920, was a unique figure in American music, with the expansiveness of a Whitman, the intellectual curiosity of an Einstein and the thought-fulness of Emerson and Thoreau. Collaer states, "He is to America what Schönberg and Stravinsky are to Europe." Combining composition with a successful career as an insurance agent in New York City, Ives was little performed and then misunderstood. He consequently abandoned music in his later years, yet his catalogue of works is a large one. Only gradually is Ives' music finding its way into print and performance, cap-turing a wider and wider audience. Belatedly, Ives was awarded a Pulitzer Prize in 1947 for his *Third Symphony,* written twenty years earlier. Until more of Ives' music is available, an accurate assessment of his place is impossible, yet there is every reason to believe that future volumes will afford him much more space, as his due.

Ives was born in Danbury, Connecticut, the son of a bandmaster who ceaselessly experimented and encouraged his son to explore acoustical and harmonic phenomena. Following graduation from Yale, where he studied with Horatio Parker, Ives went to New York, served as a church organist, entered business and composed in all his free time. In his music we find attempts to reproduce such homely New England pictures as the village band, the country-dance fiddler, the village choir with its wheezy

utilizing the most *avant-garde* techniques, though never slavishly. As in the case of Ives, Bartók has enjoyed posthumous popularity to a degree never experienced in his lifetime. Stage works from his second period (1908-1926), such as the one-act opera, *Duke Bluebeard's Castle* (1911) and the ballet, *The Miraculous Mandarin* (1919), have been successfully revived and recorded. His use of the arch form, that is, an A-B-C-B-A pattern integrating a movement or a work, for example, the *String Quartet No. 4* (1927), his tone clusters and daring string effects, his strong rhythms and his modality have not passed unnoticed by other composers.

Edgard Varèse

A most interesting and revolutionary Franco-American composer is Edgard Varèse (1885-1965), who, like Bartók, resists precise classification. Although a contemporary of Stravinsky and Schönberg, he struck out in quite a different direction after studying at the Schola Cantorum in Paris with d'Indy and Roussel. Pitts Sanborn writes:

> It is easy to relate the music of Varèse to that modern movement in the visual arts which is represented by Matisse, Picasso . . . and Brancusi. And Varèse himself has authorized us to believe that his *Hyperprism* (1923) aims its facets toward the elusive desideratum of the Fourth Dimension.

After writing (and later destroying) rather Romantic and Impressionistic compositions in Europe, Varèse emigrated to the United States in 1915 and became active in New York's musical life. He also re-examined his compositional techniques and commenced producing eerie pseudo-primitive music that exploited the upper registers of standard instruments and widened the scope of the pulsatiles. In *Hyperprism,* written for chamber orchestra and sixteen percussion instruments, including sleighbells and a siren; *Octandre* (1924), a chamber work for seven wind instruments and double bass; *Intégrales* (1925), another work for winds and percussion; and *Ionisation* (1931), scored for thirty-five instruments of "percussion, friction, and sibilation" including two sirens, we discover monuments to a unique musical imagination which document the composer's statement, "I refuse to submit myself only to sounds that have already been heard."

Deciding that nothing more was possible in musical expansion, Varèse discontinued composing until electronic equipment became available. His *Déserts* (1954) and *Poème électronique* (1958), most of the latter written directly on magnetic tape, are contributions of a septuagenarian to this new realm of music-making, often requiring that a listener, to quote Charles Ives' remark about Carl Ruggles' (1876-   ) music, "use his ears like a man." Machlis summarizes Varèse's influence as follows:

> Varèse's imagery is poetic; but the poetry derives from turbines, generators, the paraphernalia of the laboratory. His metallic music is about force and energy. His emphasis on sheer sonority presaged one of the most important trends of our era. In this respect Varèse pointed the way for the composers of electronic music. In the light of what is happening today *Ionisation* stands revealed as one of the prophetic scores of the twentieth century.

PAUL HINDEMITH

In Paul Hindemith (1895-1963) we have a musician who functioned with great success as composer, performer, conductor, theorist and teacher. Born in Hanau, Germany, and educated at the Frankfurt Conservatory, Hindemith early evinced his musicality, becoming concertmaster of the Frankfurt Opera at twenty and later traveling as violist with the Amar Quartet, an ensemble that championed new music during the 1920's. In his youth, Hindemith also had experience playing in cafés, dance halls and the like. From 1927 to 1935 he taught composition at the Berlin *Hochschule für Musik*. With Hitler's advent to power, Hindemith found himself labeled as "decadent" and his music blacklisted as unacceptable to the Third Reich. The composer spent two years (1935-37) reorganizing the musical life of Turkey. He first visited the United States in 1937, at the invitation of the Elizabeth Sprague Coolidge Foundation. In 1940 he became professor of theory and composition at Yale University where he remained for thirteen years, after which he returned to Europe, settling in Switzerland, and continuing his busy life until his death.

Hindemith was a practical musician with a thoroughly professional outlook. He wrote music to be performed. For a while he was a leader in the movement dealing with the "sociological function of music." That "music—good as well as bad—is futile if it cannot attract an audience" was the conclusion of a group of Germans who tried to find a common basis on which musicians and the public might again meet. In the nineteenth century, music had become a popular luxury, but after World War I, new conditions created a new audience and a new music was required. Radio and the sound film did their share to disseminate this music. As Hans Gutman states, ". . . the auditor is to be roused from his lethargy, stimulated and induced to make music himself, instead of uncomprehendingly following the conductor's baton." So useful or functional music (*Gebrauchsmusik*) attracted the attention of many composers and publishers, and Hindemith wrote chamber music for amateurs and school children and a "fun" cantata, *Let Us Build a City* (1930). With the advent of Hitler, however, this movement was thrown into the discard, and a completely reactionary attitude adopted, that resulted in an exodus from Germany of most of the musicians who were in any way progressive.

Hindemith's operas were considered epoch-making, not because they were so successful but because they were "different." Among the earliest are two one-act works, *Mörder, Hoffnung der Frauen* (*Murder, the Hope of Women,* 1921) and *Sancta Susanna* (1922); a Burmese marionette show, *Das Nusch-Nuschi* (1921), in which Hindemith exhibits his rich rhythmic sense in a gay burlesque; and a dance-pantomime, *Der Dämon* (*The Demon,* 1922). *Cardillac* (1926), one of the first experimental operas in pre-Nazi Germany, ". . . represents the most strongly defined antitheses to everything traditional," comments Adolph Weissmann. ". . . This is the first time that the Bach school, the school of pure music, is expressed through the medium of opera . . . The style is that which we associate with the chamber orchestra; it is contrapuntal and linear and therefore as remote as possible from the operatic convention." *Hin und Zurück* (*There and Back,* 1927), a sketch from Charlot's Revue, is a short comedy in which the second half reverses the action of the first part. Another work for the stage, *Neues vom Tage* (*News of the Day,* 1929) is a tabloid-opera of everyday life.

Mathis der Maler, 1938, Hindemith's operatic masterpiece, was written in pre-Nazi Germany. Although it is occasionally performed as an opera, it is as a *Symphony* that the work is best known. The movements represent a tryptich, the Isenheim Altarpiece by Matthias Grünewald, the sixteenth-century artist who is a central figure of the opera. The three sections of the orchestral version are *Engelkonzert* (*Angelic Concert*), the overture of the opera; *Gnablegung* (*Entombment*), an intermezzo of the final scene, and *The Temptation of Saint Anthony,* taken from the sixth scene. The grandeur of the music, the profundity of its emotion and its position in the musical evolution of the epoch mark this as one of the significant works of the twentieth century, rich in provocative overtones.

Hindemith's last opera was *Die Harmonie der Welt* (*The Harmony of the World,* 1957), based on the life of the great astronomer, Johannes Kepler. Other stage works include ballets such as *Nobilissima Visione* (1938), inspired by St. Francis of Assisi and *The Four Temperaments* (1944). Works for full orchestra number *Philharmonic Concerto* (1932), *Symphony in E Flat* (1941) and the *Symphonic Metamorphoses on a Theme of Weber* (1944), among others.

Although his early works have a Brahms-Reger-Strauss heaviness about them, for example, *Op.* 11, and although his piano suite, *1922,* with its "March," "Shimmy," "Night Piece" and "Ragtime," evidences exposure to the influence of jazz, Hindemith found his *métier* quite early in a neo-Classic, or even neo-Baroque style, that characterizes most of his music and from which he rarely deviated. His melodies reflect his interest in the medieval German popular song and his initial harmonic conception changed to an increasingly contrapuntal manner. He never relinquished the principle of tonality which he considered fundamental. However harsh his dissonance, we find cadential rest in a simple triad. Rhythmically and formally, too, Hindemith leans toward the traditional.

Hindemith wrote a great many works for chamber groups and chamber orchestras, beginning with the six compositions known simply as *Kammermusik,* I, II, etc. Noting a lack of solo literature for some instruments, the composer wrote numerous sonatas. He composed concertos for various instruments, with large or small orchestras, including *Der Schwanendreher* (1935, *The Swan-Catcher*) for viola, based on folk material. And he is responsible for a long list of duos, trios, quartets and quintets. His most Bach-like work is *Ludis Tonalis* (*The Play of Tones,* 1943), a set of twelve fugues for piano in as many tonalities, connected by interludes and prefaced with a prelude which, in retrograde, becomes the postlude.

With typical thoroughness and rationality, Hindemith studied the tonal elements of music and set forth his pedagogic and theoretical convictions in two volumes entitled *Unterweisung im Tonsatz,* published (1937-39) in English as *The Craft of Musical Composition.* In these he re-examined the overtone series and arrived at a system of tonal relationships that can function as reasonably with modern dissonance as in analyses of music of the past. Although there are certain inconsistencies in his theory, it was satisfying enough to him to occasion revision of some of his earlier compositions, notably the beautiful song-cycle, *Das Marienleben* (*Mary's Life*), written to poems of Rainer Maria Rilke. Hindemith's original version was composed in 1923. Twenty-five years later he rewrote the songs and published them with an interesting preface explaining the logic of his revisions.

We will allow Hindemith himself the last word. In his book, *A Composer's World,* he asserts:

> We must be grateful that with our art we have been placed halfway between science and religion, enjoying equally the advantages of exactitude in thinking—so far as the technical aspects in music are concerned —and of the unlimited world of faith.

*   *   *   *   *

Thus, in the music of our twentieth-century pathfinders we notice dominant tendencies that pervade the present musical scene—the new emphasis on rhythm, the dissonances of polytonality, atonality and serialism, the backward glance that revivifies old forms and ancient modalities, the expression of urban, mechanized values, the experiments with electronic instruments and the need to function within the framework of today, however difficult that may be. In our concluding chapter we shall survey representative composers of the "middle generation," whose music develops further these various idioms.

SUGGESTIONS FOR FURTHER READING

Austin, William W., *Music in the 20th Century*. New York, Norton, 1966.

Bacharach, A. L., ed., "The Twentieth Century," * Vol. 4 of *The Music Masters*. Baltimore, Penguin, 1957.

Bauer, Marion, *Twentieth-Century Music*. New York, Putnam, 1947.

Chase, Gilbert, *America's Music, from the Pilgrims to the Present*. New York, McGraw-Hill, 1955.

Collaer, Paul, *A History of Modern Music*.* New York, Grosset & Dunlap, 1961.

Copland, Aaron, *Our New Music*. New York, McGraw-Hill, 1941.

Cowell, Henry and Sidney, *Charles Ives and His Music*. New York, Oxford University Press, 1955.

Craft, Robert, ed., *Conversations with Stravinsky*. Garden City, Doudleday, 1960.

Ewen, David, ed., *The New Book of Modern Composers*. New York, Knopf, 1961.

Fassett, Agatha, *The Naked Face of Genius: Béla Bartók's American Years*. Boston, Houghton-Mifflin, 1958.

Forte, Allen, *Contemporary Tone-Structures*. New York, Columbia University Press, 1955.

Hansen, Peter S., *An Introduction to Twentieth Century Music*. Boston, Allyn & Bacon, 1961.

Hindemith, Paul, *A Composer's World*. Cambridge, Harvard University Press, 1952.

Howard, John Tasker and Lyons, James, *Modern Music*.* New York, Crowell, 1957.

Ives, Charles E., *Essays before a Sonata and Other Writings*.* New York, Norton, 1966.

Křenek, Ernst, *Studies in Counterpoint, Based on the Twelve-tone Technique*. New York, Schirmer, 1940.

Lang, Paul Henry, ed., *Stravinsky: A New Appraisal of His Work*.* New York, Norton, 1963.

Lederman, Minna, ed., *Stravinsky in the Theatre*. New York, Pellegrini & Cudahy, 1949.

Leibowitz, René, *Schönberg and His School*. New York, Philosophical Library, 1949.

Machlis, Joseph, *Introduction to Contemporary Music*. New York, Norton, 1961.

Moldenhauer, Hans, comp., *Anton von Webern: Perspectives*. Seattle, University of Washington Press, 1966.

* Available in paperback edition.

Newlin, Dika, *Bruckner, Mahler and Schönberg.* New York, Columbia University Press, 1947.

Redlich, H. F., *Alban Berg, the Man and His Music.* New York, Abelard-Schuman, 1957.

Reti, Rudolph, *Tonality, Atonality, Pantonality.** New York, Macmillan, 1958.

Rufer, Joseph, *Composition with Twelve Tones Related Only to One Another.* New York, Macmillan, 1954.

Salzman, Eric, *An Introduction to Twentieth-Century Music.** Englewood Cliffs, Prentice-Hall, 1967.

Schoenberg, Arnold, *Style and Idea,* New York, Philosophical Library, 1950.

Searle, Humphrey. *Twentieth Century Counterpoint.* New York, De Graff, 1954.

Slonimsky, Nicolas, *Music since 1900.* New York, Coleman-Ross, 1949.

Stevens, Halsey, *The Life and Music of Béla Bartók.* New York, Oxford University Press, 1953.

Stuckenschmidt, H. H., *Arnold Schönberg.* New York, Grove, 1960.

Stravinsky, Igor, *An Autobiography.** New York, Norton, 1936.

——, *The Poetics of Music.** Cambridge, Harvard University Press, 1947.

Tansman, Alexandre, *Igor Stravinsky: The Man and His Music.* New York, Putnam, 1949.

White, Eric Walter, *Stravinsky: The Composer and His Works.* Berkeley, University of California Press, 1966.

A SAMPLER OF SUPPLEMENTARY RECORDINGS

Bartók, Béla, *Cantata Profana* (1930)
    Concerto No. 2 for Piano (1931)
    Music for Strings, Percussion and Celesta (1935)
    Piano Music
    Sonata for Violin Unaccompanied (1944)
    Concerto for Orchestra (1943)

Berg, Alban, *Chamber Concerto for Violin, Piano and 13 Winds* (1925)
    Lyric Suite for String Quartet (1926)
    Wozzeck (1914-21)

Hindemith, Paul, *Concert Music for Strings and Brass* (1931)
    Marienleben, Op. 27
    Nobilissima Visione (1938)
    Mathis der Maler (1934)
    Symphonic Metamorphoses of Themes by Weber (1944)
    Requiem, "For Those We Love" (1946)

Ives, Charles, *Central Park in the Dark* (1898-1907)
    Sonata No. 2, "Concord, Mass." (1909-15)
    Songs
    Three Places in New England (1903-14)
    Variations on "America" for Organ (1891)
    Symphony No. 4 (1910-16)

Schönberg, Arnold, *Five Pieces for Orchestra* (1905)
    Pierrot Lunaire, Op. 21 (1912)
    Theme and Variations for Band, Op. 43a
    Verklärte Nacht, Op. 4
    Piano Music

Stravinsky, Igor, *Agon* (1957)
Canticum sacrum (1956)
Concerto for Piano and Wind Orchestra (1923-24)
Ebony Concerto
Firebird Suite (1910)
L'Histoire du soldat: Suite
Octet for Wind Instruments (1923)
Oedipus Rex (1927)
Petrouchka: Suite (1911)
Sacre du printemps (1913)
Symphony of Psalms (1930)
Varèse, Edgard, *Ionisation.*

OPPORTUNITIES FOR STUDY IN DEPTH

1. The most natural person with whom to compare Stravinsky is his contemporary artist, Pablo Picasso. Both have led full and long lives; both have been constant probers of problems; and both have set forth fashions that other artists have followed. Continue the comparison, as far as feasible.

2. Due to limitations of space, we have been forced to omit many interesting experimentalist composers. Investigate the music of one of the following: Julián Carrillo (b. 1875); John J. Becker (1886-1961); Alois Hába (b. 1893); or Hans Barth (1897-1956).

3. What was the significance of the New York Armory Show, held in 1913? The show was recently restaged and an informative illustrated catalogue is available. Make a study of the personalities involved and representative works exhibited.

4. We have mentioned Schönberg's friendship with Kandinsky and the fact that the composer himself was a painter who actually held several one-man shows. If practical, visit a museum and survey paintings, prints and sculptures of the German Expressionists. Or study several of the excellent monographs available on the subject. Who were the Expressionists? What were they trying to accomplish? Where did their efforts lead?

5. Stravinsky was intimately connected with Diaghilev's ballet company and his works were choreographed by prominent men such as Nijinsky, Massine and Fokine. Write a paper about the *Ballet Russe* and its importance as a branch of musical theater.

6. We have indicated the barest outline of the serial method of composition, conceived by Schönberg and carried further by his disciples. If possible, after more study and thought, devise a tone row, its inversion and retrograde and attempt a piece of music in the dodecaphonic manner.

7. Prepare a report for class presentation on some of the works of that rugged individualist, Charles Ives. Implement it with recordings or performed examples. The Cowell biography (see "Suggestions for Further Reading") will supply helpful information.

8. Read and present a book report on either of the following: Alma Mahler Werfel's *And the Bridge Was Love* (N.Y., 1958) or H. W. Heinsheimer's *Menagerie in F Sharp* (Garden City, N.Y., 1947).

VOCABULARY ENRICHMENT

"the true tradition"
noise music
primitivism
neo-Classicism
archaism
neo-Romanticism
polyharmony
polyrhythm
atonality or pantonality

serialism, dodecaphony, twelve-tone music
Expressionism
Sprechstimme
arch form
tone clusters
pulsatiles
Gebrauchsmusik
atypical chamber groups

Chapter 28.

NEW TENDENCIES—ECLECTICISM

Unlike that moment in a film when a still shot suddenly immobilizes a complete scene, a single musical moment immobilized makes audible only one chord, which in itself is comparatively meaningless. This never-ending flow of music *forces* us to use our imaginations, for music is in a continual state of becoming.

—Aaron Copland, *Music and Imagination*

As we approach the end of our journey in music through the ages, we are certainly aware that "music is in a continual state of becoming"—a state characterized by both profusion and confusion. There are many as yet unattached threads to the tapestry of musical creativity now being woven; time, the greatest art critic, will decide upon the relative value of woof and warp, after a passage of years. In the meantime, however, we may choose to examine one aspect shared in common by the multitude of diverse composers and their equally diverse productions. That is **eclecticism,** a renewed and renewing synthesis of new tendencies, intertwined into individual fabrics that delight, distort, garb and clarify experience. In this chapter we shall survey but a sampling of composers and compositions through the midpoint of the twentieth century, endeavoring to point out the nature of the weaves and the possible directions to which they move.

Just as polyphony had been an international vogue, followed by Classicism and Romanticism, Impressionism swept over the entire musical world in the early twentieth century, creating a veritable renaissance, as we have noted. Italy, growing tired of its monopoly of opera, developed a new school of instrumental composers, including Respighi, Idlebrando Pizzetti (1880-   ), Gian Francesco Malipiero (1882-   ) and Alfredo Casella (1883-1947). Albéniz went to Paris from Spain and drank deep draughts of Impressionism, which he handed on to Falla. England had Delius, Scott and Arnold Bax (1883-1953). Franz Schreker (1878-1934) and Schönberg were the heads of two opposing camps in Austria. And in America Loeffler, Carpenter and Griffes were prophets of a new order.

After World War I, however, this type of music no longer expressed world feeling. The spirit of the times demanded stronger colors and rhythms, violent contrasts, abrupt shifts of key, brutal dissonances, humor, brevity and objectivity. The general adoption of jazz was an indication of the world's fatigue and of its need for unusual stimulation. What has not been blamed on the "Jazz Age" is often blamed on the "Machine Age."

Fig. 89. "The Three Musicians"—Pablo Picasso. The spirit of the twentieth century demanded strong colors and rhythms, violent contrasts, caricature and no sentiment. (Courtesy Philadelphia Museum of Art, A. E. Gallatin Collection.)

Les Six

Nowhere was this spirit more prevalent than in the heady atmosphere of Paris, the post-war arts capital, whence so many twentieth-century milestones originated. Release from war tensions resulted in a gay, mad, confident and uninhibited *milieu* and a revival of creativity unparalleled elsewhere. The reaction against Impressionism found utterance in the music of six composers, rather arbitrarily lumped together as *Les Six* by a critic, Henri Collet, who in 1920 published an article entitled, "Five Russians, Six Frenchmen, and Erik Satie." The six Frenchmen selected were Germaine Tailleferre (1892-   ), Louis Durey

(1888-   ), Georges Auric (1899-   ), Arthur Honegger (1892-1955), Francis Poulenc (1899-1963) and Darius Milhaud (1892-   ).

Originally, *Les Six* had rallied about the banner of Erik Satie, who disavowed, however, any intention of forming a school of followers. The young composers endorsed provocative public statements of their points of view, such as those expressed by Jean Cocteau in *Le Coq et l'arlequin,* published in 1918. In this little book, Cocteau sounded a battlecry, writing, "Enough clouds, vapors, aquariums, water-sprites, and perfumes of the night; we want a music of the earth, an everyday music." To which Milhaud added, "Down with Wagner!" The preferred music was to be sophisticated, apassionate and full of vigor. A smile was to replace a sigh, so to speak. The vulgarity and economy of the music-hall offered promise.

In common with other labels, *Les Six* is basically inaccurate, as connoting a broad unity of purpose and product. Although these composers were friends and, for a brief historical moment, associated with one another, giving joint concerts and actually writing (minus Durey) a composite ballet to a script of Cocteau, *Les Mariés de la Tour Eiffel (The Couples at the Eiffel Tower,* 1921) and although they shared literary leanings that led them toward the theater, they had differing musical personalities and, as time has proved, uneven talents, analogous to "The Mighty Five." *Les Six,* to the present music lover, have become *Les Trois,* that is, three composers who have contributed substantially to the twentieth-century repertoire.

Of the others, Tailleferre, Durey and Auric, after a short moment in the sun, faded from the horizon, as far as creative influence is concerned. Germaine Tailleferre, the female member, composed ballets, such as *Le Marchand d'oiseaux (The Bird Merchant,* 1923) and chamber music. Louis Durey soon retired to Provençe and has served as a music critic, composing now and then. Georges Auric, whose ballets, such as *Les Fâcheux (The Tormentors,* 1924) and *Les Matelots (The Sailors,* 1925), were performed by the *Ballet Russe,* was to become absorbed in writing music for films, achieving a celebrity of sorts with his waltz, *"Moulin Rouge"* (1952). At present he is director of the combined *Opéra* and *Opéra Comique* in Paris. The tenuous bonds uniting *Les Six* quickly severed, leaving Honegger, Poulenc and Milhaud to pursue their individual creative paths.

Arthur Honegger, of Swiss parentage, was born at Le Havre and educated at the Zürich and Paris Conservatories, where one of his teachers was André Gedalge and one of his classmates, Milhaud. He was the first to break from *Les Six,* probably because of his Swiss-

German background. A conscientious workman with an immense technique, an admirable sense for form and a musical nature, Honegger was temperamentally drawn to Schönberg rather than to Stravinsky, whom he regarded as an extremist and therefore a danger. He disapproved of the various attempts to go back to Gounod, Rossini, and Liszt, but he admitted that two cantatas, which he had heard as a youth, drove him "back to Bach," and inspired him to become a composer. He possessed a strong sense of tradition. As he commented, "It is pointless to smash doors that one can open."

Fig. 90. "Aria de Bach"—Georges Braque. Honegger was one of many musicians of the twentieth century inspired by study of Bach's works. (Private Collection.)

Among Honegger's many works in many forms are two that caused sensations: one is *Le Roi David* (*King David,* 1921), originally incidental music to a play by René Morax, and now performed frequently as an oratorio; and the other an orchestral tone-poem, *Pacific 231* (1924), depicting tonally an American locomotive—a bit of modern realism. Another popular work of the same year as *Pacific 231* was Honegger's *Concertino for Piano and Orchestra,* which in its last movement shows the influence of jazz. His interest in athletics is evident in the ballet, *Skating Rink* (1922) and in the symphonic poem, *Rugby* (1928), characterized as are many of his compositions by its driving force. A sampling of Honegger's approximately 200 works reveals a great variety. Somewhat on the order of the large musical canvas of *King David* are *Jeanne d'Arc au bûcher* (*Joan of Arc at the Stake,* 1935), a stage oratorio; and *La Danse des morts* (*Dance of Death,* 1938). Both are excellent examples of contemporary choral writing. Moreover, Honegger has written more than a dozen operas, including *Judith* (1926) and *L'Aiglon* (1937), in addition to film music, chamber music, songs and piano pieces.

In 1951 Honegger authored a monograph, *Je suis compositeur* (*I Am a Composer*), in which he pessimistically asserts, "The vocation of composer has the distinction of being an activity and preoccupation of one who seeks to make a product no one wants." Traces of this gloom are apparent in his *Symphony No. 5* ("*Di tre re*"—"Of Three D's"), a stark anti-Romantic work introduced by the Boston Symphony Orchestra during the following year. In this we find the pathos, grandeur, massive sound, contrapuntal textures, dissonance, formal construction and rhythmic urgency that distinguish Honegger's style.

Francis Poulenc, a native Parisian, composed music of a quite different nature than Honegger's. His style was influenced by Chabrier, Ravel and Stravinsky as well as Satie, yet has a gamin quality all its own. Poulenc has written neo-Classic *salon* piano pieces, using polytonal harmony in a gracefully naïve style. His *Mouvements perpetuels* (1918) and *En Promenade* are humorous and artlessly simplified. Significant among his chamber compositions are a *Sextet* for wind instruments and piano (1932) and a *String Quartet* (1942). Of his concertos the *Concert champêtre* for harpsichord and orchestra (*Country Concerto,* 1928) and the *Concerto* for organ, strings and percussion (1936) are felicitous.

Poulenc's gift was primarily lyric. He was a born melodist. Nowhere is this more apparent than in his more than 100 songs, including the cycles, *Le Bestiaire* (*The Animal Trainer,* 1919), in which words by Guillaume Apollinaire are set for voice, flute, clarinet, bassoon and string quartet, and *Le Travail du peintre* (*The Work of Painters,* 1957), seven impressions of modern painters with text by Paul Éluard. The composer has also written many choral works, including *Mass in G* (1937); *La Figure humaine* (*The Human Face,* 1943), a secular cantata; and *Stabat Mater* (1951). Georges Auric speaks of his colleague as resisting the German occupation forces of World War II by giving recitals of contemporary song with the singer, Pierre Bernac. "No one will forget the fine courage they have always displayed in rejecting the least compromise, the least concession, the least hint of propaganda."

The stage beckoned Poulenc and he composed ballets, among which is *Les Biches* (*The House Party,* 1923), performed by the *Ballet Russe.* In addition, Poulenc wrote three operas of very different content. *Les Mamelles de Tirésias* (*The Breasts of Tiresias,* 1944), on a libretto by Apollinaire, is a farce of the first order, in which surrealist high-jinks are projected with the aid of allusions to many other composers' music and to satirical versions of music-hall favorites. On the other hand, *Les Dialogues de Carmélites* (1957) is a serious work of psychological significance, dealing with the decision of a nun to face death by guillotine rather than desert her spiritual sisters. Poulenc's last opera was *La voix humaine* (*The Human Voice,* 1958), a one-character lyric tragedy in a single act, on a libretto by Cocteau. In it the composer achieves a continuity and variety that affirms his considerable ability.

The talented Frenchman, Darius Milhaud, a Provençal by birth, lived in Paris until the Second World War drove him to America. Educated at the Conservatory, he studied with Gedalge, d'Indy, Dukas and Widor. In 1917-1918 he served as an attaché at the French legation at Rio de Janiero. This sojourn had a genuine influence on his early compositions, as seen in the piano collection, *Saudades do Brasil* (*Souvenirs of Brazil,* 1921). A frequent visitor to the United States, Milhaud finally made his home in California, where he has taught at Mills College since 1940. At present he divides his time between France and this country, teaching, conducting and composing, although severely crippled by arthritis.

Tremendously facile and astonishingly versatile, Milhaud has written over 300 opuses. For the Swedish Ballet he composed *La Création du monde* (*The Creation of the World,* 1923), his tribute to jazz. "Jazz," he remarked, "was like a beneficent thunder clap which cleaned our art-sky . . . Today jazz is not interesting . . . I once dreamed of releasing jazz from the narrow confines of the dance and of writing a symphony in this form of music. I actually realized the project in ballet form and it is *La Création du monde.*" The ballet, with costumes and sets by the artist, Fernand Léger, utilized an orchestra of seventeen instruments, including saxophones and a large selection of percussion. Its primitivism, in contrast to Stravinsky's *Le Sacre,* is extremely stylized, representing a Gallicized jazz—bluesy, rhythmically syncopated, yet somehow transformed and modified. As the composer noted, "I made wholesale use of the jazz style to convey a purely classical feeling."

Other stage works include *Le Boeuf sur le toit* (*The Bull on the Roof,* 1920), a ballet on a libretto of Cocteau, in which bizarre things happen to the characters, who are placed in an American Prohibition bar. Equally incongruous things happen in the music which is almost exclusively South American in form and feeling. His most ambitious opera was a setting of Paul Claudel's *Christophe Colombe* (1928), in which Milhaud combined cinematic effects with twenty-seven scenes, a huge chorus, fifty characters and orchestra. The chorus sings, speaks, chants; it functions somewhat like a Greek chorus in supplementing the story and commenting as spectators to the action. His interest in Hellenic themes appears in such operas as the three *Opéras-minutes—Europa, Ariadne* and *Theseus* (1927)—none of which lasts more than eight minutes; *Les Malheurs d'Orphée* (*The Misfortunes of Orpheus,* 1929); and a one-act *Médée* (1938). Historical subjects are explored in *Maximilien* (1930); *Bolivar* (1943) and a pageant-opera for Israel, *David* (1953). Quite different are his incidental music for a devout Catholic drama, *L'Annonce faite à Marie* (*Announcement Made to Mary,* 1932) and *Le pauvre matelot* (*The Poor Sailor,* 1926), a grimly realistic drama by Cocteau.

Among Milhaud's large *oeuvre* are many large and small symphonies; over twenty-four concertos, including *Concertino de printemps* for violin, viola and 'cello (1935); over 150 songs, of which *Poèmes juifs* (*Jewish Poems,* 1916) and *Catalogue de fleurs* (*Catalogue of Flowers,* 1920) are most attractive; eighteen string quartets, of which Nos. 14 and 15 are interesting, as they may be played separately or combined to form an octet, a contrapuntal *tour de force; La Suite Provençale* (1936), on popular folk airs of the eighteenth century; *Scaramouche* (1937), a suite for two pianos in which rhythmic, polytonal and lyric elements mingle in a happy manner; and a *Sabbath Morning Service* for baritone, chorus and organ (1947).

It is difficult to generalize about Milhaud's musical style, as he allowed the subject matter to determine it, whether it be a translation from the Greek, pure chamber music, the lyrics of French poets, a humorous ballet, or the ultra-modern fantasy and treatment that Claudel or Cocteau gave to the librettos he employed. In his moods, Milhaud swings from the trivial to the most profound, from gaiety to sadness, from humor to nostalgia, from spontaneous simplicity to sophisticated artificiality. Withal, he has the equipment to run the entire gamut from an utterly banal tune to the most complicated counterpoint.

Milhaud has been most closely identified with **polytonality,** but as was the case with Debussy and the whole-tone scale, the device had been anticipated by others, such as Ravel, Ives, Bartók, Satie and Stravinsky. One authority states that Milhaud's particular brand of polytonality were better termed *polymelody,* as the composer's tendency toward lyricism and his Gallic predilection for clarity led him to set off one melody from another. We have noted his love of Latin American rhythms and his use of folksong. Perhaps it is fairest to say that Milhaud has never been an adherent of any single -ism, but in true eclectic style has been able to use elements of all of them as it suited his intentions.

OTHER FRENCH COMPOSERS

Other French composers of originality are Henri Sauget (1901-   ), who "combines a pseudo-counterpoint à la Bach, with jazz rhythms and the antiquated graces of Second Empire romance," to quote Prunières; Jean Françaix (1912-   ), whose works fall into a neo-Classic style; Jacques Ibert (1890-1962), best known for his amusing piano piece, *Le petit âne blanc* ("The Little White Donkey") and the symphonic sketches, *Escales (Port of Call,* 1922); and Oliver Messiaen (1908-   ), of whom Auric wrote prophetically: "His fresh inspiration and extremely personal accent at once compelled attention . . . I shall be much surprised if we have not, in Oliver Messiaen, one of the future masters of French music."

A pupil of Dukas and an organist, Messiaen has intermingled Catholic mysticism with Oriental occultism, using strange sonorities, electronic instruments, recorded natural sounds and intricate rhythms to produce novel and exciting effects. His *Mode de valeurs et d'intensités* (1949) for piano is an attempt at "total control" (which we shall discuss in the Prologue), supplementing three twelve-tone rows with rows of attacks, dynamics and durations. Some see in Messiaen's *Chronochromie* (1960) an extension of Scriabin's interest in the relationship between color and tone. As Oliver Daniel writes, *"Chronochromie* is colorful, to be sure, and less birdie than one might expect. It is indeed a fascinating and brilliant orchestral tour de force that both pleases and exasperates." Messiaen has been very influential as professor of harmony at the Paris Conservatory, counting among his pupils, Pierre Boulez (1924-   ), one of the most important young European composers of today.

REPRESENTATIVE SOVIET COMPOSERS

Sergei Prokofiev (1891-1953) was the leading Soviet Russian composer of the second quarter of the twentieth century. A realist by nature, his earlier music shows an iconoclastic fearlessness comparable to that of early Stravinsky. His vigor and virility reveal themselves in motoric rhythms and clashing dissonances. A savage, barbaric side is exhibited in such works as the *Scythian Suite, Op.* 20 (1914). Sabaneyev comments that "Prokofiev restored to Russian music the jest and irony, the satire and laughter." He is a master of musical grotesquerie, as evidenced in *Sarcasms, Op.* 17 (1912-14) for piano, in which he indicates his polyharmonic scheme by using different key signatures for each staff, as well as in his ballet for Diaghilev, *Chout, Op.* 21 (*The Buffoon,* 1924) and his opera for Chicago, *The Love for Three Oranges, Op.* 33 (1919). Classic proclivities are apparent in his leaning toward the larger traditional forms of concerto, sonata and symphony, while neo-Classicism appears in the concise and elegant *Classical Symphony* (No. 1), *Op.* 25 (1917), composed, the creator stated, "as Haydn might have written it had he lived in our day," and in his chamber music. All these stylistic characteristics can be found in the oft-performed *Concerto No. 3 in C for Piano, Op.* 26 (1921).

After sixteen years spent in European music centers and in the United States, Prokofiev returned to Russia and from 1932 until his death was one of the outstanding Soviet composers. A change took place in his music, a simplification and directness—almost a neo-Romanticism—which did not, however, alter the verve, vitality and charm of almost everything he wrote. With the *Symphonic Song, Op.* 57 (1933) Prokofiev assumed his role of Soviet composer. Many works from the Soviet period quickly found a permanent place in the twentieth-century repertoire. They include a suite from film music for *Lieutenant Kijé, Op.* 60 (1934); the *Concerto No. 2 in G Minor for Violin and Orchestra, Op.* 63 (1935); suites from the ballet, *Romeo and Juliet, Op.* 64-bis (1935); the famous *Peter and the Wolf, Op.* 67 (1936), an engaging musical fairy tale, expertly orchestrated; a cantata drawn from film music, *Alexander Nevsky, Op.* 78 (1938); the ambitious opera, *War and Peace, Op.* 91 (1941-52) after Tolstoy's novel; *Symphony No. 5, Op.* 100 (1944), dedicated "to the spirit of Man"; a ballet, *Cinderella, Op.* 87 (1944); and the *Symphony No. 7, Op.* 131 (1953), his last. In addition there are ten piano sonatas, written in a powerful and idiomatic manner and such occasional compositions as *Ode on the End of the War, Op.* 105 (1945) for eight harps, four pianos, military band, percussion ensemble and double basses.

In 1929 a Manifesto had been issued which stated that the proletariat musician would "fight the influence of decadent bourgeois music among young musicians, impress the necessity of absorbing the best, the healthiest, and ideologically acceptable elements of the musical legacy of the past, prepare the ground for the formation of a new proletarian music."

Although the organization that formulated the Manifesto was disbanded, the accomplishments of Prokofiev, Dmitri Shostakovich, Aram Khachaturian and Dmitri Kabalevski attest to the fact that its purposes were carried out.

Communist leaders recognized the importance of using music to inspire and to entertain. They have assisted their artists by giving them economic and temporal freedom to work, even in war-time, to supply the demand for music. So the Soviet composers have created for their people not only great symphonies, choral works and chamber music, but they have written Red Army music, songs for the workers and for youth organizations. Gifted men have been encouraged to create, but to create music that would meet the political purposes of the U.S.S.R.

Dmitri Shostakovich (1906-   ) astounded the musical world when he was nineteen with his *First Symphony, Op.* 10 (1925) and many feel that it has a quality that the Soviet composer has seldom equaled. Since 1926, Shostakovich has completed twelve more symphonies. The second was the *October Symphony* (1927), celebrating the tenth anniversary of the Revolution; the third is called *May First* (1931). When the latter was introduced the composer made the statement, "I am a Soviet composer, and I see our epoch as something heroic, spirited, and joyous . . . Music cannot help having a political basis—an idea that the bourgeoisie are slow to comprehend. There can be no music without ideology." Here we see the tangible workings of the Manifesto.

The Manifesto extended ever further as far as Shostakovich was concerned, because in 1936, an article in the Moscow newspaper denounced his opera, *Lady Macbeth of Mzensk,* as an "un-Soviet perversion." It continued to state that "the listener is plunged into a mass of international discords." The composer was also accused in his ballet, *The Limpid Stream* (1935), "of treating a Soviet theme lightly, not to say frivolously." "Formalism" and "realism" in music were the subjects of heated discussions in the Soviet press. Shostakovich, an ardent believer in Soviet principles, had to recant and to reconstruct his creative work. After writing the *Fourth Symphony* (1936), he withdrew it as inadequate and immediately started the *Fifth* (1937), one of his strongest works. Its reception was an artistic and personal triumph for the young composer. His "mistaken tendencies" were forgotten, or else forgiven.

The *Sixth* (1939), *Seventh* (1941) and *Eighth* (1943) *Symphonies* followed and were successful. Shostakovich worked on the *Seventh* in Leningrad while the city was under siege. He had volunteered for the Red Army but was refused because of his value as an artist. The symphony starts as a requiem to those who lost their lives "so that justice and reason might triumph" and ends in a prophecy of victory. While the

Eighth Symphony is an appropriately serious wartime work, the *Ninth* is quite cheerful. The *Tenth* (1953) won a New York Critics' Circle Award while the *Eleventh* (1958) subtitled "The Year 1905," has an appropriately Soviet program for an inventive but restricted composer like Shostakovich, who was trained in post-Revolution Russia and has rarely left his native land. A *Twelfth Symphony in D Minor, Op.* 112, "1927," appeared in 1959 and a *Thirteenth,* for voices and orchestra, in 1962.

Shostakovich, like Prokofiev, has a keen sense of the grotesque, a quality that may have been misunderstood by his censors. It is evident in his opera, *The Nose* (1930), in his ballet, *The Golden Age* (1930), whence the well-known "Polka," and in many of the twenty-four *Preludes and Fugues* (1951). He has written chamber music of high quality, including ten string quartets. Moreover, he has also composed much incidental music and film music as well as large choral-orchestra works like the choral cycle, *Democratic Vistas* (1951) after Walt Whitman. In 1966 Shostakovich suffered a severe heart attack. What effect that will have on his future creativity we shall have to wait and see.

Aram Khachaturian (1903-   ), a native of Tbilisi, Georgia, brings to Soviet music an Armenian folk flavor. Gerald Abraham writes:

> The oriental essays of composers like (Lev) Knipper (1898-), (Boris) Shekhter (1900-   ) and Khachaturyan are the fruit of their attempts to saturate themselves in Asiatic folkmusic . . . and to evolve from it a higher type of musical organism playable by ordinary Western instruments of orchestras, yet otherwise free from the conventions of European music.

Khachaturian has written several symphonies, ballets, chamber music in which he uses native Caucasian rhythms and melodies, and attractive piano pieces. His best-known works include a *Concerto for Piano and Orchestra* (1936), which reflects Orientalism and is technically brilliant in the Lisztian tradition; *Gayne (Happiness,* 1942), a ballet in which is celebrated life and love on a collective farm and from which comes the pulsating "Saber Dance"; and a *Concerto for 'Cello and Orchestra* (1950).

A student of Scriabin and Nikolai Miaskovski (1881-1950) at the Moscow Conservatory, Dmitri Kabalevski (1904-   ) writes in a rhythmic, tonal idiom. The composer of operas, ballets, four symphonies, chamber music, songs, incidental music and piano pieces, he is represented outside the Soviet Union by his teaching pieces for children; several sonatinas for piano; the overture to his opera, based on Romain Rolland's *Colas Breugnon* (1937): *The Comedians* (1940), a suite for small orchestra; and twenty-four *Preludes* for piano (1943). Like

Prokofiev, Knipper, Wessarion Shebalin (1902-1963) and Yuri Shaporin (1887-   ), Kabalevski has written large choral-orchestral works, one of the most recent of which is a *Requiem* (1963).

In a nation which has recently witnessed the most radical social upheavals, art is still characterized by conservatism, political utility and popular accessibility. The Communist position would seem to have the same objective that Count Leo Tolstoy advocated in his treatise, *What Is Art?*

> . . . Universal art, by uniting the most different people in one common feeling, by destroying separation, will educate people to union, will show them, not by reason, but by life itself, the joy of universal union reaching beyond the bonds set by life.

REPRESENTATIVE MIDDLE EUROPEAN COMPOSERS

Bohuslav Martinu (1890-1959) has been assessed by André Coeuroy as "one of the most happily endowed musicians not only of Czechoslovakia but of all contemporary Europe." He was born and brought up in the tower of a country church. A shy youth, he had difficulty in school and later at the Prague Conservatory of Music. He studied the violin, taught music in high school, played in the Czech Philharmonic, studied composition with Josef Suk, and in 1923 went to Paris. There he studied with Albert Roussel and found himself in an environment of modern music, painting and literature which fascinated him. It was the day of Diaghilev's *Ballet Russe* and *Les Six*. Martinu was particularly influenced by Stravinsky, whose example seemed to answer many of his problems concerning the modern techniques of composition. Although he looked to Paris rather than to Vienna, Martinu continued the line of Bohemian composers, combining neo-Classicism with Czech Romanticism. He remained in Paris until 1940, when he moved to New York.

Martinu's name became known in this country in 1932 when he won the Elizabeth Sprague Coolidge Prize with a string sextet. He has written many operas, ballets, chamber-music works, orchestral compositions and an opera-film. His interest in neo-Classic forms as evidenced in the *Double Concerto* for two string orchestras, piano and kettledrums (1940), a work that had a checkered career, owing to war conditions. When he left Paris the manuscript was lost. But on his arrival here he learned that the Czech conductor, George Szell, now musical director of the Cleveland Symphony, had rescued a copy in Prague. It has had many performances since Koussevitsky first presented it with the Boston Symphony Orchestra. In America Martinu composed a beautiful elegy for orchestra, *Memorial to Lidice* (1943) and undertook writing symphonies, the sixth and last of which was introduced in 1955.

Ernest Bloch's (1880-1959) influence in America has been not through his compositions alone but also through his having taught many well-known American composers, such as George Antheil (1900-1959), Ernst Bacon (1898-   ), Mark Brunswick (1902-   ), Ray Green (1909-   ), Douglas Moore, Quincy Porter (1897-1966), Bernard Rogers (1893-   ), Roger Sessions, and Randall Thompson (1899-   ). Bloch might be called a musical prophet of the Hebrews, as he tried to capture the spirit and tradition of the Old Testament, "the sacred emotion of the race that slumbers deep in our soul." In his music is an amalgam of German, French, Swiss, Hebrew, Romantic and neo-Classic influences.

Born in Geneva, Bloch studied in Belgium, Germany and France. His opera, *Macbeth,* was presented at the *Opéra Comique,* Paris, in 1910, but was withdrawn for political reasons although the public liked it. Ironically, some twenty-five years later it was successfully revived in Italy, only to be proscribed by Mussolini. Bloch returned to Switzerland but came to the United States during the First World War. He was introduced to American music lovers with his excellent *First String Quartet* (1916), and in 1919 won a prize with the *Suite* for viola and piano.

Bloch was far from the cool constructivist; his was a music of emotion and abandon. Apart from those works directly inspired by Hebraic themes stand his *Concerto Grosso No. 1* for string orchestra and piano obbligato (1925) written to demonstrate neo-Classicism to his students at the Cleveland Institute of Music, where he served as director for five years; the impressive *Quintet for Piano and Strings* (1923) in which the composer used quarter-tones; an epic rhapsody, *America* (1926), a gesture to his adopted land in which he used jazz, American songs and Indian motives; a *Violin Concerto* (1938); a *Symphony for Trombone and Orchestra* (1954); *Proclamation for Trumpet and Orchestra* (1955); and *Quartet No. 5* (1956).

Compositions of his "Jewish Cycle" include: *Trois Poèmes juifs* (1913); *Schelomo* (*Solomon,* 1916), a rhapsody for 'cello and orchestra, with passages suggesting Oriental cantillation; *Baal Shem* (1923), for violin and piano; *Sacred Service* (1933), a magnificent work for baritone solo, chorus and orchestra; and *Suite Hebraïque* for viola and orchestra (1953). In these works Bloch fulfilled himself, for as he wrote:

> I am a Jew. I aspire to write Jewish music because it is the only way in which I can produce music of vitality—if I can do such a thing at all.

Kurt Weill (1900-1950), a pupil of Ferruccio Busoni (1866-1924), had been interested in several experiments, such as employment of the jazz idiom and *Gebrauchsmusik*. He wrote *Die Dreigroschenoper* (*Three-Penny Opera*, 1928), a modern German version of Gay's *Beggar's Opera*, which, Copland says, "used the jazz idiom to mirror the depressed and tired Germany of the twenties in an unforgettably poignant way." *The Rise and Fall of the City Mahagonny* (1930), which Weill called a *Singspiel*, was a chamber-music opera in jazz idiom. Ernst Křenek tabulated it in *Music Here and Now* as "musical surrealism."

Weill wrote a short opera for children called *Der Jasager* (*The Yes Man*), carrying out the ideas of the *Gebrauchsmusik* movement. In 1935 he settled in America, where he worked with the idea of writing music that the public would understand. He wrote incidental music for Franz Werfel's *The Eternal Road*, Paul Green's *Johnny Johnson* (1936), and Elmer Rice's *Street Scene* (1947) as well as the music for Maxwell Anderson's *Knickerbocker Holiday* (1938) and Moss Hart's *Lady in the Dark*. He also composed an opera in folk idiom for young people, *Down in the Valley* (1948).

Ernst Křenek (1900-   ), of Viennese birth and a pupil of Franz Schreker, as composer of *Jonny Spielt auf!* (*Johnny Strikes Up the Band*, 1927) won a reputation of writing light popular music, when as a matter of fact he has an enormous modern technique, and is a serious composer with an austere outlook on the latest contrapuntal style. Křenek is one of the most important composers now making use of twelve-tone serialism. His opera, *Karl V* (1933), was the most comprehensive work written under these principles to that time. Through Křenek's compositions we find a line of development paralleling that of the twentieth century in general; from Mahler (whose daughter he married), Křenek moved to neo-Classicism, atonality and jazz until he reached dodecaphony, which he adapted to his own purposes. His works include operas, ballets, choral pieces, eight string quartets, six piano sonatas, four piano concertos and five symphonies. Křenek came to the United States in 1938, and has taught at Vassar College and Hamline University. In 1963 he received the Grand Prize of Austria.

Ernst Toch (1887-1964), another Viennese, has contributed chamber music, piano, orchestral and stage works to the modern repertoire. With Schreker, Eduard Künneke (1885-1953) and Max Butting (1888-   ), Toch composed for the German Broadcasting Company, before emigrating to America, where he became a citizen in 1940 and professor of composition at the University of Southern California. Although his music is essentially Romantic and tonal, Toch has experimented with spoken voices (*Gesprochene Musik—Spoken Music*, 1930) and free serialism (*String Quartet No. 7, Op. 74*, 1957). His best-known compositions include an opera, *The Princess and the Pea* (1927); *Big Ben,* variations on the "Westminster Chimes" (1934); *Pinocchio,* "a merry overture" (1936); *Symphony No. 3* (1955), which won a Pulitzer Prize; and *Five Pieces for Wind Instruments and Percussion* (1962).

While Werner Egk (1901-   ) is primarily a composer of opera and orchestral works that utilize Bavarian folk elements, Boris Blacher (1903-   ) has written in many forms, including such splendid orchestral scores as *Concertante Music for Orchestra* (1937) and *Variations on a Theme of Paganini* (1947). With *Orchester-Ornament* (1953) Blacher began employing a system that he calls **variable meter,** a methodical organization of bars of differing lengths so combined and repeated that serial formations result. While difficult for conductor and performers, variable meter does not impede the flow of music for the listener.

REPRESENTATIVE BRITISH COMPOSERS

Two leading composers of the English school are William Walton (1902-   ) and Constant Lambert (1905-1951). Walton's early work, *Façade* (1923), a catchy chamber setting of Edith Sitwell's poems, in which the composer shows music-hall influence, was an immediate success. In 1925 a comedy overture, *Portsmouth Point,* followed. Leaning toward neo-Classicism, Walton produced a *Viola Concerto* (1929) and *Sinfonia Concertante* for piano and orchestra (1928), which caused him to be labeled "The English Hindemith." His reputation rests upon surprisingly few works. Among them are an oratorio, *Belshazzar's Feast* (1931), presenting the Biblical story in dramatic, colorful scenes, connected by a baritone narrator; a *Violin Concerto* (1939), written for Jascha Heifitz; an opera, *Troilus and Cressida* (1954) and a *Second Symphony* (1960).

The Rio Grande (1929), on a poem by Sacheverell Sitwell, set for piano, chorus and orchestra, gave Constant Lambert an opportunity to use jazz syncopations entertainingly. We see the influence in his *Piano Sonata* (1929) and the *Piano Concerto* with small orchestra (1931). Lambert served as musical director of Sadler's Wells from 1928 to 1947, and composed ballets, incidental music and music for films. His pessimistic and biting book, *Music Ho! A Study of Music in Decline* (1934), aroused much comment for its sarcastic and outspoken opinions. Edwin Evans comments:

> Lambert has no affectation, but he is an intellectual to whom craftsmanship is incidental and ancillary. Walton's interest is more narrowly musical, and therefore more directly concerned with it. They are, in fact, entirely different types.

Most brilliant among established British composers of today are Michael Tippett (1905-   ) and Benjamin Britten (1913-   ). Tippett's early interest lay in the rhythmic style of English madrigalists whose influence can be discerned in his *Double Concerto for Strings* (1939). As he has matured, however, he has increasingly freed himself from any leaning toward nostalgia for the past or Romanticism and delved into Jungian psychology in such operas as *The Midsummer Marriage* (1952) and *King Priam* (1962). The former has given us a brilliant concert piece in the "Ritual Dances" from Act II. Tippett has also composed a *Piano Concerto* (1953) which evinces an aura of otherworldliness.

Benjamin Britten has a very long list of interesting compositions to his credit, as he commenced composition at an early age and has shown enormous facility. As Hansen comments, "He seems to sum up, and to have at his disposal, all of the musical techniques and idioms of his time just as Mozart made thorough use of the ideals and vocabulary of his age." The son of a Suffolk dentist, Britten studied with Frank Bridge and at the Royal College of Music in London. He spent several years in America, during which time several of his works were heard, including an opera, *Paul Bunyan* (1941) and some beautiful settings of Michelangelo poems. Since his return to wartime England he has lived in Aldeburgh, on the seacoast of his native county.

Among Britten's many works are *Variations for String Orchestra on a Theme by Frank Bridge, Op.* 10 (1937); settings of Rimbaud's poetry, *Les Illuminations* for high voice and strings, *Op.* 18 (1939); *Serenade for Tenor, Horns and Strings, Op.* 31 (1944); the *Variations and Fugue on a Theme by Henry Purcell, Op.* 34, also known as *The Young Person's Guide to the Orchestra* (1945), in which each instrument of the orchestra and each choir is given a chance to strut in very fine idiomatic writing; and a *Spring Symphony, Op.* 44 (1949) for three soloists, orchestra and chorus. *The Ceremony of Carols* (1942) for boys' voices and harp has already established itself as a classic and the *War Requiem* (1961), using the Latin Requiem text interspersed with poems by Wilfred Owen, has aroused critical acclaim. Britten's operas, however, form the core of his output to date. They include *Peter Grimes* (1945); *The Rape of Lucretia* (1946); *Albert Herring* (1947); *Let's Make an Opera* (1948); *The Little Sweep* (1949), a children's opera; *Billy Budd* (1951); *The Turn of the Screw* (1954); *Noye's Fludde* (1958), another children's work; and, most recently, *A Midsummer Night's Dream* (1960), among others. In these he shows to best advantage his eclectic and resourceful gifts, and his sense of musical elegance.

Fig. 91. Scene from the Metropolitan Opera Co. production of Benjamin Britten's *Peter Grimes,* 1966-67 season. Britten's opera, a psychological drama conceived in *arioso-recitativo* terms, expresses "the perpetual struggle of men and women whose livelihood depends on the sea." (Photograph courtesy *The New York Times.*)

REPRESENTATIVE LATIN AMERICAN COMPOSERS

Although sharing one hemisphere, North Americans have always been more closely connected with Europe than with South America, Mexico and Central America. And Hispano-America or Latin America, the name by which it is better known, has been more empathetic to Spain, Portugal and even Italy, than with the United States or the rest of Europe. Race, religion, language, early discovery and exploration are at the root of this separation. To the outsider, the music of all Latin-American countries may sound alike, but a little study will reveal differences due to various influences and backgrounds. The chief ingredients of the music are Indian, Negro and Spanish.

With the twentieth century, Latin America came of age musically and the period of strong European influence and dilettantism was over. A renaissance took place there just as it did almost everywhere else. The conservatories and organizations of the nineteenth century reaped a rich harvest in well-trained musicians, excellent pianists and gifted composers. These became conscious of both national and international, local and regional influences.

Foremost composer of South America was Heitor Villa-Lobos (1887-1959) of Rio de Janeiro. He began his musical career early, playing the 'cello in theaters and moving-picture houses and writing popular music. After youthful attempts at composition, he became immersed in the problem of using Brazilian primitive and folk music as the basis of a national art expression. Making frequent trips into the interior of Brazil, he collected material from the Indians, and absorbed the character of his vast country from coastal cities to jungle, which he then transmuted into exotic music. Francisco Curt Lange describes Villa-Lobos as "restless and inquiring, profoundly Brazilian, endowed with a spirit of inexhaustible initiative." Lange also characterizes him as "absolutely spontaneous, witty, vivacious, humorous—a real prodigy—rather than one who creates by reflection." This last statement is borne out by the fact that the composer has written over 2000 works.

Villa-Lobos met Artur Rubinstein, the pianist, and Darius Milhaud, the French composer, in Brazil. Both had an influence on him. Rubinstein has played much of his piano music, from the *Prole de Bébé* (*Baby's Dolls,* 1918-1921) to the *Rudepoema* (1921-1926) which Villa-Lobos made into one of his most elaborate orchestral compositions. Milhaud introduced him to Debussy's music. In 1923 the Brazilian journeyed to Paris, where he remained for four years. There he drank in French Impressionism and works of the later school, including neo-Classicism and Stravinsky, as avidly as he had absorbed his own native music.

The *Bachianas Brasileiras* are nine suites combining Bach's technique and Brazilian folklore in what Slonimsky calls "an audacious, but remarkably successful experiment." Each movement has a double title, one traditional, the other Brazilian. For example, in the first suite, an ensemble of eight 'cellos, the movements are marked Introduction (*Embolada*), Prelude (*Modinha*), Fugue (*Conversación*). Other of the *Bachianas Brasileiras* are for chamber orchestra, piano and chamber orchestra, piano solo and orchestra, and voice and 'cellos. They also exist in piano form. To Villa-Lobos, Bach's universality seems to flow directly from the folk and he became an intermediary between all peoples.

Villa-Lobos, always an original thinker, wrote fourteen works which he named *chôros* (1920-1928). Although *chôros* means a street band of players of popular songs, Villa-Lobos says that he used the title to mean a composition "in which the various aspects of Brazilian music, Indian and popular, achieve their synthesis." The *chôros* are in all styles from a guitar solo, a duet for flute and clarinet, a quartet for brass instruments, a piano solo, to large works for full orchestra and native percussion instruments, and a work for piano and orchestra. *Chôros* No.

10 is for mixed chorus and is particularly successful in depicting the primitive.

A few years after his return from Paris, Villa-Lobos was made supervisor and director of music education in Brazil (1932). He has written hundreds of children's choruses and has experimented in solutions of many interesting educational problems. Each year on Brazil's Independence Day, he conducted a group of several thousand school children in what he called an "orpheonic concentration," for which he wrote original works concerned with all sorts of effects including "percussive and explosive sounds, sibilation, and clapping hands."

A contemporary and fellow countryman of Carlos Chávez, whom we discussed in Chapter 1, Silvestre Revueltas (1899-1940) began his musical career as a violinist. As a seventeen-year-old boy he went to Austin, Texas, and then to Chicago to study. He gave recitals in Mexico, and conducted theater orchestras in Texas and Alabama. After Chávez founded the *Orquesta Sinfónica de México,* Revueltas was appointed assistant conductor in 1929. He left that post in 1936 to conduct a new group, *Orquesta Sonfónica Nacional,* but his activities were interrupted by the Spanish Civil War, for he went to Spain to take part in the cultural activities of the music section of the Loyalist government. After his return home, he composed and conducted until his untimely death in Mexico City.

Chávez encouraged Revueltas to compose, and performed his early orchestral scores. "Revueltas was the spontaneously inspired type of composer," writes Copland, "whose music was colorful, picturesque and gay." He said that he loved best the music of the ranchos and villages, while Chávez's inspiration came from ritualistic music of the ancient Indian tribes of Mexico. This difference shows in their composing methods. Revueltas' rhythms and melodies are based on an urban folklore. He absorbed the spirit of his country so completely that he reproduced it without using actual popular or folk tunes. His harmony is dissonant, sometimes to the point of being brutal. His rhythmic sense is extremely complex, often giving to his works a wildness and an abandon that mark him as a unique and individualistic composer. His form is not traditional, and in his use of instruments he frequently imitates the Mexican popular orchestra. His percussion writing, which lends brilliance and color to his scores, is highlighted by the addition of many native drums and rattles. Among his compositions are *Esquinas (Corners,* 1930), *Ventanas (Windows,* 1931) and *Caminos (Roads,* 1934).

Alberto Ginastera (1916-   ) is regarded as one of the most gifted of the younger composers of this hemisphere. He has attempted a reconciliation of national and international traits. Lange states that he brings "to Argentine rhythm and melody the harmony and timbre of the modern European schools. His technique falls within a very orderly framework, and his very clear style and the fluidity of his musical utterance are extremely agreeable."

Ginastera has written ballets, one of which is *Panambí* (1940); a *Concierto Argentino* (1941) for piano and orchestra; chamber music; a *Sinfonia Porteña (Buenos Aires Symphony,* 1942); and piano pieces, such as *Danzas Argentinas* (1937). In 1943 Ginastera won a Guggenheim Fellowship. Since his stay in the United States the composer has undergone a transition period which wiped away most traces of such stylistic influences as Villa-Lobos, Stravinsky, Bartók and Copland and witnessed a personal absorption of serial techniques first found in his *Second String Quartet* (1958) and the *Cantata para América Mágica* (1960), which is scored for fifty-three percussion instruments and dramatic soprano. His opera, *Don Rodrigo* (1964), was chosen by the N.Y. City Center Opera Company to inaugurate its 1966 season at the Lincoln Center cultural complex.

We have almost forgotten that Louis Moreau Gottschalk, an American-born composer of the nineteenth century, spent much of his time and made himself famous in Latin America. Gilbert Chase calls him "the first musical ambassador of the United States to Latin America" and says that he was also its musical discoverer. Today a number of our writers and composers have "discovered" Latin America. Aaron Copland made a "good-will" trip into South America and is a frequent visitor to Mexico. "It wasn't the music I heard, but the spirit that I felt there, which attracted me." And Copland captured that spirit of the popular dance hall in *El Salón México*. Cuba attracted George Gershwin, who wrote a *Cuban Overture* (1934). Harl MacDonald (1899-1955) wrote a *Rumba Symphony,* suggested by the popularity of the Cuban dance. Paul Bowles (1910-   ) has visited Mexico and has written several *Huapangos*. Morton Gould (1913-   ) has caught Mexican rhythms in his work, *Latin American Symphonette* (1941) and Henry Cowell and Robert McBride (1911-   ) have been attracted by Latin-American folk tunes.

REPRESENTATIVE AMERICAN COMPOSERS

There is little doubt that music through the ages has not yet completely thrown off European domination; there is equally little doubt that increasingly the United States is gaining a more prominent place in the world music scene. Although we shall adopt the year 1910 as an arbitrary cutoff birth date by which to limit American composers to be discussed here, we are still forced to exclude many, many figures worthy of representation, and pay the most cursory notice to others. The reader is referred to Marion Bauer's *Twentieth-Century Music* and other specialized works for more generous and explicit information.

Highly influential upon the American musical scene today are those composers born between 1890 and 1910, most of whom are still actively creative and whose work is technically proficient, mentally and emotionally stimulating and far too seldom performed for most of us to have a genuine acquaintance with it. Included in this group are Douglas Moore (1893-   ), a student of Horatio Parker and d'Indy, chairman of the music department of Columbia University and a distinguished opera composer, among whose compositions are *The Devil and Daniel Webster* (1938), on a libretto by Stephen Vincent Benét, *Moby Dick* (1928) and *The Ballad of Baby Doe* (1956); Walter Piston (1894-   ), a pupil of the far-reaching French teacher, Nadia Boulanger, and composer of a favorite ballet score, *The Incredible Flutist* (1938), eight symphonies, several concertos and much chamber music of a moderately dissonant, polyphonic nature; Henry Cowell (1897-1965), an exhaustive researcher as well as composer, who gained renown through his experimental approach to **tone clusters,** chords built in seconds, and who has written a variety of music containing both American and exotic flavors; Roger Sessions (1896-   ), a Bloch pupil, whose music, thorny for the casual listener, includes incidental music to Andreyev's play, *The Black Maskers* (1930), an opera, *Montezuma* (1947), chamber music, the *Idyll of Theocritus* for soprano and orchestra (1956) and *Symphony No. 5* (1964); and Virgil Thomson (1896-   ), a disciple of Satie, who developed an American Romantic style characterized by simplicity and satire, as heard in his operas, *Four Saints in Three Acts* (1928), on a libretto by Gertrude Stein, the ballet, *Filling Station* (1938) and film music, such as *The River* (1937) and *Louisiana Story* (1948), as well as *A Solemn Music* for band (1949), a *Mass of 1959* and *The Feast of Love,* for baritone and chamber orchestra (1964).

Howard Hanson (1896-   ), an eminent educator at the Eastman School of Music in addition to being a prolific composer, works in a neo-Romantic idiom, stemming from Liszt, Franck and Sibelius, with an opera, *Merry Mount* (1934), symphonic poems like *Pan and the Priest* (1926), choral works such as *Three Songs from Drum Taps* (1935) and five symphonies to his credit. In contrast to the sophistication of his colleagues, Roy Harris (1898-   ), an Oklahoman who studied with Arthur Farwell, has a dynamic force, a primitive quality and something of the Western spirit of adventure in his music, which is characteristically American, melodic and often modal. His *Third Symphony* (1939), suggesting the development of music from Gregorian chant through the complexities of polyphony, is a most interesting work. Perhaps his most popular composition is an arrangement of "When Johnny Comes Marching Home Again."

Contemporary with Roy Harris, but with a tragically shortened lifespan, was George Gershwin (1898-1937), one of the few American composers to penetrate the European continent. A graduate of Tin Pan Alley and a matchless melodist, Gershwin is represented by but five large and somewhat imperfect works: *The Rhapsody in Blue* (1924); *Concerto in F for Piano* (1925), commissioned by Walter Damrosch; *An American in Paris* (1928); a *Second Rhapsody* (1931); and the folk opera, *Porgy and Bess* (1935), in which the jazz idiom was grafted to the trunk of European tradition, with moving results.

Aaron Copland, one of our most gifted Americans, was born in Brooklyn in 1900, in an urban environment "that," as he comments, "had little or no connection with serious music," an environment that this much-honored, kindly man has never forgotten nor, for that matter, blamed, as he explains in an essay, "The Composer in Industrial America." His studies in composition were made with Rubin Goldmark in New York and the very influential French pedagogue, Nadia Boulanger, who has nurtured several generations of American musicians. In Copland's early works we find a melding of sophisticated European methods of the 1920's with American jazz elements. This combination is evident in such compositions as the *Dance Symphony* (1925), which was awarded an R. C. A. Victor Company prize; *Music for the Theater* (1925), composed at the MacDowell Colony and introduced to the American public by the League of Composers, a society organized in 1923 to promote contemporary compositions; and the *Concerto for Piano and Orchestra* (1927), of which the composer wrote, "This proved to be the last of my 'experiments' with symphonic jazz . . . an easy way to be American in musical terms," yet one that was limited to two moods, the "blues" and the snappy number.

Other early music included Copland's first published piece, *The Cat and the Mouse* (1919), showing an influence of Impressionism; an unperformed ballet, *Grogh* (1923), from which he drew for later works; a *Symphony for Organ and Orchestra* (1925), written for Mlle. Boulanger's American tour; two choral works, *The House on the Hill* (from the poem of Edwin Arlington Robinson) and *An Immorality* (Ezra Pound); *Vitebsk* (1928), a study on a Jewish melody for violin, 'cello and piano; and *Symphonic Ode* (1929), one of the compositions celebrating the fiftieth anniversary of the Boston Symphony Orchestra, in which Copland's big gesture and interest in polytonality and poly-rhythms, characteristics of his early style, are epitomized.

After the *Ode,* Copland gradually came to grips with the problem that concerned the exponents of *Gebrauchsmusik;* namely, the need to lessen the gap between listeners and the contemporary idiom. In such works as *Piano Variations* (1930), *Short Symphony* (1933) and *Statements* (1935), as well as *The Second Hurricane* (1936), a "play-opera" for high school youth and the *Outdoor Overture* (1941), composed for the same group, we find a change in style, leaning on the one hand, toward conscious simplification, angularity and austerity, and on the other, toward actively enlisting the participation of young people in music-making.

A nationalistic idiom and further simplification was reached in the pages of his ballets and in his film scores. Copland's sense of rhythm, an important characteristic of his style, is completely American, as is his appropriation of cowboy tunes (*Music for the Radio* [1937], sub-titled "Saga of the Prairies"; *Billy the Kid* [1938]; and *Rodeo* [1942]): Latin American rhythms (*El salón México* [1936] and *Danzón Cubano* [1942]); and New England and Shaker hymns (*Appalachian Spring* [1944], an apotheosis of this approach which won a Pulitzer Prize). Film music includes effective scores for *Of Mice and Men* (1939); *Our Town* (1940); *The Red Pony* (1948); and *The Heiress* (1948), the latter earning an Academy Award. The lovely *Quiet City* (1940), for trumpet, English horn and string orchestra, was originally written as incidental music to a play. Copland's only opera, *The Tender Land* (1954), has not yet enjoyed complete success, perhaps because, as Machlis succinctly puts it, "Opera, like love, is best discovered before one is fifty."

Copland did not abandon his more abstract and less popular idiom during these years. His *Piano Sonata* (1941) combines the austere qualities of the *Piano Variations* with a highly developed sense of form and a percussive piano technique. It is the work of an outstanding com-poser, as is the *Sonata for Violin and Piano* (1943), in somewhat the same formal mold, although more gracious and tender in mood. Among other significant compositions are the *Third Symphony* (1946), an ex-pansive work suggesting, but not quoting, folk materials, full of con-templative lyricism, declamation, stimulating rhythms and ingenious counterpoint; *Concerto for Clarinet and String Orchestra* (1948), com-missioned by Benny Goodman, the popular clarinetist; a song cycle, *Twelve Poems of Emily Dickinson* (1950); and a *Piano Fantasy* (1958), in which Copland adopts an individual arrangement of twelve-tone principles. However rigorous the *Fantasy,* it does not exceed the starkness of the *Piano Variations* of 1930; nor does it escape the impress of a uniquely forceful musical personality.

Copland's most recent works include a *Nonet for Strings* (1960); *Connotations* (1952), an orchestral composition conceived entirely in serial technique; a ballet, *Dance Panels* (1963); and a symphonic suite, *Music for a Great City* (1964). Oscar Thompson writes:

> Harmonically spare, rhythmically strong, melodically hardedged rather than in any sense lush . . . Copland's music is always alive; even when, by a seeming contradiction of terms, its emotional content . . . yields an effect of sterility. Irrespective of whether there is lasting appeal in this music, it must be regarded as sharply representative of its day.

One of the most justly admired contemporary American composers is Elliott Carter (1908-   ), a pupil of Piston, Holst, Hill and Boulanger, and a man of intellectual breadth and rare sensibility. Possessor of an immense technique, Carter early absorbed elements of Stravinsky and Bartók, in addition to features of Renaissance and Baroque music, assimilating them into an increasingly chromatic and intricate personal style, characterized by both exuberance and sobriety. Carter has evolved a rhythmic process called **metrical modulation,** in which tempo changes "smoothly and accurately from one absolute metronomic speed to another by lengthening the value of the basic note unit," as Richard Goldman states. The process is roughly analogous to enharmonic changes in harmony. This "overlapping of speeds," to quote the composer, is found in his *Sonata for 'Cello and Piano* (1948) and the monumental *String Quartet No. 1* (1951), in which two instruments play serenely, while the other pair cavort about violently. As Carter disavows any slavish adherence to systems, the technique is handled most expressively and cannot be separated from "a large perspective of ideas."

Other significant works include the *Variations for Orchestra* (1955), of which Carter says: "As in all my works, I conceived this one as a large, unified musical action or gesture. In it, definition and contrast of character decrease during the first variations, arriving at a point of neutrality in the central variation, then increase again to the finale, which comprises many different speeds and characters"; *String Quartet No. 2* (1959), which won a Pulitzer Prize; the *Double Concerto* for harpsichord and piano with two chamber orchestras (1961), in which antiphony is gained not only spatially but in the writing itself; and an acclaimed *Piano Concerto* (1966), which Carter describes as a conflict between man and society.

Samuel Barber (1910-   ), educated at the Curtis Institute of Music, acquired his style relatively early like many lyricists. It was essentially conservative and projected with sure skill. His *Overture* to *The School for Scandal* (1932) and *Adagio for Strings* (1936) are among his best-known works. Others include two *Essays for Orchestra* (1938, 1942); *Concerto for Violin and Orchestra* (1939); and a *Capricorn Concerto* (1944) for chamber ensemble. A trained singer, Barber has written choral works, such as the cantata, *Prayers of Kierkegaard* (1954) and songs, among which is *Dover Beach* (1931), for solo voice and string quartet. As the composer matured, his Romantic style was enriched by more *avant-garde* techniques. More recent compositions show the influences of polytonality, chromaticism and newer rhythmic and melodic tendencies. Barber has written several operas, among which is *Vanessa* (1958), to a libretto by Gian-Carlo Menotti (1911-   ) and *Antony and Cleopatra* (1966), which opened the Metropolitan Opera Company's first season at Lincoln Center.

The present director of the Lincoln Center is William Schuman (1910-   ), who has had a skyrocket career despite his late start in music. An exciting teacher who drastically revised the curriculum of the Juilliard School of Music, a meticulous administrator, both at Juilliard and in his present position, Schuman incorporates his assertiveness and energy into large-scale musical works that include eight symphonies, the core of his production, in addition to several concertos, ballets, string quartets and choral works. His rhythms are forceful and he is interested in long melodic lines. Leonard Bernstein (1919-   ) writes that Schuman has "an energetic drive, a vigor of propulsion which seizes the listener by the hair, whirls him through space, and sets him down at will."

AMERICAN LYRIC THEATER, BALLET AND CANTATA

There is an encouraging development of American music in the lyric theater—in opera, Broadway musicals and the dance. In addition, eloquent choral works have occupied the American composer. In film, radio and television, the American field has potentials for a rich yield of music now and in the future.

Through the interest and appetites of university and regional semi-professional theaters, an American opera based on American themes has appeared, usually outside the periphery of the Metropolitan, whose attitude seems to turn increasingly conservative. We have already noted several distinctive contributions, to which we might add Louis Gruenberg's (1884-1964) *The Emperor Jones* (1933), on Eugene O'Neill's play of the same name. American folk operas, works characteristic of various sections of our country and those based on our literature abound, and, perhaps, the supply may create a demand. A sampling of them gives us an idea of the quantity and breadth of musico-dramatic production. Apart from those mentioned earlier are: Robert Russell Bennett's (1894-   ) *Malibran* (1935), based on an American incident in the great singer's life; Vittorio Giannini's (1903-1966) *The Scarlet Letter* (1938), after Hawthorne; Bernard Wagenaar's (1894-   ) *Pieces of Eight* (1943); Norman Lockwood's (1906-   ) *The Scarecrow* (1945), after Percy MacKaye's play; Marc Blitzstein's (1905-1964) *The Cradle Will Rock* (1936), *No for an Answer* (1941) and *Regina* (1949).

More recent operas include: Virgil Thomson's *The Mother of Us All* (1947), on a Gertrude Stein libretto about Susan B. Anthony; Lukas Foss' (1922-   ) *The Jumping Frog of Calaveras County* (1950), from Mark Twain's short story; Jan Meyerowitz's (1913-   ) *Eastward in Eden* (1951), based on Dorothy Gardner's play about Emily Dickinson; Jack Beeson's (1921-   ) *Hello Out There* (1954), after Saroyan; Gian-Carlo Menotti's *Saint of Bleecker Street* (1954); Carlisle Floyd's (1926-   ) *Susannah* (1955); Beatrice Laufer's (1923-   ) *Ile* (1958), after O'Neill; Louise Talma's (1906-   ) *Alcestis* (1959), on a libretto by Thornton Wilder; Norman Dello Joio's (1913-   ) *Blood Moon* (1961); and Martin David Levy's (1932-   ) *Mourning Becomes Electra* (1967), after O'Neill.

A related form dawning in the 1940's has rich promise, although we can but indicate it here. That is certain pieces of the Broadway musical theater, which have brought a fresh and less arty, if no less sincere, approach. Four composers have made a definite impression in works intermediate between opera and vaudeville. They are Richard Rodgers (1902-   ), with *Carousel* (1945), a version of Ferenc Molnar's *Liliom* transferred in locale from Budapest to Maine; Frank Loesser (1910-   ), a childhood friend of William Schuman's, with *Guys and Dolls* (1959), after Damon Runyon; Frederick Loewe (1904-   ), with *My Fair Lady* (1956), after George Bernard Shaw's *Pygmalion;* and Leonard Bernstein, with *West Side Story* (1957). In these musicals, the composers and librettists have stripped away clichés, formalities and stuffiness and given birth to a new form, neither musical comedy (for it is adaptable to tragedy or comedy), nor comic opera (for it has none of its artifices) nor grand opera (for it is neither grandiose nor pompous). In its essence, this form is romantic, vigorous and enthralling in its singable melodies.

Imaginative choreographers have stimulated composers to write ballet music of high quality. Agnes de Mille, among others, integrated ballet within such works as *Oklahoma!* and *Carousel.* The list of works written for Martha Graham alone is a long and impressive one. Many art years have passed since Tchaikovsky's *Swan Lake,* a landmark in modern ballet. Today the ballet is no interpolation or set of conventions or crinolined postures. In its own expansion, it has supplied the means of extending a growing form, perhaps most akin to the *dramma per musica* of the seventeenth century. Indeed, with the ballet, we have gone aeons back in a feat of reclamation, and given the dance its opportunity to express life, whether a sailor's shore leave, as in Bernstein's *Fancy Free* (1944), the elemental exposition of a ballad, as in Jerome Moross' (1913-   ) *Frankie and Johnny* (1938) or psychological insights, as in William Schuman's *Undertow* (1945). At present John Cage (1912-   ) and dancer Merce Cunningham are engaged in some interesting experiments.

Another trend that has strength is the modern cantata or choral work. Space prevents an adequate discussion, but we may cite some examples, among which are *Ballad for Americans* (1939) by Earl Robinson (1910-   ); *Folk Symphony* (No. 4, 1940) by Roy Harris; *A Lincoln Portrait* (1942), in which Aaron Copland uses a speaker instead of chorus in delivering Lincoln's words; *The Testament of Freedom* (1943) by Randall Thompson, on a text taken from the writings of Thomas Jefferson; *The Prairie* (1944) by Lukas Foss, on a text by Carl Sandburg; and *Western Star* (1944), by Dello Joio, on a poem by Stephen Vincent Benét.

*   *   *   *   *

In the preceding pages we have noted an international interest and vigor in music during the first half of the twentieth century. Amid the disparity of systems or lack of systems, we have selected the ambiguous aspect of eclecticism, that loosely binds contemporary composers into a more apparent than real unity. Actually, at mid-century, the musical scene is wide open. Some composers write with no more advanced techniques or materials than those of Sibelius; others construct personal musical idioms of expression from the resources of both past and present with a touch of the future.

But what, one may ask, of the present-day tendencies which are without direct antecedents in the past? What of the amplifications of serialism, of electronic music, of *musique concrète,* of so-called "chance" or aleatoric music, or even of computer music? What of the composers now in their forties who are just coming into prominence as figures of significance in music through the ages? We shall devote a few words to these queries in the Postlude.

SUGGESTIONS FOR FURTHER READING

Abraham, Gerald, *Eight Soviet Composers.* New York, Oxford University Press, 1943.

Austin, William W., *Music in the 20th Century*. New York, Norton, 1966.

Bauer, Marion, *Twentieth-Century Music*. New York, Putnam, 1947.

Berger, Arthur, *Aaron Copland*. New York, Dutton, 1955.

Broder, Nathan, *Samuel Barber*. New York, Schirmer, 1954.

Chávez, Carlos, *Toward a New Music*. New York, Norton, 1937.

Cowell, Henry, ed., *American Composers on American Music*. Palo Alto, Stanford University Press, 1933.

Dallin, Leon, *Techniques of Twentieth Century Composition*. Dubuque, W. C. Brown, 1964.

Demuth, Norman, *Musical Trends in the 20th Century*. London, Rockcliff, 1952.

Eimert, H. and Stockhausen, K., *Young Composers*. (*Die Reihe,* vol. 4) Bryn Mawr, Presser, 1960.

Gatti, Guido M., *Ildebrando Pizzetti*. London, Dobson, 1951.

Goldberg, Isaac, *George Gershwin*. New York, Ungar, 1958.

Hansen, Peter S., *Twentieth Century Music*. Boston, Allyn & Bacon, 1961.

Hartog, Howard, ed., *European Music in the Twentieth Century*.* London, Penguin, 1961.

Hiller, Lejaren A. and Isaacson, Leonhard M., *Experimental Music*. New York, McGraw-Hill, 1959.

Honegger, Arthur, *I Am a Composer*. New York, St. Martin's, 1966.

Hoover, Kathleen and Cage, John, *Virgil Thomson, His Life and Music*. New York, Yoseloff, 1959.

Howes, Frank, *The Music of William Walton*. New York, Oxford University Press, 1943.

Křenek, Ernst, *Music, Here and Now*. New York, Norton, 1939.

Lang, Paul Henry, *Contemporary Music in Europe*. New York, Norton, 1965.

———, ed., *Problems of Modern Music*.* New York, Norton, 1966.

Milhaud, Darius, *Notes Without Music*. New York, Knopf, 1953.

Mitchell, Donald and Keller, Hans, eds., *Benjamin Britten*. New York, Philosophical Library, 1953.

Nestyev, Israel V., *Sergei Prokofiev*. New York, Knopf, 1946.

Persichetti, Vincent, *Twentieth Century Harmony*. New York, Norton, 1961.

Sessions, Roger, *The Musical Experience*. Princeton, Princeton University Press, 1950.

Sofránek, Miloš, *Bohuslav Martinu*. New York, Knopf, 1944.

Schreiber, Flora R., and Persichetti, Vincent, *William Schuman*. New York, Schirmer, 1954.

Seroff, Victor, *Dmitri Shostakovich*. New York, Knopf, 1943.

Thomson, Virgil, *Virgil Thomson*. New York, Knopf, 1967.

Werth, Alexander, *Musical Uproar in Moscow*. London, Turnstile Press, 1949.

A SAMPLER OF SUPPLEMENTARY RECORDINGS

Barber, Samuel, *Adagio for Strings*
Blitzstein, Marc, *The Cradle Will Rock*
Blacher, Boris, *Studie im Pianissimo, Op.* 45 (1954)
Britten, Benjamin, *War Requiem, Op.* 66
Bloch, Ernest, *America, An Epic Rhapsody*
  Suites for Violin Solo

* Available in paperback edition.

Carter, Elliott, *Quartet* (1951)
Contemporary American Music Sampler
Copland, Aaron, *Quiet City for Trumpet, English Horn and Strings*
                    Appalachian Spring: Suite
Cowell, Henry, *Saturday Night at the Firehouse* (1948)
Egk, Werner, *Tentation de Saint-Antoine*
Gershwin, George, *An American in Paris*
Ginastera, Alberto, *Pampeana No. 3* (1953)
Hanson, Howard, *Symphony No. 2*, "Romantic"
Harris, Roy, *Symphony No. 3*
Honegger, Arthur, *Pacific 231*
                    King David
Kabalevski, Dmitri, *Children's Pieces, Op.* 27
                    Symphony No. 4 (1956)
Khachaturian, Aram, *Gayne*
Křenek, Ernst, *Eleven Transparencies* (1955)
Martinu, Bohuslav, *Concerto for Two String Orchestras*
Messiaen, Oliver, *Trois Petites Liturgies de la Présence divine*
Milhaud, Darius, *Création du monde*
                    Frenchman in New York (1963)
Moore, Douglas, *The Ballad of Baby Doe*
Piston, Walter, *The Incredible Flutist*
Poulenc, Francis, *Aubade for Piano and Eighteen Instruments*
                    Gloria in G
Prokofiev, Sergei, *Classical Symphony in D, Op.* 25
                    Peter and the Wolf, Op. 67
                    Piano Music
Revueltas, Silvestre, *Homenaje a Federico Garcia Lorca* (1936)
Rodgers, Richard, *Carousel*
Schuman, William, *American Festival Overture*
Sessions, Roger, *Black Maskers Suite*
Shostakovich, Dmitri, *Symphony No. 5, Op.* 47
                    Age of Gold
Tailleferre, Germaine, *Sonata for Harp*
Thompson, Randall, *Testament of Freedom*
Thomson, Virgil, *Four Saints in Three Acts*
Tippett, Michael, *Midsummer Marriage: Dances*
Toch, Ernst, *Geographical Fugue* (1930)
                    Five Pieces for Winds and Percussion (1961)
Villa-Lobos, Heitor, *Bachianas Brasileiras No. 5*
Walton, William, *Belshazzar's Feast*
Weill, Kurt, *Three-Penny Opera*

OPPORTUNITIES FOR STUDY IN DEPTH

1. In the year 1959, when Russia successfully launched the first moon rocket and Castro took over Cuba, the following compositions appeared: Boulez's *Improvisations sur Mallarmé;* Hindemith's *Pittsburgh Symphony;* Britten's *Missa Brevis;* Stravinsky's *Movements for Piano and Orchestra;* Meyer Kupferman's *On Jazz Elements;* Lou Harrison's *Suite for Symphonic Strings;* and

Ralph Shapey's *Evocation for Violin, Piano and Percussion*. Describe and compare these works.

2. Make a study of writing music for the films, perhaps with the idea of attempting such a venture as a class project. Hans Eisler's book, *Composing for the Films* (N.Y.: 1947) and periodical articles will provide illuminating information.

3. During recent years the concert band has become an important performing unit and modern composers have been using it as a medium for their creative thinking. Compile a short list of works for concert band and discuss them in terms of this comparatively new medium. Note strengths and weaknesses as compared with the standard symphonic ensemble.

4. Limitations of space have forced us to omit many significant twentieth-century composers, among whom are Luigi Dallapiccola (1904-), Ulysses Kay (1917-), Peter Mennin (1923-), Gian-Carlo Menotti (1911-) and Gottfried von Einem (1918-). Make a study of the contributions of one of these men, noting style and tendencies.

5. Prepare a bibliography of periodical literature pertinent to any one topic or composer mentioned in this chapter. If possible, briefly annotate each article cited for future reference.

6. We have gained some insight recently into Soviet music-making through cultural exchanges and post-Stalinist flexibility. What is the present function and situation of a Soviet composer? How much latitude is he allowed in writing his proletarian music? Outline findings.

7. We have stated, "Now we can see developing under our eyes American forms of music in the lyric theater." Is this true? What are they? Of what possible significance may they be for the future? Amplify.

8. Investigate the state of music in one of the less celebrated musical countries, such as Holland, Sweden, Japan or Greece. Information offices attached to national consulates in this country are very generous with materials about their achievements. Assemble a representative discography to accompany the report.

VOCABULARY ENRICHMENT

eclecticism	ideology
synthesis	variable meter
jazz age	*chôros*
machine age	tone clusters
Les Six	metrical modulation
Manifesto	American lyric theater
proletarian music	choreography

POSTLUDE

In an age of vast and startlingly swift scientific advances—of Venus shots, moon landings, quasars, laser beams, potent new chemicals and frightening insights into the nature of nature—when war for once seems mightier than pestilence and automation threatens every phase of our lives—we may well wonder how music is reacting to these constant changes and in what new directions the art is expanding to continue its function of interpreting human experience. How can a composer, engaged in his essentially solitary audiations and time-consuming manual labor (for as yet there is not even a satisfactory musical typewriter), adequately reflect the world of which he is a part and which is inescapably a part of him? The answer is now being prepared and will be consolidated in the future. It appears an exciting one, and an inevitable result of man's ability to adopt, to adapt and to break through barriers of limitation. We have noted the disintegration of systems and forms that reigned supreme for several hundred years, and pioneering attempts to replace them with new solutions. A powerful shaping force in twentieth-century music has been the development of mass media of communication and sound reproduction.

MEANS OF MUSIC REPRODUCTION

The advent of mechanical-electronic means of reproducing sound has effected a total musical revolution in our times, one that we are all too prone to take for granted because it has become so much a part of our lives. Radio, the phonograph, sound tracks, tapes and television have made all kinds of music available to all kinds of people, with, we may add, all kinds of results, not always beneficial. Never before has there been such a dissemination of music, nor such widespread interest. Refinements of the means of sound reproduction tend to obscure the fact that this situation is recent indeed. For instance, the electronic tube was not invented until 1906. The first experimental opera broadcast did not take place until 1910 when the legendary tenor, Enrico Caruso, sang *Pagliacci*. And, as we have already mentioned, the first symphony concert was not aired until 1926. For several decades thereafter the various radio networks pursued the enlightened policy of acting as patrons to stimulate new compositions and there was some reason to believe that radio might call forth a "special" kind of music based on frequency, intensity ranges, etc. The distortions and static interference of early broadcasting were corrected when F.M., developed by Major E. H. Armstrong, was introduced. As the ever-progressive conductor, Leopold Stokowski, wrote twenty years ago:

> The broadcasting of symphonic and operatic music requires a frequency range of from 30 to 13,000 cycles per second, and an intensity range of about 85 decibels. Anything less than these two ranges will not convey to the listener symphonic and operatic music with their full expression . . . Through frequency modulation these two ranges are possible. The chief engineers of any good American sound laboratory can achieve these results. The Bell Laboratories of New York and the RCA Laboratories of Princeton are examples of outstanding sound laboratories.

How dated that now sounds! Yet we still rely upon radio for live broadcasts of the Metropolitan Opera (which started in 1931) and programs of unusual contemporary music. And some of us are grateful for the memory of concerts by the N.B.C. Orchestra under Toscanini, the Sunday afternoons spent with the New York Philharmonic and recitals by the most eminent soloists and chamber-music ensembles.

In another category are "the storers," as Carlos Chávez calls them— the phonograph, the film sound track and the tape recorder. Improvements in the quality of sound reproduction achieved during the past fifty years are beyond anything one could have imagined when Edison introduced his wheezy wax cyclinders. With long playing records another milestone was passed, offering listeners inexpensive, compact, professional products and offering composers an opportunity to be heard by a larger public than that of the concert hall. During the 1940's we learned to record sound on tape, a procedure holding rich promise for today and for the future. There is now no finer way for those distant from centers of intensive music-making to enjoy music than through stereophonic recordings, which range in scope from Gregorian chant to highly sophisticated contemporary works. Furthermore, anthropologists and interested researchers have brought to us the music of little known locales and of savage tribes. These materials are of both scientific and artistic value to student and scholar alike; moreover, they provide the composer with challenging insights extending beyond the resources of our Western heritage. So significant have recordings become that there are some, of whom pianist Glenn Gould is one, who allege that live concerts will soon be things of the past due to the new technology that permits "perfect" performances and allows the executants and the listener every convenience, except that of spontaneity.

The sound tracks we hear accompanying motion pictures and television are other phenomena of our age that extend to composers almost limitless possibilities, if commercial pressures are kept to a minimum. While attempts to present standard operas have not been especially successfully, there would seem to be a potential here for compositions written specifically for the media, such as Menotti's *Amahl and the Night Visitors* (1951), the first opera commissioned for television. Colin McPhee (1901-), in *Mechanical Principles* and H_2O made interesting contributions to film music of a new order. Oscar Straus (1870-1954), composer of *The Chocolate Soldier* (1908), came to this country to write film music, as did Robert Stolz (1882-), with *Zwei Herzen im dreiviertel Takt* (*Two Hearts in Three-Quarter Time,* 1933) and Erich Wolfgang Korngold (1897-1957), among many others. Perhaps there is some truth to the statement that "operetta has not finished dying and film music is just being born." It is ironic, however, that a routine "B" movie may have an impressive score, while many large budget productions are still afloat in seas of *Schmaltz.* But the century is still young.

ELECTRONIC INSTRUMENTS

In addition to the instrumentalities of sound reproduction we have at our command modified and brand new instruments. Electrical energy early replaced manual means of inflating the bellows of an organ and of producing the proper air pressures for the propulsion of a player piano, for example. Microphones and amplifiers were attached to existing instruments, like the piano, harmonica, violin and guitar. The *vibraphone,* designed in America about 1920, has found increasing favor in contemporary popular and art music.

Among fully electronic instruments we now have an organ, substantially the product of inventor John Hays Hammond, Jr., which utilizes revolving disks and magnets to create dynamics and *timbres* that can both soothe and horrify. The electric organ has found its way into many of our homes along with the ubiquitous and perhaps iniquitous television set. The *Solo-vox,* most often used as an attachment to the piano, is a miniature version of the *Novachord,* which has twelve times its capacity. Both produce sustained tones similar to those of an organ. In 1920 Leon Theremin introduced his "hands-off" instrument, which was patented in the United States as the *Thereminovox* and created quite a stir for a while. The Theremin looks like a radio set with an upright rod projecting from the right rear corner of the cabinet and a metal loop protruding nearly horizontally from the left side. A player stands in front of it and makes nicely calculated passes in the air with both hands. He does not touch it. With his left hand moving in front of the loop he can alter dynamics; the nearer the hand to the loop the louder the tone. With his right hand passing to and from the vertical rod he alters the pitch from high to low. Another space-age instrument is the *Ondes Martenot,* quite popular with French composers, including Milhaud, Messiaen and André Jolivet (1905-   ), who composed an *Ondes Martenot* concerto in 1948. Both the *Thereminovox* and the *Ondes Martenot* produce different kinds of sounds from those to which we are accustomed.

We may probably not like the novel *timbres* of these and a host of other new instruments. Yet in music through the ages new instruments have always stimulated composers. In spite of some initial outcry, there has been a willingness to realize each new instrument's merits and place. Mozart discovered the clarinet in Mannheim and made good use of it. Berlioz used chromatic horns. Wagner added instruments to his orchestra, and so on from Monteverdi to the present. Had we heard the pianoforte in Mozart's day, many of us would have thrown up our hands and formed a society to preserve the *clavecin.* Yet, if musicians in the past had become panic-stricken, the violin itself would never have developed from any of its remote ancestors, for, remember, it was thought too brilliant, vulgar and raucous. But the violin filled the need for a more powerful instrument than the viol, when musical performances moved out of nobles' antechambers into public halls. Remember, too, Mozart used bells in *The Magic Flute*; Tchaikovsky did not hesitate to employ a *celesta;* nor were Sax's new instruments nor the Tourte bow denied places. A glimpse at any book on ancient instruments confirms where we would have remained, had we resisted the new.

From semi-electronic and electronic instruments it required but a short step to conceive of harnessing electronic means to create a new music. As Chávez writes in *Toward a New Music*:

> The new electric apparatus of music production was conceived and developed by the physico-mechanical sciences as ways of repeating or reproducing the music of today. If they are satisfactory for that purpose, they are immensely more important as apparatus for the creation of a new and unthoughtof music. What is needed is an understanding of all the physical possibilities of the new instruments. We must clearly evaluate the increase they bring to our own capacity for expression and the magnitude of the advance they make possible in satisfying man's supreme need for communication with his fellows . . . The historic evolution of musical notation indicates a tendency to make constantly more important the phenomenon of creation or musical production,

and to make the phenomenon of its performance or reproduction constantly more mechanical. That is, it indicates a tendency to make the musical work unalterable as originally conceived.

EXPERIMENTAL APPROACHES

Chávez's words are most significant when we consider contemporary experimental approaches which lean toward electronically-generated sounds, an extension of von Webern's type of serialism to total control, and, paradoxically, attempts to relax the implied immutability with creative participation either on the part of the conductor or that of the performers. All sorts of variants co-exist at the present time—some which seem only capricious and whimsical, while others are explained by their creators in the most abstract philosophical terminology, backed by an impressive knowledge of mathematics and the physical sciences.

Electronic music, that is, music generated, manipulated and reproduced by electronic means, emerged after World War II, most spectacularly in the studios of West German Radio, Cologne, under the direction of Herbert Eimert (1897-   ). There electronic devices producing pure sounds from 16 to 20,000 vibrations expanded the tonal palette of the composer to undreamed of proportions. No longer was he dependent upon the imperfect resources of nineteenth-century instruments nor our rather rudimentary schemes of notation. A whole new world of sound opened up and the composer and engineer worked as a team which ultimately eliminated the need of performers.

In France electronic music centered in Paris under the leadership of Pierre Schaeffer at *Radio-diffusion Française.* The French were especially interested in *musique concrète,* that is, electronic music derived from the manipulation of natural sounds, such as those of machines and of nature. In this aspect, *musique concrète* represents an extension of an earlier Italian concept of "noise music" in which random noises of nature and society were urged as instrumentation of the "orchestra of the future" by Luigi Russolo (1885-1947) in 1913. Initial efforts in the United States came from Columbia University where Otto Leuning (1900-   ) and Vladimir Ussachevsky (1911-   ) experimented with cutting, splicing, reversing, changing speed and otherwise exploring the potentials of magnetic tape, often deriving their basic materials from conventional instruments and the human voice, transformed, however, into what one New York newspaper called "the strangest music this side of paranoia . . ."

Since the 1950's electronic music centers have proliferated, both in this country and abroad. Composers such as Henk Badens (1907-   ), Milton Babbitt (1916-   ), Pierre Boulez (1925-   ), Luciano Berio

(1925-   ), Karlheinz Stockhausen (1928-   ) and Bo Nilsson (1937-   ) have widened the scope and deepened the breadth of electronic music. They and their colleagues, however, faced certain very difficult problems. How was this new departure to be organized? How could it be notated? Where would it lead, when even a computer can compose music, as in the *Illiac Suite for String Quartet* (1957), written under the guidance of Lejaren Hiller and Leonard M. Isaacson at the University of Illinois electronic-music console?

One answer seemed to lay in the development of "total control" over musical materials. Boulez has gone so far as to say that "since the discoveries made by the Viennese, all composition other than twelve-tone is useless." **Total control** emanated from the serialism of von Webern and resulted in extending the row concept to rows of rhythm, rows of dynamics, rows of stresses and rows of *timbres,* thereby seeking a new unity and authority in musical materials, whether restricted to the twelve semi-tones of the octave or applied to electronically-generated sounds. Another von Webern influence we may perceive is a deliberate **athematicism,** that is, the avoidance of recognizable tonal fragments, often in favor of rhythmically-organized tensions and an overall integration.

On the other side of the coin, there has been interest evinced in freeing music from the restrictions of printed page and precise rendition, and allowing it the opportunity of happy accident. John Cage, a student of Schönberg, took over where Henry Cowell stopped, engaging in the most audacious experiments, allowing players free choice of instruments, clefs and durations, and conductors the privilege of using only those parts they desired of the total complement. (Cage also shocked critics and audiences by composing a piece for twelve players and twenty-four radios, in which the radios are flicked on and off and the volume modulated as directed, with the assistance of stop watches.) In Stockhausen's *Zyklus* (1955), a single performer is encircled by forty percussion instruments and instrumentalities. The score, mounted on a revolving ring, directs the player to begin where he pleases and when he has completed a full circle to stop. In Boulez's *Piano Sonata No. 3* (1957) the performer is given certain fixed choices he may make in the arrangement of the work.

Such approaches have come to be known as "chance" or **aleatoric music** and novel though they may be, they have a validity in enlisting the active creative participation of performers, in an analogous if far more sophisticated form to that of primitive jazz. A related approach, although often less adventurous, is that of "the third stream," championed by Gunther Schuller (1925-   ) who combines principles and practices of jazz and chance music with twelve-tone serialism. His twelve-tone jazz opera, *The Visitation,* drawn from Kafka's *The Trial,* was greeted with fifty curtain calls at its premiere in Hamburg, Germany, in 1966. Nor is the chance element without representation in other arts. The popular *avant-garde* "happenings" operate on somewhat the same premises, although the onlooker also participates. And Argentinian author, Julio Cortázar, encourages the reader of his novel, *Hopscotch* (1966), to scan the first fifty-six chapters in numerical order, then skip to chapter seventy-two and from there to hopscotch about in all directions, re-reading any one chapter four times.

Evaluation of these and other experimental approaches is impossible at the moment. There is no doubt that in some cases obscurity is used to disguise the obvious; that novelty is evoked for publicity's sake; that cynical men are pulling the public's leg; that the chaos of our times is reflected by a nihilistic despair; and that insecurity breeds insecurity. On the other hand, these instances are transitory and rare. What we are now witnessing is a gradual synthesis of the many twentieth-century tendencies with the resources of technology and spatial-temporal desiderata. The future is rich for music in our epoch and there is no reason to fear new processes and thoughts any more than there was in other years of advance. The music lover should not condemn the new visions just because they are new. Imagination need know no boundaries even as ideas, as Varèse said, are not subject to protective tariff but are part of the Common Market. Perhaps André Malraux's affirmation is as good as any:

> The greatest mystery is not that we have been flung at random between the profusion of the earth and the galaxy of the stars, but that in this prison we can fashion images of ourselves sufficiently powerful to deny our nothingness.

A Sampler of Supplementary Recordings

Antheil, George, *Ballet mécanique* (1924)
Austin, Larry, *Improvisations for Orchestra and Jazz Soloists* (1963)
Babbitt, Milton, *Composition for Synthesizer* (1964)
Berio, Luciano, *Differences* (1958-60)
Boulez, Pierre, *Marteau sans Maître* (1955)
Brubeck, Howard, *Dialogues for Jazz Combo and Orchestra*
Cage, John, *Sonatas and Interludes for Prepared Piano* (1946-48)
Feldman, Morton, *Durations* (1960)
Ligeti, György, *Atmospheres* (1961)
Luening, Otto and Vladimir Ussachevsky, *Poem in Cycles and Bells for Tape Recorder and Orchestra* (1954)
Maderna, Bruno, *Serenade No. 2* (1954)

Nono, Luigi, *Polifonica, Monodia, Ritmica* (1951)
Schuller, Gunther, *Concertino for Jazz Quartet and Orchestra* (1959)
Skalkottas, Nikos, *Greek Dances*
Stockhausen, Karlheinz, *Zeitmasse for Five Woodwinds, Op.* 5 (1956)
Ussachevsky, Vladimir, *Piece for Tape Recorder* (1955)
Varèse, Edgard, *Poème électronique* (1958)

VOCABULARY ENRICHMENT

electronic tube
Frequency Modulation
Thereminovox
musique concrète

total control
athematicism
chance or aleatoric music
"the third stream"

GENERAL BIBLIOGRAPHY

REFERENCES

Apel, Willi, *Harvard Dictionary of Music.* Cambridge, Harvard University Press, 1950.

Blom, Eric, ed., *Grove's Dictionary of Music and Musicians.* New York, St. Martin's Press, 1959 (Supplement, 1961). 9 vols.

Cobbett, Walter W., *Cobbett's Cyclopedic Survey of Chamber Music.* London, Oxford University Press, 1929-30. 2 vols.

Darrell, R. D., *Schirmer's Guide to Books on Music and Musicians.* New York, Schirmer, 1951.

Julian, John, *A Dictionary of Hymnology.* New York, Dover, 1962. 2 vols.

Riemann, Hugo, *Manual of the History of Music.* Arlington, Mass., 1928. 8 vols.

Scholes, Percy, *The Oxford Companion to Music.* New York, Oxford University Press, 1955.

Slonimsky, Nicolas, ed., *Baker's Biographical Dictionary of Musicians.* New York, Schirmer, 1965.

Thompson, Oscar, and Slonimsky, Nicolas, eds., *International Encyclopedia of Music and Musicians.* New York, Dodd-Mead, 1953.

Westrup, Jack A., ed., *New Oxford History of Music.* New York, Oxford University Press, 1955. 11 vols.

BOOKS OF INTEREST

Allen, Warren D., *Philosophies of Music History.** New York, Dover, 1962.

Apel, Willi, *Masters of the Keyboard.* Cambridge, Harvard University Press, 1947.

Bacharach, A. L., ed., *Lives of the Great Composers.** Middlesex, Penguin, 1943. 3 vols.

Bauer, Marion, and Peyser, Ethel, *How Music Grew.* New York, Putnam, 1939.

Bekker, Paul, *The Orchestra.** New York, Norton, 1966.

Benade, Arthur H., *Horns, Strings and Harmony.** Garden City, Doubleday, 1960.

Berry, Wallace, *Form in Music.* Englewood Cliffs, Prentice-Hall, 1966.

Buchner, Alexander, *Musical Instruments through the Ages.* London, Spring Books, n.d.

Cheney, L. J., *A History of the Western World.** London, Allen & Unwin, 1959.

Cooper, Grosvenor, and Meyer, Leonard B., *The Rhythmic Structure of Music.* Chicago, University of Chicago Press, 1960.

Copland, Aaron, *Copland on Music.** New York, Norton, 1960.

———— *Music and Imagination.** Cambridge, Harvard.

———— *What to Listen for in Music.** New York, Whittlesey House, 1939.

* Available in paperback edition.

Dent, Edward J., *Opera.** Baltimore, Penguin, 1965.

De Silva, Anil, Simson, Otto, Hinks, Roger and Troutman, Philip, eds., *Man through His Art.* (Vol. 2. *Music.*) Greenwich, New York Graphic Society, 1964.

Dewey, John, *Art As Experience.* New York, Putnam, 1934.

Dorian, Frederick, *The History of Music in Performance.** New York, Norton, 1942.

Douglas, Winfred, *Church Music in History and Practice.* New York, Scribner, 1962.

Edman, Irwin, *Arts and the Man.** New York, Mentor, 1949.

Einstein, Alfred, *A Short History of Music.** New York, Vintage, 1954.

———— *Essays on Music.** New York, Norton, 1966.

Finney, Theodore, *A History of Music.* New York, Harcourt-Brace, 1947.

Geiringer, Karl, *Musical Instruments, Their History in Western Culture from the Stone Age to the Present.* New York, Oxford University Press, 1945.

Ghiselin, Brewster, ed., *The Creative Process.** New York, Mentor, 1952.

Grout, Donald J., *A History of Western Music.** New York, Norton, 1960.

———— *A Short History of Opera.* New York, Columbia University Press, 1947.

Harewood, Earl of, ed., *Kobbé's Complete Opera Book.* New York, Putnam, 1965.

Haydon, Glen, *Introduction to Musicology.* New York, Prentice-Hall, 1941.

Hill, Ralph, ed., *The Concerto.** Baltimore, Penguin, 1952.

———— *The Symphony.** Baltimore, Penguin, 1950.

Illing, Robert, *A Dictionary of Music.** Middlesex, Penguin, 1950.

Jacobs, Arthur, ed., *Choral Music.** Middlesex, Penguin, 1963.

Kerman, Joseph, *Opera As Drama.** New York, Vintage, 1959.

Kolodin, Irving, ed., *The Composer As Listener.** New York, Collier, 1962.

Lang, Paul Henry, *Music in Western Civilization.* New York, Norton, 1941.

Langer, Susanne, *Philosophy in a New Key.** Cambridge, Harvard University Press, 1951.

Leichtentritt, Hugo, *Music, History and Ideas.* Cambridge, Harvard University Press, 1938.

Loewenberg, Alfred, *Annals of Opera 1597-1940.* Cambridge, Heffer, 1955.

McHose, Allen I., *Basic Principles of the Technique of 18th and 19th Century Composition.* New York, Appleton-Century-Crofts, 1951.

McKinney, Howard, and Anderson, W. R., *Music in History.* New York, American Book Co., 1957.

Morgenstern, Sam, ed., *Composers on Music.* New York, Pantheon, 1956.

Mursell, James L., *The Psychology of Music.* New York, Norton, 1937.

Nef, Karl, *An Outline of the History of Music.* New York, Columbia University Press, 1935.

Nettl, Paul, *The Book of Musical Documents.* New York, Philosophical Library, 1948.

Norman, Gertrude, and Shrifte, Miriam L., eds., *Letters of Composers.** New York, Knopf, 1946.

Norton, M. D. Herter, *The Art of String Quartet Playing.** New York, Norton, 1966.

Peyser, Ethel, and Bauer, Marion, *How Opera Grew.* New York, Putnam, 1956.

Phillips, C. Henry, *The Singing Church: An Outline History of the Music Sung by Choir and People.* London, Faber & Faber, 1945.

Pincherle, Marc, *An Illustrated History of Music.* New York, Reynal, 1959.

Read, Herbert, *Art and Society.** New York, Pantheon, 1945.

Robertson, Alec, ed., *Chamber Music.** Middlesex, Penguin, 1957.

Robertson, Alec, and Stevens, Denis, eds., *The Pelican History of Music.** Middlesex, Penguin, 1960/63. 2 vols.

Sacher, Jack, ed., *Music A to Z.** New York, Grosset & Dunlap, 1963.

Sachs, Curt, *The Commonwealth of Art.* New York, Norton, 1946.

───── *The History of Musical Instruments.* New York, Norton, 1940.

───── *Rhythm and Tempo: A Study in Music History.* New York, Norton, 1953.

───── *World History of the Dance.** New York, Norton, 1937.

Schering, Arnold, *History of Music in Examples.* New York, Broude, 1950.

Seaman, Julian, ed., *Great Orchestral Music.** New York, Collier, 1962.

Searle, Humphrey, *Ballet Music: An Introduction.* London, Cassell, 1958.

Slonimsky, Nicolas. *Lexicon of Musical Invective.* Boston, Coleman-Ross, 1953.

Stevens, Denis, *A History of Song.* London, Hutchinson, 1960.

Strunk, Oliver, *Source Readings in Music History.** New York, Norton, 1950. 5 vols.

Toch, Ernst, *The Shaping Forces in Music.* New York, Criterion, 1948.

Ulrich, Homer, *Chamber Music: The Growth and Practice of an Intimate Art.* New York, Columbia University Press, 1948.

───── *Symphonic Music.* New York, Columbia University Press, 1952.

Veinus, Abraham. *The Concerto.* Garden City, Doubleday, 1944.

Westerman, Gerhart von. *The Concert Guide.* New York, Arco, 1963.

Westrup, Jack A., *An Introduction to Music History.** New York, Harper Colophon, 1965.

Wienandt, Elwyn A., *Choral Music of the Church.* New York, Free Press, 1965.

Wold, Milo, and Cykler, Edmund, *An Introduction to Music and Art in the Western World.** Dubuque: Wm. C. Brown, 1955.

INDEX